T0326649

Free and Unfree Labour

International and Comparative Social History

Issued by the International Institute of Social History
Amsterdam

Free and Unfree Labour

The Debate Continues

edited by
Tom Brass and Marcel van der Linden

PETER LANG
Bern · Berlin · Frankfurt a.M. · New York · Berlin · Paris

Die Deutsche Bibliothek – CIP-Einheitsaufnahme

Free and unfree labour
The debate continues / ed. by Tom Brass and Marcel van der Linden. –
Bern ; Berlin ; Frankfurt a.M. ; New York ; Berlin ; Paris : Lang, 1997
(International and comparative social history ; 5)
ISBN 3-906756-87-4

This work was prepared under grants from the following institutions:

The Netherlands Institute for Advanced Study (NIAS)
International Institute of Social History

ISSN 1420-5297
ISBN 3-906756-87-4
US-ISBN 0-8204-3424-8

Printed in Germany

Contents

Acknowledgements

Drafts of the papers collected in the present volume were presented at a conference organized by the International Institute of Social History (IISH), Amsterdam, on 13 and 14 January 1995. The Netherlands Institute for Advanced Study (NIAS) in Wassenaar hosted the meeting and offered infrastructural support. All the conference participants expressed their heartfelt thanks both to the IISH and to the NIAS for the quite magnificent hospitality, delightful surroundings and genial atmosphere which characterized the meeting. That is was a success is due in no small measure to the patience and considerable organizational skills of the conference secretary, Annemarie Woudstra, of whom special mention must be made and to whom our grateful thanks are hereby extended.

In preparation of the conference the IISH published a pamphlet with the title *Free and Unfree Labour* (Amsterdam, 1993) outlining the central research questions and offering essays written by the convenors Tom Brass, Marcel van der Linden and Jan Lucassen. These three essays have been reprinted below without any alterations.[1]

In addition to the authors in this volume Pieter Emmer (Leiden), Oleg Khlevnjuk (Moscow) and Prabhu Mohapatra (New Delhi) actively took part in the conference.

Aad Blok played a key coordinating role in preparing the present publication; Rob Wadman and Ineke Kellij assisted him.

Tom Brass
Marcel van der Linden

---

1. Tom Brass, "Some Observations on Unfree Labour", this volume, pp. 57-75; Marcel van der Linden, "Forced Labour and Non-Capitalist Industrialization: The Case of Stalinism (c. 1929 – c. 1956)", this volume, pp. 351-362; Jan Lucassen, "Free and Unfree Labour before the Twentieth Century: A Brief Overview", this volume, pp. 45-56.

Free and Unfree Labour: The Debate Continues

Tom Brass

This book is divided into two sections: the first deals with theory about unfree labour while the second consists of case-studies examining its presence/absence in particular contexts at specific periods. The first section is composed of seven contributions: in addition to two of the position papers (Lucassen, Brass) written for the conference, it includes five other presentations covering mainly theoretical issues (Köbben, Kössler, Steinfeld and Engerman, Roth, Grossman). The case-studies of unfree labour are grouped under five regional headings: the United States and the Caribbean (Angelo, Krissman, Shlomowitz, Casanovas), Latin America (Johnson, Martins, McCreery, Pastore), Russia (van der Linden, Craveri), Asia (Olsen, Kerr, Baak), and Australasia (Munro, Markey). A final section consists of a new contribution by van der Linden, on the rise of free labour.

The introduction itself is in four sections. The first and second outline the substance of each contribution, while the third focuses on general theoretical and methodological questions raised by the study of unfree labour. The fourth and final section of the introduction examines a number of important issues structuring the presence/absence of unfreedom (markets, profits, workforce restructuring, gender, the state and the law) raised both in the conference and by contributors to the book.

I. Unfree Labour in Theory

In a brief overview extending from classical antiquity to the end of the nineteenth century, Lucassen examines the appearance/disappearance of various forms of unfree labour in Europe, the Mediterranean and Africa. He identifies the presence in these contexts during this period of three kinds of labour: free dependent workers, unfree dependent workers, and independent workers, the latter corresponding to the labour of peasant smallholders and artisans. All these forms, Lucassen maintains, coexisted in time and space and complemented each other. He considers three kinds of explanation for the demise of unfree labour: one variant of the "from-above" cause, or the case that abolition was due to moral arguments inspired mainly by christian religion; another variant of the "from-above" cause, that slavery was abolished because it was no longer profitable; and the "from-below" cause, that emancipation was a consequence of revolutionary action on the part of slaves themselves.

Focussing on the nineteenth and twentieth centuries, Brass outlines the ways in which unfreedom has been made to "disappear" epistemologically, both by neo-classical economic theory and by postmodernism. Against the latter, which he classifies as revisionist, he explores the process of deproletarianization, a form of class composition/decomposition/recomposition which accompanies the struggle between capital and labour. Deproletarianization refers to a process of workforce restructuring that involves introducing or reintroducing unfree relations, either by replacing free workers with unfree equivalents or by converting the former into the latter. The advantages of deproletarianization are twofold. Economically, such restructuring enables capitalist producers to lower the cost of free workers by employing more easily regulated, and thus cheaper, unfree labour. Ideologically, its purpose is either to prevent the emergence of (or where this already exists, to curtail) a specifically proletarian consciousness.

Köbben examines and qualifies the labour-shortage argument of Nieboer, which links unfreedom to the presence of unsettled land (or "open resources"). The merit of Nieboer is that his approach is global in scope, he links the presence/absence of slavery to property relations, and examines unfreedom in relation to kinship. While Nieboer's argument is still useful, however, it is necessary to ask whether it can account for unfreedom in non-tribal contexts generally, in pre-capitalist contexts where resources are closed, and in capitalist contexts where the state plays an important role in regulating labour power.

The contribution by Kössler similarly accepts the distinction between free and unfree labour, but nevertheless identifies a convergence of another kind, based on factory despotism. He examines the historical roots of unfreedom in the Aristotelian concept of father as master of both a household and of slaves, a useful exercize which again permits one to link the household and slavery, a connection addressed both by Nieboer and by Orlando Patterson, for whom slavery was a form of "kinlessness". Kössler makes the important point that the shift of the workforce from private to public domain entailed a twofold restriction on factory despotism: welfare was delinked from wage-labour, and workers' secured rights under democracy.

Turning to the contribution by Steinfeld and Engerman, here the three main claims are as follows. First, that the theoretical opposition between freedom and unfreedom is constructed, and not natural. Second, that, as during the nineteenth century "neither wage labour nor contract labour had a fixed content", wage labour was essentially no different from contract labour, and consequently no real difference existed between wage (= free) labour and contract (= unfree) labour. And third, that whether or not coercion exists is ultimately a question of law (economic coercion is governed by laws).

Rather than the more usual practice of linking the emergence (or perhaps the re-emergence) of unfree labour in twentieth century Germany to the beginnings of the Nazi dictatorship in January 1933, Roth locates its origins in 1930/31. Between the latter date and the mid-1940s, therefore, unfree labour in Germany increased from virtually nothing to around 43 percent of the workforce. His argument is that fascism represented the culmination of and a continuity with the more general process of capitalist response to the economic crisis of the 1930s; an important object in the deployment of unfree labour (low-paid foreign workers, concentration camp prisoners) was to undermine working class resistance to restrictions in mass consumption, thereby permitting capital investment in rearmament. By decommodifying labour power in a context where full employment might otherwise generate pay increases, Roth argues, capital was able to hold wages down to the level of the 1930s Depression.

Grossman examines unfreedom in a post-apartheid context, and adopts a more specific conceptual definition: the right – or lack thereof – to withdraw labour power from either the production process or the market. He outlines the way in which struggles for the right to strike were conducted in South Africa from the 1930s onwards, and how by the 1980s opposition to apartheid had been transformed from individual to collective defiance of the repressive pass law system. Challenging the argument advanced by liberal critics of apartheid that (unlike small capitalists) large capitalists were opposed to an economically irrational racism, Grossman maintains convincingly that in reality no divergence existed between the apartheid principle and big/"progressive" capital. Much rather the contrary: large capitalist producers wish to train black labour in order to use it to replace the skilled and relatively more expensive labour power of whites without at the same time matching the pay and conditions enjoyed by the latter. In this regard, Grossman points out, large-scale producers in the "new" South Africa are simply coming into line with the practice of big capitalists worldwide; the ending of apartheid and the achievement of political freedom notwithstanding, black workers are now prevented from going on strike against wage cuts.

The final contribution to the volume, by van der Linden, examines the rise of free labour. Observing that wage labour was present in ancient society, and also that slavery as much as the wage relation is compatible with capitalist production, he argues that unfree labour becomes an economic problem for capital only when it confronts the latter in the market as consumer.

II. Unfree Labour in Practice

Case studies of unfree labour in the United States and the Caribbean are presented in the contributions by Angelo, Krissman, Shlomowitz and Casanovas. In her analysis of the re-creation of unfree labour in the American South following the abolition of slavery, Angelo demonstrates that not only did unfreedom continue to exist in postbellum American South but also that architect and beneficiary of this was the landlord and not the merchant. Furthermore, by keeping wages low for almost a century after the Civil War (1865-1940), the American South also created the conditions for the expansion of low cost manufacturing from the 1960s onwards.

Many of the claims made by Angelo for the American South are also made by Krissman with regard to the state of California over roughly the same timescale (1870s to 1990s). His argument is that throughout this period the profitability of Californian agribusiness remained dependent on the existence of a racially segmented rural working class, a situation which permitted capital to draw upon and super-exploit the labour power of a succession of immigrant and indigenous groups. Central to the accumulation project of California agribusiness, therefore, was the unfree and thus low cost-labour of Chinese workers during the 1870s, Japanese workers in the 1890s, Mexican workers at the beginning of this century, that of "Okies" or "poor whites" during the 1930s, and again Mexican workers under the *bracero* programme from the 1940s until the mid-1960s. Krissman shows how this process of workforce segmentation along ethic lines continues into the present, in the form of low-cost/unfree undocumented workers currently supplied to California agribusiness by farm labour contractors.

In a presentation which challenges directly that of Angelo and Krissman, Shlomowitz contrasts what he designates as the two main analytical frameworks – the (coercive) "class" versus the (non-coercive) "market" approach – for studying labour markets in three particular locations during the mid-nineteenth century: the postbellum American South, the Cape Colony (South Africa) and the British West Indies. As an exponent of the "market" approach, he maintains that in each of these contexts ex-slaves effected a successful transition to free workers, notwithstanding the (unsuccessful) attempt by employers to prevent this from happening by recourse to coercive legislation.

Focussing on coexistence of free and unfree labour among the urban workforce employed in the manufacture of tobacco in nineteenth century Cuba, Casanovas argues that such proximity in the labour process contributed to the construction of a common identity which in turn facilitated not only collective action but also the development of the labour movement. He demonstrates how white artisans gave their support to creole political parties on condition that the latter campaigned to end unfree labour, the presence of which lowered the pay and conditions of the artisans themselves.

In the first of the four contributions dealing with unfree labour in Latin America, Johnson also examines its occurrence in urban artisanal production, in this case Argentina between 1770 and 1815. His argument contrasts with that made by Casanovas for Cuba: despite the coexistence in Buenos Aires of free and unfree workers in the same kind of artisan and skilled manual urban occupations, therefore, the presence of unfree employees did not result in deteriorating wages and conditions of free equivalents. Wages remained high, however, because payment was made not to unfree labour itself but rather to its owner (the major and sometimes the sole beneficiary of wages earned by slaves).

De Souza Martins charts the resurgence from the 1970s onwards of unfree relations, particularly debt bondage, on indigenous and foreign-owned agribusiness enterprises operating in the frontier regions of Brazilian Amazonia. The object of economic expansion during this period, associated with the "Brazilian miracle", was not so much cattle-breeding but rather what he categorizes as the "production of farms". Although the military government in Brazil attempted to circumvent rental obstacles to the investment of productive capital by tax incentives and subsidies, therefore, Martins argues that in Amazonia unfreedom was – and is – a characteristic of primitive accumulation, where its reproduction is determined not by new economic activity but rather by the barrier to productive investment represented by ground rent and landownership.

Emphasizing the importance to coffee planters in Guatemala of debt peonage as a means of disciplining and cheapening labour, McCreery outlines the way in which unfree relations persisted until the transition to free labour which in his view occurred during the mid-1940s. From the early 1920s onwards, coercion took the form of vagrancy legislation whereby Indians were compelled to work on coffee plantations a stipulated number of days per annum. However, a combination of village-level resistance to such coercive measures, together with the increases in labour supply consequent on population growth, eventually rendered peonage in Guatemala unprofitable and thus unviable.

In the case of colonial Paraguay, the decline of unfree labour and the rise of a free peasantry is attributed by Pastore to the revenue needs of a predatory State. Following the discovery of silver mines in Potosí during the mid-sixteenth century, Spanish colonizers in Paraguay extracted coerced labour from enslaved indigenous inhabitants of the open frontier region where land was abundant, (private) property rights undefined and population scarce. He argues that in order militarily to defend conquered territory and also to preserve its long-term capacity for rental appropriation, the colonial State in Paraguay engaged in a twofold attempt to offset the depletion of indigenous labour power through depopulation: on the one hand by cutting back on the extent of labour coercion, and on the other by encouraging a shift to non-labour-intensive production (livestock, yerba mate) plus the settlement and expansion of a free peasantry.

The issue of unfree labour in socialist countries presents special theoretical, methodological and political difficulties, some of which surface in the contributions by van der Linden and Craveri. Examining the structure and dynamic of forced labour in the Soviet Union over a twenty-five year period from the 1930s until the mid-1950s, van der Linden identifies the origin of GULag camps in the labour scarcities which arose as a result of rapid industrialization. His argument is that the GULags epitomized the labour regime (= militarization of labour) of the Soviet Union during the period in question, and as such constitute not a deviation from but rather an extreme manifestion of exogenously-induced but state-directed/controlled economic growth.

Craveri seeks to account for the lack of solidarity among inmates of the labour camps. She attributes the absence of organized resistance to the existence of irreconcilable political differences between on the one hand Left Oppositionists who were socialists, and on the other Ukrainian and Baltic nationalists (many of whom had collaborated with the Nazi invaders). On the basis of a study of strikes carried out in 1953 by inmates of two labour camps in the Soviet Union, Craveri argues that resistance within such contexts – in the form of hunger strikes, refusals to work, and escape attempts that undermined the work regime and led to the breakdown of camp administration – was based mainly on an anti-Soviet nationalist ideology, and also became both viable and effective only after the death of Stalin.

Case studies of unfree labour in Asia are presented in the contributions by Olsen, Kerr and Baak. Comparing the approaches by Marxists and neoclassical economists to the existence of unfree labour in Indian agriculture, Olsen criticizes both. She is critical of neoclassical economics because it is ahistorical, it assumes all parties to the relation benefit, and thus it regards unfreedom as voluntary. Marxism is also criticized by her, for two reasons in particular: because it cannot predict interest rate determination, and is thus unfalsifiable; and because in her view it ignores gender-specific forms of unfreedom, and is thus sexist.

On the basis of his study of the workforce employed in building railways in India during the latter part of the nineteenth century, Kerr argues that both liberalism and Marxism privilege the concept of free labour, and that in his view the free/unfree labour distinction is not only unhelpful but disempowering. He also asks the important question of whether poor peasants and tribals recruited/controlled by local contractors by means of kinship and religion were in fact free workers offering their labour power to capital. However, he accepts that the object of coercion exercized by means of such traditional relationships may indeed have been to pre-empt proletarianization and strike activity.

Much the same kind of point is made by Baak in his contribution. After the abolition of slavery in South India during the mid-19th century, he argues, ex-slaves chose to remain in their masters' employment as *de facto* unfree workers rather than migrate to European-owned plantations. The reason for this, in his view, was that ex-slaves did well out of this arrangement, not only in the form of assured employment and food but also because they were able to bargain for higher wages and over working conditions. Baak also notes that, having been recommodified, the labour power of ex-slaves was then once again decommodified, which suggests a process of recommodification/decommodification of labour power corresponding to deproletarianization.

Case studies of unfree labour in Australasia are presented in the contributions by Munro and Markey. Focussing on the historiography about the Pacific labour trade generally, and in particular the recruitment of Melanesian workers for employment on the Queensland sugar plantations during the latter half of the nineteenth century, Munro outlines the recent epistemological and methodological shifts in this debate. The initial "from above" historiographic phase was dominated by historians of Empire, who characterized Pacific islanders as passive workers whose recruitment/employment was structured by coercion (= unfreedom). This view was subsequently revised by adherents of the "Canberra school", whose "from below" framework emphasized worker agency (= freedom) rather than oppression, and then challenged by "counter-revisionists" for whom such worker autonomy was itself negated by state control (= unfreedom). The latter position is currently disputed by "neo-revisionists", who on the basis of new methodologies (oral histories, quantification) once again place the emphasis on grassroots agency, and claim that Pacific island labour recruited for and employed in Queensland did so under its own terms (= freedom).

The impact on class formation/consciousness in nineteenth century Australia of convict labour from the British isles and indentured workers from the Pacific islands, together with the historiography about this, is also central to the contribution by Markey. The role of unfree convict labour is, like its Pacific island counterpart, is the subject of debate between those who maintain that convicts were lumpenproletarians (= criminal underclass) and those who argue that in terms of occupation and political consciousness they were part of the working class. Markey himself inclines to the latter view, and argues not only that crimes were work-related, but also that convicts were educated and skilled workers who had pevious experience of migration within the British Isles and did much the same kind of work as they had done before transportation.

III. The Debate Continues

It is a truism that, rather than being exercizes in theoretical/political/methodological synthesis, conferences merely serve to underline the extent of existing disagreements, and the conference on which this volume is based was no exception.[1] The reasons for this are not difficult to discern. That unfree labour remains a live issue in the last decade of this millennium is both surprising and yet unsurprising.

It is surprising to the degree that varieties of modernization theory have maintained that the spread of capitalism will everywhere be accompanied by the decline of unfreedom and a corresponding expansion in a free workforce (= emancipation as an automatic effect of capitalist development). In much of the recent debate about economic development, therefore, the transition from pre- or non-capitalist modes of production to capitalism is judged to have been accomplished largely on the basis of whether or not free wage labour has replaced the pre-existing unfree relationships in the agrarian sector.[2] In the case

1. Three points should be noted at the outset. First, the comments which follow address issues/themes raised by those attending the conference not just in their written contributions to this volume but also in discussions at the conference itself. Second, in an attempt (not always successful) to avoid repetition, these comments focus in the main on issues/questions not dealt with in my own contribution to this volume. Finally, and inevitably, such a commentary represents a particular view, not just about the subject in question but also about the kinds of issues this raises.

2. Such a view structured the debate on mode of production in Indian agriculture. For some contributors to this debate (such as Bhaduri, Prasad, and Patnaik), therefore, the presence of bonded labour in Indian agriculture was taken as evidence of its semi-feudal character, and the corresponding absence of capitalism. Bhaduri, "Study in Agricultural", pp. 120-37; Rudra *et al.*, *Studies in the Development of Capitalism in India*; Patnaik and Dingwaney, *Chains of Servitude*; Prasad, *Lopsided Growth: Political Economy of Indian Development*; and Patnaik, *Agrarian Relations and Accumulation*. Regrettably, the history of this debate is in the process of being rewritten, both by some of its participants and also by those at the margins of the original debate, a number of whom seem to suffer from selective amnesia. For example, because he fails to understand the connection between deproletarianization and capitalist restructuring, Breman wrongly accuses me of regarding debt bondage as a semi-feudal relation, and consequently maintains that my views are no different from those of Utsa Patnaik. Breman, *Beyond Patronage*, pp. 301-2. Breman claims further that he himself, by contrast, has argued all along that bonded labour is compatible with capitalism. *Beyond Patronage*, p. 300. About such claims at least four observations are in order. First, and in a general sense, Breman is not merely confused about what precisely constitutes unfreedom but unfortunately appears to have forgotten what he himself said about this on a previous occasion. Having originally identified debt, the employment of an indebted worker's kinsfolk, and the absence of fixed limits to work as constitutive of unfreedom, therefore, Breman now informs us that precisely this same set of characteristics has "more to do with exploitation than with bondage" (as if bondage and exploitation are unconnected!). Jan Breman, *Of Peasants, Migrants and Paupers: Rural Labour Circulation and Capitalist Production in West India* (Delhi, 1985), p. 127; *Beyond Patronage*, p. 311. Second, as even a superficial acquaintance with what I have written on this subject would reveal, my view is the exact

of India, for example, this kind of reasoning lay behind the conservative political position of the CPI: having identified unfree labour as evidence for the persistence of semi-feudal relations of production, and consequently defining feudalism and not capitalism as the principal enemy and focus of struggle in the countryside, the CPI used this as a means for postponing a socialist programme and entering into political alliance with the "progressive/national" bourgeoisie against the landlord class.[3]

It is unsurprising insofar as not only has this not happened (unfree labour being demonstrably compatible with capitalism), but also because of attempts by a "from above" and also a "from below" variety of academic discourse to revise history by claiming that past forms of unfreedom have not been as coercive and disempowering as depicted.[4]

opposite of that attributed to me by Breman: unfree labour is for me a capitalist and not a pre-capitalist relation. Third, Breman's claim to the contrary notwithstanding, it is nevertheless the case that in his earlier pronouncements he identified debt bondage as a feudal relation: if he now choses to disregard or deny this, then one must assume charitably that he has forgotten what he himself wrote on the subject of labour attachment in Gujarat. For examples of the latter, see *Of Peasants*, pp. 131, 306-13. And fourth, the extent both of the difference between my own position on the issue of unfree labour and that of proponents of the semi-feudal thesis, and consequently also of Breman's mistaken assumptions about this, emerge most clearly from a recent exchange between Utsa Patnaik and myself. Patnaik, "On Capitalism and Agrestic Unfreedom", pp. 77-92; Brass, "Reply to Utsa Patnaik", pp. 93-117. It is somewhat curious that Breman is unaware of this difference, not least because – yet again – it implies an unfamiliarity with the contents of his own writings: in a recent text, co-written with Val Daniel, he actually refers to a review by me of a book co-edited by Patnaik, where this theoretical difference between me and her is clearly delineated. Brass, Review of Patnaik & Dingwaney, pp. 120-26; Breman and Daniel, "Conclusion: The Making of a Coolie", pp. 291, 292.

3. For the politics of the CPI, see Ghose, *Socialism and Communism in India*, pp. 395 ff. The CPI(ML) also cited the bonding of poor peasants by moneylenders and landlords as evidence for the continued existence in rural India of feudal production relations. Sen, Panda and Lahiri, *Naxalbari and After*, 2, (Calcutta, 1980); Banerjee, *In the Wake of Naxalbari*, pp. 7, 32-33.

4. The combined impact of the *Time on the Cross* debate about chattel slavery in the antebellum American South on the one hand, and of the ubiquitous "everyday-forms-of-resistance" framework structured by postmodernism on the other, in terms of attempts to similarly revise the meaning of other forms of unfree labour in other areas (Latin America, India, Australia), in terms of perceptions on the part of the colonized about plantation workforce agency (= grassroots empowerment), and in terms of the need on the part of the inheritors of colonial power to present unfreedom as its "other" (grassroots empowerment = freedom) in order to have a "usable past" (a history purged of its "black legend"), are all points that have been made by this writer on previous occasions. See, for example, Brass, "Unfree Labour and Capitalist Restructuring", pp. 50-77, "Slavery Now: Unfree Labour and Modern Capitalism", pp. 183-197, "Latin American *Enganche* System, pp. 74-103, "Class Struggle and the Deproletarianization of Agricultural Labour, pp. 36-67, "Market Essentialism and the Impermissibility of Unfree Labour", pp. 225-244; "A-Way with Their Wor(l)d", pp. 1162-68, "Contextualizing Sugar Production, pp. 100-117; and Brass and Bernstein, "Proletarianization and Deproletarianization", pp. 1-40. Perhaps nowhere is this kind of epistemology more evident than in the clearly stated view expressed by Lal in a text celebrating the

Theoretical Considerations

Broadly speaking, it could be argued that there are three views about unfree labour. First, that it was unfree, it did exist and continues to do so. Second, that it was unfree, existed in the past but does so no longer – a partial denial. And third, that for a variety of reasons unfreedom was not unfree, and thus it did not and does not exist – the most absolute of denials. In this third category are to be found views which seek either to dissolve the free/unfree labour distinction or else to dismiss its significance. It is important to note that the alternative is not to argue that labour is always and everywhere fixed eternally and naturally as either free or unfree (a view based on surface appearances whereby legal emancipation automatically signals an irreversible transition). Much rather, it is to argue that a connection between free and unfree labour does exist, but not one which eradicates difference. Accordingly, in the course of class struggle (workforce de-/re-composition) labour can experience a two-way transition, both from freedom to unfreedom and vice-versa.

As always, disagreements about definitions (whether or not particular relational forms were/are unfree, together with the reasons for this) have their origin in teleologies that are themselves structured by politically distinct (not to say opposed) theories. This kind of divide was evident in the different interpretations about the meaning/existence/desirability of unfreedom advanced on the one hand by those contributors who could be defined as marxists (Brass, Grossman, Kerr, Krissman, Angelo, Roth, Martins) and on the other by adherents of a neoclassical economic framework (Steinfeld and Engerman, Shlomowitz, Pastore).[5] It is important to note, however, that the theoretical debate is not

---

contribution by Indians to the economy, society and culture of Fiji. "Over the years, many a derogatory myth has been built around the origins and character of Fiji's *girmitiyas*, and these myths have been unfairly and cruelly used on many occasions to remind their descendants of their proper place in society", he observes, "[...] the overwhelming majority [of Indian indentured migrants to Fiji were not undesirable riff-raff but] were young, productive agricultural workers [...] who had fallen on hard times and who *chose* to migrate temporarily to alleviate their plight" (emphasis added). Lal, "Fiji *Girmitiyas*: The Background to Banishment", p. 25. The theme of worker agency is also examined by Munro in his contribution to this volume, specifically with regard to the debate about Pacific island labour recruited for and employed in the sugar plantations of Queensland.

5. It should be noted that the incompatibility between marxist and non-/anti-marxist approaches to the issue of unfree labour gives rise to a large variety of contradictions, not all of which are capable of solution. Thus, for example, the theoretically eclectic attempt by McCreery to combine elements from a marxist framework with the non-marxist (or even anti-marxist) "everyday forms of resistance" approach of Scott is somewhat problematic. The attempt by Olsen to synthesize Marxism with a neo-classical economic framework is confronted by different kinds of difficulty: in particular concerning the kind of Marxism that is to be combined with neoclassical economics, and whether the latter is indeed able to theorize the bonded labour relation and the effect of unfreedom on agrarian class formation/struggle. Some

simply one between a marxist and a neoclassical economic framework: as the following examples all suggest, disagreements about the epistemology structuring the free/unfree opposition also occur within neoclassical economics and Marxism.

In varying degrees, but for different reasons, Steinfeld and Engerman, Johnson, Martins, and Kerr all question the free/unfree distinction. According to Steinfeld and Engerman, therefore, the opposition between free and unfree labour is not "natural" but constructed, the inference being that the free/unfree polarity is actually a false (= non-existent) dichotomy. However, this writer is not aware of anyone currently writing about this issue who in fact thinks the free/unfree distinction to be "natural", and while it is indeed constructed as Steinfeld and Engerman claim, they fail to say by whom, and why they agree or disagree with particular constructions.[6] More importantly, their difference-dissolving claim that no distinction exists between free and slave labour in terms of a requirement to work overlooks abundant evidence to the contrary. Similarly problematic is their claim that both free and slave labour possess the same ability to choose to work, a difference-dissolving argument that is redolent of the "choice-

of the points Olsen makes in her contribution to this volume have also been made previously by Pranab Bardhan in a similar attempt to synthesize marxist and neoclassical development economics; in his case, however, the result amounts not so much to a merger between Marxism and neoclassical economics as a takeover by the latter of the former. Bardhan, "Marxist Ideas in Development Economics, pp. 64-77; Bardhan, *Economic Theory of Agrarian Institutions.* The problem Bardhan faces is that his attempted synthesis only seems to work because what he synthesizes with neoclassical economics is in fact "analytical Marxism", which many would argue is not actually Marxism at all but rather a variant of neoclassical theory itself. Olsen faces a similar kind of problem, in that against neoclassical economics is pitted only the Marxism of those like Pradhan Prasad and Amit Bhaduri, who theorize bonded labour as a feudal/semi-feudal relation that is accordingly incompatible with capitalist accumulation. Bhaduri, "Agricultural Backwardness" and Prasad, *Lopsided Growth.* Not only is it easy to "falsify" this kind of straw person Marxism, for example by pointing to the continued existence of bonded labour in capitalist agriculture, but it also opens up a theoretical space for the consequent argument put by neoclassical economics that such agrarian relations in a capitalist context are not unfree (or bonded) but much rather free wage labour (see Brass, "Some Observations on Unfree Labour, this volume, pp. 57-75). Given that much neoclassical economic theory is structured by a concept of the choice- making individual who unproblematically exercizes preferences in a free market (= market essentialism), it could be argued that neoclassical economics does not – and indeed cannot – have a theory of unfree agrarian relations. It is therefore impossible to combine such a theoretical framework with a very different kind of marxist analysis, which argues not only that bonded labour is compatible with accumulation but also that – where alternative and better paid employment opportunities are present agrarian capitalists utilize the labour-tying mechanism to roll back the negotiating power acquired by workers in the course of labour market formation, and with this the accompanying process of proletarianization, thereby restructuring the labour process (cutting wage costs to raise profitability) by deproletarianizing labour power (or decommodifying the latter in an economic and politico-ideological sense).

6. In the field of political economy, for example, concepts of unfreedom are central to the theory of Marx, Smith, Mill and Weber.

making" individual expressing "subjective preferences" at the centre of neoclassical economic theory.[7]

In a position that superficially resembles that of Steinfeld and Engerman, Martins argues that in the Brazilian Amazon contemporary forms of unfreedom are unlike historical forms of chattel slavery, and are thus more accurately theorized as variants of wage labour.[8] Unlike Steinfeld and Engerman, who wish to erase the difference between free and unfree labour on the grounds that all employment is to some degree regulated, Martins argues that contemporary forms of peonage in the Brazilian Amazon and free wage labour are similar in terms of duration only. In contrast to Steinfeld and Engerman, therefore, Martins does not dilute or downgrade the element of coercion specific to (and indeed constitutive of) unfree relations themselves.

For yet other reasons, Kerr also questions the efficacy of the free/unfree distinction. While it is true, as he observes, that both liberalism and Marxism privilege free labour, it is however also important to note that each draws a different political conclusion from its presence. Liberals regard free labour as a vindication of capitalism (its apogee); for Marxism, by contrast, free labour signals the possibility of transcending capitalism en route to the more important process of a transition to socialism. Moreover, freedom to organize is itself a precursor of the ability of workers to combine/act collectively as a proletariat (a point made by Kössler). This difference between Marxism and liberalism on the issue of unfree labour – the significance of which Kerr challenges – and the extent to which the achievement of freedom corresponds to an authentic emancipation, is in fact central to the case made by Grossman.

Grossman's argument is that the concept of freedom which structures much of the debate about the issue of unfreedom is a bourgeois one, and thus in itself inadequate. For this reason a general, non-politically-specific, concept of "freedom" cannot be regarded as sufficient for a closing-off of the question about what is desirable as a solution to the problem of unfreedom. Like Steinfeld and Engerman, but from a radically different political perspective, Grossman problematizes the all-important issue of what we mean by "freedom": in other

---

7. As Steinfeld and Engerman themselves observe: "In the case of both the slave and the free worker, the parties may be said to have been coerced into performing labour, or to have freely chosen the lesser evil". My difficulty here is with the words "freely chosen". Free workers, whose labour power is their own property, can as a consequence withdraw from a particular employment or from the labour market altogether. By contrast, unfree workers whose labour power is the property of another, are unable to do either of these two things.

8. A variation on this position is the argument that capital binds its supposedly "free" workforce through mechanisms such as insurance plans, pension funds, etc. It is made here by van der Linden, and has also been advanced earlier, both by Bauer, "Rural Workers in Spanish America", p. 41, and by Patterson, Slavery and Social Death, pp. 24-27. For my observations on this, see Brass, "Revisionist Reinterpretations", p. 81.

words, what is so wonderful about being a free wage labourer in a neo-liberal capitalist context? What – if any – benefit accrues to the working class (as distinct from individual labourers or categories of labour) from freedom achieved under capitalism? His view – shared by this writer – is that freedom has to be considered on a collective (= workers-as-a-class) basis under socialism and not simply in individualistic terms (= workers-as-individuals) under varieties of capitalism. Hence the understandable scepticism on Grossman's part about the theoretical and political closure implied in both the fact and the desirability of a transition from unfree to free labour; as long as the latter is confined to (and defined theoretically in terms of) a capitalist mode of production, the true achievement and extent of worker emancipation must remain problematic.

Apart from its intrinsic political importance (the background being South Africa), and the fact that it focusses on epistemological issues connected to the significant "other" of unfreedom, the contribution by Grossman also forms a link between those who address the issue of free/unfree labour in capitalist contexts and those who address the same issue in socialist contexts generally and in the Soviet Union in particular. That is, the different political role and systemic impact of the market, the plan, the state, and class on the way in which the free/unfree labour dichotomy is conceptualized. The contributions by van der Linden and by Craveri both outline the way in which labour power in the Soviet Union became less free during the 1930s, findings which underline a fundamental theoretical and political difficulty: that the object of a centralized system of socialist planning is precisely to eliminate the free market exchange of all commodities, labour power included.[9]

A related problem in this regard is the issue of systemic convergence, or the implication that since it seems to be common both to socialism and to capitalism,

---

9. This issue surfaced in the debate between Kautsky and Trotsky regarding a democratic as against a revolutionary transition to socialism, and in particular the role in this process of the dictatorship of the proletariat as effected by means of the militarization of labour. Kautsky, *Terrorism and Communism* and Trotsky, *Defence of Terrorism*. The absence of a role for free labour under a system of socialist planning is clear from the following observation by Trotsky: "[...] it is necessary [...] to make clear to ourselves that the principle itself of compulsory labour service has just as radically and permanently replaced the principle of free hiring as the socialization of the means of production has replaced capitalist property [...] we [...] oppose capitalist slavery by socially-regulated labour on the basis of an economic plan, obligatory for the whole people and consequently compulsory for each worker in the country. Without this we cannot even dream of a transition to socialism [...] The transition to socialism [...] means the transition from an anarchical distribution of labour power [...] to the systematic distribution of the workers by the economic organizations of the country [...] Such a form of planned distribution presupposes the subordination of those distributed to the economic plan of the state. And this is the essence of *compulsory labour service*, which inevitably enters the programme of the socialist organization of labour, as its fundamental element." (original emphasis) *Ibid.*, pp. 126-27, 129, 131.

unfree labour appears to have more to do with the forces of production (industrialization by a technologically backward nation) than the social relations of production (the property form governing this process). This argument about systemic convergence, advanced by Kössler, implies that coercion/unfreedom is a "natural" outcome of the increase in the level of the productive forces. Such a view perceives unfree labour as a characteristic not of a pre-capitalist, a capitalist or indeed a socialist/communist mode of production so much as an effect of industrialization itself (= "the machine age", or "modernity"). Accordingly, the militarization of labour is seen as intrinsic to planning, and socialism becomes indistinguishable from capitalism.[10] It could be argued, therefore, that as with Steinfeld and Engerman, such a position dissolves the distinction not just between free and unfree labour but also (and consequently) between capitalism and socialism as emancipatory labour regimes.

Methodological Considerations

As important as questions of theory in the continuing debate about the nature of and difference between free and unfree labour are issues to do with methods. Hence the investigation of the structure and process of unfreedom, or the way in which coercion and its effectiveness is reproduced over time, is confronted with a central paradox. Since it is methodologically impossible to quantify those concepts, such as "power" and "coercion", which are central to the debate about the meaning/enforcement of unfree labour relations, in what way does one measure and evaluate the relative importance of different kinds of control, from outright physical oppression (killings, floggings, violence) to more subtle ideological forms (kinship authority).[11] It is not without significance, therefore,

10. In this connection it is important to remember that the benefits of primitive accumulation went not to the people of the USSR in the form of consumer goods, but rather on armaments to protect it from capitalism. US presidents boasted that the object of American policy was to bankrupt the USSR, and turn its people against CPSU, the success of which Gorbachev himself confirmed.

11. Part of the difficulty here is a tendency to overlook the reinforcing role of other institutional/ideological forms in the wider context which influence and thus contribute to the politico-ideological reproduction of unfreedom. In the case of coercion, therefore, it is important to be not just aware of the presence but also of the likely impact on unfree labour of institutional forms (such as the law, the state, the police, lynching, violence, kinship ideology, etc.), any component or combination of which will be supportive of those particular mechanisms actually operative in the labour process itself (such as peonage or debt bondage), and which are used specifically in order to control workers. In the case of lynching, for example, it is clear that in the fifty years after 1880 this form of extra-judicial murder had a very powerful impact in the American South as a seasonally-specific means of controlling black labour during those periods in the agricultural cycle when the demand for labour power (and consequently the potential bargaining capacity of workers) was at a peak. Beck and Tolnay, "Season for Violence", pp. 1-24.

that an important component of the discourse concerning the presence/absence/meaning/desirability of unfree labour actually turns on questions of methodology.[12]

As is clear from the contribution by Munro, methodological issues are central to the way in which recent historiography has characterized the Melanesian workforce on the nineteenth century Queensland sugar plantation as either free or unfree.[13] However, he tends unfortunately to fetishize oral history, quantification and fieldwork, all methods which are regarded as capable by themselves of providing satisfactory answers to complex theoretical questions about the free/unfree character of the workforce.[14] The implication is that the adequacy

12. A related methodological issue here is the one pointed out by van der Linden, that any attempt to analyse forced labour in the Soviet Union is confronted with a fundamental problem of the politically reactionary Cold War discourse structuring most of the secondary sources. An illustration of this difficulty is the case of a pamphlet issued by the International Confederation of Free Trade Unions (ICFTU) detailing the use of unfree labour in the Soviet Union. International Confederation of Free Trade Unions, *Stalin's Slave Camps*. The ICFTU was in fact set up and controlled by the CIA, as one of its ex-agents admits. Agee, *Inside the Company*, p. 611. However, although the opening of the Russian achives now permits researchers to focus on primary sources, many crucial documents are still unavailable for study.

13. Appearances to the contrary notwithstanding, it is important to note that Munro is in fact a protagonist in the debate about Melanesian labour in Queensland. His views about the acceptability or otherwise of the different positions taken by the participants in this debate are, in short, not neutral. Hence the arguments of "neo-revisionists" such as Shlomowitz and Moore tend to be viewed sympathetically, while those of marxists such as Graves and this writer are presented less sympathetically. For example, the work of Graves is dismissed by Munro as being that of an "outsider" intent on imposing an inappropriate African framework on Queensland, whereas this same "outsider" status is regarded as an advantage in the case of Shlomowitz and Moore. This is ironic, for the following three reasons. First, because Shlomowitz could plausibly be accused of imposing on the study of Pacific island labour migration a theoretically and methodologically problematic neoclassical economic framework used by Fogel and Engerman in their study of chattel slavery in the antebellum American south. Second, because a text in a collection edited by Munro himself deems a comparison between Africa and Melanesia to be an appropriate one. And third, because Munro endorses as "the way forward" a critique of Shlomowitz by T. David Williams which reproduces precisely the central criticism made of Shlomowitz' work by this writer! On these points, see Leckie, "Pre-Capitalist Labour in the South Pacific", p. xx; Munro, Williams and Shlomowitz, "Debate on the Queensland Labour Trade", pp. 105-36; and Brass, "Market Essentialism".

14. Not the least of the many difficulties with such a view are the following four interrelated problems. The first is its innate empiricism, an approach in which the acceptability or otherwise of any explanation is dependent ultimately on the technique of research and not on the prefiguring theoretical framework. The second is that it fails to problematize both quantitative methods and oral history in terms of what such methods do and do not disclose about unfree labour. Third, it reproduces the traditional/modern dichotomy invoked by cliometricians, whereby novel methodologies displace existing theory simply because they are new. And fourth, it also reproduces a false polarity between a "from-below" framework which emphasizes worker agency (= freedom) and a "from-above" one in which, it is

of explanation is an effect simply of the latest methods which license access to unproblematically constituted "facts", rather than theoretical rigour which asks what "facts" are in the first place. Such advocacy of fieldwork generally, and of measurement/testing and oral history in particular, overlooks two things. First, the fact that by its very nature methodological approaches to questions concerning free/unfree labour are part of the difficulty and not of themselves the solution. And second, it ignores the methodological impossibility of quantifying those concepts, such as power and coercion, which are central to the debate about the meaning/enforcement of unfree relations.

These kinds of methodological difficulty surface in the contributions by Baak, McCreery and Pastore. Thus the contribution by Baak reproduces the "subsistence guarantee" argument that can be – and indeed has been – extended to chattel slavery itself.[15] In short, the claim that the receipt of food and employment by chattels is a redeeming feature of slavery, and thus one which makes such an institution acceptable to its subject (slavery = "benign").[16] Much the

implied, workers are depicted as passive (= unfreedom). Such a view ignores the fact that, for marxist proponents of the latter view, it is precisely because workers engage in active class struggle as free wage labour that employers on farms and/or plantations resort in turn to immobilizing mechanisms/legislation. On all these points, see Brass, "Revisionist Reinterpretations", "Market Essentialism", "A-Way with Their Wor(l)d", and "Contextualizing Sugar Production".

15. As the following two examples indicate, not the least of the many difficulties with the concept "subsistence guarantee" are the circumstances in which this kind of justification has been invoked, the identity of those who have done this and the situation licensed thereby. Hence the German firms that took labour power from the Nazi concentration camps justified such action by claiming that in this way they saved workers. On this point one source comments that: "One still hears today what a defence of Krupp proclaimed almost 40 years ago: that German companies performed a humanitarian service for concentration camp prisoners by employing them at their factories, thus saving them from death in the camps." Bellon, *Mercedes in Peace and War*, p. 319 note 112. As the additional example of Mengele's justification of his medical experiments on concentration camp prisoners demonstrates, this very selfsame defence has been advanced by Nazis themselves. As was made clear in an ITV programme about Mengele broadcast on British television on 17 September 1985, Mengele justified himself to his son Rolf by saying that he *helped* those he selected for medical experiments by saving them from the gas chambers. Those who volunteered for experiments got more food, and Mengele thought Jews should build a statue in his honour to commemorate the many lives he had saved in this way. The similarity between the justification of unfreedom as a form of "subsistence guarantee" as advanced both by Mercedes Benz and by Mengele show that what can be presented by an employer (or others in a position of power) as a virtuous act of saving inmates from the concentration camp can also be seen by the "beneficiaries" of such virtue as being a method of getting cheap labour (or "volunteers" for medical experiments) that in the circumstances has little or no negotiating power. This point is neatly depicted in the film *Schindler's List*, in which a character "rescued" in this manner asks the main protagonist bluntly (and bravely): "What's in it for you, Mr Schindler?".

16. This kind of justification of (or apologia for) unfree labour is unfortunately still very common, and encountered not just in the academy but also – and perhaps more worryingly – in the

same kind of claim is made in the case of peonage on the coffee plantations of Guatemala, where according to McCreery there was little incentive on the part of the worker to escape debt since labour contractors and landholders were regarded as sources of ready cash and protection. This claim about the "benign" nature of planters, landholders and labour contractors shades into and licenses a further claim: that all the latter were actually powerless in dealings with their workforce, the inference being that peonage was unenforceable. It is then possible to argue that, because the unfree component of these relations was a mirage (unfreedom = "unfreedom" = freedom) consequently they were reproduced not "from above" by planters, landholders and contractors but much rather "from below" – by the workers themselves, because such relations were to their advantage. Indeed, McCreery himself argues that it was necessary for landholders to negotiate with workers, because the former had had little actual power over the latter.

Claims about unfreedom-as-reciprocity which in turn license images of employers as "benign" and/or "powerless" are themselves confronted with a number of methodological difficulties. It is necessary to ask, therefore, to whom precisely does unfree labour appear as a "benign" form of reciprocity (= equal exchange) based on patronage and indicative of employer powerlessness? If the answer is to the researcher, then in the absence of corroborating evidence that such a view emanates from the grassroots, it amounts to an imposed value-judgement. If the answer is to employers, then this is neither surprising nor objective. If the answer is to workers themselves, then it is important to know what is the evidence for this, how are these views obtained, by whom and in what circumstances?[17] The same kind of methodological difficulty confronts

bureaucratic apparatus of the state. In the case of India, for example, notwithstanding the outlawing (once again) of bonded labour in the mid-1970s, government officials in charge of investigating the extent of unfreedom in Bihar denied that it existed on the grounds that attached labour – the most common form of debt bondage – enjoyed better conditions than free workers in terms of assured subsistence provision (food, clothes, employment, loans). Das, *Does Bihar Show the Way?*, pp. 8-9. To a lesser degree, Markey is also vulnerable to the same kind of critique, insofar as he describes the convict labour system in nineteenth-century Australia as "rational" without saying for whom it was so.

17. In this connection it is important to remember two things regarding the quality of the sources from which indirect/direct information about unfree labour is obtained. First, it is indeed ironic that many of those who claim that unfreedom is acceptable to its subject are in fact historians, given that in the majority of instances the written records on which the historian depends contain little or no evidence about what labourers actually thought of their work situation. And second, even the reliability of contemporary oral evidence gathered directly from workers themselves must be questioned, again for rather obvious methodological reasons: for example, in cases where unfree workers are either interviewed in front of their employers, or where there is a fear on the part of bonded labourers that the fact and/or content of any such interview will be made known to an employer. In many ways still the most interesting and fruitful analysis of the methodological problems associated with the investigation of

those who maintain that unfreedom is acceptable to its subject, yet provide no corroborating grassroots evidence in support of this claim, relying instead on motive implied in economic behaviour. Hence the claim by Pastore that in the case of colonial Paraguay it was material incentives which induced bonded labour voluntarily to increase output, an idealized framework in which the impact of coercion is downgraded or ignored, and in effect replaced by a concept of the choice-making individual expressing subjective preferences.

IV. Structure of the Debate

Questions of theory and methods themselves combine to inform the debate on the specific areas/issues raised by participants, both in the conference itself and also in their contributions to this volume. While all these areas/issues are clearly interconnected, the main concerns can be grouped under four general headings: unfree labour, the market and profitability; unfreedom, frontier colonization and workforce restructuring; unfree labour and gender; and, finally, unfreedom, the state and the law.

Unfree Labour, Markets and Profits

The presence in the market of unfree labour gives rise to two sorts of difficulty. First, the low wages paid to unfree labour perpetuate correspondingly low levels of consumption, which in turn delineates the upper limit to the domestic market for commodities, and thus hastens the crisis of overproduction. In other words, capitalists cannot hope to find new purchasers for the commodities they produce and sell if at the same time the ability of those same prospective consumers to buy is constrained by low wages consequent upon unfreedom: the market remains small, and industrial capitalists do not invest. To what extent and at what point, therefore, does the presence of unfree labour constitute an obstacle to the process of market formation/expansion on which capitalism depends?

And second, since a neoclassical economic framework is premised on the voluntary supply of labour as one of the factors of production in what is – and for adherents of this particular theoretical approach only ever can be – a free exchange between individuals in the context of the market, this leads to difficulties when labour is not freely provided by the owner of this commodity.[18]

contemporary forms of unfree labour is that by Shankaran, "Methodology for Identification of Bonded Labour".

18. A manifestation of this particular difficulty is the tendency to theorize unfreedom benignly as a form of "patronage", to the advantage of bonded labour and thus freely entered into (not to say actively sought out) by its subject. A recent example of the confusion to which such an interpretation gives rise is a text by Jean-Philippe Platteau, where he announces not only

The kinds of problems to which this antinomy gives rise are evident in the contribution by Shlomowitz, which deals with the transition from unfree to free labour in the American South, the Cape Colony and the British West Indies, and in particular the way in which he theorizes the difference between "class" and "market".

The significance of unfree labour in both colonial and metropolitan capitalist contexts over the nineteenth and twentieth century, and the implications of its continued existence in many parts of the world even during the 1990s, is evident from its contradictory role (contributing to accumulation in the short-term but undermining it in the long-term) in the development process. Since the current pattern of global agrarian transformation suggests that the peasantry has no future simply as subsistence cultivators, what then are the implications for market formation/expansion and the debate about free/unfree labour of its economic role as part-time/full-time providers of cheap labour power? One argument that surfaced in the course of conference discussion was that capitalists do in fact need free labourers, since the latter embody the consuming power that in turn generates the market demand on which the former depend in order to sell commodities produced by the free workers themselves. In short, without free labour capitalism could not sell its own commodities and realize the surplus-value necessary for accumulation to continue.

This issue is actually more specific: it depends where the market is, and thus who generates the consumer demand. Both historically and contemporaneously capital has managed to exploit workers in one particular location so as to sell to markets/consumers in other locations. In what has been described as the new international division of labour, post-war economic development has been characterized by a shift in production from the metropolitan capitalist countries: initially to the newly industrializing countries (Hong Kong, Korea, Singapore,

that labour-tying by means of debt (= "patronage") is actually compatible with capitalism and thus not an archaic pre-capitalist relation but also that unfreedom is not confined to labour scarce contexts, conclusions already reached by this writer some ten years ago. Platteau, "A Framework for the Analysis of Evolving Patron-Client Ties", pp. 767-786; Brass, "Capitalist Restructuring". He purports to identify a number of scenarios whereby "patronage" (= for the worker a desirable but for the employer an economically irrational form of "subsistence guarantee") is reproduced or dissolved: it is reproduced because it is mutually advantageous, and dissolved either "from above" by "patrons" against the wishes of "clients" who wish to retain this arrangement, or "from below" by "clients" as alternative sources of employment become available. Equally predictable, but no less wearisome, is the fact that because Platteau associates labour-tying with "patronage", the decline of the latter is wrongly identified as heralding the end of unfreedom. What he fails to understand is that a shift from permanent attached labour to seasonal and/or casual work signals not the demise of unfreedom but only a change in its form. Despite casualization, therefore, what declines in such instances is the pay and not the workload of the temporary/seasonal/migrant subject who replaces the permanent labourer.

Taiwan), subsequently to yet other national contexts (the Caribbean, Thailand, Malaysia), and currently to what are now *de facto* or *de jure* ex-socialist social formations (Russia, Eastern Europe, China, Vietnam).[19]

It could be argued that all countries are now engaged in what amounts to a Dutch auction, whereby governments in metropolitan capitalist countries, newly industrializing countries, less developed countries, and ex-/actually-existing socialist countries attempt to undercut one another in terms of the cheapness and compliant nature of the workforce they are able to deliver to international capital, a process in which unfree labour plays an important role.[20] This reloca-

19. The extent of this paradox may be illustrated by the fact that both actually-existing and ex-socialist countries will be at the centre of the two main regional political economies now in the process of formation. One of these corresponds to the Pacific rim, and will involve the access by US and Japanese capital to the labour reserves of China. The other will be located in Europe, and will entail a similar access by European and other capitals to the labour reserves of Russia and Eastern European nations. Theory based conceptually on the emergence during the post-war era of a "new international division of labour" was originally associated with the work of Fröbel, Heinrichs, and Kreye, *The New International Division of Labour*, and has now generated a vast literature. For more recent texts on the subject, covering a variety of production processes in different countries, see among others Boyd, Cohen and Gutkind, *International Labour and the Third World*; Chossudovsky, *Towards Capitalist Restoration?*; Cohen, *The New Helots*; Cohen, *Contested Domains*; Deyo, *Beneath the Miracle*; Henderson and Castells, *Global Restructuring and Territorial Development*; Kaplinsky, "Export Processing Zones in the Dominican Republic", pp. 1851-65; Mitter, *Common Fate, Common Bond*; Munck, *The New International Labour Studies*; Portes et al., *The Informal Economy*; Sanderson, *The Americas in the New International Division of Labor*; Southall, *Labour and Unions*; Stichter and Parpart, *Women, Employment and the Family*. What most of the latter confirm is that the initial and continuing process of restructuring/ recomposition/relocation – and with it the globalization of the industrial reserve army of labour – has been made possible by the breakdown in "traditional" agrarian structures, the development of transportation and communication technology, the fragmentation of the labour process, and the deskilling of the workforce. Significantly, many of the workers employed in the extra-territorial or "off-shore" units (such as world market factories and export processing zones) that characterize the new international division of labour come from rural backgrounds, driven from the land as "peasant economy" ceases to be viable.

20. That such a process is on the agenda of the neo-liberal political right is clear from a recent text by Jagadish Bhagwati, an exponent of this view whose argument against protectionism and its "interference" with free trade includes among its targets not just tariffs (= protection of national capitalists) but also labour legislation (= protection of national workforces), each of which is dismissed by him as a discriminatory practice that is anti-competitive and thus an obstacle to free trade. Bhagwati, *Free Trade*. The target of the latter text – published by the Institute of Economic Affairs, a rightwing "thinktank" – is the argument that, in the name of the desirability of universal standards, international trade should take place on the basis of uniform (= international) working conditions. His view, by contrast, is that world trade ought to be conducted on the basis of the *absence* of such standards. Of particular relevance here is Bhagwati's endorsement of child labour, which in many so-called Third World contexts is unfree, and the employment of which in his view rightly permits those employers who use it to undercut and outcompete those who do not, a situation of competitive advantage

tion of production away from high wage areas/economies to low wage areas/economies while at the same time selling in the former contexts the commodities produced in the latter, also raises important theoretical questions, both about the limits to accumulation and the ability of capital to reproduce itself through access to hitherto untapped sources in non-capitalist contexts of cheap/(unfree) labour power.[21] Herein lies the source of contradiction: although contributing to the profitability of *individual* capitals in the short term, over the long term unfree labour undermines the *systemic* capacity to realize surplus-value and with this the profitability on which further accumulation depends.

Turning from a consideration of the impact of unfreedom on the market as this involves workers as consumers of commmodities, the second conceptual difficulty relates to the work of Shlomowitz and concerns the way in which the labour power of unfree workers is itself exchanged in the market.[22] Shlomowitz initially designated the "class" position as one based on conflict between capital and labour over wage levels and working conditions, whereas the "market" position by contrast maintained that the capital/labour relation was "the outcome of a free interplay of competitive forces".[23] In essence, therefore, the "market" position amounted to the proposition that labour was free, despite the fact that it circulated involuntarily in what were actually exchanges between employers.

which many less developed countries generally – but not always – have over metropolitan capitalism. Claiming that "diversity of labour practices and standards is widespread and reflects [...] diversity of cultural values", therefore, Bhagwati defends unfree labour in the name of a culturally-specific form of national "otherness". *Ibid.*, p. 28.

21. Of particular interest in this connection are the views of Rosa Luxemburg, who argued that the basic contradiction facing capitalist accumulation was the inability of consumption to keep pace with production. Luxemburg, *The Accumulation of Capital*. In other words, the necessity on the part of capital to keep down the living standards of the working class necessarily placed a limit on the demand for its own commodities. However, in the short-term a counter-vailing mechanism exists in the form of the ability of capital to unload part of its production onto populations outside the closed capitalist system; that is, capitalists can still find market outlets in non-capitalist contexts. But, she argued, the very process of capitalist expansion eventually destroys this safety valve, as increasingly acute competition for markets means that even non-capitalist contexts are ultimately incorporated into (and thus become a part of) capitalism. In the long-term, therefore, this initial tendency toward crisis cannot be avoided.

22. Ironically, Shlomowitz' claim that during the mid-nineteenth century ex-slaves effected a successful transition to free workers in in the American South, the Cape Colony and the British West Indies supports the case made by this writer about deproletarianization. If indeed ex-slaves became free as he says they did, then the subsequent increased recourse to indentured labour in both South Africa and the British West Indies during the second half of the nineteenth century and the introduction in South Africa of the apartheid system at the beginning of the twentieth century constitute attempts by employers in these contexts to roll back the gains made by free workers (= recommodification) by once again decommodifying labour power.

23. Shlomowitz, "The Fiji Labor Trade", p. 108.

Following a debate with this writer about the presence and meaning of unfreedom, Shlomowitz appears to accept both that on the basis of his original criteria it could be argued that chattel slavery itself was also free, since exchanges between planters purchasing slaves and labour contractors selling them were also "the outcome of a free interplay of competitive forces", and further that he had failed to differentiate what were in fact two relationally distinct transactions: a direct exchange between worker and employer (a market in free labour power) on the one hand, and on the other an indirect transaction involving only employers, one of whom transfers a debt-bonded worker to the other (a market in unfree labour power). The latter distinction has been incorporated into his contribution to this volume, and he has accordingly redefined the content of the "class"/"market" dichotomy. Now the "class" position consists of the view that employers collude to enserf workers, while the "market" position is that a *relatively* free market for labour exists because employers are unable either to collude or to enforce unfreedom by means of state power.

Although Shlomowitz has changed his mind, and now accepts that the existence of a free market in labour does not necessarily require the presence of free labour power, his framework is still theoretically problematic. Thus a "class"/"market" dualism has little basis in reality, not just for marxists but also for those non-marxists who are not adherents of a neoclassical economic approach. For all the latter, therefore, class is a relationship that not only includes but actually has no meaning without the additional concept of a market (in which labour power circulates). Moreover, a "class"/"market" dichotomy based on the presence/absence of employer collusion requires the kind of supporting evidence that simply is not available.[24] Most importantly, Shlomowitz' acceptance that market competition between employers does not necessarily depend on workers themselves being free has consequences for his teleology: the inability of individuals to express "subjective preferences" in the market negates the concept of the "choice-making" subject that is itself central to a neoclassical economic framework.

Many contributions to this volume contain examples of unfree labour circulating in free markets. Thus Johnson points out that historically a competitive market in what was unfree labour had a long existence in Argentina: during the seventeenth century, when illegally imported slaves were allocated by their owners to the Andean mines rather than to Buenos Aires; and also towards the end of the eighteenth, when slaves were allocated by their owners to the urban

---

24. Shlomowitz incorrectly interprets the lack of evidence about employer collusion as being synonymous with the absence of collusion itself. There is anyway plenty of evidence confirming not only employer intent but also that employers do indeed collude in order to prevent or make it difficult for unfree labour to obtain other jobs. On this point, see for example, Das, *Bihar*, pp. 18, 22; and Scott, "Explaining Abolition", p. 42.

labour market of Buenos Aires itself. That employers in Australia exchanged
what was in fact the unfree labour power of convicts is similarly clear from the
contribution by Markey. Much the same is true in the case of Germany in the
period 1930-45, where as Roth shows labour power circulated in the market
in an unfree form, leased by the SS to industrial capital. Generally speaking, the
historical connection between the prison and the factory, as embodied in the
employment by the latter of inmates from the former, is a matter of record, and
the existence of the convict lease system not just in Australia and the American
South but also in South Africa and China, all underline the economic importance of the circulation of unfree workers in the labour market.[25]

The issue of an economic link between the employment of unfree prison
labour and capitalist accumulation itself raises another point of contention which
surfaced at the conference: the profitability or otherwise of unfree labour, and
in particular the role of this in its reproduction and/or demise.[26] On this
question, therefore, the common view was that in many instances a combination
of high costs and low profits led to the replacement of unfree labour by its free
equivalent. In his contribution to this volume, for example, the demise of unfree
labour in Guatemala during the first half of the twentieth century is attributed
by McCreery to the fact that it was too expensive.[27] The implication is that
unfree labour is costly because it is well-paid, that employers are eager to replace

25. On the connection between prison labour and capitalist production, together with contextu-
    ally and historically-specific examples of this, see among others Sellin, *Slavery and the Penal
    System*; Melossi and Pavarini, *The Prison and the Factory*; Ayers, *Vengeance and Justice*; Wu,
    Laogai: The Chinese Gulag; and Lichtenstein, *Twice the Work of Free Labor*. The important point
    made by Ayers, *Vengeance*, p. 212, that the 27,000 convicts leased out to employers in the
    American South during the 1890s had a considerable negative impact on wage levels and
    working conditions of free labour employed in existing Southern industries, confirms the
    more general argument made by Angelo in her contribution to this volume. That unionized
    free workers in North America strongly and continuously opposed the attempt by the state
    and employers to undercut wages and undermine working conditions through the employ-
    ment of prison labour − in short, the process of deproletarianization − is clear from Melossi
    and Pavarini, *Prison*, pp. 139-42.
26. Although such information is and has always been difficult to obtain, there are nevertheless
    many historical and current examples that confirm the profitability of employing unfree
    labour. For the profits made by the British-owned East India Carpet Company during 1927-
    29 as a result of employing unfree child labour, see Governement of India, *Report of the Royal
    Commission on Labour*, Evidence, vol. II, part 2, Punjab, Delhi and Ajmer-Merwara, pp. 94,
    105, paragraphs B-1215,B-1369 to B-1371. For an excellent case-study from contemporary
    Tamil Nadu, see Kapadia, "The Profitability of Bonded Labour", pp. 446-83.
27. For similar arguments to that of McCreery, that in India and Australia the demise of
    indigenous contract labour migration from Bihar to the tea plantations in Assam and of Pacific
    island contract labour migration to the sugar plantations of Queensland over the latter part
    of the nineteenth century was due to the high cost of such workers, see Behal and Mohapatra,
    "Tea and Money versus Human Life", pp. 142-172; and Graves, *Cane and Labour*.

it with free labour and struggle to realize this objective, and that unfree workers are the ones who benefit from and thus struggle to retain this arrangement.

Such assumptions about the high costs and low profits of unfree labour are confronted by two difficulties. First, what are indeed additional costs for the importation/regulation of unfree labour are in many instances borne not by the employers of such workers but rather by the population as a whole, administered by the state as a subsidy to employers of unfree labour. And second, the high cost of unfree labour does not mean that the workers themselves benefit from this situation, in the form of correspondingly enhanced wage payments. The error of assuming that high costs of unfree labour translates automatically into high wages and low profits is evident not just from the examples of the lucrative employment of prison labour in the American South, foreign and/or the concentration camp workers in Nazi Germany, and labourers from penal colonies in contemporary China, but also from the contribution to this book by Johnson.[28] The latter shows that in Buenos Aires during the late eighteenth

28. The profitability of the convict leasing system in the American South during the late nineteenth century is evident from the following observation: "By 1886 the mining states of Alabama and Tennessee enjoyed the most profitable systems: convicts there brought in around $100,000 to each state annually – about one-tenth of the states' total revenue. Georgia, Mississipi, Arkansas, North Carolina, and Kentucky made the lesser but still respectable sums of between $25,000 and $50,000 each per year. Nationally, all prisons which did not use the lease system earned only 32 percent of their total expenses, while those who did take advantage of the demand for convict labor outside the prison walls earned 267 percent. In comparison with manufacturing enterprises within the penitentiaries of the North, the profitability of the lease system was real and sustained. Substantially lower overhead, more profitable products, longer hours, and the more brutal exploitation made possible by a disregard for the prisoners health and welfare generated considerable short-term profits for the state as well as for the businessman lucky enough and callous enough to lease convicts." Ayers, *Vengeance*, p. 196. That the employment of prison labour in the United States during the early part of the nineteenth century was similarly profitable is clear from Melossi and Pavarini, *Prison*, p. 140. In Europe the most notorious example of the profits gained from the use of unfree prison labour was Nazi Germany, where during the years 1942-44 companies such as IG Farben, Krupp, AEG, Telefunken, Volkswagen, BMW and Daimler-Benz took 2.5 million forced labourers from twelve different concentration camps. Ferencz, *Less Than Slaves*, pp. 112, 186-87. Given the demand for labour, therefore, "no German company had to be coerced into taking labor. On the contrary, the firms had to get all the help they needed [...] An elaborate accounting system was set up to ensure that the companies paid the SS for every hour of skilled or unskilled labor [...] the inmates of course received nothing [and] remained under the general control of the SS, but under the immediate supervision of the companies that used them". *Ibid*, p. 24. Daimler-Benz, for example, "spent approximately 710 marks a year per person in employing foreign workers during World War II [...] During the same years, the firm probably paid one of its workers 2,500-3,000 marks annually in wages, with hundreds of additional marks in social benefits. Whatever the productivity of the foreign workers (and there is reason to believe that it was good), the men and women deported from occupied Europe were a good bargain for Daimler-Benz's operations". Bellon, *Mercedes*, p. 252. Much the same is true of unfree workers from penal

and early nineteenth century legally emancipated slaves nevertheless continued to hand over either the whole wage or a proportion thereof to their ex-masters. In this context, therefore, the high wages received by unfree workers in the labour market went not to the slave him/herself but much rather to the owner of the latter's labour power.[29]

Unfree Labour and Workforce Restructuring

The same kinds of problems (profitability, costs and control) are similarly evident in what might be termed the "labour scarcity" argument about the connection between the market, an insufficiency of workers and the existence of unfree labour, a theme raised in a number of contributions (especially those on Latin America) and one that is itself linked epistemologically to concepts of frontier colonization and the closed/open resources argument of Nieboer.[30]

> colonies in China who are now engaged in producing commodities cheaply for national and international capital. Wu, *Laogai*.

29. Much the same kind of arrangement operated where an employer obtained labour power indirectly through a contractor, which also suggests that a significant proportion of what employers frequently identify as "high labour costs" actually goes to the contractor in the form of profits and not to the worker in the form of wages. That labour contractors not only withold wages but do not pass on the full payment made by employers for labour power hired in this manner is clear from the case of China, where a contractor supplying labour to the employers in the Shanghai docks paid his workers only 20-40 per cent of the wage rate he himself received from the company for their labour power. Honig, *Sisters and Strangers*, p. 117. Generally speaking, the origins, role and profitability of labour contracting remain an under-researched aspect of the literature on unfree labour. A recent and interesting exception is the monograph by Michael Tadman on the chattel slave trade within the American South during the first half of the nineteenth century, which suggests that the business of labour contracting yielded a high annual rate of profit (ranging from 60-80 percent in 1817-19 to 15-30 percent in the 1840s/1850s) and generated substantial wealth for individual traders. Tadman, *Speculators and Slaves*, pp. 204 ff. Of equal interest is the finding by Jan Breman that store owners on the plantations of the east coast of Sumatra during the late nineteenth century not only became wealthy labour contractors but this process was also linked to worker indebtedness. Breman, *Taming the Coolie Beast*, p. 110. For the background, role, and power of labour contractors in Colonial Asia, and the profitability of labour contracting in the case of the cotton mills in China during the early twentieth century, see Breman, *Labour Migration and Rural Transformation*, pp. 20 ff., and Honig, *Sisters and Strangers*, pp. 111-12.

30. It is doubtful whether it is correct to assume – as does Köbben – that the coexistence in India of debt bondage, unemployed agricultural workers, and a seasonal demand for labour is a confirmation of Nieboer's theory. Such a view implies that unfreedom is to be correlated simply with labour shortages, whereas Nieboer himself made clear that for him unfreedom was an effect of the absence not of labour *per se* but rather of property in land (= open resources). The situation referred to by Köbben is indeed common in India, and one that has for a long while now been discussed by Indian and non-Indian scholars. It has, however, a different cause, and one that is incompatible with Nieboer's central premiss: it is the absence not of property (since most agricultural labourers are anyway landless) but rather of bargaining power vis-a-vis creditor-employers that makes rural workers vulnerable to unfreedom.

Unfreedom was and is necessary in "labour-scarce" areas, it is claimed, because for economic growth to occur peasants have to be forced off the land and workers compelled to work hard. Accordingly, unfreedom is linked to the necessity on the part of capital to have to habituate its workers to proletarian status. In other words, on the frontier capitalism is acting in what might be termed a progressive fashion, in that it is actively seeking to create the proletariat both it and society needs. That such an interpretation may not be entirely satisfactory, however, is clear from some of the contributions presented here. As argued by Markey with regard to nineteenth century Australia, by McCreery with regard to early twentieth century Guatemala, and by Martins with regard to the contemporary Brazilian Amazon, therefore, unfreedom/ violence/-coercion exercized by capital has been and is necessary in all these contexts because in a region where labour is scarce employers pay low wages. That is, the absence of workers is due not so much to an unwillingness on the part of potential workers to leave the land or to work hard but much rather to the unacceptability of the low pay and bad conditions on offer. If employers simply relied on the market mechanism in such contexts, no labour supply would be forthcoming at wage levels they were and are willing to pay.

This suggests the existence in at least some of these contexts of a very different kind of dynamic: that is, instead of attempting to create a proletariat – by separating peasants from means of production and then habituating them as workers – capitalism was much rather trying to prevent this from taking place. In other words, it was not encouraging the formation of a proletariat but much rather using unfreedom as a mechanism to prevent this from occurring, or where it has already happened to curb its development, by using forced labour, peonage, debt bondage or indenture against those *already* separated from the means of production and *already* habituated to the rhythms of the capitalist labour process. That employers resort to unfree labour in situations where a free market already exists is clear from the contribution by Roth, who argues persuasively that the case of unfree labour in Germany during the period 1930-45 suggests the importation into metropolitan capitalism of a work regime historically associated with the colonial periphery.

Much the same point about the targets of unfreedom being those who were actually in the market is confirmed by other contributors to this volume. Thus Markey indicates that in nineteenth century Australia large landholders continued to lobby for the reintroduction of convict transportation, since from their point of view the problem with free workers was that they opted for more congenial and remunerative urban employment. Similarly, as Casanovas demonstrates with regard to the tobacco industry in nineteenth century Cuba and McCreery with regard to coffee plantations in early twentieth century Guatemala, the object of the *libreta* or passbook system was – as in the case of South

Africa – to prevent or restrict the free movement of workers and a corresponding ability on their part to sell their labour power for higher wages and/or to
bargain for better working conditions. As long as a worker owed debts to his
employer, a situation recorded in each worker's individual *libreta*, then it was
not possible for that labourer to seek a different job. This process of deproletarianization, or the way in which labour is constituted/reconstituted
relationally as unfree in the course of class struggle, has a very different politics.[31]
In such instances it is no longer possible to present capital as a progressive socio-
economic force, attempting to create a market in free labour.

A related issue here is the extent to which unfreedom is successful in
preventing/pre-empting workforce organization. For Grossman, therefore, an
indicator of free labour power is the right to strike, the absence of which
indicates unfreedom, whereas for Craveri by contrast it was unfree workers that
went on strike in the labour camps.[32] Agreeing with Grossman, Krissman shows
that when the *bracero* programme ended in 1964, workers from Mexico began
to organize, and Californian agribusiness responded to the increased bargaining
power of agricultural workers in the 1970s by resorting once again to the labour
contract system. Discharging a crucial role in the replacement of a free permanent workforce with unfree casual labour, contractors were employed by
Californian agribusiness specifically in order to segment the agricultural labour

---

31. A form of class composition/recomposition which accompanies the struggle between capital
    and labour, deproletarianization refers to a process of workforce restructuring that involves
    introducing or reintroducing unfree relations, either by replacing free workers with unfree
    equivalents or by converting the former into the latter. In contrast to this writer, Roth
    maintains that workforce unfreedom corresponds not to deproletarianization but rather
    subproletarianization. Although this is not a major difference, particularly since this writer
    agrees with Roth's analytical framework, a difference does exist. Theoretically, one could
    have a sub-proletariat, a term that identifies *structural* separation from the proletariat but not
    a chronological experience of the latter (apart-from but not necessarily having-once-been-
    part-of the proletariat), whereas the *process* of deproletarianization suggests relational change,
    the forcible transformation of a proletariat into its "other". In fact, Roth agrees that "[t]he
    vastly swollen ranks of the proletariat in the areas under Nazi hegemony were [...] subjected
    to a process of 'un-making'", which does indeed suggest a chronology of becoming-
    something-"other" rather than simply occupying a physical space that is relationally distinct
    from that of the proletariat (as implied in the term "subproletarianization").
32. This difference in interpretation is due in part to the kinds of political consciousness involved.
    For Grossman, therefore, as for this writer, the role of unfree labour is to prevent/pre-empt
    the emergence of a specifically proletarian consciousness. By contrast, in the case referred
    to by Craveri, inmates organize not as workers (an identity which they do not in fact possess)
    but rather on the basis of a shared national/ethnic identity. Strikes based on the latter do not
    pose questions about the ownership/control of the means of production, and are consequently
    regarded by employers as less threatening than workforce organization based on class, as the
    many examples of workforce restructuring confirm (see Brass, "Some Observations on Unfree
    Labour", this volume, pp. 57-75).

market: in short, to undermine working-class solidarity established through collective bargaining, and thus the process of trade union organization itself.[33]

Unfree Labour and Gender

The issue of unfreedom as a form of labour control raises another important question: the role of gender in this process. Claiming that analyses of bonded labour in general and those by marxists in particular have failed hitherto to problematize gender, Olsen notes that the unfree status of female labour in the Indian state of Andhra Pradesh derives from its position within the rural household (where it is subject to control by family/kinship ideology), and suggests further that future research into debt bondage relations ought to focus on the role of women's labour in meeting intra-kin group debt servicing work obligations incurred by male borrowing.[34] The difficulty with this view, however, is that it ignores the extent to which the reproduction of unfree labour relations by means of authority embedded in family, kinship, fictive kinship, and patriarchy has long been recognized – by marxists and non-marxists alike.[35]

33. The same is true of Japan in the last decades of the nineteenth century, where employer response to strike activity by young women workers in the textile mills was to impose further restrictions on the freedom of the workforce. About this process one observer comments: "Female workers [...] initiated work stoppages and wild cat strikes. They did so especially during the 1880s and 1890s before the dormitory system became widespread and employer control tight [...] The response of managers to such strikes was to build more dormitories for workers, to lock their workers more securely in these dormitories, to supervise them more thoroughly both on and off the factory floor, to strive to keep them too exhausted to unite and fight. [...] Such responses probably made strikes less likely to erupt spontaneously and harder to continue once they had begun [...] As dormitories became an integral part of factory architecture, undoubtedly it became almost impossible for outside labour organizers to reach the women in the textile mills. But there is little evidence that the textile hands 'passivity' was anything but forced upon them by their employers." Tsurumi, "Female Textile Workers", p. 17.

34. Much the same kind of claim is made by Kapadia, "Women Workers in Bonded Labour", who – like Olsen – announces that a gendered analysis of bonded labour is lacking, and also that this writer is guilty of just such an ommission.

35. The kinship/unfreedom link – albeit in a different form – is central to the contribution by Kössler, who reminds us of the Aristotelian origin of the view that slaves are located ideologically outside the realm not just of citizenship but also kinship. Interestingly, precisely this view (slavery = kinlessness) structures a number of influential contemporary interpretations of unfreedom in Africa and America. Patterson, *Social Death*; Miers and Kopytoff, *Slavery in Africa*. Among the texts published earlier this century which have attempted to address the question of a link between gender and/or kinship/family relations on the one hand and unfree labour on the other are those by Nieboer, Lasker and Douglas, and the 1931 Royal Commission on Labour in India. Nieboer, *Slavery as an Industrial System*, pp. 9–25; *Report of the Royal Commission on Labour in India*; Lasker, *Human Bondage*, pp. 16, 22, 43, 66, 90, 92, 132, 247, 292 ff.; Douglas, "Matriliny and Pawnship in Central Africa", pp. 301–313. Neither is it the case that gender and patriarchy have been absent from more recent analyses of unfree labour

For example, my own research into unfree labour, both in Latin America and in India, has examined the economic and ideological control exercized by males over the labour power of females within the same kin group, and the requirement for women to meet debt-servicing labour obligations owed to employers by males in the same household who "abscond" leaving debts unpaid. Ironically, the act of worker empowerment by men may in some instances be realized at the expense not just of women but of the woman-as-worker. Fieldwork conducted during 1990 by this writer in Purnia District, Bihar, suggests that migration, which may be empowering for a male worker, is for a female worker disempowering. Whereas an "absconding" male worker who migrates in this way (literally) escapes bondage and is accordingly transformed from an unfree into a free labourer, this process of emancipation is nevertheless achieved at the cost of a female worker who, as a result of having to meet his debt-servicing labour obligation, is herself transformed from a free into an unfree labourer.

The important role of gender ideology in reproducing unfree relations may be illustrated by reference to an episode which occurred in Purnia itself. During the course of a fieldwork interview, a weeping woman appeared and informed everyone that she had been beaten by the daughter and wife of her employer (a landholder owning between 12 and 15 acres) because, not having been paid for 2-3 months, she had dared to ask him for the back wages due her. His reply was that she must not demand things of him. She then observed that, if no back payment was going to be made, why should she continue working for him, at which point her employer instructed his wife and daughter to beat her. The significance of this episode lies in the fact that in Purnia the withholding by land-

in the Americas, Africa, Asia and Europe, as the following examples demonstrate: Indian School of Social Sciences, *Bonded Labour in India*, pp. 12-13, 85 ff.; Guy, "Women, Peonage, and Industrialization", pp. 65-90; Phongpaichit, *From Peasant Girls to Bangkok Masseuses*; Robertson and Klein, *Women and Slavery in Africa*; Rubbo and Taussig, "Up Off Their Knees", pp. 5-23; Gupta, "Himalayan Polyandry", pp. 258-81; Stoler, *Capitalism and Confrontation*; Honig, *Sisters and Strangers*, pp. 365-380; Griffith, "Nonmarket Labor Processes", pp. 838-852; Jaschok, *Concubines and Bondservants*; Beall, "Women Under Indenture in Natal", pp. 89-115; Zegeye and Ishemo, *Forced Labour and Migration*; Beckles, *Natural Rebels*; Tsurumi, *Factory Girls*; Anderson, *Britain's Secret Slaves*; and the contributions by Carter, Kelly, and Breman and Daniel in Daniel, Bernstein and Brass, *Plantations*. Nor is it true – as alleged either implicitly by Olsen or explicitly by Kapadia – that this writer has omitted to gender his analysis of bonded labour in India and Latin America; much rather the contrary is the case, since a central focus of my research has been precisely on the implications for the continued existence and effectiveness of debt bondage relations of intra-/inter-kin group power – such as patriarchal authority – embedded in discourse about family, kinship, and fictive kinship, as a consequence of which all the latter are identified by me as crucial ideological sites which license the reproduction of unfree labour. See for example Brass, "Capitalist Restructuring"; "Revisionist Reinterpretations"; "The Elementary Strictures of Kinship", pp. 56-68; "Peasant Essentialism, pp. 444-456; and "Migration, Tenancy and Bondage", pp. 283-293.

holders of wages due casual workers in order to prevent the latter from leaving their employment corresponds to a period-specific form of unfreedom, the object of which is to prevent the worker from offering his/her labour power elsewhere at the point in the agricultural cycle when it is most advantageous to do so.

In demanding the payment of wages owed her, and at the same time threatening to withdraw her labour power if this was not done, therefore, the labouring subject confronted her employer not as a woman but as a *worker*. The landholder, however, refused to recognize this class identity, and instead responded to her as a *woman* – by setting his female kinsfolk on her (= this is a woman's affair, to be settled by women as women). In other words, not only is it the employer who reconstitutes the identity of the labouring subject by shifting the identity of the latter from a threatening discourse (about class) to a less dangerous one (about gender) but this shift is for the subject concerned a disempowering one.

The example of Purnia (and, indeed, other contexts in India) suggests that the discourse about gender as a form of worker disempowerment is also connected with the distinct kinds of sanction each invites from the wider context. Whereas a worker who is female might expect to receive the support of her kin/caste group in a direct confrontation with an employer over issues of pay and conditions, the same worker could expect by contrast to be a target of hostility from this same kin/caste group in the event of an indirect confrontation with the same employer where this involved challenging/defying the right of a husband/brother/father/uncle to insist that a wife/sister/mother/daughter meet the debt-servicing labour obligations incurred by males in her household/family/kin group.

Unfree Labour, the State and the Law

Yet another contentious area of discussion in the conference was the link between unfreedom, the law and the state. On the question of the role of the state in the reproduction of unfree relations, a number of divergent viewpoints emerged, as is clear from the contributions to this volume. In the case of colonial Paraguay, therefore, Pastore ascribes an a-historical, non-class-specific agency to the state (= inherently predatory institution) which, he argues, nevertheless limited the impact of coerced labour on the indigenous population in order to preserve the latter as a source of revenue.[36] By contrast, Shlomowitz regards the

---

36. Implicit in the argument of Pastore is the view that the (non-class-specific) state fulfills a positive social role by redistributing the surpluses generated through the employment of unfree labour, investing in infrastructural improvements that benefit society at large. In other words, not only is the state regarded as "autonomous" (= above the fray, a neutral arbiter) but in the end slavery can also be perceived as a "positive good". For at least three reasons, this view is problematic. First, it is impossible to categorize the state as a "neutral" institution, particularly where its class nature remains unspecified yet agency is ascribed to it. Second,

state as being unable to prevent labour from operating the market to its advantage, whereas Steinfeld and Engerman perceive the regulatory function of the state as one that in effect blurs or eliminates the distinctiveness between free and unfree labour. Broadly speaking, any attempt to problematize the connection between unfreedom and the state must begin by addressing the issue of class power as mediated through legislative discourse and practice, a terrain which raises many theoretical and methodological difficulties.

An example of one such difficulty is evident in the contribution by Steinfeld and Engerman, which operates with a socio-economically disembodied concept of law, and thus tends to fetishize legality. While important, what the law permits or forbids may not be a very helpful guide to grassroots practice. Thus coercion may exist in law but not in fact, or in fact but not in law. More importantly, law is about the power of the state, which in turn raises the issue of what social forces are represented by and/or rule through this apparatus.[37] Accordingly, to say that the law permits or disallows unfreedom is to say nothing about why unfreedom is legal or illegal, whether legislation is enforced or disregarded, why this happens and changes, and what social forces benefit from or are disadvantaged by this whole process.[38] The difficulties raised by fetishizing legality may be illustrated by a number of instances outlined in this volume. In the case of nineteenth century Cuba, therefore, Casanovas shows how injunctions against physical coercion exercized by masters against apprentices existed in law but not in fact. Similarly, Johnson shows that in Buenos Aires towards the end of the eighteenth century, manumitted slaves were required to continue paying a proportion of their earnings to ex-slaveowners, an arrangement which suggests that legal emancipation existed in name only.

where surpluses generated by the employment of unfree labour are taxed by the state, infrastructural investment undertaken by the latter is generally designed to further capital accumulation, and thus cannot be regarded as being for the benefit of society as a whole. And third, it is necessary to ask whether at a more particular level those indigenous inhabitants in Paraguay (and elsewhere in Latin America) whose labour power actually generates these surpluses benefit in any way whatsoever from infrastructural investments undertaken by the colonial state.

37. The role of the state is also used by Steinfeld and Engerman in a geographically restricted sense, which raises the following question: in what sense is it possible to analyse labour in nineteenth century America solely with reference to the north, and without reference to relations of production in California or the American South? Similarly, is it possible to talk about free labour in nineteenth century England without reference to the way in which British capital either imposed or operated with existing forms of unfreedom in its colonial possessions?

38. This problem is one which also confronts the claim made by McCreery concerning the ending of unfreedom in Guatemala. Despite agreeing that coercion and indebtedness as means of cheapening labour power continued beyond this date, therefore, the legislative abolition in 1945 by the Guatemalan state of pass laws (*libretas*) is taken by him as evidence for the end of unfree labour and a corresponding transition to free labour.

An even better-documented example of law-as-rhetoric is the case of India, and in particular the fate in this context of successive legislative ordinances banning unfree labour. In terms of domestic human rights legislation, debt bondage has been outlawed both by Article 23(i) in Part III of the Indian Constitution, and by Point 4 (which stated that "bonded labour, wherever it exists, will be declared illegal") in the 20-Point Programme introduced during the Emergency of 1975-77.[39] In addition to the extensive provisions contained in the Bonded Labour System (Abolition) Act passed by the Congress government in 1976, numerous legislative ordinances outlawing specific and localized variants of debt bondage have been enacted at various times during this century by individual state governments.[40] With the exception of unratified ILO conventions, therefore, an impressive armoury of legislation directly relevant to the issue of unfree labour in India already exists.[41] Unsurprisingly, the problem remains largely one of legal implementation, which raises the basic question about this whole issue: the economic role of unfree labour, and thus the nature and strength of the political opposition to its eradication on the part of the capitalist class in India.

39.   Estimates for the number of bonded labourers in India during the 1980s vary from the Union government's own figure of 120,000 and the National Sample Survey Organization 1979 figure of 345,000 to the 2.6 million calculated by the National Labour Institute and Gandhi Peace Foundation joint survey carried out in 1978, and the figure of five million mentioned by the Bonded Liberation Front in 1983. The Union government figure is based on information submitted by individual states; for the NSSO figure, see "States slow on identification of bonded labour", *Hindustan Times*, 9 September 1983; for the NLI/GPF survey, see Marla, *Bonded Labour in India*, p. 154; for the Bonded Liberation Front estimate, see Morcha, *Crusade Against Slavery*.

40.   For example, the Bihar and Orissa Kamiauti Agreements Act (1920), the Bombay Moneylenders Act (1946), the Orissa Debt Bondage Abolition Regulation (1948), the Rajasthan Sagri System Abolition Act (1961), the Orissa Dadan Labour (Regulation and Control) Bill (1975), the Uttar Pradesh Landless Agricultural Labourers Debt Relief Act (1975), and the Maharashtra Debt Relief Act (1976). For an account of legislation on bonded labour, see Kulkarni, "Law and Social Change".

41.   Although both the ILO Forced Labour Convention (No. 29) of 1930 and the Forced Labour Recommendation (No.36) were accepted by the Indian government in 1954, by the mid-1980s India had still only ratified four out of the eight ILO conventions dealing with basic human rights. One of those ommitted was the Abolition of Forced Labour Convention (No. 105) of 1957, the ratification of which the Indian government claimed would prevent state governments from recruiting workers to meet emergency requirements such as famine and flood. Most significantly, the majority of the 106 ILO conventions (out of a possible 136) not ratified by the Indian government related to the employment conditions of agricultural labour, the official justification for this omission being that village level implementation was administratively impossible. Dhyani, *International Labour Organization and India*.

PART I

THEORETICAL ISSUES

Free and Unfree Labour Before the Twentieth Century: A Brief Overview*

Jan Lucassen

Introductory Remarks

In an article, published more than ten years ago, O. Nigel Bolland posed the following question: "How do we account for the fact that in some situations of labour shortage the workers are able to increase their benefits in terms of greater freedom and better remuneration, while in others the employers exercize even more powerful coercion, in the form of violence or bondage? Or, similarly, why does an expanding economy sometimes result in the greater hegemony of the ruling class, while at other times it provides an opportunity for workers to win more concessions?".[1] As Bolland and others have done, one may try to answer this question by studying a particular area during a limited period of time. The following birds' eye view takes another path in order to show that these questions can be put to many different situations before the emergence of the "modern" world.

Before doing so, however, some preliminary remarks have to be made. First, as has been said already in the introduction and as has been stated by many specialists in the history of slavery, in world history, unfree, rather than free labour is the rule.[2] This assertion has serious consequences for labour history in particular which until now nearly exclusively studies free labourers – thereby meaning those who have a free choice of an employer – since the so-called Industrial Revolution.[3] Before going deeper into the history of free and unfree labour, we must be aware that yet a third kind of labour can and should be

---

* Obviously, it is impossible to master the immense literature on this topic within these few pages. The secondary sources, used here, are restricted to some more general overviews of recent discussions and historiography. However, even with these restrictions, no attempt to completeness has been made. I wish to thank Richard Price (University of Maryland at College Park and during 1992-1993 fellow of the IISH) for his critical remarks on an earlier version of this chapter.

1. Bolland, "Systems of Domination after Slavery", p. 616.
2. E.g., Engerman, "Slavery and Emancipation in Comparative Perspective", pp. 318-319 following Orlando Patterson; also Manning, *Slavery and African Life*, pp. 27-30.
3. See Steinfeld, *Invention of Free Labour*. He argues that free labour properly conceived did not become a dominant legal ideal until the later eighteenth century and not the dominant paradigm until the nineteenth century.

distinguished: labour, performed independently from an employer. This "independent labour" takes place outside the labour market, but can be closely related to free and unfree labour and quantitatively it is a very important element in labour history.

Thus, in this essay, three kinds of labour will be treated in their mutual relationship:

– free dependent labour that is free to current legal standards. Of course this type of labour is not free of "want", because this precisely is the motor that moves free labourers into a labour relation with an employer;
– unfree dependent labour, ranging from slavery, via serfdom to indentured labour;
– independent labour, encompassing small peasant farming and cottage industry.

The functions of these three kinds of labour are not uniquely aimed at production for the market or for direct consumption by the producer or his household. In particular many unfree labourers and especially slaves had a function in conspicuous consumption – including sexual services –, rather than in the production for their masters.[4] The forms of labour functions and labour relations that are important for an historical analysis are given in figure 1.

Figure 1

FUNCTION:	dependent labour		independent labour
	free	unfree	
productive	wage labour	slavery	
		serfdom	peasant
		indentured labour	proto-industry
consumptive	domestic	slavery	0
	service	serfdom	

For labour historians the shifts of persons between the four categories are most important, as are shifts within the categories, intermediate forms, and combinations. Many a labourer had to combine wage labour and independent labour within one and the same year. Many European peasants worked in their own cottage during spring and autumn, worked as seasonal wage labourers elsewhere

---

4. This phenomenon is extensively dealt with in Patterson, *Slavery and Social Death*; see Phillips, Jr., "Old World Background", p. 48, who mentions servants, guards, sexual partners to "demonstrate the wealth and luxury of their owners".

during summer (or during winter, if stemming from mountainous parts of the continent) and spent the winter as proto-industrialist weavers or spinners.[5] Others, like indentured labourers, first spent part of their lives as unfree labourers and subsequently managed to become free or independent labourers.

Next to the changes between and within the categories, labour relations which these categories and the changes between them involve, are of utmost importance for the development of the concepts of labour history.

Not all sorts of labour, not even all sorts of unfree labour can be discussed fully in these few pages. The focus will be on productive slavery, serfdom and indentured labour in agriculture, in certain forms of industry – in particular in mining – and at the service of the state, in particular as sailors and soldiers. Geographically, the western hemisphere, by some authors recently called the "Atlantic System", including Europe, the Mediterranean, Africa and the Americas will receive the most attention.

Probably the most important distinction between free and unfree labour is "the freedom whether or not to choose one's own employer and therefore one's labour conditions, or to choose one's means of production". As with most dichotomies, in this case also there are many intermediate forms. In most historical situations free wage labourers didn't have, according to their capacities, a complete free choice of employer. Either the state, or the employers, or the established free wage labourers (and usually coalitions of all three), put restrictions on this choice, such as restrictions by the guilds until the nineteenth century in Europe, restrictions and control by the state and the employers in the form of work permits (e.g. workbooks or livrets in the nineteenth and twentieth centuries) or entry permits, linked to work permits as in most countries today[6]. Sometimes, also within a legal system of free labour, the state imposed temporary restrictions in the form of forced labour, working prisoners or press-gang. In particular around 1800 Britain and France made an excessive use of these forms, as did the Third Reich later on.

A Typology of Productive Unfree Labour

Within the Old World and the Atlantic System three main forms of productive unfree labour and, in particular, of slavery have to be distinguished:[7]

---

5. See Lucassen, *Migrant labour in Europe*.
6. This may lead to excessive power of employers over their employees, who in the case of a dispute only have the choice to leave the country; a major problem for many migrant workers.
7. The first two forms according to Phillips, "Old World Background", pp. 47 ff.

(i)   Small-scale unfree labour in homes, farms and artisan establishments,
        omnipresent in Europe up until ca. 1000 AD and in the Mediterranean
        parts until ca. 1700, in Eastern Europe until the nineteenth century, in
        the Americas from the sixteenth to the seventeenth century, in the muslim
        world and in Africa until the early twentieth century.

(ii)   Large-scale unfree labour in big enterprises like plantations or mines.
        There is some disagreement as to whether there is a continuous develop-
        ment of chattel slavery in the western hemisphere from classical Greece
        and Rome. The Belgian historian Charles Verlinden argues for a very
        close link between sugar cane production and slavery from Antiquity, via
        crusader-invaded Syria and Palestine in the eleventh century through
        Cyprus, Sicily, and Spain unto the Americas.[8] But according to Phillips
        and Solow, in the medieval Mediterranean slave labour was not a "major
        feature" of sugar cane agriculture and new sugar-cane plantations devel-
        oped on the basis of chattel-slavery on the Atlantic Islands: from ca. 1450
        on Madeira, from ca. 1500 on the Canaries and developed from Madeira
        via Sa Tome in the C16th to the Carribean and the American Continent.[9]
        However hard it may be for an outstander to assess carefully the arguments
        exchanged, undoubtedly after 1650 in America large-scale unfree labour
        outnumbered by far small-scale unfree labour, although the last form did
        continue to exist everywhere.

(iii)   Large-scale unfree labour in state-service as sailors and soldiers. The system
        of slave soldiers seems to be almost exclusively confined to muslim states
        according to Pipes.[10] All major muslim dynasties from the ninth until the
        nineteenth century and from Spain in the west to India in the east relied
        on this type of military manpower. The explanation put forward by Pipes
        is closely linked to Islam as a cultural system: "The existence of military
        slavery has almost nothing to do with material circumstances (geographic,
        economic, social, political, technical, and so on), but follows from the
        needs inherent in islamic organization." This form of military recruitment
        "existed in only one civilization and occurred there almost universally".[11]
        This conclusion has to be doubted if we include the navy in military
        recruitment in Europe. Since the high middle ages three major forms of
        recruitment occurred in that continent: compulsory recruitment of
        inhabitants, hiring of mercenaries and enslavement of sailors. Compulsory

---

8. Verlinden, *Esclavage dans l'Europe Médiévale*, Part II; see also Verhulst, "Decline of Slavery",
    pp. 195-203; Curtin, *Rise and Fall of the Plantation Complex*; and Patterson, "Slavery", p. 420.
9. Solow, "Slavery and Colonization", p. 3: "dormant in Europe for 500 years" (i.e., from 1000
    AD to 1500 roughly).
10. Pipes, *Slave Soldiers and Islam*.
11. *Idem*, p. 100.

recruitment of inhabitants by the way of militia conscription or universal service was well-known in the form of press gang in certain navies and became popular and almost universal for armies since the French revolution. Hiring of paid soldiers, called mercenaries, involved in principle free but many times indentured men. This device was popular since the high middle ages and lasted until the first half of the nineteenth century. It became a specialty of the Swiss, the Irish and the Scots. Recruitment of unfree sailors was practised foremost on the Mediterranean galleys of all catholic, orthodox or muslim powers until well into the eighteenth century. As is well-known at the battle of Lepanto all contesting powers were heavily dependent on slaves from the Balkans (Greeks, Albanians, Bosnians, etc.).

Historical Developments

In order to make the interactions between free, unfree and independent productive labour more concrete, a quick overview of developments in the western hemisphere from classical antiquity to the early twentieth century may be useful.[12]

Classical Antiquity

Although slavery antedates classical antiquity and goes back to prehistoric times – as Orlando Patterson puts it: "slavery was intricately tied up with the origins of trade itself, especially long-distance trade",[13] it is clear that it finds a first culmination point in classical Attica when at least one third or one quarter of total population of this region and even more in its centre, Athens, were slaves. Apart from domestic and agricultural slaves most notorious are the slaves employed in the silvermines of Laurion.[14] In the hellenistic period its importance grew and the Roman Empire depended heavily on slave labour as well. The main source for Greek and Roman slave trade were the Black Sea shores, to be followed by Northern and Eastern Africa.

Western Europe During the Middle Ages

The first half of the middle ages in Western Europe, although characterized by economic decline, saw no demise of slavery. Nevertheless, there was a sharp

12. This overview relies on works like Patterson, *Slavery and Social Death*, and Curtin, *Rise and Fall of the Plantation Complex*.
13. Patterson, *Slavery and Social Death*, p. 149.
14. Verlinden, *Esclavage dans l'Europe Médiévale*, pp. 7 ff.

decline from classical antiquity. According to the estimates of Orlando Patterson, and notwithstanding atrocious practices by Vikings[15] and others, the total volume of the trade at its height must have been some 7,000 annually as compared to a legal annual trade in the Roman Empire during the period of the principate of 250,000.[16] Only in northwestern Europe from about 1000 AD did slavery disappear to be replaced by large-scale servitude. Only towns knew real free labour in the late middle ages, whereas in the countryside an independent peasantry gradually came into being in Northern France, the Low Countries, Britain and some other regions.

The Mediterranean During the Middle Ages and the Early Modern Period

In christan and muslim Southern Europe slavery flourished as before. In Spain, Southern France, Italy and in the east private small-scale slavery was common – and even increased – until the sixteenth century.[17] In Italy, for example, as late as the fourteenth century, the labour shortages after the Black Death ca. 1350 caused householders to turn to slavery and indentured labourers for their labour supply.[18] In Italy thriving commercial centres like Genoa and Venice and their colonies depended heavily on private and public slavery, the latter mainly in the form of galley-slaves. In many of these countries slavery never was abolished officially, it simply died off gradually in the seventeenth, eighteenth or even the early nineteenth century.[19] During the late middle ages a partial shift took place in recruitment of slaves from the Black Sea regions to the eastern shores of the Adriatic. This change also meant a shift in terminology as from those times "slave" instead of "servus" became the common word in most European languages.[20]

It is hard to estimate the ratio between free, unfree and independent labour. Until the end of the Ancien Régime unfree labour seems to have been the rule in the christian part of the Mediterranean, whereas free and independent labour in the early modern period won ground in the cities and perhaps also in the mountainous regions.[21] For the muslim world in principle, however belated, the same holds true.

---

15. See Scammell, *World Encompassed.*
16. Patterson, *Slavery and Social Death*, resp. p. 157 and p. 152.
17. Apart from Verlinden, *Esclavage dans l'Europe Médiévale*, see also the chapters on Genoa, Venice and Portugal in Scammell, *World Encompassed.*
18. Phillips, "Old World Background", p. 48.
19. Verlinden, *Esclavage dans l'Europe Médiévale*, pp. 1020-1046.
20. *Idem*, pp. 797-798 and pp. 999-1010.
21. See Lucassen, *Migrant Labour.*

Eastern Europe[22]

Europe east of the river Elbe started in the middle ages from a similar background as the rest of Northern Europe[23] with after 1000 AD a diminishing importance of slavery as against serfdom. But from around the fifteenth century onwards socio-economic developments in central and eastern Europe started to diverge from the west. The demands of foreign trade on the one hand and a scarceness of labour in comparison to land on the other led to a reintroduction of unfree labour, called the period of the "second serfdom". In Russia this development took place in close relation to the centralization and expansion of the Russian state. This erosion of peasant freedom took place in three phases, marked by legislation in 1497 and 1649, introducing first the restriction and finally the prohibition of movement of the peasants and leading in the end to a system very close to chattel slavery. This system came to an end in Germany and Poland around 1800 and in Russia in 1861. However, this did not mean that from now on Russian labour relations were characterized by free labour. As Kolchin says: "New forms of dependency that provided the ex-bondsmen with at best semifreedom became the rule".[24]

The Atlantic World

When around 1500 demand for colonial products (initially sugar) rose spectacularly, plantation owners made a choice for unfree labour. Only African slaves were available at that time[25] as all other traditional sources for slavery in Europe were drying up. Europeans – in particular Balts and Slavs – had by now all been converted to Christianity or Islam and for that reason could no longer be enslaved by coreligionists. The Turks barred Europeans from the fertile slaving grounds north of the Black Sea. Muslims, always good to be enslaved now had been removed from the Iberian Peninsula, although of course berbers and moriscos from North Africa could be enslaved. Last, newly discovered Indians, mainly because they were not resistant to diseases from the old world, in the long run were replaced by black slaves, first in Brazil and later all over the new continent.[26]

Why did the new colonial masters make a choice for unfree labour? Why did – according to Stanley Engerman – two slaves arrive in British North America for each white immigrant before the American Revolution, or – to put it differently in the words of David Eltis – why were the Americas an extension

22. Mostly after Kolchin, *Unfree Labor*.
23. See also Patterson, *Slavery and Social Death*, p. 155 (map).
24. Kolchin, *Unfree Labor*, p. 375. See also Van der Linden, "Forced Labour and Non-Capitalist Industrialization", this volume, pp. 351-362, on forced labour under stalinism.
25. Phillips, "Old World Background", p. 57.
26. See also Curtin, *Rise and Fall of the Plantation Complex*, pp. 9 ff.

of Africa rather than Europe until the late nineteenth century?[27] Barbara Solow who quotes these authors points to the fact that there is no inherent reason why export-led growth is associated with plantation slavery. The examples she quotes are West African small holders producing cocoa, small Burmese peasants supplying rice, and later on, Canadian and Australian family farms producing wheat and wool.[28] The answer to all this questions had been given long ago by Edward Gibbon Wakefield in the 1820s, but is maybe bestknown in the form of H.J. Nieboer's classic *Slavery as an Industrial System* (The Hague 1900). His still valuable argument runs that profitable large scale export production by free dependent labour is not possible where land is abundant and therefore cheap. Indigenous populations and free immigrants alike will tend to be their own bosses, mainly in the form of peasant farming (either avoiding the market as much as possible, or owner-farmers, producing export crops). In these circumstances production of export crops, dependent on large scale capital investment – as is the case with sugar cane production par excellence – in these circumstances needs enforced labour. Only if land becomes scarce does the alternative of dependent free labour (induced by "want creation"[29] and therefore the creation of a labour market) become possible.

This theory is particularly attractive because it also offers an explanation for the widespread white indentured labour in British America that went hand in hand with chattel slavery.

Patrick Manning made a careful estimation of slaves exported from Africa and reaches a grand total of 18 million between 1500 and 1900, i.e. four millions in the first half and fourteen millions in the second half of this period, reaching its peak in the period 1750-1850.[30] The destination of these 18 million slaves was roughly 12 million to the Occident and six million to the Orient, viz. the muslim world. On top of this and in relation to slave exports, enslavement within Africa itself grew in importance, only to deminish in the late nineteenth and early twentieth centuries. It may have involved perhaps another 8 million persons.[31] Out of separate internal African, Oriental and Occidental markets, in the eighteenth and early nineteenth centuries, an integrated "world market for forced labour" as Manning calls it, came into being.[32] This market came to an end only very slowly. Notwithstanding British abolition of the slave trade in 1808 and of slavery in 1838, the western hemisphere was in urgent need of new slaves until slavery was abolished in Cuba in 1886 and Brazil in 1888. The

27. Solow, "Slavery and Colonization", p. 26.
28. *Idem*, p. 28.
29. Engerman, "Slavery and Emancipation", p. 338.
30. Manning, *Slavery and African Life*, p. 84.
31. *Idem*, p. 104.
32. *Idem*, pp. 102-103.

oriental trade continued even longer; and in Africa it only ended in 1935 with Ethiopia's denial of legal status of slavery.

As might be expected if one accepts the "free land" theory in order to explain unfree labour, the abolition of slavery in the Americas did lead to major readjustments in the procurement of labour. Freed slaves, mostly after a period of "apprenticeship" preferred to establish themselves as peasants rather than to turn into free wage labourers. The shortage of plantation labour therefore was met by another system of unfree labour: indentured labour of Asians in this case.[33] Curtin estimates that "for the Carribean as a whole the number of non-African coerced laborers" (mostly from China and India) "imported in the nineteenth century slightly exceeded the number of Africans who still came by way of the illegal slave trade".[34] This new overseas migration of unfree labour encompassed 2,5 million people between 1850 and 1920 worldwide.[35] However, contrary to the former period, this migration was not restricted to the Atlantic region, but took place everywhere plantation economy took roots, also in Asia. A well-known example is coolie labour on the tobacco plantations on eastern Sumatra.[36]

In conclusion, it is clear that unfree labour played a very important role in comparison to free and to independent labour in the Atlantic economy until very late in the nineteenth century. Maybe more important than exact percentage rates of the three forms – especially difficult to reach because we know so little about independent labour – is the fact that in general all three forms existed *next to each other*: they were not exclusive but in many ways complementary in many ways. This holds true especially for independent labourers, regularly entering and leaving the free labour market. Another complementary form is maybe temporal debt-induced participation in unfree labour by both free and independent labourers.

Disappearance and Abolition: How to Explain Unfree Labour

As has been shown in the preceding paragraph on the Old and New World up until 1900, unfree labour looms large. Its function for economic development is undeniable. It is teherefore important to ask what forces led to its demise and what reasons lay behind the varied chronology of its replacement by free labour. Three historiographical traditions on the possible causes of abolition of unfree labour have been proposed: the moral, the economic and the revolutionary argument.

33. See Galenson, "Rise and Fall of Indentured Servitude", pp. 1-26.
34. Curtin, *Rise and Fall of the Plantation Complex*, pp. 176-177.
35. Manning, *Slavery and African Life*, p. 104, quoting Engerman, who makes the subdivision of 1,6 million from India, 0,3 million from China and 0,5 from other places, like Japan and Java.
36. Breman, *Taming the Coolie Beast*.

The Moral Argument

The oldest and best-known argument runs as follows. Slavery is unwanted by moral forces outside the slave population itself.

In particular the role of Christianity and Enlightenment has been stressed. In this tradition the British Abolition Law of 1807 was "hailed by political leaders as the most altruistic act since Christ's crucifixion and as proof that Britain waged war for human brotherhood" in the words David Brion Davis.[37]

It is important to know that this kind of abolitionism was virtually absent from many christian and enlightened countries and, apart from England, only was a real force in the United States and – but for a short period – in France. In most other countries – the Italian cities of the early modern period, in colonial Denmark, Sweden, Holland, Portugal and Spain it did not play an important role.[38] Charles Verlinden has shown that Christianity and especially Catholicism did not impede slavery until very recently.[39] According to him, the gradual emergence of a carolingian *societas christana* prohibiting at least christian slaves, was a consequence rather than a cause of changing commercial streams of slaves.

Drescher has made it clear that it was less christian morality or Enlightenment and more a new economic morale in which free labour was the norm, both for employers and for employees, which led hundreds of thousands of Britons to plea for abolition. No wonder that Manchester, England's most successful boomtown of the 1780s, took the lead in the abolition movement of winter 1787/1788.[40] Thus, "the metropolitan free masses" formed "a critical new variable in the history of slaves" as distinct from Mediterranean Antiquity, medieval northern Europe, renaissance Italy and early modern Russia. Davis has a similar approach, arguing: "British antislavery provided a bridge between preindustrial and industrial values; by combining the ideal of emancipation with an insistence on duty and subordination, it helped to smooth the way to the future".[41]

The Economic Argument

This argument (also known as the Williams argument, put forward in Eric Williams' famous *Capitalism and Slavery* of 1944) states that slavery vanished because it became economically unprofitable. Recently, it met much criticism

---

37. Davis, "Capitalism, Abolitionism, and Hegemony", p. 215.
38. Drescher, "Paradigms Tossed", p. 197.
39. Verlinden, *Esclavage dans l'Europe Médiévale*, pp. 20 ff. See also pp. 1031-1032 (the occurrence of papal slaves until the late eighteenth century).
40. Drescher, "Paradigms Tossed". See also Engerman, "Slavery and Emancipation", pp. 323-333.
41. Davis, "Capitalism, Abolitionism, and Hegemony", p. 217; also p. 225 and Temperley, "Eric Williams and Abolition", pp. 229-257.

and seems to be no longer supported by most scholars. Engerman made it clear for the Americas that at the time of abolition "slavery was expanding and it took political and military action to bring it to a halt". He thinks the same argument can be applied to European serfdom, following Domar and Machina and Rudolph.[42] On the other hand, notwithstanding political action leading to formal abolition, unfree labour could continue to be the major form of labor relation, albeit in disguise. This occurred in particular where racial differences determined the division of the labourers.[43]

The Revolutionary Argument

This argument says that slavery vanished because it was unwanted by the victims. According to its adherents the most important factor in ending unfree labour systems was armed resistance and revolt. For Antiquity and the early Middle Ages this point has been defended by Pierre Dockès, not very convincingly however.[44] Robin Blackburn is a strong advocate of this theory for the early phase of abolitionism in the Americas until 1848.[45]

To conclude, nowadays scholars seem to agree that slavery has been abolished on purpose, either by the efforts of philantropists or of the victims themselves. In order to decide between the two schools of thought, the first and the third argument need a more deepened confrontation yet.

Labour History and Unfree Labour

The emergence and function of productive unfree labour has to be interpreted primarily in the framework of economic and social history. Patterson stresses its relationship with the occurrence of long distance trade and commerce, many others point to the relation between unfree labour and capitalism. A denial of this relation between labour history and economic history may lead to odd conclusions, for instance where Peter Kolchin concludes that "slavery and serfdom were fundamentally noncapitalist productive systems, increasing antagonistic to the emerging bourgeois world order, because they lacked capitalism's basic ingredient: a market for labor-power (that is, labor hire) [...] thus marked by an essential contradiction between the commercial orientation of

42. Engerman, "Slavery and Emancipation", pp. 327 ff. See also Blackburn, *Overthrow of Colonial Slavery*.
43. Baud, "Sugar and Unfree Labour", pp. 301–325.
44. Dockès, *Medieval Slavery and Liberation*. For a highly critical review by Ellen Meiksins Wood see *Social History*, 9 (1984), pp. 101–103.
45. Blackburn, *Overthrow of Colonial Slavery*.

the masters with respect to the *distribution* of their product and the noncapitalist nature of its *production*".[46] All depends on the definition of capitalism of course. As we may be sure by now that there is a strong relation between the occurrence of international economic development and unfree labour (without saying that these developments are impossible without unfree labour) and that consequently unfree labour cannot be seen as a phenomenon, restricted to some primitive or backward situations, we might do well to focus the social history of free and unfree labour to the following three topics.

In the first place a comparison between labour relations under conditions of either free or unfree labour. Here, as well as under the next point, the concept of "honour"[47] may be very useful, as it can be applied not only to unfree labour, but also to the labour consciousness of free industrial workers and artisans.

In the second place relations between free dependent, unfree and "independent" labour. Because of the complementarity, stated above, both employers and labourers for most of the period discussed in this paper had to adjust to all three forms. To what extent did free and unfree labourers compete, did they rally, did they exploit each other?

In the third place the complementarity between the three systems. There is a constant change of status of persons belonging to the three groups. Sometimes it is a tricklet, sometimes a stream. Equally important as the actual change of status is the possiblity of change, either as something to aspire at (cf. the function of manumission, as explained by Patterson; but also the function of marroon society), or as something to fear and to be avoided. These possibilities were part of the habitus of employers and employed.

Last, the three systems can have also reciprocal ideological functions, the meaning of abolition for the emancipation of workers and women being best known.

46. Kolchin, *Unfree Labor*, p. 360.
47. Patterson, *Slavery and Social Death*, p. 13.

Some Observations on Unfree Labour, Capitalist Restructuring, and Deproletarianization[*]

Tom Brass

Both historically and actually, there is a complex interrelationship between the existence of unfree labour and the process of class formation and struggle in the course of agrarian transformation. However, much current writing about rural labour in the Third World is based on three interrelated assumptions. First, that labour market imperfections are always the fault of peasants resisting the attempts of capital to proletarianize them. Second, that capitalist penetration of agriculture always transforms peasants into proletarians, in the full meaning of the latter term. And third, that where these exist (non-urban contexts, backward agriculture, and/or underdeveloped countries), unfree relations are always unproblematically pre-capitalist forms of production destined to be eliminated in the course of this process. In the Marxist approach which follows, it will be argued that each of these three assumptions is wrong.

Conversely, it will be suggested here that capitalism is not only compatible with unfree labour but in certain situations actually prefers this to a free workforce; accordingly, the interrelationship between free and unfree labour, and in particular the process of deproletarianization, is determined both historically and contemporaneously by class struggle (waged from above as well as from below). In support of this view it will be necessary to confront two interrelated revisionist interpretations of unfree production relations: on the one hand neoclassical economic theory, and on the other the "culturalist" arguments derived from moral economy, survival strategies and resistance theory, (re-) interpretations which involve either a denial or a dilution of unfree labour. Faced with the co-existence of unfreedom and capitalist production, yet unable to theorize the connection between them, one particular variant of Marxism (the semi-feudal thesis) is in some senses a mirror image of revisionism. The latter accepts the presence of capitalism, and accordingly redefines unfree relations of production as a form of free wage labour; the former, by contrast, accepts the presence of unfreedom, but redefines the mode of production itself as feudal or semi-feudal.

[*] The writer wishes to thank Henry Bernstein for a stimulating discussion of some of the theoretical issues raised in section 1.

1. *Marxism, Capitalism, and Unfree Labour*

Any definition of what constitutes an unfree production relation has to begin by focussing on the labour power of the subject as private property, and hence as an actual/potential commodity over which its owner has disposition.[1] Unlike a free labourer, who is able to enter or withdraw from the labour market at will, due to the operation of ideological constraints or extra-economic coercion an unfree worker is unable personally to sell his or her own labour power (in other words, to commodify it), regardless of whether this applies to employment that is either of time-specific duration (e.g., contract work, convict labour, indentured labour) or of an indefinite duration (chattel slavery).

For many writers on the subject, the unfreedom inherent in chattel slavery derives from property rights exercised by one person over another. All forms of work relationship that do not entail ownership of persons are consequently regarded as free. Such a view, however, overlooks additional forms of unfreedom which occur in situations where the labouring subject is prevented from entering the labour market under any circumstances (in which case labour power ceases to be a commodity), is prevented from entering the labour market in person (labour power remaining a commodity in such circumstances, but is sold by someone other than its owner), and is permitted to enter the labour-market in person, but only with the consent and at the convenience of someone other than its owner. It is precisely these kinds of unfreedom which arise in the case of convict, bonded, contract and indentured labour.[2]

Like chattel slavery, such relationships entail the loss on the part of a debtor and/or his kinsfolk of the right to sell their labour power at prevailing free market rates during the period of bondage. Unlike chattel slavery, however, where the *person* of the slave is itself the subject of an economic transaction, in

---

1. A number of important issues relating to the theorization of unfreedom in different historical/geographical contexts cannot be covered here. These include questions of methodology (the nature of the written and/or historical record, the methodological accessability of coercion, the enforcement of debt-servicing labour obligations by means of indirect pressure exercised through actual/fictive kinship and caste networks, etc.) and theory (non-economic concepts of unfreedom, defined in terms of fraud/deception/trickery, maltreatment), all of which are addressed elsewhere. Brass, "Coffee and Rural Proletarianization", pp. 143-152; "Free and Unfree Rural Labour in Puerto Rico", pp. 181-193; "Elementary Strictures of Kinship", pp. 56-68; "Unfree Labour and Capitalist Restructuring in the Agrarian Sector", pp. 50-77; "Slavery Now"; "Latin American *Enganche* System", pp. 74-103; "Class Struggle and the Deproletarianization", pp. 36-67; "Market Essentialism", pp. 225-244; and Brass and Bernstein, "Introduction: Proletarianization and Deproletarianization", pp. 1-40.
2. Needless to say, the conceptual extension of unfreedom to include labour relations other than slavery is controversial, and the subject of much debate. For more recent attempts to define unfree labour, see Miles, *Capitalism and Unfree Labour*; and Ramachandran, *Wage Labour and Unfreedom in Agriculture*, ch. 8.

the case of a bonded, convict, contract or indentured labourer it is the latter's *labour power* which is bought, sold, and controlled without the consent of its owner. Hence the frequent conflation of these arrangements with the free wage relation, notwithstanding the fact that while a free wage labourer may personally dispose of his/her own labour power (by selling it to whomsoever s/he wishes, or withdrawing from the labour market altogether), neither a chattel slave nor a bonded/convict/contract/indentured labourer possesses this right. All the latter may appear in the free labour market, therefore, but not as autonomous sellers of their own labour power.[3]

The necessary starting point for a consideration of the connection between unfreedom and capitalism is Marx's emphasis on the freedom of wage labour in the relationship between labour and capital, the social relation of production that constitutes the distinctive character of capitalism. As is well known, the designation of the freedom of wage labour has a double aspect: labouring subjects ("direct producers") are "freed" from access to the means of production that secure their reproduction, and consequently they are (and must be) free to exchange their labour power with capital for wages with which to purchase subsistence.[4]

Generally speaking, both aspects of wage labour capture the difference between capitalism and pre-capitalist modes of production. The first aspect signals the moment of *dispossession* of pre-capitalist producers, part of the process of primitive accumulation. Dispossession is the condition of the formation of a class of free wage labour which is the second aspect, or moment of *proletarianization*. The contrast here is that, whereas in pre-capitalist modes of production labour is exploited by means of extra-economic compulsion, under capitalism proletarians are owners of the commodity labour power which they exchange with capital under the "dull compulsion of economic forces".

Having outlined these familiar positions, it is useful to interrogate them a little further. First, with regard to the moment of dispossession, it is necessary to recognize that not all social subjects in all pre-capitalist formations necessarily

---

3. It is important to distinguish between a free market in labour, in which both free and unfree labour power can circulate, and a free labour market, in which only free wage labour circulates. A result of the failure to make this distinction is market essentialism (see below), a theoretical effect of which is the conflation of two relationally distinct transactions: on the one hand a direct exchange between worker and employer (labour power as the private property *of* the individual subject), and on the other an indirect transaction involving only employers (or the latter and contractors), one of whom transfers an unfree worker to the other (private property *in* the labour power of the individual subject). In the antebellum American South, for example, plantation slaves were no less such for being hired out by their owners, either to other planters or to manufacturing employers in local towns. Starobin, *Industrial Slavery*, pp. 128-37.
4. On this point, see Marx, *Capital*, I, pp. 271-272.

had property or usufruct rights in land and/or other means of production, let alone that all pre-capitalist formations guaranteed the means of subsistence. Historically, strongly differentiated pre-capitalist formations in Asia and Latin America have contained landless labourers "available" for recruitment by capitalism.[5] In short, dispossession of pre-capitalist producers was not always necessary to the (initial) formation of a class of capitalist wage labour.

This brings us to the second, and more general, moment of proletarianization. This too has an important double aspect, albeit often overlooked or confused, that is conveyed theoretically in the distinction between *labour power* and *labour*, and more concretely in the difference between *labour market* and *labour process*. Labour power is the capacity to work that is the *property* of workers (their mental and physical energies): the commodity they exchange with capital for wages. Labour is the *use value* of labour power: the expenditure of the mental and physical energies of workers in a production process controlled by capitalists, the products of which are the property of the latter and not the former. Correspondingly, the labour market designates the site in which labour power is exchanged, and the labour process the site in which labour is exploited by the imperatives of capitalist production, accumulation, and profit. Evidently, both labour markets and labour processes within capitalism exhibit a wide range of variation in their specific conditions, how their contradictions are manifested, and the forms of class struggle to which they give rise.

What is the connection between on the one hand the theoretical rationale of the freedom of wage labour and on the other the pervasive incidence of *unfree* wage labour throughout the history of capitalism? Accordingly, two suggestions are made here. First, given this interconnectedness between accumulation and unfree labour, that in particular instances it might be more appropriate to invert the usual way in which the question is posed: that is, to problematize the achievement of free wage labour rather than the existence of unfreedom. And second, that assaults by capital (actual or potential, preemptive or reactive) on the freedom of wage labour − the ability of workers to enter *and withdraw* from particular labour markets and labour processes − are a *general* feature of capitalism.[6] That is, the capitalist class as a whole (or its representatives) in some cases,

5. On the pre-colonial/pre-capitalist presence and extent of landless labour in South India, see Kumar, *Land and Caste in South India*; Hjejle, "Slavery and Agricultural Bondage", pp. 71-126. For Asia generally, see Breman, *Labour Migration and Rural Transformation*. For the presence of an extensive "ambulatory" migrant workforce, composed of landless labour, in the Central Valley region of Chile from the mid-nineteenth century onwards, see Bauer, *Chilean Rural Society*.

6. On this point, see texts by *inter alia* Kloosterboer, *Involuntary Labour since the Abolition of Slavery*; Aufhauser, "Slavery and Scientific Management", pp. 811-824; Van Onselen, *Chibaro*; Corrigan, "Feudal Relics or Capitalist Monuments?", pp. 435-463; Legassick, "Gold, Agriculture, and Secondary Industry", pp. 175-200; Mundle, *Backwardness and Bondage*;

or particular groups/types of capitalists and/or individual capitalists in other cases, seek to define and redefine the labouring subject so as to limit the exercise of his/her freedom as the owner of the commodity labour power.

Such actions and struggles on the part of capital (with their economic, political and ideological expressions) aim to bring about *deproletarianization*, in the sense of diminishing or eliminating altogether the freedom of wage labour as defined above: the ability of owners of the commodity labour power to exchange it as they choose (on which more, see below). In other words, it is precisely by means of deproletarianization that capital is able to effect a *double* dispossession of its workforce: both from the means of labour, and also from the means of commodifying labour power itself. Moreover, the ability of capital to engineer unfreedom in labour markets – to impose restrictions in the process of *recruiting* workers – has implications for the freedom of capital in *using* workers in labour processes from which they are unable to withdraw. Evidently certain historical conditions, such as those of colonial imperialism, provide capital with reasons and opportunities for waging this particular kind of class struggle against labour. In this connection we should also note that the trajectories of wage labour are often marked by competition between branches/groups of capitalists and/or individual capitalists for access to and control over labour power.

On the side of workers, this suggests that their class struggle against capital is commonly a struggle to assert, reassert or extend their freedom to dispose of their own labour power: either separately from or combined with class struggle to destroy capitalism, therefore, such actions always constitute a potential/actual threat to existing property relations.[7] Accordingly, when workers seek to defend and exercise their freedom as owners of labour power, they are also required to contest on an individual or collective basis the attempts by capital to impose/reimpose and reproduce unfreedom both in the labour market and the labour process. That the experience of the proletarian condition does not automatically generate an immediate, unambiguous or exclusive class conscious-ness on the part of workers, therefore, may in given circumstances be a conse-quence of the fact that the aim of deproletarianization is precisely to prevent, deflect or distort the development of just such a consciousness of class. For this

---

Meillassoux, *Maidens, Meal and Money*, pp. 91 ff.; Patnaik, "Introduction", Brass, "Unfree Labour and Capitalist Restructuring", and "Slavery Now"; Miles, *Capitalism and Unfree Labour*; Cohen, *New Helots*; Zegeye and Ishemo, *Forced Labour and Migration*.

7. This applied in the case of the antebellum American South, for example, where the debates on slavery taking place during the 1840s were structured by an underlying fear of a threat to property relations. Concerned that an emergent rural proletariat would ultimately demand the expropriation of the Southern landowning class, therefore, anti-abolitionists such as Cardozo and Dew advocated ruling class unity between Northern property owners and Southern planters in defence of slavery in order to counter a potential working class challenge to existing property rights. Kaufman, *Capitalism, Slavery, and Republican Values*, pp. 121 ff.

reason, the experience of *becoming* a worker in the employ of capital, or the change from class-in-itself to class-for-itself, has crucial implications for the self-perception and the perception-of-others on the part of the labouring subject, as well as the forms taken by any resulting political action. Viewed thus, unfree relations of production are an integral part of both class struggle and capitalist accumulation in the context of much Third World agriculture.

2. Revisionist Concepts of Unfree Labour

In contrast to the marxist interpretation outline above, of unfreedom as an exploitative relationship which permits the extraction of surplus labour, and which is either reconstituted or dissolved in the process of class struggle, the revisionist project which structures much recent writing on unfreedom eliminates the element of coercion from most or all agrarian relationships, and subsequently reclassifies them as free wage labour. Hence revisionist contributions to debates about rural labour theorize what marxists term unfreedom as a form of equal exchange, or a benign (and thus tension-free) arrangement to the benefit of all parties to the relation.[8] Eschewing objective definitions, these texts adopt subjective criteria when conceptualizing freedom/ unfreedom, and consequently maintain that what outside observers wrongly interpret as unfree relations derives from the voluntary entry by rural labour into "reciprocal" and essentially desirable working arrangements which provide the labouring subject with economic security in the form of a "subsistence guarantee" or "employment insurance".[9] Accordingly, revisionists theorize the debt component of relations such as indenture, peonage, contract or bonded labour as evidence not

8. Texts which subscribe to this view include, *inter alia*, Miers and Kopytoff, *Slavery in Africa*; Bauer, "Rural Workers in Spanish America", pp. 34-63; Cotlear, *Sistema del Enganche del Siglo XX*; Cross, "Debt Peonage Reconsidered", pp. 473-495; Reid, *Slavery, Bondage and Dependency in Southeast Asia*; Bardhan, *Land, Labor, and Rural Poverty*; Breman, *Of Peasants, Migrants and Paupers*; Hart, *Power, Labor, and Livlihood*; Hart, "Exclusionary Labour Arrangements", pp. 681-696; Knight, "Mexican Peonage", pp. 41-74; Taylor, "Earning a Living in Hualgayoc", pp. 103-124; Knight, "Debt Bondage", pp. 102-117. For the way in which pro-slavery ideology in the Antebellum American South projected unfreedom as beneficial to its subject ("positive good") and cast planter/slave relations in terms of "reciprocity", see Glickstein, *Concepts of Free Labor*; and Tise, *Proslavery*.
9. Among those who interpret unfreedom as a form of "subsistence guarantee", "employment insurance", and/or "patronage" are Breman, *Peasants, Migrants*, pp. 127 ff.; Bardhan, *Land, Labor*, pp. 175-176; Bauer, "Rural Workers", pp. 44, 56, 62; Cotlear, *Sistema del Enganche del Siglo XX*, pp. 37-39; Cross, "Debt Peonage", pp. 488, 490; Taylor, "Earning a Living", p. 112; and Ramachandran, *Wage Labour and Unfreedom in Agriculture*, p. 254.

of the coercive power exercised by employers but much rather of the enhanced bargaining power exercised by workers.[10]

Significantly, this revisionist view concerning unfree social relations of production is epistemologically no different from (and in some instances is explicitly determined by) neoclassical economic theory.[11] Within such an economic framework, silence on the part of the choice-making subject is interpreted as assent: accordingly, a result of a methodological inability and/or theoretical unwillingness to address non-economic aspects of unfreedom, and the consequent failure to problematize coercion, is the epistemological impermissibility of unfreedom within a neo-classical economic framework. Having banished coercion, neoclassical economics is left with a form of market essentialism, a reductionist approach whereby anything and everything involving the employer/worker relationship is *ipso facto* proof of the harmonious operation of a free (or "perfect") market in which choice-making individual labourers express subjective preferences.[12]

The fact that within this framework value is subjective and not objective, and consequently all parties to market exchanges receive the value of their own individual economic contribution and nothing more, necessarily precludes analytical categories such as exploitation, class formation/reproduction, and class struggle. Since neoclassical economic theory cannot accept that in some circum-

---

10. For an example of a revisionist text which regards unfreedom as evidence of the enhanced bargaining power of agricultural labour (= worker "self-empowerment"), see Bauer, "Rural Workers", pp. 46-47, 54. A variant of this position is the postmodern view of Prakash (see below), whereby unfree workers symbolically "win" battles in the ideological domain which in economic terms they either lose or do not fight.

11. It is not without significance that neoclassical economic theory, which emerged in the 1870s, was an explicitly anti-marxist response to the development of the labour movement. In politico-ideological terms, it constituted a project of innateness, or the dehistoricizing and reconstituting as immutable of what had been regarded by classical economic theory as terrain changed by conflict; in neo-classical analysis, such terrain became an unchanging and thus a "natural" socio-economic order.

12. For the application of a neoclassical economic framework to unfree labour, see *inter alia*, Evans, "Some Notes on Coerced Labor", pp. 861-866; Brown and Reynolds, "Debt Peonage Re-examined", pp. 862-871; Fogel and Engerman, *Time on the Cross*; Galenson, *White Servitude*; Higgs, *Competition and Coercion*; Cotlear, *Sistema del Enganche del Siglo XX*; Shlomowitz, "Markets for Indentured and Time-expired Melanesian Labour, pp. 70-91; Bardhan, *Land Labour*, pp. 61, 67, 71-72, 83-84, 86, 124-126, 157, 175; Engerman, "Servants to slaves to servants", pp. 263-294; Jagannathan, *Informal Markets*, pp. 38 ff.; Srinivasan, "On Choice among Creditors", pp. 203-220; Lal, *Hindu Equilibrium*, pp. 120-126. For critiques from different theoretical viewpoints of the methods utilized in this process, see Gutman, *Slavery*; Sutch, " Treatment Received by American Slaves, pp. 335-438; Davids *et al.*, *Reckoning with Slavery*; Greenberg, "New Economic History", pp. 131-141; Mandle, *Roots of Black Poverty*, pp. 22-27; Fox-Genovese and Genovese, *Fruits of Merchant Capital*, pp. 91 ff.; Graves, "Nature and Origins of Pacific Islands Labour Migration", pp. 113-115; and Brass, "Market Essentialism", pp. 225 ff.

stances employers prefer to recruit unfree labour, and thus may actually strive to bring about an imperfect market, it correspondingly fails to recognize the attempt by either party to change the relationship from what it is to what in the opinion of the respective protagonists it ought to be. The absence of this crucial dimension – class struggle – in effect negates the neoclassical view of the market as an arena of harmony, and undermines not only the notion of an equilibrium structuring the exchange between employer and labourer, but also the assumption that rural employers (planters, landlords, rich peasants, labour contractors) are everywhere and always interested in the operation of a free market, and strive towards its realization.

Much the same is true of the frequently invoked "survival strategies" framework.[13] Insofar as it entails an "adaptive" approach by an individual choice-making subject, therefore, the concept "survival" is similarly compatible with neoclassical economic theory. Within such a framework, moreover, there is an analogous progression in textual interpretation whereby "survival" shifts rapidly from being an end in itself to being a *positive* countervailing aspect of the agrarian context under consideration (plantation, estate, rich peasant holding), a position which then links up with the neoclassical claim that rural workers actively *chose* such (unfree) employment, which consequently could have been neither exploitative nor oppressive.[14] Significantly, the "survival strategies" framework is in many ways similar to the notion of "self-help" which structures much of the currently fashionable theory of peasant "resistance", itself strongly influenced by the work of James Scott.[15] Where resistance occurred on the plantation or estate system, the argument goes, then the unfree relations of production structuring its labour process were consequently rendered unviable; from this position it is once again a short step to the neoclassical economic argument that, as workers could have made it non-operational had they chosen so to do, the continued existence in such contexts of unfreedom was *ipso facto* chosen by the workers themselves, hence non-coercive/non-exploitative and to their advantage.

Even some variants of Marxism also overlook the fact that unfreedom is constucted and undermined by class struggle. Ironically, attempts by neoclassical theory to combat negative portrayals of black slaves on the cotton plantations of the antebellum American South through arguments about "positive" aspects of black *economic* participation/autonomy in the plantation system (material well-

---

13. See, for example, Lieten *et al.*, *Women, Migrants and Tribals*.
14. For just such a positive theorization of "survival" by female indentured labour on plantations in Fiji, see Lal, "Kunti's cry", p. 179.
15. For more recent examples of the ubiquitous "resistance" theory, see Scott, *Weapons of the Weak*, Colburn, *Everyday Forms of Peasant Resistance*, and Haynes and Prakash, *Resistance and Everyday Social Relations*. For the application by Scott of his "resistance" framework to chattel slavery, see "Domination, Acting, and Fantasy", pp. 55-84.

being, self-improvement, etc.) find parallels in attempts by left scholars similarly to challenge negative stereotypes by invoking positive images of a resilient black *culture* produced by plantation slaves themselves.[16] The difficulty faced by both these politically opposed viewpoints is that they license a discursive slide whereby the defence of blacks (implicitly or explicitly) may ultimately – as the case of Fogel and Engerman demonstrates – be transformed into a *celebration* of the plantation, and in particular its mode of unfreedom. This in turn opens up a theoretical space for anti-universalizing/decentered postmodern analysis: the latter objects to (and thus denies the efficacy/existence of) unfreedom on the grounds that, in the overarching metanarratives of colonial and capitalist discourse, free labour is privileged as the totalizing agent of universal progress. Like neoclassical economic theory, which precludes a connection between capitalism and unfreedom by redefining the latter as free wage labour, post-modernism dismisses bondage as a figment of western discourse, thereby banishing it from indigenous accumulation and simultaneously reifying unfreedom as a cultural "other".

In the postmodern framework of Taussig, for example, the debt peonage relation encountered in the Putumayo region of Peru during the Upper Amazon rubber boom of the early 1900s merges into and becomes nothing more than a specifically cultural manifestation of irreducible "otherness"/difference; accordingly, unfreedom possesses only a discursive existence, linked to the construction by colonists of a mythological/folkloric image of indigenous horror/terror (based on savagery/rebelliousness/cannibalism), and projected by them onto the tribal workforce they recruited/employed.[17] Rather than connecting the existence of terror/unfreedom in such a context to struggles over the commodification of labour power, and identifying thereby a specifically economic role for terror in the enforcement of unfreedom which in turn licenses the process of capital accumulation, he deprivileges/ banishes economics and reifies ideology.[18]

16. For the economic self-improvement/achievement of black slaves on the plantation in the American South, see Fogel and Engerman, *Time on the Cross*, pp. 108-109, 127. For examples from the other end of the political spectrum of a "culturalist" defence of slaves (*not* slavery), see James, *Spheres of Existence*, pp. 173-190; and Genovese, *Roll, Jordan, Roll*. In part, the defence of slave economic life on the plantation by those on the political right and of slave culture by those on the political left were both attempts to rescue black slaves from the negative image associated with the passive/docile "sambo" stereotype projected by Elkins, *Slavery*.

17. Taussig, "Culture of Terror", pp. 467-497; Taussig, *Shamanism*.

18. At some points Taussig maintains that in the Upper Amazon region a market for labour power was absent, and is therefore correspondingly dismissive of Casement's attribution of terror/un-freedom to a scarcity of workers; elsewhere, however, Taussig appears to accept not merely the existence of labour shortages but also the economic irrationality of destroying scarce workers and that the object of terror was in fact to increase rubber production. "Culture", pp. 475-477, 488; *Wild Man*, pp. 46, 52 ff. For Casement's account of Putumayo, see Singleton-Gates and Girodias, *Black Diaries*, pp. 201-315. In other words, terror combined

Unsurprisingly, Taussig opts instead for the non-economic/innateness of Foucault's postmodern concept of power, whereby the exercise of terror becomes an irrational end in itself; in short, a Nietzschean view of terror/unfreedom as chaotic, purposeless, and hence unchanging/unchangeable.[19] The resulting analysis oscillates uneasily between two competing discourses about debt peonage in the Upper Amazon region: one by Roger Casement condemning the use of unfree labour for rubber production, the other by employers supporting its use, and (because of "epistemic murk") neither of which according to Taussig is it possible to categorize as true or false.[20] Like other revisionists, Taussig comes near not just to endorsing the "lazy native" myth, but also to questioning both the actuality of terror – as distinct from the efficacy of discourse about this (= uncorroborated "stories" which are believed, and thus possess a materiality regardless of whether or not they are accurate) – and ultimately the reasons for together with the existence of debt peonage itself.[21]

The more recent postmodern (re)interpretations of unfreedom by Prakash and McCreery not only attempt to give voice to the mute indigenous subject of Taussig's analysis, but in so doing push the problematic theorization of unfreedom structuring his postmodern framework to its logical conclusion. Since Taussig does not address the issue of how unfreedom was perceived "from below" by the tribal worker, for him the question of a negative/positive perception of such a relation by the subject of labour does not arise, and consequently remains open. In seeking to answer precisely this question, and attempting to supply this missing voice-from-below, texts by both Prakash and

---

with unfreedom possessed a twofold economic object: to intensify output on the one hand, and on the other to warn potential absconders of the consequences of flight/disobedience. As in the case of the tobacco plantations in the Dutch colony of Sumatra, therefore, executions and floggings of tribal workers in the Putumayo region took place in the labour process itself. Breman, *Taming the Coolie Beast*; Taussig, "Culture", pp. 475-477.

19. "Culture", pp. 491, 495; *Wild Man*, pp. 27, 69, 442-443.
20. "Culture", pp. 470, 494; *Wild Man*, pp. 27-29. This equivocation on the part of Taussig is prefigured in the similarly postmodern ambiguity of de Man, who notes: "It is always possible to face up to any experience (to excuse any guilt), because the experience always exists simultaneously as fictional discourse and as empirical event and it is never possible to decide which one of the two possibilities is the right one. The indecision makes it possible to excuse the bleakest of crimes because, as a fiction, it escapes from the constraints of guilt and innocence." De Man, *Allegories of Reading*, p. 293. The outcome of this framework, in which language is decoupled from material reality, is ethical relativism, which in turn naturalizes horror/terror/(unfreedom). That such a position licenses complicity with fascism is confirmed by the cases not only of de Man himself but also of Heidegger, Blanchot, and Derrida.
21. For Taussig's views on the "lazy native", see "Culture", p. 490. Other revisionist endorsements of the "lazy native" myth are noted in Brass, "Revisionist Reinterpretations", pp. 90-91. For Taussig's questioning of the actuality of terror/unfreedom, see "Culture", p. 494; *Wild Man*, pp. 60, 65-66.

McCreery illustrate how a postmodern and revisionist concept of unfreedom is compatible with the concepts "popular culture" and "resistance" theory.[22]

Like Taussig, Prakash maintains that because it lacked a discursive form in the precolonial era, debt bondage in the Indian state of Bihar automatically had no relational existence; he concludes that unfreedom is the significant and invented other of "colonial discourse", and consequently that freedom is the correspondingly unacceptable embodiment of totalizing Eurocentric notions of human destiny.[23] Against this it is possible to make two points. First, that as with Taussig, this symptomatically postmodern outside-of-discourse/language-there-is-nothing view is a palpably idealist position.[24] And second, that – again like Taussig – Prakash fails accordingly to distinguish between an *ideology* of unfreedom (which may indeed have been absent, although precisely what constitutes proof of this remains problematic) and *de facto* unfreedom, which had a material existence that predated colonialism (regardless of whether or not it was identified by its subject as such).

Notwithstanding his claim that hierarchical inversion in oral tradition was a form of "resistance" practiced by unfree labour in the southern part of Bihar in eastern India, Prakash finally concedes that, after all, it might just be the case that "the resistance contained in oral traditions was not particularly significant; they may have made the burden of bondage a little easier to shoulder, moderated the impact of hierarchy, but did little to change the 'real' condition of the Bhuinyas [...] one may say that the oral traditions deluded the Bhuinyas into thinking that they were reconstituting hierarchy and labour relations when, in fact, they did nothing of the sort".[25] In other words, what is idealized by Prakash as a form of "resistance" may amount to no more than a contextually/historically specific form of false consciousness.[26]

---

22. Prakash, "Bonded Labour in South Bihar", pp. 178-205; Prakash, *Bonded Histories*; Prakash, "Becoming a Bhuinya", pp. 145-174; and "History and Historiography of Rural Labourers", and "Reproducing Inequality", pp. 1-46, 282-304.

23. Prakash, "Bonded Labour", pp. 197-198. Not the least of the many difficulties which confront the postmodern framework of Prakash is its refusal to countenance any alternative to a specifically bourgeois/individualist concept of freedom, thereby ignoring completely the socialist approach in which unfreedom is negated by collective freedom based on class.

24. For an instance of the application of an idealized/"culturalist" approach to the more general question of rural labour in Colonial India, see Prakash, "History and Historiography of Rural Labourers".

25. Prakash, "Becoming a Bhuinya", p. 170. Much the same can be said of his attempt to inscribe "resistence" into spirit cults in south Bihar. Prakash, "Reproducing Inequality".

26. Part of the difficulty here is that the concept "false" consciousness is itself epistemologically impermissible within a postmodern framework. Since Prakash not merely accepts but celebrates the plurality of the ideological, by definition no form of consciousness can be categorized as "false". Generally speaking, postmodernism rejects consciousness of class as an Eurocentric concept that involves an "outsider" unacceptably imputing a politically appropriate, logically

Another symptomatic text in this regard is that by McCreery, where the culturally-based "resistance" theory of Scott is combined with a "survival strategy" framework in order to invert the meaning of unfreedom on coffee plantations in Guatemala during the late nineteenth century. Despite noting that "[f]orce, the coffee planters reasoned, was what the Indian understood, force would do, and force was what the Indians got", that "[l]abor recruiters and state agents in villages jailed workers, beat and defrauded them, kidnapped their wives and children, and burned their houses", that from the 1870s "the state [...] had the ability to deliver effective and immediate violence to the countryside", and that "[l]ife on the run and cut off from [...] the community, [...] was precarious [...] [Labour contractors and village authorities], pressed to deliver labor, [...] increasingly took their search for [workers] into every corner of the municipality, making evasion more difficult", McCreery nevertheless claims that the state was powerless to enforce unfreedom on the indigenous population.[27] For this reason, he theorizes the debt bondage relation in a positive fashion, as a mechanism that enabled rural workers "to force from their employers as much money as possible"; accordingly, bonded labour is subsumed by McCreery under the rubric of "culture" which – along with folk tales, dances, religious ceremony and ritual – becomes yet another form of unproblematically successful "resistance" on the part of indigenous communities.[28]

In many ways, these different attempts to revise the meaning of unfreedom constitute a new variety of functionalism. The old functionalism of Durkheim and Parsons maintained that the survival of a particular institutional form (such as religion) was linked to its capacity to satisfy basic societal needs, thereby contributing to what was perceived as social stability; as critiques pointed out, however, this amounted to a framework in which institutions were functional-for-those-who-rule. By contrast, the new functionalism of the "survival strategies" theory and postmodernism argues that the continued existence of institutional forms such as indenture and debt bondage is similarly linked to their ability to meet basic social needs, but this time not of the subjects but rather of the objects of rule; that is, unfreedom as a relationship that is perceived as being functional-for-those-who-are-ruled.

consistent and historically necessary set of universalistic beliefs to particular socio-economic agents. However, without a concept of consciousness that discriminates between notions of "true" and "false" (which in turn entails the theorization of a *politics* that transcends the randomness of non-specific/ amorphous conflictive practices), it becomes possible to identify each and every single component of behaviour/activity (or existence) as yet another form of "resistance".

27. McCreery, "Hegemony and Repression", pp. 161, 164, 166, 168. For earlier, non-revisionist, accounts by the same author of unfreedom in Guatemala, see McCreery, "Debt Servitude in Rural Guatemala", pp. 735-59; "'Odious Feudalism'", pp. 99-117.
28. McCreery, "Hegemony and Repression", pp. 167, 169, 172.

3. Unfree Labour and the Feudal/Semi-Feudal Thesis

A major theoretical shortcoming in the revisionist thesis is the absence of a concept of agrarian class structure, and therefore class struggle.[29] Unsurprisingly, this results in turn in a fundamental misrecognition concerning the reason for the presence of unfree relations. In the case of Latin America, for example, revisionists perceive bonded labour (the *enganche* system) as a necessary element in the formation of a labour market: however, because unfreedom is regarded as a pre-capitalist relation, and thus equated with feudalism/semi-feudalism or "refeudalization", yet because the enganche operates in the context of capitalist agriculture, it is theoretically necessary to recast the debt bondage relation as a form of free wage labour.[30] Such a relationship, it is implied or asserted, was (and is) the only way in which peasants could be persuaded to sell their labour power and so be drawn voluntarily into the process of capitalist production. Since on the one hand the element of coercion has been eliminated, and on the other primitive accumulation made possible, it now becomes feasible within the revisionist framework to argue that bonded labour represents not only an economically progressive tendency (signalling a transformation from feudalism to capitalism) but also constitutes a development toward or actual evidence of proletarianization. When confronted with the co-existence of unfree labour and capitalism, therefore, revisionists respond by accepting the presence of capitalism but redefine the relation of production.

Precisely the opposite procedure is followed by the variant of Marxism held by proponents of the semi-feudal thesis. Similarly incapable of theorizing the connection between capitalism and unfree labour, in this case it is not the production relation but the mode of production which is redefined. Within such a framework, therefore, relations like debt bondage retain their feudal connotation: unconnected with accumulation, unfreedom is seen instead as an archaic survival through which unproductive landlords extract pre-capitalist forms of rent from smallholding peasant proprietors, sharecroppers, or estate tenants. Thus economic stagnation in India is attributed by Bhaduri, Prasad, and others, to an unwillingness on the part of feudal/semi-feudal landlords to install labour displacing and productivity enhancing technological improvements because this would undermine their political hold over the indebted tenants from whom they

---

29. The reasons for this are examined more fully in Brass, "Revisionist Reinterpretations", pp. 88 ff., and "Deproletarianization", pp. 37 ff.
30. Taylor, "Earning a Living", p. 120; and Albert, "Creation of a Proletariat", pp. 109-110. For other examples of the theorization of unfree labour in Latin America as a pre-capitalist/feudal/semi-feudal relation, see Bauer, "Rural Workers", pp. 53, 61; Cotlear, *Sistema del Enganche del Siglo XX*, p. 52.

obtain an income based on property rights and usury.[31] Rather than follow the "rational" economic behaviour of capitalists who employ free labour in order to maximize output and profits, therefore, the Indian landlord class is categorized as uniformly "feudal" in so far as it prefers instead to combine low growth with the continued employment of bonded labour, a situation which blocks the development of the productive forces (and hence the expansion of capitalism) in agriculture.

There are two difficulties with this view. First, such a theorization cannot account for the continued existence or indeed the expansion of unfreedom, not just in what are undeniably areas of capitalist agriculture but also in some urban industrial capitalist contexts. The use of forced labour in Europe during wartime, the continuing existence of peonage in the United States, and contract migrant labour in white South African mining and industry and the sunbelt states in the USA, together with moves towards extra-territorial production zones (where legislation protecting workers does not apply), and the replacement of welfare provision with workfare, the compulsory "training"/"retraining" schemes for youth and the long-term unemployed in metropolitan capitalist countries, all point to the opposite conclusion.[32] Rather than an archaic relational form constituting an obstacle to (and therefore destined to be eliminated by) capitalism, unfree labour is in certain circumstances an integral aspect of both the initial and continuing accumulation process.

The second difficulty with the feudal/semi-feudal thesis is that, as with other apparently "innocent" forms of conceptualizing unfreedom, this lacunae (capitalism and unfreedom are incompatible) in turn opens up a theoretical space for the neoclassical economic argument that, in a capitalist context, such agrarian

31. Bhaduri, "Study in Agricultural Backwardness"; Prasad, "Semi-Feudalism", pp. 33-49; *Lopsided Growth*, pp. 37-43. For other instances of the unproblematic equation of unfree labour with feudal/semi-feudal relations in Indian agriculture, see, *inter alia*, Bardhan, *Land, Labor*, pp. 81-83; Breman, *Peasants, Migrants*, pp. 131, 306-313; Tiwary, "Bondage in Santhal Parganas", and Chopra, "Bondage in a Green Revolution Area", pp. 180-181, 212.

32. For the use of forced labour by both parties to the conflicts of 1914-1918 and 1939-1945, see Ferencz, *Less than Slaves*; Summerskill, *China on the Western Front*; Elsner, "Foreign Workers", pp. 189-222; Sherwood, *Many Struggles*, pp. 93-130; Hayes, *Industry and Ideology*. Accounts of peonage, unfree migrant labour, and the workfare system in the USA and Canada are contained in United States Congress, *Hearings on Migrant and Seasonal Farmworker Powerlessness*, Part 1 (Washington, 1970), pp. 5-15, 28, 39-49, 66, 95-100, 108-111, 116-117, 122, 125-145, 158, 176 ff., and Part 2 (Washington, 1970), pp. 353 ff., 433-434, 450-451, 473-474; and Friedland and Nelkin, *Migrant*, and "Metamorphosis of Slavery, 1865-1900", pp. 88-99; Griffith, "Nonmarket Labor Processes", pp. 838-852; Block and Noakes, "Politics of New-style Workfare", pp. 31-58; Satzewich, "Unfree Labour", pp. 89-110. For the employment of unfree black workers in the mining and industrial sectors of white South Africa, see among (many) others, Wilson, *Labour in South African Gold Mines*; First, *Black Gold*. For the existence of unfree industrial labour in the special processing zones of China, see Yonghong, "Export Processing Zones in China", pp. 355-365.

relations are not unfree (or bonded) but much rather free wage labour. However, it is important to note that there is no disagreement with the semi-feudal
thesis as advanced by Bhaduri and Prasad regarding both the existence and the
effect of the control exercised by landlords over their workers by means of the
debt mechanism; the main objection is that, for them, such control is confined
to and indeed indicative of feudalism/semi-feudalism. As is argued, both here
and elsewhere, capitalist producers also resort to this method of workforce
control/discipline in the form of deproletarianisation; that is, imposing or
reimposing unfreedom on workers whose sole property is their labour power.

4. Unfree Labour, Deproletarianization, and Capitalist Restructuring

Generally speaking, deproletarianization (or the economic and politico-ideological decommodification of labour power) corresponds to workforce restructuring by means of introducing or reintroducing unfree relations, a process of
class composition/recomposition which accompanies the struggle between
capital and labour.[33] In contexts/periods where/when further accumulation is
blocked by overproduction, economic crisis may force capital to restructure its
labour process either by replacing free workers with unfree equivalents or by
converting the former into the latter. The economic advantage of deproletarianization is that such restructuring enables landholders/planters first to lower the
cost of local workers by importing unfree, more easily regulated, and thus
cheaper outside labour, and then to lower the cost of the latter if/when the
original external/local wage differential has been eroded.[34] In this way it is

---

33. A common form of historical and contemporary restructuring is the decentralization of the
    labour process itself, a transformation which entails the displacement of existing factory
    production by a smallscale outwork/putting-out system based on unfree sweated labour. A
    recent study of the clothing trade in nineteenth century London has argued that the
    introduction of the sweatshop system was a result of industrial growth rather than stagnation,
    and suggests that the switch to production with low-paid workers in unregulated/non-
    unionized premises during the second half of the century was a direct response by employers
    to the consolidation in the first half of a well-organized, militant and highly unionized
    workforce protected by factory legislation. Schmiechen, *Sweated Industries*. For accounts of
    a similar restructuring process in the contemporary period, see Levidow, "Grunwick", pp.
    123-171; Mattera, *Off the Books*; and Mitter, "Industrial restructuring and manufacturing
    homework", pp. 37-80. The way in which unfree relations are enforced within these
    smallscale units is outlined by Hoel, "Contemporary Clothing", pp. 80-98.
34. Instances abound across space and time of cost cutting achieved through restructuring based
    on deproletarianization, albeit frequently not theorized as such. See, for example, Hannington,
    Problem of the Distressed Areas, pp. 92-114; Dew, *Ironmaker to the Confederacy*, p. 30; Tinker,
    New System of Slavery, pp. 217-218; Santana, "Role of Haitian Braceros", pp. 120-132;
    DeWind et al., "Contract Labor in US Agriculture", pp. 380-396; Monteón, "*Enganche* in
    the Chilean Nitrate Sector", p. 66; Ramesar, "Indentured Labour", pp. 60, 65; and Brass,

possible either to maintain wages at existing (low) levels or even to decrease pay and conditions of both components of the workforce, thereby restoring/enhancing profitability and with it the accumulation projection (or linked to) the capitalist labour process.

In ideological terms, the object of the deproletarianization/decommodification of distinct forms of labour power employed by capital is either to prevent the emergence of a specifically proletarian consciousness or to curtail the latter where it already exists. Hence the utilization of unfree components from the industrial reserve army of labour not as an addition to the existing (free) workforce but rather as a substitute for – and thus competitors with – the latter has dire consequences for the development of working class political consciousness, in agriculture no less than manufacturing. There are numerous instances of racist responses on the part of an existing agrarian workforce displaced by the nationally/ethnically/regionally specific labour power of cheap/unfree migrants recruited by planters, landowners or rich peasants engaged in the restructuring of the labour process.[35]

Where an initially progressive proletarian class struggle shows signs of being/becoming effective, the attempt by capital to demobilize it by means of workforce restructuring may convert what is an actually or potentially revolutionary situation into a politically reactionary combination of nationalism and racism. Accordingly, in such circumstances the form taken by class struggle waged from above in turn affects the form taken by class struggle waged from below. Although it may continue to reproduce itself in economic terms, therefore, and thus constitute a (segmented) class-in-itself, working class recomposition takes the all-important form of class-for-itself only where/when such politico-ideological division is transcended.

In contrast to the position adopted here, which links the existence of unfree relations to issues of profitability and class struggle, the presence/absence of unfreedom is generally attributed simply either to a shortage or to a surplus of labour. The view that unfreedom derives from labour scarcity is linked to the work of Nieboer, who argued that as inhabitants of non-capitalist societies usually prefer to work for themselves rather than for others, actual or potential employers of labour power must rely on un free workers so longer as unappropriated land ("open resources") is still available.[36] Once land becomes private

---

"Class Formation and Class Struggle", pp. 427-457, "Revisionist Reinterpretations", and "Class Struggle and Deproletarianization".

35. For examples of racism as a result of restructuring, again not necessarily interpreted as such, see Beachey, *British West Indies Sugar Industry*, p. 109; Tinker, *New System of Slavery*, pp. 217-219; Hunt, "Exclusivism and Unionism", pp. 80-95; Cohen, *New Helots*, pp. 52-53, 129-130, 187, 193 ff.; Plant, *Sugar and Modern Slavery*, pp. 69-70; Baud, "Sugar and Unfree Labour", pp. 301-325.

36. Nieboer, *Slavery as an Industrial System*. This view also structures the argument in two recent

property (or a "closed resource"), unfree labour ceases to be necessary since the sale of labour power is now the only method of obtaining subsistence. However, the use of indenture or debt bondage against free workers *already* separated from means of production suggests that reasons for the existence of unfree relations are unconnected with the need of agrarian capitalists to compel unwilling and/or wholly self-sufficient peasant proprietors to sell their labour power, and raises the issue of the connection between unfreedom and worker availability. In such circumstances, the concept "labour shortage" posesses a specific politico-ideological meaning. The term is applied by employers not to an absolute unavailability of labour power (additional workers are needed, yet none exist) but to situations where market forces or political consciousness permit free workers to act as (and reap the benefits from being) proletarians.[37]

The opposing view links the occurrence of unfree relations to a surfeit of agricultural labour that has few or no alternative sources of subsistence. Many texts on rural labour in India are structured by this argument, unfree relations being seen as connected with the existence at different historical periods of

texts, where the presence of unfree labour in Russia and on the plantation systems of America, the Caribbean, South Africa, and Australia is linked to the existence in all these contexts of labour shortages. Miles, *Capitalism and Unfree Labour*, pp. 205, 214; Kolchin, *Unfree Labor*, pp. 18, 359 ff.

37. Attributing indentured migration generally to a "distaste by free labourers to bear the non-pecuniary costs of production upon the plantations", Engerman, "Servants to slaves", p. 277, implies that everywhere and at all times free labour was unwilling to undertake plantation work under *any* circumstances. Such a view overlooks the fact that planters employed unfree contract/indentured labour because locals were exercising not an absolute but rather a relative unwillingness to work, and withholding their labour power in order to secure improvements in pay and conditions for the application of this commodity on the plantation itself. In other words, the object of employing unfree labour in such circumstances was to compel free locals to accept plantation work conditions and pay levels that they would otherwise have rejected. For an excellent case-study of the latter process, see Rodney, *History of the Guyanese Working People*. Much the same kind of restructuring procedure was operated by agribusiness enterprises in the United States during the 1960s, when unfree contract labour from the Caribbean was (and continues to be) imported specifically with the object of forcing local workers to accept lower wages and less favourable conditions. About this situation the normally conservative US Congress has commented: "Growers [...] have convinced the US Department of Labour that a shortage of domestic farmworkers exists and thus offshore workers are needed. We see very little evidence of such a shortage but rather that the introduction of [unfree migrant] offshore workers has greatly hampered the domestic workers and in some cases has resulted in foreign workers displacing US workers in [...] this country. With the foreign workers' arrival, harvesting prices for US labor dropped. As a stable supply of labor was introduced, employers refused to negotiate prices to be paid to US laborers." Unlike local workers, who can negotiate for higher wages, foreign contract workers have to accept pay levels and conditions imposed by employers, who accordingly "find it much less expensive with a controlled labor force". United States Congress, *Hearings*, Part 1, pp. 178, 185.

labour surpluses in agriculture.[38] Both past and present forms of bondage are theorized as the result of economic immizerization that afflicted large sections of the rural workforce; accordingly, unfreedom is regarded as possessing its origin not in proletarianization but in peasant impoverishment which derives from high levels of unemployment. This situation is attributed in turn to demographic growth combined with a lack of industrialization and thus non-agricultural job opportunities.

It is important to note that workforce restructuring can occur in contexts where no actual labour shortage exists, or even where surplus labour is present, as well as in those where labour is scarce. In the latter case, employers will be faced with increasing labour costs because, though not organized on a collective basis, workers are nevertheless aware of the fact that labour power is much sought after, and attempt to sell this to the highest bidder. However, even in areas where the demand for labour is either met or exceeded by the existing supply, and consequently there is no competition for workers, employers may still be faced with rising labour costs: due to the levels of political consciousness and organization exhibited by workers on the one hand, and on the other because overproduction and the tendency of the rate of profit to fall in the course of capitalist competition generally requires individual producers to cut the price of labour power. Despite the differences in terms of labour availability, therefore, employer response is in both cases the same: the restructuring of the labour process.

5. Conclusion

What is significant about each of the apparently distinct views considered above is that, in their different ways, all deny the possibility of a link between unfree labour and capitalism. By redefining bondage/indenture as free wage labour, therefore, both neoclassical economic theory and the revisionist variants influenced by it dismiss the existence of a connection between unfreedom and capitalism; by categorizing bondage as a figment of western discourse, postmodern theory also rejects such a link, which by its very nature is necessarily precluded from the semi-feudal thesis. By contrast, it is maintained here that when labour begins to act individually or to organize collectively in defence of its own interests, by exercising freedom of movement to secure higher wages,

---

38. See, for example, Kumar, *Land and Caste*; Patnaik, "Introduction", pp. 9, 11 ff.; Patnaik, "Agrarian Question", pp. 781-793; and Ramachandran, *Wage Labour and Unfreedom in Agriculture*, pp. 258-259. For a critique of the argument which unproblematically links unfreedom to population density in the case of the Caribbean, see Nigel Bolland, "Systems of Domination after Slavery", pp. 591-619.

better working conditions, shorter working hours, etc., capitalist employers introduce or reintroduce restrictions on the formation or extension of a labour market with the object of shifting the balance of workplace power in their own direction. This procedure corresponds to a restructuring of the labour process, and entails either replacing free workers with unfree equivalents or converting the former into the latter. In short, a socio-economic and politico-ideological transformation which amounts not to proletarianization or to depeasantization but to deproletarianization.

Why Slavery?[*]

André J.F. Köbben

> Always and everywhere men have been in-
> clined to burden their fellow-men with
> heavy and degrading work rather than per-
> form it themselves; and the strong have
> succeeded in imposing this work on the
> weak.[1]

1. Nieboer's Treatise on Slavery

In his doctoral dissertation, written almost a century ago, Herman J. Nieboer asked himself the momentous question why it is that in some societies slavery is present whereas in others it is not.[2] Basically his answer – as is the case with most Grand Theories – is gloriously simple: Slavery tends to occur in societies with *open* resources and is absent where resources are *closed*.

In a tribal agricultural society where simple capital goods (a hoe, a primitive plough) suffice to work the soil, and where there is fertile land in plenty ("open resources") any able-bodied man can provide for himself and his kin. If therefore someone wants others to perform the necessary drudgery for him, he must coerce them to serve him and this coercion will readily assume the form of slavery.[3] As epitomized in the Ashanti saying: "We buy a slave because of filthy work."[4]

---

[*] My thanks are due to Leo d'Anjou, Gert Oostindie, Mario Pastore and Alex Schmid.

1. Nieboer, *Slavery as an Industrial System*, pp. 420-421.

2. Herman Jeremias Nieboer took his doctoral degree on 12 July 1900 at the University of Utrecht. A much expanded second edition (474 pages) of his thesis appeared in 1910; a photo-graphic reprint was published by Lenox Hill Publ., New York, in 1971. To this day most writers on the origins of slavery and other forms of unfree labour refer to his study. Apart from this *opus magnum* Nieboer published hardly anything in the field of anthropology, the reason presumably being that a professional career as an anthropologist was out of the question in those days, at least in Holland.

3. Nieboer, *Slavery*, pp. 302, 419.

4. Rattray, *Ashanti Law and Constitution*, p. 44. However, there are many slave societies where master and slave may work side by side. This is true for ancient Rome as well as for a number of tribal African societies (Finley, *Ancient Slavery and Modern Ideology*, p. 101; and Tuden and Plotnicov, *Social Stratification in Africa*, p. 13). Furthermore, under special circumstances slaves may reach prestigious positions (see par. 2.2).

On the other hand, where all fertile land is appropriated and in use, or where costly capital goods, such as cattle or sophisticated tools, are needed for one's independent economic survival ("closed resources") the landless and the poor will offer their labour to the economically privileged, out of necessity. It is then no longer profitable for the latter to retain property rights (and duties!) in others, hence no slavery. Nieboer sums up the difference as follows:

> In slave societies workers are held as property and valued as such. If a landlord loses a worker, his capital is lessened, so if the worker runs away, he eagerly tries to recover him. In countries with closed resources it is generally quite the reverse. If a workman, at least an unskilled one, leaves his service, the andlord knows that there are many others ready to take his place. Here it is not the landlord who prevents his workers from escaping but the latter who try to prevent the landlord from dismissing or ousting them.[5]

As examples of "closed resources" in the tribal world, Nieboer mentions Polynesian and Micronesian islands, "where the poor eagerly ask the landlord for employment even in the meanest work".[6]

One may well ask whether Nieboer was the first to think of this explanatory model. Not so! Here Goethe's dictum comes to mind: "*Alles Gescheite ist schon gedacht worden*": all sensible things have already been thought (and said). Nieboer himself mentions E.G. Wakefield (1849) as a precursor.[7] Although Wakefield writes about slavery in a (semi-)colonial situation rather than in tribal societies, he points to the same underlying mechanism. He does so in forceful language still worth quoting:

> It is strange that it should never have come into the heads of philosophers to ascertain the causes of the revival of slavery by all the nations of modern Europe which have engaged in colonization.
>
> Philanthropists have treated slavery as a moral and religious question, attributing it to the wickedness of the human heart. However, the spirit of the slave-master is not love of oppression and cruelty, – these are the mere effects of keeping slaves. His universal motive is in the economic circumstances: slavery is a make-shift for hiring. It happens wherever population is scanty in proportion to land. Slavery, except in some mild form as the fading continuation of a habit has been confined to countries of a scanty population.[8]

There is, however, a vast difference between Wakefield and Nieboer in the way they handled empirical data. Wakefield provided a few stray examples to demonstrate his point, whereas Nieboer canvassed all available ethnographical

---

5. Nieboer, *Slavery as an Industrial System*, pp. 419-422 (slightly reworded).
6. *Ibid.*, p. 342.
7. *Ibid.*, p. 306.
8. Wakefield, *A View of the Art of Colonization*, pp. 322-325.

sources, carefully pointing out which cases were and which were not in conformity with his basic thesis. "If we find a hypothesis", he writes in his Introduction, "that accounts for many, but not all, of the observed phenomena, our task is not finished until we have explained the remaining ones by showing the influence of additional factors"[9]. What is more, he executes this ambitious programme faithfully. In the rare cases in which he is unable to bridge the gap between his data and his hypotheses, he is the first to point this out himself.[10] I'll come back to this aspect of his work in a moment.

Nieboer's thesis may seem so obvious that it borders on the trivial. This is precisely what Evans-Pritchard suggests in a critical essay on "The Comparative Method in Social Anthropology". He duly compliments Nieboer for the care and subtlety with which he assesses his data, but judges his final outcome as most disappointing: "His conclusions take us little beyond what one might have expected: that as a rule slaves are not kept when there is no use of them."[11]

Nieboer's theory may conjure up the illusion of obviousness by being convincingly argued and aptly illustrated. The fact is, however, that in the historical and sociological literature on the rise and fall of slavery, Nieboer's "self-evident" truth is largely ignored. Giants in the field of the social sciences such as Adam Smith, Karl Marx and Max Weber could have profited greatly had they taken it into account. In the literature slavery is seen as: an inevitable phase in the evolution of mankind; as caused by "the pride and love of power of the masters" (Adam Smith); as a corollary of *Naturalwirtschaft* (barter trade) as opposed to *Geldwirtschaft* (money based economy); as indicator of a pre-industrial or a pre-capitalist mode of production; even as the consequence of *over*population.[12] Conversely, the fading away of slavery in early Western Europe is attributed by several authors to the civilizing influence of Christianity rather than to population growth gradually making unfree labour obsolete.[13]

Nieboer is to be praised for his sound and consistent logic, his intellectual integrity and his ability to separate the dross from the gold of ethnographical source material which was most uneven in quality. There is, however, one flaw in his reasoning: He presents human beings as exclusively motivated by rationality, i.e. driven by their enlightened self-interest. The same holds good for all rational choice-theorists past and present. Montesquieu (1721) has tersely formulated their basic premise as follows: "None is evil gratuitously. We do

---

9. Nieboer, *Slavery as an Industrial System*, p. xix.
10. *Ibid.*, p. 383.
11. Evans-Pritchard, "Comparative Method", ch. 1.
12. Finley, *Ancient Slavery*, pp. 28, 41, 51; Miles, *Capitalism and Unfree Labour*, pp. 2-3, 44; Nieboer, *Slavery as an Industrial System*, pp. 171, 299, 352; and Saucier, *Sub Saharan Slavery*, p. 32.
13. For an overview of the literature, see Finley, *Ancient Slavery*, pp. 13-17, 32-33.

injustices because we put our own well-being above that of others".[14] While this goes far in explaining human behaviour, it is by no means the whole story.

If Montesquieu were right, slaves would invariably be well cared for. To their masters they are capital goods. No more than that perhaps but no less either. The slave-owner who treats them badly would be like the entrepreneur who does not keep his machinery in good working condition. This is exactly the argument of Fogel and Engerman in their famous studies on American slavery, at least as summed up in a recent essay by Fogel: When slave-owners fed and housed their slaves adequately and made use of the carrot as well as the stick (whip) they did so, Fogel suggests, not so much for moral but for economic reasons.[15] Indeed, this is why the German sociologist Simmel (1900) was of the opinion that slaves were better off than the proletarians of his day: they were at least assured of their daily necessaries.[16]

However, when one recalls the reality of the slave societies of Surinam and Northeastern Brazil, to mention only two examples, one is struck not only by the cruelty but also the sheer irrationality of many slave-masters.[17] Salles quotes the case of a widow in Belém (Brazil) as described by a contemporary witness:

> The way this woman treats a young female slave reminds one of the tortures of hell and goes so far that the poor creature is no more than skin and bone. Sometimes this shrew gets so angry with her slave that she gives her no food for days. And when a compassionate soul brings her something to eat, she snatches it from her hands and rants and raves at the benefactor[18].

Although this was no standard behaviour, as witness the fact that it was commented upon by a contemporary, the author notes that it was by no means exceptional either.

Van Lier writes about Paramaribo (Surinam):

---

14. Montesquieu, *Lettres Persanes*, p. 150 (my translation).
15. Fogel, "Moral Aspects", pp. 593-596.
16. Cited from Twaddle, "Visible and Invisible Hands", pp. 1-12, esp. p. 5. Accordingly, in this paper the term "free labour" has a purely technical meaning and is not seen as a condition being necessarily better or more advantageous than "unfree" labour to the workers in question.
17. In the eighteenth and nineteenth century Surinam had the reputation of being one of the world's most cruel slave societies. In a recent article Oostindie, "Voltaire, Stedman", pp. 1-34, has argued that the Surinam slavery regime was no worse (but no better either!) than that in other tropical plantation areas. Interestingly, both in Brazil and in Surinam there were humanitarian slave owners as well (see Salles, *Negro na Pará*, pp. 130-133 for Brazil, and for Surinam Stedman, *Narrative of a Five Years' Expedition*, I, pp. 63-64, II, pp. 376-377, 213; and Van Lier, *Samenleving in een grensgebied*, pp. 136, 151). Their behaviour cannot be explained by purely rationalistic motives either.
18. Salles, *Negro na Pará*, p. 133 (my translation).

The silence of the tropical afternoon was often disturbed by the screaming and moaning of male and female slaves who were punished, sometimes for trifles such as alleged impertinency.[19]

Flogging of slaves was a daily occurrence. In the year 1832 about one thousand slaves, or three percent of the total slave population, were whipped (25, 50 or 100 lashes) by officers in an official capacity, thus excluding whippings that took place on the plantations.[20] Presumably, after one hundred lashes, a man is not in optimal condition to do his work! Other, less frequent, punishments were the amputation of a leg or the cutting of the Achilles tendons. These come down to permanently incapacitating a man for work, or in economic terms the outright destruction by the master of his own capital good.[21]

Some authors take objection to the above reasoning and argue that extremely harsh treatment of slaves ("terrorizing slaves") *is* instrumental as it keeps them from rebelling, and thus can and indeed should be seen as rational conduct.[22] This may be true for the earlier phases of a system of unfree labour. Once, however, slavery is firmly embedded in a society, such treatment will rather have the opposite effect.

Nieboer confined himself to exploring slavery in tribal ("savage") societies, with the exception of one long chapter on the fading away of slavery and serfdom in early medieval Europe.[23]

In subsequent years, scholars have argued that his theory has a wider application. It also holds good for more complex societies as well as for other modes of unfree labour.[24] Wherever labour is hard to obtain, if not slavery or serfdom, then such functional equivalents as indentured labour, debt bondage or convict

19. Van Lier, *Samenleving in een grensgebied*, p. 154 (my translation).
20. Siwpersad, *Nederlandse regering en de afschaffing van de Surinaamse slavernij*, pp. 98, 235, 242.
21. Van Lier, *Samenleving in een grensgebied*, p. 138. Here it is not the place to discuss in full the causes of such irrational behaviour. Van Lier refers to 'the fear for the multitude of slaves', which sounds quite plausible as by far the majority of the Surinam populace consisted of slaves (*ibid*. pp. 31, 51, 73, 98). Such irrational behaviour is by no means restricted to slavery societies. In Poland, under the Nazi-occupation, some German officials, even SS-officers were upset – be it not for moral reasons – by the fact that many able-bodied Jews in concentration camps were not put to good use in *kriegswichtige Arbeit* ("labour essential to the war") but instead were killed or maltreated so badly that they could no longer work properly (Browning, *Ordinary Men*, pp. 158, 171-172; Keneally, *Schindler's List*, pp. 144, 164, 264-265).
22. See in this sense Breman, *Koelies, planters en koloniale politiek*, p. 8.
23. Nieboer, *Slavery*, pp. 346-382. Domar, while praising Nieboer's work as a major contribution to the theory of unfree labour, criticizes him for ignoring the role of government. The reason for this is, I submit, the very fact that Nieboer confined himself largely to tribal societies where the role of government in shaping economic and social relationships is a relatively minor one. See Domar, "The Causes of Slavery", pp. 18-32, esp. p. 32.
24. Nieboer, *Slavery* refers on one page only (p. 420) to modes of unfree labour other than slavery or servitude.

labour tend to develop. This is especially true where commodities such as cotton, rubber, sugar, tobacco or wool are produced on a large scale.

The first to point this out was Fahrenfort in an excellent article published fifty years ago in the midst of war and occupation, which has not had the impact it deserves.[25] One of his examples refers to the Eastern coastal districts of Sumatra where in 1863 the first tobacco plantation was established, not long after the Dutch government had abolished slavery in the East Indies. A thriving plantation economy (tobacco, rubber) developed for which Chinese and Javanese labourers were imported; but never in sufficient quantities. Re-introduction of slavery was out of question but the planters convinced the government of the necessity to take special measures. In 1880 a "Coolie Ordinance" was promulgated in which a three year labour contract was introduced with penal sanctions. In combination with debt bondage it gave rise to a situation which for practical purposes equalled chattel slavery, with all its concomitant abuses.[26]

Interestingly, in the same period, on the neighbouring island of Java, with its huge labour-intensive sugar plantations most of the regulations constraining the freedom of labour were abolished as the teeming population made them superfluous.

2. Exceptions

However powerful as an explanatory device, Nieboer's proposition is by no means a "law" in the sense of a rule without exceptions. In other words, none of the four boxes in the two-by-two table below is empty.

Table 1. The Cases in Boxes I and IV are in Accordance with Nieboer's Thesis, Those in Boxes II and III Are the Exceptions

	open resources	closed resources
slavery	I	II
no slavery	III	IV

One may well ask: Why not? The facile answer would be that this is so because unfortunately in our sciences we do not work under laboratory conditions. I think, however, that a more precise answer is possible by taking the following factors into account: 1) multicausality; 2) parallel causality; 3) intervening factors; 4) cultural lags; 5) functional equivalents; 6) (mis)classification.

25. Fahrenfort, "Over vrije en onvrije arbeid", pp. 29-51.
26. *Ibid.*, pp. 36-39; Breman, *Koelies, planters en koloniale politiek, passim*, and Kloosterboer, *Involuntary Labour*, pp. 44, 49, 210.

I hope to demonstrate that discussing these six factors is no empty intellectual exercise but a way to a better understanding of the multifaceted phenomenon of unfree labour as it presents itself in various societies and periods.[27]

2.1. Multicausality

Nieboer's thesis, as explained in its barest form in paragraph 1, is a monocausal theory. In symbolic form:

What is pre-supposed here is the "other things being equal"-condition. Suppose, however, that a second factor or condition must be present to bring about slavery. Or:

Suppose further that a student tests Nieboer's thesis not realizing that X is a necessary condition as well. In the table in which he displays the results of his test, box I will contain the cases in which open resources are present, and X also happens to be present; therefore slavery is present. Box III ("exceptions"), however, will contain those cases in which open resources are present *but X happens to be absent*, so that slavery is absent as well.

In the sixties Baks *et al.* retested Nieboer's hypothesis using newer and presumably more reliable data than those available in Nieboer's days.[28] The results were as presented in table 2:

Table 2. Retest of Nieboer's Thesis by Baks et al.

	open resources	closed resources
slavery	15	2
no slavery	20	7

As is evident there is no significant correlation here. So the hypothesis in its original form should be rejected.

27. See further Köbben, "Why Exceptions?", pp. 3-34, Köbben, "Comparativists and Non-comparativists", pp. 89-98.
28. Baks, Breman, and Nooij, "Slavery as a System of Production", pp. 90-109.

But let us approach the phenomenon from a different angle. Slavery is a form of systematic coercion. Such coercion seems hardly feasible in egalitarian societies, i.e. societies in which only individual, non-hereditary differences of prestige and power are present. So Baks *et al.* postulated social stratification as a second necessary condition of slavery: slavery can only occur, or so they argued, in societies that (apart from slavery) comprize two or more hereditary classes unequal in status and power. When Nieboer's theory is separately tested for stratified and for egalitarian societies, the results are as shown in table 3.

Table 3. Retest Taking into Account the Factor of Stratification

	stratified		egalitarian	
	open resources	closed resources	open resources	closed resources
slavery	10	2	5	–
no slavery	2	5	18	2

For stratified societies, Nieboer's hypothesis is tenable, at least in the sense that a statistically significant correlation exists between the two phenomena in question. As to egalitarian societies, no less than 18 of the 25 cases examined turn out to contradict Nieboer's hypothesis. One is almost tempted to say that these are the societies that could "profit" from slavery but are not capable of introducing it.[29]

2.2. Parallel Causality

I use the term "parallel causality" if a phenomenon may be brought about by several factors independently of one another.

Suppose that slavery, apart from open resources, may be the result of other factors as well. In symbolic form:

open resources ⟶ slavery

other factors ⟶ slavery

If, then, a student tests Nieboer's thesis without being aware of these other factors, box II ("exceptions") will contain cases in which resources are closed, yet slavery occurs because (one of) these other factors happen to be present.

In eighteenth and nineteenth century Moroccan cities, there was no question of open resources, yet slavery flourished. Whatever its origin, slavery in these

---

29. Nieboer, *Slavery*, refers to a possible role of classes (hierarchical order) only in passing (p. 45, p. 385 note). He does, however, refer to "living in large groups and having fixed habitations" as contributing factors.

cities was due to two principal factors (motives). The first was *conspicuous consumption*, to use Veblen's famous expression.[30] The more slaves (domestics) one owned, the more prestige it bestowed. The Sultan had thousands of slaves, the ordinary wealthy household between one and six.

The second factor is *loyalty*. Most slaves being both dependent and vulnerable were extremely loyal to their master. Unlike kinsmen or friends they could never aspire to be his equal or rival. Slaves, therefore, often became their master's confidants and in the process could reach positions of influence, free men working under their orders.[31]

2.3. Intervening Factors

When we say: "open resources, hence slavery" or "closed resources, hence no slavery" these are shorthand expressions for what in fact are complicated psychological and sociological processes. Nieboer's arguments why slavery ensues from open resources sound eminently reasonable, yet intervening factors may change the course of events.

In the fourth century A.D. independent peasants in the outlying parts of the Roman empire were plagued by bands of invaders and robbers. This led many of them to the one available source of protection, a powerful local landlord: in return they accepted voluntarily to become his tenants.[32] Similarly, in the vast Brazilian hinterland where the impact of the central government was, until recently, negligible, peasants used to seek (and may well seek to this day) the protection of a political boss, in exchange for performing whatever tasks he assigned to them.[33] So both cases have to be placed in box III (open resources, yet no slavery or other forms of unfree labour).

Conversely, due to intervening factors, slavery may be present in a situation of closed resources. The poor, instead of doing what Nieboer expected them to do, i.e. offer their services to the powers that be, may instead decide to live from the crumbs of the tables of the wealthy. A case in point is ancient Rome where thousands of unemployed eked out a living as *clientes* of wealthy *patroni*, without, however, doing menial jobs for them. For that the patrons still needed slaves. Whereas the clients in a sense were privileged as *cives romani*, the slaves were mostly aliens.[34]

---

30. Veblen, *Theory of the Leisure Class*, pp. 42-46.
31. Schroeter, "Slave Markets and Slavery", pp. 185-213, esp. pp. 200-204; see for other examples of slaves in high positions Blakeley, "Slavery and Slavishness", pp. 76-86, esp. pp. 78-79; Conrad, "Slavery in Bambara Society", pp. 69-90, esp. pp. 75-77; and Tuden and Plotnicov, *Social Stratification in Africa*, p. 14. Nieboer, *Slavery as an Industrial System*, discusses "slavery as luxury" on pp. 284, 403-406.
32. Finley, *Ancient Slavery*, p. 148.
33. Galjart, "Class and Following", pp. 3-22, esp. p. 5.
34. Finley, *Ancient Slavery*, p. 79.

It seems not too far-fetched to compare this with the situation in modern welfare states, where the situation of the unemployed is such that they may refuse to accept dreary and poorly paid jobs.[35] One of the means for employers (at least some employers) to fill such vacancies is to recruit illegal aliens, i.e. labourers who, like slaves in bygone days, lack the protection and rights of ordinary citizens.

Intervening factors may be of an external nature, as the following case illustrates. In Surinam (Dutch Guiana) on Wednesday 1 July 1863, at six o'clock in the morning, slavery was abolished, twenty one ceremonial gunshots marking the occasion. Three days of spontaneous rejoicing followed; to the surprise of the planters no nasty incidents occurred. In the preceding months, the slaves had been carefully instructed as to their new rights and duties; the slave-owners were generously recompensed.[36]

Thus slavery came to an end in a idealtypical slave society, in which the majority of the populace were slaves and where all the conditions for the continuation of slavery for at least another generation seemed to be fulfilled.[37] Still, as from then on the Surinam case (open resources, yet no slavery) was an exception to Nieboer's rule. *All this was occasioned by a parliamentary decision in faraway Holland.*

This decision was preceded by three decades of exacerbated debate. In it the open resources-argument was repeatedly proffered by politicians to argue the alleged inevitability of slavery:

> [The slaves] have too few needs and since it is easy, given the fertility of the soil, to fulfill these, they will not be inclined, once emancipated, to do any labour whatsoever on the plantations [...] The moment of emancipation has not yet come as every-one can settle in the forest or alongside the rivers in this almost uninhabited country and, owing to the mildness of nature, can gain his livelihood without effort [...] The question of emancipation here as everywhere, is a question of population.[38]

The decade after 1863 was a period of "State Supervision", a half-hearted attempt by the government to obligate the ex-slaves by legal means to conclude labour contracts. In 1873 the first ship bringing British Indian contract labourers arrived.[39]

35. For an example see Sansone, *Schitteren in de schaduw*, pp. 59-64.
36. Emmer, "Between Slavery and Freedom", pp. 87-113, esp. pp. 89-90.
37. Contrary to general opinion in nineteenth century anti-slavery circles, modern historians are of the opinion that New World slavery societies, such as the one in Surinam, were economically viable and profitable. See Drescher, "Long Goodbye", pp. 25-27 and the literature mentioned there.
38. Siwpersad, *Nederlandse regering en de afschaffing van de Surinaamse slavernij*, pp. 7, 94, 246 (my translation).
39. Emmer, "Between Slavery and Freedom", *passim*.

The above history may have its singular elements, it is certainly not unique. Everywhere in the New World, from the US to Brazil, in the course of the nineteenth century a similar development took place. So external influences are among the main factors for occasioning exceptions.[40]

2.4 Cultural Lags

Using an almost forgotten concept coined by Ogburn (1928), I refer to a *cultural lag* when an institution continues to exist while its causal factors have ceased to be present.[41] As Wakefield said in the passage quoted earlier (p. 78): "Slavery may exist in some mild form as the fading continuation of a habit." A case in point are the tiny Dutch Antillian islands where, until 1863, slavery continued to exist despite the fact that plantations were of minor importance while there were no more open resources of any size available. Significantly, the bitter debate about abolition in the Netherlands concerned Surinam, *not* the Antilles. After 1863, no "State Supervision" was deemed necessary on these islands and no contract labourers were imported.[42]

Whereas the above is a case of "closed resources, yet unfree labour" as a consequence of a cultural lag, the opposite may also occur ("open resources, yet free labour", also as a consequence of a cultural lag). Around 1345 A.D. in most parts of Western Europe the various forms of serfdom had faded away, presumably as a result of rather heavy population pressure.[43] However, in the years that followed (1346-1350) this part of the world was struck by the first waves of Black Death epidemics, wiping out a large part of its populace.[44] The ensuing labour shortage did not, of course, lead to the re-appearance of unfree labour right away. So in, say, the year 1350 the situation by and large was one of "open resources, yet no unfree labour". Indeed, for a short time the lot of labourers may have improved as they could bargain with would-be employers and thus ensure a rise in their wages.[45] Soon, however, the landowners began to use the various means of coercion at their disposal to arrange matters to their advantage again. They did so by reinstating or re-emphasizing the old laws of servile labour as well as imposing new laws designed to keep down wages and

40. For recent discussions of abolition and its aftermath in the British Caribbean, see Sheridan, "From Chattel to Wage Slavery", pp. 13-40; Shephard, "Alternative Husbandry", pp. 41-66; Craton, "Reshuffling the Pack", pp. 23-76.
41. Ogburn, *Social Change*, part IV.
42. Hoetink, *Patroon van de oude Curacaose samenleving*, and Oostindie, "Same Old Song?", p. 167.
43. McNeill, *Plagues and Peoples*, pp. 156, 159; Hilton, *Decline of Serfdom*, p. 31; and Slicher van Bath, *Agrarian History*, p. 161.
44. McNeill, *Plagues and Peoples*, pp. 155-163.
45. *Ibid.*, p. 172; and Hilton, *Decline of Serfdom*, p. 39.

restrict the mobility of labour.[46] They did not succeed, however, in re-establishing a fully-fledged system of serfdom.[47]

2.5 Functional Equivalents

As to functional equivalents of slavery as a possible factor of exceptions, I can be short. In this paper I enumerated a number of such equivalents: servitude, indentured labour, debt bondage, convict labour, state induced forced labour; and one may note others in the literature. Suppose now a scholar tests the hypothesis that such and such factors will cause slavery to occur, and that in fact no slavery but some other mode of unfree labour comes about. Technically thereby his hypothesis is falsified, but chances are that he will not have to change his basic stance. It is only when we specifically try to assess why slavery rather than a different mode of forced labour is present, that such a falsification affects our theory.

2.6 (Mis)classification

In the opening sentence of his magnificent book on ancient and modern slavery, Finley states that "there have been only five genuine slave societies in history" (but what, pray, is "genuine"?).[48] Other authors, however, use the concept of slavery in a much wider sense, so that hundreds of societies can be characterized as "slave societies". Presumably, when testing the conditions of slavery, it makes a great deal of difference whether we define "slavery" in a narrow or in a wide sense.

The same is true for the concepts of "open" and "closed" resources. Olsen, in her article in this volume, notes the occurrence of debt bondage in regions of India where many agricultural labourers are unemployed. At first sight this seems to be a straightforward case that runs counter to Nieboer's theory ("closed resources, yet unfree labour"). However, the reason why employers see it nevertheless as profitable to have at least some of their labourers in bondage, is that these are at their beck and call even in the peak agricultural season, thus at a time when there may be temporary shortages of labour.[49] Seen in this light this case may even be interpreted as a beautiful *confirmation* of Nieboer's theory. Whether we do so or not, depends on where we lay the boundary between "open" and "closed" resources.

---

46. *Ibid.*, p. 36.
47. Domar, "Causes of Slavery", p. 28.
48. Finley, *Ancient Slavery*, p. 5.
49. Olsen, "Marxist and Neoclassical Approaches to Unfree Labour in India".

In this paper I use the concept of "slavery" in a rather broad sense, my only precondition being that one human being is the owner (proprietor) of other human
beings.[50] Apart from this criterion anything goes: I talk of tribal slavery versus
plantation slavery; of "mild" as opposed to "harsh" forms of slavery; of societies
in which the majority of people are slaves as opposed to societies where slaves
are a small minority only. I am sure, if e.g. one studies only eighteenth-century
chattel slavery in the New World, regularities may be found with fewer exceptions. However, what one would gain in precision, one would lose in scope.
In my opinion, it is worthwhile to construct a more ambitious theory in which
slavery as well as other modes of forced labour are encompassed. This paper is
meant to be one step towards such a theory.

2.8 Three Observations

I may add three concluding observations to this paragraph. The first is that in
the case of slavery as with others, our rules may have not one category of
exceptions, but a series of them, if not all six in combination. I will refrain from
giving examples in order to leave something to the imagination of the reader.
In fact, in several cases presented in this paper such a combination of factors may
be discerned.

Secondly, following a suggestion by J.B. Watson, one might think of dividing
my list of factors into two classes: human or taxonomic errors versus formal
properties of systems.[51] An example of a "human or taxonomic error" in
Watson's sense would be a multitude of spurious exceptions ensuing from too
broad a definition of slavery.

Attractive as this distinction may appear at the first sight, it is in fact pointless
if not confusing: in a way all factors can be attributed to errors of the human
mind. For example, it is not multicausality as such that makes for exceptions,
but rather the human mind's overlooking one or more of the causal factors in
question. On the other hand, a case can be made for attributing all factors to
"the formal properties of systems". In the case of exceptions resulting from a
too broad definition of slavery, it is "really", one might argue, the complex
nature of the social phenomena under investigation that makes for exceptions.

My third point is a question rather than a statement. In modern society slavery
and its functional equivalents, apart from some serious lapses, have vanished,
at least as legal systems. A temporary scarcity of labour nowadays is no longer
a threat to the freedom of labourers but rather a boon, as every trade-unionist

---

50. I fully realize that this precondition is not as simple as it sounds, as our concepts of owner
    and proprietor rarely have their precise equivalents in other cultures.
51. Watson, "Commentary", pp. 27-28.

realizes. My question is whether we can explain this historical evolution by the same set of explanatory devices as used in this paper hitherto.

My provisional answer is: No, at least not entirely so. New social phenomena should be taken into account, such as the strength of organized labour and the blurring of classlines in recent years, as also the systematic development of labour saving techniques.

Would that be all? The famous nineteenth century historian W.E.H. Lecky wrote: "The unostentatious and inglorious crusade against slavery are among the three or four perfectly virtuous acts recorded in the history of the nations."[52] This "virtuous act", once having been crowned with success, may be seen as a historical factor in itself. Or have we grown too cynical to think of morals as a possible independent agent of social change?[53]

3. Conclusions

A historian of the younger generation, commenting on an earlier version of this paper, courteously expressed his keen interest in the subject but added: "Our generation is wary of Grand Theories and 'Laws' as we are always able to think of a contrary argument or case".

I am sure they are! But then my purpose is not to formulate a grandiose and all encompassing theory of the "where A there B" variety. In the case of slavery as with most subjects in our field it is wellnigh impossible to disentangle the knot of causal factors into a (quasi-)mathematical formula. Where these are proffered on a high level of abstraction they are mostly either spurious or meaningless. My intention is simply to present a reasoned list of factors that should be taken into account when we try to assess what set of factors have given rise to slavery or any other form of unfree labour in the particular cases we happen to study.

As to comparative studies, all we can hope to establish are correlations between phenomena. Students do go to great lengths to explain such correlations. Once they have achieved this to their satisfaction, they see their task as completed. In this they are wrong. They should try and explain the exceptions as well, thereby correcting and enriching their theories. Exceptions are valuable pointers and should not – as happens too often – be ignored or be treated as anomalies or as a *saltus naturae*.

---

52. Cited from Drescher, "Epilogue", p. 245.
53. See also Lucassen, "Free and Unfree Labour Before the Twentieth Century", this volume, p. 54. Leo d'Anjou, in an overview of the literature, mentions two ideological factors in combination as contributive to the abolition of slavery: Enlightenment and new developments in Christian theology: d'Anjou, *Social Movements and Cultural Change*, ch. 4. See also Furneaux, *William Wilberforce*.

Wage Labour and Despotism in Modernity

Reinhart Kössler

Introduction

Modern societies and their unprecedented dynamic have been forged, as a central structural feature, by free labour employed in rational capitalist enterprise as Max Weber has stressed in a careful and elaborate distinction between several types both of "capitalism" and of "rationality".[1] Again according to Weber, "free labour and complete appropriation of the means of production", i.e., "expropriation of *all* the workers from the means of production", is bound to secure the requisite work "discipline" in an "optimal" way.[2] The reason for this Weber identifies in the "whip of unemployment",[3] in other words, in "a combination of the transfer of responsibility for maintenance to the workers personally and the corresponding powerful indirect compulsion to work"; the latter may be traced back to the "compulsory guarantee of the property system".[4] In Weber's extremely concise and aloof language, these points summarize much of the tension that exists between on the one hand the freedom of labour to seek employment and to dispose of its earnings, to plan lives and careers within the bounds of possibility thus defined, and on the other hand the coercive relationships that butress one of the core structures of the whole set-up of modern capitalism, and arguably the decisive one, namely the enterprise and (especially) the factory.

In this paper I shall argue that it is precisely in this basic aspect of the relationship of free wage labour that the deep-rooted despotic feature of industrial capitalism resides. And further, the despotic relationship rooted in industrialism has shaped, in decisive ways, other modern societies as well, and above all, Soviet type societies. Whereas under "normal" capitalism, the despotic relationship has been restrained, not least as a result of roughly two centuries of labour struggles, in the Soviet system, factory despotism has been projected on to a societal scale. In order to pursue my argument, I shall present a re-constructed concept of "despotism", which in some ways clearly runs counter to common usage. I hope to demonstrate, however, that my version is more rigorous than the usual notions of despoty and despotism, and that it can be rooted squarely

1. Weber, Preface of *The Protestant Ethic*.
2. Weber, *Theory of Social and Economic Organization*, p. 228.
3. Weber, "Zur Psychophysik der industriellen Arbeit", p. 127.
4. Weber, *Theory of Social and Economic Organization*, p. 243.

in classical texts. Moreover, this re-constructed concept of despoty affords a possibility of understanding the decidedly modernist content of Soviet-type forms of despotic domination. From here, a critical reading of the Bolshevik experiment becomes possible, and one that identifies the despotic character of Stalinist rule in particular, while at the same time avoiding the pitfalls of relating this to the pristine and "Oriental" features of the Russian past.[5] In what follows, therefore, the despotic character of Soviet-type societies is underlined, but it is not traced to relapses into or carry-overs from a supposedly "Asiatic" or, in Wittfogel's latter-day terminology, "semi-peripheral hydraulic" past. Rather, this despotism emerges as a corollary of a specific process of modernization, of the creation of a modern – albeit not capitalist – society.

Given the persistent crisis of modernity and also the fact that Soviet-type societies, regardless of their implosion in 1989/91, have so far represented the only forms of a version of modernity consciously set in opposition to capitalist hegemony, I hope to contribute towards a better understanding of the reasons not just for the failure of the Soviet experiment but also for the reproduction and radicalization of despotic relations of dominance which have occurred within that system, not least on account of the Bolsheviks' quest for radical modernization and rationalization.

This also precludes a perspective that has gained some popularity in the wake of the collapse of Soviet type societies in Eastern Europe; namely, to construe the ensuing transformations in terms of theories of modernization, mapping a passage from "traditional" or erstwhile "socialist" societies into "modern" ones shaped by "free market economies". Rather than thus collapsing modernity into capitalism, it is suggested here that transformation in Eastern Europe occurs within differing forms of modern societies that have for a long time now shed, in quite divergent forms and under widely different circumstances, "traditional" social relationships. Some of these transformations and their corollaries in terms of relations of power and dominance with regard to labour will form the subject of the following discussion. In addition, it is hoped that this paper will also make clear that the issue of "unfree" labour, in particular in the Soviet case, transcends the limits of forced labour strictly speaking[6] and of slavery.

---

5. Celebrated examples, although divergent in detail, for this theorem of Asiatic relapse are Wittfogel, *Oriental Despotism*; Dutschke, *Versuch, Lenin auf die Füsse zu stellen*; and Bahro, *Alternative*. For more detailed and differentiating criticism see Kössler, *Despotie*, ch. 2.
6. See also Van der Linden, "Forced Labour and Non-Capitalist Industrialization", this volume, p. 351-362.

1. *The Notion of Despoty*

To situate despotism within modernity, it is necessary to define the former in a way that goes beyond the usual notion of the exercize of untrammeled and arbitrary power. A reading of key classical texts reveals a more precise and richer, a more insightful and possibly a more disturbing content of the term. I shall not dwell on the niceties of the very intricate history of "despot" and "despotism" in classical philosophy, together with their reception both in medieval literature and from the Renaissance onwards; this has been covered sufficiently for our purpose.[7] The most important classical point of reference, however, remains Aristotle.

In his *Politics*,[8] Aristotle defines three distinct relationships that make up the household (*oîkos*) of the freeborn Athenian: *gamiké* is the relationship between the husband (*pósis*) and his spouse (*álochos*); *teknopoietiké* is that which exists between the father (*patér*) and his children (*tékna*); and *despotiké* relates the lord (*despótes*) to his slaves (*doûloi*). Thus, *despótes* is defined not just as the father of the house, which would be *oikónomos*, but as the father of the house specifically in relation to the slaves. Strictly speaking, *despotiké* here has also to be set apart from patriarchy, which would fall under *gamiké* and also *teknopoietiké*. *Despotiké*, or the despotic relationship I shall refer to in the following sections, further defines *despótes* in two functional relations to the slaves: (1) the slaves are assigned the business of securing the material daily necessities, the "things" of life (*khrematistiké*). This is the place of Aristotle's ill-famed description of the slave being by nature an "animated tool" which is connected with the idea, completely unrealistic at the time of writing, of supplanting the necessity of human labour by an "*autómaton*".[9] This conceptualization underlines the general trend informing Aristotle's deliberations about *khrematistiké*. Elsewhere, the relationship between *despótes* and slave, in contradistinction to the other two relationships that make up the *oîkos*, is seen to stand outside the *philía*, and analagous to that of "craft and tools, and of spirit and body".[10] Slaves and the relationship to them thus stand outside the central qualities of *philía* and *koinonía*; i.e., not only outside the community of the free and equal citizens of the *pólis*, but also outside human relationships properly speaking. The *despotiké* relationship is pervaded by the circumstance of necessity (*anagké*), in keeping with the slaves' task to furnish the material prerequisites of life, to secure and produce what is needed to satisfy

---

7. The most important reference is Koebner, "Despot and Despotism", pp. 275-302; see also Venturi, "Oriental Despotism", pp. 133-142.

8. Aristotle, "Politica", 1253b-1255b.

9. *Ibid.*, 1253b.

10. Aristotle, "Ethica Eudaimonia", 1242a.

the daily wants of the household members.[11] (2) This is therefore also the field of "slaves' knowledge", while "master's knowledge" pertains to the "application of slaves".[12] In this conceptualization, of course, hand and mind are separated in a very strict and rigid way. The slave is seen as endowed with a soul but not with a deliberating mind (*bouleutikón*). And it is therefore precisely by employing his slaves in a deliberate manner that the master-*despótes* is in a position to free himself from the exigencies of *anagké*; it is because the private realm of the household is structured in this way that he can take his place as a citizen among equals in the community of the free and equal. At least as important is the fact that, in moving on to an emphatic statement of the universal necessity of dominance, Aristotle stresses its functional aspects: both master and slave, as well as the soul and the body, are seen in this way: The dominant part, in Aristotle's view, is decisive in making the whole arrangement work, in forging "something common" out of parts that would otherwise be separate and disjointed[13]: Rule (*arkhê*) of some kind is thus seen as a precondition of community. Doubtlessly, this view dovetails with Aristotle's well-known aristocratic bias; but there is more to it, as we can see when we re-formulate his statement, in the sense that under conditions of dominance at least, productive functions vital both to the individual and to society cannot be carried out without a directing and dominant instance. Without this, the slaves would not be in a position to exercize their productive function.

The meaning of despotism, then, encompasses more than unrestricted power to coerce. In the Aristotelian concept, this power is (1) linked to the dimension of *anagké*, that is to the mode of securing the necessities of life by making use of the working capacities of others, and (2), to the vital role of the *despótes* in conceptualizing and organizing the process of *khrematistiké*, which is then executed by the slaves. Over and above the obvious ideological justification of classical slavery, this concept contains important insights that probably account for at least part of the persistent interest commanded by the Aristotelian text and, more importantly, can be usefully transferred to the analysis of modern societies. Of course, in the case of the concept of "despoty" in particular, this has to take into account the career of the concept itself, as well as the fundamental changes of societal contexts. At the same time, the motive of despoty has re-appeared in vital analyses of modern social and political relations. However, in general usage at any rate, the concept's focus on the form of the state is much more pronounced than in Aristotle, where it does not figure among the three forms of good government or their negative counterparts, but is used rather in contradistinction to it, *pace* some "occasional remarks" referring to the "aban-

11. Aristotle, "Politica", 1253b.
12. *Ibid.*, 1255b.
13. *Ibid.*, 1254a.

donment of lawful tradition".[14] Further, modern usage has projected "despotism" in the sense of arbitrary and unlimited power onto non-Western, specifically Oriental societies, while at the same time employing it in anti-absolutist propaganda.[15] A tendency towards this may also be discerned in Aristotle, but this aspect has been brought out really only by the authors of the Enlightenment. All the more reason why the application of the term "despotism" to a relationship that is both clearly Western and without any direct linkage to the state, the modern factory, should command more interest.

2. Despoty in the Modern Setting

From the very start, critics of the factory system have branded it as "despotic". The most celebrated version of this indictment will probably be found in the *Communist Manifesto*. At the same time, the following quote highlights the structural parallels between industrial and military organization, the absoluteness of command and of disposal on the part of the employer and his agents: "Masses of labourers, crowded into the factory, are organized like soldiers. As privates of the industrial army they are placed under the command of a perfect hierarchy of officers and sergeants. Not only are they slaves of the bourgois class, and of the bourgeois state; they are daily and hourly enslaved by the machine, by the overseer, and, above all, by the individual bourgeois manufacturer himself. The more openly this despotism proclaims gain to be its end and aim, the more petty, the more hateful and the more embittering it is."[16]

The notion of despotism is linked here not just to the market, as Michael Burawoy has suggested in his important account of a sequence of factory regimes; nor is the translation of "capacity to work" into "sufficient labour" conceptualized here by "coercion" in the sense of exercize of brute force.[17] Factory despotism, which is analysed in much the same terms in *Capital*, means something else, and the notion carries more analytical force than is commonly perceived. It recalls strikingly the Aristotelian perspective. Thus, Marx demonstrates that "capital" adresses not just an economic relationship, i.e. exploitation of workers by their employers, but rather, a *functional* relationship at the same time: "Through the co-operation of numerous wage-labourers, the command of capital develops into a requirement for carrying on the labour process itself, into a real condition of production."[18] Here, capital is seen as an instance of

---

14. Koebner, "Despot and Despotism", p. 277.
15. See *ibid.*, section IV, also Kössler, *Despotie*, pp. 70 ff.
16. Marx/Engels, *Manifesto of the Communist Party*, p. 74.
17. Burawoy, *Politics of Production*, p. 134.
18. Marx, *Capital*, I, p. 448.

dominance that is by no means incidental to, but rather a necessary precondition of, the work process. This whole process rests on the co-operative, societal integration of the workers. However: "[The] co-operation of wage labourers is entirely brought about by the capital that employs them. Their unification into one single productive body, and the establishment of a connection between their individual functions, lies outside their competence. These things are not their own act, but the act of the capital that brings them together and maintains them in that situation. Hence the interconnection between their various labours confronts them [...] in practice, as his authority, as the powerful will of a being outside them".[19] These quotations might easily be multiplied. In all of them, capital is seen as something more than "merely" the exploitative side of the wage-labour relationship: be it in the person of an individual entrepreneur or in an anonymous body, capital at the same time also creates the co-operative connection among the workers within the factory that is so vital for the functioning of the entire set-up.

In discussing the role of the capitalist, Marx refers explicitly to Aristotle in a closely related discussion. He even paraphrases the Aristotelian *Politics* and, as it were, "translates" it into the modern setting: "'the master' – the capitalist [Aristotle's *despotes*] – 'proves himself such not by obtaining slaves' – ownership of capital, which gives him the power to buy labour – 'but by employing slaves' – using labourers, nowadays wage-labourers, in the production process." This boils down to the fact "that domination, in the economic domain as well as in the political, imposes on those in power [*Gewalthaber*] the functions of dominating",[20] and this Marx postulates for "all modes of production which [...] are based on class opposition."[21]

Of course, ancient relationships and modern capitalist ones must not be collapsed into each other by a mere exchange of the terms "slave" and "wage labourer". After all, modern capitalism is, on account of the historical record, the free labour system *par excellence*. The structural analogy, then, applies only to an albeit strategic part of both societal configurations. Under capitalism, the Aristotelian *oíkos* has been split up into two distinct spheres, one geared to production and one geared to reproduction. The "disembedded" modern household, stripped of the productive functions and potential of the *oíkos*, is dependent for its day-to-day workings on continuous market access to procure material provisions.[22] To obtain the means to do so, the wage-dependent household has to realize the wage relationship on a continuous basis. It is

---

19. *Ibid.*, pp. 449-450.
20. Marx, *Capital*, III, p. 509. Marx refers to Aristotle, "Politica", 1255b.
21. Marx, *Capital*, III, p. 510.
22. The implications of this have been put in classical fashion by Polanyi, *The Great Transformation*; important updates are provided by Schiel, "Alltag und Geborgenheit", pp. 53-79.

therefore dependent, as it were, on the other pole of the former *oîkos*, i.e., on its productive functions which are now embodied in the enterprise. Only on condition that a wage-dependent household succeeds in the continuous sale of labour power, and as a precondition, in the continuous use of that labour power within the enterprise, will this household be able to perform its reproductive functions properly, to restore working capacity, to raise and socialize children. Both the individual household and the enterprise represent in principle *private* spheres with the *public* spheres of the market and the state mediating between them.

The establishment of these public spheres and their central position in the constitution and shaping of the over-all social context in capitalist societies can hardly be overestimated in terms of their consequences. With regard to the present discussion, it is by these very means that the despotic elements inherent in the enterprise as well as in the patriarchal household can be hemmed in and restrained, albeit not in a direct – and always in a precarious – manner. With respect to the despotic relationship, among the restraints to its exercize that evolved over roughly two centuries, two deserve particular mention: first, what might be called societal solidarity funds, usually guaranteed by the state (systems of social security) which, by easing the dependence of the wage-earning household on the market, also act to strengthen the bargaining position of the worker inside the enterprise, to tilt the balance of "production politics" to some extent in the workers' favour and, accordingly, to contribute towards a change in factory regimes;[23] and second, the public sphere afforded space to organize – or to win the freedom to begin the process of organization – which in turn was a pre-condition to workers' obtaining rights inside the enterprise itself, again a process guaranteed by the state.

In developments such as these, Michael Burawoy in his forceful argument for a differentiated view of factory regimes under capitalism, sees a central reason, besides the even more fundamental changes in work processes, for the transformation from "despotic" to "hegemonic" regimes. But Burawoy himself stresses the historical character of the processes he describes. He points to the rise of of a "hegemonic despotism" under the new conditions of globalization where "labour [...] makes concessions on the basis of the relative profitability of one capitalist vis-à-vis another", and where workers may be "forced to choose between wage cuts [...] and job loss".[24] In terms of the present discussion, this diagnosis by Buroway has not only been validated during recent years (especially after 1989/91) but also re-inforces the view that the despotic relationship is central to the capitalist enterprise, in-depth modifications to the latter notwithstanding.

---

23. This is detailed especially by Burawoy, *Politics of Production*, pp. 137 ff.
24. *Ibid.*, p. 150.

The existence within the capitalist enterprise of a modern despotic relationship may be linked to the private character of the former, coupled with its central importance for the lives not only of capitalists but, even more so, of wage-earners and their household members.[25] The modern concept of ownership conveys unrestricted power over the property concerned. Again, this has been modified in the case of the enterprise, but these modifications do not change the heart of the matter. The "owner" or "dominus", through his "ius disponendi de re sua"[26] has the right to dispose of his property in terms of using or changing it, or also of *not* using it. For the enterprise, this may amount not only to strategic investment decisions, to changes in the work processes, but also to plant closure. Of course the actual pressure exerted on the employees is partly rooted outside the factory – the "whip of unemployment" is mediated by the market, specifically the labour market. But inside the enterprise this is transformed into a relationship that is deeply informed by despotic traits.

As has already been mentioned, any industrial (or commercial) enterprise is not just an assembly of machines, but rather has to it the vital aspect of represent-ing the co-operative, or societal nexus. In contradistinction to the over-all context of modern capitalist society, created by the communication and exchange in the market-place and in the public sphere generally, this nexus is forged by the will and decision of the capitalist, or even of some collective body, a "Board" which represents the instance of Capital. This "immediate" form of social integration[27] is clearly contrary to the "mediated" market nexus: While the former is dependent either on coercion or – in the hypothetical case of the "free association of producers" – possibly on the direct agreement among the participants in a joint working effort, the latter functions by the co-ordination of anonymous commodity owners and therefore without coercion. Again, the coercion inherent in unmediated integration may be modified by the concrete forms of "production politics" in various historical stages, ranging from the granting of "paternalistic" favours to the institutionalized co-option of workers' representatives under "hegemonic" regimes. In addition, the industrial work process is dependent not only on formal technical arrangements but also on the functioning of informal networks of communication. These, as well as informal strategies or "games" on the part of the operators are consciously integrated into shop-floor management practices designed to ensure smooth functioning of the enterprise.[28] At present, these relationships are being transformed once more in

---

25. This point is made with particular force by Weber, "Zur Psychophysik der industriellen Arbeit", p. 155.
26. Kant, *Metaphysik der Sitten*, pp. 366, 387. The blatantly male form of this argument is taken from the original and also considered congruous with most of social reality.
27. Marx, *Capital*, I, p. 508.
28. Cf. Burawoy, *Politics of Production*, pp. 35–40, and *Manufacturing Consent*.

the course of the microelectronic revolution, with outcomes ranging from de-skilling to a widening of workers' space for their own initiative on the shop floor.[29] And in the final instance, regardless of the particulars of formal and informal communication networks, these networks depend for their existence on the continued existence of the enterprise, i.e. on the will of the capitalist proprietor(s). Any decision to close an enterprise or plant removes the basis for co-operation in the labour process as well as for communicative networks associated with it; and very likely, actual communication between the partici-pants collapses as well, once they are no longer part of the work-force. This validates the formula that it is the capitalist who brings together the workers – they stay together, as a collective of co-operating workers at least, only as long as this fits the interests of the capitalist. This is congruent with the concept of the despot outlined earlier.

This whole discussion hinges on the central point that *in spite* of all modifi-cations and of their importance, the despotic relationship has not been elimi-nated as a basic aspect of the capitalist enterprise. This is borne out by the fact, also noted by industrial sociologists,[30] that the power to dispose of the means required to maintain the co-operative nexus among the workers still rests with the capitalist and that despite all modifications, "contracting ends before the production process is entered into".[31] Regardless of its modifications and their far-reaching effects, the capitalist enterprise, by virtue of its internal structure of communication and inherent authority and by its external setting in societal property relations, is "despotic in its form".[32]

The importance of all this to our present argument lies precisely in this basic despotic content of the modern capitalist industrial enterprise. The relevance of this for a proper understanding of Soviet-type societies and their labour relations is even greater than for modern capitalist societies, although these form the indispensable background for our further argument.

3. Bolshevik Rationalization and the Unleashing of Modern Despotism

The Marxian critique of machinery and the capitalist enterprise has, despite its radical implications, never shed a basic ambiguity that has turned out to have far-reaching consequences. Machinery as developed by modern capitalism and as organized within the enterprise, was seen by Marx both as a means of exploitation and de-humanizing subjection, and at the same time as the central achievement

29. Instances are provided e.g. in Wood, *Transformation of Work?*
30. See the very explicit statement by Bechtle, *Betrieb als Strategie*, p. 62.
31. Littek, "Arbeitssituation und betriebliche Arbeitsbedingungen", p. 107.
32. Marx, *Capital*, I, p. 450.

of capitalism which would eventually usher in the universally rich society he equated with socialism.[33] This ambiguity was resolved in favour of the pro-gressivist and industrialization pole by the stress which the leading figures of the Second International – especially Karl Kautsky – placed on rational organization, supposedly epitomized in the modern capitalist enterprise. In their view, this compared very favourably with the irrationality that prevailed under capitalism on a societal scale on account of the "anarchy" of the market; it did not seem very farfetched, therefore, to hope that the ills of capitalist disproportionalities would be cured by projecting the rationality of the enterprise onto the wider society.[34] The vision of socialism during the second half of the nineteenth and the early twentieth century thus never entailed a critique of technology or of the industrial work process as such, nor a criticism of the forms under which they were organized. The authority of direction in the enterprise was stressed by Engels in his later work,[35] and it was taken for granted even by leading anarchists like Mikhail Bakunin[36] and – albeit by default – Petr Kropotkin.

The Bolshevik idea of a socialist society shaped according to the latest rationalizing feats of the German war economy was therefore quite in keeping with socialist thought then prevailing. Even the proverbial excesses of the early phase of war communism, such as the militarization of labour, can be shown to be rooted in Kautskyan concepts.[37] The idea that the latest achievements of shop organization under capitalism represent, by this very token, the pinnacle of rationality also motivated the adaptation of Scientific Management, as propagated by F.W. Taylor and – later on – the application in the Soviet Union of Henry Ford's conveyor belt methods.[38] Both moves implied violent measures to discipline the work force, and sharp changes in the power relations inside plants and enterprises.[39] In addition, the evaluation of Taylorism by Lenin, while always extolling (and probably overestimating) its rationalizing potential, underwent a clear shift shortly after the advent of the Bolsheviks to power: The former emphasis on gains for workers in terms of free time through higher productivity gave way, under the exigencies of the situation, to a stress on the exclusive rights of managers, militating against collegial forms of direction and workers' participation on plant and shop-floor levels.[40]

33. For elaboration on this, see Kössler, *Arbeitskultur im Industrialisierungsprozess*, pp. 37-49.
34. I have set this out in more detail, see *ibid.*, pp. 341-355, and "Arbeit und Revolution", pp. 96-107, with source quotations.
35. Engels, "On Authority", pp. 482-483.
36. Bakunin, *Statism and Anarchy*, pp. 198 ff., and *Gott und der Staat*, pp. 110 f.
37. This holds true in spite of the bitter exchanges between the ruling Bolsheviks and their erstwhile preceptor, see Kössler, "Trotzki zur Militarisierung", pp. 161-171.
38. Cf. Carr and Davies, *Foundations of a Planned Economy*, p. 367.
39. Cf. Süss, *Arbeiterklasse*; and Kössler and Muchie, "American Dreams", pp. 68-83.
40. Linhart, *Lénine, les paysans, Taylor*, pt. II.

The main and decisive strand in the Bolshevik experiment, however, was the fact that Soviet industrial and economic policies did not limit themselves just to an adaptation of "rational" techniques developed in the capitalist West and in the enterprise in particular. Rather, the Bolshevik project entailed the re-organization of society in the image of the enterprise in its most advanced and, therefore, supposedly most rational form. The role of societal integration, mediated under capitalism by the market, was to be changed, a process whereby the market was supplanted by the plan, which in turn entailed unmediated integration at the level of society as a whole. The Soviet system of planning, from its inception until its final demise, depended basically on planning in natural units. That means it was built on the assumption that planning meant to co-ordinate in *direct*, unmediated manner the over-all resources, both material and human.[41] This approach was criticized from the outset, not least because of its inefficiency, its wasteful production, and its failure actually to deliver the benefits promised by the concept of a planned co-ordination of societal production. Rather than "planning", it was suggested, what actually did take place in Soviet type societies was a form of "organization" within a chaotic over-all situation,[42] or of "negotiation" between the central, regional and plant levels, which however did not remove the "coercive" character of the over-all system.[43]

The comprehensive management of all the resources of society included, in theory at least, also control, as far as possible, over the work force. In the heyday of the system, it was hoped by these means to apply "American" (i.e. Fordist) production methods in such a way that the economies of scale inherent in mass production would be fully realized only under the Soviet system, whereas in the United States they would still be restricted to individual enterprises – albeit giant ones.[44] Obviously, this kind of industrial rationality was aimed at already in Lenin's considerations on the eve of the October revolution when he called for transforming all citizens into "employees and workers of a *single* country-wide 'syndicate'", namely the state[45] and when he defined as "our immediate aim" to "organize the *whole* economy on the lines of the postal service".[46] These concepts have informed Soviet labour relations, which modified modern wage labour in important respects without completely discarding its form.

The state, or rather the party-state apparatus with its leading elite on top, assumed the role of the sole organizer of an economy conceived, in principle, as one giant enterprise. The apparatus, and the elite in particular, was, therefore,

41. Conert, *Die Ökonomie des unmöglichen Sozialismus*, pt. I.
42. Ticktin, "Towards a Political Economy", p. 34.
43. Heller *et al.*, *Sowjetische Weg*, pp. 102, 97.
44. See Süss, *Arbeiterklasse*, p. 143.
45. Lenin, *State and Revolution*, p. 473.
46. *Ibid.*, p. 427.

in the first place in a position to exert enormous power over the workers, not only by means of "political" control via the party, the police, etc., but also in terms of economic might, by its virtual monopsony vis-a-vis labour power. The collapsing of the political into the economic, occasioned by state ownership and control of the means of production made each and everyone directly dependent on the state for their day-to-day reproduction. Since the separation between the home and the work-place was by and large maintained, *pace* the early experiments in communal living, this meant that on a formal level at least, control over the workers was extended far beyond the possibilities of the individual (although giant) capitalist enterprise. True, attempts at all-encompassing control, including the private everyday lives of the workers are well-known from various stages of capitalist development, be it the "company states" of the early factory masters,[47] "Kruppian" paternalism or similar concepts and designs enacted by Henry Ford in overseeing workers' habits and doings even outside hours of work.[48] But still, regardless of the considerable and at times even nearly total power thus exerted, employers remained a plurality in principle, and the relationship between the work-place and the household as the place of reproduction remained mediated by the market and thus, in the average case at least, shielded from direct intervention by the employer.[49]

4. The Contradictions of Coercion and Industrial Working Capacity

Under the Soviet system, the state as the only employer acquired a seemingly rational motive for a system of much more comprehensive control compared to the general run of individual or corporate employers under industrial capitalism. The party and state elite legitimated their actions by the "common good" of socialist reconstruction as represented and presaged by the party of the proletariat. Once the ruling party had effectively supplanted the class it claimed to represent, the path was open for "educating" workers, for a large-scale attempt to remodel them and their working capacities in that typical Soviet adaptation of Taylorism, Scientific Organization of Work.[50] Taylorism was transformed here from an approach geared to *virtuosos* of work into a mass approach which was propagated by mass campaigns, strictly centrally directed under party political control during the 1920s. Later on, these concepts re-emerged as administrative tools to effect "a combination of intensification and

---

47. Burawoy, *Politics of Production*, p. 91.
48. Arnold and Faurote, *Ford Methods*, pp. 41 ff.
49. Lucassen, "Free and Unfree Labour Before the Twentieth Century", this volume, pp. 46f.
50. Kössler, *Arbeitskultur im Industrialisierungsprozess*, pp. 399-440.

rationalization" in the economy.[51] In all these approaches, the directing centre was seen as the main locus of the application of rational methods of planning and management, which fit well Lenin's visions prior to the October revolution.

Under modern capitalism, the despotic relationship is a persistent structural feature of the enterprise; it shapes vital aspects not only of the working process but also of the "private" lives of workers and employees outside working hours, above all on account of the circumstance that the necessities of life cannot be secured without entering the "hidden abode of production".[52] But as has been indicated, the despotic relationship can be and has been restricted not only to the enterprise as the private realm of the capitalist but also by modifications inside the enterprise, due to technological changes, to state interventions, and to workers' struggles. The latter two reflect the importance of a public sphere that provides a space for independent organization and for the autonomous articulation of individual and group interests. The practices involved in developing and maintaining such organizations in turn have played a very important role in the gradual acquisition of abilities and attitudes that are necessary in order to cope, not only with the demands of modern, capitalist society, but also with those of the industrial work process.[53] It was not least through the experiences mediated through autonomous organization, self-improvement etc. that working people mastered the "rules of the game",[54] i.e., the ways and means, including modes and techniques of behaviour required both for the management of the disembedded household and as general abilities by the industrial labour process. In another context, the formation and spread of these attitudes of restricted behaviour, perseverance in monotonous tasks, long-term planning and the like have been designated as the "process of civilization".[55] The Bolsheviks' approach to the problems of worker "indiscipline" and lack of culture from the early days of Soviet rule has been strictly top-down, defining the "education" of the Soviet workers as an emphatically modernizing and civilizing mission. This is not only consistent with the basically and explicitly Jacobinian concept of party and vanguard, but also recalls similarly aimed initiatives of middle class philanthropes in industrial nineteenth-century England, and later on, in colonialist intervention.[56]

The failure to emulate the levels of productivity achieved in developed industrial capitalist countries has been both a salient indicator of the prolonged crisis of the Soviet system and a main cause for its final demise. The problem associated with efficiency of plant organization and labour, with the motivation

---

51. Tatur, *Taylorismus in der Sowjetunion*, p. 65.
52. Marx, *Capital*, I, p. 279.
53. See Kössler, *Arbeitskultur im Industrialisierungsprozess*, pt. II.
54. Hobsbawm, *Labouring Men*, p. 350.
55. Elias, *Über den Prozess der Zivilisation*.
56. On the latter see, e.g., Alatas, *Myth of the Lazy Native*.

to exert labour power and with the ability to adapt to (and to bring forth) technical innovations have been particularly pronounced after the shift to "intensive" industrialization during the mid-1950s, in contradistinction to the preceding, "extensive" period with its mass application of relatively unqualified and often forced labour.[57] The barriers to rationalization have never been really overcome within the framework of the Soviet system, and therefore, the race with the Western adversary could never be won, in any case not in the fields of industrial production, efficiency, and availability of consumer goods. Many critics have attributed these strategic shortcomings to a specific *gap* within otherwise overwhelming control, to the *lack* of the systemic coercion which also formed part and parcel of Soviet type labour relations. The statutory or at least, factual obligation for everyone to perform waged labour and "a degree of control [that] has never existed anywhere"[58] were counterbalanced, to an extent, by the absence of a "genuine labour market" as well as, due to the low effectiveness of consumer good production by the absence of real positive incentives; the plant directorates were thus stripped of "disciplinary means",[59] and the guarantee of employment made retrenchment virtually impossible and thus acted as one of the massive brakes blocking technical innovations.[60] One possible solution, besides the more and more illusory hope for the advent of "real" workers' power, was seen in the return of that "whip of unemployment" entailed by an effective labour market and in the removal both of the obligation to work and of the guarantee to be able to do so. In provocative terms, "insecurity" was thus identified by some as the necessary condition for dynamism, efficiency and progress.[61]

The above considerations may suggest a somewhat different perspective. Direct coercion and control of labour in Soviet type societies was not an isolated feature but was linked closely to the monopoly for political articulation and all kinds of organization claimed by the ruling party or rather, the elite or *nomenklatura*. This political monopoly was central both to the Bolshevik project and to the Stalinist and post-Stalinist power structure, although it may be argued that its social and ideological content, and certainly the intentions of its agents, did undergo important changes especially during the first decade of Soviet rule. The systematic ban imposed on any organization outside the close purview of the party also served to close those spaces where everyday capacities could be formed in confronting and coping with the exigencies of the new society. One of the very few attempts actually to do so was the "Time League" (Liga Vremya)

57. See Nuti, "Contradictions of Socialist Economies", pp. 228-273.
58. Ticktin, "Political Economy", p. 41.
59. Ticktin, "Contradictions of Soviet Society", p. 35.
60. Arnot, "Soviet Labour Productivity".
61. Heinsohn and Steiger, "Geld, Produktivität und Unsicherheit", pp. 2-15.

organized by P.M. Kerzhentsev during the early 1920s as a mass movement to popularize time economy in the set-up of the personal everyday lives of its members. Very soon, the league was suppressed as a useless and potentially harmful "organ for self-organized grassroots activity".[62]

Inversely, it may of course be argued that the exigencies of everyday life in Soviet type societies demanded and fostered quite different capacities in persons than those preparing them for participation in – albeit sophisticated – industrial work processes. In any case, these very few hints would suggest that the extension of the industrial despotic relationship as embodied in the "rational" enterprise onto a societal scale has proved, not only as the avenue of creating actual despotic states but also, to counter-act important preconditions for effective participation in industrial work processes.

All this may of course also be referred back to the Marxian ambiguity in evaluating machinery touched upon above. The lack of a consistent critique not only of relations, but of forces of production has fostered affirmative conceptions that did not take notice of the built-in mechanisms of domination in seemingly rational technological and administrative arrangements.

Conclusion

The Soviet experience, while demonstrating the *impossible* of strategies of socio-economic development and engineering along these lines, has very little to tell us about what is *possible* in terms of the current situation. In other words, the tendency to overlook the built-in forms of formal and informal domination, the founding of the despotic relationship inherent in all modern societies, is understandable in the face of the demise of the one competing system. It would be wrong and short-sighted, however, not to take account of the limited nature of this past challenge whose limits are apparent, not only in its own failure but in the persistent crises faced by the seemingly triumphant capitalist adversary. On account of these crises, the identification of spheres of dominance and countervailing potentials remains of central interest. And this interest is enhanced by insight into the consequences of underestimating these problems of dominance that made up part of the initial flaws of the Soviet experiment and contributed greatly to some of its most oppressive features, as well as to its strategic deficiencies.

---

62. Cf. Kössler, *Arbeitskultur im Industrialisierungsprozess*, pp. 434-439.

Labor – Free or Coerced? A Historical Reassessment of Differences and Similarities

Robert J. Steinfeld and Stanley L. Engerman[*]

I

Over the last twenty years, historians have developed a more complicated picture of the forms of labor in use in the eighteenth and nineteenth centuries. Where previously they tended to divide labor simply into free wage labor on one side, and slave or serf labor on the other, this new view has added contract labor, indentured servitude, apprenticeship, and peonage to the map of forms of labor in use in earlier centuries.[1] But the new map continues to classify these different forms of labor as coming under the basic categories free or unfree, and continues to assume that each of these forms of labor is a distinctive "type" which is supposed to have a natural core set of characteristics that sets it off from the others, and marks it definitively as either "free" or "unfree". The modern conceptual map of labor looks something like the following:

Free labor: Wage labor
Unfree labor: Apprenticeship, indentured servitude, contract labor, peonage, serfdom, slavery

This paper will argue that the above picture and the assumptions upon which it rests still need to be radically revised to capture the reality of labor relations in the past and perhaps also the present. First, it will argue that "types" of labor, like "wage labor" and "contract labor", never did possess a set of fixed, natural characteristics, but were defined by a range of characteristics and that depending upon the precise characteristics they possessed in any particular place, such labor might be considered either "free" or "unfree". By the standards of twentieth-century American constitutional law,[2] for example, nineteenth-century English wage labor" was "unfree" labor, while nineteenth-century American "contract

---

*   For comments in the preparation of this paper we wish to thank Seymour Drescher, David Eltis, Lou Ferleger, David Galenson, Sherwin Rosen, and the participants at the conference, particularly Pieter Emmer and Ralph Shlomowitz.

1. A number of the ideas presented in this paper have been developed more fully elsewhere. See Steinfeld, "Myth of the Rise of Free Labor", *Invention of Free Labor*; see Engerman, "Coerced and Free Labor", "Economics of Forced Labor", and "Land and Labour Problem".
2. See Clyatt v. United States, 197 U.S. 207 (1905), pp. 215-216; Bailey v. Alabama, 219 U.S. 219 (1911), p. 243; Pollock v. Williams, 322 U.S. 4 (1944), p. 18.

labor" was "free" labor. As this example makes clear, the different "types" of labor were, in certain respects, not nearly as discrete and discontinuous as the standard picture implies. At the boundaries the "types" of labor frequently blur and merge. Moreover, since labor force characteristics include a number of different dimensions (entry, performance, and exit among them), at times not all these aspects can be fit into the same side of the free-unfree dichotomy.

We shall argue that the classification of labor into "free" or "unfree" is an arbitrary not a natural classification. All "dependent" labor is elicited as the result of pressures brought to bear on it, pressures that are socially and legally constructed. Since variations exist in the economic, legal, political, and social aspects of these constructions, the spectrum of labor systems does not imply any equivalence in effects upon workers or hirers, and such differences remain a source of debate and struggle. Nevertheless, to call some labor elicited under certain pressures "voluntary" and other labor elicited under different kinds of pressures "involuntary" represents arbitrary line drawing that obscures the coercive content of some labor regimes, and ignores the important role of the legal system and laws in land and labor (including immigration) policy.

Further, we will suggest that a better way to understand the history of labor is in terms of a range of coercive practices utilized in different places and at different times, all constructed (but sometimes in different ways) by law, rather than by the present construct of discontinuous "types" of labor arranged under the headings "free" and "unfree". We will offer a number of examples of the ways in which different regimes can be made to achieve similar results. Finally, we will suggest that historians of labor should focus on a more particularistic set of inquiries about the particular practices that different societies and polities permitted and prohibited, the reasons for those decisions, and thus the nature and the outcome of the different varieties of what can be generally regarded as forms of labor coercion.

II

Part of the difficulty involved in the attempt to separate free from unfree labor arises from the fact that there are several different aspects to the package of labor inputs that need to be considered. The absence of legal or physical coercion in one dimension need not preclude such coercion in another. Various different forms of control may be used in the different dimensions of the labor relationship. Therefore, even when the absence of direct controls and coercion are as complete as they are under conditions of "freedom," some coercive elements may remain, which makes a definition of free labor problematic.

To better understand what is meant by various types of free and coerced labor, including slavery and serfdom, it will be useful to trace the steps involved in the acquisition and use of labor, and to describe the problems faced by users of labor as well as laborers at each step. We can regard the ruling class as desiring to have a large supply of labor with low labor costs, where and when it wants it. Low labor costs need not necessarily mean low wages or other payments to laborers, since productivity must be considered, and expensive labor with large amounts of human capital may be preferred to cheap labor with only limited skills.

Among free populations, labor force participation is influenced by the desire to consume. This desire could be due to the basic need to acquire a minimal, physically necessary, amount of goods, although in general people desire to acquire, for whatever reason, amounts above what is physically necessary. Traditionally, among mercantilists and other believers in the "backward bending supply curve of labor," it had been argued that for an increased labor force participation poverty and low living standards were needed – otherwise most people would see no need to work.[3] The advantage of free labor, it was often argued, came not only from the incentives it provided by letting workers benefit from increased outputs, but also from the effectiveness of starvation as an inducement to work. It is, of course, possible to maintain aspects of this argument even today, as some do, using changing definitions of poverty and of what a necessary standard of living is. This relation among free labor, low incomes, and labor force participation is a reminder that income levels do not always track the legal status of workers or the nature of the distribution of power within society. Thus, it has been argued that, in the past, slaves had higher incomes than did free farmers or free wage laborers, and this persisted through-out most of the nineteenth century. Even under slavery, laborers may have been able to influence the determination of some part of their labor income and effort, as when slaves worked under the task system or other similar systems which allowed them to allocate some labor time, although, as with serfs, less working time for owners sometimes meant more working time overall to achieve desired consumption levels.[4]

Clearly, subsistence income levels were not determined exclusively by nature, since they incorporate much in the way of social conventions and of individual desires above the physiologically required minimum. At various times, where labor was nominally free, attempts were made, by introducing taxation, limiting the land to be settled, increasing immigration, and other similar devices influenc-ing labor incomes and land availability, to lower incomes and change the amount

3. For discussions of this in the case of the British Industrial Revolution, see Coats, "Changing Attitudes to Labour"; and Mathias, *Transformation of England*, pp. 131-167. See also De Vries, "Industrial Revolution and the Industrious Revolution".
4. For recent discussions of slave influence on working arrangements and consumption patterns, see the essays in Hudson Jr, *Working Toward Freedom*.

and/or nature of the work free workers were "willing" to do.[5] Such considerations, for example, were central to the long-standing debate over the British Poor Laws, where the standard, and long-standing, objection to any subsidy for even the temporarily "deserving unemployed" was that workers should be maintained at poverty levels and could not be permitted to receive unnecessary subsidies from other members of society, particularly if labor could be obtained from those physically able to work.

The steps required to get labor to work when and where it is wanted include the processes of migration to place of work, getting labor into the particular work site, giving them incentives to be productive once on the job, and preventing workers from voluntarily leaving the job or region in which their labor is needed. Long-distance, intercontinental, migration to a new place of work, has been accomplished (1) by free migrations (when incomes reached an adequate level and incentives to move were there, as when industrialization over time in different parts of Europe forced people off the land), (2) by "voluntary" indentured servitude, where the initial contract (presumably but debatably entered into by voluntary choice) to pay for transport required a certain period of controlled labor and included the possibility of sale, and (3) by slavery, with the sale of labor on one continent for movement to another. In terms of the settlement of the New World prior to 1820, it was slavery that was most important, although the numbers were not as large as were to be the free migrations from Europe in the later nineteenth and early twentieth centuries.[6] In increasing numbers over time, however, there was a return flow of European migrants to their original homes, so that some aspects of the labor adjustment were more "temporary" than permanent, a situation quite different from that of slaves. These movements could be either for attachment to a specific employer in an area, or to provide a large pool of laborers in a particular area on which employers could then draw.

A type of geographic relocation historically more important for serfs, ex-serfs, and free workers than for slaves, arose with the expansion of industrial work in urban areas. Given the prior predominance of rural populations, some movement was necessary to permit modern development, a movement that led to some higher incomes but also to some dramatic changes in living and working conditions. Migration to urban areas could be either permanent or seasonal, with

---

5. "By creating conditions which restricted the alternatives available, increased labor input as well as changes in the composition of output were achieved. At the limit, the Malthusian subsistence level would determine the minimum necessary labor input, but it was possible to obtain similar results by artificial methods of social and political control. While individuals maintained legal property rights in themselves, controls over land and capital led to economic outcomes resembling those when property rights in persons belonged to others." Engerman, "Coerced and Free Labor", p.18.
6. See Eltis, "Free and Coerced Transatlantic Migrations".

quite different effects on family patterns, cultural continuities, and work habits.

Even when a sufficient population was available in a given area, problems could remain in getting people into the productive labor force or getting people to work at a desired work site, be it farm or factory. To accomplish this the ruling classes relied upon poverty, while individual employers could use positive incentives such as higher wages, shorter hours or better working conditions, or certain forms of legal or physical coercion involving specific controls or compulsions for particular work. Thus serfdom, which generally drew its labor force from people already resident, utilized the legal power of the lord to make serfs work for the lord's benefit, most frequently in agricultural pursuits, but, at times, also in industrial or service enterprises.[7] Similarly, there were controls introduced by the Spanish settlers over native-Americans that had different characteristics than African slavery, and did not involve long-distance involuntary movement of the Indians. After a brief period of slavery, the systems of *encomienda* and *repartimiento*, and then debt peonage, were used to compel working time on the estates of the Iberian estate owners. In addition, Indians were often required to make payments in the form of tribute to the government and/or to private landowners.[8] The coercion under serfdom and in the Spanish-American systems was intended to force work of a particular kind at a specific location, but the fact that these were already populated areas meant that the long-distance involuntary migration characteristic of modern slavery was not necessary.

Once in the workplace, high levels of worker output were not guaranteed, and incentives were needed to induce the desired amount of production. Some incentives, to the free workers or those coerced into the workplace, are regarded as positive (higher wages, including the use of piece wages; good working conditions, etc.), some as negative (fear of firing; physical punishments; removal of benefits; fines, etc.). The mix (since several different methods could be used together) could vary over time with the nature of legal institutions, and the kinds of incentives they intended to permit. Users of labor were frequently concerned with the morale of the labor force and its effect on output levels, whatever the legal status of labor. The most widely-cited argument on comparative incentives was Adam Smith's remark that slave labor would be less productive than free because of the lack of incentives for slave workers.[9] While this reflected the legal basis of the system, which did not require the payment of wages or the provision of other positive incentives, the point was also well-known to slave-owners, who frequently sought methods to provide incentives to their slaves to increase production, once they were on the plantation. At times the physical, psychologi-

---

7. On late serfdom, see Blum, *End of the Old Order*.
8. On the Spanish-American labor systems, see Burkholder and Johnson, *Colonial Latin America*, pp. 108-116; and Lockhart and Schwartz, *Early Latin America*, pp. 86-146.
9. Smith, *The Wealth of Nations*, p. 684.

cal, and material treatment of slaves and serfs was not as extreme as the law would permit, because of the desire to obtain high outputs from the workers.[10] Further, the need to direct and coordinate labor when working is a central concern of entrepreneurs, which requires the worker to forego certain rights during the contracted period. It has been argued, therefore, that during the work period itself the various forms of labor institutions approximate each other.[11] Clearly, the patterns of controls and punishments in the workplace would differ depending upon the legal status of labor, particularly the freedom to move from one job to another, as well as the specific nature of the job. This latter point could explain the different incentives and treatment of military in contrast to civilian labor.

An important concern of so-called free labor was the right to leave employment whenever and as soon as desired. There were some limitations on this agreed to under the terms of voluntarily accepted contracts, and there is a long history of court cases regarding specific performance, the need for reimbursement, and the measurement of loss due to premature quitting. An important example of exit restrictions has been the British Master and Servants Acts, which were carried into most of the British colonies in the nineteenth century.[12] These made the leaving of a job by "free workers" before the expiration of the agreed-upon time period a criminal offense, punishable by imprisonment. Similar examples of restrictions on quitting can be seen in what some regard as critical industries even in the twentieth century; for example, a British worker who left a munitions factory without permission in World War I would be forced to suffer six weeks of unemployment.[13] Similar legal provisions existed in other countries, particularly in the earlier stages of industrialization. In mid-nineteenth century Russia a "free" worker who left a factory without authorization was regarded as a criminal, basically similar to the status of a serf who had run away from the estate.[14] Thus even when there was freedom in hiring and in labor mobility, the ability to quit when desired, without criminal penalties, was not always available to workers.

10. See Fogel and Engerman, *Time on the Cross*, pp. 107-157; and the ensuing dicussion of slave material living standards.
11. For an early argument to this effect, see Cicero, *De Officis/On Duties*, pp. 68-69: "Similarly, the work of all hired men who sell their labor and not their talents is servile and contemptible. The reason is that in their case wages actually constitute a payment for slavery." An even earlier observation to this effect is to be found in Weber's description of Babylonian law regarding free hired labor – in *Agrarian Sociology of Ancient Civilizations*, p. 96 – "the period of work was regarded as temporary slavery".
12. In addition to the writings of Steinfeld, see also Craven and Hay, "Criminalization of 'Free' Labour".
13. See Wolfe, *Labor Supply and Regulation*, particularly pp. 217-234.
14. See Zelnik, *Labor and Society in Tsarist Russia*, pp. 21-43.

Finally, there were questions concerning the ability of even free workers to move to new locations in seeking new jobs, since such actions were sometimes restricted, used to increase the labor pool in an existing area. In the case of serfdom, labor was legally prevented from departing without the lord's permission, while the same was true under slavery. The slaveowner, however, was free to sell the slave to another person who would then control the slave's location. Neither slave nor serf was free to move of their own volition. With free labor, however, there were restrictions on mobility enforced in many different societies, and under several different arrangements. Land for sale and settlement was often restricted in countries of relatively low population density such as Australia and the United States, thus limiting the numbers of potential new settlers who might take up land and avoid wage work, providing benefits to landowners and capitalists in older, more settled areas. Similar effects restricting mobility can result from private contracts which include provisions serving to raise the costs of departure decisions. Frequently, after the ending of slavery, ex-slaves would be given small plots of land for themselves if they were willing to work for their landlords, thus presumably increasing labor availability and reducing its costs. Limitations on the incomes and nationality or ethnicity of potential immigrants and of settlers on land have existed, favoring dominant groups. Immigration laws, by influencing overall rates of settlement, have had a marked impact on returns to labor and labor supplied, even if they have not themselves had a direct, legislated effect on the incomes and locational patterns of workers. Given the frequent pattern of migrants settling disproportionately in urban areas, however, significant effects on wages and the level and structure of output resulted. We can also note that the British aid to the unemployed (poor relief) was initially intended to keep people in their original place by not letting them receive benefits if they moved elsewhere. Any such movement was also discouraged by the imposition of residence requirements to prevent aid payments in areas of in-migration.[15] By these measures the labor pool in the former area was increased, while the potential area of in-migration saved on benefit payments, albeit with a lowered labor supply available.

III

The discussion in the previous section was intended to point to several problems in maintaining the rigid distinction between free and coerced labor. First, coercion may not exist at each step of the labor acquisition and use process, but only at one or two of the stages. Thus the specific forms that coercion takes will

15. See Slack, *English Poor Law*, and Rose, *Relief of Poverty*.

differ, and what is regarded as coercion can vary over time and place. Second, the various indicators may not all go in the same direction. In particular, the distinction between the legal nature of the coercion and the relative material benefits to the coerced has long been observed. Poverty may be considered as one form of coercion of those legally free, but what some regard as poverty might have been the result of choices made voluntarily, though within a framework of constraints established by numerous factors including law. Third, it is possible to distinguish between economic coercion and legal coercion. Economic coercion results from the operation of the market, influenced by individual tastes in the face of economic constraints, but also by the legal regulations in effect. The market is itself structured by law. Legal coercion results from a more direct imposition of legal penalties and police controls. Fourth, in our focus on coercion for economic production we have omitted discussion of other reasons for coercing populations, such as military purposes, for criminal correction, for handling children and others deemed unable to care for themselves, as well as for dealing with vagrants and the unemployed who should have been capable of caring for themselves. Coercion in the economic sphere may be only a limited part of the total of society's coercive pattern.

IV

The present discussions of forced labor, concentrating on the dichotomy of free and slave is a residue of the eighteenth and nineteenth-century attacks on slavery.[16] Slavery at the time was seen as a unique evil, entailing the buying and selling of people and the absolute domination of one person by another. Whether from a religious or secular perspective, the radically unequal power and legal rights of the two parties were seen as inappropriate for modern times and modern societies. Even on grounds of economics slavery was seen as inefficient and unproductive and a system incompatible with modern economic development. In contrast, non-slave (free) labor was regarded as more productive, with its incentives generating more output per worker, as well as more morally acceptable, since it ended the legal domination over individuals by other persons. The debates over slavery posed a contrast that permitted no intermediate cases or complications in personal or legal status, a presentation useful for that particular attempt at reform, but one which has proven to be misleading as applied to the broad range of cases. For the legal, political, and economic systems have been able to provide constraints, which even if not legally as severe as slavery, serve

---

16. On the issues noted in this paragraph see, in particular, Davis, *Problem of Slavery in the Age of Revolution*, and *Slavery and Human Progress*; and Drescher, *Capitalism and Antislavery*.

to limit individual choice. While neither ideally "free" (however that might be defined) nor as coercive as slavery, these systems do constrain, by intent or otherwise, what individuals might do. Neither slave nor free, these hybrids contain elements of both. Some are based on initially voluntary agreements that constrain behavior for a period up to several years, some result as responses to legal or illegal actions undertaken by individuals, and some arose from a desire to constrain economic choices of landowners as well as workers on the land, but all do serve to limit worker rights and incomes, generally based on the control over the labor of individuals, not the full ownership of their bodies.[17]

V

The conventional dichotomy of free and coerced labor rests on a set of assumptions that have been with us for a long time. Labor is supposed to be arranged in a menu of "types": wage labor, contract labor, peonage, slavery, serfdom. Each "type" is supposed to have a set of fixed characteristics that define it as either "free" or "unfree". Wage labor is the principal "type" of free labor. Contract labor is one "type" of unfree labor. What separates free labor from unfree labor is that unfree labor is subject to physical or legal compulsion while free labor is not.

In this section, we will look more closely at these two "types" of labor in the United States and in England to show that nineteenth century wage work was sometimes elicited through legal compulsion, and nineteenth-century contract labor was sometimes not subject to this kind of pressure. Following the conventional distinction we would have to say that in these cases the wage labor was unfree labor while the contract labor was free labor. As noted above, for almost a century after the Industrial Revolution, most English wage workers could be legally compelled to perform their engagements.[18] If they tried to quit before they had completed their term of engagement they could be imprisoned and reimprisoned until they returned to work out their time.[19] During their period of engagement they could be sent to the house of correction for breaches of conduct, for disobedience, sloppy work or leaving before the work day had ended. The labor of English wage workers, in other words, was elicited under

17. The distinction between owning labor and owning the body of the laborer can be found in Blackstone, *Commentaries*, 2, pp. 401-402, and was later a part of the proslavery defense.
18. See particularly 6 Geo. III, c.25 (1766), and 4 Geo. IV, c.34 (1823).
19. The King v. The Inhabitants of Barton-Upon Irwell, 2 M. & S. 329 (1814); Ex Parte Baker, 7 El. & Bl. 697 (1857); Unwin v. Clarke, 1 L.R. 417 (1866); Cutler v. Turner, 9 L.R. 502 (1874).

the kinds of threats that under modern American constitutional law make the labor "involuntary servitude."[20]

On the other hand, contract laborers imported into the United States beginning in the 1860s could not be legally compelled to perform their agreements, even though their employers had paid their transportation expenses.[21] The law of Northern states simply didn't authorize criminal punishment for contract breaches.[22] Needless to say American employers did strive to hold their contract workers to their agreements. They incorporated numerous provisions into contracts to try to ensure their performance. Sometimes, they had groups of workers agree to be held jointly and severally liable for breaches by any member of the group. If one absconded before fulfilling her agreement, the remaining group members would be liable for the debt.[23] Or they would have a propertied person from the contract laborer's home town personally guarantee the passage debt in case the contract worker ran away.[24] Employers used these devices as substitutes for criminal punishment to try to force workers to perform their agreements.

The conventional picture of labor forms arranged under the categories free and unfree has reified labor "types." Neither contract labor nor wage labor were "things" with fixed, natural sets of characteristics, one of which was freedom or unfreedom. They were social/legal practices which could be constructed in a range of different ways. Freedom or unfreedom were coincidental rather than essential features of both. The state could decide to give criminal sanctions to employers for breach or could decide not to. Moreover, this decision was only one of numerous social and legal decisions that went into the construction of these practices. A hundred similar decisions determined the fine grained coercive content of these practices along a continuum, rather than in terms of a single yes/no (coerced/free) decision about criminal sanctions. Suppose, for example, that courts had refused to enforce contracts in which immigrants agreed to be held jointly and severally liable for breach. Judges might have taken this position on the ground that these kinds of coercive measures represented unwarranted impositions on immigrants. Or suppose the opposite. Suppose employers were legally entitled to double damages for premature departure, could garnishee future wages to collect these damage awards, as well as hold new employers responsible

---

20. See Clyatt v. United States, pp. 215-216; Bailey v. Alabama, p. 243; Pollock v. Williams, p. 18.
21. See in general Erickson, *American Industry and the European Immigrant*, pp. 1-63. See also Steinfeld, *Invention of Free Labor*, p. 172.
22. See, for example, Parsons v. Trask and Others, 73 Mass (7 Gray) 473 (1856).
23. Creamer, "Recruiting Contract Laborers", p. 46.
24. *Ibid.*, pp. 49, 53.

for the debt. A range of different possible practices of contract labor and wage labor are possible giving employers many different degrees of coercive power.

An implicit explanatory scheme underlies the contemporary map of labor "types" in which each "type" falls on one side or the other of the free/coerced dichotomy. Employers are viewed as facing an established menu of fixed labor "types". It is assumed that economic conditions explain why they choose a particular "type" in a particular place at a particular time. Unfree labor was used where the wage-labor market had not yet been created or where it had broken down, where as in the colonial periphery, labor was in short supply and land was abundant. Where there was a large population of propertyless laborers and where land was expensive, as in the mature metropolitan economies, free wage labor was the "natural" form of labor. Under those circumstances, the "dull compulsion of economic relations" could be relied upon to supply adequate labor at economical wage rates. Legal compulsion was unnecessary.

But the English and American experiences raise serious questions about this explanatory scheme. American employers did resort to contract workers largely because the domestic wage labor market had partially broken down. The military demands of the Civil War had made skilled labor very difficult to obtain at economic wage rates. But it is in such circumstances that employers are supposed to turn to unfree labor. Yet American contract labor was free labor. Why?

American contract workers were free because in the northern states into which they were imported the law did not provide criminal sanctions for contract breach. The contract rules which limited employers to money damages in northern states have to be understood as decisions taken by these polities through their legal systems to authorize certain kinds of coercion in labor relations but to prohibit others. To explain these kinds of decisions, it is necessary to undertake much more particularistic inquiries into local political (including the extent of the suffrage), legal, and cultural conditions as much as into local economic ones. The contract rules in effect in northern states were the product of a long and complex history of conflict. It is enough here to say that the outcome of this history was a collective determination reached in those states and later in the United States as a whole that slavery was illegitimate and should be prohibited and that forms of labor like slavery should be prohibited along with it.[25] The 1864 "Act to Encourage Immigration", under which some contract laborers were imported, itself makes clear why criminal sanctions for breach would play no part in this legislation. Section 2 of the act declares: "nothing herein contained shall be deemed to authorize any contract contravening the Constitution of the United States, or creating in any way the relation of slavery or servitude".[26]

25. See Parsons v. Trask.
26. *U.S. Statutes at Large*, XIII (1863-1865), pp. 385-387.

The same kind of analysis is called for in the case of wage labor, even the wage labor of the metropolitan core. Measured by comparative wage rates, American labor was in shorter supply than English wage labor throughout most of the nineteenth century. The relative abundance of English labor and the high cost of English land on one hand, and the relative scarcity of American labor and low cost of American land on the other would lead us to expect that if legal compulsion were used, it would have been used against American wage workers rather than English wage workers. But exactly the opposite turns out to have been the case. Where labor was scarcer and land less expensive in the United States, wage labor was free. Where labor was more abundant, and land more expensive in England, wage labor was unfree.

What needs explaining in the case of wage labor as in the case of contract labor is not the "type" of labor used, but the legal rules that give employers rights to certain coercive devices, permit them to use others, but prohibit them from using a range of still other possible forms of coercion. And it does not appear that these rules can be explained solely by a simple economic formula based on the characteristics of local land and labor markets. Any explanation for these rules must take into account numerous additional factors, including relative political power, the role of the judiciary, social norms, and the bargaining strength of labor.

VI

To this point, we have not directly challenged another previously mentioned basic assumption which underlies the contemporary picture of the forms of labor: the idea that labor is divided into free and unfree, and that it is natural to draw the line between the two at the point at which employers are able to compel labor by resorting to physical force or legal compulsion.

But just as we earlier criticized the soundness of the picture of discrete types of labor each with a fixed set of core characteristics, each functionally adapted to a particular stage or type of social/economic organization, at this point, we have to take a further step. We need to rethink the basic soundness of the binary opposition free/unfree labor. The line between voluntary and coerced labor has been drawn in different ways in different places at different times. For the most part, for example, the nineteenth century English did not consider their wage workers unfree. But there is a good reason that this line has been drawn in different ways. Nearly all forms of labor not performed for sheer pleasure can be characterized in either way.

When we speak about compulsion in labor relations, it is important to see that we are generally talking about situations in which the compelled party is only offered a choice between unpleasant alternatives and chooses the alternative which represents the lesser evil to him or her.[27] This kind of compulsion is present in both slavery and free wage labor. In slavery, for example, labor is not normally elicited by directly imparting motion to a slave's limbs through overpowering physical force. It is compelled by forcing slaves to choose among very unpleasant options, between, for example, death, dismemberment, torture, endless confinement on the one hand, or back breaking physical labor on the other. The labor of free wage workers is similarly elicited by offering workers a choice, for example, between life on an inadequate welfare stipend established by the polity, or in the extreme, starvation, on the one hand, and performing more or less unpleasant work for wages for an employer on the other. In the case of both the slave and the free worker, the parties may be said to have been coerced into performing the labor, or to have freely chosen the lesser evil (made a beneficial bargain, in effect, given the background set of alternatives). Either characterization is available. And that is the reason that some choices among evils can be characterized as voluntary decisions while other choices among evils can simultaneously be characterized as coerced. Where the line is drawn, from a logical standpoint, is arbitrary. One tradition of thought, for example, portrayed slavery in completely consensual terms, as an agreement in which the slave had voluntarily granted absolute control over himself to his master in exchange for his life. In fact, in certain areas at certain times, slavery and serfdom were formally initiated through agreements. (This was never a feature of New World slavery, however.)

Needless to say, the choices presented in slavery are much harsher than the choices normally presented in free wage labor, and so we may rightly say that the degree of coercion in one form is normally much greater than in the other, but there are no logical grounds for saying that the performance of labor in one case is coerced, while in the other it is voluntary. As a matter of logic we have to say either that both are involuntary in different degrees, or that both involve the free choice of a lesser evil.

Often in drawing the distinction between free and unfree labor it is tacitly conceded that there are elements of coercion involved even in free labor. The distinction then comes to turn on the different kinds of coercion involved in free vs. unfree labor. Unfree labor is coerced through the threat or actuality of "physical violence" (state authorized in most systems of unfree labor), or "legal compulsion" (state administered). Free labor is supposed to be coerced through "economic compulsion" (market based).

27. Hale, "Force and the State", pp. 149-161, and Hale, *Freedom Through Law*, pp. 189-196. Much of the analysis in the following paragraphs derives from Hale's work.

Two implicit assumptions are made that justify the separation of labor coerced in these different ways into the opposing categories free and unfree. First, the different "types" of coercion are assumed to have fundamentally different sources and characteristics. The source of "legal" and in most systems of unfree labor "physical" coercion is law. The forces of the market are supposed to be the source of "economic" coercion, and they are supposed to operate impersonally and indirectly. They "coerce" only in the way that nature may be said to coerce, if you do not work you starve, rather than in the way "law" coerces, personally and directly. The forces of the market can be interfered with, but in so far as they are left undisturbed, no one controls them, they work naturally. Law is artificial, made and controlled by men. Second, the different types of coercion are assumed to operate with radically different degrees of harshness. "Physical" violence and "legal" compulsion are viewed as much severer than "economic" coercion.

This stark dichotomy, economic vs. legal coercion, which places labor subject to one in one category and labor subject to the other in an opposite category, operates to obscure the common sources and characteristics of the two. "Economic" coercion always has its source in a set of legal rights, legal privileges and legal powers, which place one person in a position to force another person to choose among disagreeable alternatives, just as "legal" compulsion and, in most systems of coerced labor, "physical" compulsion do. Its exercize is also quite personal and quite direct.

Consider "economic" coercion in the bargaining relationship between employers and employees. Robert Hale showed that law was the ultimate source of an employer's power to force a worker to choose among unpleasant alternatives. His argument is worth quoting at length.

The owner [of private property] can remove the legal duty under which the non-owner labors [not to consume or otherwise use that property]. He can remove it, or keep it in force, at his discretion. To keep it in force may or may not have unpleasant consequences to the non-owner – consequences which spring from the law's creation of a legal duty. To avoid these consequences, the non-owner may be willing to obey the will of the owner, provided that the obedience is not in itself more unpleasant than the consequences to be avoided. Such obedience may take the trivial form of paying five cents for legal permission to eat a particular bag of peanuts, or it may take the more significant form of working for [a factory] owner at disagreeable toil for a slight wage. In either case the conduct is motivated [...] by a desire to escape a more disagreeable alternative [...] In the case of the labor what would be the consequence of refusal to comply with the owner's terms? It would be either absence of wages, or obedience to the terms of some other employer [...] Suppose, now, the worker were to refuse to yield to the coercion of any employer, but were to choose instead to remain under the legal duty to abstain from the use of any of the money which anyone owns. He must eat. While there is no law against eating in the abstract, there is a law which forbids him to eat any of the food which actually exists in the community – and that law is the law of property. It can be lifted as to any specific food at the discretion of its owner, but if the owners unanimously refuse to lift the prohibition, the non-owner will starve unless he can himself produce food. And there is every likelihood that the owners will be unanimous in refusing, if he has no money [...] Unless, then, the non-owner can produce his own food, the law compels him to starve if he has not wages, and compels him to go without wages unless he obeys the behests of some employer. It is the law that coerces him into wage-work under penalty of starvation – unless he can produce food. Can he? Here again there is no law to prevent the production of food in the abstract; but in every settled country there is a law which forbids him to cultivate any particular piece of ground unless he happens to be an owner. This again is the law of property. And this again will not be likely to be lifted unless he already has money. That way of escape from the law-made dilemma of starvation or obedience is closed to him [...] In short, if he be not a property owner, the law which forbids him to produce with any of the existing equipment, and the law which forbids him to eat any of the existing food, will be lifted *only* in case he works for an employer. It is the law of property which coerces people into working for factory owners [...][28]

So-called "economic" coercion is an artifact of law, not of nature, and operates personally and directly on individuals. There is, however, a crucial respect in which it does differ from what we normally call "legal" compulsion. "Legal" or "physical" compulsion normally confronts an individual with a highly restricted set of unpleasant alternatives from which to choose. The choice, for example, might be between going to prison, becoming a fugitive from justice, or remaining at work. In most cases of "economic" coercion, the universe of alternatives is at least potentially much wider. A worker thinking about leaving his employer can try to find another job, apply for food stamps and Section 8 housing, open a small business repairing cars in the back yard homestead in Alaska, move to Georgia where there are more jobs, emigrate to Australia, go back to school to retrain, join the army, move in with relatives, play guitar in the subway, and so forth. What is different about "economic" coercion is that it is often difficult to evaluate the universe of options which an individual faces. If most of the above options are unfeasible, as they often are, and the real choices are much narrower, remain at work, look for another job in the same line, go on welfare, become homeless, then the degree of coercion operating in this situation may even be greater than the degree of coercion operating when the threat is a mere fourteen day prison sentence. (Many nineteenth century English wage workers served such short term sentences.) On the other hand, if Australia is desperate for workers, is willing to subsidize passage over, provide housing, and guarantee a good paying job, and the unemployment rate in this country

---

28. Hale, "Coercion and Distribution in a Supposedly Non-Coercive State", pp. 472-473.

is 2%, then the degree of coercion operating in this situation may be practically nonexistent. And so it is difficult to characterize this worker's situation in the abstract, because the feasibility and unpleasantness of all the potential options involves highly context specific information. It is hard even to compile a definitive list of what all the "real" options may or may not be. It is much easier to evaluate degrees of coercion when the alternatives confronting an individual are clearly defined and strictly circumscribed. This is why "economic" coercion is so slippery and contestable.

But this difference does not make "economic" coercion "natural". The background conditions which constitute the options available to individuals and determine the degree of "economic" coercion operating in any situation are pervasively shaped by law.[29] Whether welfare is a good, bad or impossible option depends upon welfare law, on eligibility rules and payment standards. Emigrating to Australia may be hard or easy depending upon Australian immigration rules. But it is only an option at all because American workers enjoy the background legal privilege of leaving the country whenever they wish to take up work elsewhere. Alaska may be a better or worse option depending upon whether the state government has a homestead program, but it is an option because Americans enjoy the legal privilege of settling in any state in the union they wish to. Playing guitar in the subway may be more or less feasible depending upon vagrancy rules and vagrancy rule enforcement. Another job may be a better or worse option depending upon how great the demand for labor is. But it is only because a worker possesses the background legal privilege of selling or withholding his labor in the first place, i.e. is not under a legal duty to work where an employer has need of labor (as in England under the Statute of Labourers, or as in slavery), that increased demand for labor can make this a better or worse option. If a preparatory course and a license are required in order to repair automobiles, or if nuisance law or zoning regulations prohibited it, opening a small shop in your yard might be less feasible or completely out of the question. How desperate workers as a group might be for work depends in good part on how widely property is distributed. But even this situation is conditioned to a great extent by a larger set of taken for granted background legal rules. Property is so unevenly distributed in the United States in good measure because inheritance laws make it possible for accumulations of property to be preserved over generations, and so on.[30]

---

29. Kennedy, "The Stakes of Law, or Hale and Foucault!", pp. 330-334, and "The Role of Law in Economic Thought", pp. 965-967.

30. On the "artificial" or "positive" nature of the law of inheritance see, for example, Blackstone, *Commentaries*, II, pp. 10, 12: "The most universal and effectual way, of abandoning property, is by the death of the occupant; when, both the actual possession and intention of keeping possession ceasing, the property, which is founded upon such possession and intention, ought

In extreme cases, such as South Africa, where ruling elites adopted vagrancy legislation and legal restrictions on land ownership in an effort to drive Africans into wage labor, law conditioned (created) "economic" coercion may produce outcomes very similar to those achievable under regimes of direct "legal" compulsion like slavery.[31] But in all market societies, an extensive set of background legal rules establish to a significant degree the real alternatives available to working people, and hence the extent of the so-called "economic" coercion they confront. In most market societies, these numerous background rules are not put in place for a single purpose or by a single group. Nevertheless, whatever the formal reasons for their adoption, they affect the universe of possibilities open to working people. And in many cases, at least certain of these rules (welfare and vagrancy rules for example) are consciously adopted with an eye toward inducing laboring people to enter into or remain in wage work. Depending upon their precise details, the magnitude of "economic" coercion facing ordinary people can be quite different in different free market societies.

Legal rules governing bargaining behavior in the market also play a crucial role in the creation of so-called "economic" power.[32] In free markets, the state must always make a detailed set of decisions about which bargaining tactics will be permitted and which kinds prohibited. It simply has no choice. The legal system will always be confronted with claims that one action or another of a bargaining party has injured the other party. If workers are given the privilege or right of freely combining to withhold their labor, employers may enjoy less coercive power in the relationship because workers have been given legal permission to damage them through certain forms of activity. If workers are permitted to mount secondary boycotts, employers may have less power still, because workers have been given legal permission to damage them in another way. If employers are prohibited from replacing workers who go out on strike, they may enjoy even less coercive power. If employers possess the legal privilege of combining to negotiate with workers, they may enjoy more power vis a vis their employees, and so forth ad infinitum. Change one or two rules and you may change the degree of coercion slightly. Change all the bargaining rules in favor of one party and you may change the degree of coercion radically. There are numerous possible ways free market bargaining relationships can be legally

---

also to cease of course [...] Wills therefore and testaments, rights of inheritance and successions, are all of them creatures of the civil or municipal laws, and accordingly are in all respects regulated by them [...]" See also Fried, *Robert Hale and Progressive Legal Economics*, p. 41: "The Supreme Court [...] in its 1898 decision in Magoun v. Illinois Trust, [upheld] a progressive inheritance tax against an equal protection claim, on the ground that as inheritance itself was a special privilege conferred by the state, the state was free to condition it as it saw fit."

31. See Engerman, "Coerced and Free Labor".
32. The following paragraph draws heavily on Kennedy, "The Stakes of Law, or Hale and Foucault!", and "The Role of Law in Economic Thought".

constructed, all of them placing the parties in different positions to coerce one another.

In an earlier section (V), we looked at another set of legal rules that define another dimension of power in labor relationships, rules governing what contract remedies are available to the parties, and what remedies they may establish for themselves as part of their agreement. A nineteenth century American common law rule of contract provided that if a worker left his job before he had fulfilled his contractual term of service, he forfeited his legal claim to wages for the time he had already worked.[33] Where an employer had held back wages, such a rule forced a worker to choose between staying and forfeiting his accumulated wages. If he stayed because he simply could not afford to lose his back wages, the legal rule would have operated to coerce him into remaining in the same way a rule that forced him to choose between staying and serving fourteen days in prison would have. Is the compulsion of the American rule any less "legal" than the compulsion of the English rule of criminal sanctions?

So-called "economic" coercion, the coercion of the market, is not like the coercion of nature, impersonal and indirect, in numerous different ways it is a product of law, just as so-called "legal" coercion is. Thus, the effort to separate labor into opposing types on the basis of a simple opposition between "economic" and "legal" coercion does not hold up. When we examine the economic/legal distinction carefully, it dissolves into a complex account of the numerous different ways in which coercion is constituted by law.

The second assumption made about "economic" coercion that justifies placing labor coerced by the market into the category free, while labor coerced by "law" is designated unfree is that "economic" coercion is less harsh than other types of coercion. In the twentieth century, a kind of implicit scale of coercion has been developed arranged abstractly by "types", with "economic" coercion placed at one end as mild, and "legal" and "physical" coercion at the other as severe. American law certainly seems to be based on this kind of abstract scale. But doesn't the coerciveness of all "types" of coercion depend upon particular circumstances? Can't economic coercion sometimes be more coercive than legal coercion? Depending upon the precise circumstances, for example, imprisonment may or may not be more coercive than so-called "economic" threats. The threat of starvation may certainly operate more powerfully than a short prison term. 19th century English wage workers sometimes expressed a preference for a short prison term rather than forego the opportunity to obtain higher wages by changing employers. And who is to say that a fourteen day prison term is invariably a more disagreeable alternative than losing one's life savings, or home.

33. Nearly all states adhered to this rule during the first half of the nineteenth century. See Holt, "Labour Conspiracy Cases in the United States", and "Recovery by the Worker Who Quits"; see also Karsten, "'Bottomed on Justice'".

It is clear that there are numerous degrees of "legal" coercion just as there are numerous degrees of "economic" coercion. It is more accurate to think of the two in terms of two parallel scales, or a combined scale, in which both run from very severe to rather mild, rather than in terms of a single scale arranged by abstract "types". In characterizing labor relations in terms of a continuum, however, we don't mean to imply that there have not been real differences in these forms of coercion. Dramatic differences have existed and these have been the basis for profound political and social disagreements and occasional violent conflict.

VII

Where does all this leave us. First, where the opposition free labor/coerced labor is used, we have to see the line drawn between the two as arbitrary. One of our tasks should be to try to explain how such arbitrary lines came to be constructed, how certain forms of coercion were subtly legitimized by being sanctioned by law. The nineteenth century English, as we have said, considered their wage workers free for the most part. Twentieth century American lawyers and historians view the decision of a worker to remain in or return to a job because his employer threatened him with imprisonment as a coerced decision in which continued work is involuntary servitude. On the other hand, twentieth-century American lawyers and historians view the decision of a nineteenth-century worker to remain at a job because his employer threatened him with the loss of his back wages as a voluntary decision in which the continued work was consensual not coerced.

Second, if the categories voluntary/coerced, free/unfree labor are, in certain important respects, empty conceptual shells, our task becomes to offer historical accounts of labor relations in terms of specific coercive practices, all, in different ways, the product of law, rather than in terms of discontinuous "types" of labor arranged under the categories free and coerced. These accounts should attempt to explain why a particular polity adopted the rules it did, why it granted to employers or workers particular legal rights, particular legal privileges, or imposed particular legal duties, because these rules determined which coercive devices the parties would have a right to, which would be legally tolerated and which would be prohibited – from among the rich variety of possibilities. Political and legal struggle between different groups over these rules must certainly be part of these explanations. These accounts should not only describe struggles *over* rules, but also struggles *under* rules. How individuals and groups defined and pursued their interests was also a function of the set of rules within which they operated at any particular time. Change rules, and interests might well come to be redefined and pursued differently.

In writing this kind of history, we have to reject the view that history unfolds in stages with each stage a functionally coherent whole composed of a fixed block of practices and institutions all required by the first principles of that form of social/economic organization. Rather, the lesson to be learned from nineteenth century English wage labor is that the rules governing social/economic life are established in ad hoc ways out of a variety of existing and new materials, and may be changed piecemeal, the outcomes depending on the relative political power of the participants, extant social views about permissible and impermissible forms of coercion, the normative persuasiveness of different groups, and a host of other factors.

Unfree Labour in the Area under German Hegemony, 1930-1945: Some Historical and Methodological Questions

Karl Heinz Roth

Introduction

Whole libraries have been filled with the results of research into one or another aspect of unfree labour in Germany during the Depression and under the National Socialist dictatorship. To date, however, there has been no single attempt to analyse these forms of labour from an overall perspective and to bring them into the international debate on the relationships between free and unfree forms of labour. Tentative enquiries which have sought to follow this direction have, in the past, been peremptorily banished to the tabu zone.[1] This verdict has remained in force until the present day, not least because grave methodological problems obstruct any attempt at bridging the abyss between source-evidence and historical theory. In the historiography to date there has been no attempt at a satisfactory clarification of terminology, although such a clarification could serve as the basis for a systematic confrontation with the rather wide spectrum of unfree forms of labour under German fascism. From the literature of the former GDR I know of only the attempt by Götz Dieckmann to compare the exploitation of concentration camp prisoners put to work in underground factories with slavery in ancient times.[2] Enquiries to other Marxist historians on, for example, the validity of their use of the term "slave labour" often brought only the reply that they had applied the term merely in a rhetorical sense.[3] In contrast, some West German researchers tend to attribute all manifestations of forced labour in the German fascist period to the "primacy of policy" or "racial ideology", and in this way to isolate them from any socio-economic analysis; or else they proceed from the premise of the alleged unprofitability of forced labour, and categorize it as a phenomenon of terror that is fundamentally alien

---

1. Cf. Ulrich Herbert's reply to my essay on the I.G. Farben Works in Auschwitz: Herbert, "Arbeit und Vernichtung", note 6, p. 419; Roth, "I.G. Auschwitz", pp. 11-28.
2. Dieckmann, "Existenzbedingungen und Widerstand im Konzentrationslager Dora-Mittelbau", esp. pp. 341 ff.
3. I last experienced such a discussion in 1992 at an international conference on "extermination through work" in Terezin/Theresienstadt, where a paper by the North American historian David M. Luebke on the connection between concentration camp labour and the "social death" paradigm used in the historiography of North American slavery was vehemently rejected. Cf. Roth, "'Vernichtung durch Arbeit'", pp. 117-120.

to capitalism and imposed upon it from without.[4] In view of the theoretical consequences of such a challenge it is regarded as a sacrilege to enquire further into the empirical finding whereby in many cases the acceleration of gigantic investment projects of the armaments industry succeeded only through the gradual inclusion of ever larger groups of forced labourers in the construction and production phases (Freund, Fröbe, Perz, Raim, Wysocki *et al.*).[5] Furthermore, the socio-statistical data necessary for a critical examination are often lacking. These data are essential if we are to quantify the inception and growth of unfree forms of labour in the crisis management of the Presidial Cabinets, to trace and collate all forms of forced labour of the Presidial era (1930 – 1933) and their integration in the first work creation programme of the National Socialist dictatorship, and if we are to understand the subsequent economic dynamic structuring the system of terror in the concentration camps. Yet individual phenomena, such as the instrument of the drafted labour (*Dienstpflicht*), the forced labour which preceeded the mass extermination of the Jewish population, the forced mobilization of unfree labourers in the occupied areas through Organization Todt, etc., have not been examined satisfactorily.[6]

Because of these considerations, any attempt at a systematic analysis must first make clear its own conceptual framework and theoretical assumptions. What I propose to present here, therefore, are my initial reactions to the research findings and hypotheses of Western Marxist social scientists and historians during the 1980s concerning unfree labour in peripheral capitalist contexts.[7] I wish to link these findings and hypotheses with the ideas which emerged independently in 1988/89 as a result of a symposium on the Neuengamme concentration camp.[8] I am in no way concerned here with a schematic adoption, but rather with the development of a serviceable analytical frame of reference so as to expand the the angle of vision into our empirical sources on forced labour relations in German fascism.

4. Cf. above all Herbert, *Fremdarbeiter*, "Arbeit und Vernichtung"; Kirstein, *Konzentrationslager als Institution totalen Terrors*; Sofsky, *Ordnung des Terrors*.
5. Freund, "Arbeitslager Zement"; Fröbe, "Der Arbeitseinsatz von KZ-Häftlingen", pp. 351-383; Perz, *Projekt Quarz*; Raim, *Dachauer KZ-Außenkommandos*; Wysocki, *Arbeit für den Krieg*.
6. This makes even more important the new research contained in the collection: Aly, *Arbeitsmarkt und Sondererlaß*.
7. Cf. the special issue of the *Journal of Peasant Studies* 19 (1992), No. 3/4; and Brass, "Some Observations on Unfree Labour", this volume, pp. 57-75.
8. Rohwer, "Kapitalismus und 'freie Lohnarbeit'", pp. 171-185; Karl Heinz Roth, "I.G. Auschwitz".

Unfree Labour: A Definition

In accord with most recent Marxist research on the structures of exploitation of colonial capitalism, I proceed on the assumption that unfree forms of labour are basically constituted by a double dispossession of the immediate producers: namely, through the expropriation of their means of production and subsistence, and through the simultaneous elimination – in varying degrees – of the commodity character of their free labour power, in that the direct and unhindered access to and regress from the labour market is blocked. So as to avoid misunderstandings, I call this phenomenon not "deproletarianization" but "subproletarianization". By means of this approach it will be possible to comprehend more precisely the broadly differentiated spectrum of "bound labour" (contract labour, bonded labour, controlled migrant labour with enforced residence in barracks, etc.), and to contrast it with free forms of labour. In this context slave labour is also to be understood as an extreme form of unfree labour, whereby the slave-labourer is neither the exclusive personal property of the slave-owner nor a pure work machine. Such unfreedom is constituted much rather by the unlimited rights of disposal and domination over the exploited, over those rented/hired from the slave-mustering authorities, and over socially-deprived persons, rights which hinder their further social (familial and generative) reproduction and, in the final analysis, include the limitation of the individual's life-span – even to extent of "consuming" the latter in an intensified process of exploitation that is itself without limit in the existing system (extermination through work).[9] On the basis of these novel epistemiological premises, the prevailing dilemma of traditional Marxism – which in its analysis of unfree forms of labour schematically contrasts the "mute" economic power of doubly free wage-labour relationships with "extra-economic" mechanisms of dominance[10] – would no longer exist. Above all, recent research (by Tom Brass and Henry Bernstein, Jan Breman, Jan Lucassen, and Martin Murray) on the forms of bound labour in the "industrial plantations" of the 1920s and the "free production zones" of the 1970s comes to the conclusion that in mature capitalism (and therefore in its global expansion since the second industrial revolution) rapid advances in development and strategies for overcoming crises and bottlenecks are only possible on the basis of the widespread employment of unfree labour.[11] The

---

9. This possibility was obviously first actualized by German fascism. Cf. Kárný, "Vernichtung durch Arbeit", pp. 133-158.

10. Cf. Eichholtz, "Gewalt und Ökonomie", pp. 358-372.

11. Brass and Bernstein, "Proletarianization and Deproletarianization", pp. 1-40; Brass, "Slavery Now", pp. 183-197; Breman, *Labour Migration*; Lucassen, "Free and Unfree Labour before the Twentieth Century", this volume, pp. 45-56; and Murray, "'White Gold' or 'White Blood'?", pp. 41-67.

removal in this manner from the working class of its collective and unimpeded access to/and regress from the labour market as a prerequisite to annulling/minimalizing the connection between wage labour and labour productivity now no longer appears to be evidence of "semi-feudal" backwardness but much rather an instrument which is immanent in the capitalist cycle of crisis and reproduction – right up to the present day.

This approach is, in my opinion, of great significance for the study of class relationships in Germany from 1930 to 1945. It enables a broader view and a novel critical understanding of the breadth of variation in forms of unfree labour developed in this period, which extended from the state-enforced contract labour ("compulsory labour" – *Pflichtarbeit* –, "labour service" – *Arbeitsdienst* –, "land year" – *Landjahr* –, "drafted labour" – *Dienstpflicht* – etc.), through the more or less forcible recruitment of foreign workers (both male and female), to the extreme form of slave-labour by concentration camp prisoners.

Unfree Labour During the Great Depression: From Deflationary Crisis Politics to State Intervention

Unfree labour emerged in Germany not with the seizing of political power by the National Socialists on the thirtieth of January 1933 but rather from 1930/31 onwards, in the context of the labour and social policies of the Presidial Cabinets.[12] The introduction of unfree labour was an essential instrument of de-solidarization, which isolated the mass of jobless eliminated from the unemployment insurance system and subjected them to specific techniques of "decommodification". The Reich Department of Labour (*Reichsarbeitsverwaltung*) tried thereby to remove, on one hand, young persons from the general labour market ("labour service", "land year", "land aid", "community service", "girls' year of service"). On the other hand, it intended to discipline those persons excluded from the labour market and unemployment insurance by "compulsory labour", "provisory labour", and "value-creating unemployment provision" ("wertschöpfende Arbeitslosenhilfe"). On top of these came the special discriminatory steps taken against female workers. In the case of all these measures, the withholding of unemployment benefits – a sanction which was enshrined in law on the occasion of the introduction of state unemployment insurance in 1927 – could be used to force people to work.[13] The National Socialist dictatorship built upon

---

12. Cf. the following: Bartz and Mor, "Weg in die Jugendzwangsarbeit", pp. 28-94; Hemmer, *"Unsichtbare" Arbeitslose*; Homburg, "Vom Arbeitslosen zum Zwangsarbeiter", pp. 251-298; Köhler, *Arbeitsdienst in Deutschland*; Wermel and Urban, *Arbeitslosenfürsorge und Arbeitslosenversicherung in Deutschland*.

13. Kahrs, "Die ordnende Hand der Arbeitsämter", pp. 9-61, esp. pp. 17 ff.

these foundations and expanded the dual-structure of unfree labour for young people and for the long-term unemployed – which had originally been conceived for a deflationary crisis – into a package of measures designed for a state interventionist "work creation" programme for raising public deficit spending, primarily for rearmament.[14] Between 1934 and 1945 about 700,000 young persons and 600,000 adult unemployed were affected by these measures (see Tables 1 and 2). In the transition to full-employment based on an arms economy, a limited regime of compulsory labour service for young persons was consolidated,[15] while for the mass of adult workers the right to freely change their place of employment was increasingly restricted, in order to bring the rate of inflation under control (cf. the introduction of the labour record book, 1935; the restriction of free movement for qualified metalworkers and construction workers, 1936/37). These legislative instruments were gathered together in a compulsory labour order (*Dienstpflichtverordnung*) of June 1938, and between February and September 1939 resulted in the imposition of a general restriction on the right of an individual to revoke an employment contract.[16] By means of this two-pronged attack, which combined general restrictions on the free choice of employment with the selective use of the compulsory labour, the National Socialist dictatorship succeeded in decoupling wages policy from economic expansion – despite the artificially induced full employment – and to effectively destroy the possibilities for the workers' reconquest of autonomy in negotiating wage rates. When considered in conjunction with both the economic dynamic of concentration camp terror and the segmentation of the working class through the employment of foreign contract workers, the rapid growth of unfree labour already evident in the pre-war period was the decisive lever in the ultimate destruction of the German labour and trade union movements. Without the extension of unfree labour in all its forms, the efficacy of the politicial pacification of the working class via the German Labour Front remains inexplicable.

14. Syrup, *Arbeitseinsatz und die Arbeitslosenhilfe in Deutschland*, p. 132 ff.; Niess, *Geschichte der Arbeitslosigkeit*, pp. 215 ff.; Wulff, *Arbeitslosigkeit und Arbeitsbeschaffungsmaßnahmen*; and Morsch, *Arbeit und Brot*.
15. Petrick, *Zur sozialen Lage der Arbeiterjugend*.
16. Documented by Mason, *Arbeiterklasse und Volksgemeinschaft*, pp. 249 ff., 665 ff., and 744 ff.

Table 1. Unfree Labour in the Depression and Before the Four-Year Plan (millions)

Year	1930	1931	1932	1933	1934	1935	1936
Total employed	18,775	14,336	13,518	13,432	15,470	16,424	17,592
Total unemployed	3,076	4,520	5,603	4,804	2,718	2,151	1,593
Jobless forced* labourers	0,175	0,361	0,334	0,401	0,631	0,349	0,234
Labour service	-	0,001	0,144	0,263	0,232	0,224	0,221
Forced youth labour**	-	-	-	0,156	0,490	0,175	0,185
Foreign workers	0,109	0,050	0,044	0,040	0,060	0,140	0,145
Concentration camp prisoners	-	-	-	0,027	0,010	0,009	0,007
Proportion of unfree labour to a) Employed	1,51 %	2,87 %	3,86 %	6,60 %	9,20 %	5,46 %	4,50 %
b) Unemployed	9,23 %	9,12 %	9,32 %	18,46 %	52,35 %	41,70 %	49,72 %

* "duty labour" (*Pflichtarbeit*), "provisory labour"(*Fürsorgearbeit*), and those employed in "value-creating unemployment benefit" (*Wertschöpfende Arbeitslosenfürsorge*), excepting youth forced labourers ("labour service", "land year", etc) and concentration camp prisoners.
** "land year", "land aid", domestic service year for girls, excepting labour service.
Source: Bundesarchiv Abteilungen Potsdam, 39.01 (Reichsarbeitsministerium); Statistical Yearbooks 1931-1937; Statistical Handbook of Germany 1928-1944, München 1949.

It is clear from the structural aspects of this whole issue that the years of the Depression and the subsequent National Socialist dictatorship in fact form a single historical unit. Unfree labour emerged as the free market was subject to increasing restriction, and became an essential condition for overcoming the Depression and securing an artificially-induced armaments boom against the bargaining risks of full employment. Even if the proportion of involuntary male and female workers remained small in relation to the overall employment figures in the pre-war period, it nevertheless reached almost fifty per cent of the figure for the unemployed between 1934 and 1936. It is therefore of particular epistemological significance that the "decommodification" of the labour force was an effect of two contrasting economic strategies: rooted in the logic of a deflationary "deregulation", this led finally to the deficit financed "labour battle" of the National Socialist dictatorship.

Slave-Labour, Extermination through Work, and the Economic Rationale of the Concentration Camp System

In terms of economic policy, the restrictions imposed on free workers were complemented by unfree labour generated within the terror-system of the concentration camps. Qualitatively, but not quantitatively, the forced labour of concentration camp prisoners presented – in its radical destructiveness – the epitome of unfree labour relationships under German fascism.[17] In the first phase of development, and in the transition stages to 1937/38, the function of the concentration camp system and in particular its systematic use of terror was both to break the imprisoned cadres of the workers' movement and to deter the whole working class from undertaking large-scale resistance. Thus the presence in the camps of an average of 10-15,000 prisoners was "sufficient" until the era of the four-year-plan. In the context of military expansion, full employment generated by the arms economy, and the intensified persecution of the Jewish population, from 1938 onwards the disciplinary role of terror was ever more closely bound up with the enhancement of labour productivity. To prevent the working class from using full employment to resist (and thus endanger) the war plans of the dictatorship, the concentration camp system was centralized and expanded. In the final years before the war, the annual average of 25,000 prisoners who found themselves behind the electrified fences of the concentration camps were increasingly "utilized" in the construction and quarrying projects of the SS. From these beginnings the SS developed a system of forced labour which had an impact not just on the whole Jewish population within the expanding area of German hegemony but on all social groups showing any signs of resistance. The human booty, dispossessed and divested of its rights by special institutions of the *Reichssicherheitshauptamt*, was transformed into a living work-machine for the benefit of the expanding SS enterprise, and from 1941-42 onwards it was allocated to the state and private arms manufacturers for employment on a number of spectacular construction projects.[18] During the phase of "total war", this system of exploitation was transformed into a fully developed slave economy. Folllowing the collapse of the forced-recruitment system developed by Sauckel (about which more below), the SS transported prospective work-slaves from the whole of Europe to Department-group D of the SS *Wirtschafts-Verwaltungshauptamt*. Those components the booty viewed as unfit for work (children, the disabled, the elderly) were killed upon arrival at the concentration camps; those deemed fit for work were hired out to the armaments industry and, after the spring of 1944, to the arms industry for the

17. Cf. to the following *Sozialpolitik und Judenvernichtung*; Kaienburg, *"Vernichtung durch Arbeit"*.
18. Cf. fn. 4; further Hamburger Stiftung, *"Deutsche Wirtschaft"*.

construction of its underground storage projects. This system of hiring out was eventually standardized as a form of leasing. The SS and the private employer had to pay the Reich a set fee for the daily labour of each prisoner; the daily fee, which was at first higher for private concerns but after 1944 was also charged to the SS, was in the order of 6 and 4 Reichsmark for a skilled worker and an unskilled worker respectively, whilst the prisoner him/herself was not paid for the work. The employing concerns had, in addition, to provide food, accommodation and clothing, whilst guard-duties were performed by SS units. Absences, public holidays, etc., were not allowed and those prisoners who became unfit for work were transported back to the concentration camps, where, after the spring of 1942, they were mostly consigned to the gas chambers. The leasing system considerably shortened the individual lifespan of this unfree workforce, since there was only a slim chance of survival for those prisoners whose labour was utilised in production processes. For prisoners employed in construction, the average survival time was a mere 3 months. The result of reconfiguring the concentration camp system in terms of a surplus-yielding economic regime was a drastic rise in mortality: from 1943/44 onwards the dominant watchword was "extermination through work", whilst those selected as unfit for work were henceforth immediately killed. The prerequisite for such a system was a steady increase in the numbers of those sent to the concentration camps. Between 1939 and the summer of 1942, the number of concentration camp prisoners quadrupled, reaching a figure of 98,000 in July that year. By May 1943 the figure was 203,000, and by August 1944 approximately 525,000; in January 1945 it reached a peak of some 750,000 prisoners. Despite this, the proportion of slave-labourers to the overall work force was only around one per cent during the war years.

The Extension of Unfree Labour Relationships into the "Greater European Economic Area"

The way in which German labour policy was extended to cover the "Greater European Economic Area" in the period 1938-45 entailed local variations/adaptations: in the annexed territories, in the occupied territories, under "indirect rule" in satellite regimes, as well as measures which remained at the planning stage, such as those drawn up for the restructuring of colonial forced labour relationships in Central Africa. The enforced mobilization of labour power on a European scale was to be conducted by three specific institutions:

a)   recruitment for work in the occupied territories (occupational administration and collaborationist regimes) was carried out under the aegis of Organization Todt;

b)   deportation into the Reich area (initially on the basis of bilateral agree-
      ments or by operations-staff of the German administration) was conducted
      from spring 1942 onwards by the *Generalbevollmächtigter für den Arbeits-
      einsatz*; and

c)   deportation of European Jews for "extermination through work", initially
      in the concentration camp archipelago and from 1943-44 onwards in the
      armaments industry, was conducted by the *Reichssicherheitshauptamt*.

This co-ordinated direction of labour operated on an inter-state basis, combining
the Sauckel "Shanghai" system and the slave-hunt; from the beginning of the
war, therefore, the mass of unfree labour relationships involved the recruitment
of male and female foreign workers.[19] The first phase of recruitment, itself a
response to the full-employment regained during 1936/37, was characterized
initially by bilateral agreements between the German authorities and their allies
or satellite regimes.[20] The contracts were of a collective nature, the benefit to
Germany being secured by compensatory trade agreements (mostly in the form
of the exchange of contingents of foreign workers for shipments of coal). Within
the system of directed migration thus created, the unfree elements the labour
relationship – a ban on any change of workplace, a penalty system for breaking
of a contract within a six- or twelve-month period, the unilateral extension of
the contract period, predominantly camp accommodation, etc. – were combined
with, in part, a highly developed political guarantee enabling the socio-economic reproduction of the work force. Under this bilateral agreement not only
was the right of foreign workers to payment secured in law but it was also
possible for them to send a portion of their earnings to their families back home.
In the pre-war years the number of migrant workers subject to these forms of
contract rose from about 150,000 in 1937 to around 301,000 in August 1939.
Although this bilateral contract system survived the war, from 1942 onwards
its importance declined.

The recruitment of male and female Polish workers began in October 1939,
and from the start of 1940 the unfree element of these labour relationships was
reinforced.[21] In the context of the deportations which followed the annexation
of the Polish western province, and after the introduction of a requirement to
work under the General Government, the recruitment process acquired within
the space of a few months a compulsory nature. In addition, the limited
protection afforded by the bilateral contracts lapsed, and the social security
payments were increasingly swallowed up by taxes. The result of this utilization

---

19. For the current research situation, see Herbert, *Europa und der "Reichseinsatz"*.
20. Kahrs, "Verstaatlichung der polnischen Arbeitsmigration", pp. 130-194, esp. pp. 171 ff.;
     Mantelli, "Von der Wanderarbeit zur Deportation", pp. 51-89.
21. August, "Entwicklung des Arbeitsmarkts", pp. 305-353.

of low-paid foreign workers, who were not only subject to racist discrimination but also denied both the right to a wage and thus the capacity to secure the socio-economic reproduction of their families, was the subproletarianization of the German working class. Then, of course, there were also the prisoners of war — who were held in a special camp system and from there hired out to industrial concerns and compelled to work. This forced mobilization of Polish migrant labour, above all for the benefit of German agriculture, was of an experimental character. It represented the violent polar opposite of the bilateral contract system operating within the fascist Axis.

As the area under German hegemony expanded during the years of the *Blitz-krieg*, so the system of recruitment of foreign labour was extended to the newly occupied countries; each national population conquered was placed precisely within a broad spectrum of working arrangements, ranging from extreme contract-labour to open forced-labour relationships.[22] The resulting variations in contract-compulsion, reproduction guarantees and restriction of freedom in the production process and/or in the camp system, projected a racial hierarchy in relation to the German working class. At the bottom of this hierarchy were the forced labourers from Poland and the Soviet Union (Eastern workers).

In the transition to "total war", the then system for the recruitment of foreign labourers from the occupied territories and the satellite regimes proved to be disfunctional. The recruitment bodies, which competed with each other and were dependent on the special interests of the occupation authorities, were placed under the authority of a single co-ordinating department in March 1942: the "General Administrator for the Mobilization of Labour" (*Generalbevollmächtigter für den Arbeitseinsatz*). The latter standardised the mobilization procedures to fit the interests of the German armaments industry, forced through a scale of priorities valid for the whole of the area of German hegemony, and generalised the enforcement methods which had been tried out successfully in the East.[23] With the help of the "Sauckel system", an enormous increase in the scale of mobilization was achieved by autumn 1943, feeding some seven million workers and prisoners of war into the production and distribution system. In this way a coolie-system was introduced within the area of German hegemony, one which intensified the process of subproletarianization. However, this model, which was described by the General Administrator, Fritz Sauckel, as "Shanghaiing", soon provoked resistance in the occupied territories and eventually failed in the spring of 1944 after a final "mass action" had seen the transfer of about 600,000 Italian special status military internees – the transfer being performed outside the bounds

---

22. Drobisch and Eichholtz, "Zwangsarbeit ausländischer Arbeitskräfte in Deutschland", pp. 1-25.
23. Eichholtz, "Vorgeschichte des 'Generalbevollmächtigten für den Arbeitseinsatz'", pp. 339-383, *Geschichte der deutschen Kriegswirtschaft*, II, pp. 179 ff.

of international law on the conduct of warfare.[24] Even the increased mobilization of labourers for the collaborationist armaments enterprises in the occupied countries failed to alleviate the situation, despite the fact that astonishing high recruitment figures were achieved. Under pressure from the State and from the private armaments manufacturers, therefore, the economic regimentation of the concentration camp system was now perfected, the object being to secure an increase in the production and storage of armaments whatever the price.

Table 2. Unfree Labour in the German Reich, 1937-1945 (in millions)

Year	1937	1938	1939	1940	1941	1942	1943	1944	1945*
German free workers	18,88	20,11	20,81	19,60	20,17	19,72	18,81	20,61	19,42
Jobless German unfree workers**	0,13	0,08	–	–	–	–	–	–	–
Foreign workers	0,15	0,25	0,30	0,80	1,75	2,65	4,84	5,30	4,90
Prisoners of war	–	–	–	0,35	1,32	1,49	1,62	1,83	1,78
Concentration camp prisoners	0,01	0,02	0,03	0,04	0,06	0,10	0,20	0,52	0,75
German Jewish forced workers	–	–	0,01	0,02	0,04	0,03	–	–	–
German drafted workers	–	0,25	0,80	0,24	0,18	0,16	0,41	0,63	0,49
Labour service	0,27	0,28	0,25	0,24	0,23	0,24	0,25	0,26	0,21
Youth forced labour***	0,08	0,08	0,09	0,10	0,09	0,08	0,09	0,08	0,06
Service year for girls****	0,02	0,21	0,32	0,34	0,35	0,33	0,34	0,32	0,29
Proportion of unfree workers (in %)	3,50	5,82	8,65	10,87	19,93	25,76	41,20	43,38	43,67

* March 1945
** "Obligatory workers" (*Pflichtarbeiter*), "provisory workers" (*Fürsorgearbeiter*), and those employed in *wertschaffende Arbeitslosenfürsorge* ("value creating unemployment provision").
*** "Land aid", "land year" (excepting labour service and the service year for girls).
**** Obligatory year for girls
Source: Bundesarchiv Koblenz, R 41, R 163; Statistische Jahrbücher 1938–1944; Statistisches Handbuch von Deutschland 1928–1944, München 1949.

24. Cajani, "Italienische Militär-Internierte im nationalsozialistischen Deutschland", pp. 295-316.

Methodological Questions

In the historical analysis presented here, it has been argued that the overall labour constitution of the National Socialist dictatorship moved unambiguously in the direction of unfree labour relationships. The three main foci of this process are as follows. *Firstly*, in the transition from deflationist deregulation to an armaments economy and deficit spending, segments of the unfree-unemployed were separated from the broad mass of wage-labourers and then deployed by the state in its own work-creation programme. When the arms economy resulted in a move towards full employment, these segments returned to the normal labour market; the latter, however, was itself now increasingly subject to a process of decommodification, an objective achieved through measures for controlling and limiting the free movement of labour. *Secondly*, this move away from a free labour market was accompanied by the introduction of slave-labour, as the concentration camps adopted an economic regime the outcome of which was the rapid-use-up and hence the destruction of labour power. And *thirdly*, the whole European labour market was adjusted to the needs of and the transformation occurring in the Third Reich, and accordingly subjected to a system of migration control that became increasingly coercive. As the two tables show, the proportion of precisely defined unfree labour relationships rose between 1930/31 and 1944/45, from a few per cent to around 43 per cent. This extensive regrouping was accompanied within the three main sectors of the transformation process by an increasing fragmentation of the resources of labour power subjected to enforced mobilization. The vastly swollen ranks of the proletariat in the areas under Nazi hegemony were simultaneously ethnicized and subjected to a process of "un-making". Against this general historical background of the "decommodification" of labour relationships in the "Third Reich" I shall, in conclusion, try to define more precisely the methodological questions which I sketched in my introduction.

1. The Connection between Unfree Labour and Mass Extermination

The unfree labour power of concentration camp prisoners, at first exploited as the property of the Economic Administration Headquarters of the SS (*Wirtschafts-Verwaltungshauptamt*) for the benefit of SS itself and later hired out mainly to private and public armaments factories, was characterized among other things by the absence of any regard on the part of its controllers and/or employers for its reproduction in the medium or long term. This can only be explained by reference to the industrial destruction in the extermination camps of all those inmates who were either initially deemed unfit for work, or who eventually became unfit for work. For an historical understanding of labour relationships under the National Socialist dictatorship, the structure of this leasing system is of particular significance: there was in fact a close connection between the various gradations of unfree labour and its most extreme manifestation, the slave-labour of concentration camp prisoners. The capacity of unfree male and female labourers to resist must be contextualized in terms of a constant confrontation with "social death" on the ramps of the concentration camps and a subsequent physical extermination through work. Similarly, the "work-reeducation camps" introduced after 1940 as one more element in the constellation of instruments of compulsion bore down upon the whole of the working class, also threatening its free components with a limited period of "social death" should they too contemplate rebellion. This radical procedure involving the rapid use-up of labour was described in some documents as "scrapping":[25] in order to make possible the desired acceleration in economic expansion, therefore, the life span of whole generations of forced labourers was reduced to just a few years, and with it the period necessary for the reproduction of the individual worker.

The extreme manifestation of the economic regime developed by German fascism emerged most clearly in the form of a rapid and genocidal "consumption" of slave-labour by the German arms industry, now engaged in the dispersal of production so as to avoid or reduce the effects of enemy bombing. Together with the wide range of and differences in unfreedom, this fact enables one to make a number of suggestions concerning the connection between on the one hand the employment of slave-labour and on the other productivity increases generated by advanced capitalism. *First*, it is known that the construction within a matter of a few months of large industrial projects depended centrally on the consumption of labour power coerced by extreme terror, in particular the ever-present threat of the gas-chamber (as was the case with I.G. Farben in Auschwitz).[26] *Second*, this system of coercion was itself combined with "rewards" for performance, whereby prisoners who exceeded their work-norm extended thereby their period of survival. In the Salzgitter complex of the Hermann Göring concern, for example, boards were set up at the end of each shift with the performance figures for that shift: if the following shift could outperform them, they would receive a basic premium.[27] *Third*, the exploitation of slave-labour took the form of highly stratified time-work policed by a double system of overseers: the concerns' own overseers and SS guards from the concentration camp, whose power to enforce work performance was itself based on sanctions such as the ever-present fear of maltreatment, the withdrawal of food, and

---

25. Thus the "scrapping" of "undesirable" Slavic population groups-for example, those of the Baltic region-over a 15-20 year period through a process of forced industrialization was considered more than once in the discussion of the SS "General plan for the East" (*Generalplan Ost*).
26. Cf. Levi, *If This is a Man and The Truce.*
27. Wysocki, *Arbeit für den Krieg*, p. 212.

ultimately death (Adlerwerke, Frankfurt on Main; Siemens Division, Ravens-brück).[28] *Fourth*, towards the end of the war there emerged piece-work groups consisting of German and Polish slave-labour in highly modern assembly lines: in this case work performance was determined by the fact that prisoners could be accused of sabotage, and sabotage was punishable by death.[29] And *Fifth*, in rare cases – and always in the interests of consolidating production – there existed the possibility of a genuine improvement in survival chances, as prisoners' living conditions slowly approached the very low levels that characterized the existence of unfree foreign workers.[30] Thus the life chances of the concentration camp slaves were dependent on the particular stage of development reached by an investment project : gangs of prison labour employed in the construction phase were characterized by a very high mortality rate, whereas for prisoners used at a later stage there were better chances of surviving (as in the case of the Dora Mittelbau).[31] However, even the latter was not always the case, as Kárný has shown in his study of the underground factories of the Osram and Auto Union concerns at Leitmeritz in Protektorat Böhmen und Mähren.[32]

2. *The Socio-Economic Determinants of Unfree Labour Relationships*

The astonishing variety and breadth of unfree labour in Germany from 1930 to 1945 is obviously based on the fact that the economic and administrative elites were able to restructure and stabilize class relations in a favourable context of mass unemployment, yet a few years later they had to cope with the re-emergence of full employment, the result of deficit spending and the policy of re-armament. They coped with this transition from a situation of deflationary deregulation to a potentially inflationary policy of full employment by means of the phased mobilization of three kinds of unfree labour: that of Germans, the forced labour of foreign workers, and the slave-labour of concentration camp prisoners. Accordingly, *unfree labour was an integral part of the political economy of German fascism*: despite the transition to full employment, therefore, the object was to decommodify labour power in order to fix wages – and with this the capacity of the working class to reproduced itself socio-economically – at the level of the Depression of the early 1930s. In short, unfree labour made it possible to combine a programme of deficit spending for full employment in an armaments race with a policy of deflationary restriction of mass consumption. This macro-economic model for combatting the Depression in isolation from

28. Kaiser and Knorn, "Adlerwerke und ihr KZ-Außenlager-Rüstungsproduktion", pp. 11-42; Rolfi and Bruzzone, *Donne di Ravensbrück*.
29. Koppenhöfer, "KZ-Arbeit und Gruppenakkord bei Daimler-Benz Mannheim", pp. 11-45.
30. Kaienburg, "Zwangsarbeit für das 'deutsche Rohstoffwunder'", pp. 12-41.
31. Dieckmann, "Existenzbedingungen und Widerstand im Konzentrationslager Dora-Mittelbau".
32. Kárný, "'Vernichtung durch Arbeit'", pp. 37-61.

the forces of the world market, with a subsequent balancing of the budget at the cost of the conquered countries, had as a precondition the subjugation and destruction of the workers movement – a precondition which could only be realised through the suspension of ever larger segments of the free labour market in Germany and later in the occupied territories.

3. Unfree Labour and the Capitalist Enterprise

The beneficiaries of this suspension of the free labour market were above all the public concerns founded in the four-year-plan phase (Reichswerke Hermann Göring; Volkswagenwerk GmbH), the agricultural enterprises, the large private industrial concerns and for a time the SS. In the transition from an armaments-economy to a war-economy the unfree forms of labour were increasingly transferred to the private and public conglomerates of the armaments industry, as soon as the acute lack of manpower had been compensated for, above all by Polish male and female forced labourers. Given the mobilization of three kinds of unfree labour (the drafting practices of the German labour administration; the coolie-system of the General Administrator for the Mobilization of Labour; and the slave-hunting of the SS), large industrial concerns soon went over to employment arrangements that combined these different forms of coerced labour relationships. Free labour was increasingly confined to a strata of German foremen/women and supervisors. Next in the hierarchy came those Germans who were drafted to work or restricted to their workplace, the foreign contract workers from the satellite regimes, and the skilled foreign workers from Western Europe and Scandinavia. Coercive methods were used against the Eastern and South Eastern European workers and the prisoners of war (gang-work, special departments, special control and punishment techniques, barrack accommodation on the work-sites or camps near the works, etc.). The lowest position in this hierarchy was occupied by the concentration camp prisoners, above all those used either in the construction of new factories or as production workers in special works near concentration camps. From 1942-43 onwards, concentration camp external-detachments (KZ-Außenkommandos) were set up in the dispersed or underground factories of the armaments industry.

The inescapable conclusion is that the employment of forced, coerced and slave labour accompanied an intensive rationalization of production and an accelerated construction of new, mostly highly modern, works in the area of the capital goods industry. Unfree labour was a fundamental precondition for the reconstruction of capital accumulation achieved by German fascism in the phase of arms build-up and warfare. The renewal of potential production capacity which was done at the expense of internal consumption and the consumer goods sector took place in hierarchically stratified total institutions, within which unfree labourers often composed as much as 80 per cent of the workforce. As a manager of the Siemens corporation remarked in 1942,[33] the art of running a concern consisted of harmonizing the process of rationalizing production with a rapidly changing workforce structure, which in its social, multi-ethnic, cultural and skills composition resembled ever more closely the segmented workforces of peripheral capitalism.

4. Unfree Labour in Germany: An International Comparison

Together with the deployment of unfree labour, the systematic mass extermination by German fascism of Jews, Gypsies, the disabled, the "a-socials", and the Eastern European leadership strata was undoubtedly unique in a global context. Yet it would be a mistake to assume the singularity of this historical event, since this would pre-empt the possibility of fruitful comparison and explanation: what we are dealing with here, therefore, is a synthesis of most of the unfree forms of labour exploitation known in the capitalist world-system during the 19th and 20th centuries. It remains to be seen how far they were consciously applied, and the extent to which they came into into being as the result of a silent economic imperative, so to speak, behind the backs of those who were ostensibly responsible. Following the general restrictions imposed on the freedom of the German working class, the latter was subjected to a process of subproletarianization through the use of foreign contract- and forced-labourers, as well as (after 1942-43) the rapid-use-up of slave-labourers as a result of the economic rationalization of the concentration camp system. It could be argued, therefore, that the kinds of unfreedom and coercion usually associated with the colonial capitalist system on the periphery (agro-industrial plantations, indentured migration, etc.) were actually reimported into the metropolitan centre, where they licensed amidst full employment an accumulation process based on deficit-spending, the purpose of which was re-armament and warfare.

Comparisons can also be made with unfree labour utilized in the accumulation model of the Stalinist Soviet Union.[34] The system of unfree labour that emerged there – from the Kolchos system, through the industrial settlements, to the work camps of the Gulags – differed from the German model of reconstruction and expansion of a developed economic structure because the Stalinist model was based on repressive disciplinary measures applied to a broad agricultural process of subproletarianization rather than – as in the German model – to the mass extermination "through work" of already subproletarianized population groups. Apart from this, any comparison must take into account the fundamentally different political-economic conditions: here the radicalization of a failed

---

33. Roth, "'Chinawerke' im 'großdeutschen' Herrschaftsbereich", pp. 7 f.
34. Van der Linden, "Forced Labour and Non-Capitalist Industrialization", this volume, pp. 351-362.

Taylorist imitation on the territory of "late-comers" surrounded by the imperialist world-system, there the strategy of a ruling elite in a fully-developed capitalist country to overcome economic depression through a predatory war and the concommitant export of unfree labour relationships into the expanding area of hegemony, with genocidal consequences.

It is possible to conclude, therefore, that the case of Germany, where unfree labour was deployed by National Socialism for the purpose of capital reconstruction and expansion, was a specifically metropolitan example of an increasing and worldwide tendency towards the use of unfree labour that has been taking place since the second industrial revolution. Unfreedom and coercion are accordingly phenomena that are not external but internal to the historical and socio-economic development of modern capitalism. Nowhere has the utopia of classical political economy, which saw the advance of capitalism as a "law" for the general forcing through of free wage labour, been so comprehensively contradicted as in Germany between 1930 and 1945.

The Right to Strike and Worker Freedom in and beyond Apartheid

Jonathan Grossman

Problematizing the Idea of Transition from Unfree to Free Labour

The world has recently watched what must surely be one of the most dramatic advances in the struggle for democratic rights. Millions of black South Africans, until recently denied even the right to move in their own country have just cast their ballots. Nelson Mandela, until recently waiting in jail to die has been elected State President. Unionists, until recently facing every possible form of threat, victimization and attack are government ministers and respected partners in new state structures of co-determination and tripartism. Demonstrations and marches, until recently subject to brutal repression by the South African Police (SAP) and South African Defence Force (SADF) are now escorted and protected by the same SAP (now SAPS) and SADF (now SANDF). To those who watch – and surely more particularly to those who have participated – the scale of the change which all of this represents is in some ways nothing less than incredible.

The international media has been filled with images of blacks and whites standing together waiting to vote. There have been moving accounts of farmworkers standing with farmers, domestic workers with madams in a "catharsis" of convergence in a newly born equality and freedom. For so many who watch and so many who have been more directly involved, nothing would be more wonderful than to be able to agree completely with Archbishop Tutu and President Mandela when they echo Martin Luther King: "Free at last. Free at last."

The world has pronounced the elections in South Africa free and fair. Fundamental democratic rights – to vote, to organize, to unionize, to speak, to strike, inter alia are embodied in an Interim Bill of Rights. There is now constitutional protection against servitude and forced labour. The changes are taken to mean that black workers, previously victims of one of humanity's most brutal systems of control, are now also free to enjoy equal human rights.

There is a developing conventional wisdom which argues that the changes in South Africa represent a transition from unfree to free labour with a convergence of the anti-apartheid pragmatism of capital and the anti-apartheid struggle of the South African masses.[1] Is that conventional wisdom an accurate reflection of what is really happening?

Just as unfreedom in South Africa is multi-dimensional and complex with each aspect demanding thorough investigation, so too the transition, its causes and components. A comprehensive investigation of the freedom and/or unfreedom of labour in South Africa would demand full investigation of the history of slavery, indentured labour, child labour, prison labour and other forms of forced labour. There can be no doubt that such an investigation would uncover continuing examples of different forms of forced labour. My focus in this paper is more limited: I am concerned specifically and only to problematize aspects of the conventional wisdom by a general investigation of continuity and change in freedom and unfreedom from the specific vantage point of the classical Marxist understanding of free labour, through a specific focus on the issue of the right to strike.

The capacity to exercise formal freedoms in the capitalist labour market, whether free or unfree, depends on the capacity of workers to exercize particular forms of collectivism – specifically the freedoms to unionise, bargain collectively and take industrial action. Capital has systematically interfered with those rights, using repression, legality, ideology and economic pressures. South African history has involved an ongoing struggle by workers to secure those rights – a struggle apparently ended with the new Bill of Rights. I will be arguing that, despite the changes which have been won, there are continuing unfreedoms specifically in relation to the right to strike. Moreover, there is a particular vision of labour history, infested with the distortions of bourgeois ideology, which obscures such actual continuities, while fabricating an ex post facto historically continuing tension between apartheid and capitalism. The beneficiary of that vision is capital which is seen both currently and historically as championing a struggle against the fetters of apartheid. The victims of that vision are the millions of workers who not only remain tied within the unfreedoms of capitalism, and a racially structured division of labour and set of structured social inequalities, but have their role in challenging and changing some of those unfreedoms devalued. In practical political terms, that ideologically distorted view of history underlies, and has been translated into, practical political institutions in such a way as to give to capital the political capacity to effectively veto any extension of the workers' right to strike.

---

1. It is reflected and developed in many ways. These include the insistence that a leading capitalist should be Minister of Finance; images of ANC leaders and union leaders embracing leading capitalists; the insistence that leading capitalists should be seen as patriots; a widespread image of consensus politics and shared goals.

The Unfreedom of Free Labour under Capitalism[2]

For Marx, there were two key factors involved in the constitution of free labour under capitalism of special relevance to this study. First, through the process of proletarianization, people were removed from dependence on the land as means of subsistence; secondly, they were then free in the specific sense of having the capacity to place the commodity they owned – labour-power – onto the labour market in exchange for wages.

Even at the most general and abstract level, free labour under capitalism involves essential limitations and unfreedoms.

– Free labour is constituted as such by violence, conquest and compulsion. Its freedom emerges out of imposed necessity, not voluntary choice. At the daily experiential level, workers are forced to work for employers – they do not choose to do so. They are forced to work in certain jobs – maybe they would choose to work in others.
– In exercizing their freedom to sell labour power on the market, workers are involved in an exchange between unequal parties. The exchange, nominally voluntary and between equals is, in fact, taking place in a real set of social relations characterised by the final power and control of capital over labour. The "playing-field" is never actually "level".
– Free labour is exploited and alienated labour in a set of social relations which involve a range of different forms of oppression including racial and gender oppression. There is a set of social and political unfreedoms which can and have co-existed with economically free labour – for example, the denial of the right to vote to white women in South Africa.
– In addition to these general historical and inherent limitations on the freedom of free labour, there are always actually specific limitations in each situation. Perhaps most notable amongst these is the widespread existence of legally bounded migrant labour. In other words, even where there is free labour in developed capitalist economies, there is unfree labour within those same economies.

In the period under discussion in South Africa, there has been a combination of free and unfree labour in the classical sense. In general, labour classified as white by statute was free; labour classified as African was unfree.[3] Amongst other limitations, black workers have been denied the ability to choose where to seek

---

2. See Marx, *Capital*, I, pp. 271-2. For a discussion of forced labour in South African history see Legassick "South Africa: Forced Labor, Industrialization and Racial Differentiation", pp. 229-270.
3. I generally use "black" as a label, unless it is necessary to specify that part of the black community to which particular conditions and laws apply.

to sell their labour-power, to whom, and, in the contract system, when to withdraw from that sale. Apartheid legislation, and more importantly the industrial colour bar (racial division of labour), systematically denied black workers access to certain skills and jobs. Legislation either did not recognise, or made illegal, independent collective organization (unions) and collective action (the withholding of their labour) by black workers.[4]

It is important to note that the unfreedom of labour had to do primarily with restrictions around the sale of labour-power, rather than with a continuing link to the land as means of subsistence. Apartheid legislated a political link to the rural "homelands" long after the land had been removed as a means of subsistence. That political link was, in fact, legislatively imposed on people born in the urban areas who had never seen the "homelands". Employers and the government continued to ideologize a link to the land both politically and as providing a subsidy to wages – thereby "legitimating" the extra-cheap labour system. In the same way, that link to the land was invoked to justify the denial of state-funded social services (housing, child-care, education) in the urban areas. The imposed and ideologized link sometimes struck a chord amongst migrant workers in romanticised notions of a return to the land. In reality, in the great majority of cases, that return was to a dumping ground which received no state social services, nor provided means of subsistence to those who were dumped there. In millions of cases the romanticized notion of a return turned into a return forced by the repressive machinery of the state.

While these features of apartheid did not mean that labour was unfree in the sense of being tied to the land, they did mean that the bargaining position of black workers on the labour market was undermined – in relation to white workers, but more importantly in relation to capital. As a system of labour control, apartheid specifically denied black workers the legal right to defend themselves on the labour market and secure improvements in wages and working conditions through the franchise, collective organization, and action. The struggle of black workers against apartheid was therefore bound up with the struggle for freedom to bargain meaningfully on the labour market.

The Focus on the Right to Strike

The freedom of labour involves the extent to which workers have "the ability (as) owners of the commodity labour power to exchange it as they choose".[5] "Ability" is meaningful as the real capacity; "as they choose" is meaningful to

---

4. For a history of the legal restriction on black workers see Corder, *Focus on the History of Labour Legislation*; and Kraak, *Breaking the Chains*.
5. Brass, "Some Observations on Unfree Labour", this volume, p. 61.

the extent that it involves bargaining over the terms, rates and conditions of exchange and the working conditions in the processes in which labour power will be used (the labour market and the labour process).

The notion of "free labour" posits the individual worker seeking to exchange his/her labour power in return for a wage from the individual employer. It is embodied in the notion of the contract between worker and employer freely entered into by both parties. As such, it embodies an essentially formalist notion of freedom and an individualist notion of the worker – extending that individualism into competition, not simply between the worker and employer over terms, but also between one worker and another worker. This can take the form either of competition over terms of employment and conditions of work (undercutting); assets embodied in the commodity (access to education, skills-training); and over who will actually succeed (and not succeed) in selling the commodity (competition for scarce jobs).

While workers were forced into competition against each other as individuals and groups, generally in order to exercize freedom in the fullest sense of free labour (to secure the best possible wages and conditions), it is necessary for labour to collectivize and assert itself as a collective force against capital. This involves organizing (unionizing); bargaining; and if necessary taking industrial action. A capacity to use the right to strike is an essential component of the capacity of labour to be free even in the limited sense of freedom under capitalism. Similarly, the capacity to use that right is an essential component of meaningful collective bargaining.

The Struggle for the Right to Strike[6]

During the 1930s and early 1940s, there was a rapid expansion of the manufacturing sector of the economy. Black workers made up an increasingly large component of the manufacturing workforce and of the urban population. In 1942/1943 there was a combination of a strike wave amongst industrial black workers and the development of an organised squatters' movement in the rapidly

---

6. My understanding of the history of working-class struggle is developed in Grossman, "Class Relations". For a general history of trade unionism see Lacom, *Freedom From Below*. On working-class struggle in the 1940s and the emergence of apartheid see Fine with Davis, *Beyond Apartheid*, pp. 1-103 *passim*, and on the Defiance Campaign, pp. 118-126. On the 1956 labour legislation see Lambert, "SACTU and the IC Act", pp. 25-44. For an intensive account of developments in the trade union and workers' struggle between 1970 and 1984 see Friedman, *Building Tomorrow Today*. On strikes in the period 1977-1984 see Bonner, "Strikes and the Independent Trade Unions", pp. 55-61. On labour legislation in the same period see Maree and Budlender, "State Policy and Labour Legislation".

growing urban concentrations of South Africa's industrial heartland. Workers faced obstacles in going on strike on at least four different levels:

- lack of historical experience;
- economic factors which favoured capital, for example accumulated wealth and the availability of reserves of labour;
- the law which made such strike action illegal and the threat of repression from employers and the government;
- political factors inside the workers' movement which led to opposition to strikes in favour of production for the war effort.

By 1994, aspects of that situation had changed fundamentally. Primarily through a collective determination to organize and strike, whether legally or not, workers had built up a strong legacy of organizational and strike experience. Through the same process, workers had forced changes in the law which removed several of the historical legal restrictions. Economic factors, however, still create advantages for capital. And, as will be discussed below, there is a renewed opposition from inside the workers' movement to workers actually exploiting the hard-won right to strike.

The United Party government responded to the 1942/43 strike wave with two War Measures. The effect has been described as making all strikes illegal in all circumstances. Even without these War Measures, strikes by black workers were illegal. Miners had been dissuaded by union, ANC and Communist Party leaders from striking during the war. In 1946, in less favourable conditions, after the strike wave had run its course and additional repressive measures had been placed on the Statute books, black miners went on the then biggest strike by black workers in South African history. The strike was ended through brutal repression and a wave of arrests. After the electoral victory of Afrikaner nationalism in 1948, apartheid measures were imposed against black workers weakened by the smashing of the miners' strike.

In 1953, as part of apartheid repression directed specifically at tightening control over black workers, strikes by black workers were (again) specifically made illegal. The Defiance Campaign of that time targetted apartheid measures but did not focus on the 1953 legislation. The 1955 Freedom Charter made no specific demand for the right to strike. At a formal political level, the Congress Alliance focused its resistance on apartheid as the denial of equal rights, not specifically as a system of labour control. In so doing, it reflected the dominance of the black petty bourgeoisie in defining the political programme of the Congress Alliance. In 1956, legislation was introduced which formalised the legal exclusion of African workers from the collective bargaining system, and thereby from the procedures making possible eventual legal strikes. The reality of this period was that the demand for the right to strike in law was made most vocally not at a formal political level through the codified programmes of the dominant political organizations but by workers actually appropriating the right to strike through illegal action. That perhaps explains why additional legislation was introduced to outlaw already illegal collective action. Similarly, the most effective defiance lay in the daily defiance of workers against the Pass Laws through illegal squatting, rather than in the symbolic protest of the Defiance Campaign.

Widespread political and industrial action was brought to a head by the Sharpeville massacre, the state of emergency, and the movement of SACTU, the ANC and PAC into exile and the armed struggle.

The "golden era of apartheid" between 1963 and 1973 was one in which white workers were effectively tied up in bureaucratic unions increasingly under the political control of Afrikaner nationalism, and there was no systematic open mass trade union organization of black workers. In this coincidence lay the specific political features of apartheid as a racist differentiated form of labour control over both black and white workers.

The next major mass political challenge to the consolidation of apartheid came from a spontaneous strike wave in 1973. This strike wave is regarded as heralding the resurgence of the workers' movement and the phase of development leading to the 1990 political reforms. The government responded to the 1973 strikes in part by beginning the reform of the industrial relations system as it involved African workers and, in the process, extending a legally severely limited right to strike to some African workers. Workers on mines, farms and in domestic service were excluded.

Analysis of the second half of the 1980s has focused on the call and programme of ungovernability. On the ground, that call coalesced with, rather than created, an already existing and growing widespread reality of mass defiance of key features of apartheid control. The history of black workers under apartheid (and other forms of oppression before it) is one of resistance which was continued, albeit in atomised and individual actions and inactions, by millions of workers, even when there was no mass open political or trade union organization. Chief amongst these were the daily breaking of the Pass Laws and the daily programme of industrial sabotage and simply working slowly and badly by millions of workers. What was significant about the second half of the 1980s was that individual acts of defiance coalesced into a movement of defiance systematically eroding key features of apartheid control.

– Forms of industrial resistance exacerbated a growing economic crisis which for capital was constituted by "low productivity".

– A massive proportion of the working class was squatting illegally in the urban areas.

- Working-class youth was in rebellion to demand educational rights in the urban areas.
- There was systematic non-payment for services which the government had been forced to provide.
- Through steps such as the formation of the United Democratic Front, the extensive acceptance of the Freedom Charter and widespread shows of mass support on the ground, the ANC was effectively being unbanned.
- In 1987, an extra dimension was added to that movement of resistance. As the most consciously, tightly and nationally organised component of the mass movement, more than half of the membership of COSATU took illegal strike action.

The maintenance of law and order, economic stability, profitability, the fabricated connection to the land and the apartheid limitation on government spending on social services were under explosive challenge.

The historical formula of state response to the mass resistance of workers involved varying combinations of repression, further legal restrictions and the extension of tightly controlled "rights" in law which had already been assumed in practice. A recurring response from employers to strikes was mass dismissals. In the 1987 miners' strike, Anglo American Corporation acquired the international record as the private employer responsible for the biggest single dimissal of striking workers. In the context of an already existing State of Emergency, the government emerged with proposed amendments to the Labour Relations Act (LRA) which would, inter alia, have made all solidarity and supporting action illegal and the unions financially liable for any losses incurred as a result of strikes. This provoked in June 1988 the then biggest stay-away in South African history. In the face of the stay-away, and the general movement of resistance, for the first time in South African history, government was forced to move away from plans to respond to a massive strike wave with legislative attacks. Similarly, employers were forced to step back from their initial support for that plan.

COSATU launched the campaign for a Workers' LRA and a Workers' Charter of Rights. The systematic demand for the right to strike in law was increasingly a conscious and vocal component of struggle on the ground. The struggle to defy the LRA was developed into an organised struggle for laws which reflected the interests and needs of workers. Through that process, extra impetus was given to the sometimes historically suppressed demands for the unbanning of organizations, and the demand for the right to vote was given clearer content as the demand for a government which would make laws which served workers.

Through mass defiance and the systematic creation of a set of realities on the ground, black workers dismantled key features of apartheid:

- through unlawful organizing they forced de facto, and then legal, recognition of organization;
- through illegal strikes they forced de facto, and then legal, recognition of the right to strike;
- by illegal squatting they forced de facto, and then legal, recognition of the right to freely enter the labour market (concretely, the right of African workers to be in the urban areas and work for whoever they chose);
- through boycotts they forced the state to pay for social services.

Together, these developments affected core features of apartheid as a system of labour control. With the major addition of the denial of formal political rights to Africans, these were precisely the features of the system of labour control which were historically charged with securing adequate supplies of cheap labour with a weak bargaining position at restricted cost in terms of social services.

Capital and government were forced to recognize that the existing systems of control were incapable of securing stability. Exploiting other political factors which created pressure from within and on the movement of opposition to enter into negotiations and accept power-sharing, State President de Klerk announced the reforms of 1990 and moved into the negotiating process which led to the elections of 1994. In the period 1990-1994, there were important changes to the LRA as it concerned the right to strike. Some of these were in line with demands of the COSATU Workers' Charter and Workers' LRA campaigns. Important limitations on the right to strike in the public sector have been removed. The limitation on the right to strike in essential services has also been restricted through a much narrower legal definition of essential services. Farmworkers have been given a severely circumscribed right to strike. While all groups of workers face legal limitations on their right to strike and some – notably domestic workers – do not have that right, legalised racial discrimination has been formally removed as a factor in such limitations. At a formal legal level, black workers are now as free to strike as white workers. These changes all became law before the elections of 1994. The right to strike has been further legally entrenched through inclusion in the Interim Bill of Rights.

In the process of struggle leading to this situation, there was, in the history, no stage of development in which workers were "given" the right to strike. Each advance in winning that right in law depended in large part on workers appropriating the right through illegal strikes in practice. Such action often met with repression from the government; employers used a variety of measures to try to interfere with, undermine, obstruct and break strikes. Nor has there been a stage when the right in law was fully conceded. Each advance in terms of the right to strike came with legal limitations on the exercize of that right. When initially forced to deracialize the right to strike, the government imposed the same procedural limitations on that right onto black workers as had historically been imposed on white workers. The procedure involved in a legal strike today is far more complex than at any other time in South African history.

At a formal juridical level, parallel to the extension of the legal right to strike, the restrictions on free labour constituted by apartheid have been removed. While there is internal migration, there is formal freedom of movement. An historically constituted racial division of labour persists in reality, but is outlawed as such by both a new Bill of Rights and specific measures to extend training to black workers. Compound systems persist on the mines and farms, but the legal compulsion and penalties of the contract system have been removed from the statutes.

Numerous factors came into play in the movement of the apartheid regime towards real political reforms. These include the armed struggle, sanctions, and the internal economic crisis. None of them makes historical sense without full recognition of the agency of millions of workers and youth in effectively defying apartheid. The reality is that the processes of mass resistance had effectively undermined apartheid as a system of labour control and rendered it historically incapable of enforcing stability – even before negotiations began and while apartheid laws remained.

Conflicting Views of the Right to Strike

Through the history, capital and the government have responded to pressure by looking for ways of constructing forms of "collective bargaining" which are stripped of the meaningful right to organize independently (1953 legislation) and the effective right to strike. For workers, the right to collective bargaining stripped of the rights to organize independently and strike is collective bargaining stripped of any real collective strength. In the experience of workers, employers do not reward workers who do not appropriate those rights - they simply exploit the situation. Nor do workers simply comply when such rights are denied in law. Eventually they can and have defied through illegal organization and action. A feature of the 1987 strike wave was the extent to which the strikes involved trials of strength, rather than only a demonstrative/protest character. For workers, the right to strike is made meaningful to the extent that it strengthens their bargaining position, increasing their capacity to pressure employers and/or government to do something which they would otherwise not do. As such, the meaningful right to strike is more than the individual right to withhold labour, in terms of which capital often seeks to define the freedom of the free labour market. It is the right to take organised action whose value lies primarily in the extent to which it is collective and disruptive of what would normally happen – the normal process of production, provision of services and profit-making.

Viewed in that way, the right to strike necessarily involves the rights to picket, organize solidarity action, freedom from intimidation and victimization, and protection from scabbing.[7] It requires a speedy, simple and straightforward legal procedure and non-interference by government and courts. Anything which actually undermines these things is interfering with the meaningful right to strike in a context in which employers already have economic advantages.

Working-class experience in strikes is of precisely such interference and limitations, even where the right to strike exists in law. Interference can involve, and has involved, a range of factors including threatened and actual eviction, dismissal, physical attack, cutting off of credit, repossession of hire purchase goods – all in the context in which workers are already losing wages through strike action. Capital can, and does, do all of this while sometimes conceding the formal right to strike. This is partly because that right is reduced, in a bourgeois conception of freedom and a bourgeois notion of the free market contract, to the individual right to withhold labour, rather than the collective need to strengthen and assert a bargaining position.

In 1991, there was a forerunner of the type of clash which is occurring in the new South Africa between two views of the right to strike, underpinned by two different visions of freedom. Workers at the University of Cape Town (UCT) went on strike primarily to demand higher wages. The employer was in advance of legislation and employment practices in terms of formally agreeing to the right to strike without dismissal. The employer also agreed to the right to strike in a sector which was then legally excluded from striking. In those senses, the employer was the advance guard of changes to apartheid-era industrial relations. There was apparent agreement between employers and workers around the right to strike – an example of the type of "convergence" against apartheid-era restrictions which will be discussed further below. Except at the most formal and abstract level, however, there proved to be little of substance in the apparent agreement. In fact, in lived political reality, the agreement gave way to sharp and bitter conflict. Essentially in the situation, differing priorities and views of the meaning of rights came into conflict. The employers operated in terms of a clear hierarchy of rights: first, the rights of management to manage (maintain law and order and normality); second, the rights of paying consumers (the rights of students to study); third, the rights of workers (the right to strike provided

7. The new Minister of Labour has spoken of the need to make access to courts more simple and quicker; his proposed new legislation is likely to make lengthy and complex procedures less complex in some cases. The Goldstone Commission made recommendations which would severely restrict any picketing. In the recent Pick 'n Pay strike, a court interdict ordered strikers to keep at least 500 metres from any Pick 'n Pay shop. The managing director of Pick 'n Pay (a publicised contributor to the ANC) is leading a campaign for mediation to be made effectively compulsory before there can be a legal strike.

that neither of the more important sets of rights was interfered with). The rights of workers in that situation were made conditional on other rights first being satisfied – a process which effectively rendered the rights of workers meaningless. Teaching and learning had to continue "as normal" without any form of disruption. The effect of this position was to deny the meaningful right to strike, under the mantle of an ideology of non-disruption.

Under this mantle, what was a clash of political priorities was ideologically represented as a clash between those who defended human rights and freedom and those who had no respect for either. Workers were charged with having no respect for human rights – a charge broadened more recently into "no culture of human rights". Linked to that is the argument that amongst workers there is no tradition of democracy and no culture of tolerance. The reality is that, in the same way that a concretised vision of the right to strike was developed out a struggle using that right, even when it was illegal, so a concretised vision of other rights has also developed in a climate which involved the systematic denial of those rights. So, for example, there has developed an understanding of the right to work as involving the actual creation of jobs and a solution to unemployment; the right to vote as involving the actual capacity to assert control over government decisions affecting your life; the right to housing as actually involving the building of houses; at the same time, internal trade union life, for example, despite all the problems, has involved forms and levels of mass participatory democracy which are unique in South African history.[8]

That working-class culture of rights is experientially derived, developed through struggle on the ground, emerging from the experience of social deprivation imposed by apartheid capitalism and the process of struggling to meet basic social needs. At the core of this culture is a resistance to imposed control from "others", a set of second-generation rights, and the right to the collective organization, action and the vote necessary to defend against oppression and exploitation, and to pursue those second-generation rights. It involves the enrichment of rights with a vision of the social conditions under which they can be enjoyed and made meaningful.

Together, these factors are important parts of a vision of freedom which has been a central part of the driving force of mass struggle in recent history. Sometimes it has been consciously understood as a socialist vision; more often it is precisely that vision in terms of which socialism has itself been given meaning. This came into conflict with a different vision of rights – ultimately deriving from the protection of private property and the inequalities which it generates. It is a vision which, to the extent that it addresses the actual rights of ordinary people in day to day life, rests on the freedom to get whatever you

---

8. I have discussed the development of working class democracy, collectivism and the tradition of tolerance in Grossman, "Individualism and collectivism".

pay for. In the reality of the situation, this involved prioritizing the rights of students to buy advantages and privileges (at state-subsidised rates) over the right of workers to bring a meaningful challenge to management.

Against that reality, the claim that there is no culture of human rights – and the associated claims – most often reflects another set of charges which have to do with conflicting priorities reflecting conflicting class interests. A position which prioritises second-generation rights is being dismissed as the absence of a culture of human rights. A position which prioritises the collective right to strike is being dismissed as a lack of respect for freedom. In an actual dispute over rights, it is those with wealth (and the power it gives) who determine which rights should be prioritised and which should be made conditional and secondary. Consistent with the historical functioning of bourgeois ideology, a concretised working-class vision of meaningful rights and freedom is ideologically dismissed as a challenge to rights and freedom per se.

In fact, the UCT strike embodies the two conflicting cultures of rights reflecting two conflicting sets of class interests. To a greater or lesser extent, these two conflicting views of the right to strike and the meaning of freedom more generally have continued to come into play in each major strike in the new South Africa. What is at issue is not merely a clash between different viewpoints. It is the extent to which formal changes are also socially meaningful; and the extent to which the formal freedom of labour in the capitalist labour market involves the actual freedom of workers to secure, through the most effective means possible, the best possible terms and conditions of exchange.

The Distorted View of Anti-Apartheid Convergence

In the same way that a vision of rights in conflict with the bourgeois notion is ideologised as reflecting a clash between the defenders of ageless freedoms and a mob with no respect for freedom, so a continuing determination by workers to exercize their hard-won right to strike is presented as the clash between the objectively determined "needs of the economy" and irrational and even destructive forces. Both conclusions are partly based on a distorted view of the roles of capital and the working class in the anti-apartheid struggle for concretely meaningful human rights.

I argued above that it was above all else mass resistance which rendered apartheid unable to maintain stability. The government unsuccessfully tried to decisively break that resistance through a long and bitter period of repression, while the working class was also suffering under the economic attacks of capital in crisis. The fact that apartheid had been rendered essentially unworkable did not mean that it simply fell away. In a sense, the instability and vulnerability of apartheid made its continued maintenance even more horrific in terms of human costs. Nonetheless, continued mass resistance placed that instability and vulnerability inescapably on the political agenda in front of the state. That is a reality which was imposed on capital and the government.

This meant that the state was forced to look at the option of serious change, even as it sought to secure particular continuity. The response is reflected in the change from the "conventional business wisdom" that "the business of business is business" to the view of a leading capitalist that "the business of business is to stay in business".[9] The continuity which capital sought lay in the protection of private property and the maintenance/restoration of capitalist law and order to serve the goal of profitability and increasing profitability. In searching politically for continuity and stability, capital did not have a free choice of options precisely because of working-class resistance.

There is, however, an ideologically authoritative view (coming to assume the proportions of a developing conventional wisdom) which sees continuity, change and agency in a fundamentally different way. In this view, "enlightened" or "progressive" capital (which tended to be discovered or rediscovered towards the end of the 1980s) is seen as leading capital in general into an anti-apartheid convergence with the liberation movement. Capital has sponsored a view that apartheid's ideological irrationality was a longstanding impediment to capitalist economic development in South Africa and that capital has a longstanding commitment to basic human rights. While liberal historiography has long repeated this position, it has more recently been forced into popular consciousness not by the analytical apologists of capitalism, but by a conscious mass media campaign funded by big business. At less cost, it is now also being repeated in various forms by sections of the leadership of mass organizations.

Some "left" analysis, while critical of the liberal view of deep-rooted historical conflict between capital and apartheid, nonetheless lends a form of support to the developing conventional wisdom with the view that economic pragmatism has forced capital into opposition to apartheid.[10] The conventional wisdom of convergence is normally traced back analytically to the 1970s. In the context of a developing economy, with large foreign investment and one of the highest growth rates in the world, it is argued that the further development of that economy faced an apartheid-imposed shortage of skilled labour. The picture created out of this is that "normal" capitalist development was in conflict with

---

9. Barlow Rand Chairperson Mike Rosholt, quoted in Consultative Business Movement National Team, *Managing Change*, p. 1.

10. See for example Kraak, "Human Resources Development", p. 409, where he refers to analysts who have applied regulation theory to explain the South African crisis and states: "[T]he continuation of a racist division of labour and racial E[ducation and] T[raining] proved to be incompatible with the requirements of capitalist growth by the late 1970s."

apartheid. Capital is currently emphasizing the needs for training in order to increase productivity. It seems this represents a continuity with the historical position of championing the lifting of the industrial colour bar so that black workers could be trained. Ideologically, an ex post facto straight line is constructed between the need for more skilled labour in the 1970s and the need for more skilled labour in the 1990s.

But it is not true that the need for skilled labour simply created an anti-apartheid imperative. From the perspective of capital, what was seen as optimal was a combination of the easing of restrictions on the training of black workers with the maintenance of a racially structured and differentiated labour system which helped secure cheap labour. The maintenance of the apartheid unfreedom of labour demanded a state machinery which would impose migrancy through influx control, place severe restraints around working-class collective bargaining and action, and maintain law and order in urban areas which were dramatically socially underserviced. On the basis of that, a select group of blacks in the urban areas would be given residential rights and access to skilled jobs. The government attempted to move in that direction during the 1980s.[11] The outstanding issue in the reform package was the political position of Africans with residence rights in the urban areas. When it was relatively free to choose, capital, continuing to exploit cheap labour, was ready to try to deal with the problem of a shortage of skilled labour by exploiting such apartheid-mainstream measures as subsidised white immigration. On the ground, employers championed a situation in which black workers were effectively trained to do the work of skilled (white) workers - without being given formal certification or being paid for that skill. This reflected inside South Africa precisely what was happening internationally. "Enlightened" employers internationally were making use of the cheap labour which apartheid repression provided in South Africa. Capital was perfectly able to combine the exploitation of free labour in one context with the exploitation of unfree labour in another. It was precisely for this reason that capital, in the period in which it was meant to be beginning its long struggle against apartheid, was systematically seeking to destroy the emerging black trade-union movement. Even when it was forced from that objective by the consolidation and the defiance of that movement, "enlightened" capital responded to the miners' strike of 1987 with the biggest-ever mass dismissal by a private owner, and welcomed the initially proposed LRA amendements of 1987/1988. The continuity involved is a continuity of the maximum possible set of constraints on the collective organization and action of workers with the maximum possible tightening of belts and increase of productivity of those who were employed.

11. On the reforms emerging out of the Wiehahn Commission see Friedman, *Building Tomorrow Today*, pp. 149-203. On the reforms emerging out of the Riekert Commission see Kraak, *Breaking the Chains*, pp. 16-19 and Bekker and Humphries, *From Control to Confusion*, pp. 23-41.

Throughout the 1980s, it was perfectly open to capital to invest in increasing the level of skills of black workers; neither apartheid legislation nor the industrial colour bar were actual obstacles.[12] But capital decided not to make such investment. The solution to its economic crisis which capital actually championed included training a limited number of black workers, coupled with mass retrenchments, pressures for wage restraint, speed-up, and pressure on government to cut taxes and government spending. For capital, a reformed apartheid system of labour control accorded perfectly with that approach. It involves skills training to drive up the productivity of a part of the labour-force, combined with increased control and decreasing social expense on the (expanding) "unemployable surplus".

All else being equal, such a solution was consistent both with the needs and interests of capital and with a reformed apartheid.[13] Capital was certainly capable of "living" with such a solution as the history shows. But all else was not equal. Workers were in widespread and systematic defiance against key features of apartheid as it had developed. The simple fact is that the kind of reform initially envisaged when the economy was growing rapidly and then re-packaged in the context of an economic crisis is exactly the kind of reform which the working class defied and made unworkable. Attempts to reform apartheid were not allowed to provide capital with the solution which it sought. The interests of capital and its plans are not uniquely responsible for the course of history. When the state embarked upon the reforms which the economic dictates of capital suggested (embodied for example in the 1987 LRA), that path was blocked by the improved collective bargaining position of black workers and, more importantly, the political determination to use working-class collectivism in defiance of repressive legislation and measures. Capital was forced to modify its approach in the light of the reality of that resistance, not by a simple reading of economic imperatives.

Like all conventional wisdoms which can begin to capture part of the popular imagination, this developing conventional wisdom of historical anti-apartheid convergence between capital and labour is not unconnected to actual history. There is obviously a set of agreements between employers, unions and the government (old and new) which are new features of the situation. But continu-

---

12. It is true that the Bantu education system of apartheid imposed a lack of formal education on black workers. Any programme of training would have had to deal with that apartheid imposition. It is equally true that employers in general resisted union demands for facilities and resources for adult education.

13. I am not suggesting that this set of reforms would have solved the capitalist crisis. There is not a contradiction-free solution to any capitalist crisis. The point is that capital did not move away from these limited reforms because of economic imperatives. In fact, capital's initial reading of economic imperatives had led it precisely in the direction of those reforms. It encountered pressure to move decisively beyond those reforms because of resistance to them.

ing turmoil shows that such agreements cannot be reduced to genuine convergence between workers in general and employers.[14] The idea of anti-apartheid convergence obscures, on the one hand, the extent to which the state was forced to modify its position and, on the other, the extent to which capital has been able to use its control of economic wealth to impose its economic programme on the new South Africa. The role of mass resistance on the one hand, and the very different role of the political consequences of private ownership of the economic wealth on the other are both obscured. Agreements are "explained" ex post facto as emerging out of a historical process of opposition which obscures the historical connivance between capital and the apartheid regime. They are presented as having a solid foundation in a history of anti-apartheid opposition which masks clashing class interests and positions (as we have seen in the UCT example).

The conventional wisdom recognises continuity in the situation, but locates that continuity in capital's need for more skilled labour, not capital's search for control appropriate to maximum profits. It recognises change which is imposed, but locates the pressure for that change in the process of economic development at the expense of full recognition of the role of mass defiance and struggle. It recognises the importance of economic forces in the historical process, but strips these from the social relations of class conflict in which they exist. It recognises real aspects of the legacy of the apartheid past for the present and the future, but, in asserting that legacy, strips it of its essence as a particular form of capitalist labour control. In contrast to the imposed social relations of apartheid, the social relations of capitalism are fetishised so that what is actually imposed through force comes to be seen as the result of voluntary agreements freely entered into – the contract between capital and free labour. History becomes the march of economic forces – interrupted only by irrational and short-sighted politics of the right (apartheid) or of the left (workers striking for their needs). We arrive at a situation – and this has happened – where workers are seriously being told that they must stop striking for a living wage and even accept wage cuts and wage restraint because they now have freedom from the cheap labour system of apartheid.

Projected into the present and the future, the argument asserting an historical anti-apartheid "convergence" suggests that the removal of apartheid means normal capitalist development; and, to complete the circle, any problem of development is either part of the legacy of apartheid, or (from the "left")

---

14. I would argue that the agreements are in fact the product of a balance of forces which allows capital to impose aspects of its programme onto labour. The imposed nature of such agreements – and hence their inherent instability – is often recognised. But that recognition seems equally often to be left behind in the light of the agreements which come to be described and then welcomed politically as "convergence" and the new "consensus".

evidence that apartheid is still with us. So, for example, if workers continue to demand the second-generation rights which they demanded in opposition to apartheid, it is because of the "legacy of apartheid". Similarly with strikes, the refusal to pay for services, the expectation of fundamental changes in their lives and low productivity. The implication of this is that, in the post-apartheid era, there are no problems caused by capitalism. Any problems which exist are because apartheid has impeded capitalist development and has left a legacy of impediments. Anything which seems to come into conflict with the dominant view of capitalist development is therefore itself a problem. The problem of the legacy of apartheid quite quickly becomes the problem of workers who are unrealistic, disruptive, expect too much and are not properly willing to tighten their belts. The solution to the problems of that legacy in its different expressions is the economic programme of capital – fiscal discipline, higher productivity and harder work, and the measures of labour control necessary for the implementation of the programme. The real consequences of this are mass retrenchments, speed-up, casualization, enormous pressure on government spending, and the search for forms of wage restraint and an "agreed" moratorium on strikes.

By this process, the fabricated anti-apartheid history is turned into a continuity of hard-nosed economic pragmatism – clashing with apartheid historically, clashing with striking workers currently. Overall it means that the strikes of the past are being devalued and the strikes of the present and future are being discredited. Because the convergence itself is seen as the driving force which produced and maintains the process of change, strikes which are the most obvious expressions of non-convergence are seen as disruptive. In any event, strikes are seen as unnecessary – because workers now have the higher freedom of the right to vote. Even the lack of political morality and conviction in capital's supposed anti-apartheid history gets turned to its advantage. It is not, in the dominant ideological vision, a question of choices about right and wrong, but a question of objective fact concerning "the needs of the economy". In the age-old fashion of bourgeois ideology, the needs of capital are reified and given the guise of the unarguable needs of all. Capital is freed of any responsibility for its actual historical role and its current actual political and economic programme – because these were and are dictated by the "needs of the economy".

Out of this, capital is ideologically provided with a legitimacy in its past and current opposition to strikes. Capital can pose as the champion of the removal of apartheid unfreedoms, even while its is using the same ideologised notion of the "needs of the economy" to actually secure the continuation of unfreedoms in the post-apartheid situation. What is happening is that the ideological distortions of the history of change are becoming the ideological underpinnings of a vision of the present which legitimates continuing and reconstructed unfreedoms. Invoking both its anti-apartheid credentials (legitimated through convergence) and its economic agenda (legitimated as the needs of the economy) capital is continuing to seek to undermine the right to strike. The idea of convergence is now politically practically institutionalised in structures such as the Government of National Unity generally and the National Economic Negotiating Forum and the National Manpower Commission more specifically. Through its participation in these structures which try to operate through consensus, capital has influence over legislation far in excess of its electoral support. Convergence has been transformed into a political practice which gives to capital the effective power to continue to ensure legal restrictions on the right to strike. In that, it is establishing a continuity with its position during apartheid where it has historically used apartheid laws and apartheid repression to bolster the advantages it already has through ownership of the wealth in seeking to obstruct and break strikes.

Capitalist Restructuring, Government Reconstruction Programme, and Restructured Limitations on the Right to Strike

Perhaps the starkest way of problematizing and challenging simplistic notions of the content of the transition in South Africa is to look at continuities in everyday working-class experience of racial inequality and economic exploitation and poverty. If the transition is to involve meaningful change in these areas, then that change is still to be implemented. It is similarly possible to problematize and challenge simplistic conflations of formal juridical rights with the actual capacity to enjoy those rights by looking at strikes. The simple fact is that even with the right to strike now in the Bill of Rights and important limitations removed, the majority of strikes taking place are still illegal.

In reality, even with the freeing of labour, that right is limited in a series of ways:

- There are the same procedural obstacles which were developed to obstruct strikes under apartheid. (While proposed new legislation is likely to remove some of the procedural obstacles in some instances, the same legislation is likely to have the effect of extending the issues which are covered by collective bargaining agreements with the consequence that strikes on those issues will become illegal for the period of the agreement.)
- Capital has the same economic advantages which it enjoyed under apartheid.
- In line with the kind of conventional wisdoms I have discussed, there is an increasingly powerful ideology of non-disruption which is effectively a position making the right to strike secondary and conditional.

- While the right to strike is now guaranteed in law, law also guarantees other rights which, in the climate of the ideology of non-disruption, effectively undermine the right to strike. These include recourse to lock-outs for employers[15] and, most importantly, the guarantee of private property which gives capital its apartheid-era and post-apartheid economic advantages.
- While direct repression through the South African Police Services is not likely to be generally sanctioned by the government, there remains a range of repressive measures available, including the use of "private security" forces such as mine-police. There are also cases of police attack despite current government policy.
- Employers are increasingly turning to court interdicts as a means of pre-empting strikes; there are growing pressures for more complex and lengthy procedures before there can be a legal strike.
- there are signs of a renewed policy of responding to strikes through mass dismissals (AECI, King Edward Hospital).
- In addition, the right to strike legally is, in effect, denied to large sectors of the workforce.[16]

It is not clear precisely how capitalist restructuring will develop. What is clear is that there are already features and trends of that restructuring, sometimes within the Reconstruction and Development Programme (RDP), which will further undermine capacity to meaningfully exercize the right to strike. These include an increase of casual labour as a proportion of total labour; pressure to place tighter legal restrictions on "foreign" migrant labour, likely to mean increasing illegality rather than decreasing migrancy; an increase of small businesses with massive pressure for exemptions from protective and minimum standard regulations; further development of the informal sector;[17] a development of government training schemes (for youth and the unemployed) with no-strike rules; the extension into reconstruction of sectors of the massive South African National Defence Force which is denied the right to strike; pressure for

---

15. Brassey has argued that the recourse to lock-out is legally a freedom rather than a legally more powerful right. The point is that employers can and actually have used lock-outs to pre-empt strikes. See Brassey, *Labour Relations*, pp. 21-22.
16. These include all workers on non-work related issues, domestic workers (both likely to be changed by proposed new legislation), child-labour, workers in essential services (more broadly defined than International Labour Organization definitions), employees of the SANDF and SAPS. Proposed new legislation would make all strikes on the issue of dismissals illegal; similarly strikes on socio-economic issues not called by a registered trade union or federation. While technically possible, it is almost out of the question that farm-workers, non-unionised workers and large groups of casual workers and illegal migrants could ever strike legally.
17. For discussion of small business development, the pressures for de-regulation and "informaliza-tion", and the impact of this on collective bargaining see Theron, *Rethinking Industrial Councils*.

widescale re-introduction, through the RDP, of piecework; the expansion of sub-contracting with special measures including exemptions from protective and minimum standards. Taken together with the overall economic programme of capital, all of this is heading inexorably in the direction of no-strike "agreements", and moratoriums on strikes. The political conditions are being created for capital to exploit the support for reconstruction in order to obstruct and interfere with strikes which in any way challenge capital's programme of restructuring. The political climate of non-disruption promoted by government and important union leaders helps to facilitate exactly that process.

It could be argued that, in general, the anti-strike pressures pointed to above are coming from capital internationally. That is precisely the point: they are not unique in any way to the South African situation, just as the unfreedoms of free labour are also not unique in any way to the South African situation.

In a formal juridical sense, none of these trends bears on the formal freedom of labour. In reality, they bear directly on the capacity of large parts of the working class to exercize that formal freedom, even within its own inescapable limitations. As the unfreedoms of apartheid labour controls were central to the actual process of capitalist development, so there are now features which undermine the freedom of newly free labour which are central to the actual post-apartheid process of capitalist restructuring. In the process of restructuring, heavy emphasis is being placed on small and medium businesses and the "informal" sector. Inextricably linked with that are pressures for deregulation and acceptance of the more or less permanent existance of a mass layer of "casual labour".

Deregulation, Free Labour Markets, and Meaningful Freedom for Workers in the Labour Market

A labour market which actually maximised the freedom of workers under the constraints of capitalism would, in addition, necessarily be highly regulated in particular aspects. While there would be a minimum of regulation and maximum simplicity of procedure to legalize strike action, there would be a maximum of regulation embodying protection and minimum standards. Anything less than this would amount to labour being denied the accumulated benefits of the collective bargaining, organization and action of the past and being reduced in reality to the formal legal situation of the individual contract. Resting on that basis, the freedom of the labour market comes to involve maximum regulation limiting the actual capacity of workers to operate collectively, and minimum regulation protecting the standards which have been won through collective action.

In a formal juridical sense, deregulation does not interfere with the freedom of labour. In fact, it is aggressively argued that deregulation is necessary to free the market – the site of exchange of labour power. In the actual situation, deregulation frees the employer from having to operate according to the gains which working-class collectivism has previously won. Capital is released from restrictions on its capacity to manipulate the market and labour process exclusively to its own advantage. It means that historical gains won very often through illegal strikes cannot be entrenched, secured and protected – but have to be re-contested and re-won again and again. All of that is done in terms of the mythical notion of the free and fair exchange of the market. In fact, it frees capital to operate exclusively in terms of the unequal balance of forces which exists in any capitalist society. In effect, deregulation outlaws the effective operation of working-class collectivism within the labour market. Without that collectivism, workers are turned into competitive individuals, in unequal competition with capital over conditions of the sale and exercize of labour power and in bitter competition with each other over scarce jobs.

It is estimated that no more than one third of the economically active population is formally employed labour. The rest are either unemployed, casuals, or a "floating category" in the informal sector. This means that casual labour is not a peripheral or even minority sector of the workforce: it is as casual labour that most workers are actually forced to make their labour power available for exchange on the market. The social reality of the deregulated free market for casual labour can be observed each day down the road from where I live. Unemployed workers travel long distances to wait on pavements to "exchange their labour power". Under apartheid legislation many of them would not have been allowed to be in the urban areas without work. They would have come to the urban areas under contract and faced legal sanction if they broke that contract. They would have been liable to arrest under the pass laws for standing on the pavement. Legally they would only have been allowed in the urban areas for 72 hours without formal employment. Beyond that, they would have been liable to summary "deportation". In the Western Cape, where I live, they would have faced the additional apartheid restriction of a "Coloured labour preference policy" in terms of which Africans were only employed if there were no willing "Coloureds". Legally, and in terms of government policy, all of that has been transformed. The same unemployed workers are perfectly free in the sense that there is no legal restriction on where they choose to work; they are legally unrestricted in choosing to sell their labour power to a particular employer or not; and to withdraw from any such exchange when they choose. I do not want to trivialize those changes. To do so would be to trivialize the struggle which forced and won them and the role of those who fought that struggle. It would be to trivialize the size of the obstacles which stood in the way of that struggle and it would ignore the emotional meaning of those changes in the hearts and minds of so many of the workers whose collective action won them. But neither can I ignore the continuities of aspects of experience, the continuities in the size of obstacles still to be overcome – essentially, the continuities in the experience of unfreedom; or what is the same thing – continuities in the experience of the limitations of the freedom of free labour under capitalism.

The reality now is that, notwithstanding the size of the changes, they stand in the same place, in the same poverty, waiting for the same employers to ab/use them or not for the same wages as they did when they were not free labour. Their freedom to sell their labour power is a choice between doing that or starving, as it was when they were not free labour. They can choose to work for the employers who stop to pick them up in trucks or go and starve instead, as they could when they were not free labour. When a truck stops to buy a bit of labour power, workers sometimes start to fight with each other over who will do the selling. If they overcome all the individualizing, disorganizing pressures and go on strike to struggle for better wages and working conditions, their strike will be illegal under democratically agreed law – not apartheid law. And the employer will simply employ someone else, as happened under apartheid. That is an important part of the real situation of millions of black workers who are now free labour in capitalist terms.

To understand the actual situation of any of those workers, it is necessary to explore also the actual conditions of unfreedom which are essential to and attendant upon their status as free labour in a capitalist economy. It is not enough to find these limitations and argue either that apartheid has not been abolished, or that capitalism has not been "properly" developed. The limitations are inherent in the way in which apartheid has been abolished and the way in which capitalism has been developed. The unfreedoms are there because the abolition of apartheid has been incorporated into the process of capitalist political and economic restructuring. That restructuring and the unfreedoms which it involves are the way in which capitalism is being developed. Pressures for deregulation, wage restraint, and a moratorium on strikes, are all essential parts of the actual process of capitalist restructuring. Together, they constitute the new challenges to the capacity of labour to bargain meaningfully on the labour market.

Conclusion

It is clear that, even in terms of free labour under capitalism, labour remains, in particular senses, unfree. The transition from apartheid to post-apartheid involves the movement from actual and formal unfreedoms to formal freedoms

and changing and continuing actual unfreedoms. The nature of the democracy established through so much suffering and struggle still means, inter alia:
– capital can effectively veto legal extensions to the right to strike;
– the private ownership developed under apartheid, which is the basis of the inequalities against which workers strike, is guaranteed in the new constitution; that private ownership can be, and is, still used by capital to its advantage in resisting and seeking to break strikes;
– even with so much in law and in terms of the economy to its advantage, capital is still given the right to lock-out – to "balance" the workers' right to strike.

It is neither simply the vestiges of apartheid nor the limitations of capitalist development which limit the freedom of labour; it is precisely the fact of capitalist development and post-apartheid capitalist restructuring which involve continuing and restructured unfreedoms. Reintegration post-sanctions into the world economy means, amongst other things, that capital has the World Bank and the International Monetary Fund as additional agencies through which to impose its own programme. It is a programme cloaked in the rhetoric of anti-apartheid, but embodying continuing and changing features of control over labour which apartheid was historically designed to maintain. These include the insistence on cuts in government spending, restrictions on wage increases, marginalization of those who can not be useful to the generation of profits, privatization, and a set of economic and political limitations on the right to strike and hence on the strength of labour in collective bargaining. In all of that, there is continuity with the historic approach of capital. The ownership and control of the wealth remaining in the hands of capital post-apartheid give it immense power to impose its economic programme and exert a political influence which, in its content, is at the root of continuing and restructured unfreedoms. The victory of mass struggle in overcoming apartheid unfreedoms is being misappropriated as part of capitalist restructuring, just as a plan for a post-apartheid South Africa reconstructed to serve the needs of the masses is being subsumed under capital's programme to restructure for political control over labour and capitalist profits.

However much the conventional wisdom of a new South Africa born out of a common anti-apartheid history and translating into a shared determination to deal with the "needs of the economy" is popularised, there are still two visions of that new South Africa and the freedom it should embody which are clashing and will continue to clash.

Categorizing labour as "free" or "unfree" tells us little about the actual conditions of working-class life and struggle and the future clash between those two different visions. The legacy of apartheid means, by and large, that the beneficiaries of apartheid continue to benefit and the victims of apartheid continue to be victims. The collaborators, functionaries and beneficiaries of apartheid seem able to ideologize this situation in such a way that they can now accuse their victims of yesterday of having no respect for human rights, no culture of democracy and no willingness to work. Partly because of the political agreements reached, primarily because of the power deriving from private ownership of the economic wealth, capital is significantly able to frustrate and dictate to the majority – while bemoaning its lack of productivity and insisting that it tighten its belt. There is a growing insistence that freedom from the cheap labour system of apartheid should involve surrendering the actual right to strike for higher post-apartheid wages.

Is there something wrong, then, with a concept of freedom which can analytically argue that such continuities of unfreedom and injustice can nonetheless be part of a transition from unfree to free labour; and which analytically describes as free labour a lived reality which is experienced as continuing oppression, exploitation, alienation and unfreedom? Marx has told us already that philosophers have done enough to understand the world: the problem and challenge is to change it. The problem does not lie in the Marxist understanding of free labour under capitalism. The problem lies in the reality that the freedom of free labour under capitalism is a limited freedom, bound up with unfreedoms. In that, it is similar to bourgeois justice or democracy or equality. They are different from bourgeois injustice and totalitarianism and inequality, but they are less than the justice and democracy and equality which human beings can conceptualize and create. Free labour under capitalism is exploited and alienated. The fact that it is free does not mean that it has jobs or decent living conditions or a living wage or political rights – or the capacity to actually meaningfully enjoy any such rights. In specific historical circumstances, the freedom of free labour under capitalism can and does mean unemployment, starvation wages and terrible working conditions. That is part of historically normal capitalist development, not evidence of pre-capitalism or non-development. To the extent that such freedom is won and used to the benefit of workers, it depends on workers – their collective organization, bargaining and action. It is part of the normal development of capitalism, in conditions where labour is unfree and where labour is free, for capital to seek to undermine working-class collectivism. But that is not the end of history. In asserting collectivism against the obstacles, through a set of different struggles, workers on the ground have taken rights into their own hands and developed a more concrete vision of rights and freedom. It is a vision of freedom whose meaning derives from the concrete experience of unfreedom of the hungry and the unemployed and the homeless and the exploited many, not the privileged, owning and exploiting few who can pay to make abstract freedoms individually meaningful. As such, it is a freedom far broader than the limits created by the attendant and inherent unfreedoms of free labour under capitalism. To the extent that there seems to be a problem with a concept of freedom which is characterised by changing and continuing unfreedom, the problem does not lie with the concept. It lies with capitalism, which cannot construct a freedom for labour which is not character-ised by unfreedom, exploitation and alienation.

PART II

CASE STUDIES

Old Ways in the New South: The Implications of the Recreation of an Unfree Labor Force[*]

Larian Angelo

Southern Labor Markets: Perfect Imperfect or Regimented?

The issue of persistent regional wage variation has posed serious questions for both economists and policy makers in the United States. In general, theories of regional wage differentials assume that factor mobility, at least in the long run, will even out local differences in factor endowments and therefore, equalize factor rewards across regions. Yet, the South has remained a low wage region for over 100 years, in spite of the enormous changes that have occurred in both the Northern and Southern economies.[1]

Until the first quarter of the twentieth century fundamental markets in the South – the markets for labor, land, and credit – showed little tendency towards convergence with the rest of the U.S. Further, southern agriculture, a key sector in the region, presented the most paradoxical and contradictory market. Throughout the nineteenth and early twentieth century, the South had the highest percentage of its labor force in agriculture, the lowest average income for farmers, the highest dependence on a single crop, cotton, the highest incidence of tenancy and was the only region in the U.S. where renting for cash did not predominate.[2]

These facts of Southern history are perplexing for the economic historian of either the right or the left because they are not easily reconciled with the assumption of a functioning market mechanism, especially for the commodity labor-power. The market mechanism that frames the analysis of capitalism for both Marxist and neo-classical economics requires free factor mobility in response to price changes and a minimum of political coercion among economic agents. The desire for profit must be capital's incentive for production and only the "whip of hunger" can be used to drive workers into the labor force.

[*] I would like to thank Donna Keren for her intellectual and editorial help. A longer version of this paper was published in the July 1995 issue of the *Journal of Peasant Studies*.

1. Rones, "Moving to the Sun", pp. 12-19; and Stamas, "Puzzling Lag in Southern Earnings", pp. 21-36.
2. For a discussion of southern agriculture in the nineteenth and twentieth centuries see, Kuznets *et al.*, *Populations Redistribution and Economic Growth*, and Goldenweiser and Truesdale, *Farm Tenancy in the U.S.*

With free factor mobility, economic theory would predict that southern agriculturalists would respond to low returns by either moving out of cotton production, leaving agriculture and/or leaving the southern region. Yet, by and large, this did not occur. The almost 100 percent wage differential that existed between the wage rate in southern agriculture and Northern industry for unskilled labor between 1880 and 1910 should have, but apparently did not, induce large migratory flows. Only 50,000 Southerners (both black and white) left the region each year, compared to the 500,000 to one million European immigrants that entered the U.S. annually in the same period.[3]

This situation is even more perplexing when it is put in the context of the extraordinary growth rates for Northern industry in this era. The 1890-1910 period is generally considered the era of the homogenization of the labor process and a period in which the U.S. economy experienced substantial growth. About five million new unskilled and semiskilled manufacturing jobs were created in the North during these three decades, with 75 percent of these jobs filled by European immigrants and their offspring. Native born white and black Americans constituted only 20 and 5 percent, respectively, of the new industrial labor force of the U.S.[4] Clearly the impoverished southern farmers (of either race) were not migrating to these jobs, nor were the jobs migrating to them. Given the large "push" of southern poverty and the strong "pull" of increasing demand for labor in the North, the relatively low rates of southern out-migration provide implicit evidence for barriers to inter-regional factor mobility. While what might be termed "the perfect market school" of Southern history has attempted to explain the low rates of return in southern agriculture through the use of standard neo-classical assumptions on productivity, they have not addressed the lack of interregional mobility.[5]

In contrast to the "perfect market" school of Southern history, the works of Ransom and Sutch, Gavin Wright, Mandle, and Jaynes view the anomalies of southern economic development and the problem of southern poverty as the logical outcome of market imperfections.[6] Yet both the perfect and the imperfect

---

3. Average annual income for a black rural family in 1913 was $290, or $24.00 per month, see Johnson, *Negro in American Civilization*, p. 18. According to *Report of the U.S. Immigration Commission, 1910*, Part 23, vol. 19, p. 111, the average monthly wage for a black industrial worker was $43.92. It must be remembered that $24.00 per month represents the return to the labor of the entire family while the industrial wage is the return to the labor of a single working member of the family. See Dan Lacey, *White Use of Blacks in America* (New York, 1972), p. 99, for a discussion of immigration flows.
4. *Ibid.*
5. The "perfect market school" is best represented by De Canio, *Agriculture in the Post Bellum South*; Higgs, *Competition and Coercion*; Reid, "Sharecropping as an Understandable Market Response", pp. 106-130; and Temin, "Freedom and Coercion", pp. 56-63.
6. Good examples of the "imperfect market" approach are found in three works by Ransom and Sutch, "Lock-In Mechanism and Overproduction", pp. 405-425, *One Kind of Freedom,*

market approaches assume that market forces dominated the allocation of land, labor and credit without questioning whether the political and social institutions of the postbellum South were designed to create markets in these fundamental commodities. By limiting their view to the degree to which the Southern market approximated perfect competition, both approaches limited their investigations into the actual causes of southern poverty.

This paper does not focus on whether the return to the southern agricultural laborer was equal to the productivity of that laborer at the margin, but rather whether that laborer had sufficient control over the quantity of labor supplied to the market such that we can assume he was a "free wage worker". Was the agricultural worker or tenant in the South free to migrate among firms or regions in search of higher wages, and free to alter the quantity of labor supplied to the market in response to changes in wage rates? Was there a general juridical equality between capital and labor, equality of bargaining power between the classes and an absence of physical coercion in the labor market? In short, did the South have the social, legal and political institutions that are necessary for the operation of a free wage-labor market where autonomous market forces generate an equilibrium between marginal productivity and wages?

In this paper I argue that the uniqueness of Southern history and development can be explained by the fact that after the Civil War, the South was an economy in which the price of the region's principle output (cotton) but not the alloca-tion of its inputs (labor and credit) was determined by market forces. In a fully functioning market, the price of an input, and therefore its allocation among competing uses, is determined by the price of final output. While the wage of the agricultural producer may have been equal to his productivity at the margin, there is no evidence that the volume of labor required to generate the region's cotton output would have been forthcoming at this low wage.

Unlike what might be termed the "perfect market school" of Southern history, I believe that the legal and extralegal barriers to labor mobility were so stringent that it would be difficult to call the southern method of labor allocation a "free wage labor market". I also argue, in opposition to what might be termed the "imperfect market school" of Southern history, that the landlord, not the merchant, class was the chief architect and beneficiary of the debt peonage system. It was necessary for the planter class to inhibit the formation of a free labor market after the emancipation for the same reason it had been necessary to expand slavery after the invention of the cotton gin; the labor shortage that existed in the U.S. would have driven up wages in the cotton fields to the point

and "Credit Merchandising in the Post-Emancipation South", pp. 64-89. Three works by Wright can be included: *Political Economy of the Cotton South*; *Old South, New South*; and "Economics and Politics of Slavery", pp. 85-111. Mandle also contributed two important works, *Roots of Black Poverty*, and "Black Economic Entrapment".

where cotton production by large scale plantations would have been unprofitable.

Yet an unfree labor system based on debt peonage requires a fundamentally
different set of social, economic and political institutions than one based on
either slavery or free wage labor. The next section will discuss the concept of
the social structure of accumulation and its application to the Southern unfree
labor system established in the post-Civil War South.

The Southern Social Structure of Accumulation in the Post Civil War Period

Because this paper investigates, rather than presumes, the existence of a free labor
market, it is necessary to use a methodological framework that focuses on the
ways in which political and social institutions influence the direction of capital
accumulation. The "social structure of accumulation" model was chosen as a
framework because it focuses on the institutions that coalesce in, and provide
support for, the firm in an economic environment. It is defined as

> [...] the specific institutional environment within which the capitalist accumulation
> process is organized. Such accumulation occurs within concrete structures; firms
> buying inputs in one set of markets, producing goods and services and selling those
> outputs in other markets. These structures are surrounded by others that impinge
> upon the capitalist accumulation process; the monetary and credit system, the pattern
> of state involvement in the economy, the character of class conflict [...]. We call
> this collective set of institutions the social structure of accumulation.[7]

The "social structure of accumulation" model is used in this paper to: 1) examine
the institutions of both the inner and the outer boundaries of the plantation
economy, 2) periodize post Civil War history in the South, and 3) investigate
the connections that may exist between the evolution of social institutions and
economic development. Specifically I argue that the Emancipation forced the
South to create a new social structure of accumulation that differed in both the
"inner boundary" of activities of profit-making firms and the "outer boundary"
of legal, political, financial and social structures in fundamental and crucial ways
from both the contemporary North and the pre-War South.

---

7. The concept has been defined by Edwards, Gordon and Reich in, *Segmented Work, Divided
   Labor*, p. 9. They suggest that each era can be divided into a period of exploration, where
   experimental solutions are tried, a period of consolidation, where a structure has been found
   that permits an economic expansion, and a period of decay, where prior solutions begin to
   prove inadequate. However, their specific periodization explicitly pertains only to the
   capitalist economy in the North and not necessarily to the South. If the principle of the social
   structure of accumulation were applied to periodize Southern history, I would argue that
   it would compare to the economic development of the North as outlined in Appendix 1.

In the "inner boundary" the most important firm, or unit of production, in the South was the plantation and this firm faced a variety of problems in gathering inputs, the production process and the selling process in the post Civil War period. Much of the "outer boundary" of the South's social structure of accumulation was created to respond to the plantation's production needs for a stable reliable stream of low cost labor.

The only way to ensure this low cost labor supply was to recreate, within the limits of the Emancipation, a new type of unfree labor force in Southern agriculture. This recreation of an unfree labor force occurred in roughly the same time period, 1865 to 1940, that is associated with the homogenization of the labor force in the North.

The Southern unfree agricultural labor force was created and reproduced through three interlocking mechanisms: 1) the forms of tenancy dominant in the region, particularly the distinction between share tenant and share cropper, 2) the limited number of credit institutions and general lack of access to capital, and 3) contract labor laws that made breech of contract a criminal offense. In every state in the "core" South,[8] share croppers were defined as wage workers who did not have title to the crop but who did not receive payment for their work until the end of the crop cycle. This forced the cropper to go into debt to create his own "wage fund". Within the South the crop lien was the standard form of collateral and because the cropper did not have title to the crop he had no independent access to credit. This virtually forced the cropper to meet his subsistence needs with a loan from the landlord. The South's contract labor laws brought breach of contract between employer and employee within the scope of criminal rather than civil law. If the cropper accepted even partial payment for, but did not complete, his annual contract he was subject to criminal sanctions and time on the chain gang. If the cropper finished the year in debt, contract labor law treated this as payment accepted for next year's work and the cycle of debt peonage was complete.

The first part of this paper will discuss the construction of the South's post Civil War social structure of accumulation and the methods used to recreate an unfree labor force in agriculture. The second part will analyze the impact that the institutions that created the unfree labor force had on industrial development and wage rates in the nineteenth and twentieth centuries.

8. For a discussion of the states comprizing the "core South" see Angelo, "Wage Labor Deferred", p. 626. Also Wright, *Political Economy of the Cotton South*, provides a good analysis of the distribution between the plantation belt and the upcountry in the U.S. South.

Recreating the South's Unfree Labor Force: The Period of Exploration, 1865 to
1880 and the Period of Consolidation, 1880 to 1915

Before the closing of the frontier, the United States was considered the classic
example of what Marx has described in *Capital* as the free colonial economy.

> The essence of a free colony [...] consists in this, that the bulk of the soil is still
> public property, and every settler on it can therefore turn part of it into his private
> property and his individual means of production without preventing later settlers
> from performing the same operation.[9]

Evsey Domar arrived at the same conclusion when he said "free land, free
peasants and non-working landowners – any two elements but never all three
can exist simultaneously".[10]

The Southern region of the U.S. solved the problem of labor shortage and
became the most advanced and extensive expropriating class in America through
the use of slave labor. In the period of Reconstruction, the Southern plantation-
owning class initiated what was to become a "period of exploration" in the
recreation of an unfree labor force. This period of exploration included experi-
mentation with a variety of forms of organization of the labor process and
various unfree labor forms, including the notorious "Black Codes". As Reconstruction drew to a close, the basic forms of labor regulation, credit and tenancy
that were to predominate until the twentieth century took shape.[11]

Farming continued to dominate the Southern economy after Reconstruction
and, as might be expected, the social structure of accumulation that was created
in the post-bellum period of "Consolidation", 1880-1915, primarily served the
needs of the agricultural sector. While the rural nature of the economy provided
a certain degree of unity, the distinction between the Black Belt and the up-
country persisted well into the twentieth century. I will focus on the process
that contributed to the creation and maintenance of a class of largely black,
landless tenants in the plantation belt because these black tenants were the
plantation owners' chief target for the extraction of surplus value. In the
following section the "inner" and "outer" boundaries of the Southern social
structure of accumulation is described and an estimate for the total number of
unfree agricultural laborers is generated.

---

9. Marx, *Capital*, I, p. 934.
10. Domar, "The Causes of Slavery or Serfdom: A Hypothesis", p. 21.
11. Excellent discussions of the "Black Codes" and the period of Reconstruction can be found
    in Foner, *Reconstruction*; Trelese, *White Terror*; and Cohen, "Negro Involuntary Servitude",
    pp. 31-60. For a discussion of the Black Codes as a period of exploration in the southern
    social structure of accumulation see Angelo, "Wage Labor Deferred", pp. 588-589.

The Inner Boundary: The Production Process

Until the 1950s, cotton was one of the most labor intensive crops in American agriculture, requiring about 63 percent of its total labor input during the harvest. Contemporary wisdom as articulated by Rupert Vance stated that "it was a well known fact that the amount of cotton a farmer can plant is limited by the amount he can pick". Cotton must be harvested in about three months and Brown estimated that, on average, a worker could be expected to pick about three bales during the harvesting season. Because of the structure of the cotton harvest, the labor of women and children was absolutely essential if the crop planted was to be picked. However, after the Emancipation, black children and in particular black women began to reduce the hours of labor offered for sale in the market. This reduction in labor supply threatened the planters' ability to expand their output.[12]

In spite of the planters' initial objections, allowing the freedmen to move from wage labor to tenancy was the only way the planter could guarantee that all the crop he planted would be picked. Unlike the wage worker, the tenants' income rises with output. Therefore any form of tenancy tends to fit the tenant family into the typical pattern of small enterprise where the labor of the entire family is used to maximize production. Thus tenancy allowed the planter to draw upon the labor of black women and children as he had done under slavery. With this secure, increased labor supply, a larger crop could be planted and harvested.

The Outer Boundary: The Southern Credit System

In the immediate post-War South, credit was scarce and expensive. The abolition of slavery and falling land prices reduced the available collateral against which planters could borrow. The pre-War cotton factors, who both extended credit and provided the necessary brokerage and vending services, had been bankrupted by the wartime blockade. While a post-War credit crisis is not unusual for the side that lost the war, what distinguishes the U.S. South is that the region never recreated a viable banking system.

Before the War, fifteen percent of all U.S. banks were located in the South, but by 1870 the region accounted for only two percent of all American banking institutions. While, "in 1870, out of 1,600 National banks, fewer than one hundred were located in the southern states. There were none at all in Mississippi and Florida and only twenty-six in Arkansas, Texas, Louisiana, Alabama,

---

12. Mandle, *Roots of Black Poverty*, p. 92; and Vance, *Human Factors in Cotton Culture*, provide good studies of cotton production, although the ultimate source is Brown, *Cotton: Its History*; Ransom and Sutch, *One Kind of Freedom*; and Brooks, *Agrarian Revolution in Georgia* provide good discussions of tenancy.

Georgia and the Carolinas combined."[13] It is often argued that Southern banking was a casualty of the National Banking Acts of 1863-1864 (the Confederacy was not represented in Congress when the Acts were passed) because the new banking laws favored industrial, capital-abundant regions over poor rural areas. Clearly, the Acts' high minimum start-up capital requirement and the prohibition against holding real estate were two effective barriers to the development of Southern banking. Yet in other rural, capital poor, regions a variety of financial institutions were created as alternatives to the National Banking structure. The real question in the history of Southern credit was not how the National Banking Acts limited Southern credit but why the South chose, as its only credit alternative, the local merchant.

The financial system of the South was primitive, even in comparison to other rural regions, and I would argue that its primitiveness helped to force tenants into debtor relations with the chief Southern employer – their landlord. This was to become a crucial link in creating a regimented labor force in agriculture and ultimately the region's lack of credit proved to be an asset to the planting class. Clearly, the plantation-owning class had tremendous influence in State and local legislative and judicial bodies, but, banking and finance were regulated by the Federal government and the South had little influence in national affairs until the turn of the century. Yet the voting patterns of Southern representatives in the national government does not indicate that there was strong pressure from regional elites to improve Southern banking institutions.[14]

As a result of the South's backwardness in finance, it was the only region whose interest rate did not converge to the national average by 1900.[15] Whether the planters actively worked against a broadening of the variety of available financial intermediaries or passively profited from the limited credit possibilities in the region, the South's underdeveloped financial system was a key component in the creation of the unfree agricultural labor force.

The Outer Boundary: The Forms of Tenancy and the Structure of Class Struggle

Tenancy and poverty have been closely associated in the economic relations of the South, yet being a tenant does not, in and of itself, imply poverty and low productivity. In fact the tenant farmer was the model capitalist in the paradigms of Smith and Ricardo, and in other parts of the U.S. tenancy was the first step in the farm ladder. However, the nineteenth century English tenant functioned

13. The numbers for the period prior to 1870 were taken from Ransom and Sutch, *One Kind of Freedom* and the quote is from Trescott, *Financing American Enterprise*, p. 58.
14. For a discussion of the National Banking Acts, the creation of alternative financial institutions in other regions, and the voting positions of southern elected officials, see Trescott, *Financing American Enterprise*; and Davis, "Investment Market 1870-1914".
15. Davis, "Investment Market 1870-1914", p. 388.

within a social structure of accumulation that was radically different from the one that was created in the post-War South. In the American "cotton states", four distinct forms of tenancy (cash tenant, standing renter, share-tenant and sharecropper) coexisted, with each form holding a different place in the social structure of accumulation.

The Southern tenant who most closely conformed to the classic model of the entrepreneurial farmer was the *cash tenant* (see Table 1). Under this legal framework, the landlord sold his right to the productivity of the land for a fixed cash amount and it was the tenant, not the landlord, who owned the output at the end of the production process. Because the tenant bore all the risk and reaped all the reward, less the rent payment, the landlord had no right to supervize the production process of the tenant. The tenant in this situation needed sufficient capital to purchase means of production and means of subsistence for the entire production period. This form of tenancy occurred least often in the 1880-1910 South, perhaps due to the fact that so little cash credit was available. Ransom and Sutch's interpretation of the 1880 Census, suggested that 16.5 percent of farmers of both races fell into this category.[16]

A second and rare form of tenancy involved paying a fixed amount of the crop grown rather than a cash rent. Here the *standing renter*, like the cash tenant, provided all necessary capital and shared some of the risk of price fluctuations with the landlord. This gave the standing renter the status of entrepreneurial farmer. Standing and cash renters tended to be lumped together and by 1920 these two forms of tenancy accounted for 25 percent of all black and 13.6 percent of all white tenants (see Table 2).

Another form of tenancy originated in the up-country among white yeoman farmers and is known as *share-tenancy*. In share-tenancy, sometimes referred to as working for thirds and fourths, the landlord furnished one-third or one-fourth of the fertilizer and the tenant provided all other capital. The landlord received either one-third or one-fourth of the product. The tenant, however, retained all entrepreneurial rights, especially the right to the crop in the ground. In discussing this form of tenancy, the 1880 Census again proves useless because it did not distinguish between sharecropper and share-tenant. The 1920 Census indicates that almost forty-one percent of all tenants farmed under the share-tenant system.

---

16. Ransom and Sutch, *One Kind of Freedom*, p. 295.

Table 1. The forms of tenancy

LANDLORD FURNISHES*	CASH	STANDING	SHARE-TENANT	SHARE-CROPPER
	Land	Land	Land	Land
	House	House	House	House
	Fuel	Fuel	Fuel	Fuel
			1/3 to 1/2	1/2 Fertilizer
			Fertilizer	Tools
				Work Animals
				Feed
				Seed
TENANT FURNISHES	Labor	Labor	Labor	Labor
	Work Stock	Work Stock	Work Stock	
	Feed	Feed	Feed	
	Tools	Tools	Tools	
	Seed	Seed	Seed	
	All	All	2/3 to 3/4	
	Fertilizer	Fertilizer	Fertilizer	
				Fertilizer
LANDLORD RECEIVES	Fixed Amount in Cash		1/4 or 1/3 of the Crop	1/2 of the Crop
LEGAL STATUS	Entrepreneur Full title to Crop	Entrepreneur Full title to Crop	Entrepreneur Full title to Crop	Wage Worker No Title to Crop
CREDIT SOURCE	Merchant	Merchant	Merchant	Landlord

★ *Source:* Starred sections after Goldenweiser and Truesdell, *Farm Tenancy in the U.S.*, p. 131.

The final form of tenancy and the most important for understanding the position of blacks in southern agriculture was the *sharecropper*. Under this system the landlord furnished all the working capital as well as one-half of the fertilizer. The cropper brought nothing to the production process except his labor and the labor of his family. It was often the case that the landlord also provided the cropper with the means of subsistence during the production period. Again the limitations of the 1880 Census make it impossible to determine how many southern tenants worked under this form of tenancy, but by 1920, 611,091 or thirty-eight percent of all tenant families were croppers.

The distinction drawn between sharecropper and share-tenant in Southern law created a *class division* between the two forms of tenancy.[17] Because the landlord supplied all necessary means of production, the sharecropper was a *wage worker whose form of wages was a share of the crop*. Unlike the cropper, the share-tenant brought his own capital to the production process and therefore was legally an entrepreneur with title to the crop. This legally created class distinction

17. Woodman, "Post Civil War Southern Agriculture", pp. 319-337; Mangum, *Legal Status of the Tenant Farmer*; and Cohen, "Negro Involuntary Servitude".

forced share-tenants and sharecroppers to find fundamentally different sources of credit. Further, the two types of agricultural contracts were regulated by a different set of laws, with the share-tenant-landlord relationship governed by *civil law* and the cropper-landlord relationship governed by *criminal law* (see below). This difference in source of credit and contract regulation was to prove crucial in the formation of the Southern unfree agricultural labor force.

The cropper was effectively cut off from access to credit when the Southern legal system asserted that the landlord, and not the cropper, owned the crop in the ground. However, the cropper still had to bear the risks of price fluctuation and crop damage even though he was legally a wage worker. In effect the cropper was forced to share in the risk of commodity production without ownership of the commodity he produced. The sharecropper might be termed either an "entrepreneur without assets" or a "worker who provides his own wage fund". The precarious nature of this position, rather than low productivity, inadequate human capital or "imprudence" may have contributed to the high rate of indebtedness among the sharecropping population.

Historical evidence also indicates that the forms of tenancy were not neutral in terms of race. Again, the 1880 Census did not distinguish between sharecropping and share-tenancy nor did it divide tenants by race. The first full collection of data by the Census in 1920 reveals that, in fact, many black tenants were disguised wage workers, i.e., sharecroppers who did not own the means of production and did not have title to the crop they grew (see Table 2).

In 1920, 53.5 percent of all white tenants were share-tenants – they held the lowest rung on the entrepreneurial farm ladder – while only 25 percent of black tenants fell into this category. On the other hand, 47 percent of all black tenants were croppers while only about 25 percent of white tenants worked under this form of disguised wage-work contract. If all forms of entrepreneurial tenant (i.e., tenants who had title to the crop they grew) are compared by race, it will be found that only 52.6 percent of all black farmers who were classified as "tenants" by the Census could actually obtain a loan from the local merchant without the intervention of their landlord. On the other hand, 74.4 percent of all white tenants worked under a form of tenure that granted them legal title to the crop grown and therefore access to credit (see Table 2).

The conflict between traditional planters and the rising merchant class centered around which group would be able to exploit the credit needs of the black population. In Georgia, the ability of the merchant to extend credit to the cropper changed four times between 1869 and 1874. The Georgia Supreme Court settled the issue by defining the cropper as a wage worker with no title to the crop and therefore no collateral to offer the merchant. In 1871 the

Table 2. Forms of Tenure by Race

	White tenants	
	Farms	Percent
Share-tenants	474,513	53.1
Share-Croppers	227,378	25.6
All Share	701,891	79.1
Share-Cash Renters	14,465	1.6
Cash & Standing Renters	145,985	13.6
Unspecified	25,223	2.8
Total	887,56	100
	Black tenants	
	Farms	Percent
Share-tenants	176,711	25.1
Share-Croppers	333,713	47.4
All Share	510,424	72.5
Share-Cash Renters	8,207	1.2
Cash & Standing Renters	178,199	25.3
Unspecified	6,725	1.0
Total	703,555	100

Source: Goldenweiser and Truesdell, *Farm Tenancy in the U.S.*, p. 124.

Alabama State Legislature declared that the landlord had a lien that was superior to the lien of the merchant. This not only secured the landlords' rent payment but also declared that any loan extended to the tenant by the planter would be repaid before any loan extended by the merchant. In 1875 Alabama law prohibited the merchant from transacting any business with a tenant after sunset. Since the normal working hours for tenants extended from sunrise to sunset, the tenant was effectively forbidden from trade with the merchant, even if the trade was in cash. By 1884 the merchant was legally unable to take a crop lien in two-thirds of the counties in Alabama, most of them located in the Black Belt.[18]

While Ransom and Sutch claim that the rural merchant prevented Black progress, the legally created class distinction between cropper and share-tenant, combined with the fact that blacks more often than whites fell into the cropper category, makes the claim unlikely. The legal status of most blacks as disguised wage workers without collateral limited their access to the credit facilities offered by the merchant. Further, it is unlikely that black tenants had much contact with the merchant even as a cash supplier because most Southern states had laws

18. For a discussion of the conflict between planters and merchants in Georgia see, Brooks, *Agrarian Revolution*. For a discussion of this conflict in Alabama, see Weiner, *Social Origins of the New South*, pp. 113-33.

prohibiting cash trade between merchants and croppers after dark. The structure of Southern landlord-tenant relations in this period forced the cropper to utilize the credit facilities of the landlord, not the merchant, to obtain means of subsistence. Sometimes the landlord chose not to "furnish" the tenant himself and assigned part of his credit line to the tenant. This allowed the tenant to make purchases on credit at the merchant's store, but even then, the tenant was legally indebted to the landlord and not the merchant.

The Outer Boundary: Contract Labor Laws and the Creation of Debt Peonage

Contract labor laws forged the final link in the chain that created the South's unfree labor system. At one extreme a sort of "public-sector" regimented labor force was created through the use of convict labor,[19] but non-criminal agricultural workers in the private sector were the real basis of the Southern unfree labor system.

In general, agricultural work was done under a yearly contract which prevented workers from taking advantage of the seasonal peak in the demand for labor during the picking season. More importantly, the widespread use of contract labor allowed the state to erect a legal structure of contract enforcement in wage labor. Under usual circumstances breach of contract involves the parties in a civil procedure where monetary damages are assessed against the loser. In a unique combination of circumstances during the 1880-1910 period, the South instituted criminal penalties for breach of contract by agricultural workers. The one-sided law had no penalties for the employer who broke his contract with a worker, and contracts between parties who were not in an employee-employer relationship remained within civil jurisdiction. The overt rationale for criminal penalties for breach of contract by workers was that they were too poor to pay monetary damages.

If a worker broke his labor contract he forfeited the right to all payment, even for work already performed. If the worker had accepted some payment for work and broke the contract, the law would view him as having defrauded the employer of the money advanced. The yearly contract system meant that the worker was paid just once a year after the crop was harvested and sold. This yearly payment system was legitimated by the fact that the majority of agricultural workers were called "tenants". As we have seen, being termed a "tenant" in the post-War South often meant sharecroppers who were required to provide their own "wage fund" during the production period but denied title to the crop in the ground. Without access to cash the cropper was forced to turn to the credit system to maintain his family. Since the only collateral in the South was the crop lien, the worker who did not have title to the crop he was producing

19. Daniel, *Shadow of Slavery*, pp. 24-25.

could not turn to the merchant for supplies on credit. He was forced to turn to his landlord for subsistence during the production cycle.

The law did not view the landlords' "furnishing" the cropper as a form of wages but rather as a debt contracted by the worker from the landlord. This legitimized the landlord's charging an interest payment on the worker's wages and left the worker indictable for fraud if he left before completing his contract. If he finished the year in debt he was viewed as already having accepted payment for next year's work and was again obliged to remain with the same landlord, or risk being indicted for fraud. The U.S. government began to erode the legality of debt peonage through the courts in 1857 (Jaramillo v. Romero) and with Federal legislation in 1867. However, the use of fraud rather than debt in Southern legal codes circumvented the Supreme Court decision and debt peonage appeared to be essentially legal and went unchallenged. Appendix 2 summarizes the most outstanding or typical laws and cases that created the regimented labor force in the seven states of the deep South. In these states the law was in a continued state of flux due to constitutional challenges, case law modifications and changing circumstances.[20] States in the peripheral South often enacted similar statutes which have been left out of this Appendix for the sake of brevity.

Every state in the cotton South maintained similar statutes (see Appendix 2). South Carolina and Arkansas fraud statutes' were not struck down until 1907 (Smith v. U.S. 157 Fed. 721 (C.C.A. 8th 1907)). North Carolina's peonage law was not found unconstitutional until 1911 (N.C. State v. Griffin 154 N.C. 611 70 S.E.). Alabama's fraud statute was struck down the same year in the famous Alonzo-Bailey case. Mississippi's was not struck down until 1912 (State v. Armstead 103 Miss. 790, 60, So. 778). Louisiana's peonage law was dismantled in 1918 and Georgia's law remained in force until 1942. The Federal government outlawed any form of statute that led to peonage in 1944 and Florida's statutes remained in effect until that time. Thus Justice Jackson's famous "sword and shield against forced labor" was not in place until the end of World War II.

To further restrict labor mobility, most Southern states had laws that prohibited a second employer from hiring a worker already under contract to another employer. Most states had legislation forbidding the movement of the workers' own household goods off the plantations between the hours of sunset and sunrise in order to prevent the escape of peon labor. Finally, to protect their labor supply from Northern labor recruiters, most Southern states required labor

---

20. For a more complete discussion of the legal distinctions between croppers and tenants, see Woodman, "Post Civil War Southern Agriculture", pp. 319-337; and Mangum, *Legal Status of the Tenant Farmer*. For a more detailed discussion of anti-enticement legislation see Cohen, "Negro Involuntary Servitude", pp. 31-60; and Scott, *Negro Migration During the War*. Cohen and Daniel also provide good summaries of the vagrancy laws while Daniel, Mangum, and Woodman provide an analysis of the false pretense-peonage laws.

recruiters to pay high fees (from $1,000 to $25,000) and obtain letters of recommendation from local businessmen and ministers. The weight of evidence indicates that the thrust of Southern states' regulation of the capital-labor relation was to prevent labor mobility and inhibit the market from establishing an equilibrium. This structure of law meant that any wage laborer who was not hired by the day or the week was eligible for debt peonage.[21]

Given the evidence I must conclude that the inability of the black tenant to gain access to the credit facilities of the merchant made it difficult for him to advance to the next rung in the farm ladder because he had to rely on his landlord for means of subsistence as well as means of production. The combination of legal status as wage worker with continued indebtedness to the landlord was to prove fatal to the freedom of the black farmer. On the other hand, the white up-country farmer, who was a landowner or a share tenant, did deal with the local merchant as an independent entrepreneur.[22]

The forms of tenancy peculiar to the South and its backward credit system were necessary additions to the contract labor laws in the creation of an unfree labor force. The absence of any of these three aspects of the social structure of accumulation would have made debt peonage impossible. It was necessary for the tenant to have a debt connection to the landlord and for his relationship with the landlord to be regulated by contract labor laws rather than the standard commercial code. If the Southern credit structure had resembled the variety of financial institutions that evolved in other rural regions, credit in cash would have been more available to poor farmers. In the South this would have put most landless farmers into the entrepreneurial category of share or cash tenant. The establishment of his entrepreneurial status removed the farmer from the contract labor law system altogether. Furthermore, if sharecroppers would have been legally defined as entrepreneurs rather than as wage workers, they would have had title to the crop and therefore been in a position to offer collateral to financial intermediaries, even if the only available credit facility was the local merchant. This would have broken the essential link in the tenancy-peonage system because the tenant would have been in debt to someone other than his landlord. In fact the cropper remained in debt to the landlord throughout the nineteenth century and the Southern contract labor laws turned that indebtedness into peonage until the boll weevil infestation of 1915-1927.

21. For a discussion of the southern laws prohibiting the bidding away of labor see Zeichner, "Legal Status of the Agricultural Laborer", pp. 412-428; and Cohen, "Negro Involuntary Servitude", pp. 31-60. For a discussion of legislation forbidding movement after sunset see Daniel, *Shadow of Slavery*; and Shugg, *Origins of Class Struggle in Louisiana*. The discussion of prohibitions against northern labor recruiters is outlined in Zeichner and also in Cohen.
22. See Hahn, *Roots of Southern Populism*.

The Scope and Practice of Peonage

Although the system of labor regulation described above leaves no doubt that the South lacked the legal framework necessary for a free labor market, the existence of legal categories does not tell us how many southern tenants were actually caught in the system of peonage. Unfortunately lack of hard quantitative evidence makes a reliable estimate of the number of Southern workers held in peonage difficult.

In spite of the data limitations, it is important to have some concept of the scope of Southern peonage and I believe that by 1900, approximately 343,000 tenant families were potential peons and could be legally held on the plantation if the landlord needed their labor.[23] To put this number in perspective, it must be remembered that in the South in 1900 there were only 2.5 million in farms total (including plantations and small owner-operated family farms). It should also be remembered that the figure used above refers to tenant *families* with each family having about four persons.

It is difficult to view the South as a free labor market when virtually all wage laborers and thirty-eight percent of all tenants could be denied the mobility that is essential for market forces to establish a wage equilibrium. The fact that a large segment of the agricultural work force was subjected to the system of debt peonage must be expected to alter the results and interpretation of any model of Southern economic development. De Canio found, for example, that the South's concentration on cotton production was not a misallocation of resources because cotton's low cost of production yielded the highest rate of return.[24] However, a major cost of cotton production was agricultural labor which would not have been so cheap if the worker had been given greater rights of mobility.

The structure of law that established the planter's ability to bind his laborers to the land in this period of Southern history is well documented and there is little evidence to indicate that employers did not exercize their right to restrict mobility in the agricultural sector in times of labor shortage. Both Shlomowitz and Wayne present evidence for inter-plantation mobility prior to the 1880 period but there is no discussion of inter-plantation mobility after the 1880s and, more important, no discussion of mobility out of the plantation system and into industry.[25]

Although Grogh asserted that one-third of all tenants moved each year he did not substantiate this figure,[26] and certainly, some amount of mobility within the

23. For a complete discussion of the methodology used to arrive at this estimate see Angelo, "Wage Labor Deferred", pp. 600-601.
24. De Canio, *Agriculture in the Post Bellum South*.
25. Shlomowitz, "Bound or Free", pp. 569-596; and Wayne, *Reshaping of Plantation Society*.
26. Grogh's assertion in, *Black Migration*, pp. 36-37, is disputed by Mandle in *Roots of Black Poverty*, p. 127.

plantation economy would not be incompatible with a peonage system. Many southern tenants were not croppers and therefore would have had the right to terminate their tenure. In addition, within the Southern labor system geographical movement is not necessarily indicative of the mobility of free wage laborers. A worker's debt could be "sold" among employers and there is evidence that the pre-War internal slave trade between the upper and lower South was replaced in the post-War period with a lively trade in peons.[27]

In fact, all contemporary accounts indicate that peonage was a central pillar of Southern agriculture. Mr. Hoyt, a U.S. Justice Department official, estimated that one-third of the planters in Georgia, Alabama, and Mississippi with five to 100 plows practiced peonage. The Justice Department found peonage in every county in Alabama in 1903 and by 1920 every state in the South was involved in a major peonage case with Federal authorities.[28] In the early twentieth century, the Federal government began to challenge, albeit timidly, the institution of agricultural peonage but, the system remained an accepted form of labor service in the South until the first quarter of the twentieth century.

However the debate on Southern debt peonage has tended to focus on whether the planters could actually "hold" their labor on the land, with an emphasis on the viability of restrictive mechanisms. While this is, of course, an important point, it is also important to remember that peonage was not slavery. Not every agricultural worker was a debt peon and, more importantly, not every peon remained in peonage his or her entire life. I will argue that it was the very porousness of the system, the ability to escape peonage more easily than slavery, that distorted the industrial development of the South in the nineteenth and early twentieth centuries.

The Results of Unfree Labor: Industrial Development

As early as 1860 the South emerged as an area that was industrially backward. In that year the South accounted for thirty-five percent of U.S. population, but only ten percent of manufacturing employment. One hundred years later, in 1960, the Southern industrial base was at least approaching proportionality with its population, but the region had come to specialize in low-wage manufacturing. As late as 1978, the industrial mix of the modern South was still geared towards low-wage manufacturing industries.[29] In this section I explore how the

27. Wallace, *South Carolina*, p. 646.
28. Daniel, *Shadow of Slavery*, pp. 108-122.
29. In 1960 the South had 31.5 percent of U.S. population and 23.6 percent of all manufacturing employment. North, *Growth and Welfare in the American Past*, p. 115. Also see Browne, "How Different Are Regional Wage Rates", pp. 33-43, for a discussion of industrial mix.

interaction of the South's peculiar geography and system of unfree labor channeled the region's development toward only those industries that would not endanger labor supply in the plantation sector.

After the Civil War the planters refused to make the transition to a free labor force in agriculture but lacked the power fully to recreate slavery. The result was a debt peonage system that could only be reproduced if sharecroppers had limited access to cash. Industrial wage work threatened the plantation economy because it could put cash into the hands of the South's debt peons and endanger the link between indebtedness and contract labor law that was at the heart of the region's social structure of accumulation. This implied that the South could not industrialize along the Northern path of relatively free economic growth but was also unable to pursue the "Prussian Road" of the German Junker.[30] Instead of using the power of state and local governments to promote full-scale industrialization, the planters used their disproportionate influence in state government to promote the growth of *only* those industries that would not threaten their hold on the agricultural labor force.

The social and geographical separation of the "white upcountry" from the plantation belt created areas where industrial development could occur without utilizing labor from the black belt. However the upcountry village could provide a labor force of limited size which, in turn, limited the region's economic development to industries that could operate efficiently with small firm size. This made the development of high wage "core" firms, like steel, auto and large scale food processing, impossible in the white upcountry.

It has been argued that the policies of the planter-dominated state and local governments played a crucial role in promoting the growth of the textile industry and inhibiting the growth of the steel industry.[31] I will extend that argument to show that the South's modern specialization in low-wage industries is the inevitable consequence of planter opposition to *all* large-scale enterprise. This opposition flowed from the threat large-scale, or what came to be "core", industries posed to the peculiar unfree labor force in southern agriculture. Planter control of state government reached its zenith in the 1880-1910 period, and unfortunately for the region, this was precisely the period in which the Northern industrial base was erected. After 1910, when the plantation economy began to decline, it proved difficult for the South to compete with the already established core industries in the North.

---

30. An in-depth discussion of theories of economic development in the context of the U.S. South is provided in Angelo, "Wage Labor Deferred", pp. 602-605.
31. Oates, *Role of the Cotton Textile Industry*, Appendix I and chapter 4; and Wiener, *Social Origins of the New South*.

Industrial Development: Textiles and Iron, Core and Periphery

Although textiles would seem to be a logical industry for the South because it represents a vertical integration of the cotton industry, it is doubtful that the sector would have flourished without the government support it received. While many southern textile firms were owned by the planter class the mills were not located near the leading cotton producing regions like Alabama and Mississippi, but rather in the states with declining cotton production like the Carolinas and Georgia. Given the high cost of shipping within the nineteenth century South, the pattern of locating mills far away from raw materials seems at odds with the concept of economic efficiency.[32]

This geographical pattern for textile mill location continued into the 1960s. If the four leading mill states of North Carolina, South Carolina, Georgia and Alabama are examined by county it will be found that, as late as 1960, the top six counties (or two percent of the counties) contained thirty percent of all southern mills. The next six counties contained eleven percent of all mills.[33] As late as 1960, not a single leading mill county was or is located in the Black Belt where labor would have been cheaper and transportation costs lower. The mill owners apparently decided to locate near the industrial labor force of choice:

> Before the turn of the century, the southern mills relied heavily upon white tenant farmers residing in the piedmont. Until the rapid expansion of the industry after 1900 it was possible to locate a plant in virtually any upland area of the Carolinas, Georgia or Alabama and be certain of an adequate labor supply.[34]

Historical evidence indicates that the pattern of Southern industrial development was dictated by the desire to exclude black labor from manufacturing employment. For the 146 counties in the leading mill states of North and South Carolina, the pattern described by Blicksilver seems to have persisted into the twentieth century. There is a correlation coefficient of 0.31 in these counties between the number of mills in a county and the percentage of the population that is black in the county, using employment data from the 1963 Census of Manufacturers and population data from the 1960 Census.[35]

The generous support granted to the Southern textile mills contrasts sharply with the generally hostile reception which greeted the developing steel industry in Alabama. While Birmingham was an ideal site for metal production, Ala-

---

32. For a discussion of the factors contributing to the development of the southern textile industry see Copeland, *Cotton Manufacturing Industry*, p. 35; and Blicksilver, *Cotton Manufacturing*, p. 2.
33. See Appendix 3.
34. Blicksilver, *Cotton Manufacturing*, p. 28.
35. See Angelo, "Wage Labor Deferred", p. 604, for a discussion of the correlation between race and textile mill location; and Oates, *Role of the Cotton Textile Industry*, p. 131 for a similar analysis for the years 1900, 1920, and 1940.

bama's vigorous and focused anti-industrial policy managed to overcome the region's natural advantages in steel production.

The iron industry had historical roots in the region but, by 1893 the South produced only fourteen percent of the nation's pig iron. The Southern textile industry had a smaller market share before its take-off period in 1860, but, unlike the rapid growth of textiles, the next twenty years produced only stagnation for the southern iron industry.

In contrast to the support obtained by the textile industry, the iron industry in the South encountered opposition from the planter class. A typical statement of the planter position on the development of the iron industry is quoted in Weiner: *The Selma Times* stated in 1866 that the region would be "better off if all its furnaces were torn down, its mines filled with dirt and its inhabitants put to planting cotton". It would be hard to imagine a more open declaration of hostility.[36]

The origin of the hostility of the planter class to the iron industry may lie in the fact that the plantation belt in Alabama is not as geographically separated from the up-country as is the case in the eastern states of the Carolinas and Georgia. Of more importance, the iron industry must be worked on a larger production scale than textiles. In 1880 the average size firm in the Alabama iron industry employed 203 workers. In the same year, the average southern textile mill employed only 104 workers. In addition, the size of the average firm in the steel industry was rising, and by 1905 the average Birmingham steel mill employed 300 workers, while the average size firm in Pittsburgh had risen to 400 workers.[37]

The pressure to keep firm size small seemed to be a function of the need to keep black labor within the plantation economy. A textile mill could be located in a predominately white up-country county and obtain an adequate labor force because of its small scale of operation. On the other hand, iron and steel production requires a large, flexible labor supply. The Alabama iron manufacturers often complained of labor shortage, and according to *The Report of the Commissioner for Immigration for 1910*, the larger iron producers in the Birmingham district had trouble assembling a year-round labor force of sufficient size.

---

36. Wiener, *Social Origins of the New South*, p. 157.
37. In textiles the advantages of large-scale production were achieved at a firm size of between 50,000 to 75,000 spindles and one to two thousand looms: see Copeland, *Cotton Manufacturing Industry*, pp. 140-145. In 1905 the Southern textile industry averaged only 27,000 spindles per firm in South Carolina, 15,000 in Georgia and 11,000 in North Carolina. These figures imply that the southern industry resisted achieving efficient firm size even in this small-scale industry.

The largest employers of labor in the district, state that under normal conditions [...] the ordinary labor supply which may be relied upon continuously affords about fifty percent of the total necessary to operate all plants at full capacity.[38]

The labor shortage in the large Birmingham firms forced the city's steel mills to break the color bar and employ black workers in industrial, often skilled, jobs. By 1910 blacks comprised thirty-nine percent of the Alabama iron workers.[39]

The planters complained that black labor was being drawn off the plantations into the iron works, explaining much of the hostility towards the industries. In general "core" industries tend to resemble the iron industry in their need for a large flexible labor supply that can vary with the business cycle. In fact size is one of the chief distinguishing characteristics of the core firm.[40] This need for a large labor force would, inevitably, pose a threat to the labor supply of the southern plantation. It is therefore not surprising that the iron industry encountered opposition from the planter class. In the face of state and local opposition large-scale, high wage "core" industries had difficulty developing in the South, even when they had the advantage of location near inputs as was the case with the Birmingham steel industry. There would be little reason to assume other core industries, with less pressure to locate near raw materials, would choose to locate in the South.

By the second decade of the twentieth century the South found itself trapped in the pattern of an underdeveloped economy, supplying raw materials and low value manufactured goods to the industrial North. To make matters worse, any attempts at industrial development in the South after 1910 encountered opposition from an already established and powerful industrial North.

The Results: The Creation of a Reserve Army of Labor During the Period of Decay in Southern Agriculture

The boll weevil infestation of the 1910-1925 period only added to the region's chronic problems of soil depletion and agricultural market instability. When westward expansion could no longer alleviate the former, and generally depressed prices exacerbated the latter, these classic problems of mono-agriculture culminated in the Southern agricultural crisis of the 1930s.

---

38. The *Report* went on to state that the native white labor force seemed to be available only in winter months and in any case was too small to support the steel industry. *Report of the Commissioner*, 9, p. 151.
39. *Report of the Commissioner*, 8, p. 17.
40. Averitt, *Dual Economy*, p. 1.

The war economy of the 1940s presented a challenge that the plantation owner found more difficult to deal with than the depression of the 1930s.[41] World War II pulled the Southern labor force out of agriculture and into the military and industrial work. At the same time the War increased the demand for cotton products and strained the ability of the plantation economy to meet the required higher level of output. It is generally agreed that the combination of increased demand for output, increased competition from other fibers, and increased demand for labor finally broke down the plantation economy.[42]

The low level of technological progress associated with the plantation economy was the necessary mirror image of the low standard of living obtained by agricultural labor, both black and white, in the South.

> The stultifying effect of Southern social and economic institutions had been a greater factor than the existence of technical difficulties in explaining the slow rate of progress in the mechanization [...] and in the general rationalization of Southern agriculture [...]. The availability of a routinized, poorly educated, and politically ineffectual rural labor force [...] rendered sustained inventive and developmental interest in labor-saving farm machines economically pointless.[43]

Yet when agricultural mechanization began in the 1940s the labor input necessary to bring in a bale of cotton fell to a fraction of its former level. One bale of cotton required about 160 person-hours using the typical Southern pattern of mule plowing, hand chopping, weeding and picking. If a tractor was used, the labor requirement fell to about 140 hours, providing little incentive for mechanization of plowing unless the chief labor bottleneck at picking time could be broken. When picking and chopping were mechanized the labor requirement fell to about twenty-six person hours per bale. The increased use of tractors along with the Agricultural Adjustment Act (AAA) subsidy did reduce the number of sharecropping families between 1930 and 1950 but the introduction of the mechanical cotton picker in the 1950s cut the number of cropping families in half in one year.[44]

The magnitude of the exodus off the land, for both black and white farmers, can be seen in the reduction in total population on Southern farms. In 1940 there were 16 million people living on Southern farms. By 1960 the Southern

41. For a summary of the impact of the Agricultural Adjustment Act on southern tenants see Mandle, *Roots of Black Poverty*, especially Ch. IV; and Mertz, *New Deal and Southern Rural Poverty*.

42. Street, *New Revolution in the Cotton Economy*, tends to focus on the strains that the increased war-time demand placed on the product market. Mandle, *Roots of Black Poverty*; and Wright, *Old South, New South*, tend to focus on the strains that increased labor market demands placed on the cotton economy.

43. Street, *New Revolution*, p. 34.

44. For a discussion of changes in the labor requirement after mechanization see Street, *New Revolution*, p. 170, and for changes in population see Mandle, *Roots of Black Poverty*, p. 95.

farm population had dropped to 6.53 million. The combination of tractors and mechanical pickers reduced the number of share cropped farms by 90 percent between 1930 and 1959.[45]

After almost 40 years of ill health, the plantation system finally died and for all concerned it must be viewed as a mercy killing. The needs of the plantation economy had condemned millions of blacks to 100 years of overt and almost 100 years of covert slavery. However the effects of the plantation economy reached beyond the black population and also created the poorest class of white farmers in the nation. Further, the existence of literally millions of poor agriculturalists helped to depress Southern industrial wages to notoriously low levels, and, in spite of the Sun Belt boom of the 1970s and 1980s, a Southern wage differential still exists.

Clarence Heer traced the lower per capita income of the South to the dominance of southern agriculture:

> Wages in the South are low because the sole source of livelihood of nearly one-half the population is a particularly unprofitable agriculture. If agriculture could be made to yield a more adequate living to the present masses of southern farm dwellers there would be a corresponding rise in the level of industrial wages [...] If industry could be expanded to the point where it is capable of absorbing the submarginal worker on the farm, the wage differential between the South and the rest of the country should disappear.[46]

Unfortunately, the timing of the push off the land was unlucky for most of the farmers in question. Between 1880 and 1910, when there was a labor shortage in Northern industry, Southern farmers were not free to migrate. Between 1920 and 1960, when Southern farmers were free to migrate, there was little demand for their labor in Northern industry. In effect, a large agricultural surplus population was "trapped" in the South, 90 years after the Civil War.

The historical legacy of planter domination of Southern politics was a regional economy of low-wage manufacturing industries, low-wage service industries, and excess labor supply. This large reserve army of labor had the effect of depressing wage rates relative to wage rates in comparable industries outside the region. The results of regression analysis of the southern regional wage difference are discussed below.

---

45. According to Musoke, "Mechanizing Cotton Production", p. 348, the number of mechanical cotton pickers in the South increased from 1,522 in 1948 to 15,550 in 1953. Between 1952-1965 the average annual increase in the number of pickers was 3,400.
46. Heer, *Income and Wages in the South*, p. 42.

The Results: The Southern Reserve Army of Labor and Manufacturing Wage Rates

The model presented below tests the influence of the size and composition of the regional reserve army of labor on the wage income obtained by individuals in each region of the U.S. in 1950, 1960 and 1970. The standard determinants of wage differences were tested in an equation that also contained estimates of each regions reserve army of labor. Estimates of the size of the various components of the reserve army of labor in each region were obtained and substituted for the regional dummies.[47]

The equation took the following form:

$$1nWAGE = A + B_1ED..........B_7IND + B_8STAG + B_9AGRI + B_{10}FLOAT + B_{11}UNAB$$

where: the dependent variable is the natural log of wage income obtained by an individual and the first seven dependent variables are:

1) a measure of quality of education in the individual's region, 2) a measure of years of schooling obtained by the individual, 3&4) years of work experience and experience squared accumulated by the individual, 5) a measure of "coreness" for the industry in which the individual works, 6&7) the race and gender of the individual. These first seven variables function as "control" variables in the equation. The influence of the various components of the reserve army of labor are then measured after controlling for all other influences on wages. The reserve army of labor variables are presented as follows:

FLOAT = the floating reserve army = the proportion of workers who are attached to modern industry but who are temporarily unemployed in the individual worker's region

STAG = the stagnant reserve army = the proportion of workers in an individual's region who are employed in low-wage industries

UNAB = the unabsorbed latent = the proportion of adults who have been thrown off the land but who have not yet been absorbed into the labor force in the individual worker's region

AGRI = the latent proletarian = the proportion of workers who are employed in the agricultural or latent proletariat in the individual worker's region.

Econometric evidence indicates that variations in the size and composition of the regional reserve army played a role in decreasing the bargaining power and therefore the wage rates of Southern workers in manufacturing as a whole and in "core" industries in 1950, and 1960. By 1970, when the differential in the

---

47. A full discussion of the econometrics used can be found in a separate publication being prepared by the International Institute of Social History.

size of the regional reserve armies had diminished, the regional wage differential, had on average, also diminished. However the Southern reserve army of labor retained the power to lower wages in core industries in the South.

Conclusions

In the context of large regional wage and income differentials, the lack of labor mobility between the North and the South prior the First World War is a perplexing fact of U.S. history. While several plausible explanations have been presented for this lack of mobility, I believe that the evidence points to a system of law and custom designed to prevent mobility for a large segment of the South's laborers and share croppers. This unfree labor force was tied to the plantation economy through a set of institutions that closely resemble a system of debt peonage.

The post Civil War social structure of accumulation created several interlocking mechanisms that, taken together, bound the worker to the land for as long as his labor was needed. Tenancy, rather than daily payment for wage work, became the predominant method of reconstituting the plantation as a unit of production. Tenancy not only gave the planter access to the labor of the tenant's entire family, it encouraged the use of the annual contract, with payment occurring once a year after the harvest. One peculiar form of tenancy, sharecropping, created a class of disguised wage workers who had to provide for their own wage fund and share risk with the landlord, but who, by law, did not have title to the crop in the ground. In a credit system where the crop lien was the major form of collateral, the designation as wage worker without legal possession of the crop pushed the cropper into a debtor relation with his landlord. The South's contract labor laws and fraud statutes forced the tenant to complete his contract if he had accepted any payment from his employer, with an unpaid debt seen as a claim on the tenant for next year's crop cycle.

Ironically the social structure of accumulation that created the unfree labor force had a variety of consequences for the economic development of the region as a whole. The institution of debt peonage not only limited the mobility of tenants, it also limited the region's industrial development to only those sectors that could operate without tapping into the agricultural labor of the plantation belt. This led the region's state and local governments to support industries that could operate with a small labor force that was located in the largely white, non-plantation counties of the upcountry. High-wage core industries that must be worked on a large scale were discouraged by State policy. The locational pattern of upcountry textile mills persisted through the 1960s and, more importantly, the industrial structure of the region remained heavily weighted toward low wage, non-core industries throughout the twentieth century.

Finally, much of the South's late twentieth century wage differential can be traced to the existence of a regional reserve army of labor that was noticeably larger than the reserve army in other regions in the U.S. The system of unfree labor trapped tenants in an inefficient agricultural sector, maintaining a large latent proletariat until the 1950s.

The South's post Civil War social structure of accumulation was intended to limit the mobility of agricultural (particularly black agricultural) labor. Yet, ironically the planter class' stubborn attachment to unfree labor led to the underdevelopment and impoverishment of the region as a whole.

Appendices

1. Application of the "Social Structure of Accumulation" Model

The North		The South	
Initial Proletarianization 1820–1890		Creation & Expansion of slavery 1800–1860	
Exploration	1820–1840	Exploration	1800–1820
Consolidation	1840–1870	Consolidation	1820–1840
Decay	1870–1890	Decay	1840–1860
Homogenization of labor 1870–1918		Recreation of Unfree Labor 1865–1940	
Exploration	1870–1890	Exploration	1865–1880
Consolidation	1890–1920	Consolidation	1880–1915
Decay	1920–1940	Decay	1920–1940
Segmentation of Labor 1920–Present		Initial Proletarianization 1940–1960	
Exploration	1920–1940	Exploration	1920–1940
Consolidation	1945–1970	Consolidation	1940–1960
Decay	1970–?	?	1960–1980

Source: Periodization of the North from Edwards, Gordon and Reich, p. 12.

2. Laws Limiting Labor Mobility

STATE	ANTI-ENTICEMENT	FALSE-PRETENSE	CROPPER-TENANT	VAGRANCY
MI	Laws 1865 (p. 85)	Acts 1884-1885 (p. 142 code; sec. 1148)	Betts, Trustee v. Ratcliff 50 MI 561 (1874)	Laws 1904 (pp. 197-203)
GA	Acts 1865-1866 (pp. 153-154)	Acts 1903 (pp. 90-91)	Appling v. Odom 46 GA 583 (1872)	Acts 1895 (p. 63)
SC	Acts (pp. 36-37)	Acts 1889 (pp. 391-392)	Carpenter v. Strickland 20 SC 1 (1883)	Acts 1889 (pp. 381-382)
NC	Public Laws (Spec. Session 1886, pp. 122-123)	Laws 1889 (pp. 423-424)	All tenants like croppers Landlord Tenant Act 1876-1877	Public Laws 1905 (pp. 412)
VI	Acts 1865-1866 (p. 83)	n.a.	Parrish v. The Commonwealth 81 VA 1 (1884)	Acts 1902-1903 (pp. 3-4)
LA	Acts 1865 (Extra Session) (pp. 24-26)	n.a.	Lalanne Bros. v. McKinney 28 LA Ann. 642 (1876)	Acts 1908 (p. 308)
AL	Acts 1865-1866 (pp. 111-112)	Code 1886 sec. 3812	Act 9 Feb. 1877 (Abolished, code 1923), all treated as tenants	General Laws 1903 (p. 244)

MI = Mississippi, GA = Georgia, SC = South Carolina, NC = North Carolina, VI = Virginia, LA = Louisiana, AL = Alabama

3. The Distribution of Textile Mills among Southern Counties, 1963

Counties		Mills	
cumulative (%)	number	cumulative (%)	number
1	4	23	467
2	8	34	687
3	12	42	850
4	16	48	961
5	18	53	1055
10	40	69	1363
100	369	100	1985

Source: U.S. Census of Manufacturing, 1963.

California's Agricultural Labor Market: Historical Variations in the Use of Unfree Labor, c. 1769-1994

Fred Krissman[*]

Introduction

Although California is generally regarded as an urban state best exemplified by a number of "high-tech" economic sectors (such as aerospace, computer hardware and software, defense, and entertainment industries), it is the state's agricultural industries that together comprise California's single largest economic and employment sector.[1] Furthermore, the multiplier effect of the state's farm production produces a ripple-effect throughout the economy, generating an estimated 45 billion dollars (US) in economic activity and providing one out of five Californian jobs.[2]

While California's agricultural sector is labor-intensive, its agribusiness[3] firms are as innovative in their production techniques as any other advanced capitalist industry, generating capital accumulation that rivals that of the most competitive urban-based businesses.[4] One contradiction to this picture of modern capitalist

* Research funding has been provided by: the Wenner-Gren Foundation; UC Berkeley's Agricultural Personnel Management Program; UC Santa Barbara's Anthropology Department, Center for Chicano Studies, and Graduate Division; and, UC San Diego's Center for US-Mexican Studies. I am indebted to Bong-Hyun Chun and the participants in both the Conference on Free and Unfree Labor and UCSD's Writers Workshop for their comments.

1. On an annual basis more than 700,000 farm workers produce about 250 Californian crops valued at more than $ 22 billion; see Palerm and Urquiola, "Bi-national System of Agricultural Production", pp. 314, 315.
2. An updated estimate of the impact of agriculture on the Californian economy first provided in Scheuring, *Guidebook to California Agriculture*, p. viii.
3. "Agribusiness" is used to distinguish the contemporary corporate Californian farms, which are the employers of the vast majority of the state's farm workers, from the US "family farm"; see Martin, "Labor in California Agriculture", p. 11.
4. Even during the national (and state) economic downturn of the past few years, California's agricultural sector has continued to expand in both output and revenues, the only state sector to accelerate its performance in that period; see *Los Angeles Times*, "Farming: California's green economic oasis [...] sector may be the most prosperous" (11-9-1992), p. D1; and "A Growth Industry: state's agribusiness rides out recession, insects and bad weather" (7-26-1993), p. D1. For example, in 1993 Dole Food Co. alone generated 3.5 billion dollars in revenues from the production of about 28,000 peak season farm workers, and paid out total compensation of almost 1.8 million dollars to its Chief Executive Officer in 1993; see *Los*

production might appear to be the nature of the agricultural labor market (the ALM), which has generally been comprised of unfree labor.[5] Whereas agribusiness profits are consistently rising, its labor force continues to languish in endemic poverty, both unorganized and threatened with both formal and unofficial repression. However, the contradiction is only apparent – it is the unfree character of the state's farm labor force which permits Californian agribusiness to maintain its preeminent position within the world economy.

This article provides an historical-structural analysis of the role of unfree labor in the successful development of California's agricultural sector. The principal goals are threefold: first, to provide theoretical linkages between the development of California's agricultural sector and its ongoing dependence upon unfree labor; second, to note the relationship between the types of farm labor utilized and the concurrent socioeconomic and political conditions within the region, as well as within the world economy; and third, to document shifts within the ALM from the occasional use of free labor back to the preferred utilization of unfree labor. In order to accomplish these goals the article is divided into three parts. First, theoretical perspectives are outlined that explain the continued demand for unfree labor by labor-intensive capitalist industries such as Californian agribusiness. Second, the trajectory of California's ALM is presented within the broader historical-structural context of each era. Third, California's contemporary ALM (1965-present) is examined to illustrate why and how capitalist industries may deproletarianize their labor force in order to increase capital accumulation.

I. The Theoretical Bases for the Ongoing Demand for Unfree Labor

The historic and contemporary demand for unfree labor within advanced industrialized nations is due to the advantages capitalist producers derive from the use of non-proletarianized workers in many labor-intensive industries, especially in capitalist agriculture.[6] In the case of California, "white' workers have had alternatives to the ALM: until at least the 1870s whites were free to

Angeles Times, "The Times 100: the best performing [public] companies in California" (4-26-1994), special business supplement, part II; and "Special Report: executive pay" (5-29-1994), p. D5.

5. See the Editorial Committee, "Free and Unfree Labour", p. 1.
6. Most labor-intensive crop industries in a number of nations under various production regimes and in different eras demand a large number of highly seasonal workers, preferring a non-proletarianized labor force which can sustain itself *via* subsistence production while not employed; see Brass, "Class Struggle", p. 37; Goldschmidt, *As You Sow*, pp. 15-21; Lianos and Paris, "American Agriculture", pp. 550-577; and Kautsky, *Agrarian Question*; and Fisher, *Harvest Labor Market*, ch. 1.

become independent direct producers (especially by claiming surplus government land for homesteading or free-hold mining); and, in the subsequent 125 years white workers have been able to obtain waged employment within labor markets that offered better conditions than the ALM. Therefore, the principal labor sources targeted to fill the ALM have consistently been non-white populations; and, tapping non-white labor has permitted agribusiness to create and maintain class fractions between farm workers and other workers, as well as within the ALM, based upon race, ethnicity, and citizenship status.

1. Race, Ethnicity, and Citizenship to Structure Divisions within the Working Class

Until the post-World War II era, all non-white workers in California were formally less free to sell their labor-power than white workers.[7] With the gains of a nation-wide civil rights movement consolidated in the 1960s, the final vestige of the many formal barriers to non-white labor freedom became non-citizenship status – the last surviving formal bulwark to the maintenance of an unfree labor force in the US. Regardless of the target focus, throughout a 225 year period the demands of capitalist development have determined the degree of non-white "unfreedom", while the specific strategies devised within particular industrial sectors have typically been supported by the State,[8] the ideological apparatuses,[9] and the more privileged sectors of the labor force.

Over the past 225 years the various States and their myriad institutions, as well as religious institutions, and the local, regional, national, and global elites together have created and reified categories of race, ethnicity, and citizenship

---

7. State legislation such as restrictions on citizenship, land ownership, and business licenses, as well as through less formal mechanisms such as vigilante violence, together kept non-white labor unfree; see Menchaca, "Chicano Indianism", pp. 583-603; Chan, *This Bittersweet Soil*, pp. 39-41; Acuña, *Occupied America*, chs 2-6; and Barrera, *Race and Class in the Southwest*, pp. 48-51. The relationship between race/ethnicity/citizenship status and class is crucial to this discussion; see Balibar and Wallerstein, *Race, Nation, Class*, ch. 12. The definition of who is "non-white" has varied considerably in order to ensure an adequate pool of unfree labor under varying historical-structural conditions within the US; see Roediger, *Wages of Whiteness*, ch. 4. And, citizenship status and gender have determined the wage levels of workers within the contemporary ALM (although gender is also manipulated by agribusiness in order to keep labor unfree, I will not focus upon this portion of the unfree labor force in the essay); see Thomas, *Citizenship, Gender, and Work*, ch. 2.

8. The "State" is used herein to refer to any of a diverse number of government branches, departments, bureaus, and agencies that implement policies and enforce regulations *via* resort to the legal means of repression, whereas "state" (uncapitalized) denotes a specific level of government, i.e., between the county and federal levels (e.g., California).

9. Ideological apparatuses together maintain a system in which the preponderance of the population (workers) have their labor exploited by a tiny minority (capitalists) without need for constant overt repression; see Althusser, "Ideology and Ideological State Apparatuses", pp. 6, 7, and 16-22.

for non-white populations as mechanisms of political subjugation and social control, as well as for the purposes of capital accumulation through capitalist production. Therefore, the specific strategies utilized by capitalists are shaped by the particular historical and structural conditions prevailing within the region, as well as in the larger world economy. Historically these determining variables are first revealed in an analysis of the non-white labor targeted for confinement within the ALM – *domestic* labor until 1870 and *immigrant* labor since then up to the present. Once immigrant labor was resorted to, the specific foreign labor targeted was also determined within this context. The free and unfree labor perspective permits the contextualization of the role of each historical labor source by examining case studies such as California's ALM.

2. Free and Unfree Labor Theory – Distinguishing between Domestic and Immigrant Workers

After the conquest of California, the labor of the indigenous population was harnessed by the colonial Spanish, as well as their Mexican and US successors. Ideological justifications supported a white minority's coercive use of force to expropriate natives' lands and labor-power, constructing a system of production with more than a passing resemblance to chattel slavery. Indeed, a coercive labor system was required to achieve the colonists aims since plentiful subsistence resources permitted the targeted labor force alternatives to dependent labor, including the availability of land to maintain a free and independent status as either gatherer-hunters or direct commodity producers.[10] However, the measures required to induce the *domestic* population to labor under unfree conditions helped undermine the basic productive and reproductive activities of the indigenous population, leading to a rapid demographic decline. The dramatic contraction of the domestic supply of unfree labor occurred at a time when California was increasingly integrated into the world economy as a result of major geo-political and technological change. California's rapidly expanding capitalist industries, including those in the agricultural sector, sought new sources of replenishable unfree labor.

Since the indigenous non-white labor supply was now inadequate to the demand, the state's growers resorted to the importation of non-proletarianized labor. Political conditions within the US ruled out California's importation of African slaves; nevertheless, the agricultural sector did use race to mark its unfree labor force. Growers targeted non-white *immigrants* because white workers continued to have alternatives to the arduous and low paying ALM.

Growers were able to structure the non-white immigrant labor force as unfree by constructing and reinforcing what neo-classical economists refer to euphemis-

---

10. Brass, "Some Observations on Unfree Labour", this volume, p. 73; Cheng and Bonacich, *Labor Immigration Under Capitalism*, p. 151.

tically as labor market "imperfections".[11] Imperfections such as "segmentation" and "displacement" keep workers divided by criteria that differentiate access into different labor markets. For example, non-white immigrant labor can be forced into and trapped at the bottom of a labor market by imposing onerous socio-political controls on such workers, segregating non-white immigrant workers from white workers; various unfree labor arrangements have been used to reinforce the captive character of non-white immigrant workers, as well as domestic non-white minorities in the US.[12] The forms of unfree immigrant labor within California's ALM during the past 125 years have included: indenture, contract, "guest", and undocumented. All of these forms have been captured within the ALM, as well as prohibited from accessing many types of regular or emergency social services available to free workers that could cushion the low wages and frequent unemployment periods that characterize farm labor. California's ALM is so pernicious that it has been compared to South Africa's former Apartheid system.[13]

Furthermore, capitalists have found that labor markets that rely upon immigrants are particularly easy to de-proletarianize.[14] Without even the nominal rights of the domestic labor force, immigrant workers can be easily recruited, controlled, terminated, and even deported at the whim of the employer and/or the State. And, since the use of immigrant labor promotes the development of constantly swelling immigrant streams from impoverished "labor-sending" countries,[15] new reserves of non-proletarianized labor are readily available to displace those workers attempting to struggle for improved labor market conditions. In practice, labor-intensive industries utilizing immigrant workers engage in periodic campaigns of de-proletarianization to maintain a low cost work force. The history of California's ALM is one of continuous deproletarianization through the recruitment of new immigrant workers, including during the contemporary period; de-proletarianization does not require the complete displacement of the established labor force, but merely the introduction of sufficient new immigrants to undermine attempts to improve the labor market. In the ALM a key strategy to ensure an unorganized labor force has been to divide the work force into competing class fractions, generally by race, ethnicity, and citizenship status.

---

11. See, for example, Gordon, Edwards, and Riech, *Segmented Work, Divided Workers*, ch. 5.
12. An immigrant labor system was adopted in the US southwest due to the impracticality of introducing the contemporaneous slave labor system practiced in the US southeast; see Lamar, "From Bondage to Contract", pp. 310, 311.
13. Burawoy, "Functions and Reproduction of Migrant Labor", pp. 1050-1087; and West and Moore, "Undocumented Workers", pp. 1-10.
14. Brass, "Some Observations on Unfree Labour", this volume, pp. 71f.
15. Massey *et al.*, *Return to Aztlan*, pp. 316-319.

While a focus upon free and unfree labor provides a clear micro-level analysis of the "relations of production" within the ALM, higher levels of analyses are also required in order to contextualize why *immigrants* have been the preferred source of unfree labor to Californian agribusiness during the last 125 years. I have found dependency/world-systems theory useful at providing links between the relations of production of immigrant workers in California's agricultural sector and international relations between the US and specific nations that produce strong labor flows to California, while articulation (of the modes of production) theory analyzes the additional benefits to capitalists of using immigrant, rather than domestic, workers.

3. Dependency/World-Systems Theory

"Dependency/world-systems" underscores the macro-level asymmetrical economic exchanges between developed and underdeveloped nations.[16] The former nations enrich themselves by using their greater political (military) and economic power against the latter to obtain at a low cost the raw materials and natural resources required for production processes. Low-cost labor is one of the most abundant and mobile resources available within most underdeveloped countries that can be tapped by developed nations.[17]

Dependency/world-systems links the ongoing imperialism/(neo-)colonialism practiced by advanced capitalist nations throughout the world to the needs of its industries for low cost productive "inputs" (including labor), as well as for markets for its finished commodities. For example, US international behavior during the past 150 years is replete with imperial and (neo-)colonial actions against underdeveloped nations in order to promote the mobility of their labor, including to the US.[18] The largest flows of immigrant labor into the ALM before 1910 were from China and Japan, in both cases the targets of forceful US efforts

---

16. See, for example, Machuca, *Internacionalizacion de la Fuerza*; Frank, *Dependent Accumulation and Underdevelopment*, ch. 6; Wallerstein, *Modern World-System*, chs 6 and 7; and Rosa Luxemburg, *Accumulation of Capital*.

17. The division of international labor into both proletarian and non-proletarian fractions for the purpose of increased asymmetrical exchanges among regions within the world-system has been recognized; see Wallerstein, *Modern World-System*, ch. 6. However, a strict focus on colonial empires and modern nation-states as the gatekeepers for containing each type of labor within specific boundaries is increasingly anachronistic, as is underscored in the present essay, and as has been demonstrated in recent work; see Sassen, *Mobility of Labor and Capital*. Dependency/world-systems theorists can fill a critical void in macro-level analyses of contemporary internationalized labor systems such as that which provides the workers for California's ALM.

18. The US has repeatedly resorted to military and trade pressures to influence political policy, including to increase labor out-migration, in the cases of China, Japan, and Mexico; see Cheng and Bonacich, *Labor Immigration*, pp. 160-162; and Acuña, *Occupied America*, p. 147.

to "open up" their economies to US penetration. Paradoxically, nineteenth century Mexico-based immigration was retarded by even more forceful US aggression; the demonization of the "enemy" during the Texas Succession and the US-Mexican War era in the mid-nineteenth century made it difficult for US industries to justify opening the southern border to their immigrants. However, the unparalleled US imperial and (neo-)colonial policies directed at Mexico[19] did facilitate equally unparalleled non-white labor mobility from Mexico into California's ALM during most of the twentieth century.

4. Articulation (of Modes of Production) Theory

Whereas dependency/world-systems analyzes macro-level international interactions, the "articulation" perspective provides a mid-level analysis, linking the types of production undertaken by households containing immigrant workers in both "labor -sending and -receiving" nations to the increased capital accumulation of industries employing such labor.[20]

Articulation theorists have noted a singular distinction between the bulk of the developed nation's domestic working class and the immigrant workers imported from underdeveloped countries. The proletarianized working class within developed nations depends primarily upon wages for subsistence. One example, provided above, documents the decline of the indigenous work force under extreme unfree conditions. California's agricultural sector contributed to the elimination of a domestic ALM by refusing to provide the minimum means of subsistence/reproduction within California.

However, most immigrant workers come from households that are forced to continue to depend upon a number of complementary income and subsistence strategies within their rural communities of origin to supplement the low level of wage savings that can be remitted by (im)migrant members of the household. For example, many thousands of Mexican households articulate two different

---

19. The history of US imperialist/neo-colonial behavior toward Mexico is too long to elaborate in detail here; illustrative examples of its intensity include: 1) the expropriation of 40 percent of Mexico's territory in a series of wars, intrigues, and forced sales during the mid-1800s in Monroy, *Thrown Among Strangers*, p. 177; 2) heavy capitalist investments in infrastructural and extractive industries in both the late 1800s and during the post-World War II eras in Cardoso, *Mexican Emigration to the US*, ch. 1; and in Hansen, *Politics of Mexican Development*, chs 4 and 8; 3) ongoing interference in Mexican internal political affairs in Katz, *Secret War in Mexico*; in Smith, *US and Revolutionary Nationalism*; and, 4) continued pressures for government restructuring and neo-liberal reforms in Kim and Peters, "From Trade Liberalization to Economic Integration" (presented at Latin American Studies Association meeting in Los Angeles, 1992).

20. See, for example, Meillassoux, *Maidens, Meals and Money*, part II; Wolpe, *Articulation of Modes of Production*, "Introduction"; and Palerm, *Modos de Producción y Formaciones Socioeconomicas*.

modes of production in order to obtain their total annual subsistence needs:[21] the non-capitalist (as direct producers, usually on subsistence plots in Mexico) and the capitalist (for example, as wage earning farm workers in California). By examining production in both nations, articulation theory reveals that capitalists garner an economic subsidy through the partial subsistence of their labor, as well as the reproduction of their labor supply, within the domestic economy of the labor-sending nation. Therefore, Californian agribusiness, for example, benefits by the separation of the labor-power within the ALM from the reproduction of that labor, which continues to occur in rural Mexico.[22]

5. Unfree Labor and the Accumulation of Capital

Together, the three theoretical perspectives provide macro-, mid-level, and micro-analyses into why capitalists seek unfree workers for labor-intensive industries. In the case of Californian agribusiness, one result of the ongoing use of unfree workers has been the extraordinarily rapid and lucrative development of the state's agricultural sector. This remarkable development would not have been possible without the level of "superexploitation"[23] permitted by the use of unfree labor for farm work for more than two centuries.[24] Although Californian agribusiness has utilized a variety of labor sources, free labor use has predominated *only*: 1) under extreme structural conditions (i.e., during the world depression, under extraordinary pressures exerted by the State and labor unions); 2) for short historical periods (e.g., a decade or less in length); and, 3) several times over the course of 225 years.

In the contemporary period, the relationship between the ongoing profitability of Californian agribusiness and that sector's predilection for unfree labor is

21. Goodman and Redclift, *From Peasant to Proletarian*, ch. 6.
22. Krissman, *Californian Agribusiness and Mexican Farm Workers*, ch. 7.
23. See Marx, *Value, Price and Profit*, chs X–XII, on capitalist production and the superexploita-
    tion of labor (i.e., increasing productivity in the face of stagnant or even declining wages).
    The superexploitation of California's farm workers is demonstrated by the fact that overall
    wages have been stagnant for more than a decade (wages have declined absolutely in a
    number of major labor-intensive crop industries), while productivity has been rising; Zabin
    et al., *Mixtec Migrants*, pp. 71, 77.
24. Monroy, *Thrown Among Strangers*, p. 240, notes that the earliest Yankee settlers in Mexican
    California recognized that the indigenous population did all the work within the agrarian
    society. Cheng and Bonacich, *Labor Immigration*, ch. 3, argue that what became the US
    southwest developed into an area of unsurpassed advanced capitalist production as a result
    of the use of immigrant labor. Martin, "Network Recruitment and Labor Displacement",
    p. 87; and Goldschmidt, *As You Sow*, p. 8, note that the availability of low-cost immigrant
    labor has been capitalized into the value of Californian farmland – curtailing access to this
    labor would result in a severe devaluation of farm land prices, which, often heavily leveraged
    through loan obligations to governmental, banking, and/or corporate food processing
    institutions, could result in a major regional economic downturn.

inferred from data that document a dramatic upswing in the production and profitability of labor-intensive agricultural crops on the one hand, and the number of undocumented immigrant workers within the ALM on the other hand.[25] This conjunctural increase in agricultural production and unfree labor availability is particularly remarkable in light of a shift in State policy during the same period to restrict the continued use of new immigrant workers. Even when the State has attempted to reform the ALM to regularize its labor practices, Californian agribusiness has been able to subvert these reforms and increase the vulnerability of its labor force by targeting undocumented workers as its preferred labor source.

The general trend of State collusion to assist agribusiness to obtain a steady supply of low cost immigrant labor and a recent shift in State policy to oppose the entry of new immigrant workers should not be viewed as a surprise – the State is riven with contradictory policies as a result of its attempts to respond to divergent political constituencies that must be served simultaneously.[26] The history of the ALM is replete with successful efforts by groups that oppose immigration to shift State policy during sustained recessionary periods (e.g., the 1870s, 1900s, 1930s, and 1980s). However, history also documents the success of Californian agribusiness to maintain access to new immigrant flows despite potent domestic opposition.

In Part III the resurrection of a labor system in the contemporary period that continues to provide undocumented immigrant labor to agribusiness will be described. Labor intermediaries have permitted agribusiness to evade State regulation, undermine a once powerful farm labor movement, and ensure the continued ready availability of an ample and well disciplined low cost non-proletarianized labor force. First, Part II documents the relationship between the historical development of diverse labor sources in California's ALM and larger historical-structural conditions in the state and throughout the world.

II. Variations within California's Agricultural Labor Market, 1769-1964

In Part II the historical trajectory of California's ALM is described within the context of regional, national, and global phenomena. This trajectory is remarkable in regard to the use of race, ethnicity, and citizenship as principal markers to divide the labor force into competing class fractions over a two century

---

25. See Palerm, *Farm Labor Needs*, chs 1-3 on these trends throughout California, as well as an ethnographic study of three representative counties, and Heppel and Amendola, *Immigration Reform*, p. 78, for similar trends nation-wide.
26. Majka and Majka, *Farm Workers, Agribusiness, and the State*, pp. 13-19; see an elegant summary of their argument in Chan, *This Bittersweet Soil*, pp. 298-301.

interval. Although the tendency of one ethnic group to come to dominance within the ALM in a specific epoch is pronounced, it must be noted at the outset that the state's vast farm labor force has generally been heterogeneous in terms of race, ethnicity, and citizenship status; indeed, the very heterogeneity of the farm labor force has been used by growers as a principal mechanism for keeping workers divided and unorganized. In the development of an agrarian economy in California, the single sharp discontinuity is from the initial utilization of a domestic indigenous population to a succession of diverse, but still non-white, immigrant groups. All of these non-white farm workers faced both formal and informal structural conditions that ensured their status as unfree labor in California.

1. Colonial Origins – Racializing a Low Cost Labor Force, 1769-1821

At the time of European contact in 1769, the total indigenous population in what was to become California has been estimated at between 100,000 and 300,000.[27] The indigenous inhabitants resided in innumerable clans within a score of loosely grouped linguistic territories. These clans had developed a sophisticated non-agrarian economy which emphasized gathering, fishing, and hunting for subsistence, yet were suitably clad, sheltered, and fed.[28]

The principal colonial force engaged in the subjugation of the native population represented two distinct but co-operative world powers, the secular Spanish royalty and the ecclesiastical Roman Catholic Church.[29] These European emissaries were determined to transform the region's native population into productive subjects of the Crown in Castile and loyal disciples of the Pope in the Vatican. Adapting procedures first developed to settle the non-agricultural populations along the northern fringe of Mesoamerica,[30] the Spaniards imposed the presidio/mission system on the native population of coastal California. This system undermined the natives' lifeways and replaced them with the socioeconomic system preferred by the Crown and Pope.

In the initial phase, the new colony was overly dependent for foodstuffs and other basic necessities upon shipments from coastal San Blas, some 1,500 miles

---

27. Lamar, "From Bondage to Contract", p. 300; and Cook, *Conflict Between the Californian Indian and the White Civilization*, 1, pp. 161-194.

28. In fact, the Spanish representatives in early California argued that the favorable natural ecology had made the natives indolent, unable to live as responsible adults; Monroy, *Thrown Among Strangers*, p. 22.

29. These emissaries sailed up from New Spain (Mexico); the English, French, and Russians, as well as representatives of the fledgling US government, also had designs upon, or even settlements within, Californian territory during the early colonial era; Harlow, *California Conquered*, ch. 5; and Chapman, *Founding of Spanish California*, ch. VIII.

30. Powell, *Soldiers, Indians, and Silver*, ch. 2; Blakewell, *Silver Mining and Society in Colonial Mexico*, ch. 1; and Pelayo, *Haciendas y Comunidades*, ch. 5.

to the south. The isolation of the Californian missions required the very rapid development of a local agrarian infrastructure – hungry soldiers threatened rebellion or desertion and the original settlers clamored to return south.[31] However, colonial California would not be developed by the labor of *conquistadores*, who saw their role as supervisory; regional development required the active participation of the indigenous peoples. Indeed, Spanish colonization throughout the New World was predicated on the assumption that it was the non-white indigenous population that would serve as the workers.[32] Therefore, the racialization of the working class emerged out of the circumstances of the conquest and the development of a colonial structure; a rigorous racial caste system was promulgated in order to install a rigid hierarchy in order to legitimize subjugation, colonization, and access to the labor power of non-white workers.[33]

The presidio (or military compound) was manned by up to a score of Spanish soldiers, equipped with their awesome firearms and intimidating steeds. The presidio occupants used selective force to dispatch native clan leaders reluctant to submit to the Spanish usurpation of the native's land and labor;[34] episodic local disorders and several regional rebellions kept the small contingents of soldiers busy and the colonizers under considerable stress.

While the presidio's soldiers provided the overtly coercive apparatus in colonial California, the missions' friars provided the primary ideological apparatus within which the natives' clans could be refashioned into a more complex agrarian society.[35] The friars offered unsuspecting natives a few trinkets, a handful of alien foods, and a sprinkling of baptismal waters. Those natives that accepted any of these offerings were considered by the friars to be duly "christianized" – these converts were henceforth forced to accept mission direction over their lives. Within a decade many thousands of natives were thus compelled to work each day under the threat of flogging and kept captive at night in locked dormitories.[36] The presidio's soldiers policed the labor force, hunting down and

31. See Chapman, *Founding of Spanish California*, chs 5 and 6.
32. Wolf, *Sons of Shaking Earth*, ch. IX.
33. However, a racial category could be altered as the result of economic payments to the appropriate authorities; see Castañeda, *Soldaderas y Pobladores*; and Cline, "Mexican Native Language Documentation" (presented at University of California, Santa Barbara, 19 November 1987).
34. Lamar, "From Bondage to Contract", pp. 299, 300; and Monroy, *Thrown Among Strangers*, pt. 1.
35. Although there are a number of institutions that serve as ideological apparatuses to justify the maintenance of an asymmetrical system of power relations within different societies, Christianity has been singled out as the key apparatus in areas under European domination between the Middle Ages and the beginning of the twentieth century, supplanted as a result of the demands of the industrial revolution for a more skilled labor force by the institution of education; see Althusser, "Ideology", p. 25.
36. Monroy, *Thrown Among Strangers*, pp. 44-68.

returning recalcitrant runaway natives who had no freedom to withdraw their labor. During such actions soldiers had incentives to capture whatever natives they might encounter, even those still living independently of the mission system.[37] Under this unfree labor system the missions expanded dramatically and boosted agricultural productivity – in fact, within a decade the friars had mounting surplus stocks.[38]

The Californian missions, much like their counterparts in other regions of New Spain, the ecclesiastical "haciendas",[39] operated as self supporting agrarian communities. The missions produced a wide variety of fruit, vegetable, grain, and livestock products to provide subsistence for the indigenous labor force, and bounty for the increasingly affluent friars and the presidio's soldiery. However, additional surplus production was soon being traded to sailor merchants that plied the coast with manufactures to exchange for agricultural commodities, principally cattle hides and tallow.[40]

Although the Crown tried to restrict such trade to taxable transactions among its subjects, English, French, and American traders were making ever more frequent visits to the missions. Foreigners became principal trading partners with the Californian friars, who desired the sumptuary goods that these traders supplied in abundance.[41] As a result of rapidly increasing trade, the missions were not long the only agricultural enterprises in colonial California. Early settlers, and especially retiring presidio soldiers, received land grants in reward for their services to the Crown. A secular "rancho" system soon developed, specializing in land-extensive livestock production. Within a few decades tensions between rancheros and the missions over access to both developed land and low cost labor reached a fevered pitch.

2. Continuity – Indigenous Labor in the Mexican and Early US Era, 1821-1860

With Mexican independence from Spain in 1821, political pressures to secularize the mission system became overwhelming. Although the native mission labor force was technically to be the beneficiaries of at least half the total mission properties, the increasingly powerful rancho owners managed to obtain the bulk of the valuable mission properties in the 1830s.[42] Whereas the Mexican government "freed" native peoples from their dependent status of the paternalistic

---

37. *Ibid.*, pp. 36, 37.
38. *Ibid.*, pp. 66, 67.
39. See Taylor, *Landlord and Peasant in Colonial Oaxaca*, ch. 5, for information on what he refers to as Church estates.
40. By 1827 the missions owned more than 300,000 head of cattle, and traded an average 35,000 hides annually; Acuña, *Occupied America*, p. 99; Monroy, *Thrown Among Strangers*, pp. 68-78.
41. Monroy, *Thrown Among Strangers*, pp. 73, 154-162.
42. *Ibid.*, p. 96; and Acuña, *Occupied America*, p. 99.

colonial era, California's indigenous population was not prepared (or permitted) to exercize its new franchise. The rancho owners were quick to ensnare the manumitted laborers through a variety of debt bondage schemes, depending on the region and the labor demands of each enterprise.[43]

During the brief period of Mexican sovereignty over California, the province's farm commodities became increasingly important within the world economy, one principal factor in the increased efforts by the US to obtain the territory from Mexico;[44] while the US was aiding secessionists in Texas, the US ambassador to Mexico City was attempting to purchase California. Although the Mexican government was well aware of US intentions along its northern tier of provinces, internal and international conflicts combined to relegate these concerns to a low priority until it was too late to stop the "Yankees".[45]

After the US conquest of Mexican California in 1846 the state's political, socioeconomic, and demographic indices all underwent a number of fundamental changes. One major political change was the application of US land law in 1851 to Spanish and Mexican era land grants.[46] Rancheros were forced to prove their land claims valid; the legal fees were high and the administrators of the new Land Act were not too sympathetic to Spanish-speaking claimants.[47]

A major economic change was the full commodification of production assets, including land, its products, and the "inputs" to production.[48] Many rancho owners were unprepared for the ruthless application of market dictates within a fevered boom/bust capitalist economy. For example, a boom in cattle prices that accompanied a series of gold strikes in the state led rancheros to invest heavily in expanding their herds; subsequent climatic disasters and a glut of beef on the market plunged the owners into debt.[49] As a result of a combination of the political and economic post-conquest changes, within two decades of US annexation, the bulk of Californian ranchos were firmly within the hands of a new elite of Yankee carpetbaggers and speculators.

A third major set of changes were demographic. As a result of the gold rush Yankees outnumbered the former Mexicans in California by almost 10 to 1 as early as 1849.[50] With the completion of a transcontinental railway, Spanish-

43. Monroy, *Thrown Among Strangers*, p. 151; and Acuña, *Occupied America*, p. 98.
44. Acuña, *Occupied America*, p. 98.
45. Harlow, *California Conquered*, ch. 5; and Monroy, *Thrown Among Strangers*, p. 175.
46. Acuña, *Occupied America*, p. 101.
47. Monroy, *Thrown Among Strangers*, p. 203.
48. *Ibid.*, pp. 240, 241.
49. *Ibid*, pp. 224, 225.
50. Acuña, *Occupied America*, p. 98.

speaking Californians went from the vast majority to a marginalized minority within two decades.[51] However, while Mexicans became marginalized, the indigenous population was utterly devastated.

Whereas native groups had been declining steadily since initial contact with the Spanish, the influx of Yankee miners and homesteaders brought with it the usual American practice of widespread genocide against indigenous peoples.[52] Only natives working on the Yankees' recently acquired ranches were provided a degree of personal security,[53] but within the ranches the system of indenture slipped back toward slavery. For example, in Los Angeles a number of vagrancy and public drunkenness laws permitted periodic sweeps of most indigenous peoples; they remained in jail until bailed out by ranch owners who demanded repayment in a week of low cost labor; after the natives were discharged, they were typically rounded up by the constable again.[54] The native population slid from 83,000 in 1850 to only 17,000 by 1880.[55] By the turn of the century only several thousand natives, relegated to a few remote and desolate reservations, could be found within the state.

From the standpoint of the state's earliest capitalist industries – the railroads, industrial mines, and agricultural sector[56] – the demise of the native population was a potential catastrophe. Yankee settlers recognized that native labor was the mainstay of California's economy.[57] Where were these developing capitalist industries to find replacements for the low cost domestic work force that had provided the labor to develop California's agricultural sector for almost a century? The Yankee land barons demanded a solution. The abundant natural resources and raw materials of California could not be converted into commodities that generated a high rate of capital accumulation without a ready source of low cost labor.

3. Importing Non-White Workers – China-Origin Contract Labor, 1860-1880

By 1860, Yankee capitalists now in control of the bulk of California's old rancho economy wanted to enter into competition to build a transcontinental railway. The potential rewards were enormous, as the US government bestowed "right-

51. Except in the then sparsely populated southern portion of the new state; see Acuña, *ibid.*, pp. 104, 105.
52. Monroy, *Thrown Among Strangers*, p. 189; and Mitchell, *Modern History of Tulare County (California)*, pp. 15-17.
53. Monroy, *Thrown Among Strangers*, p. 192.
54. *Ibid.*, pp. 185, 186.
55. Cook, *Conflict*, p. 96.
56. Cheng and Bonacich, *Labor Immigration*, pp. 140, 141.
57. Acuña, *Occupied America*, p. 101; and Monroy, *Thrown Among Strangers*, p. 240.

of-way" acreage bonuses for each mile of track laid.[58] In order to be competitive with the established eastern companies, the railway speculators stimulated the first large-scale importation of non-white immigrant workers to California by engaging labor recruiters to provide a large China-origin work force. Chinese out-migration emerged in this period as a major phenomena largely due to the chaos in China that had resulted from ongoing European and US imperialism.[59]

Although European-origin labor had deluged the new US southwest in the aftermath of its annexation from Mexico, "white" labor was free to enter the better labor markets in the state, or even to remain independent (by home-steading federal land or mining for gold). The railway needed a captive labor force, unable to escape the wretched conditions prevailing during the construc-tion of the transcontinental line. Legislation limiting immigrant naturalization, and the many rights of citizenship, to white workers obstructed Asians from legally engaging in most types of independent economic activities, forcing them to work for low wages in the developing capitalist industries in the US west.[60]

Along with the State-sanctioned differentiation of labor by race, capitalist industries also sought to tie unfree workers to their employers by permitting the establishment of coercive contracts. The typical would-be Chinese immi-grant was destitute, unable to self-finance passage to the US. Therefore, most of the Chinese arrived in California *via* an indenture system.

Labor recruitment in rural China and job placement in the US occurred under the auspices of multi-tier ethnic organizations headed by Chinese merchants based in San Francisco. Workers remained indentured until the recruiter's exorbitant service and interest charges for recruitment, transportation, and job placement were paid out from the low wages earned. Indenture forced these immigrants to work under the most extreme conditions,[61] while their non-white racial status restricted their ability to escape these conditions. To enforce labor contract obligations the labor contractors imposed strict discipline on their labor force, using the coercion of both their agents and the State.[62]

While the vertically structured ethnic labor organizations did not hesitate to wield repressive means when necessary, the contractors also offered their marginalized laborers vital assistance as well. Aside from recruitment, transport, and placement, contractors also protected the immigrants from violence at the

---

58. Indeed, the Southern Pacific Railway became the owner of over 11 million acres of land in California – 20 percent of the total state acreage in private hands; Acuña, *Occupied America*, p. 102.
59. Chan, *This Bittersweet Soil*, ch. 2; and Cheng and Bonacich, *Labor Immigration*, pp. 60-78.
60. Cheng and Bonacich, *Labor Immigration*, pp. 130-185.
61. Chinese rail workers were regarded as expendable. Untold thousands died to keep construc-tion schedules as safety was subordinated to competition between construction firms for claims to lucrative right-of-way federal land; see Saxton, *Indispensable Enemy*, pp. 60-66.
62. *Ibid.*, pp. 7-10.

hands of white "nativists",[63] as well as providing an array of support services important to the new immigrant workers. The assistance that the contractors provided helped retard the development of horizonal, class-based relations between Chinese workers and white workers.[64] The Chinese contract labor system was so efficient in providing an ample immigrant labor supply that it served as a template for the future recruitment, training, and control of subsequent influxes of non-white immigrant workers into California – racially distinct indentured workers that were carefully supervised by ethnic contractors who enforced exploitative labor contracts for the mutual benefit of the contractor and his capitalist employer.

California's farm labor contractor (FLCs) system arose out of the railroad's labor system, and was augmented upon its completion; the Chinese foremen shifted their crews into the burgeoning agricultural sector in the 1870s.[65] The increased demand for labor-intensive agricultural commodities was met by the ready availability of the Chinese indentured labor force; large land owners were able to maintain their holdings intact even as they shifted from land-intensive livestock to the labor-intensive production of high-value export crops such as citrus and grapes.[66] Indeed, the expertise of the Chinese, most of whom came from an area in rural China long associated with the labor-intensive cultivation of vegetables and fruits, was crucial to the preparation of the land, the introduction of private irrigation projects, and the successful planting and harvesting of many new crops in California.[67]

Although the Chinese never comprised more than 50 percent of the total ALM,[68] as the single largest group of farm workers their availability permitted the continuation of the substandard working conditions in the agricultural sector. Furthermore, about 6,000 Chinese became tenant farmers for large landowners, permitting many estates to remain intact. The Chinese tenants tapped their FLCs to assist in the development of irrigation works, land drainage, and labor-

---

63. Acuña, *Occupied America*, p. 131, defines the nativist movement as follows: "Historically speaking it refers to anti-immigrant sentiments [...] an ultranationalist group of Anglo-Americans who considered themselves the true Americans, excluding even the Indian." Cheng and Bonacich, *Labor Immigration*, pp. 151-156, and Roediger, *Wages of Whiteness*, especially ch. 4, explain white worker racism as due to a fundamental distrust of capitalism and a determination to maintain a free waged labor force.

64. Saxton, *Indispensable Enemy*, pp. 7, 8.

65. The new railroad system was a principal stimulus to the development of labor-intensive industrial sectors such as agriculture in the western US, permitting commodities such as perishable crops to be transported profitably to eastern population centers; Monroy, *Thrown Among Strangers*, pp. 249, 250. In the aftermath of the railway's construction, the demand for Chinese labor accelerated; see Cheng and Bonacich, *Labor Immigration*, p. 163.

66. Saxton, *Indispensable Enemy*, p. 232.

67. Chan, *This Bittersweet Soil*, chs 2 and 8.

68. *Ibid.*, p. 278.

intensive cropping tasks, all of which added value to the landowners' assets. Although waves of rural anti-Chinese violence followed in the wake of the economic recession of the 1870s, its intensity in rural California may have been tempered by the roles played by the Chinese in facilitating, rather than dominating, crucial aspects of the agricultural economy.[69]

Indeed, China-origin immigration actually accelerated dramatically in the aftermath of the completion of the transcontinental railway.[70] The Chinese came to comprise an astounding 25 percent of California's total labor force, and one eighth of the state's total population, within two decades.[71] However, even with the ongoing influx, the Chinese never completely dominated the ALM due to the terrible conditions in the agricultural sector. Exploitative as the labor contract system was, Chinese workers continued to escape the substandard conditions in the ALM by paying their debts, necessitating their constant replacement with newly indentured Asian workers. Therefore, even as the ALM became an increasingly important labor market, it also became characterized as one that required "revolving door" entry of new immigrants to replenish those that abandoned it as a result of persisting poor conditions for the work force.

The enormous and ongoing Asian influx into California, fueled by the demands of the growers, agitated white residents. The entrance of emancipated Chinese farm workers into urban labor markets during a regional recession in the 1870s escalated the nativist movement and finally led to the enactment of the Chinese Exclusion Act in 1882.[72] One focus of the new law was to restrict the immigration of Chinese women in order to reduce the level of Asian reproduction within the US and to encourage the mostly male labor force to return to China after a few years of work in the US. With the revolving door to new indentured Chinese immigrants closed, as well as official legal sanctions and unofficial violence directed at the resident Chinese population, the importance of China-origin labor declined rapidly and ceased to be a major proportion of the state's total labor force by 1900.

As the revolving door entry of new Chinese workers ground to a standstill, those Chinese still working in the ALM engaged in labor actions to increase wages, assured that they could not be easily replaced with new boat loads of immigrants from their homeland.[73] Therefore, Californian growers desperately sought a new source of indentured immigrant workers.

69. *Ibid.*, p. 406.
70. Cheng and Bonacich, *Labor Immigration*, p. 163.
71. Saxton, *Indispensable Enemy*, p. 7.
72. Cheng and Bonacich, *Labor Immigration*, pp. 74-76; and Saxton, *Indispensable Enemy*, pp. 229-234; for a definition of nativism, see n. 63, above.
73. Chan, *This Bittersweet Soil*, pp. 332, 333.

4. Substituting Other Immigrants – Japanese Labor, 1890-1907

Japan-origin immigration mushroomed in the aftermath of the Chinese Exclusion Act, a pattern that has subsequently recurred in the aftermath of the political repression of other non-white immigrant groups.[74] Growers' contracts to provide immigrant labor shifted from Chinese to Japanese immigrant merchants. Following the pattern of the Chinese, resettled Japanese merchants established powerful, vertically structured organizations to recruit laborers in their homeland and control the labor force through an indenture labor system. However, the resulting Japanese FLCs were more successful than had been the Chinese in promoting ethnic labor solidarity in the face of unremitting racism in California.[75]

The Japanese FLCs gained considerable autonomy from the growers by arranging monopolistic regional agreements among themselves and manipulating the critical harvest labor force to obtain substantial wage increases;[76] nonetheless, the working and living conditions of Japanese farm workers were still far worse than those of the workers in other state labor markets.[77] The Japanese were not content to remain farm workers, nor even tenants of wealthy white landowners. The FLCs persisted in bettering working conditions, and many foremen marshalled their crews to farm in direct competition with white growers. The ethnic growers tapped their well trained labor force to reclaim previously "worthless" swamp lands and turn them into some of the most fertile fields in the state.[78] Furthermore, the Japanese worked for their patrons at lower wage rates than for adjacent white farmers.[79] As Japanese FLC agents became farmers, they passed on the mantle to their most hardworking crew members, accelerating labor mobility up and out of the ALM and into head-to-head competition with white farmers.[80]

---

74. Cheng and Bonacich, *Labor Immigration*, ch. 2.
75. There may be a relationship between the relative power of the "labor-sending" state to protect the interests of its emigrants and the ethnic solidarity of its emigrants in the US; Cheng and Bonacich, *ibid.*, pp. 160-162, point out that whereas the weak Chinese government was all but powerless under the relentless imperialist pressures put upon it by a variety of western nations, including the US, Japan was much stronger at home, and was able to extend that power to a concern for its nationals abroad.
76. Trujillo, *Parlier*, p. 24.
77. Fisher, *Harvest Labor Market*, ch. 2.
78. McWilliams, *Factories in the Field*, ch. 7.
79. Trujillo, *Parlier*, p. 24.
80. Chan, *This Bittersweet Soil*, pp. 328-341, gives considerable evidence that the Japanese were actually following in the well-worn footsteps of their Chinese predecessors in these regards, providing a major revision to a century of research on the ALM. Previous scholarship claimed that the Chinese had not established the ethnic solidarity displayed by their successors in the ALM.

Under these circumstances, many white farmers joined with urban Californians that had long decried the new "yellow peril" in order to reassert control of the labor market. As nativist violence escalated, the Japanese government, fresh from its astonishing military upset of the Russians, sought US permission to declare war on California without engaging federal forces.[81] Denied this avenue to vent its frustrations, Japan settled for an accord that temporarily reduced bi-lateral tensions over the immigration issue. A series of restrictions between 1907 and 1924 were placed upon Japan-origin immigration and on Japanese immigrants.[82] Growers were forced to renew their search for a replenishable source of low cost non-white immigrants.

5. Entrenchment of the Immigrant Labor Model – Mexico-Origin Labor, 1910-1929

The farm labor contract system had been successful in providing agribusiness with low cost labor for four decades at this point. Attempting to maintain this model, other Asian nationals were indentured for work in the US west.[83] However, the political potency of the west coast nativist movement strictly limited the entrance of new Asian workers by the 1920s, culminating in the implementation of the restrictive Immigration Act of 1924.[84] Reluctantly, growers abandoned hopes of securing a sufficient replenishable supply of Asian labor.

Instead US growers eventually settled upon the tens of thousands of Mexicans dislocated as a result of a half century of liberal development policies carried out by the Mexican State, including the acceleration of foreign capital (mainly US) penetration, and by the famine and revolution that those policies spawned.[85]

81. Kenneth Starr, in an interview on National Public Radio's *Which Way LA?: The Immigration Backlash*, (KCRW, Santa Monica, April, 1994).

82. The later restrictions on immigrant rights contributed to ongoing US-Japanese tensions. Finally, with the onset of World War II white growers had their revenge. After the Japanese bombed Pearl Harbor, Californian growers added their voice to the pressures on the government to intern *all* Japanese, including US-born citizens of Japanese ancestry, forcing Japanese American farmers to sell their properties at fire-sale prices or have them confiscated. The Japanese were not reimbursed (nominally) for these abuses for four decades.

83. For example, thousands of south Asians and Filipinos were imported through the indenture system after the turn of the century; Leonard, *Making Ethnic Choices*; and Cheng and Bonacich, *Labor Immigration*, pp. 60-77.

84. The Act of 1924 was the result of nation-wide nativist pressures. A deluge of immigration from central and eastern Europe was slowed to a trickle by the Act's provisions. One result was that European Jewry and others persecuted by Fascist movements were trapped in Europe; see Marrus, *Unwanted*.

85. Of course, the US southwest actually had "inherited" a hundred thousand Mexican nationals by way of conquest in the mid-1800s; see Acuña, *Occupied America*, pt. I. These new US residents were systematically marginalized to capture their labor at the bottom rungs of the region's labor markets, including regional agriculture; Monroy, *Thrown Among Strangers*,

A new ideology was required to re-fashion these recent foreign enemies into a desirable source of low cost labor; a great deal of effort was expended to create a revised image of Mexicans in the public mind.[86]

Tens of thousands of Mexicans were hired to construct US-owned railroads in north Mexico in the 1880s;[87] thousands were offered jobs on rail maintenance crews in the US, and the new north-south railways facilitated migration through the north Mexican desert. By 1900 shanty towns of Mexico-origin immigrants had arisen wherever railway hubs were located.[88] As conditions in Mexico continued to deteriorate, large-scale immigration to the US began. Mexican immigrants were used to break steel and meat packing industry strikes in the US mid-west; eventually most of these Mexicans migrated to California, while continued privation within Mexico increased out-migration directly into the US southwest.[89] By 1920 Mexicans had become the dominant ethnic group in California's ALM.

However, Mexico-origin labor was not as tightly bound through an indenture system as that which had disciplined their Asian predecessors so effectively. The costs of travel from Mexico were relatively low,[90] the southern international border was effectively open to unlimited Mexico-origin immigration and circular migration,[91] and many of the new FLC agents were not ethnically linked to the new source of labor.[92] Labor recruitment occurred at the border or within each region requiring farm labor rather than in the communities-of-origin. Furthermore, the new FLCs principal method of labor control was crude coercion; cut off from the labor force culturally, few FLCs provided sufficient labor services to balance their unremitting exploitation. Without the mediating influx of traditional intermediaries the agricultural sector was rocked by frequent, widespread, and sometimes effective labor actions, generally led by Mexico-origin workers.[93] The increased levels of labor organization, as well as the first State-sponsored efforts to regulate the FLCs, indicated the possible conditions

---

ch. 5. However, it proved difficult to keep this domestic labor force captive from generation to generation; Barrera, *Race and Class*, ch. 6.

86. Fellows, *Economic Aspects of the Mexican Rural Population*, pp. 30, 31, 72, 73.

87. Cardoso, *Mexican Emigration to the US*, pp. 13-17.

88. Garcilazo, "Mexican Railroad Workers".

89. Acuña, *Occupied America*, pp. 126, 127.

90. Fisher, *Historical Study of the Migrant*, p. 13.

91. US agricultural interests put great efforts into keeping the border open to Mexican labor in the face of stricter restrictions on immigration; Fellows, *Economic Aspects*, p. 28.

92. Fisher, *Harvest Labor Market*, p. 48.

93. Indeed, much of the labor force had already been radicalized by the ongoing class struggle within Mexico; on Mexico-origin farm labor activities after the turn of the century; see Weber, "Struggle for Stability"; Chacon, "Labor Unrest and Industrialized Agriculture"; Acuña, *Occupied America*, pp. 196-213; and Barrera, *Race and Class*, ch. 4; and, Fisher, *Harvest Labor Market*, ch. 3.

for the transformation of the characteristics of the ALM during the 1920s. However, the world-wide economic depression of the 1930s short-circuited the momentum of the Mexico-origin union movement and flooded the ALM with an increasingly diverse population.

6. "Racializing" White Labor – Turning US Citizens into "Okies", 1930-1940

The global depression pushed unemployment rates in the US above 30 percent, while low food prices and drought conditions pushed tens of thousands of US farm families off the land, especially in the lower mid-west. Californian growers finally showed a willingness to shift, at least partially, to a domestic labor force, for the first and only time in more than a century.[94] As had been the case with the Asians before them, Mexicans suddenly found themselves "excludable"; close to half a million were extra-legally deported south of the US-Mexican border in the early 1930s.[95] Mexicans were blamed for the bad times, and politicians argued that "Americans" should get their jobs. Many of the deported *were* Americans – Mexican Americans, including Californians with roots in the state going back generations. However, to white vigilantes these Americans *looked* and *sounded* "Mexican".[96]

During the depression, conditions in the ALM remained grim in spite of the shift to a largely white domestic work force. John Steinbeck's *The Grapes of Wrath* dramatizes the poor working conditions and the grower-incited violence of the period, which were a reflection of the history of the ALM. The "Okies", migrants from the mid-western state of Oklahoma, had been attracted to the state by grower recruitment propaganda distributed throughout the US, but found the ALM grossly oversupplied. Californian government officials refused to provide even the most basic of social services for citizens when confronted with the newest immigrant influx. Instead, police blockades turned back indigent US migrants on major interstate arteries into California. A renewed nativist sentiment was now directed at white US citizens, and a progressive candidate for governor was defeated at the polls, in part, due to his defense of the rights of fellow Americans, the newly racialized Okies.[97]

94. Buchanan, *Understanding Political Variables*, p. 19 n. 2, notes that (only partial) exceptions such as this can "prove the rule", the "rule" being that Californian agribusiness prefers highly vulnerable, disenfranchised immigrant labor; only in the face of a massive economic downturn were growers willing to use white non-immigrant labor, effectively marginalized by the huge increase in the national unemployment rate.
95. Acuña, *Occupied America*, pp. 137-142; and Hoffman, *Unwanted Mexican Americans*, ch. 7.
96. The Mexican government was forced to marshall very scare resources to receive the often penniless deportees, but was powerless to do more than write diplomatic protests to its powerful neighbor; see Cardoso, *Mexican Emigration*, ch. 8; and Acuña, *Occupied America*, pp. 136-143.
97. Indeed, the depression era characterizations of the Okies paralleled the de-humanization

Although the state's agricultural sector used the newest influx as merely another source of low cost labor, the plight of a predominantly white domestic migrant work force drew a high level of sustained national interest. California's growers, like other US capitalists,[98] were ultimately unsuccessful in keeping white workers segmented within a racialized labor market. As public opinion mounted for the Okies, both growers and farm workers (including union organizers), blamed the FLCs for the bulk of the farm workers' grievances.[99] Great pressures were exerted to reform the ALM into a free labor market by extending labor rights to farm workers. However, the depression era gave way to a war-time boom, permitting the Okies to flee the ALM for jobs in the expanding manufacturing sector, and in the armed forces. Without a mechanism to maintain the subordination of white labor within the ALM, Californian growers demanded a renewal of the Mexico-origin labor supply.

7. Institutionalization of a Non-White Immigrant ALM – the State Steps In, 1942-1964

Due in large part to the ferment generated by the abuses heaped upon a white citizen labor force,[100] the State became increasingly involved in directly regulating the ALM. Furthermore, the extingencies of putting the nation on a war footing permitted agribusiness to lobby the State to quickly adopt new procedures to assure the efficient recruitment and control of an ample and docile *non-white immigrant* labor force for the ALM. In the process, the main role of the FLCs was usurped, as the State itself took on the role of provisioning immigrant labor for the Californian agricultural sector. In negotiations between the US and Mexican governments to implement the *bracero* program, an agreement was reached for direct intervention by the State to provide workers to the growers, bypassing the traditional labor intermediaries.[101]

Although the Mexican government hoped that federal intervention would reform the notorious ALM, Ernesto Galarza's classic *Merchants of Labor* documented the checkered history of the State-sponsored program. The State was supposed to regulate the worst labor abuses within the agricultural sector – minimum standards of transport, housing, wages, and other living and working conditions were mandated in the bracero accord. However, State enforcement

campaigns previously targeting Asians and Mexicans; see Goldschmidt, *As You Sow*, pp. 51-68.
98. Roediger, *Wages of Whiteness*, ch. 7; and Gordon et al., *Segmented Work*, pp. 171-192.
99. For example, testimony at the Conference on Agricultural Labor held in Bakersfield, California in 1938; see the Kern County California Free Library mimeo files; and Fisher, *Harvest Labor Market*, pp. 33-38.
100. The 1938 Conference on Agricultural Labor included 350 representatives from various State agencies, the professions, academics, as well as the public; see the Kern County California Free Library mimeo files.
101. Acuña, *Occupied America*, p. 146.

of these provisions were typically best observed in the breach. Furthermore, the State wielded a variety of legal means to enforce strict discipline upon the immigrant work force, including arbitrary enforcement of immigration at the border, as well as selective regulation of the use of immigrant labor within the US. Braceros were assigned work without choice, under threat of deportation at the whim of the State or growers, and marshalled to break strikes by non-bracero farm workers.[102]

The State hoped to capture the bulk of immigrant labor within the bracero program by increasing enforcement at the international border. However, the program actually stimulated undocumented immigration by desperate immigrants who had traveled hundreds of miles to the border but were unable to obtain bracero papers, as well as by former braceros (encouraged by growers) unwilling to accept the program's constraints.[103] Recourse to an ample and well disciplined labor force permitted growers to keep wages for all farm workers low; in fact, farm wages throughout the inflationary 1950s remained static.[104] Although no longer indentured, both the State-contracted and undocumented immigrant farm workers were nonetheless "unfree", segregated apart from the domestic labor force, without any of the rights of US workers, and even available for use as a tool to discipline domestic labor.

While the State took over, and improved upon, the traditional FLC functions of recruitment and control, the role of the growers also expanded. Agribusiness industries were required to organize co-operative associations to assess seasonal labor needs, as well as to supervise the workers. Over the course of the twenty-two year program, large agribusiness operations even developed internal personnel departments to facilitate the employment process. Meanwhile, the government tried to hobble the FLCs with new regulatory controls mandating licensing procedures and business standards. Therefore, the State, co-operative grower associations, and agribusiness firms together took on many of the long-time functions of the FLCs. By the time the State finally terminated its role as an institutional labor intermediary in 1964, the FLC system was all but extinct. Furthermore, a new and more innovative farm labor movement was emerging; indeed, the demise of the bracero program was its first major victory.[105]

102. Galarza, *Merchants of Labor*, ch. 16.
103. By the mid-1950s there were more undocumented farm workers in the US west than there were braceros, resulting in the first militarization of the immigrant issue – including "Operation Wetback', which coincided with grower efforts to break strikes; see Galarza, *Merchants of Labor*, ch. 7; and Acuña, *Occupied America*, pp. 156-162.
104. Galarza, *Merchants of Labor*, pp. 207-210.
105. Turner, "No Dice", pp. 14-32.

III. The Contemporary Agricultural Labor Market, 1965-1994

When the bracero program ended, growers feared an impending shortage of farm labor. In fact, due to the development of grower associations and agribusiness personnel departments during the bracero-era, a proletarianized farm labor force finally emerged.[106] Growers pressured the State to provide US residency status to tens of thousands of former braceros to retain their current labor supply; many former braceros, along with their families, even re-settled within California. However, no longer subject to automatic deportation, farm workers began to demand working and living conditions comparable to those of other workers in California; agribusiness resisted efforts to improve the ALM at their expense.

1. Reform and Reaction – The State, Labor Unions, and Agribusiness, 1965-1975

In the battle to extend the bracero program in 1963, the State shifted to an interest in curtailing further immigration from Mexico without disrupting California's premier economic sector. With the termination of the program in the following year, the State played a major role in attempting to integrate California's newly documented farm workers into the overall labor force. State programs were initiated over the next decade to supplement the low annual wages of seasonal farm workers. Among the most important that now targeted farm workers were: unemployment benefits, migrant education and health care, subsidized housing, as well as a number of other social services. Together, these policies sought to "sedentarize" a farm labor force in rural California[107] in order to eliminate the many socio-economic problems caused by the continuing revolving door entry of new immigrant workers into the state's farm labor market.

Californian farm workers were not satisfied to remain permanently impoverished, dependent upon seasonal work at low wages, and supplemented by government poverty programs to make ends meet. A sustained class struggle ensued, pitting the United Farm Workers union (UFW) against Californian agribusiness. Severe losses were sustained by both growers and workers; growers suffered commodity losses in the fields due to strikes, and in the market due to consumer boycotts, while farm workers lost crucial income, sacrificing cars and homes to repossessors,[108] and going without regular meals and wearing worn out clothes. The first sustained round finally culminated in labor gains after nearly a decade of struggle. Along with a flurry of union contracts with growers, representing about ten percent of the ALM, California finally mandated a set

106. *Ibid.*, pp. 29-32.
107. Palerm, *Farm Labor Needs*, ch. II.
108. Acuña, *Occupied America*, p. 271.

of labor laws for the protection of its farm workers in 1975 and the state Agricultural Labor Relations Board (ALRB) was created to enforce them.[109] The organization of farm workers promised to integrate this previously unfree labor force with that in other state labor markets.[110] The mere threat of labor organizing drove up wages throughout the agricultural sector and lifted a portion of the state's farm workers out of the ranks of the "working poor".[111] Those with union contracts also obtained improved working conditions, the introduction of non-governmental fringe benefits, and the establishment of union hiring halls to re-employ seasonal workers based upon seniority rosters. The ALM was undergoing organization into a structured work force comprised of free labor, with both better living and working conditions that could sustain families raised within the US.

However, determined to keep the cost of labor low, agribusiness adopted strategies to combat labor market integration.[112] "Labor relations" firms advised agribusiness in the use of legal, extra-legal, and even illegal and violent tactics to prolong the process by which elections and collective bargaining could be undertaken.[113] If a company had not been successful in suppressing union sentiments through a combination of co-optation and repression, "sweetheart" contracts were often signed with unions preferred by the company. Finally, if an independent union such as the UFW was recognized by the ALRB as the workers' representative, companies often restructured the organization of production to permit the termination of in-house workers and the sub-contracting of labor needs to FLCs.[114]

Agribusiness responded to the escalating demands of the labor force by reviving the system of labor intermediaries; indeed, the creation of new FLCs often occurred at the behest of agribusiness firms, headed by newly independent former company supervisory personnel.[115] In the 1970s, even though the state's total farm labor force grew as a result of a marked increase in the production of labor-intensive fruit and vegetable crops, the FLCs' share of that market suddenly rose from long stagnant single digits to more than fifteen percent.[116]

109. Agricultural Labor Relations Board, *Handbook*; and Majka and Majka, *Farm Workers*, ch. 11.
110. The United Farm Workers union alone organized as many as 110,000 members by its peak in the late 1970s, while the Teamsters, as well as a score of smaller unions, also negotiated contracts to represent tens of thousands of farm workers; Jenkins, *Politics of Insurgency*; Majka and Majka, *Farm Workers*, ch. 10; and Edid, *Farm Labor*, pp. 48-50.
111. Edid, *Farm Labor*, ch. 1; and Martin, *Seasonal Workers*, pp. 24-30.
112. Jenkins, *Politics of Insurgency*, chs 6 and 7.
113. Edid, *Farm Labor*, pp. 45-47.
114. Cesar Chavez, "Farm Labor Movements in the US", notes from Chicano Studies course 191HH, taught at UC Santa Barbara, Spring 1992.
115. Krissman, "Farm Labor Contractors", pp. 7, 9.
116. Rosenberg *et al.*, *Farm Labor Contractors*, pp. 2, 3.

2. Retrenchment – The Resurrection of the FLC System, 1976-1985

By the mid-1970s charges of widespread unfair labor practices and good faith bargaining violations bogged down the new ALRB bureaucracy. Many farm workers were forced to accept their new employment status as contract labor in order to provide for their families. Although the great diversity of the state's thousands of FLC firms makes generalizations difficult to make, the following can be said with confidence. The vast preponderance of FLC management agents are Mexico-origin immigrants, with a smaller minority of Mexican Americans and a few top-level white managers.[117] The ethnic composition of the management structure is a reflection of the composition of the vast majority of the labor force during the past half century; the ethnic affinity between management and labor permits easy access to bi-national "migrant networks", which fuel ongoing immigration.[118] As in the past,[119] it is the common ethnicity of the FLC agents and the labor force that undergirds the success of the contemporary FLC system.

The FLCs generally maintained the wage rates previously paid by the grower in order to minimize labor turmoil during the transition. However, all non-government mandated benefits, only recently won through collective bargaining, were usually eliminated in order to supply labor to agribusiness at a competitive price, while allowing the FLC an average 5-7 percent profit margin.[120] Indeed, the very low profit margins permitted by agribusiness encouraged FLC owners and their low paid management agents to elaborate supplemental income-generating activities by providing services for a fee to their workers.

FLC agents offer services that mimic the reciprocity provided within migrant networks, including the provision of migration and subsistence loans, housing, transportation, and, of course, employment. These processes are so well entrenched within the FLC system that the State has developed regulations that cover FLC agents that provide any of these services[121] (as well as those that supervise the workers' labor in the fields). Unlike the participants in migrant networks,[122] FLC agents charge very high fees and utterly usurious interest rates

---

117. *Ibid.*, p. 19; and Martin and Taylor, "Immigration Reform", p. 242.
118. Martin and Taylor, "Immigration Reform", p. 250; and Massey *et al.*, *Return to Aztlan*, pp. 287-311; and Mines, *Developing a Community Tradition*, pp. 34-45.
119. Bonacich, "A Theory of Middlemen Minorities", pp. 583-594.
120. Cavazos, "A View of Farm Labor Contracting in California", p. 79; Martin and Taylor, "Immigration Reform", p. 259; and Lloyd *et al.*, *The Ventura Citrus Labor Market*, p. 15.
121. State regulation of FLCs occurs at both the state and federal levels, with some distinctions in the service providers regulated; see 29 USC sec. 1802 and Cal. Labor Code sec. 1682. However, many Californian FLCs are subterranean operations that remain completely unregulated, while the regulation of even the licensed FLCs is best observed in the breach; Rosenberg *et al.*, *Farm Labor Contractors*, p. 11; Martin and Taylor, "Immigration Reform", pp. 244, 250, 259.
122. See, for example, Hirabayashi, *Cultural Capital*, p. 23.

of up to 30 percent *per month* for their services.[123] Furthermore, many agents engage in extreme practices to control labor, often carefully monitoring their new workers both on and off the job, limiting their contacts even with family and friends, or even keeping them captive, at least until their debts are repaid out of their meager wages.[124]

The proportion of in-house agribusiness employees began to dwindle as the use of FLCs became a preferred agribusiness strategy to distance growers from a restive labor force. By the early 1980s the proportion of FLC-provided labor reached 20 percent statewide even as the total size of the ALM continued to expand.[125] The use of FLCs as an agribusiness strategy put a great deal of pressure on farm worker unions – newly organized agribusiness operations merely shifted to contracting their labor needs to unorganized FLCs.[126] Indeed, FLC expansion emerged earliest, and has been greatest, in those regions of California which had experienced the most conflict between growers and the labor force.[127]

The resurrection of the FLCs was also facilitated by UFW losses in the political sphere. Whereas the ALRB initially had demanded quick resolution of management-labor conflicts, pro-grower legislators balked at providing the necessary funds to administer the process in the late 1970s.[128] Then a candidate who was heavily financed by agribusiness succeeded to the state house as governor in 1982; a chief campaign promise was to "balance" what growers claimed was a "pro-union" ALRB. By the mid-1980s the ALRB decision-making process had slowed by up to several years, while decisions swung decidedly in favor of growers. As the ALRB cases piled up and violence re-ignited in the fields, the UFW faced a critical juncture – to redouble the class struggle on the farms or to focus on political lobbying. UFW union president Cesar Chavez chose to curtail field organizing and focus on consumer boycotts of non-union commodities.[129]

---

123. Krissman, "Farm Labor Contractors", p. 5.
124. Slavery operations still occur; see *Voice of the Fields* (Sacramento, 11-16-1993), p. 2. Even more common are relatively short-term captive situations: Krissman, "Farm Labor Contractors", p. 12.
125. Rosenberg *et al.*, *Farm Labor Contractors*, pp. 2, 3; Commission on Agricultural Workers, "Employment Trends in the US", p. 822; and Martin and Taylor, "Immigration Reform", p. 241.
126. See *Los Angeles Times*, "A Growing Influence: With Decline of UFW, Labor Contractors Have Become a Powerful, Sometimes Abusive, Link in Food Chain" (10-17-1993), p. A3.
127. Especially in the San Joaquin Valley; Majka and Majka, *Farm Workers*, ch. 9. Almost half the state's total farm labor is employed in the Valley; California Agricultural Employment and Earnings Bulletin (Sacramento: Employment Development Department, September, 1994), p. 6. At least 60 percent of the Valley's farm labor is provided by FLCs; Rosenberg *et al.*, *Farm Labor Contractors*, p. 10.
128. Edid, *Farm Labor*, pp. 50-54.
129. Chavez, *Farm Labor Movements*; *Los Angeles Times*, "Cesar Chavez, Founder of UFW, Dies at 66", (Los Angeles: 4-24-1993), A1; and Edid, *Farm Labor*, pp. 54, 55.

*3. Deproletarianization – The Decline of the Unions and the Shift to FLCs in the
1980s*

The strategy to back away from direct class struggle and rely upon consumers,
organizations, and politicians ultimately proved to be a failure. UFW members
under contract plummeted from a mid-1970s high of 110,000 to as few as 6,000
by 1990. Chavez engaged in a thirty-eight day fast in 1988 to protest the anti-
union onslaught and may have permanently damaged his health. In the aftermath
of Cesar Chavez' death in 1993 at the age of 66 the union has attempted a
comeback in the fields. Although it is too early to determine whether the UFW
may renew its once enormous influence within the ALM, the initial signs are
not promising. While the news headlines proffer a great deal of hope, the
"victories" obtained thus far are a pale reflection of the UFW's heyday. Between
January 1990 and September 1994 elections have been held in 84 firms; 40 voted
for the union and 44 for no union.[130] Only a handful of the successful elections
have yielded negotiated contracts with the obstructionist growers. In a labor
market with more than 7000,000 seasonal farm workers, contracts obtained in
hard fought struggles during 1994 represent a total of less than 2,000 jobs.[131]

As the FLC system spread throughout California between the early 1970s and
1980s, a large proportion of the established labor force was displaced along with
the unions. First, agricultural labor, always primarily a young person's occupation due to its physical demands,[132] experienced even higher rates of employee
"retirement" due to the deterioration of working conditions under the FLCs.
Second, FLCs generally bypassed experienced farm workers, preferring to
replenish their crews with young, strong, and vulnerable new immigrant
workers, especially new undocumented workers who work hard, fast, and
without challenging management practices.[133] Third, a sharp rise in the estimated
number of undocumented border crossings fueled this process of labor replenishment; between the mid-1960s and the mid-1970s undocumented apprehension
rates quadrupled to more than 800,000 annually,[134] and reached about a million
by the early 1980s. And, fourth, the largest agribusiness firms, with dispersed

---

130. Sutter, "Agricultural Labor Relations Board Statistics", p. 3.
131. Villarejo, "Elections Signal Revived UFW", p. 2.
132. Martin, *Seasonal Workers*, p. 17.
133. Zabin *et al.*, *Mixtec Migrants*, pp. 43-56; and Mines and Anzaldua, *New vs. Old*, pp. 111-113.
134. The rising levels of undocumented rates in the 1970s are documented in Rodolfo Acuña,
     Occupied America, pp. 168-171. In fact, the UFW itself fell into a nativist reaction during the
     1970s, reporting to the Immigration and Naturalization Service (INS) strikebreaking FLCs
     suspected of using undocumented workers; Garcia, *Memories of Chicano History*, pp. 249, 250.
     Although the subsequent INS raids sometimes hindered grower efforts to harvest a field, the
     union's use of the State's repressive apparatus damaged relations between the UFW and the
     new immigrant workers who have since become an important proportion of the labor force
     that the union wants to represent.

operations in varied ecological niches throughout the US southwest, shifted to migrating FLCs comprised of cross-border "commuter" workers based in north Mexico towns, displacing resettled immigrants that used to harvest these crops seasonally within each region.[135]

Furthermore, many long-time farm workers also abandoned the ALM, discouraged by the decline of the farm labor movement, the loss of their hard won benefits, and the capriciousness of FLC management.[136] Therefore, the composition of the labor force shifted from Mexican Americans and former braceros (and their offspring) to groups of newer immigrant workers.[137] These newer immigrants first entered the US during the 1970s or later, missing the opportunity to obtain visas in the aftermath of the bracero program.[138] In the past two decades these undocumented immigrants came to dominate many crop industries and even entire regions of the state's ALM.[139] In fact, 5-10 percent of the ALM came to be represented by indigenous peoples from south Mexico, many of whom do not speak Spanish.[140] New class fractions emerged within the ALM, marked by increased heterogeneity in race, ethnicity, and even language, but underscored by non-citizenship status.

In sum, the termination of the State-sponsored bracero program in 1964 did not end the use of unfree immigrant labor; instead, after a brief hiatus, Californian agribusiness resorted to the use of FLCs again in order to undermine a nascent proletarianization process by obtaining a new supply of unfree labor marked by citizenship status. Some established immigrants have moved up the economic ladder by providing new immigrant workers to agribusiness, taking advantage of the socio-cultural and socio-economic needs of this unfree labor.[141] Furthermore, the displacement of hundreds of thousands of legal farm workers by new undocumented workers has augmented the already powerful "pull" of US jobs upon a largely underemployed rural Mexican populace,[142] stimulating even more undocumented immigration to the US and more marginalized and unfree labor for the ALM.

135. Rosenberg et al., Farm Labor Contractors, p. 16; and Carlos and Espinoza, "The International Economic System" (presented at Society for Applied Anthropology meeting in San Diego, 1983).
136. See, for example, Los Angeles Times, "The Grapes of Wrath Revisited: squalor and poverty have again become common for farm workers in California" (9-29-1991), p. A1.
137. Mines and Anzaldua, New vs. Old, pp. 82-91.
138. Hutchinson, Legislative History, pp. 366-382.
139. Taylor and Espenshade, "Illegal Immigrants", p. 10; and Martin and Taylor, "Immigration Reform", pp. 251, 252.
140. Zabin et al., Mixtec Migrants.
141. Krissman, "Farm Labor Contractors", pp. 10-14.
142. Latapi, "Connection at Its Source".

4. Restructuring – The Increased Use of Immigrant Labor throughout the US Economy in the 1980s

Many labor-intensive US industries appear to have noted that agribusiness continued to obtain unfree immigrant labor after the end of the bracero program. As part of a process of restructuring during a prolonged recessionary cycle since the 1970s, the use of immigrant labor increased dramatically in the urban US, while the proportion of union-represented labor plummeted by more than half, from its 1950s high of about 35 percent to under 15 percent.[143] Therefore, whereas the ALM used to account for the bulk of undocumented Mexico-origin workers, the urban sector provided 85 percent of the US jobs taken by undocumented workers by the early 1980s.[144]

Undocumented workers have become essential within many labor-intensive industries throughout the US southwest and beyond, especially in labor markets that traditionally had a high rate of unionized labor. Undocumented workers have made significant inroads in construction, garment manufacture, meat packing, landscaping, janitorial services, domicile services (such as gardeners and housekeepers), "hospitality" industries (such as tourist facilities, restaurants, and hotels), electronics, and even high-skill professions such as nursing and computer programming.[145] However, the increased visibility of, and abuses to, undocumented immigrant workers renewed debate over immigration policy within the US. The result was a broad revision of US immigration policy in 1986.[146]

After focusing for decades on "supply side" interventions (i.e., the arrest and deportation of an unending flow of undocumented immigrants), the State finally conceded the necessity of imposing "demand side" restraints.[147] In the mid-1980s "employer sanctions" (both civil and criminal) upon firms using undocumented immigrant labor ultimately became politically palatable as apprehension rates of undocumented immigrants soared to an annual average of over 1 million

---

143. Edid, *Farm Labor*, p. 2; and Gordon *et al.*, *Segmented Work*, pp. 215-227.
144. Cornelius, "What Role Does Mexican Labor Play", p. 2.
145. See Zlolniski, "Informal Economy"; Martin, "Network Recruitment", pp. 78-80; *Los Angeles Times*, "Around the World and Back at the Speed of Light: [...] major implications for jobs and labor migration" (10-1-1991), p. H6; "Guess? Pact to Curb Sweatshop Abuses Praised: [...] question whether apparel maker sill diligently police its contractors" (8-6-1992), pp. B1 and D3; "Unions get a Wake-up Call as Drywallers Achieve a Victory" (11-8-1992), p. D3; "Creating Hi-Tech Sweatshops: firms find skilled – and cheap – programmers abroad" (11-15-1993), p. A1; and "$260,000 paid by Disneyland in Immigration Records Case" (6-22-1994), p. B6.
146. Fuentes, *Impact of the Immigration Reform*, pp. 1-3; and Bean *et al.*, *Opening and Closing*, pp. 20-24.
147. California tried to implement employer sanctions in the 1970s, but the state law was struck down as infringing on the immigration prerogatives of the federal government; see Acuña, *Occupied America*, p. 171.

persons.[148] However, the threat of employer sanctions has had an impact that was the opposite of the one intended.

5. Escalation – Both State "Border Control" and Undocumented Labor Use Increase after 1986

The principal aim of the Immigration Reform and Control Act of 1986 (IRCA) was to curb the uncontrolled importation and use of new immigrant labor.[149] However, many experts reprised their post-bracero predictions of doom for California's dynamic agricultural sector if cut off from their current undocumented labor force. These pundits tacitly acknowledged the farm sector's continued reliance upon new immigrant labor in spite of two decades of State policies to reform the ALM. In response to renewed pressures exerted by agribusiness, several provisions were inserted into IRCA to provide residency status to the current undocumented farm labor force, analogous to the efforts undertaken during the post-bracero documentation a generation earlier.[150]

More than three million immigrants were documented under IRCA, over a million of whom qualified under the special provisions specifically targeting farm workers.[151] The farm worker applications processed exceeded both State predictions and the total estimated farm labor force in California. However, agribusiness has continued to pursue practices that push the newly documented out of the ALM. After the documentation of more than a million long-time undocumented farm workers in the late 1980s, much of the current farm labor force is still believed to be undocumented in the early 1990s.

Post-IRCA agribusiness practices are revealed by their greatly increased reliance on FLCs. Despite grower promises to improve pay and working conditions for the newly documented labor force in order to stabilize a legal, integrated work force, agribusiness actually accelerated their shift to the use of FLCs, which are acknowledged to provide the worst conditions for farm workers.[152] The growth in the use of FLCs suddenly quadrupled on the eve of the imposition of IRCA-mandated employer sanctions, and has sustained high

---

148. See *Los Angeles Times*, "Holding the Line: at the border, rules of the game have changed" (11-20-1993), p. A28.
149. Commission on Agricultural Workers, *Report of the Commission*, pp. 4-8; and Fix, *Paper Curtain*, pp. 1-11.
150. See Heppel and Amendola, *Immigration Reform*, ch. 1; and Fuentes *Impact of the Immigration Reform*, pp. 8-20; however, this time agribusiness obtained new restrictions upon this group's access to social services in order to keep this newly documented labor force captive to the seasonal labor needs of the ALM.
151. Bean *et al.*, *Opening and Closing the Doors*, pp. 37-41.
152. Commission on Agricultural Workers, *Report*, p. 121; and Heppel and Amendola, *Immigration Reform*, chs 1 and 2.

average growth rates since then.[153] By 1990, the FLC-provisioned proportion of the farm labor force had expanded dramatically, doubling from the early 1980s to about 50 percent. Furthermore, in the Imperial and San Joaquin Valleys FLCs now dominate the ALM, providing as much as 75 percent of all farm workers. Researchers now predict continued steady growth of the use of FLCs into the foreseeable future.[154]

Agribusiness representatives say that the principal reason for their increased use of FLCs is to evade IRCA-mandated "paperwork" requirements.[155] However, the aim of these requirements is to ensure that employers have made "good faith" efforts to employ only workers legally eligible to work in the US.[156] Rather than demonstrate their good faith by abiding by IRCA's provisions, agribusiness has chosen to increase the use of FLCs, passing on good faith requirements to the under-regulated contractors.[157] Not co-incidently, the ALM continues to be dominated by undocumented labor, in spite of IRCA's mandates.[158] One result of these trends is the increased superexploitation of farm workers.[159] Therefore, the lack of legal work and residence papers has become a principal marker of farm labor – those who obtain papers seek to improve their living standards by finding better employment than is typically offered within the ALM. However, as new undocumented immigration has continued to

153. Commission on Agricultural Workers, *Case Studies*, p. 836.
154. Taylor and Martin, "Immigration Reform", p. 239; and Rosenberg *et al.*, *Farm Labor Contractors*, pp. 1-3.
155. Rosenberg *et al.*, *Farm Labor Contractors*, p. 37.
156. *Ibid.*, p. 5; and Howard Rosenberg and Eagan, *Labor Management Laws*, pp. 33-36.
157. In California, only 12 field investigators regulate both the state's agricultural sector and the garment industry combined; *Los Angeles Times*, "Complex Laws, Lean Staff, Heavy Load Challenge Labor Commissioner" (8-30-1992), p. D2. Furthermore, agribusiness continues to use FLCs as a shield in spite of its responsibility for its workers; Linder, *Migrant Workers and Minimum Wages*. Several court cases have held some growers complicit with their FLCs under specific conditions; *Los Angeles Times*, "Hired Guns Boom in the Workplace: [...] growing number of one-time employees [...] lacking benefits and protections: (2-2-1993), p. A1. As a result, agribusiness lawyers have been touring the state, tutoring growers on how to avoid crossing the legal line which makes them responsible for their FLC-provided work force; for example, see Lundrigan, "The Grower" (presented at FLC Personnel Management Conference in Visalia, California, 1993).
158. Heppel and Amendola, *Immigration Reform*, pp. 45-50.
159. The federal Commission on Agricultural Workers reported that farm wages and working conditions have declined since 1986; *Los Angeles Times*, "Farm Workers Losing Ground, Report Says" (4-3-1992), p. D5. This report does not consider the even steeper decline from the zenith in wages, benefits, and working conditions attained at the height of the farm workers' unionization movement in the late-1970s; Edid, *Farm Labor*, pp. 34-47.

accelerate to unprecedented proportions,[160] in part to fuel the ALM's revolving door, California's nativist sentiments have re-emerged.[161]

Suddenly immigration has become a "front page" issue. In the midst of a global economic downturn California has been hit harder than the nation as a whole during the past few years.[162] Individuals and *ad hoc* organizations have started acting out against non-whites they believe to be immigrants.[163] Politicians have jumped on the bandwagon, prohibiting undocumented immigrants from accessing an array of social and emergency services.[164] In fact, serious discussions are underway in the federal Congress to curtail access to social services even by *legal* immigrants. However, anti-immigrant organizations have succeeded in pushing politicians even further to the right during the last election cycle by promoting the worst anti-immigrant legislation since the official confinement of Japanese Americans during World War II – California's Proposition 187.

6. Separating Production and Reproduction – A Nativist Resurgence in 1994

Aside from a "representative" legislative process, the Californian constitution also permits direct citizen-approved legislation *via* ballot votes on "propositions". The system allows individuals and groups to circulate proposition petitions before state-wide elections. If sufficient registered voters sign a petition, it is placed on the ballot for a vote. Although once a rare occurrence, ballot propositions have proliferated in California during the prolonged recession of the past two decades, as legislation has been increasingly brought directly to the voters.[165]

---

160. Sanctions have been judged a failure; *Los Angeles Times*, "The Illegal Worker Problem: do hiring sanctions work?" (11-26-1991), p. A5. Undocumented border crossings and fatalities linked to these crossings are both at record setting levels; *Los Angeles Times*, "Arrests Rise for Illegal Immigrants: the 1.1 million figure is the highest in four years [...] fading influence of employer sanctions" (11-19-1991) p. A3; *News-Press*, "Growers [and FLCs] cited for labor violations" (Santa Barbara, California, 12-27-1992), p. A1; and *Los Angeles Times*, "2 Immigrants Killed Crossing I[nterstate]-5: a record 15 pedestrians have died in 1990 near [...] border check point" (12-26-1990), p. A.

161. See *Los Angeles Times*, "Immigrants: Hostility Often Greets Newcomers" (11-14-1993), p. A1; and *Los Angeles Times*, "Job Market a Flash Point for Natives, Newcomers: are immigrants taking away work?" (11-15-1993), p. A1.

162. *Economist*, "California on Its Back." (London, 12-14-1991), pp. 23, 24.

163. The murders of border crossers by the Border Patrol and by US residents living along the border, the beatings and robberies of immigrants by gangs and by paramilitary organizations, and vigilante border actions such as the "Light Up the Border" movement have all become part of the daily fare in California"s newspapers. For example, recent incidents along the San Diego-Tijuana border are innumerable; see Chavez, *Shadowed Lives*, chs 1 and 9; and *The Nation*, "The Mexican Border War" (11-12-1990), pp. 557-560.

164. After the 1990-91 California agricultural freeze, after the Los Angeles 1992 "Civil Disturbance", and after the Los Angeles 1992 earthquake; Krissman, *Removal of the Safety Net*.

165. Whereas only a dozen propositions had gone before the state's voters before 1979, more than 170 have appeared on the ballot between then and 1994.

Proposition 187 was promoted as a way to stop "illegal alien" immigration. However, its provisions actually seek to further marginalize immigrants, including legal immigrants that fear increased discrimination.[166] 187's three principal goals are to: 1) increase penalties for the sale and use of fraudulent immigrant documents; 2) increase police powers to discover and deport undocumented immigrants; and, 3) terminate all public social, health, and educational services for the undocumented, and their children. Perhaps most dramatically, under the third category of prohibitions the providers of such services are *required* to determine the status of the parents of even qualified (US-born citizen) children. Thus even a group of US citizens will not be able to receive a broad range of services for fear of causing the discovery and deportation of a parent in the US without documents.[167]

As critics note, not one provision is actually aimed at stopping undocumented immigration; rather the aim is to separate labor production from the sites of labor force reproduction.[168] Production with immigrant labor is expected to proceed; in fact, the day after its approval in California, federal Republican Congressional leaders called for both a federal version of 187 *and* a renewed bracero-style "guest" worker program for agribusiness and other labor-intensive industries dependent upon low cost immigrant labor. Indeed, regional newspapers have anticipated this sentiment, calling for a new bracero-style program months before the election.[169] However, as noted in Part II, the previous bracero program actually fostered undocumented immigration, as well as military-style anti-immigrant "operations" that served primarily to keep all Mexico-origin labor from obtaining the status of free labor.

Nonetheless, 187 supporters convinced the State's voters that it will "Save Our State".[170] The proposition passed by a wide margin (59 to 41 percent) although it was opposed by virtually all organizations and agencies that provide law enforcement, health, and education, as well as every major state newspaper and

166. In fact, 187 was written and partly funded by groups that promote the elimination of virtually all non-white immigration to the US. For example, a principal financial backer of the proposition is the Pioneer Fund, whose roots lie in the racist eugenics movement of the 1920s; Los Angeles Times, "Prop. 197 Creators Come Under Closer Scrutiny" (9-4-1994), p. A1; and Los Angeles Times, "Make it "SOS' for Snake-oil Salesmen: who's behind this noxious nostrum?" (9-15-1994), p. B7.

167. Anecdotal reports have begun to appear in the media (even though a federal court order has stalled the implementation of all but the first two types of provisions) about preventable deaths due to a fear of medical personnel informers; escalating absenteeism in schools within predominately immigrant communities; and, tips to the police and Immigration Service concerning "suspicious' immigrant neighbors, co-workers, and customers.

168. Chavez, "Proposition 187"; and Kenny, "The Feminization of Immigration, pp. 3-80.

169. For example, Los Angeles Times, "Anyone for Adult Solutions to Mexico-US Border Problem?" (7-18-1994), p. B6.

170. Proposition 187 backers have designated the initiative "SOS" (Save Our State).

the Democratic Party.[171] The voters discounted the common assertion of critics from across the US political spectrum (such as Jesse Jackson, Bill Clinton, Jack Kemp, and William Bennett) that the measure is laden with racist overtones, instead accepting the claim that the proposition will merely preclude people that are in the state "illegally" from accessing costly social services.[172] However, 187's supporters can only maintain this fiction by resolutely disregarding California's history of alternatively recruiting and then castigating non-white immigrants in concert with the state's economic boom/bust cycles of the past 135 years.

Conclusion

Many of California's most important labor-intensive capitalist industries have been developed through the use of non-white unfree labor during the last two centuries. After exhausting the productive and reproductive power of the indigenous population, capitalist industries shifted to the importation of non-white immigrant workers 125 years ago. Both important fractions of the domestic and immigrant labor force have been marked for unfreedom based upon race, ethnicity, and citizenship status within the US economy in order to increase capital accumulation and fuel the rapid development of major economic sectors in the state, including the single largest set of industries – California's agricultural sector.

My article has attempted to contribute to a general understanding of the reasons for the ongoing use of unfree labor within advanced capitalist nations such as the US. In particular, I have endeavored to document five issues. First, the concept of unfree labor was applied to an analysis of the relationship between the historical pattern found in California's ALM and the development of this state's agricultural sector into the most lucrative in the world. The unfree labor concept has proven useful in explaining the enigma of the use of unfree labor by dynamic and highly advanced capitalist crop industries. While the conditions endured by the state's farm workers have consistently remained substandard to those in any other sector of the state economy, ranging between enslaved to merely marginalized, agricultural industries have prospered. The history of the ALM documents the myriad ways in which a series of non-white immigrant

171. The Republican Party provided funds to place the initiative on the ballot, and most of its state candidates embraced the increasingly popular proposition during the last few months of the election campaign; *Los Angeles Times*, "Stressing GOP [Republican Party] Unity, [Governor] Wilson backs Prop. 187" (9-18-1994), p. A3.

172. However, the ability of undocumented immigrants to obtain most types of services is grossly overstated; see *Los Angeles Times*, "Who's on the Dole? It's not illegal immigrants" (8-3-1994), p. B7.

groups have been denied political freedom, and how that unfreedom has deprived these workers of their labor freedom. Indeed, the formal and informal repressive mechanisms which have been brought to bear by both the State and agricultural interests upon the work force have had the primary effect of keeping wages and other labor costs very low; however, the low remuneration to farm workers has also ensured that this labor force has only be reproduced – generation after generation – abroad.

Second, an examination of the ALM also demonstrates the importance of both historical and structural conditions in the evolution of the state's farm labor force. The colonial legacy, the incorporation of California into the developing world system, and the ascendence of the US to the pinnacle of economic and military world power, have all helped to shape the state's ALM. However, the persistence of specific capitalist economic structures have had a crucial impact upon the succession of marginalized farm workers as well. There have been important variations in the composition of the ALM as a result of specific public policies (such as which immigrants are allowed entry, and even whether immigrants should be permitted to enter), economic cycles (e.g., expansions and recessions), and the organizational capacities of the workers (i.e., the Japanese FLCs and the UFW). Nonetheless, the powerful agribusiness sector has maintained absolute control over its non-white work force during the past 225 years. Therefore, a study of the ALM reveals the ability of the owners of the means of production, especially with the collaboration of the State, to define and maintain a vast labor force as unfree in spite of historic change.

Third, this essay has shown that factors such as race, ethnicity, and citizenship status can supplement an economic, materialist interpretation of class relations. California's growers have been able to adroitly maintain a very high level of worker exploitation through the creation and maintenance of working class fractions within the ALM. The general public has most commonly lashed out against the victims of this labor system. Furthermore, FLCs have been tolerated and even encouraged under contradictory State policies which have had the effect of undermining the State's labor and immigration policies. While the material interests of a major economic sector have been a primary motor driving this inequitable system, race, ethnicity, and non-citizenship status have been used as ideological justification for an ongoing system of unfree labor use within the US.

Fourth, my study demonstrates that the ALM is a product of a highly developed capitalist mode of production. Although farm labor has been long thought to be an anachronism, soon to be mechanized out of existence, California's agricultural sector demonstrates the ongoing importance of labor-intensive production within the most advanced capitalist nations. Indeed, the very competitiveness of the modern agribusiness sector is predicated upon ongoing access to immigrant labor from Third World nations, that is, the continued articulation of two modes of production.

Fifth, recent trends in other US and global economic sectors accentuate the importance of a study of California's ALM. The type of unfree labor described here is being emulated by many other labor-intensive industries. What makes the case of California's ALM so compelling is the evidence that similar practices exist worldwide, including in Europe, the Middle East, and East Asia, indeed, wherever labor-intensive production occurs in regions with relatively tight domestic labor markets. Therefore, although this article is a case study of one US labor market, its theoretical and empirical implications are much broader. Furthermore, even under the best of conditions the struggle of immigrant workers to attain a free labor status have proved to be problematic in the face of persistent efforts to keep such labor unfree.

The case study of the contemporary ALM is a case in point. In the aftermath of a pivotal civil rights movement in the 1960s, the Mexico-origin farm workers engaged in a fierce and sustained struggle to obtain the benefits of a free labor force. Their initial success led to a nascent proletarianization of the ALM, with a marked improvement in wages, benefits, working conditions, and rights for all farm workers. However, agribusiness was able to use the undocumented status of the immigrants that are provided to the ALM by the resurrected FLCs as a new marker to delineate labor unfreedom. Ethnic intermediaries have been reinserted by agribusiness between itself and labor in order to defuse class struggle, evade scrutiny by the State, and increase the superexploitation of labor. Although the intermediaries can achieve upward mobility for themselves in such a system, the prospering agribusiness sector benefits the most from the current deproletarianization of the ALM.

As revealed in this article, the FLC system contains several crucial elements that ensures its success. Because of the increasing importance of contract labor throughout the world, these characteristics are reviewed here. First, management agents share a common ethnicity with the target pool of labor. Second, conditions within the labor-sending country are so impoverished that the target populations are desperate for waged income, willing to endure indenture in order to overcome the high costs associated with transport to, and job placement in, the distant US. Third, there is an ample replenishment pool, permitting the continual importation of new immigrants to replace those that escaped their indenture status. Fourth, these new immigrants are set apart by race and culture from the dominant society, facilitating their segmentation within the ALM. Finally, the State has institutionalized their inferior legal status by legislation that restricts their socioeconomic mobility and political rights; often these restrictions are even made to apply to their US-born "citizen" children. Such a system is intended to ensure that the targeted labor source continues to reproduce the work force abroad.

Furthermore, the overall economy in California has become dependent upon undocumented workers, and almost all the state's residents benefit from the low cost labor provided by these unfree workers in numerous labor-intensive industries. However, these workers are members of families and communities, with spouses, children, and extended families who inexorably become part of the migrant network process that facilitates immigrants access to waged work. And, a lot of other people whose roots in the US precede those of most white Californians *look* and *sound* a lot like these new immigrants. Nonetheless, a resurgent nativism has been orchestrated by organizations and politicians. A principal aim of the current nativists is much the same as in the past – to push out "surplus" immigrant labor, along with most of their dependents, during the current economic downturn. Regardless of the motive, this nativism has the effect of re-legislating the separation of labor production from the sites of its reproduction, further deproletarianizing the immigrant work force.

Considering the recurrent waves of past intolerance toward non-white immigrants, in which individuals, groups, and even the State have often lashed out against immigrants, the question must be asked: will the current attempt to target undocumented immigrants for the state's woes result in renewed racist incidents, including against legal residents and even citizens? In the aftermath of the passage of Proposition 187, the current wave of "blame the victim" seems likely to follow historical precedent, resulting in officially-inspired violence or even official racial discrimination similar to the many past incidents that are part and parcel of the history of unfree labor in California.

The Transition from Slave to Freedmen Labor in the Cape Colony, the British West Indies, and the Postbellum American South: Comparative Perspectives[*]

Ralph Shlomowitz

Introduction

In the study of free and unfree labor, a distinction can be made between free markets in labor and free labor: whereas *free markets in labor* refer to labor markets whose outcomes are determined by the competitive forces of demand and supply rather than by collusion on the part of employers and/or workers, *free labor* refers to workers who voluntarily enter into labor contracts which are not enforced by specific performance or penal sanction.[1] The existence of free markets in labor, accordingly, does not necessarily imply the use of free labor. Scholars have documented, for example, the existence of free markets for various types of unfree labor such as slavery and indentured servitude. And as late as 1875, British manual workers entered into labor contracts under Masters and Servants Acts that were enforceable by specific performance and penal sanction, and so can be considered unfree labor even though they voluntarily entered these contracts in free markets. Manual workers in the North American colonies, in contrast, were by the 18th century no longer constrained by criminal sanctions against departure, and so can be considered free labor.[2]

This paper uses this distinction between free markets in labor and free labor to investigate the transition from slave to freedmen labor in the postbellum American South and in post-emancipation British colonies.

[*] I am indebted to Eric Foner and other participants of the American Studies of Southern Africa Symposium at Durban, (South Africa) in July 1994; and to Pieter Emmer, Stanley L. Engerman, Robert J. Steinfeld, and other participants of the Conference on Free and Unfree Labour organized by the International Institute of Social History at Wassenaar (The Netherlands) in January 1995; and to David Eltis, Farley Grubb, Robert Ross, and Nigel Worden for comments on an earlier version of this paper.

1. On the defining characteristic of free labor as voluntary labor not subject to specific performance or penal sanction, see Steinfeld, *Invention*, pp. 10, 13.
2. *Ibid.*, pp. 50-51; Tomlins, *Law, Labor and Ideology*, pp. 239-258; Bush, "'Take This Job and Shove it'", pp. 1398-1400.

Postbellum American South

There have been two basic approaches to the study of agricultural labor markets following the emancipation of the slaves in the American South, and these have been called the "class" and "market" approaches. According to class analysts, employers colluded to set the terms that they would offer the ex-slaves, usually called freedmen, and through the use of debt, and the enactment of vagrancy and contract-enforcement laws, the ex-slaves were made into peons, bound in servitude to specific employers. The class approach, accordingly, emphasises the inequality in power between the ex-slaves and their employers, that employers were united, and that employers set up an extra-market coercive apparatus to procure, hold, and exploit the labor of the ex-slaves.[3]

The market approach, in contrast, disputes that employers were united and so able to collude, and emphasises that employers competed against each other for the labor of the ex-slaves. And this competition was set in the context of a labor shortage, occasioned by the ex-slaves reducing their labor supply as a consequence of emancipation. The market approach also points to the lack of success of employers in attempting to use state power to set up a coercive legal apparatus to enforce labor contracts and limit the mobility of the ex-slaves. And evidence of considerable mobility places doubt on the view that the ex-slaves were made into debt peons. The market approach, accordingly, emphasises the coming into existence of a free market for labor, and that this placed constraints on the ability of employers to coerce and exploit the ex-slaves.[4]

In sum, the class approach places emphasis on coercion and non-market mechanisms of allocating and rewarding labor, while the market approach places emphasis on the operation of the free market for labor. These two approaches were formalised in the 1970s, and initially coexisted due to a lack of a sustained effort to obtain empirical evidence to distinguish between them. That by the early 1980s, these were still largely untested hypotheses is reflected in Foner's dismissal of the view that there was a "free market" for labor in the postbellum

3. The class approach is most clearly enunciated in the work of Wiener and Mandle, while Cohen, Novak, and Daniel reach similar conclusions. See Wiener, *Social Origins of the New South*; Wiener, Higgs and Woodman, "AHR Forum", pp. 970-1006; Mandle, *Roots of Black Poverty*; Cohen, "Negro Involuntary Servitude", pp. 31-60; Novak, *Wheel of Servitude*; Daniel, "Metamorphosis of Slavery", pp. 88-99. The terms class and market approaches were used by Wiener, "AHR Forum".
4. Higgs, *Competition and Coercion*; DeCanio, *Agriculture in the Postbellum South*; Reid Jr, "Sharecropping as an Understandable Market Response", pp. 106-130. Ransom and Sutch take an intermediate position: they acknowledge the role of free market forces in the labor market, but argue that the ex-slaves were exploited in the credit market. See Ransom and Sutch, *One Kind of Freedom*; Sutch and Ransom, "Sharecropping", pp. 51-69.

South as a "massive abstraction".[5] Yet during the next few years, a number of scholars assembled an overwhelming body of evidence showing the competitive behaviour of employers; the failure of their few and isolated attempts at collusion; extensive labor mobility; and the variety in contract terms which reflected the bargaining process between individual employers and workers in free markets.[6] That the free market was not an abstraction but accurately described postbellum reality, was later acknowledged by Foner in his overview of the period of Reconstruction, and, more recently, Mandle and Cohen have also changed their positions.[7]

Although a free market in labor became established, the labor of ex-slaves was constrained. For the first four years after the ending of the Civil War, 1865-1868, the ex-slaves were employed on a contract labor system supervised by the Freedmen's Bureau, an agency of the Northern army. Although it appears that the ex-slaves voluntarily entered into annual contracts and were free to leave at the end of these contracts, there were unfree elements in this system: employers were given the authority to levy fines for lost time and unsatisfactory work, and if workers attempted to leave before the completion of the contract, Bureau officials could enforce the contract by sending the ex-slaves back to work. The fine system persisted after the Bureau ended its involvement in the labor market, and disputes between ex-slaves and employers over the implementation of the fine system became a major impetus to the adoption of the sharecropping arrangement, as the positive incentives associated with the sharecropping arrangement made the day-by-day monitoring of work performance, and the associated system of fines, redundant. Later in the century, contract-enforcement provisions were included in numerous statutes enacted by post-Reconstruction southern states, but it is not clear if they were widely used.[8]

5. Foner, *Nothing But Freedom*, p. 37.
6. Shlomowitz, "'Bound' or 'Free'?", pp. 569-96, Shlomowitz, "Planter Combinations and Black Labour", pp. 72-84 (and references cited in note 22); Wright, *Old South, New South*, pp. 64-70.
7. Foner, *Reconstruction*, pp. 139-140, 401; Cohen, *At Freedom's Edge*, pp. 275, 291; Mandle, *Not Slave, Not Free*, p. 20.
8. Shlomowitz, "Genesis of Free Labour", pp. 213-215, "Origins of Southern Sharecropping", pp. 558-60, "On Punishments and Rewards", pp. 98-9, and "'Bound' or 'Free'", pp. 589-91. See also Nieman, *To Set the Law*, pp. 65, 172-90, 210-21; and Foner, *Nothing But Freedom*, p. 53.

Cape Colony

It is possible to draw on the insights gained from this recent literature on the postbellum American South to consider the development of labor markets following the effective emancipation of slaves in British colonies in 1838, official emancipation in 1834 being followed by a four-year period of apprenticeship. In particular, the paper will attempt to assess the conclusion of Foner that "in the literature" on "postemancipation adjustments" in British colonies, "[...] the free market [...] is conspicuous by its absence. Dominant classes everywhere feared the market in labor [...] and used political power to suppress, as far as possible, its operations".[9]

In considering post-emancipation labor market adjustments in British colonies, the focus in this paper will be on the Cape Colony (South Africa) and the West Indies.[10] The slave population of the Cape Colony, which numbered about 36,000 at the time of emancipation, had mainly been procured from India, the East Indies, Central Africa, and Madagascar, and had mainly been used in the production of wheat and wine on relatively small-scale farming units.[11] After the ending of the apprenticeship system in 1838, the labor of the ex-slaves and other workers, particularly the Khoi – known by whites as the Hottentots –, became regulated by the Masters and Servants Ordinance of 1841: labor contracts of the ex-slaves were to be no more than one year in length, and, as in similar legislation in Great Britain, breaches of labor contracts were made a criminal offence. In 1856, an amended Masters and Servants Act, passed by the newly-elected Cape parliament, strengthened the contract enforcement provisions of the Ordinance of 1841.

A number of scholars have studied the post-emancipation labor market adjustments in the Cape Colony from a variety of perspectives, though these have not been formalised as "class" and "market" approaches. Saunders and Ross, for example, emphasize the continuity in labor control and exploitation. For Saunders, "the benefits of the transition from slavery to freedom were marginal", and "in assessing the nature of the transition from slavery to freedom, the emphasis – at least so far as conditions of labour were concerned – should be on the side of continuity rather than discontinuity".[12]

---

9. Foner, *Nothing But Freedom*, p. 37.
10. It is intended to extend the framework adopted in this paper to Mauritius at a later stage, as the secondary literature on post-emancipation labor market adjustments in Mauritius does not address the concerns of this paper. See North-Coombes, "From Slavery to Indenture", pp. 78-125; Worden, "Diverging Histories", pp. 3-25; and Carter, "Transition from Slave to Indentured Labour", pp. 114-30.
11. Worden, *Slavery in Dutch South Africa*; Mason, "'Fit for Freedom'".
12. Saunders, "Liberated Africans", pp. 238-9.

Ross agrees. Emancipation, according to Ross, led to "little alteration in the actual relations of production" and "the position of a large proportion of these labourers did not change to any great extent", so that "in a sense" emancipation was a non-event. Continuity in "the subservience of labour to employers" was effected by the contract-enforcement provisions of the Masters and Servants Ordinance of 1841, which became the legal vehicle for labor control. And farmers also used a variety of extra-legal "techniques of holding their labourers under control [...] refusal to allow labourers to leave with the stock they had been paid as wages, debt bondage [...] and alcohol addiction [...]" Only a small number of workers, however, were so "tied" to specific employers by contracts under the Masters and Servants Ordinance and extra-legal means. Besides this permanent core of laborers on each farm, seasonal peak labor requirements were met by "a large pool of men and women travelling round the countryside and working where they were needed at any given moment". Although Ross concludes that there "seems to have been no possibility of a free-market in labour", he does not, however, substantiate this conclusion with an analysis whether employers colluded over pay and working conditions, or whether these were determined by competitive market forces.[13]

Whereas for Ross there was no possibility of a free market for labor, other scholars disagree. For Worden, the system of combining contract and seasonal labor "operated in the context of a 'free market' in labour", such that "farmers often found after the ending of apprenticeship that they frequently had to offer advance wages, or grants of land or cattle, to induce labourers to remain on the farm".[14] Rayner also cites the claims of farmers "that they were now forced to advance wages at the beginning of a contract to induce servants to remain with them", and suggests that the ex-slaves "apparently managed to gain some control over the terms of their employment [...] Few labourers were apparently willing to make contracts, other than oral agreements from day to day or by the month at the most."[15] Marincowitz concurs that a "free labour market" developed in which their "mobility as casual and day workers, placed many proletarians in an unprecedentedly strong position in relation to their former owners and employers", leading to a rise in casual wages.[16]

Bradlow, however, has provided the most comprehensive documentation on the development of a free market for the labor of the ex-slaves. She points to the competition among employers for labor and the ex-slaves exercizing their

13. Ross, "Pre-Industrial and Industrial Racial Stratification", p. 85, "Origins of Capitalist Agriculture", pp. 79, 81, and 83, "Emancipations and the Economy of the Cape Colony", pp. 142, 144-5, and *Beyond the Pale*, pp. 44-49.
14. Worden, "Adjusting to Emancipation", p. 37.
15. Rayner, "Wine and Slaves", pp. 315-6.
16. Marincowitz, "From 'Colour Question' to 'Agrarian Problem'", pp. 154, 161.

"freedom of choice", in a context of labor shortage. This labor shortage was attributable to both demand and supply forces: on the side of demand, slave compensation funds increased the money supply which stimulated growth, while on the side of supply, emancipation was associated with a reduced supply of labor. And the labor shortage resulted in rural wages rising "appreciably" after the end of the apprenticeship period, and the isolated instances of employer collusion did not prove to be effective. Moreover, the contract-enforcing provisions of the Masters and Servants Ordinance of 1841 were not effective in holding labor, as is shown in their mobility in "going from farm to farm to improve their employment prospects." The ex-slaves, accordingly, used the free labor market to their advantage, and this was acknowledged by contemporary commentators. In 1841, for example, it was reported that "many almost make their own terms with their employers [...] They are in reality, at the present moment persons of the first consideration", while in 1849, the "competition [...] all over the colony, is between masters for laborers, not servants for work"; "*masters* are more dependent *on their servants* than the servants are dependent on the *masters*"; and with "the present scarcity of labor, and as the law now stands, servants are lords over their masters and hold them in perpetual fear [...]"[17]

A review of the primary evidence provides further support of Bradlow's conclusion that the ex-slaves possessed considerable bargaining power in the free market which developed after the end of the period of apprenticeship, and they used this bargaining power to their advantage. In 1839, for example, the editorial writer of *The South African Commercial Advertiser* reported that there was "general competition for laborers" and that the "farmers must give [...] what the laborer considers equals to the wages he can obtain by other kinds of employment", while in 1840, it was acknowledged that employers had not colluded over wages, and he advised against such collusion: "Any combinations among masters to keep down wages [...] would only be productive of disap-pointment and mischief." And that the ex-slaves were not "tied" labor is shown by their considerable mobility. In 1841, for example, a letter to *The Grahams Town Journal* reported "native servants leaving suddenly when we feel most the want of their services. This is one of the worst, as well as most marked traits in the character of the colored classes in this Colony".[18]

In 1848, a committee of the Legislative Council sent a questionnaire on the working of the Masters and Servants Ordinance of 1841 to a wide variety of people, including magistrates, and the answers to this questionnaire were

---

17. Bradlow, "Capitalists and Labourers, Part I", pp. 59-60; *ibid.*, "Capitalists and Labourers, Part II", pp. 62-63. For an earlier contribution reaching similar conclusions to those of Bradlow, see Marais, *Cape Coloured People*, ch. 6.
18. *The South African Commercial Advertiser*, 23 March 1839 (editorial); 29 February 1840 (editorial); 15 May 1841 (extract from a letter to *The Grahams Town Journal*).

published in 1849. This is a unique document for seeing the actual operation of the post-emancipation labor market. The answers given to the questionnaire provide ample evidence that the labor market was significantly opened up to competitive market forces. Respondents told that there was competition for labor, that workers were mobile, and that wages were determined by the forces of supply and demand. It was acknowledged that "to fix the rate of wages is difficult" and that it "is a commodity which regulates its own price", so "the less this is interfered with, perhaps, the better". Other respondents, however, recommended a vagrancy law to increase the supply of labor, and collusion – effected through Agricultural Societies – to fix a maximum rate of wages and a requirement that employers refuse to engage a worker without a certificate of character. Such recommendations are further collaborative evidence that employers were then being faced with a mobile labor force and wages were then being determined by market forces. What is also clear from these responses is that the contract-enforcement provisions of the Masters and Servants Ordinance of 1841 were not effective in binding the ex-slaves to specific employers either during their contracts or for longer periods.[19]

Whereas scholars are divided on the effectiveness of the Masters and Servants Ordinance of 1841 in binding the ex-slaves to their employers, there appears to be general agreement that the Masters and Servants Act of 1856 was able to accomplish this objective. According to Rayner, for example, the Act enabled farmers to lock "former slaves and other black labourers into a nearly perpetual servitude".[20] But this conclusion has not been based on detailed studies of the working of this Act, and this suggests a major gap in our knowledge of the actual operation of the post-1856 labor market.[21]

British West Indies

In contrast to the relatively smooth transition in the Cape Colony, the transition in some British West Indies colonies, particularly Jamaica, was characterised by a contest between planters and ex-slaves over post-apprenticeship labor arrangements. In the first few years after the end of the apprenticeship system, planters in Jamaica formed combinations to set maximum wage levels and used labor-for-rent schemes to tie the ex-slaves to their estates. Under such schemes, planters charged exorbitant rents for the use of cottages and provision lands with

19. Cape of Good Hope. *Master and Servant. Documents on the Working of the Order in Council of the 21st July 1846* (Cape Town, 1849), pp. 19, 24, 25, 74-5, 99, 100, 103, 153, and 204.
20. Rayner, "Wine and Slaves", p. 323. See also Fredrickson, *White Supremacy*, pp. 181-2.
21. One attempt to help fill this gap is the work of Scully. See her "Criminality and Conflict", pp. 289-300.

occupancy made dependent on work on their estate. A contemporary reporter commented:

> The mixing up the questions of tenancy of land, and rent, and wages together, has been the cause of much heart-burning and discord [...] In case of any misunderstanding between the overseer and the labourers, on the subject of the work, either as to its duration, or price, threats of ejectment have followed. These threats in many cases have been put in forcible execution [...] plan of doubling or trebling the rent, or even multiplying it fourfold, upon the arbitrary decision of the employer [...] to compel labour. Sorrowful to say, this plan has been practised through the length and breadth of the island.[22]

In the context of the labor shortage that was associated with emancipation, however, the ability of planters to implement these coercive policies was constrained. This limitation to planter power is well brought out by a contemporary reporter:

> On a negro refusing to work in the cane-fields, the planter might oust him from his cottage and garden-land; but the only result of such a proceeding would be, loss of the rent which he would have paid; a new tenant would not be readily procured, and probably he would demand as favourable, if not more favourable, terms than were enjoyed by him dispossessed. The planters are at the mercy of the negroes; [...] legislation can avail nothing. The demand for labour is greater than the supply of labourers, and any attempt to regulate the market could be productive of mischief and increased difficulties.[23]

There is a considerable body of evidence showing that the attempts of planters to collude over wages were not successful, and by 1842 their attempts to charge exorbitant rents, and tie the ex-slaves to their estates by labor-for-rent schemes, had generally been discontinued. The labor market had become relatively free, dominated by competitive market forces. Contemporaries reported, often with regret, the "high wages which the insufficiency of the supply of labour, and their competition with each other, naturally compel the Planters to pay [...]"; the "baneful, ruinous competition between different properties [...]" for the *worst* subjects"; and that "a combination of circumstances [...] have conspired to place his recent master in a sort of subjection to him: the tables have been turned [...] he may now consult his own taste as to any employment which he may think proper to apply himself to [...]".[24]

22. "Prosperous State of the British West India Colonies, No V, Jamaica", *The Colonial Magazine and Commercial-Maritime Journal*, IV (January-April 1841), p. 467.
23. "Jamaica and Its Prospects", *The Colonial Magazine and Commercial-Maritime Journal*, V (May-August 1841), p. 274.
24. "Report from the Select Committee on West India Colonies", *British Parliamentary Papers*, 1842, Vol. XIII (479), p. iv; Ross, "Tenantry and Allotment System", p. 23, and "Difficulty of Obtaining", p. 570. On the short-lived coercive attempts of planters and the gaining of

The response of a majority of the ex-slaves to the coercive policies initially adopted by planters was to reject full-time employment on the estates. In contrast to the Cape Colony where few ex-slaves had the opportunity to acquire land, the ex-slaves in many of the colonies in the West Indies had this option: some collectively purchased estates; some purchased or rented individual lots of land on estates and supplemented their income with seasonal estate labor; while others formed village settlements on vacant land. Scholars, however, differ on whether the ex-slaves were "pushed" from the estates by planter coercion, or "pulled" by the attraction of a more independent lifestyle.[25]

In the relatively free labor markets which eventually came into operation in the West Indies, demand and supply conditions – and hence wage rates – varied widely among the various British colonies: wage rates were highest in British Guiana and Trinidad, and lowest in Barbados, Antigua, and St. Kitts. Such differences in demand and supply conditions meant that planters in areas where labor was relatively abundant, such as Barbados, were much less dependent on Masters and Servants Acts to hold their labor, than planters in areas where labor was relatively scarce, such as Trinidad and British Guiana.[26] But in both labor-scarce and labor-abundant colonies, planters had little success in persuading the ex-slaves who remained on the estates to enter into written contracts under various Masters and Servants Ordinances, and disputes between planters and ex-slaves were seldom brought before magistrates. The ex-slaves usually opted to enter verbal agreements on a daily basis. Contract laws, accordingly, were not effective in holding the ex-slaves to the estates.[27]

ascendancy of free market forces, see Adamson, *Sugar Without Slaves*, pp. 165-6; Curtin, *Two Jamaicas*, pp. 128-9; Green, *British Slave Emancipation*, pp. 188, 198 and note 26, 297-8, 300 (note 11); Hall, *Free Jamaica*, pp. 20, 23, 44, 168; Mandle, *Plantation Economy*, p. 22; and Wood, *Trinidad in Transition*, pp. 53-4.

25. Green, *British Slave Emancipation*, pp. 299-301; Riviere, "Labour Shortage", pp. 5-6, 9; Hall, "Flight from the Estates Reconsidered", pp. 7-24; and Marshall, *Post-Slavery Labour Problem Revisited*.

26. On inter-colonial differentials in wages and land/labor ratios, see Riviere, "Labour Shortage", pp. 29-30; and Engerman, "Economic Adjustments", p. 196. For a challenge to this explanation and ensuing debate, see Bolland, "Systems of Domination", pp. 591-619; Green, "Perils of Comparative History", pp. 112-9; and Bolland, "Reply to William A. Green's", pp. 120-5.

27. Green, *British Slave Emancipation*, p. 175; "Report from the Select Committee on the West India Colonies", for Trinidad (pp. 43, 87, 93); Barbados (pp. 116, 119); British Guiana (pp. 145, 172); Jamaica (p. 403).

Conclusion

This paper has investigated the circumstances under which the transition from slave to freedmen labor took place in a number of British colonies and in the postbellum American South. In this investigation, a distinction is made between free markets in labor and free labor. Using this distinction, the paper questions Foner's view that free markets for labor did not come into existence in post-apprenticeship British colonies and in the postbellum American South. Although employers did attempt to use their political power to suppress the coming into existence of a free market by enacting coercive labor laws (including laws relating to vagrancy), in British colonies these were set aside by the metropolitan government and in the postbellum South these laws were set aside by the victorious Northern authorities. And without the use of such state power and in an environment of labor scarcity, planters were unable to collude effectively, so preventing the coming into existence of a relatively free market for labor. In this labor market, the ex-slaves were voluntary participants, free to contract with employers, but there were unfree elements relating to contract-enforcement sanctions present, though the extent to which these legal provisions could be enforced differed widely from region to region.

The most interesting finding of the paper is that although both British workers in Great Britain and the ex-slaves in the Cape Colony and the British West Indies were employed in the 1840s under Masters and Servants Acts which allowed for contract enforcement through penal sanctions, these sanctions were applied much more extensively against British workers than against the ex-slaves. One possible explanation for this differential rate of enforcement lies in the relative lack of policing resources on the colonial frontier, but this begs the question why more policing resources were not made available in the colonies. An alternative explanation for this differential rate of enforcement may lie in the role of public opinion in Britain: the humanitarian lobby appears to have been much more concerned about the condition of the ex-slaves on the colonial frontier than about working conditions at home.[28]

---

28. I am much indebted to Pieter Emmer for suggesting these possible explanations.

Slavery, the Labour Movement and Spanish Colonialism in Cuba (1850-1898)[*]

Joan Casanovas

The existing historiography on nineteenth-century Cuban labour has mainly focused on rural slavery, while urban workers have been largely neglected.[1] Little is known about the transition to free labour in Cuban urban centres. In addition, studies of organized labour in Cuba offer few insights into the connection between free and unfree labour in these centres.[2] However, the history of labour cannot provide a complete explanation for social change in Cuba without considering all "urban popular classes", both free and unfree, as interconnected and in constant evolution.

Until the 1980s, most historical analyses contended that the increasing need for skilled labour could not be satisfied with slave labour; thus, the development of production techniques provoked the elimination of slavery in Cuba.[3] Recent studies argue that the need for skilled labour was not the reason for abolishing slave labour on this Caribbean island. They contend that planters tried to use slave labour as long as they could, despite changes in production techniques. It was the slaves' struggle for freedom that made slavery unviable.[4] The examination of working conditions in tobacco growing and urban trades reinforces this

[*] This article was originally presented as a paper to the Conference on Free and Unfree Labour held at NIAS, Wassenaar, The Netherlands, January 1995, and organized by the International Institute of Social History in Amsterdam. It was published in the *International Review of Social History* 40 (1995), pp. 367-382. The present version has been revised again and includes some new data. I would like to thank Magdalena G. Chocano, Temma Kaplan, Brooke Larson, Clara E. Lida, Nicolás Sánchez-Albornoz, Rebecca J. Scott and Barbara Weinstein for discussing with me many of the ideas developed in this article.

1. For works focusing on sugar slavery in Cuba, see Cepero Bonilla, "Azúcar y abolición", pp. 11-171; Muñiz, "Esquema del movimiento obrero", VII, pp. 247-300; Knight, *Slave Society in Cuba*; Scott, *Slave Emancipation in Cuba*; Barcia, *Burguesía y abolición*; and Bergad, *Cuban Rural Society*.
2. See, for instance, Spalding Jr, "Workers' Struggle", pp. 3-10; Aguirre, *Eco de caminos*; Hidalgo, *Orígenes del movimiento obrero*; Plasencia Moro, "Historia del movimiento obrero en Cuba", pp. 88-183; and Instituto de Historia [...] de Cuba, *Historia del movimiento obrero cubano*.
3. This current is best exemplified in Cepero, "Azúcar y abolición"; Fraginals, *El Ingenio*; and Knight, *Slave Society*, pp. 178-182.
4. Scott's *Slave Emancipation* and Bergad's *Cuban Rural Society* best represent this current.

view. Tobacco growing and manufacturing, the most important areas of production after sugar, required a highly skilled labour force, and yet slaves were used massively in this production. The fact that slaves could be used as skilled labourers meant that free and unfree labour coexisted in all productive sectors.[5]

Following this latter line of analysis, I contend that the working conditions that slavery and Spanish colonialism created in Cuba's urban centres drove the urban popular sector to build class ties across divisions of race and ethnicity. Slavery and colonialism were not only used to extract the slaves' labour, they also helped the elite in Cuba to harden labour relations for free or partially free labour in urban centres. Slavery was the labour model of the elite in Cuba, who considered it essential to enforce rigid racial segregation to sustain it.[6] When slaves could not be used, the socio-economic elite sought to have the closest equivalent, i.e. indentured servants, apprentices, soldiers, prisoners, etc. Moreover, as the historian Julio Le Riverend claims, the presence of this unfree or semi-free labour was used to pressure free labourers into accepting harder working conditions.[7] Until the 1880s, free labourers in Cuba faced the constant threat of being replaced by forced labourers. Therefore, free labour co-operated increasingly with unfree labour in eliminating the combination of slavery and colonialism.

The Impact of Bond Labour on Free Labour in the Mid-Nineteenth Century

Nineteenth-century Cuban colonial and slave society sharply divided its inhabitants by race and ethnicity. Despite differences between the Spanish and the Creole elites because of the preferential treatment that the Spanish administration gave to wealthy Spaniards, both elites considered that in Cuba non-Whites had to be enslaved or have their freedom severely curtailed. Until the end of slavery in 1886, most of the Creole elite, especially in western Cuba, consented to Spanish military rule as the guarantor of this order, which gave *Peninsulares* (Spanish residents on the island) a preponderant position. Among poor Whites, Peninsulares also had some privileges. They filled the ranks of the better-paid jobs in many workshops and tobacco factories, and the administration gave them preferential treatment. Even shopkeepers could be invited to receptions in the palace of the governor of Cuba in Havana.

The Spanish and Creole elite never succeeded in creating a society totally segregated according to race and ethnicity though. The coexistence of free and unfree labour was particularly intense in urban centres. In agricultural produc-

5. Casanovas Codina, "Labor and Colonialism", pp. 32-53.
6. For the relationship between slavery and racial segregation, see Martínez-Alier (or Stolcke), *Marriage, Class and Colour in Nineteenth Century Cuba*.
7. Le Riverend, *Habana*, p. 310.

tion, it was easier than in urban trades to have free and unfree labour working separately, even when these two kinds of labour were doing the same task. Strong labour demand and the small spaces used for manufacturing meant that in Cuba's urban centres free and unfree labourers were in constant contact, often doing the same tasks in the same workshops or factories, and under the same masters or overseers. Proximity helped urban labourers of different social ranks to build a shared identity and acknowledge their common interests, the basis for developing collective action.[8] Moreover, the very intense militarization of Cuba created an atmosphere of harsh political repression for the popular sector as a whole.

With the expansion of the urban economy from the 1830s on, the socio-economic elite in Cuba looked for more coercive forms of labour. Responding to the interests of this elite, the colonial administration created legal mechanisms to coerce juridically free labour. One example of the relationship between this pro-slavery socio-economic elite and the Spanish colonial administration is the apprentice system established in Cuba between the late 1830s and the mid-1870s. This system contributed to the hardening of work conditions for apprentices, many of whom were juridically free labourers, as well as for urban labour in general. It was devised and implemented precisely when labour demand increased in Cuba's urban centres because of the tremendous economic growth of those years.[9] In the words of the Creole intellectual Antonio Bachiller y Morales, who conceived the new system in 1835, it was a system not for reviving the European "ancient and discredited guild organization" but for mitigating "vagrancy" and "stirring up a judicious emulation among artisans".[10]

The disappearance of the trade *cofradías* at the beginning of the nineteenth century did not eliminate the tradition of placing apprentices under the orders of an artisan master by oral contract. The old contracts, in the times of the cofradías, established that the apprentice would work without wages in a workshop for two to five years in exchange for learning the trade. Both slaves and free labourers could be apprentices. However, in 1837, following the suggestions of Bachiller from the Sociedad Económica, the government ruled that all apprentices had to be indentured, and that the Sociedad Económica was in charge of supervising apprentices and their masters in all major Cuban centres through a Junta de Aprendizaje (Board of Apprenticeship). Moreover, the Junta

---

8. Howard in "Culture, Nationalism, and Liberation", p. 226, contends that in the 1880s "white and black urban labourers in some cities shared similar socioeconomic experiences", which led them to develop joint collective action. However, Howard does not provide information about the working conditions that increasingly drove these "white and black" workers together.
9. Le Riverend, *Economic History of Cuba*, pp. 158-159.
10. Marrero, *Cuba*, XIII, pp. 147-150.

de Aprendizaje was in charge of directly indenturing children who were orphaned, abandoned, or whose parents or owners agreed to this system in exchange for the training and maintenance of their indentured dependents. The Sociedad Económica could place these indentured apprentices in the workshops that it created expressly for them or in any other workshop, even without the master's consent. As in previous times, apprentices did not get wages for several years, but now they had to remain as apprentices even after learning the trade well enough to take the journeymen exams that the Sociedad Económica supervised.[11]

The new set of regulations the government established in 1849 reveals how much slavery affected this apprenticeship system. Females could be indentured for up to ten years and males up to twelve. To break restrictions on the number of individuals in a trade, each master had to accept up to two indentured apprentices from the Sociedad Económica per journeymen he employed. An official delegate monitored apprentices and commented on their performance in a booklet that every apprentice had to have. If the apprentice had been sick or disobedient, his term was extended. Another punishment was to send apprentices to a penal institution. If this could not break the apprentices' will, they were sent to work in the fields. This was the same punishment meted out to rebellious urban slaves. Female apprentices were subject to these regulations as well, but with an additional clause: if they got pregnant, they had to compensate their master for their services.[12] The instructions also forbade masters from employing corporal punishments against apprentices, but the use of the whip and stocks and fetters continued to be common practice.

In the mid-1850s, apprentice conditions continued to worsen with the founding in Havana of a large workhouse known as the Taller General Correccional de Aprendices (General Correctional Workshop for Apprentices). This was a factory-prison in which orphans and indentured apprentices worked alongside the children that the police arrested as "vagrants" or the apprentices sent there as punishment. In the Taller there were sharp differences along racial lines. Only white apprentices were allowed to go to evening classes in geometry and instrument drawing in one of the Sociedad Económica's schools, which reflects the official interest in blocking Afro-Cubans' access to education.[13]

It is difficult to evaluate the impact of the apprentice system introduced in the

11. For the workshops of the Sociedad Económica, see de la Pezuela, *Diccionario geográfico*, III, p. 267; and Gordon, *El tabaco en Cuba*, pp. 36-37. These workshops seem to copy the English new "Workhouses" or "Bastilles" established after the Poor Law of 1834, just two years before Bachiller's proposal, and which Thompson has studied in *The Making of the English Working Class*, pp. 266-268. For apprentices remaining as such long after learning the trade, see Rivero Muñiz, *Tabaco*, II, pp. 263, 272-273.
12. Cuba, *Reglamento para el aprendizaje*.
13. Cuba, *Proyecto de Reglamento de la Junta*; Lopez de Letona, *Isla de Cuba*, pp. 57-58.

1830s. The socio-economic and administrative elite wanted as many indentured apprentices as possible because they were a cheap form of unfree labour, and because more apprentices meant more journeymen, both free and slave, and lower wages in the future. In placing orphaned, abandoned and poor children into workshops and factories as indentured apprentices, it probably increased by one fourth or more the number of apprentices in Havana, who already numbered more than 4,000 in the late 1830s.[14] The regulations for the apprentices that the administration directly indentured effectively helped to harden labour conditions for the apprentices privately indentured by their parents or owners.[15] During the mid-1860s, a labor weekly published a short story caricaturing this form of apprenticeship: "Well sir, this was a man that [...] at ten entered as apprentice in a press and when he was forty he had learned as much as the first day. When his overseer realized that he was old and useless, it was thrown out of the workshop."[16] Indentured apprenticeship lasted until shortly after the end of the Ten Years' War in 1878,[17] and severe physical abuse persisted at least until the turn of the century.[18]

Another official coercive device closely connected to the apprenticeship system was the *Libreta del tabaquero* (journeyman cigar maker's booklet) used in Havana from the early 1850s to the early 1860s. The administration instituted the Libreta del tabaquero in 1851 in response to tobacco manufacturers' complaints that high labour demand allowed journeymen cigar makers to "abuse" employers. Specifically, manufacturers argued that cigar makers did not return the money given to them in advance of their wages to insure that they work in their workshops and factories. Under the rules of the Libreta system every journeyman cigar maker, both male and female, had to register with the Sociedad Económica's "Industry Section" – in fact, the same section that was in charge of monitoring apprentices. The cigar maker's workplace, place of birth, home address, physical traits, and possession or otherwise of a journeyman's title were

14. For an assessment of the number of apprentices that the Sociedad Económica indentured in the 1840s and 1850s, see Marrero, *Cuba*, XI, p. 81; *ibid.*, XIII, pp. 147-150; "Resumen estadístico de la población, riqueza agrícola, comercio, industria, y fomento de la isla de Cuba", p. 30 (in *Comisión de Estadística, Cuadro estadístico de la siempre fiel Isla de Cuba, correspondiente al año de 1846* (Havana, 1847)); and Wurdemann, *Notes on Cuba*, pp. 235-239 (transcribed in Pérez, *Slaves, Sugar, & Colonial Society*, pp. 141-142).

15. *La Aurora* 2:33 (30 December 1866), 1.

16. "Cuentos de Salon", *La Aurora* 36:1 (24 June 1866), 4.

17. For the decline of the indentured apprenticeship system after the Ten Years' War, see Rivero Muñiz, "Lectura en las tabaquerías", p. 228.

18. On physical punishments to discipline apprentices, see Rivero Muñiz, "Lectura en las tabaquerías", pp. 252-253; Instituto de Historia, *Historia del movimiento obrero*, I, p. 19; "Partes de novedad de la Jefatura Superior de Policía, 1883-84", Ultramar, Archivo Histórico Nacional, Madrid (hereafter, AHN), exp. 2, leg. 5917; and the periodical *El Productor* (Havana and Guanabacoa, 1887-92).

recorded in the Libreta. No cigar manufacturer could accept a free worker or a slave hiring himself out without the *Libreta*.[19]

Whenever the journeyman found employment, the employer kept the *Libreta*. In it, the employer could annotate the amount of money he advanced to the employee. If the employer noted that the employee owed him money, the worker could not leave the factory. Obviously, the Libreta was a mechanism to "tie" the worker to the job similar to the "debt peonage" system used in plantations in several Latin American countries. It was also similar to the Libreta established in Puerto Rico between 1849 and 1873 for rural workers. It was the employer, not the administration nor the employee, who annotated the workers' debt. Because cigar production decreased every year form January to July, many cigar makers accepted cash advances form employers during these months; but when labor demand and wages raised from July to December, those cigar makers who had accepted advances had no choice but to work for their creditors at low wages, instead of earning higher wages in other workshops.[20]

In 1859, Captain General José Gutiérrez de la Concha tried to extend the Libreta system to all trades and even to rural workers throughout the island. Concha, who governed Cuba between 1854 and 1859, argued that the high demand for labour in Cuba gave free labourers too much leverage over employers. As he cynically put it,

> [In Europe] the difficulty is that money capital, relatively more scarce than labour capital, constantly tends to abuse the latter by exploiting the need of the worker to subsist: here [in Cuba], on the contrary, the limited number of free workers easily impose their free will on the owners of workshops, and have in their hands the fate of these shops by leaving one workshop owner to employ themselves in another one because they know that their replacement is difficult or impossible.[21]

---

19. "Libreta para oficiales artesanos dispuesta por el Superior Gobierno en resolución de 25 de julio de 1851", (transcribed in Portuondo, *'La Aurora'*, pp. 102-105). Cuba, *Proyecto de Reglamento de la Junta y Ramo de Aprendizaje*, p. 7; and *D. del G. de 22 de Diciembre de 1856, previniendo que las libretas de oficiales de tabaquería se expidan por la junta de aprendizaje de artes y oficios* (transcribed in Erénchun, *Anales de la Isla de Cuba*, p. 736). Although Rivero Muñiz in *Tabaco*, II, p. 276 states that the Libreta del tabaquero system did not last long, it lasted in fact more than a decade.
20. "La libreta de los tabaqueros", *Revista de Jurisprudencia* 4:1 (1859), pp. 509-17. Two excellent studies on the Libreta system in Puerto Rico are Fernando Picó, *Libertad y servidumbre en el Puerto Rico del siglo XIX: los jornaleros utuadeños en vísperas del auge del café* (Río Piedras, 1979); and Andrés Ramos Mattei, "Technical Innovations and Social Change in the Sugar Industry of Puerto Rico, 1870-1880", in Moreno Fraginals, *et al.*, eds., *Between Slavery and Free Labor* (Baltimore, 1988), pp. 161-63.
21. "Circular" no. 1829, signed by Captain General Concha on 16 March 1859 (transcribed in Portuondo, *"La Aurora"*, pp. 105-107).

Nonetheless, Concha's project failed and the Libreta system could never be extended beyond the tobacco industry. During the early 1860s, the Libreta del tabaquero fell into disuse. This did not stop the administration from continuing to debate the possibility of creating "workhouses" and of reimplementing the Libreta to limit vagrancy and to help employers discipline the workforce.[22] Even after the end of slavery in 1886, the colonial administration unsuccessfully tried to implement the same Libreta system for domestic servants, many of whom had been slaves.[23]

Legal mechanisms to coerce juridically free labour into semi-free labour were also used against Peninsulares. This was the case with shop and factory assistants (*dependientes*), whose life was similar to that of the apprentices. The great majority of dependientes were poor Peninsular immigrants who lived and worked in extremely oppressive conditions. Most of them were employed in small stores and workshops, but some were employed in tobacco factories. Dependientes usually lived in the workplace, often with some apprentices, slaves or indentured Chinese labourers, with whom they did similar tasks and shared many of their working conditions. Their regular working day was sixteen hours long, without a break even on Sundays, and their freedom of movement was severely limited. However, unlike slaves and indentured Chinese labourers, most dependientes could leave the workplace once every two weeks. Still, to work or to find employment in another store, dependientes needed official authorization,[24] and they suffered severe corporal punishments as well. Even after the end of slavery in 1886 and up to the twentieth century, this group of workers remained semi-free and continued to endure very harsh working conditions.[25]

Spanish troops also suffered the consequences of the hard working conditions in Cuba, they became semi-free workers who engaged in a variety of procuctive activities. As the Peninsular brigadier and ex-governor of a Cuban Province Antonio López de Letona wrote in 1865, this phenomenon was much more extensive in Cuba than Spain because "the lack of hands that this country expierences in all sorts of jobs and industries". Thus, army officers allowed rank-

22. For the debate on the use of the Libreta to discipline the workforce, see Velasco, *Guerra de Cuba*.

23. [Roig] "La patria y los obreros", *El Productor* (Havana) (hereafter *E.P.H.*), II (63) (12 May 1889), p. 1; J., "La libreta y 'La Lucha'", *E.P.H.*, 2nd series, I (2) (12 Sept. 1889), pp. 1-2.

24. On the working conditions of the tobacco factory dependientes and apprentices, see Rivero Muñiz, *Tabaco*, II, p. 272. For the authorization dependientes needed in order to change their place of work, see "1854. – Noviembre 30. – Decreto del Gobernador Capitan general declarando las resoluciones que correspondan á la Secretaría del Gobierno político de la Habana", in Rodríguez San Pedro (ed.), *Legislación ultramarina*, X, p. 71.

25. For the "semi-free" status of dependientes in tobacco factories after the abolition of slavery, see Rivero Muñiz, *Tabaco*, II, p. 307; Rivero Muñiz, "Bosquejo Histórico de la Sociedad de Escogedores de Tabacos", p. 11; Iglesias Pantín, *Luchas Emancipadoras*, I, pp. 17-18; and García Galló, *Biografía del Tabaco Habano*, pp. 71, 75, 83.

and-file soldiers "to work in public and private contructions, and even in domestic service." The proportion of off-duty soldiers was so large that when the Ten Years' War broke out in 1868, only a third of the Spanish troops in Cuba were prepared to fight. From the mid-1850s on, captain general Concha intensified the use of troops to work under military discipline in public works or private enterprises, just as the state would do with prisoners, and sometimes the differences were minimal. Besides military rule, the administration used misery in the barracks to force soldiers to search for jobs outside the army. Therefore, most of the rank-and-file soldiers were constantly off duty working, mainly as cigarette and cigar makers but also as painters, bricklayers, domestic servants, farmers, cane cutters or any other possible wage earning job. Letona was so committed to un-free labor that he proposed sending troops to work alongside *emancipados* and prisoners to build a projected railroad linking eastern and western Cuba (the so-called "central railroad").[26]

The Early Cuban Labour Movement

Fostered by favourable political conditions, the Cuban labour movement that emerged in the late 1850s became stronger during the following decade. In the 1860s, the Spanish government and the socio-economic elite in Cuba felt compelled to embark on a process of colonial reforms. The growth of Peninsular immigration and international pressure against the slave trade, mainly from the United Kingdom and the United States, until its extinction in 1867, increased the proportion of Whites in Cuba. In 1862, for the first time in nineteenth-century Cuba, a population census revealed that there were clearly more Whites than Afro-Cubans. Thus, the traditional colonial policy based on the threat to the Creole elite that "Cuba would be either Spanish or African" lost credibility.

Traditionally, in Cuba the administration had systematically favoured the Spanish party. This party was an informal network of Peninsular merchants, tobacco-factory owners, and some planters who monopolized local politics on the island. In the 1860s, however, the administration allowed the Creole elite to debate colonial reforms through the founding or enlargement of many associations and periodicals. The Creole elite welcomed this policy shift and used it to promote colonial reform by setting up a political movement known as the Reformist party, although it was never established as a formal political party because Spanish colonial law forbade it. This movement supported free trade to foster Cuban exports, White immigration, and the immediate end of the slave

26. López de Letona, in *Insla de Cuba* (Madrid: Imp. de J.M. Ducazcal, 1865), 98–101, describes in detail the use of soldiers in all sorts of jobs. On the proportion of troops ready for combat in 1868, see Marrero, *Cuba*, 15: 296.

trade, but not of slavery itself. Because all these reforms were specific to Cuba, the Reformist movement claimed that Cuba ought to have an autonomous government. As was to be expected, to preserve its privileged position vis-à-vis the colonial administration the Spanish party initiated an aggressive anti-reformist campaign.

To compensate for the near total absence of merchants and tobacco-factory owners in its ranks, and to weaken their opposition, the Reformist movement sought the backing of white artisans by reducing its support of slavery. Free white workers were opposed to the use of unfree labour in the factories and workshops because it helped employers to harshen working conditions. The Reformist movement therefore began to present itself as being closer to abolitionism by expressing support for the Union in the American Civil War.[27] Moreover, reformists began to propagate the idea that artisans ought to have better access to education and culture, that they should form co-operatives and trade unions, and that they had the right to resort to collective bargaining and to elect their delegates for this purpose.[28] Relaxation of press censorship from the early 1860s until 1866 even allowed reformists to debate socialist ideas for the first time in Cuba.[29]

Among the popular classes, the rise of reformism created a political atmosphere favourable to labour mobilization, and many white artisans joined the Reformist movement. Already in 1848, a few Spanish artisans had founded a recreational centre in one of Havana's neighbourhoods, and in the late 1850s the administration authorized some mutual-aid associations, which were racially segregated, in western Cuba as well as in Camagüey, in the eastern half of the island. Nevertheless, in 1865 a wave of strikes broke out for the first time among the tobacco workers of Havana. Not surprisingly, they voiced their demands through the reformist press. A few months after these strikes, printers founded an association for all the white members of the trade in Havana, while tobacco workers sought to follow this path. The administration stopped this latter attempt, however, and only allowed associations for tobacco workers of the same neighbourhood. Furthermore, Havana's artisans founded the first labour periodical, *La Aurora*, a weekly closely linked to the reformist *El Siglo*, a daily.

Difficulties in extending labour organization due to official repression led the editors of *La Aurora* to concentrate on the education of artisans. Thus, one of *La Aurora*'s first campaigns was to promote the reading of books and periodicals during working hours in the tobacco factories. This latter venture – known as the *lectura* – consisted in having a person read aloud while his fellow cigar makers

---

27. *El Siglo*, 2 (378) (4 Dec. 1863); *ibid.*, (2) (379) (7 Dec. 1863); *ibid.*, (3) (163) (23 Aug. 1864).
28. Cepero, "El Siglo", pp. 189–193.
29. For *El Siglo*'s exposition of socialist ideas, see Cepero, "El Siglo", pp. 191–192. See also de Fuentes, *Estudios económico-sociales*.

rolled cigars. Soon, it became the most important cultural institution among tobacco workers in Cuba for nearly a century. Despite tobacco manufacturers' opposition, by mid-1866 the lectura was a daily event in most of the larger factories and workshops in Havana and surrounding towns. Regarding the rapid spread of the lectura, La Aurora acknowledged the help of the Reformists: "The daises in the workshops followed those in the *Liceo*" [the bourgeois clubs].[30] Besides the lectura, Havana's artisans began to found schools to educate their children and themselves.

Both the strikes and the lectura helped to blur divisions of race and status among workers. Since free and unfree labour worked together in tobacco manufacturing, non-Whites and even self-hired slaves participated in the strikes. Furthermore, slaves, indentured Chinese labourers and free Blacks became part of the audience during the readings in the factories. Despite censorship from the administration and the manufacturers, through the lectura unfree workers could hear the open or covert denunciations of physical abuse in the factories. They also might have heard abolitionist proclamations from the Spanish Abolitionist Society founded in 1865 in Madrid, or from the Cuban separatists in exile. The labour movement of the 1860s, nevertheless, never gave explicit support to abolition.

The rapid spread of the readings and associations in the tobacco factories and the growth of Reformism infuriated most manufacturers. One of their moves was to claim that there was a shortage in leaf tobacco in order to fire thousands of workers until they accepted lower pay or worse working conditions. The tension between the Reformist and the Spanish parties reached a peak in May 1866, when reformists won all the seats in a commission to negotiate colonial policy changes in Madrid. After a theatre event, these two parties clashed in downtown Havana, an event known as the "Tacos del Louvre". The fact that in this clash many tobacco workers of all races and ethnicities sided with the Reformists reflects the popularity of Reformism, while the Spanish party showed that it could mobilize cart and coach drivers, most of them Peninsulares.

Events like the Tacos del Louvre were one of the main causes that prompted a policy shift from the Spanish administration. The lectura was forbidden and soon few Reformist clubs and periodicals remained operational. On the other hand, the Tacos del Louvre exposed strong divisions within the popular sector. During this period it seems that clashes between artisans supporting Spanish rule and artisans supporting Cuban autonomy or independence became more frequent. Spanish artisans occupied privileged positions in the tobacco factories. Most of the overseers were Spaniards and the better paid trades were in their

---

30. "Utilidad de las tribunas en los talleres", *La Aurora*, 1 (27) (22 April 1866).

hands. Thus, with the growth of labour mobilization, Creoles and non-Whites sought to improve their respective positions.

Spain's reactionary policies after the Tacos del Louvre and the failure of Reformism helped separatists to rally the necessary popular support to unleash the Ten Years' War in October 1868. Since the dominant form of separatism until the 1860s had been pro-slavery annexationism to the United States, until then cigar makers participated little in the separatist conspiracies. However, repression of the labour movement, and the shift toward populism and abolition-ism of a sector of the separatist leadership, led many white and non-white artisans to become separatist.[31]

The Formation of a Two-Pronged Labour Movement

The outbreak of the Ten Years' War gave the Spanish party the opportunity to regain much of its lost power. Spain's military and political weakness, due to the beginning of a six-year revolutionary period in the Peninsula, compelled the colonial administration to rely on the Spanish party to sustain colonial rule. Parallel to the growth of the separatist campaign, the Spanish party broadened its base by arming most Peninsulares and compelling or forcing them to join the *Voluntarios*, an irregular militia founded some years before the war that grew from 10,000 in 1868 to 70,000 in the early 1870s.

The violence the Voluntarios unleashed forced scores of Creole workers to go into exile, most of them to southern Florida and New York. This mass exodus led to the formation of two branches of the Cuban labour movement. Despite repression and the increasing militarization of Cuba's urban centres, participation in the Voluntarios allowed some Peninsular artisans to participate in mutual-aid and recreational associations. On the other hand, emigré workers in the United States used their experience from the associations established in Cuba from the 1850s on to develop their own labour movement. Although these two branches of the Cuban labour movement had a common past in the labour struggles of the mid-1860s, the war determined their independent evolution for ten years. As in past periods in which the colonial administration was strongly repressive, throughout the war Peninsulares became the dominant group within the popular associations. Therefore, it was only in the exile communities in the United States that Creoles could occupy leadership positions in popular associations. Overall, these associations served as the bedrock from which the labour movement could expand after the war.

---

31. For the acceptance of separatism among the popular sector in Havana, see García del Pino, "Habana en los días de Yara", pp. 149-172.

The evolution of these two branches of the Cuban labour movement shows that the urban popular sector, both in western Cuba and in the exile communities, sought to overcome the strong limitations that the war imposed on organized labour. Inside Cuba, despite the heavy militarization of this colonial society, workers sought to curtail the power of the Spanish party. Although wealthy Peninsulares filled the officer ranks of the Voluntarios, the massive participation of lower-class Peninsulares in this irregular militia meant that at least part of the labour force retained some bargaining power when dealing with the administration. This helped lower-class Peninsulares to establish guilds, mutual-aid societies, and cultural centres, as well as to participate in the founding of regional associations. For instance, in one application a group of Peninsular artisans claimed that as Peninsulares and Voluntarios they deserved to be authorized to found a society:

> The ones signing below, natives of Asturias and Santander, all of them members of the Voluntarios' Institute, eager to establish a recreation centre where artisans will be able to expand and relax their minds with useful and honest entertainments, which will avoid their attending of other places with atmospheres not so conducive to purifying their spirit, [...] [have] the purpose of founding a society named "Artisans' Institute" of mainly artistic and literary character.[32]

Favourable political circumstances during the Spanish Republic of 1873 helped the Peninsular-led labour movement to radically challenge the leadership of the Spanish party. A principal aspect of this confrontation was the abolitionism of federal-republicans, who proposed the franchise and abolition granted to Puerto Rico in 1873 as a reform model for Cuba. This abolitionism, nevertheless, did not mean the absence of racism. Clearly continuing the traditions of the Reformist movement, which was always very worried about the possible "Africanization" of Cuba, a labour weekly declared: "We want the growth of the [Cuban] population, and yet we want it to be of the white or European race."[33]

The fall of the Spanish Republic was a serious setback for the republicans in Cuba, but despite repression the federal-republican labour movement persisted. Thus, when the transformation of colonial society due to the Ten Years' War forced Spain to start reforming the colonial system before the end of the war, federal-republicans re-emerged and, in 1877, they established the *Recreo de Obreros*, which evolved into the most important centre of the labour movement in Cuba. Due to these metropolitan policy changes at the end of the war and the reduction in the number of slaves, even non-Whites succeeded in establish-

32. "Exp. prom. por el Gobernador Político dando cuenta del espediente instruido á consecuencia de la solicitud de D. Saturnino Martínez, para establecer una Sociedad que se titule 'Instituto de Artesanos'", Ultramar, AHN, leg. 5899.
33. "Inmigración Asiática", *La Unión*, 20 (12 Oct. 1873), p. 2.

ing associations after nearly two decades of prohibition. Therefore, when Cuban separatists and the Spanish army signed the Treaty of El Zanjón in 1878, there already was a network of popular associations that served as the basis from which the labour movement expanded rapidly.

On the other hand, working-class exiles did not participate in the separatist movement unconditionally. Due to the hostile position toward labour demands of the conservative wing of the separatist leadership, the Aldamistas, exiled workers joined the Quesadistas, the left wing of the movement, and made contact with the International Working Men's Association (First International). As the Spanish consul reported from New York in 1872, "a great number of Cuban separatists, especially the Quesadista Party, belong to the society [known as] 'The International,' and they declare that 'the cause of the commune' is the cause of 'Independent Cuba' [...]".[34]

As in Cuba, the Treaty of El Zanjón triggered a deep transformation of the Cuban working-class exile communities. After the war, freedom to enter and leave Cuba gave exiled tobacco workers a better bargaining position in labour disputes at the tobacco factories, which in most cases were owned or managed by people with strong links to the separatist leadership. In 1878, many of these workers returned to Cuba, while the separatist movement dwindled, and from then on they joined their counterparts on the island in the building of a new labour movement, one that incorporated the experiences of the two labour struggles Cuban workers had engaged in throughout the war.

A New Cuban Labour Movement

The Treaty of El Zanjón, signed in February 1878 between the Spanish and the separatist armies, marked the beginning of a period in which Spain attempted a substantial transformation of the colonial system by granting a degree of freedom never experienced before in Cuba. The Spanish party and the old Creole reformists formed political parties, the Party of Constitutional Union (UC) and the Liberal Party of Cuba (PLC) respectively. Press censorship, furthermore, was loosened. These colonial policy changes had a profound impact on the labour movement. The decline of slavery until its total abolition in October 1886, and Spain's transformation of the repressive apparatus used to sustain slavery, aided the emergence of many working-class societies. Most of these associations were

34. "Carta del Ministro Plenipotenciario de España en Washington al Ministro de Estado. Manifestación de comunistas franceses y emigrados cubanos, La Internacional, la Alianza", 27 Jan. 1872, Colección Caballero de Rodas, doc. 858, vol. IV, pp. 270-271, RAH. On the support that separatists in New York expressed for the Communards, see Instituto de Historia, *Historia del movimiento obrero*, I, pp. 37-39.

the mere surfacing or transformation of already existing associations, many of them clandestine or semi-clandestine. During the war they had been able to operate by declaring that their main purpose was to offer education, cultural activities and mutual-aid services for their membership. With the political reforms that followed El Zanjón, however, many of these associations took on a more radical character and legal labour unions emerged for the first time in Cuba. Again, Creole Whites began to occupy some leadership positions alongside Peninsulares. Parallel to the emergence of these associations, and often in connection with them, Afro-Cubans founded a myriad of associations, which suggests that Afro-Cubans had a quite limited role in the main trade unions.

Initially the two political parties of the socio-economic elite, the PLC and the UC, followed political lines to which this growing popular associational movement felt little attraction. A crucial issue was the very moderate or insincere abolitionism of both parties, and the limited interest that they showed for the situation of urban labour. The impact of the short-lived but openly abolitionist and separatist uprising known as the Guerra Chiquita (1879-80), and the deepening of colonial reforms after it, allowed the reformist-led labour movement to participate in the republican Democratic Party experiment of 1881. Although this party could not win representatives at the polls due to the highly restrictive electoral system in Cuba, not lack of popularity, it propelled the PLC toward radical abolitionism. The increasingly marginal position of the PLC, despite its elitism, prompted this party to make overtures to the republicans. Until the end of slavery in 1886, republicans kept pressuring the autonomists on the abolition issue. Thus, the republicans, with the aid of the labour movement, substantially contributed to generating a political and social atmosphere favourable to abolition.

The growth of the labour movement and the evolution of party politics probably accelerated the decomposition of slavery. The colonial administration continued to treat the labour movement very harshly, precisely because it feared that the growth of organized labour would prompt unfree labour to become more militant. The dissimilar evolution of the slave emancipation rate in Havana and Santa Clara provinces and the labour struggles of free and unfree workers on some western Cuban plantations show that in areas closer to centres of labour mobilization, such as Havana city, emancipation proceeded more rapidly.

After the Treaty of El Zanjón, the decline of slavery and the repressive apparatus to maintain it had a great impact on urban labour relations: it allowed labour militancy and unionism to grow and successfully improve working conditions. For instance, the largest union established after El Zanjón, the Gremio de Obreros, effectively transformed labour relations in the tobacco factories and workshops. To counter this tendency, employers could no longer count on the same degree of intervention from the colonial administration as before the Treaty of El Zanjón. Tensions along class lines were so intense that people of different race and ethnicity increasingly participated in strikes together. For instance, in 1885 a coopers strike broke out in western Cuba, and in it "The Spaniard as well as the Cuban and [the] mulatto fraternized." Even Spanish soldiers sided with the strikers, which led the United States consul in Matanzas to conclude that,

> This significant action convinced the authorities that the army could not be relied upon in an emergency; and two days after when a leader from Havana addressed the strikers here and used incendiary and threatening language, referring personally to high Government officials, and when Spaniard, Cuban, and mulatto alike cheered the speaker to the echo, then it was that the demands of the strikers were granted.[35]

Therefore, employers founded associations such as the Gremio de Fabricantes de Tabaco to better protect their interests regarding labour discipline, but, due to the strong bargaining position of tobacco workers in this period, the success of this syndicate appears to have been rather limited.

It was in this climate of class confrontation that anarchist propagandists first emerged publicly in Cuba and began to attract a growing number of workers to their side. However, the colonial administration's turn toward more repressive policies and the sudden economic crisis that began in late 1883 hindered the spread of socialism among workers. In this repressive atmosphere the reformist labour leadership attempted to counter the growth of socialism by collaborating with employers' organizations and the colonial administration. This approach failed completely however. The administration refused to accept any of the demands of the reformists and, despite their anti-separatist propaganda, it even intensified its repressive policies against them. With the reformists severely discredited, once the economy began to grow again and Spanish liberals came back into office in the mid-1880s urban labour began to elect anarchists to the most important leadership positions in the labour movement. The disastrous role of the reformists in a very large strike by tobacco workers in 1886 further accelerated this evolution.

The end of slavery, the main barrier dividing the popular classes and the main reason for the state's extreme interventionism in labour relations, fostered the rapid expansion of the labour movement. Through the mass mobilization of people of diverse race and ethnicity, the labour movement eliminated most of the residual methods of disciplining labour from the slavery era, and contributed to the rapid transformation of colonial society. During this period, anarcho-

---

35. Frank H. Pierce, consul at Matanzas, 5 March 1886, "Labor troubles in Cuba", in U.S. Congress, House, *Reports from the Consuls of the United States, April-December, 1886*, House of Representatives, 49th Congress, 2nd Session, 1886-1887, *Miscellaneous Documents*, 55, vol. 4 (Washington, 1886), p. 266.

collectivist propaganda reached a broad sector of the urban popular classes in Cuba, especially in the west of the island, but even workers in eastern towns were aware of the growth of collectivism. Colonial authorities used the exceptional power that colonialism gave to the military to do whatever was possible to contain the expansion of the anarchist-led labour movement. Nevertheless, the particular approach that anarchists developed to colonial politics and class struggle outmanoeuvred both the colonial administration and the employers on several occasions. By remaining independent from any political force, the labour movement incorporated workers with divergent political sympathies, from those supporting Spanish rule, among them most lower-class Peninsulares, to those who yearned for an independent Cuba. Furthermore, as an independent political and social force, the labour movement developed a strong bargaining position in Cuban politics. The big strikes and lockouts that tobacco workers won in 1887 and 1888 in Havana, and in 1889 in Key West (an island off southern Florida, seventy miles from Cuba), showed workers the validity of the anarchists' approach to class struggle and colonial politics.

Conclusion

The evolution of organized labour in Cuba illustrates how the popular sector became increasingly interested in eliminating slavery and the colonial status of Cuba. The situation of indentured apprentices, the Libreta del tabaquero and the working conditions of Peninsular dependientes suggest that slavery and colonialism hindered the struggle for better working and living conditions of juridically free labour. In its initial steps during the 1860s, the Cuban labour movement opposed the use of slave labour in factories and workshops. Despite the fact that during the Ten Years' War Peninsulares dominated the branch of the labour movement inside Cuba, from the 1870s on the labour movement explicitly supported abolition. In the 1880s, the two branches of the labour movement, the one inside Cuba and the one in the United States, became increasingly intertwined. Creoles could occupy leadership positions again, while non-Whites increasingly began to fill the ranks. These circumstances gave new force to the labour movement, which succeeded in compelling the PLC to take on abolitionism as one of its main causes. Post-emancipation party politics and colonial reformism provided an atmosphere of greater freedom, in which the labour movement could mobilize the popular sector as it had never done before. In a few years, Cuban labour successfully fought against the residual methods of disciplining labour from the era of slavery, such as racial discrimination against non-Whites and the physical punishment of apprentices and dependientes.

The Competition of Slave and Free Labor in Artisanal Production: Buenos Aires, 1770-1815

Lyman L. Johnson

Little attention has been paid to wage labor in the history of colonial Spanish America. Yet, across the empire, wage labor was increasingly important in urban manufacturing and service sectors and in mining from the mid seventeenth century. By the late eighteenth century, the skilled trades of the empire's largest cities and towns relied primarily on wage laborers. Both transportation and construction were also largely dependent on wage labor. Although some urban economies retained their early dependence on the coerced labor of Indians and slaves, the most dynamic urban economies of Spanish America were moving dramatically in the direction of wage labor by the end of the colonial period. Nevertheless, the coerced components of both rural and urban production have received much greater attention from historians and other social scientists. Slave labor and the coercive labor systems imposed on indigenous peoples such as the Andean mita have attracted the interest of some of Spanish America's most distinguished historians. In particular, the slave labor systems of the major Iberian sugar-producing plantation societies of Brazil and Cuba have been explored in depth. In addition, there are a number of excellent studies of the plantation sectors of colonial Venezuela, Ecuador, and Peru. A similar concentration on forms of coerced labor is found in the social historical and economic scholarship devoted to mining and manufacturing enterprise in late eighteenth-century Spanish America. The Potosí mita and the use of coerced Indian workers in the textile obrajes of New Spain and Quito have also attracted re-examination. But what is known of the wage workers who labored alongside these coerced workers? And, more broadly, how did these two systems of allocating labor interact in response to changes in these colonial economies?

Despite more than forty years of intensive interrogation of the region's economic development in the late colonial period, there are only a handful of wage and real wage studies. As a result, we know little about changes in labor demand or, alternatively, changes in compensation and living conditions experienced by the mass of wage laborers. Other issues associated with wage labor such as recruitment, employment patterns, training, and work discipline have been similarly ignored. In cities like Buenos Aires where wage laborers provided the majority of both skilled and unskilled labor pools, our knowledge of both social structure and economic performance are obscured by these limitations in the literature.

Although coerced labor of various kinds (including debt peonage and convict labor) remained important, if not central, to export agriculture in Spanish America well into the national period, wage labor came to hold an important place in the production process even in plantation zones. On the sugar plantations of Cuba and the cacao plantations of Venezuela, for example, skilled jobs were often filled by wage laborers by 1800. Outside the plantation economies free labor was proportionally more important. Although slaves were present in large numbers until eventual abolition of slavery in 1861, the agriculture and livestock sectors of the province of Buenos Aires and neighboring Uruguay depended more on free than slave labor.

In this essay I offer an analysis of the relationship between slave and free labor regimes in the city of Buenos Aires and its immediate agricultural hinterland during the period 1770-1815. I begin with an overview of the region's economic history in the late colonial period and then turn to a more-detailed discussion of labor supply and workforce distribution. The integration of slaves in the urban wage labor force and the impact of increased numbers of slaves on wage rates will be discussed. In a brief postscript, I trace the region's labor history to the final abolition of slavery in the Province of Buenos Aires in 1861.

The Early Economy of Buenos Aires

Although Buenos Aires was permanently settled early in the colonial cycle in 1580, the city's growth was retarded by imperial policies that placed narrow limits on direct trade with Europe and with interior provinces. Until the last half of the eighteenth century, Atlantic trade was monopolized by merchant guilds in Seville and a small number of American colonial cities. Only in 1778 did the merchant guild of Lima lose its control of Buenos Aires' commerce. This cumbersome and costly dependence on Lima restricted the city's commercial links with the developing Atlantic market and slowed economic development. Nevertheless, Lima's commercial monopoly serviced the Spanish Crown's desire to limit the illegal exchange of American bullion for contraband goods provided by European rivals. Because the region's major products (livestock by-products and yerba) were burdened by a low value to bulk ratio, these trade restrictions nearly eliminated the possibility of legal trade for Spain's South Atlantic colonies. Only the hugh profits from the illegal trade in silver kept commerce alive by drawing Spain's European rivals to the Río de la Plata.

Commercially marginalized by Crown policy, the city, along with Montevideo and Colonia on the east bank of the estuary, eventually won a niche in the Atlantic market as a center of contraband. Despite increased efforts by Spain to control trade to the region by augmenting coast guard and customs service scrutiny, French, Dutch, English, and Portuguese merchants continued to exchange prohibited imports for silver produced at Potosí and a significant share of the region's production of low-profit livestock by-products that served in effect as ballast on the ships returning to Europe with silver. As a result, foreign goods dominated the regional market until the founding of the Viceroyalty of Río de la Plata in 1776.

Slaves were among the prohibited goods imported at Buenos Aires. Official records indicate that a total of 22,892 slaves entered the city between 1595 and 1680.[1] The vast majority of these slaves were imported by foreign merchants with the connivance of Spanish officials who permitted foreign captains to off-load and sell slaves after claiming their ships had been damaged by storms. In other cases, slaves were "confiscated" and sold by Crown officials who then compensated foreign merchants under the table. Many scholars believe the actual number of slaves entering Buenos Aires during this period may have been double the official count.

Regardless of the actual volume of the slave trade before 1700, it is clear is that very few slaves remained long in Buenos Aires or its immediate hinterland. The majority of slaves followed the trail of illegal silver back to its origin in Potosí. The disproportionate flow of slave labor to the Andean zone effectively represents the competitive labor demands of Buenos Aires and the Andean mining zone. Although Potosí and other Andean silver mining regions experienced a steep decline in production in the seventeenth century, the expensive labor of African slaves continued to be allocated by market forces to the Andean region rather than to Buenos Aires.

The distribution of slaves in the labor force of the city of Buenos Aires confirms this summary judgement. In the early eighteenth century, less than twenty percent of all slaves were concentrated in the city's artisan shops or employed in the nearby agricultural sector. Instead, the majority of the Río de la Plata region's slaves were placed as household servants. That is, slave labor was more associated with establishing the status of elite households than with producing income. The limited profitability of manufacturing and agriculture before the Bourbon Reform era could not sustain reliance on this form of expensive coerced labor.

---

1. Andrews, *Afro-Argentines of Buenos Aires*, p. 24.

The Economy in the Era of the Bourbon Reforms

The Río de la Plata region benefitted enormously from the altered geopolitical and economic policies of the Bourbons. After 1700 the port of Buenos Aires was incrementally opened to direct trade with Spain and other Spanish colonies. In an effort to staunch the flow of contraband silver and thwart Portuguese military and commercial ambitions in the region, the Spanish Crown made Buenos Aires the capital of a new viceroyalty in 1776. By including the mining region of Alto Peru (Bolivia) in the viceroyalty, the Crown both recognized the city's historic role as exporter of Potosí's silver and provided the means to pay for the city's greatly expanded civil and military responsibilities. In 1778, as part of an empire wide commercial reform, Ordinance of Free Trade, Buenos Aires was given greatly expanded commercial access to Spain and to Spanish colonial markets.

The impact of these reforms is reflected in the growth of urban population. From a population of approximately 9,000 in 1720, Buenos Aires grew to more than 60,000 in 1810, rivaling in size the ancient viceregal capital of Lima.[2] While rural population growth lagged behind the city's upward trajectory, increased urban demand for food and expanded access to European and Western Hemisphere markets for livestock by-products created new economic opportunities in the countryside as well. Between 1781 and 1798, the frontier town of Chascomús, for example, grew from 374 to 1,000 inhabitants. This rate of growth was general in the region with the rural commercial center of Luján growing five-fold to over 2000 inhabitants in this same period.

Slaves and Wage Laborers in the Viceregal Economy

In both the city and countryside, economic expansion after 1776 initiated a long period of chronic labor shortage that persisted until the era of large-scale immigration in the 1880s. This labor shortage, and resulting high wages, was a constant theme in the reports of colonial officials, the records of the town council (cabildo), and in the official and private correspondence of local merchants and foreign visitors. Both local and viceregal governments debated, and in some cases attempted, an array of schemes to meet the region's labor needs. As these pressures mounted, Crown officials effectively suspended longstanding imperial prohibitions that barred the immigration and residency of foreign nationals and actively petitioned for direct participation in the slave trade.

2. See my "Estimaciones de la población de Buenos Aires", pp. 107-120.

Because references to labor shortages are so common in the documents, nearly every scholar of the late colonial period has mentioned the issue. Yet there have been very few substantial efforts by colonial economic and social historians to examine labor supply in the Río de la Plata region. Among the small number of scholars who have discussed the regional labor market, research has been concentrated on rural labor supply in the era following independence.[3] A similar concern with rural labor supply has also dominated the much more limited literature devoted to the colonial period.[4] As a result, the discussion of colonial labor supply is most commonly illustrated by the efforts of viceregal and municipal governments to provide harvest labor by compelling the short-term labor of Paraguayan Indians, convicts and beggars. Larger issues, like the effect of high wages on regional development, have been largely ignored.

The Urban Labor Market to 1815

Slaves provided an important component of the city's labor force to the end of the colonial period. Between 1696 and 1750 the Crown granted monopoly control of the slave trade to Buenos Aires to a succession of foreign companies. The Portuguese Caheu Company held the monopoly initially, but was forced to relinquish control due to poor performance in 1701. The monopoly was then granted to the French Guinea Company. Following the War of Spanish Succession, the British South Sea Company exercized the monopoly until 1748. During the period of the French and British monopolies, a total of approximately 14,000 slaves legally entered Buenos Aires.

As was true in the seventeenth century, the majority of slaves imported before 1750 were quickly shipped to other destinations. Of the approximately 11,000 slaves imported by the British monopoly between 1715 and 1738 only 30 percent, or approximately 3,300, stayed in Buenos Aires and its rural hinterland.[5] The majority were sent to interior towns, to the Andean mining zone, or to Chile. Both Chile and Alto Peru took slightly larger shares of total slave imports than Buenos Aires.

Legal importations of slaves totaled approximately 28,000 in the period 1750-1806. Actual importations probably reached 50,000 due to continued contraband. As illustrated in the following table, legal slave imports were very limited

3. Slatta, *Gauchos and the Vanishing Frontier*, especially ch. 7.
4. Among the many recent contributions see, Mayo, "Estancia y peonaje"; and Salvatore and Brown, "Trade and Proletarianization".
5. Data for the last decade of the British *asiento* are fragmentary. See Scheuss de Studer, *Trata de negros*.

through the 1770s.[6] Slave imports then increased in response to the economic stimulus provided by the creation of the new viceroyalty and the opening of direct trade with Spain and other Spanish colonies. Although European wars disrupted trade repeatedly during the period 1790–1806, slave imports increased steadily as local merchants were permitted to enter the direct trade with Africa and as the ships of neutral nations were granted access to the Buenos Aires market. Slave ships captured by local privateers also contributed to this rising tide of slave imports. As a result, 82 percent of total legal slave imports for the 57 year period 1750–1806 landed during the final seventeen years.

Table 1. Legal Slave Imports to Buenos Aires, 1750–1806

Year	Total	Per Year
1750–1759	1214	121
1760–1769	397	40
1770–1779	475	48
1780–1789	2806	281
1790–1799	9013	901
1800–1806	13256	1326

Sources: These figures are based on my search of *Aduana* and *Consulado* records held by the *Archivo General de la Nación* in Buenos Aires, Argentina.

Unfortunately, we lack records for the period after 1778 that would allow us to confidently compare with earlier periods the percentage of slave imports retained by the city and its hinterland relative to those re-exported to other locations. However, the surviving evidence seems to suggest that at least a majority of slaves that entered Buenos Aires after 1778 stayed in the city or the nearby countryside. Contemporary census records provide the outline of this altered pattern in the slave trade. The city's black and mulatto population (slave and free) increased from 16.9 percent of the population in 1744 to 33 percent in 1810. During this same period, the percentage of slaves in the black and mulatto population of the city of Buenos Aires rose from 75 to 86.3 percent.[7] Nevertheless, even while the labor needs of this rapidly expanding urban economy promoted the expansion of slave holding in Buenos Aires, a steady stream of men and women gained their freedom through manumission and

6. These sources clearly underrepresent actual arrivals. Some scholars have put the total for the period 1740–1822 at more than 45,000. The importance of the contraband slave trade is suggested by the altered racial distributions found in contemporary censuses. These sources indicate that the African-originated population of the city rose from 17 percent in 1744 to 29 percent in 1778. See Goldberg and Mallo, "Población africana, pp. 15–69.

7. See Johnson and Socolow, "Población y espacio", especially pp. 332–34.

entered the pool of free labor.[8] Moreover, large numbers of those who remained in bondage operated with substantial independence in the local labor market, seeking work and negotiating wages with little direct supervision by their owners.

That is, the expanding economy of late colonial Buenos Aires produced seemingly contradictory results relative to our common assumptions about the competition between slave and free labor. The long period of sustained labor demand and high wages initiated by imperial reforms made the purchase of large numbers of costly slaves feasible for the first time in the city's history. But the same expansion that promoted the growth of the slave population seems to also have produced significant opportunity for manumission and remarkable levels of independence for those who remained in bondage. Moreover, the expansion of slavery generally and the integration of slaves into artisanal and other skilled manual occupations apparently occurred without depressing the wages or limiting the employment opportunities of free workers.

The importance of slavery to the economy of late colonial Buenos Aires is indisputable. Nearly every contemporary account by a foreign visitor or Crown official noted the importance of slave and free black labor to the city. Many simply stated that blacks and castas dominated all the urban trades, including the most-skilled artisan crafts, the urban service sector, and domestic service.[9] In each of these employment sectors, slave participation expanded rapidly after 1790.

Travelers as well as local residents commonly drew attention to two additional features of the local slave regime. Although there were some substantial slave holdings in the city, as was true in all the Spanish American capitals, there were very large numbers of slave owners in late colonial Buenos Aires who owned only a single slave. Within the slave owning population, a small number of wealthy individuals did own large numbers of slaves. Wholesale merchants, high-ranking royal officials, and some artisan manufacturers (especially bakers and owners of brick factories) had the largest holdings, in some cases owning more than thirty slaves.[10] However, the emerging character of this slave regime

---

8. It is difficult to assert with confidence a manumission rate for Buenos Aires, or any other colonial city, but a close analysis of the surviving notarial records indicates that by the last decades of the colonial period just under 1.5 percent of the slave population gained freedom each year. See my "Manumission in Colonial Buenos Aires", pp. 258-279.

9. Most of these sources suggest that only 20 percent of the urban population was white. The difference between the census counts and the perceptions of visitors to the city reflects the necessarily imprecise line that separated "white" from "mulatto" in colonial Buenos Aires. Where visitors saw mulattoes, locals often saw whites. See Goldberg and Mallo, "Población africana", p. 18.

10. The concentrated nature of the distribution became very clear when the governing junta sought to conscript slaves during the independence struggle. See Goldberg y Jany, "Algunos problemas referentes a la situación del esclavo".

resulted more from the startling high number of slave owners with only one or two slaves.

Large numbers of slaves, perhaps a majority of the city's slave population, were owned by men and women of very modest means. As one visitor put it in 1794, "[...] you should know that there is an increased number of slaves in the city and many families have no property other than their slaves. [...] [T]hese the law obligates to provide their owners with a daily payment [...]".[11] Many owners, in fact, were completely dependent on the wages of their slaves.

This generalization can be corroborated from a variety of sources. In the manumission documents of the period it was common for slave owners to unambiguously acknowledge their dependence on the earnings of one or more slaves. As a result of this dependence, many slaves gained freedom conditionally, burdened by the requirement to continue making weekly or monthly cash payments during the owner's life time.[12] The city's political institutions also clearly recognized the importance of these transfer payments. In 1789, during a debate over efforts to create a guild of shoemakers, the town council unambiguously asserted the importance of slave wages to families and individuals of limited means. The shoemakers had submitted a guild constitution to the town council that prohibited slaves from attaining the rank of master. The city fathers summarily rejected this constitution singling out the proposed limitation to the advancement and, therefore, earnings of slaves. This, the councillors noted, "[...] is prejudicial to the Republic, it being apparent that there are many widows and families in this city that sustain themselves with the daily wages of their slaves [...]".[13]

As slave arrivals increased after 1790 slave prices declined slightly thus drawing a larger pool of potential buyers into the market. In 1802, Buenos Aires's first periodical, the *Telégrafo Mercantil*, offered the following short summary of the city's slave market. "[...] every day there arrives in our port a frigate with three or four hundred slaves who will be disembarked on our shores. With notice of the arrival, people who wish to begin living a lazy life congregate to seek those who will work in their place. To accomplish this end, each comes with one or two thousand pesos to spend, departing for their home [with a slave or two] very satisfied. Within a few days they obligate their new slaves to walk the streets to find a day's labor that will pay four or five reales."[14] We know that "three or

11. De Aparicio, "Relación de un viaje", p. 236.
12. Archivo General de la Nación, Escribanía, Registros 1-7, *anos* 1776-1810. Approximately 11 percent of all the manumissions granted during the viceregal period required that the slave continue making a weekly or monthly payment to the owner.
13. Archivo General de la Nación, Interior, Legajo 26, Expediente 4, 25-25 vta.
14. "Telégrafo Mercantil", pp. 191-196. This article is somewhat misleading on the price of recently-arrived African slaves, *bozales*. During the last two decades of the colonial era, the price of African males in Buenos Aires fluctuated between 200 and 250 pesos. A slave who became a master artisan could bring as much as 600 pesos.

four hundred slaves" did not arrive daily in 1802. Nevertheless, it is clear from surviving accounts that as the volume of imports rose and opportunities for hiring out increased slave ownership did in fact become more common among people of modest means.

It seems unlikely that many recent arrivals from Africa or Brazil were sent into the local labor market with the minimal cultural equipment suggested in the *Telégrafo Mercantil* article. Unable to speak Spanish and without knowledge of local wage and price custom or knowledge of monetary values, a recent arrival was certain to be a target for abuse and fraud. Of more direct concern to owners was the likelihood that unassimilated and inexperienced slaves would be unable to locate employment at standard rates and would, therefore, fail to provide the adequate return on invested capital. We should presume that only those owners completely overtaken by sloth or completely absorbed in their own affairs would fail to supervise directly the employment contracts of newly-arrived slaves. Indeed, the notarial copybooks seem to suggest that, in longer labor contracts, wages, minus estimated living expenses, were commonly paid directly to slave owners by employers of hired slave labor.

These same records indicate that, rather than sending newly-purchased slaves out on their own, it was more common to place them as apprentices or as helpers with established artisans or lesser-skilled wage workers. At the cost of some lost income, owners delegated direct supervision of their slaves to these employers for a period of two to six years, depending on the trade. As was the case with free apprentices, apprenticed slaves lived in the home of a master who provided room and board and, sometimes after the first year, a small wage. Master artisans were also responsible for instruction in the Catholic faith and discipline. Although less formal arrangements were the norm in the brick kilns, bakeries, stockyards, and construction gangs that employed thousands of the city's workers, it was also customary for slaves in these occupations to share meals and sleeping arrangements with free workmates. Nearly every workplace and most workers' housing in late colonial Buenos Aires integrated free and slave workers.[15] Since the youngest, least-skilled slaves had only limited earning potential, slave owners sought to reduce the cost of skill acquisition and subsistence by transferring these burdens to an employer. As slaves gained experience and acquired skills their income potential grew. Owners generally responded to enhanced earning potential by granting slaves greater freedom to negotiate employment and determine living arrangements. For thousands of slaves in late colonial Buenos Aires, slavery meant weekly, or less commonly monthly, cash payments paid to their owners. Owners were able to both ratchet

15. This conclusion is drawn from a close examination of a number of matriculations of artisans from 1780 that show residence arrangements. See the census of Albañiles, for example, in Archivo General de la Nación, Tribunales, Legajo 66, Expediente 15.

up the amounts of these cash payments and increasingly make slaves responsible for their own subsistence as they acquired skills and gained cultural sophistication. In its mature form after 1790, slavery in Buenos Aires was not the paternalistic social system that historians have generally found in other Spanish colonies. Overwhelmingly, the slave owners of Buenos Aires regarded their slaves as investments that they expected to produce regular dividends.

Although the volume of free immigration was consistently inferior to that of the slave trade, free immigrants also entered the Buenos Aires labor market in large numbers after 1776. Unfortunately, colonial officials made no effort to record the arrival of immigrants. Any effort to estimate the scale of immigration, therefore, must rely on population counts compiled for other purposes. These records suggest that the vast majority of free immigrants were young males. According to census counts, the native-born portion of the city's white male population declined from 58 percent in 1744 to 31 percent in 1810.[16] Among manual workers, immigrants were disproportionally found in the skilled artisan trades. Table 2 provides the origins of a cross section of the city's artisans in 1780. Unfortunately, many artisan occupations and all of the city's lesser-skilled trades (bakers, brick manufacturers, laundresses and others) are excluded from these records. Given what we know of the recruitment practices of the trades excluded from these records, the table probably overrepresents the importance of European immigrants in the total workforce. Nevertheless, these matriculations provide the most reliable information available for the origins of the *porteño* working class. Forty-five percent of the city's artisan community were native-born in 1780 and one ninth of these were free blacks. Nearly 41 percent of all artisans were European immigrants while immigrants from other Spanish colonies in the Americas contributed another 14 percent.

Among master artisans the importance of immigrants is even clearer. In 1780, fifty-nine percent of all master artisans were immigrants with slightly more than two thirds of all immigrants originating in Portugal or Spain. No comparable records exist for the last decade of the colonial period, but since free immigration clearly increased after 1780, it is probably safe to conclude that the proportion of immigrants at the upper end of the skill hierarchy changed little before 1810. At the bottom of the skill hierarchy among apprentices and laborers, on the other hand, slaves and the free native-born contributed slightly more than 80 percent of the total in 1780.

16. Portions of the 1810 census have disappeared and, as a result, my estimate of the percentage of native-born based on this census is less reliable than that for 1744. The best analysis of the 1810 census is found in Belsunce *et al.*, *Buenos Aires*.

Table 2: Origins of Artisans of Buenos Aires, 1780 (N = 1,045)

Born in Spain or other European Nations	41%
Born in other American Colonies	14%
Born in Buenos Aires or Hinterland	45%

Source: Archivo General de la Nación, Tribunales, Legajo 13, Expediente 15; Tribunales, Legajo 66, Expediente 37; Interior, Legajo 9, Expediente 5; Justicia, Legajo 9, Expediente 177; Interior, Legajo 9, Expediente 5; and Tribunales, Legajo 13, Expediente 15.

Wages and Employment

An upward-ascending wage curve in the city and its hinterland made possible the deep integration of slave and free labor regimes after 1778.[17] Anticipating that local demand for both skilled and unskilled labor meant that slaves could be quickly placed with employers, men and women of modest means confidently borrowed money to purchase slaves. Wealthier residents also participated in the development of this new labor market. The greater resources available to the elite meant that its members could purchase and hire out larger numbers of slaves. In some cases prosperous merchants combined their ownership of labor resources with investments in small manufacturing enterprise: brickyards, bakeries, hat factories, and bronze foundries.

Table 3 provides a wage index for the period 1774-1815. The region's wage history is divided into three periods, each initiated by significant wage increases. The period 1774-1779 began with a decline in wages. The large-scale military activity that accompanied the creation of the viceroyalty forced down wages, especially for the lesser-skilled. Military wages were low and often in arrears. As a result, off-duty soldiers and sailors entered the local labor market in large numbers, bidding down local wage custom. Once the commercial reform and growth in local public sector spending had taken effect after 1780, wages moved upward, at first hesitantly and then with some strength. A new round of commercial liberalization after 1792 led to a second period of rising wages. Finally, after the British invasions of 1806 and 1807, a rapid expansion in regional military manpower requirements exacerbated chronic labor supply problems and inaugurated further increases in the cost of labor.

It is important to note that most of the increase registered by the wage index coincided with periods of greatest slave imports. This suggests that the scale of regional economic expansion and the effects of military manpower requirements allowed Buenos Aires to absorb coerced laborers in large numbers without forcing down the wages of free laborers. In fact, notarial records for the period

17. See my "Salarios, precios y costo de vida", pp. 133-158, for a preliminary analysis of wages.

Table 3: Weight Index of Wages (1776 = 100)

1774	105.3	1788	105.2	1802	124.6
1775	100.3	1789	107.7	1803	139.6
1776	100	1790	105.2	1804	139.6
1777	100	1791	107.7	1805	139.6
1778	100	1792	107.7	1806	148.1
1779	100	1793	105.2	1807	151.7
1780	107.5	1794	107.7	1808	152.4
1781	101.9	1795	107.7	1809	152.3
1782	101.9	1796	108.4	1810	177.3
1783	101.9	1797	117.1	1811	177.3
1784	107.7	1798	124.6	1812	177.3
1785	107.1	1799	115.9	1813	177.3
1786	105.2	1800	123.4	1814	172.3
1787	105.2	1801	123.4	1815	172.3

Note: Weights were assigned to the wage histories of individual occupations based on their proportional importance in contemporary census records. This index includes the wages of carpenters, bricklayers, iron-workers, caulkers, ship carpenters, armsmakers, sailors, urban peones, and rural peones.

suggest that there was no measurable wage discrimination experienced by slave workers (or, put more accurately, by the owners of these slave workers). Moreover, because slaves in Buenos Aires commonly had significant discretion in contracting for employment and retained portions of their income, the urban labor force remained flexible and productive even as the numbers of slaves increased.

By 1800 nearly every manual occupation, every skill level, and nearly every job site in the city hosted an integrated workforce of slave and free laborers. However, the documents suggest that racial affinity and racial discrimination played an important role in distributing workers among employers. Legal status seems to have acted in a less intrusive and predictable manner. A close examination of workforce recruitment among the city's artisan shops suggests a deep interpenetration of slave and free labor. There is only one surviving craft census that allows us to confidently assign racial identity, a *visita* conducted on a shop-to-shop basis by a group of master shoemakers and a representative of the cabildo (town council). This *visita* demonstrates that a clear majority of free nonwhite apprentices and journeymen worked under the supervision of black master artisans.[18] Among slave apprentices and journeymen who negotiated their own

18. Archivo General de la Nación, Interior, Legojo 41, Expediente 14, 11-17vta.

employment, a majority were found in the shops of white master artisans. This suggests to me that free black and mulatto artisans sought to limit discriminatory obstacles to skill acquisition and advancement within their trades by avoiding white employers. Slave artisans, on the other hand, were found in greater numbers in the shops of the more prosperous white masters because the likelihood that these shops would offer more secure employment and pay higher wages was the key to eventual manumission.

In the brickyards and bakeries that employed large numbers of workers, every employer mixed free and slave labor. Among artisans, slave and free craftsmen worked together in all but the smallest shops that employed only one or two apprentices or journeymen. Most commonly, free master artisans supervised the labor of a mixed workforce that included both slave and free helpers. Many of these master craftsmen owned the slave apprentices and journeymen they employed. There were also many examples in late colonial Buenos Aires where slaves who had achieved the rank of journeyman or master directed the labor, and even disciplined, free apprentices, or lesser-skilled laborers.

Given the culture of artisan production, the boundaries between slave and free were obscured when free apprentices worked in shops with slave journeymen or masters. In these cases, the slave's authority derived from mastery of skills tended to override the cultural presumption that the free apprentice held higher social status. This inversion was exaggerated in those shops where enslaved master artisans supervised the labor of free journeymen and apprentices. In cases like these we need to pause before assigning traditional labels of free and unfree to the late colonial workforce of Buenos Aires.

The expanded military requirements provoked by the British invasion of 1806 initially drew down free labor supply only. However, with the beginning of the struggle for independence in 1810, the region's revolutionary governments sought to draw slaves into the military. At first, slave-owners were encouraged to enlist their slaves as a patriotic contribution. In 1813 these indirect means were abandoned as the government began the conscription of slaves. Those slaves who survived their terms of military service were promised freedom. At the same time the region's new political leadership took the first hesitant step towards the eventual abolition of slavery, the 1813 *Ley de libertad de vientes*. This law declared that all children born to slave mothers after January 31, 1813 would be granted freedom after a mandatory period of supervised apprenticeship.[19] The combination of slave conscription and a rising tide of abolitionist sentiment undermined the links that had earlier tied the Atlantic slave trade to the skilled

---

19. These *libertos* were to gain their freedom upon marriage or upon reaching the age of 16 for women and the age 20 for men. They were all required to serve their masters without salary until the age of 15. From the age of 15 until emancipation 1 peso per month was to be deposited on their behalf with the police.

trades of Buenos Aires. As a result, the mass of slave purchasers, many dependent on borrowed capital, who had sustained demand for slaves before 1813 exited the market.

As urban demand for slaves declined, rural producers, especially *estancieros* (large-scale ranchers) became primary players in a slowly collapsing slave market. Slavery gained a new lease on life in the countryside as rural labor demands supplied new momentum to the faltering institution. And, as a result, the institution survived for decades after the first efforts at comprehensive abolition were undertaken in the city. However, the employment of slave labor in the Province of Buenos Aires after 1815 diverged in character from the urban slave regime that had developed in the last two decades of the colonial period. Unlike the city where slaves commonly arranged their own employment contracts and lived outside the homes of their masters, slaves in the countryside worked for their masters under much closer supervision. With most of the slaves employed in the countryside of Buenos Aires province distributed among ranches and small farms, there was no likelihood that the oppressive system of social control found in plantation zones would appear. Still, this was a fundamentally new work regime for the region: Rural slave owners unlike their urban contemporaries sought labor power, not rent.

Rural Production/Postscript

The region's livestock industry lagged behind competitors across the estuary in what is now Uruguay and in the interior provinces to the west. Throughout most of the colonial period, unbranded cattle and horse herds grazed freely on the province's open range. Grazing lands in the province of Buenos Aires had little monetary value before the 1780s. Hides and other by-products like tallow were produced freely by entrepreneurs who purchased the necessary licenses and then organized groups of rural laborers for intense short-term harvests. That is, the cost of producing the region's exports was largely determined by the cost of labor.

As the value of these products increased following liberalization of trade in 1778, land ownership became more important, land values rose, and systematic efforts were made by landowners to retain a permanent labor force capable of protecting herds and extracting product. By the 1790s, colonial authorities had required rural workers to carry cards proving employment under pain of conscription or incarceration. These changes in land values and labor practice coincided with significant new investment in rural property. Especially after 1809 when direct trade with Great Britain overwhelmed traditional commercial arrangements with Spain, important local merchant families began to invest in rural properties. Not only did these investments intensify the demand for rural labor, but these politically powerful families were also capable of bending the coercive powers of the state to meet their needs. As foreign demand for the region's products expanded in the 1820s, rural workers were forced to accept even more draconian labor laws. Ranchers and their foremen were granted *de facto* control of courts, jails, and corporeal punishments to discipline and compel the labor of free men and women.[20] Rural slaves faced a work regime that was even more coercive.

The labor shortages of the city between 1780 and 1810 and the countryside after 1820 both led to increased dependence on slave labor. Yet, the slave systems that evolved in the city and countryside were very different. Unlike the labor market of the late colonial city, both slave and free workers in the early national countryside were prevented from negotiating improved employment conditions or higher wages by contract and license laws imposed by the state. Rural slaves were also generally denied the opportunities for manumission that had been associated in the city with the acquisition of skills and improved income that came from employment in artisan and other skilled trades. In addition, rural slave owners also would prove to be more effective in slowing the progress of abolition than urban masters.

Without significant new slave importations, slave labor declined in relative importance after 1830 as free immigration expanded. Nevertheless, the residual slave population continued in the relentless grip of the estanciero class. Slave owners used various schemes to keep their slaves, despite government emancipation laws. Few of the *libertos* "freed" by the 1813 law, for example, actually experienced freedom before middle age. Many were held in bondage illegally when the police records that contained their birth dates, and therefore the date of their emancipation, conveniently disappeared in 1831.

As the political power of the rural elite increased after 1820, the *estanciero* class initiated efforts to import new slaves. Thousands of slaves seized from Brazilian shipping by local privateers during wartime were admitted to the province in clear violation of a 1825 treaty with Great Britain that had abolished the slave trade. Then, despite British protests, the powerful governor of the province, Juan Manuel de Rosas, briefly legalized the slave trade in 1831. But these schemes added only a few thousand new slaves, commonly identified by the euphemism *libertos*, to the provincial workforce. Following Rosas' overthrow in 1852, the new national constitution of 1853 abolished slavery unambiguously. But, again, liberation was denied to the province's small remaining slave population when the local political elite revolted against the national govern-

---

20. Many authors have written on this topic. See Slatta, *Gauchos*, especially ch. 7; and Lynch, *Argentine Dictator*, especially ch. 3.

ment. As a result, slavery was not finally abolished in Buenos Aires until 1861 when the province finally rejoined the national union.

The labor history of the Province of Buenos Aires, 1776-1850, suggests that slave and free workers could be compatibly integrated in both urban manufacturing and service sectors and in rural livestock and small farming production. Moreover, the Buenos Aires case indicates the blurred boundaries that separated free and slave workers, especially in urban occupations. In an artisan culture where slave journeymen arranged their own labor contracts and free apprentices were sometimes supervised by slaves who were master artisans, the distinctions between free and coerced labor are stipulated only with great difficulty. What is needed, especially in the regions outside the plantation economies of the Americas, is additional research that places the experiences slaves in a broadened context to include wage workers as well.

The Reappearance of Slavery and the Reproduction of Capital on the Brazilian Frontier

José de Souza Martins

I

The small and fascinating historical and sociological literature concerning the persistence or the renewal of forms of slave labour in different societies forces researchers to face certain dilemmas that are very difficult to solve. The main one is the very concept of the type of labour that, in a country like Brazil, has simply been defined as slave labour. Another one, whose solution is not so difficult, is its historic insertion or, more controversially, the mode of production that such relations are part of.

In this paper, I prefer to follow a different route. Instead of getting lost in a useless attempt to classify these relations, I believe it is more sensible, when considering the Brazilian case, to begin by describing them, exposing the complex and contradictory web of connections that gives them life and meaning. Especially because one can easily verify that the type of slavery to which I refer – debt bondage – is found in different economic activities, organized according to extreme and varying degrees of economic and technical modernization. On the one hand, there are economies that still follow 19th and even 18th century standards, like certain sectors of Amazon extractivism, especially rubber extraction. On the other, there are activities – namely the new cattle-breeding farms in the Amazon – developed by modern companies, some of which are linked to powerful and wellknown international economic groups. We are not, therefore, only facing the phenomenon of the persistence of archaic labour relations that, at first sight, have often been defined as pre-capitalist. What we observe here is that modern capitalist companies that invest in agriculture and cattle-breeding ventures in the huge region of the Brazilian Amazon (more than half the territory of a country with approximately eight and a half million square kilometers) have routinely resorted to debt bondage in some of their activities.[1]

---

1. An as-yet incomplete list of enterprises whose farms use slave labour includes the following: Bradesco – Banco Brasileiro de Descontos S.A.; BCN – Banco de Crédito Nacional; Banco Bamerindus; Sílvio Santos; Bordon; Liqüifarm; Daniel Keith Ludwig; Manah; Camargo Corrêa: Eletronorte; Café Cacique; Volkswagen (that afterwards sold its farm in the Amazon to the Matsubara group); Supergasbrás and White Martins S.A.

My objective, therefore, is to suggest that a sociological comprehension of the persistence of such relations, and especially of their renewal in the last thirty years, as a practice adopted by companies whose economic logic, characteristically capitalist and modern, makes us suppose that the adoption of slavery by such companies would be contradictory and irrational. I prefer, therefore, not to follow the path already competently trodden by other researchers, who believe that they can base their analyses of the problem on the very concept of these labour relations. An *a priori* definition can be a trap that will make us lose sight of details and diversities of the problem that are essential for its comprehension.

Although we are dealing with a variation of peonage or debt bondage I prefer, in the Brazilian case, to consider it as a form of *temporary debt bondage*. It is similar to slavery in that it rests on the belief that the boss may physically dispose of the worker, as his authority includes life and death. The difference is that even during the period of legal slavery the murder of a slave by his master did not exempt the latter from crime he committed and its judgment although, once in court, he could count on the goodwill of his peers. In addition, at that time slaves were an investment, and it was therefore irrational to kill or mutilate them even if they committed a grievous fault. In today's situation debts are manipulated and the peons are not, strictly speaking, the property of their bosses, nor do the bosses claim this. They are expendable workers, which attributes to this form of unfreedom the nature of temporary slavery whose duration is regulated by the farm's labour needs. In some farms in Brazil the argument that has justified the persecution, capture, torture – and even murder – of peons who try to escape is that, as they were advanced money or foodstuffs by their boss, they are the repositories of the boss' property, and any escape is considered attempted theft. It is, in fact, the moral factor that makes many of these workers submit themselves for some time to the captivity to which they are subjected.[2]

2. Even before this debt bondage in the Amazon rubber plantations was a matter of record, and the subject of well-founded accusations. On this point, see for example the series of essays by da Cunha, written at the beginning of the century, and also the classic novel written by de Castro in 1934. Da Cunha, *Á Margem da História*; Castro, *A Selva*. Ferreira de Castro himself lived and worked in a rubber plantation, and personally witnessed the events described in his book involving enslaved rubber tappers. The press has periodically denounced cases of slavery in Brazil; in 1913, for example, a working-class newspaper reported the occurrence of slavery in the tea plantations of the Cia. Mate Laranjeiras, in the Paraná State: "Horrendous worker enslavement in the State of Paraná", 32, 1913, p. 1. Silence about modern slavery or bondage in Brazil was broken by the Pastoral Letter written by father Pedro Casaldáliga in 1971, when he became the bishop of São Félix do Araguaia, in Mato Grosso. See Casaldáliga, *Uma Igreja da Amazônia em Conflito com o Latifúndio e a Marginalização Social*, pp. 104–118. It was also broken by the journalist Lúcio Flávio Pinto, whose accusations concerning this issue were subsequently published in book form. Pinto, *Amazônia: No Rastro do Saque*, pp. 99–104. After 1975 the occurrence of bondage was systematically denounced by the Land Pastoral Commission. More recently, international human rights organizations have conducted their own investigations

The isolation and size of most farms accused of employing slave labour and the fact that unfreedom has been illegal in Brazil since 1888, made direct collection of data on the subject at the sites charged with holding workers captive almost impossible. Even inspectors from the Ministry of Labour have found it difficult to investigate the accusations of slavery that reach the Regional Labour Departments.

The broadest and most systematic source of data has been information published by newspapers when the accusations are investigated by the Federal Police, legally in charge of repressing the slave trade. Most of the period studied corresponds to Brazil's military dictatorship (1964-1985), when the press was censored by the police. In major newspapers, especially between 1970 and 1984, news about slavery was, in fact, news about the results of actions taken by the police to investigate accusations of enslavement. This means that in a way the instances were confirmed by the police; this fact allowed them to be divulged. Important alternative sources for this and for later periods are newsletters and internal publications of Catholic dioceses and parishes and the newsletters of the Pastoral Land Commission, both the one published by the national secretariat and by its regional agencies.

The most reliable information are precisely the data collected systematically after 1975 by the Pastoral Land Commission of the National Conference of Brazilian Bishops, that continued the work conducted along these lines by a few bishops and their pastoral agents. The data have a somewhat individual nature, being classified by each farm, and are based on accusations made directly by workers who flee and, pursued and threatened, who usually seek the protection of priests or bishops in nearby villages. Usually the priests register the cases in writing, often authenticating them with the signature or fingerprint of the worker concerned – if possible with witnesses. Sometimes the document is registered with an official notary, the idea being to ensure the possibility of subsequent legal proceedings against the persons responsible for violating the labour legislation. Then the workers are sent to the appropriate trade union and to the local police authorities, so that legal measures can be taken. At other times the workers go directly to the trade union or seek help from the local police. The trade unions usually pass this information onto the National Trade Confederation, in Brasilia, which in turn generally submits the case formally to the Federal Police so that the latter can, following its mandate, order the regional police departments to take the measures necessary to free the workers still enslaved at the farm charged. Usually the intervention of the Federal Police is in favor of the workers, and thereafter the information gets to the newspapers.

into unfreedom in different regions of Brazil, and have published useful reports about this. See Watch, *Violência Rural no Brasil*, pp. 102-117; Sutton, *Slavery in Brazil*.

Information on all these cases, both that obtained from Church and from other sources, are classified and filed at the Pastoral Land Commission in Goiânia and at the respective regional agencies of the States where the problem occurs.

In addition to extensive use of data from this archive I also used detailed notes by Father Antonio Canuto and other pastoral agents about instances of peonage at the prelacy of São Félix do Araguaia after 1970; the prelacy covers a large part of north Mato Grosso. Several cases of debt bondage were registered, especially during the 1970s. I also used the detailed notes made by Father Ricardo Rezende and pastoral agents of the diocese of Conceição do Araguaia, that covers a large part of the south of Pará. These two areas comprise the part of the Brazilian Amazon where the most typical and notorious cases of debt bondage have occurred.

I analyzed all the cases in detail, and eliminated those without sufficient proof of physical intimidation to keep the peons captive at the farms. I also excluded cases involving instances of marked and inhuman exploitation of workers not necessarily through debt bondage.

In addition, I personally interviewed young peons who had escaped from Cascalheira, in the north of Mato Grosso. I also interviewed men known as "gatos" ("cats"), contractors who arrange slave labour for the farms; and I interviewed prostitutes in Porto Alegre do Norte, also in Mato Grosso, as they are often subordinated in ways similar to the peons, and are among the first people the latter contact when they manage to recover their freedom and get to a village.[3] The peons usually tell the prostitutes about the violence they underwent. Often the prostitutes are privileged sources of information about what happens to workers on the farms, information to which researchers have no access. In one case, after initial agreement, my attempt to accompany one of the slave labour contractors to the jungle where he held a group of workers captive failed, and I was left "forgotten" by a road for several hours until someone from a nearby village told me that the "gato" had left well before the time agreed on, taking several new workers with him.

Based on the number of workers – approximately 85 thousand – whose unfreedom was denounced and documented after 1970, compared to other indications concerning the total number of workers employed in specific farms during the same period for deforestation, I estimated that the real number of

3. I am grateful to Jan Rocha, who let me use some of her own data about peonage; to Ana de Souza Pinto, who made very valuable suggestions concerning contacts and interviews in Ribeirão Cascalheira, in the North of Mato Grosso; and also to Sister Mercês, who provides prostitutes with assistance and religious counselling in Porto Alegre do Norte – in the same State – where she works as a missionary and a nurse, and who drew my attention to the link between peonage and prostitution.

the peons trapped in temporary bondage during the period concerned was between 250 thousand and half a million.

II

The repeated accusations after 1970 of the occurrence of slavery in Brazil – especially in the Amazon region – suggest the necessity of critical theoretical reflection on the extensive diversity of labour relations in capitalist society. They suggest moreover that capitalist relations are not necessarily defined by a typical, rational and legal standard, that is, that they are unproblematically contractual, presupposing a juridically equal treatment among entrepreneurs and workers.[4]

The situation that makes this supposition feasible began to develop in 1966, when the military dictatorship put in place an extensive program for the economic development of the Brazilian Amazon on a supposedly modern basis. Although historically a slow, spontaneous process of settlement, occupation and development "of the West" and – after the mid-fifties – of the Mid-West and North of the country, the military regime decided to speed up and define the characteristics of this settlement, and to control it. The objectives were economic, but also – and especially – geo-political. The axiom of the dictatorship was to "integrate" (the Amazon to Brazil) "so as not to deliver it" (to supposedly greedy foreign powers). The military spoke of "occupying the empty areas", although the region was actually already occupied by dozens of indigenous tribes – many of them never contacted by whites – as well as by a dispersed but settled peasant population which had been in the area since at least the 18th century.

In view of these concerns the type of occupation proposed was contradictory: cattle-breeding, an economic activity that waives labour and empties territories. Estimates were that a maximum of only forty thousand new jobs would be created in all that huge area. Not to mention that, because of the type of

---

4. Both Marx and Weber emphasized the centrality to the reproduction of capital of the free wage relation based on the commodification of labour power by the worker concerned. On this point, Marx observes: "In and for itself, the exchange of commodities implies no other relations of dependence than those which result from its own nature. On this assumption, labour power can appear on the market only if, and in so far as, its possessor, the individual whose labour power it is, offers it for sale or sells it, as a commodity. In order that its possessor may sell it as a commodity, he must have it at his disposal, he must be the free proprietor of his own labour-capacity, hence of his person." Karl Marx, *Capital*, I, pp. 270-271. In a similar vein, Weber notes: "It is a contradiction to the essence of capitalism, and the development of capitalism is impossible, if such a propertyless stratum is absent, a class compelled to sell its labour services to live; and it is likewise impossible if only unfree labor is at hand. Rational capitalistic calculation is possible only on the basis of free labour [...]". Weber, *General Economic History*, pp. 208-209; see also Weber, *Protestant Ethic*, p. 22.

occupation proposed, the indigenous tribes would suffer – as indeed they did – heavy demographic losses through the contact with white men and their diseases. A few tribes lost up to two-thirds of their population in these few years.[5] Not to mention that thousands of peasants would have to be expelled from the land they worked – as indeed they were – so that large grazing areas could take over their land.[6] Many of these peasants ended up migrating to towns in that same region, to live in misery, underemployment and slums. The new economic activities created the large modern landholdings, linked to powerful Brazilian and foreign economic conglomerates.

To achieve this end the Federal Government gave large companies, both Brazilian and multinational, tax incentives, that is, the possibility of a 50% rebate on the revenue tax owed by their ventures in the country's more developed areas. The condition was that this money would be deposited in the Banco da Amazônia, a federal bank and, after the approval of an investment project by government authorities, it would constitute 75% of the capital of a new company, either related to agriculture and cattle-breeding or to industry, always in the Amazon region. It was in effect a donation, not a loan.

The government acted thus to ensure the profitability of the new investments since, on principle, major entrepreneurs from banks, the industry and commerce had shown no interest in extending the activities of their capital to agriculture and cattle-breeding. This was not only due to the traditional characteristics of Brazilian agriculture, where the highest profit has always been obtained through the commercialization of agricultural produce, and not its production, but also to the ownership of land and thus the existence of ground rent, the classic obstacle to the expansion of capital in agriculture. As we know, the price of land represents a deduction from capital, thereby reducing the amount available for productive investment – the effective capitalist investment. The military government offered entrepreneurs in other sectors the reward of this donation of 75% of the capital they needed for the new venture. The entrepreneurs, in turn, would contribute with 25% of their own resources, or join large landowners to establish the new economic activities.

This was also a political option: by this means the government ensured the economic and political survival of the landholding oligarchies that controlled the regional power in the states of the Mid-West and North of Brazil. Thus they were not deprived of ground rent, a deprivation that would be an alternative solution, through an agrarian reform that would open the territory to capitalist expansion. The military government socialized the costs of capitalist occupation

5. See Martins, *Nossos Índios, Nossos Mortos*; Davis, *Victims of the Miracle*; Carelli and Severiano, *Mão Branca Contra o Povo Cinza*; José Porfírio Fontenele de Carvalho, *Waimiri-Atroari*.
6. See Casaldáliga, *Creio na Justiça e na Esperança*; Kotscho, *O Massacre dos Posseiros*; Figueira, *A Justiça do Lobo*, Figueira, *Rio Maria – Canto da Terra*; Souza, *O Empate Contra Chico Mendes*.

of the Amazon, transferring the price of the non-realization of agrarian reform to the whole of society. The meaning of that decision lies in the very fact that the class of landowners and the traditional oligarchies with a landholding base were an important social base to sustain the *coup d'état* and the military regime. The coup took place to deter a supposedly agrarian revolution with Communist leanings, begun by poor peasants, basically from the Northeast of Brazil.[7]

The rapid expansion of the pioneer front towards the Amazon occurred in a totally different context from what usually takes place in countries that serve as models for the discussion of the topic, like the U.S., for example. Instead of constituting an opening of the territory based on the values of democracy and freedom, the expansion was supported by the closed framework of a military dictatorship, repression and lack of political freedom. Above all, in an anti-Communist context where the working class, both in the towns and fields, became automatically suspect of subverting the political order whenever it reacted to the poor living conditions imposed by the regime. This repressive environment, associated to the fact that landowners and entrepreneurs were the main allies and beneficiaries of the military regime, created a highly adverse situation for both peasants and rural workers. In a country where the personal authority of large rural landowners is still the power of life or death, this engendered a situation where the exploitation of labour depended markedly on the will of the farmer or his proxies. In fact, the institutions of justice and of the police were severely weakened, when they did not openly connive with the enslavement of workers and the expulsion of peasants from the land, as is traditional in several remote areas of the country. Large landholdings have always been enclaves, governed by their own specific, although illegal, criteria of justice; places subject to the will of the landowners, who consequently became, and are still, the owners of consciences and of human beings.

This extraordinary power was consolidated by the transformation of large entrepreneurs into landowners, as well as the size of landholdings. The fact that the new rural landowners came from an urban, a modern and a more properly capitalist tradition in no way prevented their farms from reproducing the type of domination, repression and violence associated historically with agrarian property and power. This was partly because modern landowners were physically absent, and therefore tended to delegate authority and with it the responsibility for the management of their property to intermediaries – the managers and overseers – who were steeped in the tradition of personal power. The latter was also compounded by the financial power these landowners wielded.

---

7. The issues that, prior to the military coup, defined and polarized the peasant movement of the Northeast of Brazil are described by two protagonists involved in the events: Julião, *Cambão*, and Moraes, "Peasant Leagues in Brazil", pp. 435-501.

I believe that a description of what occurred on the 431 farms, where it is known that there was slave labour between 1970 and 1993, and in regard to which I was able to collect information, is an appropriate starting point to analyze the problem of debt bondage in contemporary Brazil. Of these farms, 308 are in the Amazon and 123 elsewhere. Specifically on these farms it was estimated that, taking into account the accusations made at different times, more than 85 thousand workers were enslaved. This is a conservative estimate, in that at least this many workers could be said to be held in captivity. The figure itself was arrived at from statements made by peons who managed to escape from these farms, and who made accusations to the authorities (like the Federal Police, legally responsible for eradicating slave labour and any trade in human beings, and the local or regional agents of the Labour Ministry). This figure, however, is well below the real figure. In their excellent study of the pioneer front, Branford and Glock estimate that at the start of the seventies, there were 250–400 thousand peons working on farms in the Amazon during the dry season. The government of the state of Maranhão estimated that in 1975 there were approximately one hundred thousand peons originally from that state working on farms in the Amazon.[8] A single farm, Suiá-Missú, employed approximately three thousand peons during the phase of deforestation. Its project foresaw that, once this phase ended, there would only be 250 fixed employees on the property of almost 700 thousand hectares, of which approximately 217 thousand hectares were included in agricultural and cattle-raising activities.[9]

Almost nine thousand workers managed to escape from captivity, mostly from farms in the Amazon. They constitute 10.2% of the peons whose plight as unfree workers was denounced all over the country, and 13.1% of those in the Amazon. In 18.3% of the farms peons were murdered, usually when they tried to escape, pursued by gunmen. The proportion is higher in the Amazon: 22.7%. In addition, peons were tortured in 33.4% of all the farms, and in 37% of the farms listed in the Amazon. In spite of these adverse conditions, all over Brazil rebellions by peons were recorded in only 5.6% of the farms denounced for enslaving their workers, and in 6.5% of those in the Amazon.

III

I believe that these data suggest, from the start, that the main issue is not whether or not this is slavery. The situation certainly does not suggest that we are in the presence of what theoreticians call "free labour". It is equally clear, however,

8. See Branford and Glock, *Last Frontier*, p. 55.
9. See Müller *et al.*, "Amazônia, Desenvolvimento Sócio-Económico e Políticas de População", p. 161; Casaldáliga, *Uma Igreja da Amazônia*, p. 49.

that we are in the presence of what is undeniably a capitalist system. I agree with authors who consider that today's slavery is a component of the very process of capital accumulation. One of these is Brass, who says that "capitalism is not only compatible with unfree labour, but in certain situations prefers it to a free workforce".[10] I agree with Brass' view that capital may actually prefer unfree labour, and his conclusion that deproletarianization is determined by class struggle. But I believe that this depends on the circumstances of the development of capital, and on its reproduction on an extensive scale; that is, the reproduction of the social, political and cultural circumstances of accumulation, the historical consequences, and also the circumstances surrounding class struggle. The conceptual usefulness of deproletarianization is that it explains the active involvement of capital in establishing coercive forms of labour which can encompass, in a case like Brazil's, a conduct that will *prevent* the full and definitive conversion of peons into a proletariat.[11] This is especially true in contexts of major ethnic and social conflict, such as the struggles taking place in the Amazon regions that involve either indigenous populations or peasants.

We can say that capital both removes and dissolves social (and production) relations that block its reproduction on an extensive scale when it includes to its reproduction persistent relations that, even if temporarily, cannot be substituted. In this sense capital in effect *re-creates* them, but now as a moment of its reproductive process. The relations seem the same, but they are now different; that is, they are a social form bearing new determinations that result from the mediation of capital at the moment of its reproduction on an extensive scale.

In fact, the problem of the persistence or the renewal of contemporary forms of slavery has the sociological importance of an analyzer-revealer[12] that allows us to extend our understanding of what capitalism is a century after Marx' analysis, when these differences could be attributed to the social, economic and political structures of a past that was still very close. Misleadingly, they often seemed to be mere survivors of a non-capitalist mode of production not yet totally destroyed by capitalism, when they were actually being reproduced by capital itself.

The most notable component of this incorporation (and, therefore, not a transition) was the capitalist re-definition of ground rent and the very genesis of capitalist land ownership. This type of ground rent was preceded by labour

---

10. See Brass, "Some Observationson Unfree Labour", this volume, pp. 57-75.
11. The concept "deproletarianization" is central to the analysis of unfree labour developed by Brass in a number of texts. Brass, "Slavery now", pp. 187.
12. According to Lefebvre, certain situations of social crisis serve as analyzers and revealers, not only because they allow a better sociological understanding, but also because they very clearly show the social contradictions. See Lefebvre, *Survie du Capitalisme*, p. 16. See also Lefebvre, *De l'État*, IV, p. 232-233; and Gutterman and Lefebvre, *Conscience Mystifiée*, p. 3.

rent, by rent in kind and by money rent. Money rent is not always capitalist ground rent because it preserves the nature of a personal tribute, a deduction from the gain of the work on the land, paid by the peasant to the landowner. Capitalist ground rent appears, obviously as money rent, when it stops being a personal tribute and becomes a social tribute. This is only possible when part of the total surplus value is transferred to the landowner in the price of the products sold and added to the surplus value he extracted from his own workers. This is made feasible by the different organic composition of capital in agriculture and industry. The difference between the average and low organic composition of capital in agriculture appears in ground rent, as if nobody paid it, while in fact the whole of society now owes this tribute to the landowner due simply to the fact that he has a deed of ownership and, therefore, charges for the use of his land.[13]

Capitalism is certainly not constituted only by the oppression and violence inherent in peonage in today's Brazil. But capitalism is emphatically also the sum total of the social processes, the procedures and the situations that this kind of relationship reveals. To explain this we must understand that the time of capital is not concretely only the unilinear time of progress, of modernization, of rational conduct as regards aims and development. We cannot attribute to moments, circumstances and specificities of the process of capital reproduction formal characteristics whose validity fundamentally refers to its overall process and, especially, to its overall trends, identified in the models of interpretation and in theory. The time of reproduction of capital is the time of contradiction; not only a contradiction of opposing interests, like those dividing classes, but of mismatched temporalities and, therefore, social realities that develop at a different pace, even if based on the same basic conditions. Henri Lefebvre suggests, very appropriately, that the interpretation of capitalism contained in Marx's *Capital* is based on the idea of *equal development* and that *Grundrisse*, from the same author, is based on the idea of the *unequal development* of capital, where the components of the process are not governed by the same pace and temporalities. Productive forces develop more quickly than social relations; in capitalism, the production is social, but the appropriation of the results of production is private. This fundamental contradiction announces the historic mismatch between material and social progress. The inequality of development is expressed in clashes that reveal diversities, and not uniformities, within the same economic and social reality.[14]

This characteristic of the process of capital accumulation, even in industry, often appears in the technical mismatch of the different moments of the labour

---

13. See De Souza Martins, "A sujeição da renda da terra ao Capital", pp. 151-177.
14. See Lefebvre, *Pensée de Lénine*, pp. 206 ff.

process. Each moment's technological development is different and therefore implies different social forms of extracting the economic surplus and hence the exploitation of the worker directly involved in this. It is necessary, therefore, to know *what tasks currently employ slave labour,* so as to *understand it as a moment of the process of capital.* My data indicate that in the Amazon 72.7% of the peons are employed in the deforestation of virgin forest for the subsequent creation of pasture for cattle. Outside the Amazon, only 26.2% of the peons are occupied in deforestation or reforestation. Both activities concern developing farms; that is, transforming raw nature into the basis of a profitable economic venture, a process that is not so dramatic, long-lasting or extensive as in industry. Throughout the country, 53.3% of the peons enslaved were employed in such tasks. In the Amazon, only 12.2% of the peons were used for permanent work in agriculture and cattle-raising; that is, in routine activities on already existing farms. All over Brazil, 34.4% of the enslaved peons were employed in these occupations.

Comparing two different periods – that until the end of the dictatorship in 1984, and the post-dictatorship period from 1985 on – the annual average of denunciations of slavery almost doubled, leaping from 13.5 to 25.1. In the Amazon the number rose from 9.8 to 17.7 cases a year. At the same time, when we consider the specific case of the Amazon, it is possible to observe that the occurrences move progressively from the Mid-West to the North, following the movement of the pioneer front: in 1970-1973, 52.5% of the cases related to the Mid-West, while in 1990-1993 only 36.8% of the cases occurred there. By contrast, occurrences in the North rose from 47.8% to 63.2% in those same years.

Thus, on the pioneer front, slave labour is being used mainly outside the labour process; that is, external to the normal and permanent process of effective capitalist production. In that sense, it is the use of work in the specific tasks of a situation of *primitive accumulation.* This concept is better defined if, in addition to considering the expropriation that forces the return of the workers to the labour market, we also consider that at this moment of expropriation of the means of existence is prolonged in the overexploitation of the workforce. That is, when the object of work is their own survival, or that of their families; when they are denied even the possibility of securing basic needs and subsistence, by having to work more than the normal working hours, even beyond the additional work extorted under the guise of the wages and the contractual nature of the relationship between employer and employee. This is clear when, at the end of several months' work, the worker has nothing coming to him in the form of wages; much rather the contrary, he must himself still pay something to the person who employed him. It is, in fact, a procedure that is part of the same confiscatory framework where the worker is deprived of the means of production he still retains, like the land and tools, because overexploitation introduces difficulties (diseases and indebtedness, for example, or even his death) that slowly incorporate him and/or his family into the so-called industrial reserve army of labour, the workforce available for capital.

This type of exploitation of labour translates into primitive accumulation, because it is, in part, the production of capital within the process of reproduction of capital on an extensive scale. This is clear if we understand that, historically, we can talk about capitalist *reproduction* of capital, a reproduction of capital based on formally capitalist production bases. But we can't really talk about *capitalist* production of capital, because the production of capital involves mechanisms and procedures that are specific to primitive accumulation. It involves, therefore, the conversion of non- or pre-capitalist means and situations into tools of capitalist production itself; that is, the production of surplus value. Essentially, what defines the process is not the result, but the *way, or mode* it was obtained; that is, the mode of production of the economic surplus. The result is a capital that is unambiguously capitalist, but the way of obtaining it is not itself recognisably capitalist. What peonage has promoted on the pioneer front, at least since the expansion of Brazilian coffee plantations towards the West of São Paulo in the nineteenth century, is the production of farms[15], and not, essentially, the production of goods from farms for the consumer market. In other words: *especially in recent cases, peonage has produced the means of production to be used by capitalists to produce goods.* And neither properly nor directly the actual goods themselves. In that sense, the recent Brazilian case shows that the *territorial expansion of capital* and its extension to agricultural and cattle-breeding activities do not occur either exclusively or predominantly as the result of the reinvestment of capital in a new economic sector. On the contrary: it is based on tax incentives and government subsidies, and on the non-capitalist use of labour necessary for the actual founding of the new venture.[16] In other words: in these instances, the reproduction of capital on an extensive scale includes non-capitalist production of capital.

15. De Souza Martins, "A produção capitalista de relações não-capitalistas de produção", pp. 9-93.
16. A survey conducted in 1970 showed that in the north of Mato Grosso, in the Mid-West region, 66 companies had already obtained the approval of the Federal Government and were installing themselves in the region, all of them with 75% of their capital coming from tax incentives (that is, government donations). The total area occupied by 51 of them was almost 2.2 million hectares (an average of 43 thousand hectares each). See Casaldáliga, *Uma Igreja da Amazônia,*, pp. 49-59. Dennis Mahar has made some calculations about the economic impact of cash payment on the running costs of a "seringal" – a rubber-tree plantation where latex is extracted – when compared with the truck system (worker indebtedness linked to the "barracão", or the farm store). In the case of cash payments, the revenue of the rubber plantation was 7.7% below its costs. In the case of the truck system, by contrast, the revenue was 22.5% higher than the costs. In other words, by paying wages such an enterprise would suffer losses, whereas peonage would yield a handsome profit. See Dennis J. Mahar, *Desenvolvimento Económico na Amazônia*, p. 207.

This characteristic of the peonage system has been recurrent in Brazilian history, even at the time of chattel slavery, when slaves were an expensive investment for farmers. While the farms were being developed free workers were used, instead of slaves; the former worked as contract labour, in exchange for the right to cultivate food products. On the other hand they were obliged to clear the land and plant the young coffee bushes supplied by the farmer. They could also, for a time, plant corn and beans for their own consumption and eventually for sale, as well as the farmer's coffee. In short: with this phase of the formation of landholdings, farmers preferred to reduce their overall financial expenditure so as to invest it principally in productive operations, even if it meant the purchase of black slaves. This characteristic continues in the case of the current Amazon and the pioneer front.

If, especially during the recent period, peonage has been the predominant way of exploiting labour for the formation of new farms, there have been – and still are – other situations where it was and is the regular form of exploitation of labour in the routine production process. I refer to the so-called truck system employed in the production of rubber and Brazil nuts in Pará, in the Amazon region, a system of labour that was widely adopted especially after the 1870s and still persists, with alterations, in a few areas. Similar to peonage, the truck system has a variety of characteristics. As Teixeira observed in his excellent study on the rubber plantations, there are various, "relationships that develop under the aegis of the truck system".[17] Especially as this is the normal and permanent way to exploit labour, it produces social results that cannot be observed in the existing peonage system. The truck system has become not only a system of labour exploitation but also a system for political domination and the manifestation of personal power. In truth, it now totally regulates the social relations of workers in the rubber plantations. It has consolidated as a model of a relationship between workers and employers based on unequall access to property and assets. In the truck system, the core of the labour relations seems to constitute variations of a double *system of credit without money*, both banking and commercial,[18] where interest is charged extortionately in a chain of credit extending from the company that exports rubber to the rubber worker. Long-standing mechanisms of extortion and usury are in place; recent instances where the labour relations in the rubber plantation appear as form of land rent paid in kind, either with the entire production or with part of it, make it appear as if the core of the lien system was that of autonomous work, as if the worker were a peasant.[19] It also appears as exploitation effected indirectly at the level of circulation, and not directly as the exploitation of labour in the production process.

17. See Teixeira, "Aviamento e o Barracão", p. 3.
18. See the excellent study by Santos, *História Econômica da Amazônia*, pp. 155–175.
19. See Zanoni, "Os Seringueiros", p. 63.

The recent period of the development of peonage, at the start of the 1970s, was also the time of the so-called "Brazilian miracle", a time of great economic growth. The expansion of the frontier coincided with the expansion of investment alternatives in other economic sectors where, apparently, the profitability of capital was greater and quicker than in agriculture and cattle-breeding. It was even suggested, at the time, that there was a clandestine transfer of the tax incentives obtained by companies from the pioneer front to the more developed and industrialized area of the country, the Southeast, especially for financial investments. The creation of farms (or industries) in the Amazon was thus a way to obtain resources from the tax incentives. But this depended on antiquated and archaic mechanisms of exploitation of labour and accumulation of capital, with peonage and the violent dispossession of the original occupants of the land – the indigenous populations and the peasants or *posseiros*. The territorial expansion of capital could not depend on actual capital, attracted to more profitable sectors, re-establishing mechanisms and processes of primitive accumulation. The occupation of the frontier was therefore a marginal part of the process of reproduction of capital on an extensive scale, and the territorial expansion of capital itself a correspondingly diverse and specific form of its reproduction on an extensive scale. The objective of territorial expansion was not cattle-breeding but the production of farms.

The expansion of peonage in areas of traditional settlement and away from the pioneer front and from the Amazon region suggests, in principle, that this system of labour is by no means confined to labour-scarce areas of recent territorial occupation, although it is characteristic of them. In the non-Amazon areas, for example, 26.2% of the peons have been working in activities connected with setting up farms. It is, therefore, a phenomenon similar to the pioneer front and, in a way, a residual and belated indication both of the transition of the pioneer front into an area that is itself part of the domestic economy of the implementation of new economic activities – such as reforestation – in already settled areas. Farms employ 73.8% of the peons in permanent activities, including rural industries such as brick kilns, this being true of 4.9% of the peons employed outside the Amazon region. In agriculture these workers are employed to cut sugarcane, harvest coffee and forage grass for the subsequent creation of pastures. Such activities are seasonal, and wage labourers are generally employed. Their living conditions have been repeatedly denounced by trade unions and other agencies as being below levels necessary for the survival of workers and their families.[20] The appearance of cases of slavery in this type of

---

20. A study of the nutritional conditions of wage labourers who cut cane in the hinterland of São Paulo emphasizes that "the anthropometric examination of the families of wage labourers reveals a very poor physical condition in both adults and children, most of whom show signs of a first-degree deficiency in protein and calories". De Oliveira and De Oliveira (organizers),

work indicates not only the intensification of the exploitation of rural workers but also that *current slavery is, at its limit, an extreme variation of wage labour.*

The fact that its use occurs in sectors of the agricultural economy especially geared to the domestic market and to exports makes one believe that, in these cases, we are not dealing with the exploitation of labour by large capital enterprises engaged in primitive accumulation. My hypothesis, however, even in regard to non-pioneer regions, is that mechanisms and procedures of primitive accumulation may expand within the very process of capitalist reproduction on an extensive scale, especially in sectors on the margin of those with a greater vitality and economic profitability. We are, in fact, dealing with a situation of overexploitation. Capital can extract surplus value beyond the limits set by the reproduction of the workforce, paying the workers wages that are not enough even to replace their physical strength after a full day's work. In such instances, the insufficiency of the wage endangers the very survival of the worker and his family, and thus of the workforce as a whole; this disregard by capital for the physical survival of individual workers is possible only when the existence of an industrial reserve army makes it easy to substitute and/or discard labour.

What seems to explain the marked reduction of these workers' living standards is that they are employed in activities that are already part – even if only marginally – of a modern capitalist economy, where there is a great investment in the plantations or equipment. Theoretically, such ventures should have a high organic composition of capital; that is to say, the amount of variable capital (or capital used to buy labour power) should be proportionally less than the amount of constant capital (the capital expenditure on machinery, equipment and technology).

Due to the insertion of these new activities into the dynamic sectors of the economy, like industrial capital and financial capital, the yield of agricultural activities thus linked is determined by a given interest rate higher than the venture's real profit rate. This is so because the organic composition of capital of these new companies is in effect less than it should be. Precisely because of that the weakest sector in the ensemble of economic elements involved – the workforce – receives a residual remuneration when compared with the returns to capital, the profit rate being as a result on a par with that in the modern sector. Strategies to reduce wages are implemented without at the same time resulting in the development of productive forces and, consequently, do not lead to a reduction in the actual amount of work. These strategies allow the

---

"Bóias-frias", uma realidade brasileira, p. 112. The same team conducted evaluations of the physical conditions of the children of wage labourers, and concluded that "there is malnutrition among the teenage children of wage labourers, and that their growth and development, and similarly their physiological responses – including the capacity for work – were much reduced, when compared to 'wealthy' teenagers"; *ibid.*, pp. 128-129.

simultaneous reduction of the relative participation of variable capital compared to the constant capital in the organic composition of the company's capital. Although these sectors really have a small organic composition of capital, they operate as if they were sectors with a high organic composition of capital. In the end, this means that peons bear the burden in the form of increased levels of surplus – or unpaid labour – extracted.

This process is already in place in the case of wage labourers, whose labour power is frequently over-exploited. When this process of appropriation is aggravated due to the need on the part of capital to reduce its variable component – that is, the expenditure on wages – the exploitation of labour easily changes into peonage and the accompanying repressive mechanisms of debt bondage. This explains some of the labour problems in the sugar cane plantations of the sugar mills in Mato Grosso do Sul.

Basically, the mechanisms of unfreedom are the same as those which exist in the pioneer front for the specific purpose of setting up new farms in the Amazon area. In the latter context, however, it is obvious that labour scarcity is one of the reasons for employing coercive and violent methods to keep the workers on the farms. Enterprises in non-Amazon areas resort to peonage because they find it difficult to recruit workers at the low wages they are prepared to pay, especially as they operate in a context where many farms are competing for existing labour. Even so, *the reproduction of capital* on an extensive scale is guaranteed by the rapid use-up of labour power to a degree that undermines the physical reproduction of the workforce. This is achieved by the insertion of certain sectors and economic activities into the process of capitalist production, even if such sectors/activities do not themselves conform to the expected standards/conditions that usually structure relations between capital and labour.

IV

The Brazilian case suggests that the relationship between unfree labour and capital accumulation can be linked to the diverse functions that peonage discharges, a point which explains the extensive and persistent occurrence of debt bondage on large Brazilian farms, especially in the Amazon region.

In this connection it is important to point out substantial differences between the new forms of unfreedom and the historical form of chattel slavery, abolished in 1888. Chattel slavery was defined by customs and law, and made sense insofar as unfree workers were legally considered as goods, and thus property which could be disposed of by its owner. In the current situation, and depending on the nature of the circumstances, peons might or might not become goods in the sense of being the-property-of-another. *Peonage, therefore, is not an institution.*

This makes it difficult to understand the situation when the merely conceptual aspect of the problem is emphasized. In my case studies there are instances of slavery of short duration, the most common ones being those that occur during the dry season in the Amazon, a period when the forest is torn down and burned before the rain and the land is cleared to sow the forage grass. After this has been completed, the workers are free to leave. But there are also cases in the Amazon like that of the Tükuna indians, who in 1985 denounced two farmers for having enslaved them for two generations, a period of more than twenty years. Equally, there are instances of employers who, once their own work has been completed and on the pretext of cancelling labourers' debts, sell workers who owe them money to other farmers. In addition to such cases of the "chattelization" of human beings, there are others where the mechanism of indebtedness does not prevent the peon from retaining a little of the money he has earned during his period of employment. This is probably the most common occurrence. On occasion the peon is allowed to go to a nearby village at the week-end or once a month, which suggests that in such cases the debt mechanism is used to ensure that the peon will return to or continue with his work, and is thus not central to the process of capital accumulation. There are yet other instances, however, when peons are forbidden to leave the farm and/or the labour process even if they are suffering from malaria and need to go to hospital or see a doctor. Gunmen hired by the employers are responsible for preventing the peons from leaving. For example, at the Codeara Farm, in Mato Grosso, at the beginning of the 1970s, it was possible for a worker to leave only if he had a safe-conduct.

If it is necessary to explain peonage by the mechanisms of capital accumulation, as a part of the global process of accumulation, it is also necessary to understand that a large part of its dynamic is linked to what might be called *petty accumulation*. I refer here to the importance of peonage in the profits generated within the immediate world organized around its existence: the labour contractors who are responsible for recruiting workers, for the latter's initial indebtedness through cash advances given to the family of the peon, and who later on sell the peons to the farms; the owners of whorehouses in the area where the peons stay (who establish with their prostitutes a relation of unfreedom very similar to that linking employers to peons), where the peon who manages to save a little money from his wage spends a large part of this; the petty traders and/or merchants who sell clothes and other items (radios, watches, sunglasses); the owners of lodging houses where peons stay when they have run out of money, who sell them to a new contractor or recruiter looking for workers; the police, who at the request of a contractor arrest strangers at night, confiscate their belongings and then illegally charge them with the cost of their incarceration, a prison debt settled by the contractor who buys them and in this manner initiates a new cycle of debt and unfreedom; the gunmen, employed by the labour contractors and the farm overseer, who watch and punish the peons when they run away. There have been cases where these same gunmen killed the peons once the latter had been paid, ambushing them as they left the farm with their wages.

It is within this small universe that the complex web of social relations is created. This web reproduces the peon's unfreedom and changes over-exploitation into slavery. In this small universe slavery is reproduced, first of all, because it is especially within its ambit that the indebtedness of the peon is reproduced, and not necessarily on, or at least not always on, the farms themselves (because the latter need the workers only temporarily). Farms do not anyway appear as contexts *immediately* responsible for the enslavement of the peons; nor do they seem to be the main beneficiaries of the exploitation to which the peons are subjected. Within the farm economy, however, are to be found the mechanisms which determine the over-exploitation of the workers and, ultimately, their enslavement. That is; all these relations occur within the process of the reproduction of capital on an extended scale, but not always immediately within the capitalist work process itself.

Some of these petty accumulators on the pioneer front of Brazil go on to become firmly established merchants. At least one of them, who transported peons by airplane to the deforested clearings in the forest so as to establish new farms, organized a small air transport company that ended up becoming one of the most important regional airlines. Others migrated, following the dislocation of the pioneer front and of the peons. In truth, there are two totally distinct situations: that of smallscale economic activities which result from the money placed in circulation as a result of the peons who manage to pay their debts; and that of the intermediaries involved in recruitment and repression, who are a burden to the farms' payroll as they add to the cost of labour and are responsible for reductions in the real or nominal payment received by the workers.

The scarcity of labour in the areas where peonage has been employed is an important factor contributing to its reproduction. It is not, however, the only or the most important one when considered from the standpoint of the workers themselves. Basically, what the contractors do is to transfer workers from areas where there is a labour surplus to areas that need them. Because of the lack of data it is impossible to calculate accurately where the peons who work on farms accused of promoting enslavement come from and where they go.

It is, however, possible to group the farms by reference to the sites of origin and destination of the peons, taking into account only those for whom this kind of information exists. Of these farms, 74.1% are in the Amazon, and 25.9% in other regions. Of the farms in the Amazon, 59.2% recruited their peons in the Amazon itself, and 49.8% elsewhere. But it is always important to consider that recruitment in the Amazon nearly always means that a peon from the Amazon who works in a farm in Mato Grosso, for example, was probably recruited in the State of Goiás. That is, far from their original homes. Of the farms that are not in the Amazon, 0.5% of their peons were recruited in the Amazon, and 92.5% elsewhere. However, only 29.7% of the farms throughout the whole of Brazil have recruited their workers from the South and Southeast; that is, from the more modern areas, where workers enjoy permanent agricultural employment. Such workers are usually employed in these same regions, generally as wage labourers. It is therefore unusual to find them employed on farms elsewhere as unfree labour subordinated by means of the debt mechanism.

If we add the Mid-West, the North and the Northeast to the list of places where workers are recruited, we see that 70.4% of the farms all over Brazil that have slaves seek their peons in these particular regions (31.1% of farms recruit peons from the Northeast, the largest source of unfree labour in Brazil, and especially of peons recruited for the Amazon region). As has been suggested elsewhere, peons recruited from these areas come from small, impoverished farms,[21] and consequently hire themselves out in distant locations as seasonal wage-earners. Young family members do this between the end of the harvest and the beginning of the sowing season, for a number of different reasons. First, so as not to burden their family budget during this period of un- or under-employment. And second, in order to earn a little money for purchasing consumer items (a radio or clothes). The fact that an additional payment is frequently made by the labour contractor to the family for the work that one of its members will undertake not only constitutes the first step in what becomes a cycle of indebtedness but also makes the family itself an accomplice in this process of recruitment and enslavement.

All these reasons make it difficult to maintain that unfreedom is simply a way for farms to ensure a labour supply. The hypothesis that peonage emerges where there are no available lands, and where workers as a result do not have the possibility of becoming or remaining farmers[22] is not one borne out by evidence from the Amazonian frontier region. Since it is an area where so-called "free lands" still exist, and are therefore available for settlement by new farmers, the peons could ostensibly choose to work for themselves as farmers. This doesn't happen, however, for a number of reasons, all to do with the way peonage enters workers' lives. First, because of family ties, since kinsfolk elsewhere are waiting for them to return, preferably with money. Second, because the reason

21. See Esterci, "Campesinato e peonagem na Amazônia", p. 138; Esterci, "Peonagem na Amazônia", p. 125.
22. Bergad suggests that, in the case of nineteenth century Puerto Rico, the scarcity of workers was responsible for peonage; the latter emerged in order to prevent or pre-empt the potential access by workers to land. Bergad, "On Comparative History: A Reply to Tom Brass", pp. 154 ff. According to Bergad, therefore, the "closing of the frontier" in Puerto Rico put an end to the availability of free land and thus led to the proletarianization of workers. This argument has been challenged by Brass, "Free and Unfree Labour in Puerto Rico", pp. 187 ff.

for leaving the family is precisely to escape patriarchal power exercized over what is surplus (family) labour in a peasant economy; the only way of doing this is to work for someone who can pay cash for the peon's labour power.

Information obtained thus far, both by other researchers and also by myself, indicates that a large number of peons who have worked in the new farms in the Amazon are mainly young men who come from peasant families in the Northeast and Mid-West. There are, however, also cases of enslaved peons who were recruited in towns, or even large cities like Goiânia and Teresina.[23] Given the historical importance for peasant economy of the family cycle, and in particular the creation of new households as younger children leave the peasant family,[24] there will always be at such moments a powerful need for money on the part of a new generation. This origin in the cyclical nature of the peasant household seems essential to an understanding of why, despite accusations of violence and enslavement, peonage continues as a means of recruitment/ reproduction of the farm workforce. Peasants believe that they are migrating temporarily, to obtain an additional amount of cash at a moment when there is no work in the places they come from.

One of the reasons why workers accept the supposedly temporary condition of a peon is that *not all peons become slaves*. Probably most of the peons that have moved to the Amazon frontier, in spite of the dreadful working conditions there, do not effectively become slaves. The system in fact *works*, in that *the workers do not always end up in a system that they recognize as unfree*. Moreover, they enter a system of labour relations that is usually no worse than the one they are used to.

Peonage, therefore, is to be found at one end of a spectrum containing work relationships that are different from it. Peonage occurs when the unfree nature of labour dominates the relationship between peon and farm (which may explain why those who worry about the violation of human rights easily extend their denunciations to situations that cannot be formally qualified as peonage). The material I have assembled about peonage indicates that a worker only becomes aware of his condition of slavery when he realizes that he is not free to leave the farm; unfreedom is therefore not linked even to debt, since the surrender by the peon of wages earned can itself be justified ideologically by the condition of indebtedness (it seems "natural" in other words). Hence the awareness of unfreedom emerges when the gunmen at the farm show their weapons, or in front of others torture workers who have tried to escape without paying their

---

23. This was the case of 42 men recruited in July, 1984, at the Vila São Francisco, a poor quarter in Teresina (state capital of Piauí), with many underemployed workers, to work in the deforestation of the Fazenda Santa Rosa, in the south of Pará. See "Em busca de salário e comida", pp. 40-45.

24. See Esterci, "Campesinato e peonagem na Amazônia", p. 127; Esterci, "Peonagem na Amazônia", p. 124; Esterci, *Conflito no Araguaia*, p. 169; Esterci, *Escravos da Desigualdade*, p. 107.

debts. Awareness of unfreedom is also hightened both when gunmen kill a runaway and leave his body exposed for all to see, or when they cut him up and feed the pieces to the pigs. The object of such actions is precisely to highten the awareness of unfreedom, since it is by this kind of demonstration that other peons are terrorized and disuaded from running away, as happened in the Jandaia Farm, State of Pará, in 1990.[25] The awareness of unfreedom that produces criticism of labour relations and classifies them as slavery is a fluid awareness. Despite the fact that labour conditions are identical, such awareness may appear in one context but not in another; its emergence depends therefore on a large variety of circumstances which define the peon's consciousness.

This suggests a situation in which rural labour relations combine ideological innovations and a tradition of exploitation with diversified times and histories. That is, there is an apparent persistence of components of past unfreedom that were not totally abolished or overcome, because their conditions of reproduction also persist. Among the latter is the fact that a certain culture of servitude and personal dependence is still evident among the urban and rural poor. It is no exaggeration to recall that poor peasants in areas where peonage occurs themselves display both a contempt towards and a fear of peons, and consider them rootless, feckless and "dangerous" – the same attitudes in fact as those which structured the perception of black slaves in Brazil until the 19th century.[26]

Farms prefer to employ peasants on a temporary basis, during a period when their labour power is not required elsewhere. Such workers, therefore, tend not to make demands for improvements in (or complain about) this employment, its conditions and remuneration. Furthermore, in this case the workforce does not circulate following the rules governing a perfect market,[27] because the supply of work is only partially determined by the conditions of worker survival. This situation is widespread in Brazil, and includes people who work temporarily in towns, in civil construction and other heavy and badly paid jobs, just so as to contribute to the family income.[28] Especially prized is the temporary freedom that younger children obtain between harvests; the opportunity of working on

25. See "Fazendeiro mantém trabalho escravo em Xinguara (PA)", p. 6; *O Estado de S. Paulo* (São Paulo, 26 July 1990), p. 22.
26. See Esterci, "Campesinato e peonagem na Amazônia", p. 134; and Lisansky, "Santa Terezinha", p. 215. People still recall that during the sixteenth and seventeenth centuries the term "peon" applied to those who – being too poor to afford a horse – were forced to go on foot, and to walk without shoes. Hence the word identified a basic difference in the social hierarchy, between those who gave orders and were waited upon, and those who obeyed orders and did the waiting. In the culture of the Brazilian poor, this kind of symbolism is an important indicator of social position (and the presence or absence of domination linked to this).
27. In his study of peonage in Mexico, Peru, Argentina and Colombia, Bauer concludes that its existence indicates the presence of an "imperfect labour market". Bauer, "Rural Workers in Spanish America", pp. 34-63.
28. See De Oliveira, *Nordestinos em São Paulo*.

their own behalf instead of for the family. In this situation, modern companies, especially in the agriculture and livestock sector, can take advantage of a temporary supply of surplus and unqualified labour that would be unavailable on a permanent basis. Away from their homes and from the vigilance and discipline of parents – and, therefore, also of wives[29] – the worker is more vulnerable to recruitment, and complacent about poor labour conditions, low payment and violation of labour rights.

Of course this also occurs as a consequence of the poverty and lack of job opportunities in the peons' home area. But it is the consequence, above all, of the growing need for money, itself a result of increasing commodification linked to a decline in the terms of trade between produce sold and consumed by peasants. It is therefore clear that overexploitation affects not only the peons themselves but also their entire family group, and thus the basis of their reproduction as a workforce for capital. Finally, by these very means, capital takes advantage of the differences in price, cost and need between different regions and sectors of the economy.[30] This is the shape taken by the difference between those sectors totally dominated by the mediation of capital and those sectors only externally affected by this mediation. In the latter case, the reproduction of the workforce only tangentially depends on the resources produced directly by means of capital. Capital therefore obtains a competitive advantage from the deadening of the awareness of its peons when they use as a measure of the value of their labour power the notion of play and superfluousness.[31]

---

29. See Esterci, *Conflito no Araguaia*, pp. 145 and 167; Esterci, "Campesinato e peonagem na Amazônia", p. 130.
30. In my view, the situation is similar to that of African workers in France, immigrants from the former colonies, whose labour power is purchased below its value. See Meillassoux, "Desenvolvimento ou Exploração", pp. 57-70.
31. Noting the role of labour contractors, Esterci comments that they "can give 'bonuses' – cash advances – either for 'fun', as they call it, [for workers] to have a good time before going back to work, or to pay off the debts already contracted, or for the upkeep of their [the workers'] families when they leave their homes to go and work". Esterci, "Campesinato e peonagem na Amazônia", p. 128.

Wage Labor, Free Labor, and Vagrancy Laws:
The Transition to Capitalism in Guatemala, 1920-1945[*]

David McCreery

> [P]roperty in money, means of subsistence, machines, and other means of production does not as yet stamp a man as a capitalist if the essential complement to these things is missing: the wage-labourer, the other man, who is compelled to sell himself of his own free will.[1]

During the early 1920s a debate broke out in the Guatemala City newspapers over the need for labor reform in the coffee export sector. This is of interest not only because in past years material of substance rarely appeared in the press, but because labor was, and had been for half a century, the coffee elite's most vexing concern. Whereas the country possessed abundant land for coffee and since the 1870s had received a substantial inflow of foreign capital, *brazos* ("arms" = workers), planters complained unceasingly, were in constant short supply. Whether such shortages were real or imagined, and whether, if real, they persisted because of population declines, because workers fled from the abusive practices of the *fincas* (coffee estates) and the state, or because of an innate reluctance of the Indian to abandon a life of sloth and vice was much discussed after 1920, as was what should or could be done about it. The debate waned in 1924 when coffee prices revived, only to appear again in 1928-29 with the first indications of the Great Depression. This unprecedented airing of the labor question set the framework for a major overhaul of the laws governing rural workers in the 1930s. The operation of these laws, in turn, helped expose conditions that prompted an end to legal extra-economic coercion and the transition to capitalist free labor in 1944-45. Why, in a period of little more than

---

[*]   The author wishes to thank William Roseberry, Charles Bergquist, Chris Lutz, and Steve Webre for their comments. Research in Guatemala was carried out under a Fulbright Research grant. This paper appeared first in a slightly different version in William Roseberry, Lowell Gudmundson, and Mario Samper (eds), *Coffee, Society, and Power in Latin America* (Baltimore, 1995).

1.   Marx, *Capital*, 1, p. 932.

twenty years, did Guatemala's landed elite abandon a four hundred year old system of labor mobilization and control that apparently had served them well?

From the Conquest, the cash/export sector of Guatemalan's agricultural economy had relied on coerced labor.[2] Though black slavery was of little consequence and abolished soon after independence, the colonial system of forced labor drafts called *repartimientos* or, after 1821, *mandamientos*, as well as debt peonage persisted into the twentieth century. When agricultural elites shifted from cochineal to coffee in the 1860s and 1870s, export production expanded to an unexampled degree, engrossing large areas of the country until then little touched by export agriculture. A new generation of Liberals rode the coffee boom to power in 1871, organizing a relatively efficient, centralized state that rested on a professionalized army and *ladino*[3] militia and that was able to project an unprecedented presence into the countryside. To mobilize workers for coffee the state expanded the use of *mandamientos* and peonage and pushed the search for labor deep into the western highlands and the Alta Verapaz, where most of the majority indigenous population lived. The two labor forms of forced drafts and debt peonage made an interlocking system: under the 1894 general labor law[4] only a debt of at least $15 *pesos* for work on an export *finca* exempted the Indian, in law if not always in fact, from the hated *mandamientos*. This was a powerful incentive. A few Indians for personal reasons abandoned their communities and took up residence permanently on the fincas as *colonos* (resident workers), but most continued to live as subsistence farmers and handicraft manufacturers or traders in the highlands and to go reluctantly to the fincas two or three months a year to clean the groves and to collect the harvest.

Coercion worked, and it helped to guarantee substantial profits for Guatemala's coffee producers, but the uncertainties attendant on World War I and the price instabilities that followed made planters increasingly uneasy about the condition of the economy. Exports had peaked in 1906 and stagnated thereafter:

2. Material on agricultural labor before 1920 is drawn from two articles by McCreery, "Debt Peonage in Rural Guatemala", pp. 735-759, and "Odious Feudalism", pp. 99-117, as well as McCreery, *Rural Guatemala*, chs 3, 7 and 8. Except for rare instances when women were drafted as cooks, forced labor and vagrancy laws applied only to men; women could and did enter into debt peonage relations, either by contracting their services or as a result of relations with a male relative, but men overwhelmingly predominated in this category too.

3. In Guatemala, a *ladino* is an individual of "national" or "Spanish" culture, though the differences are often expressed in racial or even "caste" terms. Ladinos hold themselves superior to Indians and use this supposed superiority to belittle and exploit the indigenous population. On *ladinos* see, Colby and Van den Berghe, *Ixil Country*; and Warren, *Symbolism*.

4. Mendez, *Leyes vigentes de agricultura*, pp. 203-8.

Table 1. Coffee Exports (5 years average quintales)

1900-1904	681,368qq	1920-1924	930,983qq
1905-1909	807,914qq	1925-1929	992,516qq
1910-1914	773,765qq	1930-1934	963,979qq
1915-1919	845,282qq	1935-1939	990,249qq

Sources: Chester Lloyd Jones, *Guatemala, Past and Present* (Minneapolis, 1940), p. 210; Grieb, *Guatemalan Caudillo*, p. 147. 1 *quintal* = 100 pounds

While world prices for coffee in these years tended to swing in wild and unpredictable arcs:

Table 2. Guatemalan Coffee Prices (U.S. Dollars per quintal)

1915	13.63	1924	24.74	1934	10.31
1916	13.47	1925	27.89	1934	12.11
1917	11.83	1926	26.95	1935	9.31
1918	14.23	1927	25.10	1936	9.73
1919	26.26	1928	25.33	1937	11.10
1920	20.36	1929	22.54	1938	9.38
1921	14.58	1930	16.55	1939	9.45
1922	16.52	1931	15.20		
1923	17.83	1933	11.82		

Source: International Institute of Agriculture, *The World's Coffee*

A decline in the value of the country's paper money against gold, from 6 *pesos* to the United States dollar in 1900 to 54 *pesos* in 1922,[5] generally benefitted the planters, who sold abroad for hard currency and paid their production expenses at home in increasingly devalued *pesos*.[6] But by the late teens the *peso*'s gyrations had become so violent and so unpredictable that growers and merchants alike found it increasingly difficult to plan or to calculate costs and profits.[7] These problems, together with the government's dismal performance in the wake of a major 1917 earthquake and the 1918 flu pandemic, prompted many of the urban poor and middle groups, segments of the elite, and foreign diplomats to come together in 1920 to bring down long-time dictator Manuel Estrada Cabrera.

5. Young, *Central American Currency*, p. 39.
6. Real wages for agricultural workers fell sharply in these years: McCreery, "Debt Servitude", p. 749; on the advantages to the planters of a depreciating exchange rate see: Ministerio de Fomento, *Memorias-1902*, p. 136.
7. Bulmer-Thomas, *Political Economy*, p. 12.

The fall of Estrada Cabrera touched off a decade of uncertainty and change.[8] Among the first things to be ended were the *mandamientos*. If some writers argued that corvée labor was an embarrassment to a modern nation and a symbol of the hated past regime,[9] for most planters the real problem lay elsewhere. Above all, they lamented the *caciquismo* (bossism) that allowed state officials to manipulate the drafts to their own profit and the monopolization of labor by the more wealthy, and especially foreign, growers.[10] Most planters were happy to see *mandamientos* go. And debt peonage remained. By the 1920s most highland Indians owed money for labor to coffee plantations, but whatever their debt none would leave each year until they received a further advance from the *finca's* representative. The effect, together with *finca* and recruiter fraud, was that Indians rarely worked off what they were said to owe. Typically, their debt rose to far more than the nominal $15 pesos the law demanded, as Table 3 makes clear:

Table 3. Average Debts Sample of Workers on South Coast Fincas, 1929

Mocaya: $928	Olas de Moca: $4,027
Santa Abundancia: $1246	La Patria: $972
El Regalo: $2,252	Milan: $1,823

Source: AGCA, Jefe Político, Sololá, 1929

While some have interpreted such large debts as evidence of hopeless "slavery"[11] to the fincas, the laborers and many *finqueros* (*finca* owners) understood the situation more clearly. The workers hated peonage and sought at every turn to escape its demands, but to be without a debt to an export *finca* was to be liable for *mandamientos* (until 1920), military recruiting, forced road work, and other extortions of the state and state agents. Only a *patron* ("patron" = employer) offered some protection from such demands. Too, the recruiter was usually the Indians's only source of ready or emergency cash. This gave little reason to seek to escape debt. The imperative, in fact, was quite the opposite. It was to the worker's advantage to extort as much money from the *finquero* as possible, to, in effect, build up the employer's investment in him. A bigger debt, rather than

8. On the politics of the 1920s see: Pitti, "Jorge Ubico"; and U.S. State Department, "Documents Relating to the Internal Affairs of Guatemala", 1910-1929, microfilm rolls #3-9.
9. For example, *El Imparcial* (Guatemala City), 26 June 1920.
10. *Diario de Centro América* (Guatemala City), 1, 4 and 12 February, 3 May, and 20 September 1919; and Rodriguez, *Guatemala en 1919*, p. 104.
11. The government in 1923 set the daily minimum wage on public works at $8 pesos a day: *El Imparcial*, 19 July 1923. Wages for agricultural work in the mid to late 1920s were generally in the range of $10-$15 pesos, though some individuals working off old contracts received considerably less. On the "slavery" of finca labor, see: *Diario de Centro América*, 30 April 1921 and *El Imparcial*, 26 September 1922.

being a burden, gave the *mozo* leverage. If pressed too hard by a *finca*, he could almost always find another ready to buy his debt, or he might simply run away, change his name, and seek work in another area. In their scramble for workers, planters routinely, and rather short-sightedly, hid run-away workers or provided them false papers to evade past obligations. Indians also crossed into Mexico or Belize to escape *finca* and state pressures and to earn higher wages. The power of a specific *finca* owner over any given individual in his work force – as opposed to the power of one class over another – was extremely limited, forcing him into constant negotiations. One obvious result of this was the Indians' ability to push their debts to unexpected levels.

The collapse of coffee prices after 1919 turned the attention of the growers to the need to improve production efficiency. This attention focused on labor. A few planters dared to suggest that local custom squandered workers:

> Such is the system of making our *mozos* work, without getting the profit from them that we should, that we are, on the one hand, wasting thousands and thousands of *jornales* (days' work) on each *finca*, and, on the other, failing to take advantage of thousands and thousands of *jornales* that we could get from the workers we manage to obtain.[12]

Most, though, felt that their problem was quite the opposite and lay in a shortage of available workers.[13] There had been no published census since 1893,[14] so no one had a clear idea how many Indians in fact there were in Guatemala. Some expressed the opinion that the absolute number had declined in recent decades, the result of alcoholism and disease and emigration prompted by the abuses of the Estrada Cabrera regime. Others argued that the problem was not the size of the population but the mobilization and control of workers.[15] How, then, might more and cheaper labor be obtained?

The process of the primitive accumulation of capital[16] in late nineteenth century Guatemala had stopped short of converting all production factors into full market commodities. The Liberals ended restrictions on interest rates, encouraged the formation of banks and the growth of commercial lending, and welcomed foreign capital. The new regime eased access to land for commercial production by selling off public and church lands, and regularizing measurement,

12. *El Imparcial*, 30 November 1922.
13. *Diario de Centro América*, 20 September 1919; and *El Imparcial*, 6 July and 30 November, 1922 and 9 June 1923.
14. In 1916 the U.S. Embassy in Guatemala reported that President Estrada Cabrera considered census material a military secret and did not allow it to be published: U.S. State Department, "Internal Affairs of Guatemala", microfilm roll #20.
15. Compare, for example, *El Imparcial*, 25 November 1922 with 30 November 1922.
16. This best introduction to the much-talked about but little studied process of primitive or original accumulation remains Marx, *Capital*, 1, part eight.

titling, and transfer.[17] Even so, precapitalist restrictions continued to weigh on land. Not only did Indian community *ejidos* (communal lands) survive largely intact in many areas, but the Liberal state allowed and assisted the villages to expand these.[18] Those few villages unfortunate enough to be in the direct path of coffee's advance were overwhelmed and their population converted into *colonos* and day laborers,[19] but most Indians lived not in the piedmont where coffee flourished but in the adjacent highlands. Their cold, dry *ejidos* were of little immediate use to coffee growers,[20] and the state usually confirmed and titled these to the villages, as well as granting or selling them additional lands from the public domain.[21] The villagers typically held this land in a peculiar hybrid form of ownership, with a general municipal title registered with and recognized by the state, under which individuals enjoyed private property or life tenure or shifting cultivation depending on local custom.[22]

The Indian peasantry of the western highlands and the Alta Verapaz inhabited a socio-economic formation structured by the articulation of subsistence and petty commodity production with a superordinate and exploitative export sector. Precapitalist relations of production/exploitation predominated in the export economy, although cash wages tended to disguise these. It is important to be clear on this. There is some tendency to confuse capitalism with the accumulation of money, the mechanization of production, and, especially, the presence of cash wages. But capitalism rests not on a pool of money or the existence of modern productive equipment but on a specific social relationship of production exploitation. Guatemala had been caught in the toils of international capitalism – first in the guise of merchant capital and then as industrial and finance capital – since the

17. McCreery, *Rural Guatemala*, ch. 6.
18. On land in the period 1820-1930 see: McCreery, "State Power", pp. 96-115.
19. See, for example, the example of Pochuta: Instituto Indigenista de Guatemala, "Pochuta, monografía", #264 (Guatemala, n.d.).
20. McCreery, "State Power". The exception was the Alta Verapaz where coffee and community lands more directly overlapped and where Indian communities aggressively resisted the expansion of the *fincas*: for example, see San Cristobal Verapaz, Archivo General de Centro América (AGCA)-Sección de Tierras (ST), 7/3.
21. The area of Pamaxán and Panan on the south coast seem to have been less sought after for coffee than the Costa Cuca to the west or Escuintla to the southeast see (McBryde, *Cultural,* map following page 14) and, therefore, more readily available to highland towns seeking to title hot country land: AGCA, Ministerio de Gobernación (MG), 28658/108 and 190 and titles in the AGCA-ST for, among many other communities, Santiago Atitlán, San Pedro La Laguna, San Martín Sacatepéquez, Concepción Chiquirichapa, Totonicapán, Santa Catarina Ixtahuacán, Santa Lucía Utatlán and Momostenango.
22. Bunzel, *Chichicastenango*, p. 16 gives a good summary of what was probably the typical pattern for land holding in the villages by the 1920s and 1930s; for a slightly different situation, or at least interpretation see: McBryde, *Cultural*, pp. 9 ff. An excellent recent study of historical patterns of land tenure is Davis, "Land of Our Ancestors".

sixteenth century, but this integration or articulation[23] took place initially only at the level of circulation. With the second generation Liberals which came to power in the 1870s capitalism came to dominate the ideological superstructure of the elites and the state, but it failed to penetrate to any serious degree, much less revolutionize, productive relations. Whereas cochineal growers (1830-70) flirted with capitalist free labor, the spread of coffee after 1871 prompted the reimposition, tightening, and generalization of extra-economic, or direct, coercion. The dominance of the local economy by a capitalism external to Guatemala, whether in the form of the cacao boom of the sixteenth and seventeenth centuries or of coffee in the nineteenth century, had the effect of strengthening rather than weakening precapitalist work relations in the countryside.

By the early 1920s the solutions to the problem of *brazos* put forward in editorials and letters to the editor focused increasingly on *trabajo libre* (free labor). This was not capitalist free labor. Such was impossible, the argument went, because Indians lacked the "civilized needs" that would draw or drive them into the wage labor market.[24] Most of the rural inhabitants of early twentieth century Guatemala remained "unfree" in the capitalist sense not only because of direct coercion but because they still had access to land or similar resources. The Indian communities controlled the means of their own reproduction and retained the ability impeded, to be sure, by the effects of coerced labor, to set these means in motion. They used cash, and in some instances they actively sought wage labor, but most were not yet dependent on either for subsistence. Indeed, no theme was more persistent among the elites than that of the drunken, lazy Indian who would not work because he had no need to.[25] As long, it appeared, as he was satisfied with "a rude shack, almost without clothing, crammed together with the family in a space of two or three meters, in nauseating promiscuity, victim of a thousand superstitions, getting drunk at every opportunity" coercion would be required.[26]

Pejoratives aside, this was an essentially correct analysis of most Indians' situation before the 1920s. So long as the indigenous population could supply its subsistence (including ritual) requirements from its own resources, it had little reason to labor in someone else's coffee fields. If an individual voluntarily looked for cash wages, this was almost always for a specific purpose, e.g., to pay for a ceremony or to buy food to tide him and his family over until the next harvest.

---

23. On "articulation" see: Foster-Carter, "Can We Articulate Articulation", pp. 210-49, and Wolpe, *Articulation of Modes*, "Introduction".
24. *Diario de Centro América*, 17 June 1920; *El Imparcial*, 26 June, 1920, 18 May, 1921 and 6 July 1922.
25. For example, *Diario de Centro América*, 26 June 1920 and 18 May 1921 and *El Imparcial*, 6 July 1922.
26. *El Imparcial*, 6 July 1922.

Higher wages meant he would work less. What resulted was the well-known "backward bending labor supply curve",[27] the despair of nineteenth century colonial administrators and export producers the world over. The highland Indian understood and responded to the opportunity for higher wages[28] but not to that of simply making more money. As a result, some elites argued the Indian was hopeless and must either be eliminated as the North Americans had done or swamped by the immigration of "healthy elements".[29] Others, a minority, believed him to be the victim of past treatment, treatment that had brutalized him and taken away his incentives, and thought that he might yet be educated to economic rationality.[30]

Why did the Guatemalan state not confiscate village *ejidos*, smash the communities, and free up land and labor for capitalist production as did the elites of neighboring El Salvador?[31] One explanation commonly offered for the survival of precapitalist socio-economic formations articulated with capitalism is that capitalism essentially functionalizes such communities, allowing and even assisting them to survive in order to produce and reproduce cheap labor power for the export economy.[32] The villages also supply cheap food and handicraft manufactures, and they offer a potential market only partially tied to the wages of the export sector. The more astute planters in Guatemala recognized the value to them of the highland villages as food producers and labor reserves, and the land policies of the Liberal state reflected this. Given the availability of direct coercion for worker mobilization and the different types of land involved, the preservation of the *ejidos* cheapened labor and pacified the countryside.

But to reify "capitalism" into an historical actor obscures more than it illuminates. Individual planters, the elite as a group, and the state they controlled, operating within a framework set by the changing conditions of the national economy and international capitalism, plainly sought to create and maintain relations of exploitation which would return them the greatest profits. However, the cross currents and contradictions at work in this environment were enormously complex and not easily reduced to schematic representation.[33] As a result,

27. Arrighi, "Labour Supplies in Historical Perspective", pp. 185-224.
28. For an eighteenth century example of Indians shifting from lower to higher wage areas, see: AGCA, A3 224 4033 (1774).
29. On this, see a series of articles by Carlos Wyld Ospina in *El Imparcial*, 31 January, 6 February, 10 February 1928 and 22, 23, and 28 November 1929.
30. *El Imparcial*, 7 April 1923. An earlier, more systematic exposition of this point of view is to be found in Juaregui, *Los indios*, pt. 3.
31. Browning, *El Salvador*, p. 208; Menjivar, *Acumulación originaria*; and Lindo-Fuentes, *Weak Foundations*.
32. This explanation is developed most thoroughly, with an extensive bibliography, in chapter one of De Janvry's *Agrarian Question and Reformism*.
33. For a look at more recent state autonomy and intra-elite conflict, see: Berger, *Political and Agrarian Development*.

whatever theory might have dictated to be in their best interest, some *finqueros*, and particularly those with excess land available on which to colonize permanent workers, did hope to break up the communities and shake out the inhabitants.

What stopped them was Indian resistance. The villagers were ingenious, tenacious and, on occasion, violent in defense of community resources and in opposing egregious exploitation on and by the *fincas*. Overt opposition to government policies by the indigenous population had fallen off dramatically after the 1870s, a logical response to the growing power of the Liberal state,[34] but it burst into the open again in the 1920s during a decade of political instability. Reports of "uprisings", resistance to state and *finquero* authority, and the ominous news that the Indians in the countryside were organizing against their long-time oppressors filled the newspapers.[35] *El Imparcial* reported strikes and unrest in the coffee areas of Colomba, Coatepeque, Xolhuitz, and Chocolá, as well as attacks on *ladinos* and land battles in Ilón, San Lucas Sacatepéquez, and other communities.[36] Peasants and urban workers came together to press joint demands.[37] The change in atmosphere from the apparent tranquility of the Estrada Cabrera years may have been in part one of perception, for the newspapers now reported occurrences which in the past they might have ignored or concealed.[38] But it reflected also both the temporary weakness of the central state, which allowed accumulated grievances to bubble to the surface, and the influences of contemporary events in Mexico and Nicaragua.

If such unrest reminded elites of the limits of their power, coercion nevertheless would continue until an adequate number of Indians offered themselves spontaneously for wage labor. In the context of 1920s Guatemala, when growers advocated *trabajo libre* ("free labor") they meant that work could be of free selection but it would be obligatory. The *mozo* "may choose between obligatory labor on public works, military service, or *trabajo libre*, which for an Indian could not be other than work on the *fincas*".[39]

34. McCreery, "State Power", and "Land, Labor, and Violence", pp. 237-249.

35. *Diario de Centro América*, 11 October 1921; *El Demócrata* (Guatemala City), 17 July 1922; *El Imparcial*, 29 November, 1922, 24 October, 1923, and 14 February 1928.

36. AGCA, Jefe Político (JP)- Sololá, 1920: *finqueros*-JP, 12 June, 1920 and 2 September 1920 and 10 July 1923 and many similar from this and other departments; *El Imparcial*, 1 and 29 November, 1922, 24 October, and 1 July 1924.

37. AGCA, JP Sololá, 1929, Federación Obrera de Guatemala-Ministerio de Gobernación, 24 April 1929; *El Imparcial*, 14 February, 1928, 25 April, 27 April, and 2 May 1929.

38. The bloodiest attack on *ladinos* in the half century before 1930, the uprising at San Juan Ixcoy in 1898, rated barely a mention in the national press, see McCreery, "Land, Labor and Violence". A major catalyst to good reporting in the 1920s was the founding in 1921 of Guatemala's first modern newspaper, *El Imparcial*.

39. *El Imparcial*, 18 March 1926.

Enforcement would require a strong vagrancy law. An 1870s law remained on the books,[40] but it defined vagrants as "those who do not have a profession, trade, income, salary, occupation or means of support by which to live". This was a measure for urban crime control not the mobilization of agricultural labor. If the threat of punishment as a vagrant was to be made to serve effectively to coerce rural workers, a new law aimed specifically at the countryside's population was needed, together with effective instruments for its implementation. To police rural areas the state relied on *ladino comandantes locales* (local military commanders) and small and poorly trained, but well-armed militia detachments, recruited from *ladino* villages and among the local *ladino* officials, shop keepers, and labor recruiters living in Indian communities. To back these up, a full-time rural police similar to El Salvador's National Guard was needed.[41] There was also the problem of how to keep track of individual workers. Indians in the highlands caught up in forced wage labor commonly adopted "*ladino* names" for use with government officials and recruiters. They changed these when convenient and lent each other documents to evade the authorities. Most of the indigenous population, too, lived not in the central part of the villages but in outlying hamlets[42] where authorities found it difficult to keep track of them. The solution most commonly proposed was that all Indian males be made to carry, in addition to the debt record, or *libreta*, the existing law demanded, a registered *cedula de vecindad* (identity card).[43]

Transition to *trabajo libre* also presented the problem of what to do about existing debts. Should these be abolished at once or worked off, and if worked off, over how long a time period? Might the *mozos* be allowed pay in money what they owed for labor? Should new advances be made? Though planters complained in other circumstances of the cost of carrying *mozo* debts,[44] when opposing their abolition they rarely brought up the losses they would suffer should this occur. This tended to confirm the suspicion that much "debt" was little more than fiction, the result of creative bookkeeping by the *fincas* rather than any real outlay of capital. The *finqueros* protested, instead, that abolishing debts would reward *mozos* who had failed or refused to work off what they owed.[45] Employer resistance to ending debt peonage was above all, it appeared, a moral question! While comments in the newspapers suggested that most

40. Decree 222, 14 September, 1878, *Recopilación de Las Leyes de Guatemala*, II (Guatemala, 1881), pp. 201-04.
41. *El Imparcial*, 7 October 1922.
42. On the spacial structure of highland Indian municipalities, see: Tax, "The Municipios of the Midwestern Highlands", pp. 423-444.
43. For example, *Diario de Centro América*, 21, 29 April, 10 and 19 May 1921 and *El Imparcial*, 17 March 1923.
44. Alvarado, *Tratado de cafecultura práctica*, II, p. 470.
45. *El Imparcial*, 7 April 1923.

planters opposed the immediate end to labor debts and rejected also the idea that Indians be allowed to pay back debts owed for labor in money,[46] they had much more in trouble agreeing upon a scheme for genuine reform.

A number of proposals for a new labor law surfaced in the years 1920-24. Because most varied only in detail, it is sufficient to look briefly at just two, one put forward in 1921, and subsequently slightly modified, by the newly created Ministry of Agriculture, and a second advanced by the planters' *Asociación de Agricultores Guatemaltecos* (A.G.A). "All labor will be free", proposed the Ministry of Agriculture, with the restrictions that no contracts could be made for work outside the country[47] and no *mozo* might be taken on by a *finca* unless he could exhibit a *boleto de solvencia* (written proof of having cleared all debts with previous employers). Debts contract for work might be paid off in money. Public officials were not to work as labor recruiters, but they could grant a worker a *boleto de solvencia* if such was due and an employer refused it. Any individual claiming to be looking for work would be punished as a vagrant if he did not find employment within a specified time.[48] The Ministry withdrew the draft in response to planter protests and returned it a year later with several changes.[49] The new version made it more difficult to repay with money advances that had been made for labor, specified and tightened the conditions under which a worker might leave a *finca* when his contract expired, and shifted responsibility for patron-worker disputes from the courts to the municipal officials of the *finca*'s municipality.

Complaining, nevertheless, that the government was meddling in affairs of which it was ignorant, planters through the A.G.A. presented their own project. Existing debts would to be worked off over no more than two years and future advances limited to the equivalent of sixty days labor. Banned too were contracts for work outside the country, the activities of *tratistas* (free lance labor recruiters) that drove up labor costs, and labor recruiting by public authorities. No worker in debt to one employer was to be contracted by or to receive an advance from another. Only in the case of severe illness would a *mozo* be allowed to repay labor debts with money. Every worker was to carry a *boleto de trabajo* (a work ticket) with his name, the amount of work done each month, and the *finca* to which he was in debt; failure to produce this would be taken as proof of vagrancy.[50] With its provisions for ending long-terms debts and for limiting

46. *Diario de Centro América*, 30 May 1921.
47. Planters, especially those in San Marcos on the Mexican border, were obsessed with the drain of labor across the frontier: AGCA, Fomento letters volume # 14928, Jefe Político San Marcos-Ministro de Fomento, 12 November 1921. On why the workers fled to Mexico, see *El Imparcial*, 14 October 1922.
48. *Diario de Centro América*, 1 June 1921.
49. *Diario de Centro América*, 30 May 1921 and 24 April 1922.
50. *Diario de Centro América*, 17 March 1923.

advances, the A.G.A.'s proposal would have moved more aggressively than Agricultura to cheapen the costs of labor recruiting and in the direction of *trabajo libre*, But there were no major or substantive conflicts between the two proposals nor between these and any of the others seriously entertained in these years.

When coffee prices rebounded in 1924, the elite's uncharacteristic self-examination faded from the press. No new labor law emerged. Custom asserted itself, with the results one writer described:

> We Guatemalans continue to be the most disorganized in the world as regards wages and working conditions. Our *caja* ['box' = the measure used in harvest labor] of coffee varies [among *fincas*] from 70 to 185 pounds and hardly two *fincas* are the same. Wages run 10 to 60 pesos a task.[51] On some *fincas* they do not provide food while on others they provide without cost meat, milk, chile, beans, corn, lye, and salt. The majority of *fincas* cajole workers with dances, clothes, alcohol and many presents, in addition to our disastrous system of unlimited advances.[52]

Only in 1928 did the doubts resurface. Although prices continued to be good in that year, dealers sold much coffee forward, and futures prices anticipated the Depression.[53] Instead of rationalizing production in the recent bonanza years, planters efforts to expand production to take advantage of market opportunities had thrown them into frantic competition for workers, driving up production costs. Efforts to attract labor depended less on increasing money wages than on offering the much more powerful incentive of free or below market price corn. Levels of corn production remained fairly constant in these years:

Table 4. Corn Harvests and Imports, Guatemala, 1921-1940

1921	3,132,412	1928	1,966,594	1936	3,280,096
1922	2,989,298	1929	2,803,618	1937	(a) 6,182,224
1923	2,488,972	1930	3,436,621	1938	6,182,224
1924	2,492,973	1931	2,921,379	1939	7,020,628
1925	2,403,440	1933	2,954,679	1940	10,019,980
1926	1,967,310	1934	2,848,061		
1927	2,386,190	1935	3,074,760		

Source: Ministerio de Agricultura, *Memorias, 1922-1940* (Guatemala).
(a) See McCreery, *Rural Guatemala*, ch. 10 regarding the apparent jump in production in 1937 and after.

51. Guatemalan coffee plantations traditionally assigned and paid for work either by the day or task. In theory the two involved approximately the same amount of labor but in fact wide variations were occurred, usually to the worker's disadvantage: McCreery, "Debt Servitude".
52. Alvarado, *Tratado* II, p. 456.
53. Bulmer-Thomas, "Central America", p. 284. This was in large part a result of the enormous Brazilian harvest of 1927/8.

But corn prices and, more significantly, corn imports soared:

Table 5. Corn Price Indexes/Corn Imports, Guatemala, 1920-1935

	Price index	Imports (Kilograms)		Price index	Imports (Kilograms)
1920	67		1928	160	22,346,58
1921	84		1929	145	18,458,42
1922	87		1930	95	1,083,493
1923	100	975,072	1931	60	2,057
1924	103	491,086	1932	55	40
1925	100	240,727	1933	67	579,436
1926	127	8,109,606	1934	68	20,119
1927	101	427,015	1935	46	834

Source: Ministerio de Fomento, *Memorias, 1922-1936* (Guatemala); Ministerio de Agricultura, *Memorias, 1923-1936* (Guatemala).
Index, 1923 = 100

Coffee planters brought in large quantities of grain to secure "their" *mozos* and to be used to entice workers away from other employers. For a short time the Indians must have enjoyed a paradise of corn! Even with these increases and additional expenses, however, Guatemalan wage costs remained below those of their competitors in other nearby countries, or so writers claimed in the late 1920s. Even so, low local levels of productivity, the result of outdated machinery, inadequate and monopolized communications, and a reluctant, coerced labor force, kept Guatemalan planters' real production costs high.[54]

Worried by this competition and offended by their workers' evident affluence, Guatemala's *finqueros* again rehashed in the newspapers many of the problems and proposals for labor mobilization and control raised in the early years of the decade.[55] State officials and *tratistas* continued to prey on them, they complained; the end of *mandamientos* had not stopped *caciquismo*. Competition from the big *fincas*, and particularly those controlled by the resurgent German companies,[56] drove up wages and monopolized labor. Lazy, ignorant Indians defrauded their

54. By the 1930s International Railroads of Central America, a subdivision of the United Fruit Company, controlled all but a few miles of Guatemala's rail system and owned the chief Atlantic port. It used this control to favor its banana exports at the expense of other shippers. For a brief treatment of transport problems in these years, see Grieb, *Guatemalan Caudillo*, ch. 9. On the costs of coerced labor, see *El Imparcial*, 27 April 1929 and 26 August 1943; Alvarado, *Tratado* II, p. 459.
55. For example, *El Imparcial*, 12 June 1928, 25 October 1929, and 2 January 1930.
56. On the formation of the best-known of these, the Central American Plantations Company [CAPCO], see Wagner, "Actividades empresariales", p. 120.

employers and the state – the irony here seems to have escaped the planters – by continuing to run up multiple debts with various *fincas* and then evading work. Proposed solutions repeated the familiar ones of free but obligatory labor, a vagrancy law requiring a minimum number of days work a year, an end to wage advances, and the imposition of improved instruments of control.

A new element evident in the debate of the late 1920s was an awareness among the coffee planters of the growth in the nation's population. A census taken in 1921, but not published until the end of 1924,[57] revealed that, far from declining as many had claimed to fear, the size of the indigenous population had increased markedly in the decades since 1893.

Table 6. Guatemalan Population Statistics

Sample Indian Departments	1893	1921	% increase
Sololá	70,039	104,283	48%
Sacatepéquez	42,712	46,453	9%
Quiché	92,753	138,076	49%
Huehuetenango	117,127	137,166	18%
San Marcos	89,322	176,402	49%
Total indian population	883,228	1,299,927	47%
Total population	1,356,678	2,004,900	48%

Sources: Dirección General de Estádística, *Censo de la República de Guatemala* (1921) and *Censo general de la República de Guatemala levantado en 26 de Febrero de 1893.*

As the Depression took hold, the possibility began to work its way into elite consciousness that in a growing number of communities the inhabitants no longer had access to enough land or other resources to support themselves without recourse to the wage sector. Increasingly, Indians voluntarily sought work on the *fincas*, work which, at least in the early years of the Depression, was often not to be had.[58] Ecological degradation, population growth, and new tastes acquired on the plantations or with plantation-earned cash had begun to create new needs among the inhabitants of the highland villages. To the employers' mind the problem of *brazos* came to focus more on control than simply on numbers.

In general, the coffee growers of Guatemala weathered the Depression remarkably well.[59] There was a burst of panic selling of properties in 1930, but the market soon stabilized.[60] After a brief hesitation,[61] planters responded aggres-

---

57. Dirección General de Estadística, *Censo de la República.*
58. Ministerio de Agricultura, *Memoria-1933; El Imparcial,* 7 January, 12 February, and 1 October 1930.
59. Bulmer-Thomas, *Political Economy of Central America,* chs 3 and 4.
60. This is evident in the yearly mortgage/sales records published in the *Memorias* of the

sively to the fall in coffee prices by increasing production and attempting to reduce labor costs. Employers, for example, cut wages, or, rather than pay wages at all, only credited a worker's debt, and they tried too to limit advances or, with less success, put an end to the practice altogether.[62] The government lowered interest rates, made small amounts of cheap credit available to hard-pressed planters, and issued a stop law to prevent creditors foreclosing on properties.[63] Most of the business houses and banks did not wish, in the event, to take over debtors' property but instead rolled over existing financing to keep the owners in business and paying on their debts.[64]

With the seizure of power by General Jorge Ubico in 1931, serious debate again disappeared from the newspapers.[65] It is thus impossible to outline the specific sequence of events or decisions which led up to a general overhaul of rural labor laws in May, 1934, but the reforms followed directly from the arguments of the preceding ten years. Decree 1995, enacted on 2 May, 1934, ended long-term debt servitude, and Decree 1996, issued six days later, put in its place a new vagrancy law specifically intended to mobilize cheap labor for the rural *fincas*.[66] The state abolished debts because of "the constant conflicts between employers and workers resulting from disagreements over debts provoked by the activities of recruiters and because advances restrict the freedom of work and convert the laborer into an object of undue exploitation by those who contract his services."[67] Decree 1995 outlawed the activities of the infamous *'tratistas*, prohibited future wage advances, and allowed *mozos* two years to work off existing debts. In effect, planters gained two years free or nearly free labor in the worst years of the Depression at the cost of the partial loss of debts of often dubious provenance. They soon discovered, however, that law or not the inhabitants of the highland communities would not work without advances, and that prohibition came to nought. But by having the courts refuse to uphold contracts to the contrary, the state did succeed in limiting advances to what could be worked off in a single season or year.

Ministerio de Gobernación and in the histories of individual *fincas* available in the Registros de Propiedad Inmueble, Guatemala City and Quezaltenango.

61. Bunzel reports, for example, that many planters "did not bother to pick the 1932 harvest", Bunzel, *Chichicastenango*, p. 11.
62. For example, *El Imparcial*, 29 October 1930; Ministerio de Agricultura, *Memoria-1932*, p. 509; AGCA, B119.21.0.0, 47790/86; Bulmer-Thomas, *Political Economy of Central America*, p. 49.
63. Grieb, *Guatemalan Caudillo*, pp. 58-59.
64. Interviews with retired *finqueros*; mortgage records of individual *fincas* in Registro de Propiedad Inmueble.
65. On Ubico, see: Grieb, *Guatemalan Caudillo* and Pitti, "Jorge Ubico", ch. 8.
66. Mendez, *Leyes*, pp. 214-215 and pp. 244-247.
67. Mendez, *Leyes*, p. 244.

The struggle for control of labor power continued transmuted but unabated. Few of the Indians had the cash or the desire to pay off what they owed and sought instead to work as little as possible or to evade the *finca*'s grasp entirely until the two years elapsed. Some of the labor recruiters, for their part, sought to convert debts originally contracted for labor into common debts of money at interest, for which the Indian would still be liable after the Decree 1995 deadline passed.[68] *Finca* agents tried in other cases to foreclose on any real property, particularly land, that the worker possessed. Such efforts did not always proceed smoothly. In the town of Nebaj, for example, a recruiter conspired with a local notary to rewrite labor contracts into debt notes and deceived illiterate Indians into signing these. When a delegation of town elders led a large crowd to the local *comandante* to complain, he panicked and threatened them. In the scuffle that followed an Indian hit him with a broom. The crowd quickly disarmed the small garrison without injury, but, knowing what was sure to follow, most of the Indians fled to the *monte* (hills). The government rushed troops to Nebaj, arrested seven of the supposed leaders, and threatened to try 138 of the local population for sedition.[69] More typically, and for obvious reasons, Indians adopted a less confrontational approach, seeking simply to stay out of sight and hand until time ran out.

In addition to the traditional definitions, the new vagrancy decree labeled as a vagrant anyone without sufficient property to provide an "adequate" income, anyone contracted for work on a *finca* but who had failed to comply with their agreement, and anyone without a contract for agricultural labor who did not cultivate at least three *manzanas*[70] of coffee, sugar or tobacco, four *manzanas* of corn, wheat, potatoes, vegetables or other products, or three *manzanas* of corn in the hot country giving two harvests a year. Few Indians had access to such relatively large amounts of land.[71] Subsequent clarification[72] provided that those who cultivated ten or more *cuerdas*[73] of land, but less than the amount that gave a labor exemption, were to work one hundred days a year for wages. Those with less than ten *cuerdas* owed at least one hundred and fifty days. The law also

---

68. For example, AGCA, B119.21.0.0 47800/71.
69. Jackson Lincoln, "An Ethnographic Study of the Ixil Indians of the Guatemalan Highlands" [1945], Manuscripts in the Microfilm Collection of Middle American Cultural Anthropology, University of Chicago; Colby and van den Berghe say the seven were shot: Colby and van den Berghe, *Ixil Country*, p. 155; for a dramatic memory of these events, see: Stoll, "Evangelicals, Guerrillas, and the Army", p. 101.
70. A *manzana* equals approximately 1.7 acres.
71. For the benefits that the new vagrancy law brought the better-off indians, see: Warren, *Symbolism*, p. 150.
72. Stadelman, "Maize Cultivation", p. 94.
73. In rural Guatemala what is a *cuerda* varies according to local custom between twenty five and fifty square *varas* (Spanish yards).

required that all agricultural laborers now carry a new form of *libreta*, to be renewed each calendar year, in which employers were to record the number of days worked for wages. Those convicted as vagrants would be jailed or fined.

At the same time that the state reformed the labor laws, Ubico further tightened control over the countryside. He replaced elected local officials with appointed intendants, usually an individual from outside the community, put into effect the much-discussed identity cards, and stepped up the activities of the Treasury Police (the *Montada*).[74] Those arrested as vagrants commonly fell into the hands of the authorities at check points as they entered or left town or during sweeps of the outlying hamlets carried out by the *Montada* or local police and village authorities. The courts took as proof of vagrancy the failure to produce an up-to-date *libreta* or certificate of exemption. Those accused usually attempted to defend themselves by claiming that they never had worked on a *finca* and did not to have a book – a holdover defense from the old peonage system that did not address the demands of the new vagrancy law – or by claiming that they had a profession that gave them a living or access to enough land in their home community or elsewhere to exempt them from compulsory labor. Certainly the most ingenious, if unsuccessful, defense was that of the individual who affirmed that "in his heart he did not consider himself a vagrant!"[75] Others said they were *tinterillos* (scribes/fixers), between employments, or that they worked as local or traveling merchants. The courts went to considerable lengths to attempt to verify the prisoners' claims, usually telegraphing the authorities in his home community or giving the individual the opportunity to retrieve documents. They regularly exonerated those found not liable under the law.

The most frequent complaint of that part of the rural population that had a profession or access to land was that local authorities obstructed their efforts to obtain the necessary certification.[76] Intendants sought to generate the maximum number of workers possible from their communities to satisfy their superiors and to curry the favor of powerful *finqueros*. As a result, the villages protested, officials ignored their work or trade or purposefully undermeasured their plantings. Although there was no legal basis for this, some intendants refused to accept land cultivated in the village common as meeting the requirements of the law. Chamelco, for example, began for the first time to charge rent for

---

74. Except as specifically cited, the following paragraphs are based on a large amount of material in the records of the courts which heard appeals of vagrancy cases. See, for example, Archivo General de Los Tribunales [AGT], Huehuetenango, Juez de Paz, 1932-38 and 1942-44, Quiché, 1937-40 and 1943-44, Sololá, 1938-1944, and Chiquimula, 1940.
75. AGT, Juez de Paz, Quiché, criminal, 1937-38, leg. 15, #673.
76. AGCA, B119.21.0.0 47800/53 and 75 and 47804/19.

the use of *ejido* land, apparently in order to establish a firmer basis of individual possession to satisfy the vagrancy law.[77]

But even efforts such as Chamelco's were no guarantee against abuses if, as communities protested, the intendants continued to respond chiefly to bribes from planters and recruiters. The inhabitants of Comitancillo, for example, complained that instead of being allowed to work on the *fincas* they wished, the intendant was forcing them go to the estates he favored and by which, presumably, he was being bribed. When they resisted, he jailed and beat them.[78] The Indians of Aguacatán repeatedly pointed to similar abuses by their intendant, apparently without gaining much relief.[79] By the late 1930s and early 1940s the recruiters' usual tactic was to denounce as vagrants men contracted to work on their employer's *finca* but who had, or so it was claimed, failed to appear or to complete the agreed-upon tasks. The courts refused to convict a man of vagrancy if he could show that he had worked the number of days for wages required by law, even if not on the *finca* that had entered the case against him, but they also usually ordered him to fulfill any outstanding contracts. Judges handling vagrancy cases ruled repeatedly that no one could be forced to commute their sentence, but some intendants pressured convicted Indians to accept work offered by preferred recruiters or planters, who were only to happy to pay the Indians' fines. In effect, some intendants sold *mozos* to the highest bidder or briber.

The villages resisted the vagrancy law as they always had fought state pressure, with appeals to *tata* ("grandfather") *presidente*, evasion, fraud, and, rarely, violence.[80] But resistance was muted not only by the effective coercive power of the Ubico regime but also by a sense among the indigenous population that the law was much fairer than had been those of the Estrada Cabrera years.[81] They recognized that Decree 1996 extended the requirements of *trabajo libre* to the non-Indians as well as Indians among the rural poor, and the police swept up *ladino* and Indian "vagrants" alike. This was a welcome change from the petty tyrannies of the past half century. It did not mean, of course, that they submitted to labor demands willingly.[82] Those who could afford it paid off the intendant to obtain genuine or fraudulent certifications of cultivation or merchants' exemptions. *Tinterillos* did a lively business in forgery. Indian and *ladino* employ-

77. Antonio Goubaud, "San Juan Chamelco", Chicago Mesoamerica Microfilm, #23.
78. AGCA, JP San Marcos, Administrativo #17, 1936, Municipio Comitancillo-Presidente, 21 August 1936.
79. AGCA, B119.21.0.0 47801/1 and 47802/64.
80. AGCA, JP Sololá, 9 September 1936; JP San Marcos, Administrativo #17, 21 August and 25 November 1936; *El Imparcial*, 13 August 1943.
81. Warren, *Symbolism*, pp. 150-151.
82. On ways to "beat the system", see: *El Norte* (Cobán), 5 June 1937 and *El Imparcial*, 13 August 1943.

ers struck deals with laborers to work for less than the required number of days for nothing or only food, in exchange for a notation of the required one hundred or one hundred and fifty days as needed.

One group of *ladinos* immediately and adversely affected by the new laws were the recruiters and tavern keepers who dominated the cash economy of all but the most isolated of highland Indian towns. Most had arrived late in the nineteenth century specifically to profit from the opportunities created by labor recruiting and the cash generated by the coffee boom.[83] They had survived, and a few had prospered, by dispensing large quantities of alcohol during the recruitment season, trafficking in *mozos*, and selling cheap consumer goods. These sources of profit now were both reduced and made more precarious. The end to indefinite labor debts generally weakened the network of credit by which the *ladinos* kept and exploited their clientele, and the Depression brought lower wages and smaller advances for their customers to spend. The abolition of debts probably had little real economic impact on the *fincas*, but it wiped out many shop keepers and *tratistas*.[84] The Indians, they lamented, were "only wait[ing] for the month of May to arrive without working, because that is the date Decree 1995 goes into effect".[85] One effect of these changes was that the 1930s the flow of *ladinos* into the highland villages began to reverse itself. Trade and commerce were re-indianized in some communities.[86] *Finqueros* tended to see the *tratistas* and other village *ladinos* as parasites who complicated recruitment and raised labor costs and did not regret their passing. In addition, Ubico's ambitious road building program meant that the state could increasingly rely on full-time state agents for internal repression and had less need of the old *ladino* local militia units.

The laws which ended long-term debts and imposed a new definition of vagrancy hastened a process of socio-economic differentiation within the indigenous population already accelerated by forced participation in the coffee economy. Rich, by local standards, Indians could now more easily avoid *finca* labor, by owning or cultivating enough land, by obtaining a merchant's exemption, or by bribing the intendant.[87] The eagerness of poor Indians to avoid having to leave the community meant that anyone with land available could easily obtain cheap labor. The exit of *ladinos* opened new commercial opportuni-

---

83. Colby and van den Berg, *Ixil Country*, ch. 2.
84. Tani Adams, "San Martín Jilotepeque: Aspects of the Political and Socio-Economic Structure of a Guatemalan Peasant Community" (unpublished manuscript in the files of the author), p. 32.
85. AGCA, JP Sololá, 13 April 1936.
86. See, for example, the history of changes in San Pedro Sacatepéquez (San Marcos) outlined in Smith, *Fiesta System*, and the life of the protagonist of Sexton's *Son of Tecun Uman*, and *Campesino*.
87. Brintnal, *Revolt Against the Dead*, p. 112; and Warren, *Symbolism*, p. 150.

ties. Indians moved into the formerly *ladino*-dominated areas of shop keeping and mule and truck transport, and former *caporales* (Indian foremen) took over labor recruiting directly. These opportunities, if less attractive than they had been to the *ladinos*, were valuable to Indians both for the profits they promised and the exemptions they offered. Finally, and perhaps unexpectedly, the new laws may actually have increased Indian access to land. To stabilize their labor force, the *fincas* registered plots of land of the requisite size for their workers, whether on the lowland plantation itself or on highland labor reserves known as *fincas de mozos*.[88]

When anthropologists in the 1930s undertook the first generation of intensive field studies in highland Guatemala, they found land shortages to be widespread. Raymond Stadelman,[89] for example, in his investigation of corn production in the department of Huehuetenango, calculated that villages needed one and a half acres of arable land per inhabitant for subsistence agriculture to be viable. On this basis, only three or four of the twenty three towns he surveyed had enough.[90] At the same time, an evident emerging balance of supply and demand, and even over-supply, of labor for the export sector could be read in government *libreta* figures, as Table 7 shows.

Table 7. Libreto Sales, 1937-1942

	Indian Departments	Ladino departments	Total
1937	100,597	49,828	150,425
1938	182,875	59,948	242,823
1939	165,084	69,142	234,226
1940	89,270	31,671	120,941
1941	123,308	48,550	171,858
1942	142,029	48,932	190,961

Sources: Ministerio de Agricultura, *Memorias, 1938-1944* (Guatemala)
Note: These figures do not include the Department of Guatemala. The selection of "Indian" vs. "Ladino" departments is necessarily somewhat arbitrary but relects population composition as recorded in the 1921 census.

88. See, for example, *matriculas de mozos* (registries of workers) of San Juan Ostuncalco (Municipal Archive) and Sumpango (AGCA).
89. Stadelman, "Maize Cultivation", pp. 105 and 134; See also Wagley, "Economics of a Guatemalan Village", p. 74. This contrasts with the picture Ruth Bunzel paints for Chichicastenango in these years: *Chichicastenango*, p. 43.
90. Some communities had other resources, e.g., salt springs,engaged in handicraft manufactures and trade, or rented land from more fortunate municipalities, but the overall growing shortage of local opportunities was clear.

Sales of the work cards indicated a yearly availability of an average of some 180,000 to 200,000 agricultural laborers. By contrast, the number of workers needed to make the crop in the 1930s was not more than 140,000 to 150,000 a year, based on only 100 days labor per *mozo*.[91] Clearly, state-enforced extra-economic coercion of labor was less and less necessary, and less and less economic. Still, the planters resisted giving up their guarantees, and the vagrancy law continued in force on into the 1940s.

Ironically, it was in the death throes of the repressive Ubico regime that direct coercion of agricultural labor also breathed its last. Under rising pressure from students and the urban middle and working classes, Ubico abandoned office in 1944, turning government over to a junta headed by one of his followers, General Frederico Ponce. It was Ponce, an unlikely reformer if ever one could be imagined, who "in a desire to pander to (i.e., gain the support of) the rural population" arbitrarily suppressed the *libreta* (i.e., the vagrancy law system).[92] But this by no means ended the matter. Ponce, in turn, fell to the October, 1944 Revolution which for the first time brought genuine popular reform to Guatemala and life back to the newspapers. Again, the question turned to labor, and the old complaints of the "lazy" Indian and warnings that an end to coercion would mean labor shortages reappeared. But the indigenous population now found many more public defenders: "Capitalism thinks of the Indian as forever the trash collector, but many times it is the traveler [in the highlands] who feels small when confronted by the noble spirit, the high morality and the grace of these men of the mountains, so poorly understood."[93] Finally, in May, 1945 the Congress passed yet another rural labor law as part of its efforts to end Guatemala's "feudal" agriculture.[94] This did away with *libretas* and required no specific number of days labor per year. Now vagrants were simply those without work or a profession or without an income or property adequate to sustain them. The new regime wrote this into the 1945 constitution. Free labor had come to Guatemala.

Precapitalist labor forms had persisted in Guatemala from the first days of the colony to the 1920s because they served the interests of the planters in the cash and export sectors and because the indigenous peasant communities resisted commodification of their work and material resources. The post-Estrada Cabrera governments ended *mandamientos* not so much to relieve the burden on the villages as to limit the extortions of the *fincas* by departmental and local officials, ultimately with marginal success. Debt peonage continued but was the subject of intense debate whenever the economy stumbled. The turning point came

91. This is based on a assumption of fifteen days' labor per *quintal* of coffee.
92. *El Imparcial*, 22 January 1945.
93. *El Imparcial*, 22 May 1945.
94. Decree 102, 22 May 1945 in Gil and Lucerno, *Resumen de leyes*, p. 255.

in the late 1920s and early 1930s with, on the one hand, the awareness among the elites of the population growth which the belated publication of the 1921 census made clear, and, on the other, when the initial cut backs in production during the first years of the Depression revealed to the *finqueros* and the villagers alike the existence of more Indians seeking work than was, at least temporarily, to be had. Centuries of exploitation had created a situation of "reproduction-destruction"[95] in the countryside. The communities persisted but suffered a downward ecological spiral and increasingly needed the *finca* wages for survival. However, a ruling class as conservative as that of Guatemala was not yet ready to abandon coercion. Instead, in 1934 the dictator adopted the halfway measure of free but obligatory labor enforced by a new definition of vagrancy. The sale of *libretas* under this law gave the first reliable count of available *brazos*, of those without sufficient land or handicraft manufacturing or trade to support themselves. It revealed an emerging sufficiency of labor. Only in 1944 and 1945 did the state and the planters finally abandon legal extra-economic coercion. Short-term debts persisted, as did the use of real or threatened coercion and violence to discipline and cheapen labor, but in the 1940s the basis of exploitation shifted from extra-economic coercion to economic necessity, to free labor.

95. On this, see Foster-Carter, "Articulate".

Staples, Endowments, Institutions and Development in Agrarian Frontiers: A Neo-Institutionalist Analysis of Sixteenth- and Seventeenth-Century Paraguay[*]

Mario Pastore

Soon after silver was discovered in Upper Peru in 1545 the cooperative arrangements that initially prevailed in lowland, land-abundant Paraguay between the Spanish "huestes" and friendly indigenous people were abandoned. Several forms of coerced indigenous labor and attendant military structures adapted to the frontier were then successively imposed, and economic activity accelerated, particularly after the mercury amalgam process was introduced in Potosí in 1570. However, the indigenous population decreased more rapidly, coerced indigenous labor and the military organization based on it began to decline, and economic activity contracted, progressively more as the crisis of the 17th century set in and hostile Indian attacks as well as Portuguese raids for Indian slaves took their toll. A considerable share of the military services required to defend the colony were now furnished, on the one hand, by a militia predominantly drawn from a growing mestizo small peasantry, which was saddled with onerous military service obligations but was free from coerced labor obligations and, on the other, by armies staffed by indigenous people from the growing Jesuit missions whose coerced labor obligations were commuted for a money payment they obtained by exporting yerba mate to the regional market. As the seventeenth century wore on both became progressively more prominent in this relatively distant colony, which mercantilist trade restrictions further isolated. As coerced indigenous labor declined imports of African slaves increased, but these remained a small proportion of the population during this century.[1]

The above evolution of staple production, labor structure, military organization, and economic activity may be accounted for — I contend — within a neoinstitutional staples model, by changing foreign demand structures, relative

---

[*] I presented several previous versions of this paper at different scholarly gatherings, most recently at the Latin American Studies Colloquium Series, Cornell University, Ithaca, NY. For their comments and suggestions on previous drafts I thank Robert Higgs, Tom Davis, Stanley Engerman, Evsey Domar, Branislava Susnik, Luis Galeano, Luis Campos, Jerry Cooney, Douglass North, John Nye, Elyce Rotella, Eni Mesquita and two anonymous referees. Remaining deficiencies are "mea culpa".

1. This deliberately brief description has been culled from several standard references. It is offered only to suggest the stylized behavior of the phenomena of concern. Here, stress will be laid on accounting for the described phenomena in terms of economic theory.

factor prices, and public finance constraints. Sketched by Smith, and used by Innis, Watkins, and North to account for the early economic development of Canada and the United States, respectively, the staples growth model was formalized by Caves as a Ricardian construct made up of a mature region to which a resource-rich, empty land is added; capital and labor migrate to the new region, to produce resource intensive goods tradeable for the mature region's manufactures and resource intensive goods not produced in the new.[2] Consistent with the staples model, Spanish colonization of the New World added a resource-rich if not empty land to more mature European economies; factor migration and trade patterns similar to those suggested by the staples growth model ensued as well. Despite the many similarities between British and Spanish America, their economic performance differed, because their institutional nature differed – many have argued. Consequently, if the staples growth model is to account for the experience of Spanish America, it must take the institutions peculiar to it into account, those which concerned labor and collective action in particular.[3]

Particularly helpful for our purposes will be two signal contributions by North and Thomas and by Domar, respectively.[4] So will subsequent advances in the

2. See Smith, *Wealth of Nations*, 2, pp. 66-158; Innis, *Essays in Canadian Economic History*; Watkins, "Staple Theory", pp. 141-158; North, *Economic Growth of the United States*; and Caves, "'Vent-for-Surplus'". In Caves' formulation, two interrelated sectors make up the economy of the first region; one produces output with capital and labor under constant returns to scale; the other additionally requires resources in fixed supply, and is therefore characterized by diminishing marginal productivity. Most of the subsequent contributions to this literature is surveyed in McCusker and Menard, *Economy of British America*, pp. 17-34.
3. Institutions as a causal factor of differential growth patterns in the Americas were emphasized as far back as the eighteenth century by Adam Smith, *Wealth of Nations* and more recently by Glade, *Latin American Economies*; Coatsworth, "Obstacles to Change"; and North, *Structure and Change*, among others. Instructive though it may be, a comparison of these approaches to institutions cannot be undertaken in the space available here.
4. North and Thomas' analysis of western Europe between 1100 and 1800 relied on a Malthusian staples model explicitly based on Caves and augmented by Coasian transactions costs, introduced to restore the institutional features that Caves formalization of the model had stripped off. North and Thomas made changes in the state a function of exogenous innovations in military technology. However, they regarded the serf-lord relationship as a contractual arrangement freely entered into, which was severely criticized. Domar's reading of Russia's experience – where a free peasantry was enserfed both de facto and de jure by mid seventeenth century – stressed that relative land abundance was neither a necessary or a sufficient condition for serfdom or slavery. He instead emphasized the need for government intervention, which he regarded as exogenous. Domar ascribed little or no role to demand for output, domestic or foreign, and the derived demand for labor. See North and Thomas, "Economic Theory", pp. 1-17; and *ibid.*, "Rise and Fall of the Manorial Economy, pp. 777-803; Domar, "Causes of Slavery or Serfdom", pp. 18-32. For critiques see Fenoaltea, "Rise and Fall of a Theoretical Model"; and Engerman, "Coerced and Free Labor", pp. 1-29.

analysis of coerced labor and predatory rule.[5] Though clearly relevant, these advances have been all but ignored by most students of colonial Spanish America, who favor other approaches.[6] The proposed theoretical synthesis may compare favorably with alternative and kindred ones.[7]

In the following sections I will describe the phenomena of interest in more detail and interpret them in terms of the proposed framework, which I will develop progressively, as the need for it arises. Section One discusses the pre-Columbian background, American and European, as well as the early relations between Spaniards and American Indians. Section Two focuses on the early colonial expansion and Section Three on the seventeenth century crisis. Section Four draws conclusions.

5. For early examples, see, in the first connection, Barzel, "Economic Analysis of Slavery"; in the second, North, "Framework for Analyzing the State in Economic History"; Barry Baysinger et al., "Mercantilism As a Rent-Seeking Society"; and Batchelder and Freuden-berger, "On the Rational Origins", pp. 1-13. The subsequent literature in both connections is referred to in Eggertsson, Economic Behavior and Institutions; Engerman, "Coerced and Free Labor"; and Root, Fountain of Privilege.

6. Among the few who built on the neoinstitutionalist literature is Hunt's "Economics of Haciendas", Assadourian's Sistema de la economía colonial asserts that Caves' model is "perfectly applicable" to the colonial context (p. 134) but goes no further. Disciples or students of his who analyzed colonial Paraguay in whole or in part, like Garavaglia, Mercado interno; and Whigham, Politics of River Trade, ignored his clue. Brown's Socioeconomic History of Argentina explicitly focused on staples and linkages but ignored the neoinstitutional literature and centered on the nineteenth century. Studies of the area of concern favoring alternative approaches are Hall's "Geographic Factors", (paper presented at the Social Science History Association Meetings), (Baltimore, MD, November 5-7, 1993), which uses Wallerstein's approach. Focusing on the nineteenth century are Baretta and Markoff's "Civilization and Barbarism", pp. 587-620, and Salvatore's "Modes of Labor Control", who opt for approaches favored by Foucault and Brenner, respectively.

7. Brenner is skeptical of both population and trade-driven accounts of labor coercion, and prefers explanations based on class conflict. However, trade and population are both linked to relative scarcity and, therefore, to the development of property rights, without which Marxian classes or class conflict cannot be defined. Furthermore, the free rider problem severely restricts the possibility of class action. Boyd's analysis of Serbia seeks to compare the explanatory power of North and Thomas versus a synthesis of Domar, Blum, and Pettengil. However, Domar's model is a special case of Caves'. It has a strong version with scarce labor and abundant evenly fertile land and a weak version with scarce labor and capital and abundant land. The strong version is a special case of Caves' region II, the weak identical with Caves' Region II. Both models are of Ricardian inspiration. Given that the staples model includes Domar as a special case, it makes little sense to oppose North and Thomas to Domar. See Brenner, "Agrarian Class Structure"; and Boyd, "Evolution of Agrarian Institutions", pp. 36-55.

I. Pre-Columbian Backgrounds and the First Encounter

The vast area between South America's Atlantic coast and the foothills of the
Andes was sparsely occupied by the Guarani-speaking Carios. Early conquest
accounts report, and anthropologists confirm, an aboriginal tendency to concentrate more heavily along the periodically flooded, more fertile river banks (the
varzeas, so-called) of large rivers, to a density of 33 persons per 100 kilometers
along the Upper Parana river and 28 persons per hundred square kilometers in
Central Paraguay.[8] This suggests a tendency for population to be more dense
where the greater fertility of land gave rise to what may be called a higher land
rent, than on the more rapidly exhausted forest lands.

In addition, forms of political organization also seem to be more complex
where rent is higher. The forms of political organization that characterized forest
communities were relatively simple. They wage war to capture slaves and wives
but do not fight for the possession of land, which is abundant. When population
grows, these forest communities simply split, the new groups moving on to a
previously unoccupied spot of the forest. This suggests that population growth
on any given spot of the forest leads to decreasing marginal product of labor and
competition, which if land is abundant can be resolved fairly peacefully by the
spread of small population groups throughout the forest. Abundant resources
earn no rent and do not justify defining property rights over them, defending
these rights, or engaging in disputes over them, which will therefore tend not
to arise. Land abundance and the associated lack of competition for it will reduce
the need for a military and a legal apparatus aimed at protecting landed property
rights and resolving disputes between competing land claimants. The virtual
absence of the state is also consistent with the findings of game theory that
wealth maximizing players will usually find it worthwhile to cooperate with
other players when the game involves few players, they possess complete
information about other players' past performance, and the play is repeated.[9]
Waging wars to capture slaves and wives and the minor scale of slavery are
consistent with the scarcity of labor relative to land and the relatively limited
coercive capability of private agents and collective action organizations to
prevent flight.

More complex forms of state tend to appear where there are varzeas, to
exclude some of the groups that compete for them.[10] More complex forms of

---

8. On the settlement pattern see Service, *Spanish-Guarani Relations*, p. 14; the density estimate
    is by Steward, *Handbook of South American Indians*, 5, pp. 659, 662, Map 16, cited in Service,
    Spanish-Guarani Relations, p. 14.
9. North, *Institutions*, p. 12.
10. See Carneiro, "Theory of the Origin of the State", pp. 733-738, which suggests that
    something similar seems to have occurred in the highlands of Mexico and Peru, where more

state also seem to arise in forest areas where agglomeration obtains, and for similar reasons. Both of these observations are consistent with the theoretical expectation that the absence of property rights will lead to the dissipation of differential and locational rent and, therefore, that incentives will exist for more complex forms of state and taxation to arise, to define and enforce property rights as well as to prevent resource overexploitation and rent dissipation. It was on such a setting that the Spanish colonization of Paraguay imposed itself.

Innovations in the technology of war led to political centralization and mercantilist expansion in early modern western Europe,[11] Spain under Isabella and Ferdinand being one of the first instances. Neoinstitutionalism views mercantilism as the fiscal system of predatory states which use their position to maximize net revenue through the sale of rent-creating regulation at prices that reflect their price-discriminating ability. A predatory state will have two objectives: the first, to provide a set of property rights that will maximize rents to the ruler, the second, to lower transactions costs in order to permit output and tax revenues to increase. Both may lead to regulations that restrict entry and supply, and to comparatively slower growth. However, less efficient rulers may be forced by competition to innovate the property rights structure so as to lower transactions costs and allow growth to take place. Institutional innovation may also arise from changes in relative factor prices or from new technologies of coercion, production, or transacting. Rulers may be more likely than constituents to effect institutional innovation because the free rider problem will discourage private collective action.[12] These are most appropriate terms in which to conceptualize the early modern Spanish monarchy.

The Catholic Kings' de facto appropriation of the natural and labor resources of America by right of conquest was sanctioned by Pope Alexander VI's bull of 1493. In exchange the crown assumed the Church's responsibility of converting the aboriginal Americans to Catholicism and of collecting the ecclesiastical tithe, of the proceeds of which it could keep the so-called "two-ninths".[13] The terms of this agreement were reflected in the contractual arragement referred to as the Patronato Real.

As a private proprietor, the crown may be expected to have sought to maximize the discounted future stream of net income its New World assets could yield.[14] To that effect the crown could assume the risks of conquering,

complex forms of state and labor coercion also seem to have arisen first where the scarcity of land made itself felt earlier.

11. See Batchelder and Freudenberger, "Rational Origins".
12. See North, "Framework to Analyze the State".
13. That New World assets were indeed privately owned by the kings of Castile and Aragon has been pointed out by numerous historians. See, for an example, Hanke, *Spanish Struggle for Justice*.
14. It has also been argued that "(r)iskiness to conquistadors would have made it irrational for

colonizing, and exploiting the resources, hiring individuals under a wage contract, monitoring their activities, and so on. Alternatively, the crown could cede its rights over these resources to private entrepreneurs in exchange for either a lump-sum payment or for a share of the profits that the resources would yield. The crown's choice would depend on its attitude towards risk, ease of access to information about conquest opportunities, and ability to monitor agents as compared to those of individuals. Even if the crown was subject to greater risk than conquistadors, under information asymmetry and costly monitoring it would have been in its interest to share profits with them – which is what happened – as opposed to employing them under a salary contract or selling them conquest rights for a lump sum payment.[15] The conquest and colonization of America, therefore, was a joint venture between the Spanish state and private entrepreneurs. To raise the rate of return on investment in exploration, conquest, and colonization the crown established the so-called "system of monopolies", which created economic rents that the crown and individual entrepreneurs could share. The crown's share usually took the form of a tax payment, which in the case of mineral ores was the royal fifth, twenty per cent of the refined metal extracted.

The American lowlands and the highlands differed in their factor endowments. In the lowlands land was relatively abundant but deposits of precious metals in short supply in the growing European economies of the long sixteenth century were more scarce than in the highlands; the lowland indigenous population was sparse, population groups were much smaller, nomadic or semi-nomadic, and more thinly spread; labor productivity was comparatively much lower. Taxation could produce sufficient revenues to sustain only a very simple form of state and religious organization. In the highlands, by contrast, the indigenous population was relatively more dense, had a more highly evolved division of labor, and higher agricultural and artisanal labor productivity. Highland systems of public finance and labor coercion had supported a fairly large pre-Columbian state and religious bureaucracies and were easily adapted to Spanish aims.[16]

In the lowlands, the relatively high land-to-labor ratio suggests that had property rights been well defined and enforced rent would have been very small

---

the crown to sell off conquest rights for a lump-sum payment and not share in the returns, assuming the returns are sufficiently detectable." See Baltchelder and Sanchez, "The Encomienda and the Maximizing Imperialist", p. 11.

15. See Service, "Indian-European Relations in Colonial Latin America", pp. 411-25.

16. This is not to say that one would not expect labor coercion to emerge in the highlands. Labor coercion may arise even if land has become scarce, as Domar's "Causes" contends was the case in the Russian Ukraine. That the incentive of the lowlands paled by comparison to that offered by the highlands is suggested by the fact that, between 1535 and 1598, direct migration from Spain to the River Plate through the Atlantic (not Peru) was not much above the minimum of 3087 calculated by Konetzke, "Emigración española al Río de la Plata", p. 428.

or zero, most or all of the output would have accrued to laborers as wages, and the state could derive comparatively fewer revenues from land rents relative to the cost of revenue collection. The nomads of the lowlands were typically harder to conquer. Furthermore, lowland colonies were more open to encroachment by mercantilist rivals and more difficult to defend. On the other hand, mineral land may be viewed as a more fertile grade of agricultural land yielding a differential rent that the crown could tax. In addition, mineral-rich colonies tended to be populated by more settled peoples, which were more easily subdued. These colonies were also inland and in the highlands, and were therefore more easily defended.

Highland and lowland colonies, therefore, had different combinations of expected profitability and risk attached. The crown, therefore, may be said to have faced a portfolio choice problem. Given that the expected rate of return on investment was higher, and risk lower, in the more densely populated highlands than in the lowlands, portfolio choice theory would have led one to expect the crown's portfolio to be concentrated in highland colonies, which is what in fact happened. However, supplying and defending the more profitable domains of Mexico and Peru from encroachment by competing rivals – indigenous and European – required frontier colonies to be settled. To induce private agents do so the crown had to offer them sufficient incentives which, for revenue-maximizing reasons, had to be furnished by New World resources. In frontier regions only labor could, in general, produce rents, land had little or no value. Consequently, inducing Spanish colonists to remain in the frontiers implied some form of labor market regulation by coercion, since only thus could the mobility of indigenous labor be curtailed and the wage rate and the marginal product of labor be made to diverge so that the difference could be appropriated by Spanish non-laborers in both the private and the public sectors.[17] Employers who forcefully curtail the mobility of labor effectively create a labor market monopsony. In the system of monopolies the labor market appeared as coerced labor.

Curiously, however, the early Spanish military "huestes" in Paraguay first sought to attain their aims mostly by voluntary associations with friendly American Indians. While trying to reach Peru they generally traded with the Carios for the labor services and goods they needed. This was the so-called "first service". The mutually beneficial alliances Spaniards and Carios formed were cemented in the customary indigenous manner, that is, by trade and the polygamous marital unions of Cario women to Spanish men.[18] From these arose

17. On the "huestes", see Velázquez, "Organización militar de la Gobernación", pp. 28-31. The Carios valued iron tools highly, and quickly substituted them for their own stone instruments. On the "first service", see De Aguirre, "Diario del capitán Juan Francisco de Aguirre".
18. Documents characterize the scenario as "Mohammed's Paradise". According to them, some

a mestizo population and kinship ties between Spaniards, Carios, and their mestizo offspring. Particularly important among these kinship relations were those between in-laws, which had mediated the exchange of voluntary, reciprocal labor services among indigenous tribes and initially served the same purpose between Spaniards and Carios. For this reason the resulting system of reciprocal labor services came to be known as the "cuñadazgo".[19] Polygamy had an economic rationale for both Spaniards and Carios. The more indigenous wives, the more indigenous in-laws a Spaniard had, and the more permanent and occasional help he could obtain. Exogamy benefitted the Carios as well, since it turned a potentially devastating enemy into an ally, albeit at a price.[20]

This voluntary "primer servicio", however, came under pressure, and began to yield to enslavement. The western "entradas" so-called required outfitting and porters, which made indigenous women became particularly valuable because they were responsible for performing agricultural and other heavy chores in their own communities. Pressed to reach Peru before other Peninsulars did so from the Pacific the Spaniards in Asunción quickly turned the "cuñadazgo" into a vehicle for coercively exacting progressively greater amounts of labor from their Cario "relatives".[21] In particular, they came to use their "wives" as slaves, ex-changing them freely among themselves for clothing, horses, etc. These increased Spanish demands were responsible for some indigenous uprisings against the Spaniards.[22] In addition, the joint military expeditions to the west produced numerous captives that Spaniards and Carios divided up as slaves among themselves.

II. The Early Colonial Economy to the 1630's

This section will first discuss indigenous slavery, which in Paraguay arose in earnest after being legally abolished from the Spanish American empire as a whole. However, it was replaced in short order by forms of coerced indigenous labor inspired in those imposed in the center of the Spanish empire but peculiarly adapted to the frontier, the "encomienda de la mita" and the "encomienda yanacona", different from the classic forms the encomienda, the mita, and the yanaconazgo took in Peru, the "congregación", whose frontier form also differed from that in Peru, and the "mandamientos de repartimiento", all terms

Spaniards were said to have had up to seventy or eighty wives, while "one who is poor" had only five or six. Service, *Spanish-Guarani Relations*, suggests an average of three indigenous women per Spaniard (p. 34).
19. From the Spanish, "cuñado/a" = brother-in-law/sister in-law.
20. On exogamy see Clastres, *La société contre l'état*, pp. 43-68.
21. See Garavaglia, *Mercado Interno*.
22. Among them that of 1545, which the Spaniards put down with the aid of two thousand loyal Indians. See Service, *Spanish-Guarani Relations*, p. 22.

whose meaning will soon become clear.[23] It will also consider the question of the indigenous population decrease.

A. Indigenous Enslavement, Depopulation, and Public Finances

Once Potosí was discovered in 1545, enslavement of American Indians in Paraguay increased in scale and was linked to production. Disregarding that the enslaving of indigenous people had been legally abolished from the Spanish empire in 1542, Spaniards began openly to raid what up to then hand been friendly indigenous communities.[24] Their raids sought women in particular, and formally stretched until 1555.[25] Indian slaves built Asunción, raised the American roots and legumes and the European cereals, sugar cane, and grapes that made up the diet of the early Spanish colonizers, and also processed the derivative sweets, rum, and wines they consumed.[26] Indigenous slaves were also exported to São Vicente, on the Atlantic coast, where they were sold to Portuguese sugar cane producers.[27] However, the trade in indigenous slaves must have been small, for Cario slave hunters located nearer the Atlantic coast had a comparative advantage.[28]

The previous description suggests that the Spaniards in Paraguay expected mining in highland Peru to result in a derived demand for inputs that they could meet given a sufficient supply of slave labor. We know, in addition, that they kept hoping to eventually find mines locally as well. Furthermore, the poor

23. On the abolition of indigenous slavery see Konetzke, "Esclavitud de indios como elemento", pp. 257-294.
24. Historians have time and again described Mexican and Peruvian – as well as frontier – forms of coerced labor. Though fewer, studies of frontier colonies abound as well, even in the case of comparatively little researched Paraguay. Among the most prominent of these are, in addition to Service, *Spanish-Guarani Relations* and and Garavaglia's *Mercado Interno*, Susnik, *Indio colonial del Paraguay*; Zavala, *Orígenes de la colonización*; Saeger, "Survival and Abolition", pp. 59-85; and Velázquez, "Caracteres de la encomienda paraguaya", pp. 115-163.
25. On the slave raids ("malocas" or "rancheadas") see Susnik, *Indio colonial*, vol. 1, *El guaraní colonial*. Their former indigenous allies reacted against these raids with a generalized resistance that Spaniards bloodily repressed, by fleeing, as well as in other ways. See Roulet, *Resistencia de los Guaraní del Paraguay*, pp. 57-64 and 203-232. For a chronology of Indian uprisings see Necker, "Réaction des Indiens Guarani".
26. Livestock was very scarce, horses being comparatively much more numerous than cattle. Municipal herds ("manadas concejiles") were kept in areas where they would not cause much damage to plantings, like the western plains across the Paraguay river from Asunción, as well as on the eastern bank.
27. See Paoli, *Economía colonial*.
28. It is not a necessary condition because so long as the gap between the marginal product of labor and the subsistence needs of labor is relatively large, serfdom may obtain even though free land may have disappeared, as happened in the Ukraine in the eighteenth century. It is not a sufficient condition because – as will be seen in detail below – land abundance may result in a small free peasantry.

delineation and enforcement of property rights would have led one to expect enslavement to arise: the demand for output would have generated a relatively greater derived demand for labor under the assymmetrically defined and enforced property rights structure that obtained than under well delineated and enforced rights. Assuming that private property rights are defined and enforced on capital and labor but not on land, capital and labor will be used until their rates of remuneration equal the average, not the marginal value product of labor and capital. Thus, the demand for labor will be greater under common than under private land ownership and, for an upward-sloping supply of labor, the equilibrium wage rate will be higher.

However, employers will have to pay these higher wages only if property rights on labor are well defined and enforced. Should the distribution of violence potential between prospective employers and employees be uneven, and absent private or state enforcement of property rights on labor and land, employers may be expected to use their greater coercive capability to reduce laborers' mobility, shift their labor supply curve to the right, and reduce the real "wage rate", that is, the portion of output turned over to laborers. Furthermore, competitive behavior in the face of a scarce resource over which no property rights are defined typically involves a rush by some demanders to appropriate the resource before others do, for the same reason that we do not expect apples in open access orchards to ripen.

Labor coercion will force the laborers off the labor supply curve that would represent their free labor-leisure choice, leading them to furnish a larger labor input than they would have provided voluntarily at every wage rate or, alternatively, reducing the cost of any given amount of labor to "employers". The shifted labor supply curve retains its positive slope, implying that material incentives could induce bonded laborers to move along their coerced labor supply curve and raise the amount of output produced. In addition to punishments, therefore, systems of coerced labor may be expected to include rewards, that is, incentive structures devised to induce laborers to voluntarily increase effort.[29] Conversely, positive inducements in this monopsonistic labor market create additional labor rents that laborers and employers may appropriate and/or the government may tax.

---

29. For these incentives to be effective, the laborers' rights to enjoy them will have to be somehow recognized, and slaves will – in general – have to be capable of property usufruct or ownership, which is inconsistent with their legal status as chattel. This contradiction will reflect itself in the law and cultures of societies based on labor coercion. However, the ambiguity will have positive implications for the coerced laborer's capacity to accumulate wealth, derive an income from that wealth, and spend it, whether on consumer goods or on repurchasing his/her freedom. On the question of ambiguity see Davis, *Problem of Slavery*. For the differences between Spanish American and US slave systems, see Klein, *Slavery in the Americas*.

This suggests that enslavement may have benefitted not only private entrepreneurs but the crown as well. Tax revenues the crown obtained from enslavement helped support officials of the royal bureaucracy in the area. Furthermore, to the extent that indigenous labor rents could help support a local settlers' militia, the crown would have to commit fewer resources of its own to colonial defense and could save revenues. Moreover, settlers had predictably expressed a clear preference for being rewarded with grants of labor and would remain in the area if incentives remained attractive. Thus, if only the crown would divert towards them part of the labor rents of indigenous people settlers could permanently provide for colonial defense at little or no public expense. Conversely, outlawing slavery would have been both costly for the crown to enforce and, if enforced, detrimental to royal interests. It is for these reasons, I submit, that indigenous slavery arose in Paraguay, and persisted in overt or disguised form, as in Chile, until much after the New Laws of 1542 abolished it elsewhere in the Spanish American empire.[30]

Consider now the related question of depopulation. The indigenous population reduction began as a result of the first military expeditions to the west, the polygamous marriages of Spaniards with indigenous women, and European diseases. However, the rate at which the indigenous population decreased seemed to have accelerated when the Spanish increased the labor services they exacted from the so-called "friendly Indians" and enslaved them. Resistance, repression, and flight compounded the problem. That is, indigenous depopulation may originally have been exogenously induced, but was endogenously compounded subsequently.

Enslavement of indigenous people by Spaniards implied in effect that the militarily superior private Spaniards – if not prevented by state intervention- could treat indigenous people as a common property resource, and could transform them into private property. The effects of enslavement on the indigenous population, therefore, can be understood by resorting to the economic theory of common property resource use, and by noting that the nature of enslavement affected the ability of indigenous commmunities to reproduce themselves. Though private poverty may be expected to be conserved, a very high rate of interest may cause slaveowners to use slaves more rapidly than they can be replenished.[31] Moreover, enslavement may destroy some part of the common property resource. Even if enslavement could be effected without destroying part of the population in the process, should the stock from which slaves are obtained be regarded as common property there is no incentive to economize its use, the resource in question is overused, the rents that would

---

30. See Velázquez, "Organización Militar", p. 32; and Konetzke, "Esclavitud de los indios".
31. See Clark, "Economics of Overexploitation", p. 630.

have accrued to it dissipate, and the resource itself is depleted.[32] In general, therefore, while the effect of slavery on those enslaved may be ambiguous, we would expect enslave hunting to unambiguously deplete the source population. Whether conservation or depletion will prevail may not be established a priori.

Hunting for indigenous slaves in Paraguay led to indigenous depopulation because Spaniards preferentially enslaved women and affected the ability of the stock to reproduce itself. The drastic reduction in the proportion of women of child bearing age among the population reduced fertility while simultaneously increasing child mortality. It also diminished the output of agricultural products and reduced the indigenous community's ability to produce its sustenance. Worsening nutrition in turn increased susceptibility to illness – already high because of low indigenous resistance to European illness – and morbidity. The indigenous population, therefore, experienced what an anthropologist has called a "vertical descent".[33]

Enslaving American Indians eventually had deleterious public finance implications as well. Although Spaniards were required to pay a head tax per indigenous slave they captured, free American Indians also had to pay a tax, for the protection they theoretically enjoyed from the crown, and would have had to pay it had they remained free. Thus, indigenous enslavement's short term benefits to the crown could be more than offset in the long run by the enslavement-induced decline of the free indigenous population and consequent shrinking of the tax base. As the conquest of Mexico and Peru was completed, therefore, the crown curtailed the political and economic powers it had granted to the conquerors and ultimately replaced them by salaried officers of the royal bureaucracy. The conflictive political struggle through which that transition was accomplished preceded the economic struggle for control of the indigenous labor force. That is, once a certain region was conquered, the crown sought to change the distribution of labor rents in its favor. How the crown went about it will become clear in the next section.

What of the abolition of Indian slavery? Domar suggested that slavery would disappear for economic reasons, as a result of population growth. Another approach suggests that abolition may come about as a result of political measures. In Paraguay, the abolition of Indian slavery came about in the context of depopulation, as a result of state measures motivated both by economic and

---

32. Thomas and Bean, studying the African slave trade, noticed a clear link between slave hunting and depopulation. They suggested that slave hunting could be seen as analogous to fishing in open access fisheries, that depopulation could be likened to the depletion of fish stocks that ensues from excessive entry, and that these and other aspects of the problem could be analyzed in terms of the economic theory of common property resources. See Thomas and Bean, "Fishers of Men", pp. 885-914.

33. Susnik, *Indio colonial*.

ideological reasons. Private Spaniards favored the continuation of Indian slavery, but the Church condemned it, for reasons that some have argued were partly economic in nature.[34] Indigenous slavery was abolished when the crown sided with the Church and forced slavery to be replaced by the encomiendas.

B. Indigenous Encomiendas (Entrustment) and Congregación (Confinement)

To indigenous enslavement and depopulation the crown responded in mid 16th century by instituting the "encomienda de la mita" and the "encomienda yanacona", also known later as the "encomienda originaria", as well as the "congregación". Both forms of the encomienda were absolutist adaptations to New World frontier conditions of the Castilian institution used during the Spanish Reconquest and of pre-Columbian forms of labor control in Peru.[35] The Paraguayan encomienda de la mita and the encomienda yanacona, however, differed from the encomienda, the mita, and the yanaconazgo in Perú, and from the corresponding form of those institutions in Mexico. The Paraguayan congregación also differed in some respects from that in Perú and Mexico. In the sequel I will describe the encomiendas and the congregación in detail and interpret them in terms of the proposed theoretical framework.

i) Encomienda de la mita. From previous experience elsewhere in the New World royal officials in Asunción expected that enslavement would lower the indigenous population, that royal finances would suffer, and that so would their salaries, for they were paid from taxes collected locally. Consequently, from early on they pressed the ruling lieutenant governor to do away with enslavement and introduce the encomiendas, which they claimed would at the same time protect free indigenous vassals from enslavement and depopulation as well as provide private Spaniards access to indigenous labor. He finally stopped supporting the kinship system of obtaining indigenous labor the settlers favored once the king conditioned his appointment as Provincial governor to the institution of the encomiendas, which the lieutenant governor imposed at last in 1556. That year alone, he assigned in encomiendas mitarias 27,000 able-bodied, adult males (the equivalent of a population of about 100,000) among a fraction (320) of the Spaniards in Asunción.[36] Those left without encomiendas set out for other areas where unentrusted indigenous settlements were known to exist, the Guayra area east of Asunción most notably, where the process was repeated.

34. Batchelder and Sanchez, "Encomienda and the Maximizing Imperialist".
35. The Quechua term "yanacona" was brought to Paraguay by men escaping the repression that followed Pizarro's revolts in Perú. It was used early in the colonial period but later yielded to the term "originario", used to refer to American Indian outside his town of origin. Mita comes from "mit'a", Quechua for "turn". See Garavaglia, Mercado interno, p. 272.
36. See Susnik, Indio colonial, vol. 1. Guaraní colonial.

The grant of an encomienda was a transaction between the crown and private Spaniards whose terms were embodied in a contract the courts recognized as legally binding. The encomienda mitaria required American Indians subject to it, in lieu of paying tribute, to take turns providing specified labor services to their masters, the so-called "encomenderos" or "vecinos feudetarios", for a period that initially extended to six months per year but that by the early seventeenth century had been reduced to two.[37] In exchange encomenderos were to protect, convert, and acculturate their Indian charges; fix residence in a given Spanish American town; pay certain taxes to the crown;[38] and contribute at their own expense to the colony's defense against internal and external enemies, i.e., take on police and military functions. An encomendero could hold an encomienda mitaria for his life time and bequeath it to one, or in very unusual circumstances, two consecutive generations of his or her descendants, that is, always less than the perpetual grant to which encomenderos aspired.[39] Encomenderos were not supposed to trade on their encomiendas in any way and were specifically barred from selling and renting them. The encomienda became "vacant" at the end of the number of generations ("lives") for which it was granted, if the beneficiary died without heirs, or if he or she abandoned the encomienda. A vacant encomienda reverted ("escheated") to the crown, which could reassign it to other worthy Spaniards of its choice. The crown could also assign encomiendas to royal officials in pursuit of public aims.

Encomenderos in Spanish America, unlike those in Spain, had no judicial powers, nor could they arm the indigenous people entrusted to them. That is, their powers were restricted relative to those of their Peninsular counterparts. Furthermore, the Paraguayan encomienda de la mita, as its name suggests it, was actually a synthesis of the encomienda and the mita of Peru. Like early versions of the encomienda elsewhere, the Paraguayan encomienda required payment in labor services and goods. Like the mita, the Paraguayan encomienda mitaria remained a rotatory, draft labor service institution until the very end of the colonial period. Unlike the mita, however, it did not require payment of a money wage. In Peru, military services were required of recipients of encomienda grants but not of recipients of mita grants.[40]

---

37. See Saeger, "Survival and Abolition", p. 60.
38. The taxes in question were the "media anata" and the "año de demora". See Saeger, "Survival and Abolition", pp. 59-85.
39. An encomienda mitaria was a temporary grant of specified, restricted labor services; it was not a land grant, nor did it necessarily imply such a grant. In Paraguay, extraction from royally owned lands of yerba mate for export, the most profitable use to which encomenderos could devote their labor grants, did not require the ownership of any land at all, only the purchase of a license. However, output can generally not be produced with labor alone and, therefore, encomenderos also tended to seek, and receive, separate grants of land.
40. For the wage payment the Peruvian mita required see Tandeter, Coacción y mercado.

The encomienda de la mita was a tax-farming scheme by which the crown leased out the right to collect in labor services the indigenous tribute, which royal officials would otherwise have had to collect.[41] Farming out the collection of the tribute benefitted both the crown and encomenderos. American Indians of the tropical lowlands, owing to their comparatively lesser degree of agricultural development and practically non-existent commerce, had a much lower ability to pay taxes than highland indigenous communities. In the tropical lowlands, the costs of collecting taxes in kind frequently exceeded the value of tax collections, owing to high transaction cost: local auction markets for agricultural produce were relatively thin, revenues in kind were perishable, and the high cost of land and water transportation made it difficult to transport them to other regions of America or to Spain, where they might be more advantageously auctioned off. The Spanish colonists, on the other hand, could devote the output of indigenous agriculture to more profitable use than the crown. They could not only consume in situ the provisions indigenous people furnished, but could also raise indigenous labor productivity significantly, by introducing production processes previously unknown locally, setting indigenous laborers to work with iron tools (which the indigenous people themselves recognized to be superior to stone tools and sought eagerly) and subjecting the indigenous labor force to a more disciplined – if involuntary – work regime. The encomiendas de la mita, therefore, could increase Spanish output and taxable income. However, they significantly skewed income distribution relative to what it would have been had property rights on labor and land been enforced.

In addition, the encomenderos' contributions to defense saved the crown the costs of supporting a standing army devoted to that end, which costs could be quite high given the colony's location on both the Indian and Portuguese frontiers.[42] Encomenderos were also fewer and more stationary than indigenous tributaries would have been had they remained free, which also reduced the crown's tax collection costs. Entrusting Indian vassals to encomenderos also saved the crown the costs of fulfilling its commitment to the Pope to protect, convert, and acculturate its indigenous vassals.[43] Thus, the encomiendas were

---

41. See Pastore, *Lucha por la tierra*, p. 12. By farming out the collection of taxes rulers generally exchange a future stream of revenues for a present lump sum payment. Tax farming, therefore, is a substitute for government borrowing in a thin or non-existent capital market (that is, a capital market innovation) or for an inefficient or nonexistent tax collecting bureaucracy. For the suggestion that "capital is a prerequisite, not a cause, of tax farming", see Levi, *Of Rule and Revenue*, p. 78.

42. However, provincial defense could not be satisfactorily organized with encomenderos alone and it became necessary to resort to the compulsory recruitment of all men capable of wielding arms even if they were encomenderos. Velázquez, "Organización Militar", p. 33.

43. The crown delegated onto encomenderos all the functions that it had committed itself to perform on behalf of the Church.

but a particular case of tax farming by which the crown increased revenues and reduced expenditures, that is, maximized fiscal revenues.

ii) Encomienda yanacona or originaria. "Recalcitrant" indigenous people who had resisted or attacked the Spaniards or who, after 1556, had refused to peacefully submit to entrustment, could be the object of "just wars". The captives thus obtained were kept under close supervision in the homes and farms of the Spaniards and served them continuously in all sorts of tasks, that is, were enslaved. Following the first distribution of encomiendas mitarias in mid-sixteenth century, these slaves came to be regarded as belonging to another encomienda, the encomienda "yanacona" or "originaria".[44] Given the nature of their tasks, yanaconas may be said to have supplied the demand for year-round labor, "mita Indians" the demand for seasonal labor. Encomiendas yanaconas or originarias, like the mitarias, could not legally be traded; they had to revert to the crown before being reassigned. The encomienda yanacona thus disguised and prolonged indigenous slavery, but in a restricted form, since yanaconas could not legally be sold or rented. These ownership restrictions would suggest that holders of encomienda yanaconas may have had incentives not to conserve their labor grant similar to those facing holders of encomiendas mitarias and, in fact, the number of days that yanacona Indians owed their masters increased from four to five per week between the late sixteenth and the early seventeenth centuries.[45] However, indications can be found that Spaniards treated yanaconas comparatively better than they did "mita Indians", perhaps because, in practice, trades and rentals of yanaconas did take place. This may have been facilitated by the fact that encomiendas yanaconas were more mobile than encomiendas de la mita, since neither encomenderos nor the indigenous people subjected to them were constrained by residency requirements.

iii) Congregación. Following the Toledo reforms in Upper Peru, that is, from the 1570's onwards, "indios de la mita" were also subject to the "congregación", a policy that involved their resettlement, concentration, and confinement in supervised, segregated towns to which only encomenderos and a few additional persons could have access.[46] Contrary to what was the case in highland, relatively land-scarce areas of the Spanish empire, in land-abundant Paraguay the colonial administration assigned these towns fairly extensive amounts of land, though these were fewer than those indigenous communities had considered their own.

---

44. See Zavala, *Orígenes de la colonización*.
45. Garavaglia, *Mercado interno*, p. 273.
46. Until their confinement to towns, many indigenous people whom the Spaniards had notified that they were subject to the encomienda but did not effectively control would simply not come to render the services expected of them. These were the "encomendados por noticia". See Mora Mérida, *Historia Social del Paraguay*. Clearly, entrusting indigenous laborers was insufficient; the laborers' ability to flee had to be forcefully curtailed as well, which is precisely what confining them to towns accomplished.

Town dwellers were to work these lands collectively to support themselves and their overseers but could not alienate them either individually or as a community. In addition, Indian town dwellers could only trade with those allowed access to the towns, in particular, royal officials and their encomendero(s), who had a monopoly on the meager market for consumer goods that Indian towns offered. That is, product and factor market restrictions applied.[47] Finally, Indian town dwellers were collectively responsible for individual tributary obligations. Under the system of monopolies, therefore, indigenous people faced monopoly and monopsony in the product market and monopsony in the labor market. Furthermore, they could have usufruct of the land, but could not privately own it, whether collectively or individually. Finally, the congregación allowed collective taxation to be imposed.[48] Clearly, this incentive system discouraged indigenous economic activity and encouraged flight.

Viewing the enslavement-induced indigenous depopulation from the point of view of the economic theory of common property resources would have suggested that the crown needed to reaffirm its property rights on the indigenous labor force and reduce its rate of utilization, which is precisely what the crown in fact did. Thus, the crown first declared it illegal for individual Spaniards to enslave its indigenous vassals except in cases of "just wars", that is, it denied individuals the right to appropriate by force indigenous labor power without royal authority.[49] Secondly, the crown not only outlawed the damaging slave raids but for a fee licensed selected individuals to use indigenous labor services under specified conditions.[50] The process by which the crown granted encomiendas allowed it to price-discriminate among those who demanded them, that is, improved the crown's bargaining position vis-à-vis private "employers" and tilted the terms of the transaction in favor of the crown. Third, by comparison to what was required of indigenous slaves, the encomiendas mitarias reduced the length and the range of labor services that mita Indians were obliged to render their masters, and progressively curtailed the length of required labor obligations from

47. Entrustment of the indigenous population could – and did in fact – take place independently of its confinement to towns, especially in the beginning. Thus, while some temporary indigenous towns were founded by private Spaniards even before the first encomiendas were granted in the 1550s, the first permanent indigenous towns were not founded until the 1580s, by Franciscan missionaries. For the early founding of Indian towns by private Spaniards, see de Azara, *Descripción e historia del Paraguay*. Franciscan missionaries would typically found a town and, after a period of time, leave it to a member of the secular priesthood to go found another town elsewhere. See Estragó, *Presencia Franciscana*, pp. 93-164.
48. On the economics of collective taxation see Hansen, "An Economic Model", pp. 473-519.
49. The crown, however, did allow a loophole. It permitted Indian enslavement in cases of "just war", which itself was supposed to require previous government approval.
50. Allowing worthy individuals alone could receive encomiendas was a way of discriminating in the sale of the grant.

around a half a year to two month.[51] Concomitantly, the crown segregated Spaniards and "mita" Indians to towns of their own.[52] That is, the crown protected indigenous people from Spaniards – thus reducing the depopulation caused by enslavement and pathogens – and restricted their freedom of movement, a condition for extracting labor rent. Many of the features of the encomienda and the congregación can be more fully appreciated when viewed in this light.

In the theoretical framework presented, changes in relative factor prices should have given rise to changes in production techniques. Those previously considered efficient should have been displaced by others which more intensively utilized the relatively abundant, cheaper factor. These changes should have been reflected in the composition of output and the structure of exports. In the context under consideration, we would have expected a move away from labor intensive techniques and towards land intensive techniques; goods produced by such techniques should have begun to predominate among exports as well. This is exactly what we observe. Until the 1570s, the economy was based exclusively on indigenous agriculture. All production was for local consumption, there was no production for export. As the indigenous population decreased, however, and the regional economy built around Potosí silver mining expanded, interest in cattle raising increased, beginning in the late fifteen sixties and the early fifteen seventies.[53] The expansion of cattle raising – in turn – led to the search for lands to the south more apt for cattle raising than those of Paraguay and closer to the Potosí market, to the founding of new cities, and to the development of regional and foreign trade. Exports first consisted mostly of cereals, sugar, and wines, which presupposed a relatively labor intensive agriculture, but the structure of exports began to change early in the seventeenth century. By the 1630s, the early exports began to be displaced by yerba mate, which did not need to be cultivated and could simply be harvested from forests northeast of Asunción. Yerba mate gathering, furthermore, also required inputs of cattle and cattle byproducts, which could also be produced by labor-saving methods.

C. Mandamientos de Repartimiento

As the crown progressively curtailed the mita obligations of town Indians, the leisure time available to them increased. Documentary evidence dating back to

51. Thus, the encomiendas originally granted in mid sixteenth century were much more onerous than those of the early seventeenth century. See De la Fuente Machaín, *Gobernador Domingo Martínez*.
52. Only the encomenderos, the town supervisor, and the priest that was supposed to christianize the residents could have access to Indian towns.
53. Although a few heads of cattle were introduced as early as 1555, it is not until the late 1560s that plans to introduce sizeable quantities of cattle are evident. See Cuevas, *Ganadería en el Paraguay*.

the mid seventeenth century indicates that the crown then imposed a new coerced labor requirement on town Indians, the so-called mandamientos, by which the state rented out indigenous laborers to private entrepreneurs. The crown established the wage that employers would have to pay indigenous laborers for the mandamiento tasks they performed. Town Indians seem to have preferred the remunerated mandamientos to the unremunerated mita, even though they received a wage lower than the going market wage and, in addition, had to turn over half of it to the town's "treasury".[54]

Mandamientos seem to have become more common once yerba mate exports began to increase. Spaniards resorted to them to build and man vessels to transport yerba mate down river to Asunción, as well as for other commercial activities. As exports increased the number of laborers sent out under the mandamientos rose and so did those who did not return to their towns of origin, either because Spaniards kept them from returning or because the town Indians themselves used the mandamientos as an excuse to escape from the towns to which they were confined and avoid the variety of obligations that weighted upon them there. The colonial administration then appointed a special supervisor, the "alcalde de sacas", to enforce mandated extraction ceilings and assure that indigenous laborers on mandamiento assignments returned to their towns.

This phenomenon may be interpreted in the following terms: Increased exports will shift the demand for labor outward, giving rise to excess demand and putting upward pressure on laborers' remuneration. The more inelastic the demand for labor, the greater would be the labor rents that a given rightward shift of the demand for labor would generate and encomenderos would capture, and the higher the opportunity cost to the state of encomiendas in private hands. The state therefore had reasons to regulate or "tame" the encomienda and impose the mandamientos. Revenues to the state would clearly have been greater under an "encomienda cum mandamientos" system than under a system of encomiendas alone. Indigenous laborers may also have benefitted from this system since they would have appropriated some of those rents.

D. Coercion, Confinement and the Continued Indigenous Population Fall

The "new" system of the encomiendas, congregación, and mandamientos did not protect the indigenous population as well as it had been expected to. By the early seventeenth century the indigenous population had been reduced to a fraction of its original size and both forms of the encomiendas had declined

---

54. In addition to their mita and mandamiento obligations, town Indians, could be called upon by the state to perform corveé labor, that is, to build and repair roads, bridges, forts, and public buildings. See Garavaglia, *Mercado interno*, p. 309; and Velázquez, "Rebelión de los indios de Arecayá", pp. 20-56.

noticeably, despite the fact that confinement to towns had been largely accomplished and that three successive sets of royal ordinances of the late sixteenth and early seventeenth centuries noted the abuses and legislated against them. Contemporary sources suggest that the indigenous population was reduced to one tenth of its original numbers by the early sixteenth century. A more conservative estimate is given by Garavaglia (1983) who suggests a fifty percent reduction.[55] Contemporaries attributed the problem to the system of incentives built-in the encomiendas. They specifically mentioned that the grant was not perpetual, that it could only be held for the grantee's lifetime and one or two generations of their descendants;[56] and that it could not be freely traded or rented out. Encomenderos shifted indigenous people subject to the encomienda de la mita to the encomienda yanacona, or exceeded the terms of the mandamientos, to which ends they bribed the Spanish corregidores of indigenous towns if necessary, a practice that became more common in the course of the seventeenth century, as the Hapsburgs' sale of offices became commonplace. For these and other reasons the decline of the indigenous population continued.

III. The Seventeenth Century Crisis: Stagnation of Encomiendas, Rise of Jesuit Missions and of the Small Peasantry

An early seventeenth century source puts the number of adult Indian males "who were serving or could potentially serve" at 28,200 in Asunción and its environs and at 115,170 in Guayra and the eastern region, for a total of 143,370. On the other hand, a 1674 survey of eighteen Indian towns found that they contained only 3,783 "service Indians".[57] That is, the indigenous population subject to the mita and reduced to towns continued to decline. In addition, the number of encomiendas mitarias decreased, although the number of indigenous people per encomienda increased. This reduction in the number of encomiendas also lowered the number of encomenderos who could be counted on to furnish military services to defend the colony. Furthermore, encomenderos evaded rendering the military service to which their grant obliged them by purchasing government offices which exempted them from that responsibility.[58]

---

55. The contemporary sources are quoted in López, "Shipbuilding in Sixteenth Century Asunción del Paraguay", pp. 59-85; for the ordinances see Chaves, "Ordenanzas de Ramírez de Velasco", pp. 107-120.
56. Mora Mérida, "Demografía colonial del Paraguay", p. 54, asserts that the report dates back to 1610.
57. See Mora Mérida, "Demografía colonial del Paraguay", p. 59.
58. See Saeger, "Survival and Abolition, p. 74.

Partially in response to the continued indigenous population decline, the local authorities requested the Jesuits to found missions in Guayrá, east of Asuncion, which they began doing in the 1610s, with indigenous people already entrusted to Spaniards.[59] However, São Paulo enslavers raided the Guayrá Spanish settlements and Jesuit missions, destroyed three Spanish cities and fourteen towns of Guaraní Indians, and forced them to move to areas farther west and south west, respectively.[60] The missions resettled in what became their "locus classicus", the area astride the Parana and Uruguay rivers. The pursuing Portuguese "bandeiras" were decisively defeated in mid seventeenth century by Jesuit-led indigenous armies which the king authorized the missionaries to train and equip with firearms.[61] In recognition of their success, the crown exempted the Jesuit missions from the encomienda between 1660 and 1680. In addition to rendering military service, exoneration from the encomienda required indigenous people to pay the tribute in cash, which the Jesuits raised by exporting yerba mate to the regional market and paid punctually. Attempts by Paraguayan encomenderos to extend the encomienda to Jesuit mission towns, observed at this time, generally failed.[62] Thereafter, the indigenous population of Jesuit missions grew despite periodic bouts of the plague.

Thus, the stock of indigenous labor evidently yielded much higher returns when congregated in missions under Jesuit oversight, segregated from Spaniards, and exempted from the encomienda than when subjected to the encomienda and confined to the less isolated towns Franciscans had founded. The crown had no reason, then, to yield to encomenderos and reimpose the encomienda on the Indians of the Jesuit missions, and did not. The following report of 7 november 1715 from the Royal Treasurer to the crown regarding the wisdom of subordinating the Jesuit missions to the authority of the Spanish colonial administration is clear on the effects that such a measure was anticipated to have, on fiscal revenues as well as in general:

> Such great injury may result from changing the governance of those Indians, putting Spanish governors and Justice to rule them, that there is not the slightest doubt of the risk to which those settlements, where such a (large) number of Indians dwell, would be exposed, [...] it being worthy of all attention that, if for any accident said Indians became restless, they would abandon the missions [...] even if none of this were to happen and the Spaniards could quietly and peacefully begin to govern [...] given the [...] poverty of those lands and the tribute [...] which each Indian

59. For the funding of the first Jesuit mission towns in the Guayra see Cardozo, *Antigua provincia*. The fact that the Jesuits formed missions with Indians already entrusted to Spaniards would later serve as the excuse for disputes with Paraguayans.
60. See Velázquez , "Organización Militar", p. 27. The name and location of the Guayrá towns destroyed may be found in Hemmings, *Red Gold*.
61. See Velázquez, "Organización Militar", pp. 41-43.
62. See Armani, *Ciudad de Dios*.

contributes to His Majesty, the Treasurer would not expect much of an increase in Royal revenues, given how general is the covetousness, especially in those parts, of those who come to govern, who only care for their own interests [...] a bull will be issued to the Audiencia ordering it not to allow any change in the government which for such a long time have had said Indian settlements.[63]

Much like the Jesuit mission Indians, the small mestizo peasantry became more important as the seventeenth century depression generally set in. Farms owned by Guarani-speaking small peasants spread over the lands indigenous people had vacated at a rate that, given the absence of immigration, must have been similar to the rate of population increase. Three issues need to be addressed here in so far as the small peasantry is concerned. First, how does one account for its appearance? Second, how does one explain the fact that mestizo peasants were – on the one hand – exempt from coerced labor obligations when the drastic indigenous population decrease would have led one to expect encomenderos to seek to extend the encomienda to mestizos? Third, why did the crown rely so heavily on them for colonial defense?

The rise of the free mestizo peasantry may be accounted for in terms of a simplified Ricardian model similar to that Domar used to account for the rise of the free Russian peasantry before serfdom, that is, of a model that embodies the scarcity of labor relative to land common to both the Eastern European and Latin American scenarios. For simplicity we may assume Lockean conditions, v.g., that labor is homogeneous and property rights on labor have emerged and are vested on the laborers themselves. Land, on the other hand, is infinitely abundant, equally fertile everywhere, and of open access. The model may or may not abstract from capital. Labor and land are initially assumed to be the only two factors of production. Being scarce, labor will fetch a price; if it is abundant and we abstract from locational advantages, land will not fetch a price or earn rent. That a free, small peasantry will arise under these conditions so long as property rights are well defined and enforced follows from implicit assumptions about the nature of the technology of production and of property rights delineation and enforcement. For as long as land remains abundant land rent will be zero. Landowners, therefore, will not hire laborers, nor will laborers hire themselves out to landowners for less than they can earn working land of their own, which under the assumed conditions they can readily obtain; consequently, land will be worked by individual proprietors without the help of hired labor. We would not expect to observe a wage labor force or share cropping, since both presuppose that land has become scarce. Property rights on commodities will be vested on the laborers, and the exchange of final goods, if it exists, will take place according to their labor content. The same goes for the means of

63. Kruger de Thomas, "Asunción y su área", p. 41.

production. By the same logic that we envision all final output belonging to the laborers, we can envision the laborers holding – if labor and land are complementary in production – private property rights on the land. Although techniques of production will tend to be land intensive, there will be little point in peasants accumulating more land than they can work alone or with the help of their families. Therefore, in addition to being owned by those who work them, farms will tend to be small and fairly equal in size, that is, the structure of property rights on labor determines the land tenure system, not the other way around. The number of peasant holdings will increase with the population, which will grow at a rate rate that may be expected to be a direct function of the difference between output and the peasantry's subsistence requirements – ceteris paribus.

The preceding results clearly depend on property rights being enforced at zero cost. Without costless enforcement the free peasantry that will arise is not likely to remain free. An uneven distribution of coercive capabilities among the peasants may lead some to attempt to enslave or enserf others, to appropriate some portion of the difference between the marginal product and the subsistence requirements of labor. Should the distribution of coercive capabilities among peasants be initially equal it will tend to become unequal, because incentives will exist to innovate the technology of coercion to appropriate some of the labor rents of those that do not innovate. Thus, even though a peasantry will arise in the absence of a state, it is not likely to remain free without state enforcement of rights.

The Paraguayan peasantry remained free of coerced labor obligations when economic forces would have led one to expect its enserfment because the state intervened.[64] The colonial administration enforced the Paraguayan peasants' rights to their own labor against encomendero pretensions, I argue, partly because it relied heavily on peasants to staff the militia necessary for colonial defense, demand for which was acute in the seventeenth century.

Nomadic Indians from the plains west of the Paraguay river became a fearsome enemy once they adopted the horse, just as the plains Indians of the United States did later. Their raids north and south of Asunción, in the absence of military fortifications, restricted the land effectively occupied by Spaniards to a narrow strip running east from Asunción along the central mountain range. In the decade of the 1660s efforts were made to set up fortifications north and south of Asunción

---

64. When their Spanish fathers recognized them as their children and the provincial governor concurred, acculturated mestizos were exempt from the encomienda, an exemption the courts enforced. For an instance see Velázquez, *Breve historia*, pp. 29–30. In fact, acculturated mestizos could themselves hold encomiendas. Moreover, due to the absence of immigration, "criollos" and mestizos actually occupied public offices supposedly reserved for Spaniards, though encomiendas and public offices continued to be assigned preferentially to Spaniards.

to defend against these attacks, but they secured only 25 to 30 kilometers of coast. Portuguese slave raids that stretched from the 1630s to the 1670s forced Spanish settlements from the Guayrá to relocate to the jurisdiction of Asunción. For that privilege they paid a high price, the division of their encomiendas among Asunción "vecinos".[65] Henceforth, these former Guayrá settlers were regarded as "poor peasants", that is, peasants without encomiendas, and were obligated to contribute to colonial defense through membership in the militia.

The organization of the provincial militias was apparently consolidated a little before or in the middle of the seventeenth century, and remained unchanged for 150 years.[66] By the late seventeenth century, most of those recruited for military service against Portuguese invasions were "soldiers without fief", and the proportion of these soldiers in the provincial militias increased as time went on.[67]

By the late seventeenth century, then, yerba mate had clearly emerged as the region's most important staple. The scarcity of labor relative to land influenced the choice of production technique and of product quality in different sectors of the yerba mate industry. Paraguayans, who continuously complained of the scarcity of indigenous labor, for the most part produced a coarser variety of the tea that required less processing. They never went beyond harvesting natural yerba mate forests to developing yerba mate plantations. The Jesuit missions, on the other hand, had relatively more numerous indigenous laborers as well as large cattle ranches in the northern reaches of what are now the Uruguayan prairies, and were known for producing a variety of yerba mate that required more labor intensive processing. They developed plantations near the missions as well.

The late seventeenth century pattern of territorial occupation is one of two Spanish and sixteen Indian towns, each with lands their inhabitants could own privately and collectively, respectively, and a small peasantry, all amidst vast royal lands containing the stocks from which yerba mate was produced.[68] The military structure had clearly changed as well. Indian armies from the Jesuit missions and an increasingly peasant based militia furnished most of the necessary defense services.

---

65. See Cardozo, *Antigua provincia.* Some of the Guayrá settlers preferred to join the Paulista "bandeirantes", thus the kinship between Paraguayan and Paulista families of today. See Monteiro, "São Paulo in the Seventeenth Century".

66. See Velázquez, "Organización Militar", p. 34.

67. *Ibid.*, p. 32. Militiamen were furnished the equipment necessary for the rotatory service they were required to render. For the expeditions they undertook against the Chaco Indians they were compensated by being allowed to share among themselves as slaves the indigenous prisoners they made. Domínguez lists 35 Chaco "entradas" between 1601 and 1700 according to Velázquez, who asserts that the list is not complete. See Domínguez, *Expediciones paraguayas al Chaco,* cited in: Velázquez, "Organización Militar".

68. Among Indian towns there were nine non-Jesuit Indian towns, and seven Jesuit Indian towns. See Velázquez, "Población del Paraguay", Appendix.

IV. Conclusions

Anticipated demand for staples, relative labor scarcity vis-à-vis land, an unequal distribution of violence potential between private agents, and poorly delineated and enforced rights by the state led to the displacement of cooperative relations by large scale indigenous enslavement. The distribution of labor rents initially favored private Spanish slave owners rather than the state. However, exploitation by private entrepreneurs of crown-owned indigenous labor along common property resource lines contributed to the depletion of the labor resource and the dissipation of rents that would otherwise have accrued to it. As labor became more scarce and, therefore, more valuable, the crown imposed the encomiendas – a tax farming scheme intended to regulate the exploitation of Indian labor and provide for colonial defense – to prevent further depletion and rent dissipation as well as to tilt the distribution of rents in its favor. As demand for export staples increased, the crown tamed the encomiendas and also imposed the congregación and the mandamientos de repartimientos. However, the system did not work well, because of reasons traceable to the incentive structure and monitoring costs. Jesuit missions became the preferred institutional arrangement to collec taxes and provide defense once it became clear that indigenous people contributed more to colonial defense and crown coffers when gathered in Jesuit missions and exempted from the encomiendas than when entrusted to encomenderos.

The small mestizo peasantry emerged and eventually predominated over the forms of coerced indigenous labor that preceded it for two reasons. First, land was initially abundant and became even more so as the indigenous population declined and was confined to towns, i.e., factor proportions were the required ones. Once the still unentrusted indigenous population disappeared the mestizos had to rely on their own labor and the still abundant land for a livelihood, that is, they became peasants. Second, as the indigenous population declined, encomenderos failed to extend the encomienda to acculturated mestizos. The state enforced regulations making mestizos legally ineligible for subjection to the encomienda partly because the free peasantry formed the basis of the militia that provided colonial defense. Thus, the peasantry remained free when economic forces would have led to its bonding due to state intervention consistent with the maximizing view of the state advocated here.

Forced Labour and Non-Capitalist Industrialization: The Case of Stalinism (c. 1929 – c. 1956)[*]

Marcel van der Linden

It is especially through the works of Alexandr Solzhenitsyn[1] that the term GULag (Chief Administration of Camps) became universally known, although the better-informed public had known about the new department of the secret police, set up at the beginning of the 1930s, for decades. The horrors of forced labour have now been extensively documented in numerous memoirs and in the many testimonies of witnesses collected by the Russian organization of historians, Memorial. After a short description of the growth and decline of the forced labour system I shall make some comments on the specific nature of forced labour relations under Stalinism and the historical place of forced labour in Soviet society.

1. Some Basic Observations[2]

Although certain types of "corrective" labour and the first concentration camps were already in existence just after the October Revolution, the beginning of the large-scale application of forced labour can be dated at around the end of the 1920s – that is, the years described by Stalin as "The Great Turning Point".

The most important and notorious form of forced labour was that found in the concentration camps (the *lager* – hence GULag). The precise number of workers held in concentration camps (meaning the camps administered by the GULag, a new department of the OGPU/NKVD) from the first Five Year Plan

---

* The following notes are based exclusively on secondary sources. They do not present new facts, but are meant to contribute to the setting up of a historical-theoretical framework for these data. Leo van Rossum carefully read and critized an earlier draft; I hope that he will forgive me for not always having followed his advice.
1. Solzhenitsyn, *Archipel Gulag*, 3 vols.
2. Unless indicated otherwise I am plundering the following works: Dallin and Nicolaevsky, *Forced Labor in Soviet Russia*, ch. 5; Schwarz, *Labor in the Soviet Union*, esp. chs 2-4; Barton, *Institution concentrationnaire en Russie*, pp. 255-388; Swianiewicz, *Forced Labour and Economic Development*; and Rossi, *Gulag Handbook*. Naturally, I am aware of the fact that most of these works have been written from a clear anti-Communist perspective and may therefore be biased. However, more reliable studies are not yet available.

– (from 1928) is a subject of controversy. Rosefielde published the following estimates a number of years ago:[3]

Table 1. The Proportion of Soviet Population, Labour Force and Non-Agricultural Workers in Concentration Camps, 1929-1977

Year	Population (%)	Total Labour Force	Non-agricultural Workers
1929	–	.5	–
1930	.5	.9	3.8
1931	1.4	2.3	8.7
1932	2.1	3.4	10.8
1933	3.5	5.6	16.4
1934	3.8	6.2	18.1
1935	4.2	6.7	18.7
1936	4.5	7.2	19.3
1937	5.5	8.9	20.6
1938	6.3	10.6	22.9
1939	6.1	10.4	22.3
1940	5.7	9.9	22.8
1941	5.3	–	–
1950	7.6	12.4	23.2
1953	6.0	–	–
1956	3.0	–	–
1959	1.9	3.7	6.2
1977	1.6	2.9	3.8

Although some experts regard these figures as more or less precise,[4] others consider them too high. Rosefield's most important critic, Wheatcroft, for example, concluded that "some four to five million is the maximum number of concentration camp labourers who could have existed in 1939".[5] At the same time this author indicated clearly that, despite his lower estimates, for him too there was no question of the social importance of forced labour.[6] In short, whether one holds to a "pessimistic" or an "optimistic" perspective, the extent and social importance of forced labour was considerable.[7]

3. Rosefielde, "Assessment of the Sources and Uses of Gulag Forced Labour ", pp. 1, 51-87, 75.
4. For example Conquest, "Forced Labour Statistics", pp. 434-439.
5. Wheatcroft, "On Assessing the Size", pp. 265-295, 286; see also: Wheatcroft, "Towards a Thorough Analysis", pp. 223-237.
6. Wheatcroft, "On Assessing the Size", pp. 287, 291.
7. A survey of recent Russian contributions on these matters has been given in Ahlberg,

The GULag workers were mostly men, roughly between 35 and 50 years old; the percentage of women in the camps was around ten. Swianiewicz estimates that on the eve of the German-Soviet War more than two-thirds of forced labour was concentrated in construction, non-ferrous metal mining (including gold and platinum), and lumbering. His data in Table 2[8] indicate the following distribution pattern.

Table 2. Distribution of Soviet Forced Labour

Construction	3,500,000
Mining	1,000,000
Lumbering (incl. felling, floating and sawmills)	400,000
Agriculture	200,000
Various	200,000
Hiring out to other institutions (excl. hiring for mining)	1,000,000
Construction and maintenance of the camps (incl. clothes and footwear	600,000
Total	6,900,000

A second form of forced labour was forced settlement: people were displaced to another part of the country and did not have the right to move anywhere else or to do any other work than that which was allocated to them. They were not regarded as prisoners and their wages were at the same level as those of "free" workers. In the course of time large groups of Poles, Ukrainians, Balts and Bessarabians were forced to resettle. In an economic sense these people were probably less important than the GULag workers: most of them were elderly people, children, intellectuals etc., who for one reason or another had been defined as "undesirables" in certain regions of the country. There was little point to forcing them to take part in concentration camp labour, because they would probably produce less than the cost of their upkeep.

Beside these two major forms of "unfreedom"[9] it should be noted that "normal" free labour was becoming less and less free in the nineteen-thirties. Two factors resulted in the shaping of new labour policies in the "free" sector: (i) the scarcity of labour, resulting from rapid industrial growth and the collectivization of agriculture (which reduced the supply of labour power from the farms); and (ii) the lack of commitment and discipline of the working class (high turnover rates and enormous absenteeism).[10] To combat these problems the rights of

"Stalinistische Vergangenheitsbewältigung", pp. 921-937.

8. Swianiewicz, *Forced Labour and Economic Development*, p. 39.
9. I am here ignoring the large numbers of prisoners of war taken between 1941 and 1945.
10. This cluster of problems has been given widespread attention by social historians in recent years. See: Van Rossum, "Western Studies of Soviet Labour", pp. 433-453.

"normal" workers were systematically encroached upon. Here are some examples.

– In October 1930 a decree *The immediate employment of the unemployed* was published. Through this decree benefit payments to the unemployed were stopped immediately. Some clauses of the decree merit special attention: "The unemployed are to be given jobs not only within their vocational qualifications but also other work requiring no special skills." And: "With the sole exception of sickness attested by a medical certificate, no reasons for refusing work shall be accepted." Finally: "Applicants refusing work will be stricken from the rolls of the labor exchanges" – that is, in many cases deprived of any chance of work.

– In 1938 the very unpopular work-books were introduced. Work-books were issued by plant management and, once issued, accompanied the employee from plant to plant. For the duration of employment they were in the safe-keeping of management, which made all entries. Every instance of being late for work "without valid reason" was now punishable, as was every case of knocking off early for lunch or at closing time, every kind of "loafing" on the job, etc. The penalties were: warning; reprimand; severe reprimand coupled with a warning of further steps, especially dismissal; transfer to lower-paid work for a period of up to three months. The imposition of these penalties was not discretionary but mandatory for the plant manager.

– In 1939 it was decreed that social insurance rights were tied to the length of employment in one establishment. Full sick benefits (100 percent of wages lost) were not to be due until after six years in a plant, and then only for union members. Non-union employees were to draw half the union rate, that is 50 percent of lost wages.[11]

– The year 1940 marked the end of free wage labour in the Soviet Union (until the 1960s). A decree of the Presidium of the Supreme Soviet (June 1940) dealt with "prohibition of workers and employees from quitting their jobs of their own accord". Quitting a job, as well as taking a new one, was now unlawful unless approved by plant management. Employees quitting the plant of their own accord were imprisoned for two to four months. Truancy (unjustified absence from work) also was made a criminal offence punishable with "corrective labour" (i.e. forced labour with confinement, as mentioned above).

With these provisions, employment ceased to be a free contractual relationship. Once employment had begun, it became a relationship founded on the principle of compulsory labour, unless the contract expressly specified a limited duration.[12]

---

11. Between three and six years in the plant entitled employees to 80 (40) percent of full benefits; between two and three years, to 60 (30) percent; less than two years, to 50 (25) percent.
12. Naturally, this did not mean that all these draconian measures were effective and accepted by

Against this background the GULag may be seen, not as a "deviation" from an otherwise different type of labour system, but as the most extreme form of a far broader tendency towards bonded labour. But why was the *general* disciplining of the working class not considered sufficient and why was part of it subjected to even more severe repression? Five factors appear to have been important. In the first place the *zeks* (forced labourers) could be employed in those places where other workers were not prepared to go: "GULag labor was used mainly [...] at sites to which free labor could not easily be attracted."[13] In the second place forced labourers were extremely mobile: "When they have completed the construction of a highway or a plant, the working prisoners are immediately shipped to some other region of Russia to begin work on a new project. On arrival, the prisoners themselves construct barracks, barbed-wired fences, and watch-towers for the guards, while the bulk of the labor force immediately attacks its major assignment."[14] In the third place, it was possible to suppress indiscipline and absenteeism: "The director of a labor camp, who is simultaneously general manager of a great industrial enterprise, knows precisely the size of his labor force; and the system of a camp is in itself a guarantee that the inmates will show up for work. Working hours are no problem in a forced labor camp, nor is Sunday work, when necessary. Even an insufficient food supply does not prevent the prisoners from reporting for work and staying at it as long as ordered."[15] In the fourth place the existence of concentration camps and forced labour in exile serves as a threat and therefore disciplines the other, the "free" workers.[16] And in the fifth place the existence of forced labour had an important influence on the market of consumer goods: the fact that the *zeks* "could not influence the conditions of demand because they had very little money" reduced the pressure of demand for consumer goods and contributed to a situation in which, despite the full employment of resources, certain consumer choices for the "free" population could exist.[17]

At the same time there were also disadvantages attached to concentration camp labour. Three become immediately apparent. In the first place it was difficult (but not always impossible[18]) to teach the *zeks* to handle delicate apparatus. Just

the workers without opposition. For this see: Filtzer, *Soviet Workers and Stalinist Industrialization*.

13. Hunter, "Economic Costs", pp. 588-592.
14. Dallin and Nicolaevsky, *Forced Labor in Soviet Russia*, pp. 91-92.
15. *Ibid.*, p. 91.
16. Jakobson, *Origins of the GULAG*, p. 143.
17. Swianiewicz, *Forced Labour and Economic Development*, pp. 199-201.
18. "Perhaps the most honourable application of prisoners' labour was scientific research. When I stayed in Moscow prisons I heard several times from my fellow prisoners that the NKVD possessed excellently equipped laboratories in which quite important research was carried out. The conditions of food and accomodation for prisoners assigned to this kind of work were quite comfortable." Swianiewicz, *Forced Labour and Economic Development*, p. 39.

like all unfree labourers they lacked interest in their labour. In the second place the output per individual forced labourer was far lower than that of a "free" labourer. And in the third place there were, naturally, costs derived from the control of the forced labourers: every guard was not just withdrawn from the productive sector but also had to be maintained by this sector.[19] In the course of time a fourth disadvantage of the GULag became apparent: the dislocation of the demographic balance. In 1959 Barton noted: "Substantial regions suffer from a stark shortage of women, while there are other regions where the male population increasingly consists of children and the elderly. In fact, the regions practically populated by men only coincide with the concentration areas populated by prisoners and ex-prisoners."[20]

These disadvantages of forced labour began to weigh heavily in the nineteen-fifties. It was not only necessary to avoid a demographic catastrophe; the rapid industrialization of the country was also leading to a growing need for highly educated labour and more productive labour relations, as well as for expanded possibilities for consumption. The long-term influence of these trends was strengthened by two non-economic changes. In the first place Stalin's death in 1953, which led to a general crisis of authority. In the second place the changing composition of the camp populations, which in the beginning of the nineteen-thirties had still consisted primarily of deferential peasants. During and after the war there was an increasing percentage of "dissident" Bolsheviks, Ukrainian partisans and other militant groups. Within the camps these two influences strengthened one another, which resulted in a wave of strikes in a number of *lager* in 1953-54.[21]

All these factors contributed in the nineteen-fifties to a substantial reduction in the number of forced labourers in the camps which, just like in the 1920s, were given a primarily political function.[22]

However, these were exceptions to the rule.

19. On the social and power structure of forced labour camps see Karklins, "Organisation of Power", and Coser, "Forced Labour in Concentration Camps", pp. 162-169.
20. Barton, *Institution concentrationnaire*, p. 260. There is an interesting parallel here with the slavery of pre-colonial Africa, studied by Meillassoux: "Stripped of their demographic growth [...] the pillaged populations could reconstitute themselves only at a slower rate than that of the slave-owning societies which preyed on them. [...] In the long term [...] the flow of supplies to the slave markets could only dry up." Meillassoux, *The Anthropology of Slavery*, p. 314.
21. *Ibid.*, pp. 305-350; Schlögel, *Renitente Held*, pp. 47-78; Graziosi, "Great Strikes", pp. 419-446.
22. The partial dismantling of the concentration camps did not take place without opposition from within the state apparatus and was therefore not a linear process.

2. GULag Labour: Slave Labour?

The labour relations within the GULag camps have sometimes been described as "real slavery".[23] Is that description justified? In order to clarify this question let us make a comparison between chattel slavery in the south of the United States until 1865 and GULag labour. We can observe the following *similarities*:

1. In practice both the slaves in the USA and the forced labourers in the USSR were without any rights; in the American judicial system this was also formally the case, while the lack of rights in the Soviet Union was mostly informal.
2. Both the slaves in the USA and the forced labourers in the USSR did mainly simple manual labour.

The following *differences* may be noted:

1. The American slave owner gained slaves either by natural reproduction (as descendants of those who were themselves slaves) or through the market (by purchasing them from slave traders). The GULag, on the other hand, gained its forced labourers by "catching" them. The consequence of this was that the costs of acquiring a slave in the American situation were considerably higher than in the Soviet case. This was the reason why American slave owners looked after their "human capital" more carefully than the Soviet authorities, who had in fact made few investments and therefore suffered little disadvantage from exhaustion and a high mortality rate among the prisoners.
2. While under the conditions of "normal" slavery slaves received enough food to reproduce their labour power from day to day, in the GULag camps material incentives were introduced, which were normally derived from the system of free wage labour and then modified. Food rations, for example, were tied to the individual labour output of the *zek*.
3. In the United States the condition of slavery was more or less permanent, while in the Soviet Union forced labourers could – if they survived their punishment – regain their freedom. However, sentences were in practice often extended and people were not allowed to return to their original place of residence after completing their period of forced labour.
4. While slaves in the United States were the private property of private entrepreneurs, the forced labourers in the USSR were under state control.
5. While the slaves in the United States produced commodities for the world market (cotton, tobacco), the forced labourers in the USSR were espe-

---

23. Brandt, "Soziale Revolution", pp. 299-301.

cially used for developing the country's infrastructure (dams, dikes, highways, etc.) and the minerals sector (mines).

6.   While slavery was regarded as a "natural" phenomenon in the south of the United States, forced labour was not generally accepted in the Soviet Union and was for that reason immersed in mystery. This attitude of non-acceptance was gradually being overcome,[24] but during the 1950s this trend was interrupted.

What can we conclude about the nature of forced labour under Stalinism on the basis of these similarities and differences? De Ste. Croix has quite rightly defended the proposition that the essential nature of slavery is *not* the result of the fact that "the slave is the *legal property* of another", but of the fact that "the *powers attaching* to the *right of ownership* are *exercised over him*" [or her] – for "the essential elements in the slave's condition are that *his [or her] labour and other activities are totally controlled* by his [or her] master, and that [s]he is virtually without rights, at any rate enforceable legal rights".[25] Seen in this way, the forced labourers in the GULag can certainly be characterized as slaves, with the understanding that (a) their situation did not necessarily last their whole life; (b) their work was not usually directed at profitable production for the market; (c) they received material incentives; (d) their "master" was a state institution and (e) their separate status was not (yet) accepted as a natural one.

3. GULag Labour and Soviet Society

The rise and fall of forced labour in the Soviet Union can only be understood by abandoning the national and limited perspective of the internal relations of the USSR and instead looking at international relations.

Many authors have already pointed out that the international industrial capitalism which came into being for the first time in Great Britain in the eighteenth century developed in a combined and uneven fashion. No single country repeats the development of another country: not just because the pre-capitalist social, economic and political heritage is different everywhere, but also and especially because each new industrializing country changes the conditions of later industrialization for other countries.

24.   "By the beginning of the 1940's the administrative staff in the camps treated the prisoners as inferior creatures, any contact with whom on a footing of equality was insulting to the dignity of a free man. It was considered inadmissible for a citizen of the Soviet Union to eat with a forced labourer, to sleep under the same roof, or to have any kind of friendly relations with him, though it was permissible to work under his direction if he possessed some particular qualifications." Swianiewicz, *Forced Labour and Economic Development*, p. 22.
25.   Croix, *Class Struggle in the Ancient Greek World*, p. 135.

This unavoidable condition has two important consequences. In the first place, the chasm between "pioneers" and "rearguard" becomes greater as time passes. The first have a more profitable agriculture, industry is more productive, the infrastructure more efficient and the human productive forces are more highly developed. Hence, under "normal" conditions, when pioneers and "followers" compete on the world market, the last are doomed to go under. Not just as far as commodity exchange is concerned, but also in other areas (like science).

This does not, secondly, mean that followers can never have any success in the struggle of capitalist competition. The most important condition for a successful industrialization under capitalist conditions seems to be that the state succeeds in distancing itself from those internal forces which block industrialization. This is, for example, what happened – during a relatively short period – in Japan during the Meiji restoration: in the face of a great foreign threat, combined with the disintegration of the internal order and the growth of nationalist movements, a number of high state functionaries were prepared to carry through a "revolution from above" and systematically encourage the breakthrough to capitalism.[26] However, as the capitalist system develops further and the international chasm increases, such attempts at catching up become more and more difficult – although they certainly remain possible, as is shown by the recent history of South Korea and Taiwan.[27]

In the course of the twentieth century alternative attempts at solving the problem of the gap have been undertaken in numerous countries. Often, a revolutionary state power came to the fore, which attempted to separate the national economy from the world market as much as possible and tried to organize an independent "modernization". Senghaas, who has extensively studied this subject, describes such attempts as a "very desperate remedy [...] for which there is only one alternative: a type of development which we can today see in the Third World".[28]

If we now look at the Soviet Union and its history in the light of these general insights, a number of things become clearer. The tsarist economy on the eve

---

26. See the analysis by Trimberger, "State Power and Modes of Production", pp. 85–98. For Germany see Steinmetz, "Myth and the Reality", pp. 239–293.

27. Closer analysis of the factors which made possible the rapid industrialization of South Korea and Taiwan since the nineteen-sixties shows that here too, the relative autonomy of the state was of decisive importance. Jenkins points at (a) the absence of influential large-scale landowners (because of Japanese colonialism and the post-war land reforms), (b) the very young industrial bourgeoisie, (c) the lack of a strong and militant labour movement, (d) the massive financial aid from the USA for the state apparatus, which enabled it to gain a large degree of independence from the local ruling classes, and (e) the assumed presence of a powerful military threat (from North Korea, and especially the Chinese People's Republic), which made a broad consensus on the need for strong economic growth possible. Jenkins, "Political Economy of Industrialization", pp. 197–231.

28. Senghaas, "Sozialismus", pp. 22.

of the 1917 revolutions may be described as "structurally crippled capitalism",[29] suffering from weaknesses of which the following were the most important:

- A conservation of the agrarian mode of production, which excluded an agricultural development (like in Denmark);
- A financial policy which continually resulted in new debts, carried out by a state which did not regard it as one of its tasks to invest the available means in general capitalization and transformation of the productive relations.
- A militarization of social production, which resulted in large parts of industrial production being tied directly to the state. Overall accumulation was weakened by the production of military goods.

Capitalism in Russia in 1917 was therefore in part quite highly developed, but at the same time very insular.

The enforced industrialization attained since the start of the Five Year Plans may be seen as a deliberate attempt to overcome this stunted economy.[30] It was not, however, a type of "auto-centred development", taking place quite separately from international capitalism. It is true that the country had been able to escape the direct influence of the laws of the market since 1917, but the international capitalist influence continually made a truly autonomous development impossible. This unremitting pressure was of course most noticeable in the military field. In the USSR the arms race – in contrast to its effect in capitalism, where under certain circumstances it could have a dampening effect on the business cycle or increase growth – continually braked and stunted economic growth. But in other areas the imperialist influence was of course also present – I refer not just to the technological dependence.[31]

> The ties to capitalist accumulation resulted in a situation in which the law of development of Soviet society was determined from the outside. True, it was not accumulation for the sake of accumulation, as in the capitalist system, but instead accumulation for the sake of keeping up seems to be the law to which all other social aims were subordinated.[32]

---

29. Scherer, *Aufbruch aus der Mangelgesellschaft*, pp. 235, 256-258.
30. I am here ignoring the question of the historical alternatives for the Stalinist path of development. For this question see: Van der Linden, *Von der Oktoberrevolution zur Perestroika*, pp. 239-245.
31. Right from the beginning the Soviet Union was to a large degree dependent on Western technology. Endogenous innovations largely took place in the military sector. Entire plants, separate production processes and products were imported again and again, mainly paid for with minerals and semi-manufactured goods. Spohn, "Technologische Abhängigkeit", pp. 225-259.
32. Pietsch, "Stalinismus als Phänomen", p. 380.

In other words: Soviet society was not driven primarily by endogenous (coming forth from society) but exogenous laws of development, enforced by the capitalist system.[33] If one does not accept this, then the development of Soviet society can only be understood in a historical-voluntarist sense, as the result of strivings by the elite, motivated either by a certain "interpretation of socialism"[34], or its "personal interests".[35]

Stalinism – once described by Oskar Lange as "a war economy *sui generis*" – in a certain sense did carry out a *partial* primitive accumulation, if we accept Marx's definition, according to which the process of primitive accumulation is "nothing other" than "the process which divorces the worker from the ownership of the conditions of his own labour; it is a process which operates two transformations, whereby the social means of subsistence and production are turned into capital, and the immediate producers are turned into wage-labourers."[36] Although the "social means of subsistence and production" did *not* become the property of capitalists (but were placed at the disposition of the bureaucratic elite), the producers were indeed robbed of the ownership of the conditions of their own labour. This happened primarily through proletarianization (the producers became workers), but also through their enslavement.[37]

The use of forced labour started as a form of political repression, but soon developed its own economic dynamics. "In the first stages of the development of the forced labor system the labor camps were a consequence of certain political measures resorted to by the government, such as the collectivization of agriculture. Later on, cause and effect were intermingled. In the later 1930s, and particularly during the war, the NKVD took certain political measures because of its need for fresh human material."[38]

Some authors refuse to recognize the economic aspect of forced labour. Mandel, for instance, wrote: "A regime based neither on the political support of the labouring masses nor on the satisfaction of their material needs, must resort to terror which becomes the main state institution. That is the most striking aspect of the Stalinist concentration camps, and not the supposed 'economic'

---

33. Within Soviet society the exogenous law of movement resulted in conflicting trends. These have been explored extensively in: Füredi, *Soviet Union Demystified*.
34. Rotermundt, *Sowjetunion und Europa*, pp. 42-43.
35. Mandel, *Marxist Economic Theory*, p. 589. If Mandel were right, then the bureaucracy would systematically have given priority to the production of luxury goods for its own comfort, and there would never have been "an exaggerated rate of accumulation" (*ibid.*).
36. Marx, *Capital*, I, p. 874.
37. It is very probable that this enslavement was partially possible because banning and forced labour were part of an old repertory of repression methods, familiar to both the people and the elite. More generally a partial "return of the modernizing Soviet state under Stalin to the models and trappings of earlier tsardom" could be observed in a number of spheres (cultural, social and political). Lewin, "Social Background of Stalinism", p. 124.
38. Dallin and Nicolaevsky, *Forced Labor in the Soviet Union*, p. 104.

contribution that prison labour is said to have made on the industrialization of the USSR."[39] Such an analytic reduction is, however, not very convincing. Although estimates of the phenomenon vary, even the lowest calculation makes an exclusively political explanation incredible. The enormous number of forced labourers and the great contribution they have made to the industrialization of the Soviet Union clarify the *economic* weight of the phenomenon (although I naturally do not deny its political importance). Furthermore, Mandel's reasoning is logically untenable. For in the post-Stalinist period from the end of the 1950s onwards the bureaucratic regime did not rest on the political support of the population and did not meet their material desires; nevertheless there was a drastic reduction of forced labour. Apparently forced labour was just one of a number of possibilities for the elite. The fact that it was given priority for a number of decades makes one suspect that there was a causal relation with forced industrialization.

The use of forced labour initially had great advantages: it was a very cheap way of mobilizing labour in regions and economic sectors where "free" wage labourers could only have been attracted with great difficulty (and if successful, for very high wages). It was a type of labour mobilization which fitted well into the stage of extensive industrialization which lasted into the 1950s.

---

39. Mandel, "Solzhenitsyn, Stalinism and the October Revolution", p. 53.

The Strikes in Norilsk and Vorkuta Camps, and their Role in the Breakdown of the Stalinist Forced Labour System*

Marta Craveri

When Stalin died, 2,500,000 prisoners worked in the camps and colonies of forced labour (ITL and ITK), depending directly on the USSR Ministry of the Interior (MVD). Prisoners would work either in the mines, in building yards, in factories owned by the MVD, or were "rented"[1] from it to other ministries to do all kinds of work.

In February 1948 the USSR Council of Ministers ordered the creation of some special camps for holding 200,000 particularly dangerous political prisoners, such as "traitors to the nation", spies, terrorists, Trotskyists, Menshevists and Social-Revolutionaries. The MVD[2] had to organize these camps and, by the end of 1949, nine of them were already working.[3]

All prisoners accused of being "traitors to the nation" were condemned during and immediately after the second World War. They were essentially members of nationalist organizations and partisans from western Ukraine, Bielorussia, from the Baltic states, and Polish prisoners of war. Officers and soldiers of the Red Army taken prisoner by the Germans, and who were sent to camps in Poland and Germany, returning to their homeland were considered as traitors and

* This article was made possible thanks to the Fondazione Einaudi of Turin and Fondazione Feltrinelli of Milan. I would like also to thank N. Formozov, A. Graziosi and A. Romano always prepared to offer suggestions and help. I am grateful to E.S. Hritsiak, leader of one of the strike committees of Norilsk, for giving me his detailed and precious testimony. Translated by Alessandra Osti, and revised by Tom Brass.

1. The MVD made their prisoners available for heavy work or to go and work in regions where there was a manpower shortage. We use the verb "to rent" because for each prisoner given, the MVD accepted money from other ministries.
2. The documents consulted for this article are kept in the Gosudarstvennyi Arkhiv Rossiiskoi Federatsii , Moskva [hereafter, GARF], GULag Fund (n 9414), Prisons Administration Fund (n 9413), MVD Decrees Fund (n 9401), Public Prosecutor's Office Fund (n 8131), Supreme Soviet Fund (n 7523). From now on we will refer to the documents of this archive as: GARF, f. for fund, op. for opis, d. for delo, l. for list.
3. These camps were the Bereglag, the Gorlag, the Dubrovlag, the Dalag, the Kamyshlag, the Mineralag, the Ozerlag, the Peshanlag, the Rechlag and the Steplag, and were placed in several republics and regions such as Kolyma, Kazakhstan, the Independent Republic of Komi and Siberia.

sentenced to forced labour. Only a small number of them were sent to the special camps.

In 1953, 218,142 prisoners were serving in special camps and in MVD jails. Ten percent (22,203) of them were condemned for spying, 13.5% (29,468) for having taken part in antisoviet organizations, and 30.4% (66,424) for activities considered against the interests of the nation.

Ukrainian and Baltic nationalists represented 40.2% (87,794) of the prisoners, while political opponents (Trotskyists, Bukharinists, Social-Revolutionaries and Whites) formed only 1% (2,596).[4]

There was a dramatic difference between this group and the political prisoners of the 1930s, who were actually peasants who had opposed collectivization, workers and members of the party who became victims of Stalin's purges. Many of them had never really opposed the regime. The majority of them considered themselves victims of a miscarriage of justice, but were surrounded in the camps by true "enemies of the people". Along with the deep cultural and social differences that divided the prisoners, this made it impossible to develop solidarity and, consequently, to resist the abuses committed by those administering the camps.

Prisoners arrested during or after the war – mostly Ukrainians, Balts and Poles – had always been enemies of the Soviet power, because they had witnessed its ferocity during the occupation of their countries after the Ribbentrop-Molotov pact signed in August 1939. They were partisans or members of nationalist organizations, well versed in war and with a long experience in clandestine operations. Though officers and soldiers of the Red Army had not always been against the regime, they became opposed to it during the war and when they returned home. There are several reasons why these thousands of prisoners became such strong opponents of the regime: the way Stalin and his counsellors led the war during the first months of the conflict; the terrible conditions in which Soviet prisoners of war were kept, without the assistance of the Red Cross (Stalin refused to sign the Geneva Treaty); and mainly the future awaiting them once back in their homelands. To escape death from starvation in a Nazi camp, or because of their political views, some of them enrolled in the Vlasov army,[5] or in the special army corps fighting against partisans in occupied areas – both in the east and west.

The entry of these prisoners into the camps signalled the beginning of the political and economic crisis of the forced labour system in the Soviet Union. The prisoners formed many clandestine nationalist organizations, the aim of

4. GARF, f. 7523, op. 85, d. 80, l. 5.
5. For information about General Vlasov and the creation of the ROA (Russkaia osvoboditelnaia armiia) by Germans after the defeat of Stalingrad, see Andreyev, *Vlasov and the Russian Liberation Movement*, pp. 19–88.

which was to resist the authorities in the camps and to destroy the spy system (used by the camp administration to maintain control).

The main problems facing the administration became the constantly increasing number of prisoners who refused to work or who attempted to escape, gangster-ism, and the murder of suspected spies. In 1951, 1,022,291 working days were lost because prisoners refused to work.[6] In a letter addressed to the camp administration, General Dolgikh (head of GULag) underlined the worsening the situation. The number of those refusing to work had doubled during the year, while in the Norilsk camp it had increased fifteenfold,[7] and 32% of workers there broke the rules governing production.[8] In 1953 alone, 135 murders, 60 cases of sexual violence and 1,559 escapes[9] were recorded.

This systematic resistance had political and economic consequences. In 1953, seven out of the ten special camps were operating at a loss, which meant that the cost of running the camp and feeding prisoners was higher than the income generated by the prisoners' work.[10] Only Gorlag, Rechlag and Steplag (where in summer of 1953 and 1954 strikes took place) were self-sufficient in this regard.

Social-Revolutionaries[11] were the first to use strikes as a means of resistance. Together with the Mensheviks, the White Guards and the few surviving Anarchists, they had been among the first to be imprisoned in camps during the 1920s. To guarantee respect for their rights as political prisoners (rights that they had been granted in Tsarist prisons), they would periodically go on hunger strikes. This represented the only possible form of strike, since it was only in the late 1920s that prisoners were forced to work. At first these strikes were effective, but from the beginning of the 1930s the most active prisoners organiz-ing such action were shot. The rest had to learn how to live with the new order.

During the 1930s and the period of the war, attempts at resistance, hunger strikes[12] or armed escapes were immediately repressed, or met with summary executions. In the years from the end of the war to Stalin's death, hunger strikes, armed escapes and rebellions[13] clearly reflected both the crisis taking place inside

---

6. The number is calculated on 174 ITL, ITK, OITK (ITK sections) and UITLK (Camps and Colonies Administration). GARF, f. 9414, op. 1, d. 1668, l. 171.
7. GARF, f. 9414, op. 1, d. 1666, l. 38.
8. GARF, f. 9414, op. 1, d. 1666, l. 20.
9. GARF, f. 8131, op. 32, d. 4459, l. 50. Figures of 1954 show the growth of these violations: 254 murders, 80 cases of sexual violence and 2,233 escapes.
10. GARF, f. 9414, op. 1, d. 2376, ll. 30-34.
11. Olitskaia, *Sablier*, pp. 207-216.
12. Mainly Trotskyists used this way of striking.
13. N.A. Formozov, an expert on problems connected with the resistance inside GULag calculated on the basis of accounts that there had been about 50 strikes, revolts, and armed escapes in the 1930s, but mainly in the 1940s and 1950s.

the concentration camp system and the lack of a solution to this. The official response to such actions consisted of enlarging the spy system and increasing the political educational programme inside the camps.

Only after the dictator's death were prisoners able to obtain real concessions by going on strike. On the basis of the available materials,[14] it is my intention to examine the origins and outcome of prisoners' strikes which took place in the special camps of Norilsk (Gorlag) and Vorkuta (Rechlag) during the summer of 1953, together with their impact on the labour camp system. I will focus on the role of prisoners belonging to different nationalities, because for them resistance to Soviet power was inseparable from the rebirth of national pride. Revolts, strikes and armed escapes thus became a way not only of demonstrating their opposition to the regime but also of showing their refusal to renounce their national independence. This is why strikes in the Soviet camps had a political nature.

The Gorlag was created in 1948, not far from the town of Norilsk, where since 1935 there had been a camp. The latter was composed of six sections (*lagotdeleniie*) and two *lagpunkts*. Twenty-three percent of the prisoners worked in the coal mines, 24% in concrete and brick factories, and 52.3% in constructing buildings and roads.[15] In May 1953, 16,532 men and 3,013 women were imprisoned there, 53% of whom had been sentenced to ten years' forced labour and 21.8% to twenty-five years.[16] Precise figures on the number of different nationalities are not available. There are, however, testimonies of prisoners from which it is clear that Ukrainians represented more than a third of all the prisoners.

In September 1952, prisoners who arrived by train at the Gorlag, mainly from Ukraine and the Baltic States, had already formed themselves into clandestine organizations. Each national group had chosen its own delegate to a "board of directors", the prisoners' executive which authorized and organized activity in the camps: this included the fostering of solidarity among prisoners and the encouragement of resistance to the administration; the identification of informers and collaborators of the MVD, and their elimination; and the creation of a fund to assist prisoners in difficulty.[17]

The administration of the Gorlag had been informed about the need to control

---

14. Materials are essentially archive documents and memories of survivors. Memories regarding strikes that have been examined in Norilsk are: Ciszek and Flaherty, *Spia del Vaticano*, pp. 213-257; Hritsiak, *Istoriia Norilskogo vosstaniia*, pp. 13-97; Klimovich, "Vosstanie v Gorlage", p. 7; and Shumuk, *Life Sentence*, pp. 77-142; memories regarding strikes in Vorkuta are: Buca, *Vorkuta*, pp. 40-122; Noble, *Un americain au Gulag*, pp. 189-211; and Sholmer, *Vorkuta*, pp. 162-223.
15. GARF, f. 9414, op. 1, d. 2598, ll. 85-86 and d. 557, l. 3.
16. GARF, f. 9414, op. 1, d. 2598, l. 96.
17. GARF, f. 9413, op. 1, d. 159, ll. 134-135.

this group of prisoners, and rumours spread concerning their dangerous nature, and the fact that they were "recidivists" who had been condemned a second time during imprisonment for crimes committed in the camps. They were given new numbers and the letters U and F,[18] so that everybody could recognize them and avoid all contact, and also so that they could be identified and controlled more easily by spies. Towards the end of 1952, and through winter 1953, these prisoners joined existing clandestine organizations in eliminating spies (at least ten), and resisted the administration as best they could.

Many the norms governing the detention regime were then violated by the camp authorities. Prisoners had to work more hours than those established by law, or were transferred arbitrarily to punishment cells and beaten. These violations, committed by prisoner escorts, guards and members of the administration generally, were a cause of concern to the Public Prosecuter, who conducted a number of inquiries in the camps during the period 1953-55.[19] What emerged from these investigations was that the situation had reached the very limit of legality. The required level of technical safety was not observed, and the number of industrial accidents – often fatal – was increasing.[20] According to the Public Prosecutor, beatings and use of weapons against prisoners, together with a disregard for their complaints, only generated more extreme forms of resistance (such as refusal to work and mass disorder).

At the end of 1953 the Director of Public Prosecution of the Soviet Union, Rudenko, wrote a long letter to the Ministry of Justice. He underlined the need to take immediate measures to restore legality in the camps: "first of all", he wrote, "we must focus on the fact that the majority of people working in the administration of the camps, such as supervisors and escorts, commit brutal abuses against prisoners, offending and humiliating these persons; it also happens that weapons are frequently used against them".[21]

What made the revolt explode in Gorlag, as in the other camps, was the provocation and aggressive behaviour on the part of the administration. The latter provoked open rebellion so as to be able to justify subsequently the elimination of most dangerous prisoners. After Stalin's death it was no longer possible to continue with such arbitrary acts, but what precipitated the disorder was the arrest of Beriia during the strike. In official documents written by the Commission charged with ending the strike, emphasis is placed on the important

---

18. The idea of assigning a letter and number to prisoners to be printed or sewn on their caps and jacket was introduced with the creation of special camps. It was particularly humiliating for the prisoners.
19. GARF, f. 8131, op. 32, d. 3024 and 3027.
20. Unfortunately the extent of these accidents is not specified within Public Prosecution reports, nor are exact figures capable of making a feasible analysis of the situation, given.
21. GARF, f. 8131, op. 32, d. 3030, ll. 272-276.

role of propaganda and the pressure to resist exerted on other prisoners by "banderists";[22] there is only a vague reference to the main cause, however, which was the continuous abuse by escorts and supervisors.

On May 21, as a consequence of the murder of some prisoners by other inmates (who were serving sentences for non-political crimes, and had been armed with knives by the administration so as to cause maximum disorder), the second section composed of 2,739 prisoners refused to work for five days. On May 25, while a group of sixteen inmates was being transferred from the isolation compound (in the fourth section) to the fifth section, the escort killed a prisoner. The following day one of the escorts shot prisoners of the fifth, and women of the sixth section, simply to make them stop talking. Seven men were wounded and one killed. The fifth section, comprizing 1,520 prisoners, then refused to work, and asked to talk to a commission from Moscow. To show their solidarity, 2,901 women prisoners did not go out to work either, and went on a hunger strike. The night shift of the fourth section did not go back to the camp, while the morning shift of 2,966 prisoners refused to go out. Strike committees were formed immediately. A representative was chosen by the largest national group of the section. However, leaders of clandestine organizations were not automatically chosen, because they often preferred not to be known to the authorities. It was necessary for them to continue to guide the group and maintain secret contacts between camps, a network that had taken years to create.

On May 27 the strike of the second section ended with the arrest of fifty activists, and in July the 2,636 prisoners in the first section went on strike.

On July 14 a group of prisoners assaulted the jail and set twenty-four prisoners free. Among them was Ivan Vorobev, an officer from Leningrad who had a legendary reputation because of his many escape attempts. The escort fired, killing five and wounding fourteen. On July 5 the third section went on strike too. All the 14,074 prisoners in the Gorlag had by then stopped working, except for those in the second section, prisoners in hospital, and the inmates of the two *lagpunkts*.

On July 6 a committee led by MGB Colonel Kuznetsov, head of the administration of prisons, arrived by plane from Moscow and began talks with the prisoners. The fourth section was the first to be visited by the committee. The prisoners' delegates consisted of a Russian, Vladimir Nedorostkov, a Ukrainian, Evgenii Hritsiak, and a Bielorussian Grigorii Klimovich. The first thing Hritsiak said was that there would be no discussion in front of General Semenov, the director of the camp. Kuznetsov turned towards the latter and said: "Did you

22. Followers of Stepan Bandera, leader of the revolutionary section of OUN, cf. Armstrong, *Ukrainian Nationalism*, pp. 31-72.

hear that? Go away!". Hritsiak[23] maintains that on hearing this, they immediately knew something had changed. It was clear that the camp administration was in a very weak bargaining position if a colonel, even one who belonged to the MGB and sent by Moscow, could talk in this manner to a general in the presence of prisoners. The episode meant a lot to the strike committee. They presented their request without any fear, outlining how the administration had been responsible for provoking the disorder, and declared that not a single prisoner would go back to work if their demands were not met.

The committee then went to the fifth section, and on the following days to the sixth and the first. Everywhere prisoners made the same complaints about the administration and the same set of demands.

As a result, the committee was compelled to agree to the removal of numbers and letters from clothes, to allow the prisoners to write and send money home once a month (rather than twice a year), to work no more than eight hours per day, to undertake to remove iron bars from windows and to leave the doors open at night, and finally to set the disabled free.[24]

After being granted these concessions, on June 9, prisoners of the fourth, fifth and sixth sections went back to work. However, those in the first and third sections remained on strike because their main demand had not been met: namely, the revision of political prisoners' sentences.

In the third section prisoners formed a strike committee to maintain order in the camp and to stop theft.[25] Former Red Army officer Boris Shamaev was elected head of the committee. Three departments were created in this section: one to supply prisoners, another to defend the camp from raids by the administration, and a department for propaganda. The purpose of the latter was to write leaflets and distribute them (by kite!) to the local population and soldiers on escort duty.[26]

On June 13, the administration threatened to send armed soldiers into the first section, as a result of which the prisoners – fearing a massacre – capitulated. The leaders, members of the strike committee, and the more active prisoners were arrested and transferred to isolation cells.

On June 14, Vavilov, a high official connected to the Attorney of USSR, arrived from Moscow. On June 15 he spoke with the prisoners of the third section and tried to persuade them to surrender. The prisoners gave him a letter

23. I met Hritsiak in Moscow, in June 1994, and he told me about this episode.
24. GARF, f. 9413, op. 1, d. 159, l. 165.
25. Camps had been created for political prisoners, but often thieves and murderers would be imprisoned there too, accused of political crimes.
26. Some of these leaflets are kept in the Public Prosecutor's Office fund. They must have been used as a charge when those accused of the disorders in the third section were tried. GARF, f. 8313, op. 32, d. 3025, ll. 85-93.

to the government, in which they asked for a "true and qualified" committee to be sent to the camp, formed by members of the Government and of the Party, and not merely by nominees of the MVD and the MGB. Vavilov promised that he would personally give it to K. E. Voroshilov.[27]

The prisoners of the third section continued their strike alone until June 24, when the fourth, fifth and sixth sections went on strike again, this time to protest against the arrest of some of their comrades. On June 26, Beriia was arrested in Moscow. Prisoners heard of this event only on July 10, when the Moscow committee hurriedly left Norilsk following the publication of the news. The third section continued on strike, taking advantage of the power vacuum. Again it did so alone. During the first week of July, the Moscow committee had actually supressed disorder in the fifth and sixth sections, while the fourth had spontaneously gone back to work to avoid useless slaughter. Repressive measures were being drawn up against the disorder in the third section, but the sudden departure of the Moscow committee delayed their application.

Heads of the strike committees were arrested and taken to the tundra, while more than 1,500 prisoners were transferred to the special camp of Kolyma, the Berlag. Hritsiak says that in the tundra they were first beaten ferociously and then left for hours in shackles. Finally, they were returned to jail, but were never tried. Only women who had directed the uprising of the sixth section, and members of the strike committee of the third section, were regularly tried and sentenced for "criminal responsibility". Hritsiak was treated differently, probably in order to undermine his will to resist: he was taken by soldiers into a cell and subjected to a series of mock executions. He was deeply changed by this experience, and abandoned clandestine organization forever: he spent the remaining years of imprisonment[28] studying the history of Indian independence, yoga meditation and practices (thanks to prison libraries, where material[29] on these topics was available). From being a member of the OUN, he became a pacifist and follower of Mahatma Gandhi, and has remained such to date.

Towards the end of July, the committee from Moscow returned to the camp. Measures were taken to supress the strike in the third section. During the night of August 3, soldiers surrounded the camp and ordered the prisoners to come out. Thinking it was a ruse, as there had been many such incidents during the previous two months, the prisoners remained where they were. Accordingly, they were all still asleep when soldiers and armoured cars entered the camp, killing 57 prisoners and wounding 98. The latter is justified in official docu-

---

27. The information was taken from a letter of Shamaev to the association "Memorial" of August 1991.
28. Freed in 1956, he was imprisoned again after a short while, and had to serve another five years.
29. Many "forbidden" books were left in prison libraries, probably due to negligence.

ments, which insist that the prisoners put up fierce resistance, and that consequently soldiers were forced to fire on them. In his letter to "Memorial"[30] of
August 1991, Shamaev writes that unarmed prisoners, unable to defend themselves, were attacked by soldiers who killed or savagely beat them. In the second
half of July there had been a friction within the strike committee of the third
section: Shamaev had ordered the closing of the laboratory organized by
Vorobev, where weapons to be used against the administration were made. In
his letter, Shamaev repeats several times that the presumed "armed resistance
led by prisoners crying Hooray!" had been a lie, and that the committee was
using this to justify the repressive measures taken against the strikers. He himself
was wounded, and was taken to a punishment cell rather than to hospital.

The only prisoners punished for going on strike were those of the sixth and
third sections.[31] The articles of the penal code under which they were sentenced
to additional periods of imprisonment, were both political and non-political:
sabotage, antisoviet propaganda, and criminal responsibility. Many of the
prisoners would never be cleared of this accusation.

Six women from the Ukraine (Zelznskaia, Petrashuk, Nich, Iaskiv, Mazepa
and Koval) one from Latvia (Dauge), one from Esthonia (Tofri) and a Bielorussian (Safranovich) formed the strike committee of the sixth section. They were
all very young, born between 1922 and 1929, of peasant origin, and without
a formal education. They had all been arrested after the war, while some of them
were still adolescents, and were sentenced to serve between ten and twenty-five
years in the forced labour camps for having betrayed the nation. Many of these
girls were probably arrested because during the war UPA (*Ukrains'ka povstans'ka
armija*) officers, or perhaps officers of the German Wehrmacht, had stopped off
in their homes to eat. Members of NKVD carried out indiscriminate round-ups.
It seems that all men, women and teenagers who could work were then arrested.
It is said[32] that officers of NKVD would go to schools to find out who were the
cleverest and most promising students, in this compiling lists of those who were
to be arrested. In the eyes of the NKVD, such persons represented a serious
obstacle to the subjugation of the Ukraine.

Many of those arrested in the Ukraine, the Baltic States and Bielorussia were
of peasant origins. Listening to some of their testimonies it would appear that
life in the camp has been for them an education and a political awakening.
Young men and women who had hitherto lived traditional peasant lives, had
now to live among opponents of the regime, such as Social-Revolutionaries

30. About the origins and history of "Memorial" Association, see Ferretti, *Memoria mutilata*, pp.
    343-390; and Adler, *Victims of Soviet Terror*.
31. GARF, f. 9413, op. 1, d. 159, ll. 181-188 and f. 8313, op. 32, d. 3025, ll. 111-114.
32. Anna Andreevna Michailevich, member of the committee of prisoners during the Kengir
    revolt in Summer 1954, told me about this when I met her in Moscow in May 1993.

who had survived as partisans and who had fought against both the Germans and the Red Army. Many of these prisoners from a rural background received a political education, as a result of which they themselves became intransigent nationalists, enemies of the Soviet state and of the Russian people.

Rechlag was created in November 1948[33] near Vorkuta, a mining town in the independent Republic of Komi where, since 1938, there was already a camp for both political and non-political prisoners. Rechlag was the most densely populated special camp: in April 1953 there were 37,067 prisoners (33,265 men and 3,802 women), 32.2% of whom were sentenced to terms exceeding twenty years duration. Ukrainians and Balts made up almost half of all prisoners: there were 10,495 Ukrainians, 1,521 Estonians, 1,075 Latvians, and 2,935 Lithuanians. All had been sentenced as "traitors to the nation".

In the sixteen sections of the Rechlag, 73.4% of the prisoners were classified as capable of performing heavy labour, 17.2% as being capable of light work, and 9.4% as unable to work; 67.6% of prisoners worked in the coal mines, 12.3% in building work, and the rest of them in building roads and brick factories.[34]

As with the other special camps, the Rechlag had serious disciplinary problems. During the first four months of 1953, 1,182 crimes were recorded: these covered escape attempts, gangsterism, "relations with the local population", refusal to work, and murder.[35]

In a letter written in May 1953 to Derevianko, head of the Rechlag, Kuznetsov, director of the administration of prisons, expressed concern about the situation in the special camp. He complained that the number of crimes committed both by prisoners and soldiers was constantly increasing, that no political reeducation was being carried out, that nothing was being done to prevent the detention regime from being flouted, and that wardens were continually infringing Soviet law by beating and killing inmates.[36]

The arrival of two new groups of prisoners, one thousand men from Kamyshlag and 350 men from Peshanlag (a special Kazakhstan camp), contributed to the worsening situation. The MVD promised higher wages and increased freedom to prisoners who volunteered to work in the coal mines of the north. In Kazakhstan, in fact, a better climate made imprisonment less arduous. Once they arrived at Rechlag and were transferred to the second section (mine Nr. 7), prisoners realized that the camp administration would not have to keep the promises made by Peshanlag administrators. On July 19 inmates decided not

---

33. Some sections of Rechlag were built during 1948-53. By 1949 eight sections were already working.
34. GARF, f. 9414, op. 1, d. 2612, ll. 2-8.
35. GARF, f. 9414, op. 1, d. 2613, l. 36.
36. GARF, f. 9414, op. 1, d. 2613, l. 32.

to go out to work and asked to talk to a member of the government or of the Central Committee. Two days later they refused to talk to Komi, vice-minister of Internal affairs of the Republic. They said they did not trust members of the MVD. On July 23, the 2,946 prisoners of the second section went on strike; on the 24th, sections three and sixteen joined them to show their solidarity with the protest. There were now some 8,700 prisoners who refused to work, bringing the operation of mines and building areas to a halt and causing considerable losses to the production of the camp.[37]

The danger of the strike spreading, news being transmitted to the different units by free workers, thereby bringing production to a halt not only in the camp but also and consequently in the factories of Leningrad, persuaded the camp administrators to make concessions, which they did after receiving a telegram from Kruglov, Minister of the Interior. On May 24 prisoners were told that the working day had been fixed at ten hours, that they could write a letter home every month, and that they could send money to their families and receive a visit from them once a year. They were also allowed to remove both letter and number from their clothing.[38]

However, the prisoners refused to go back to work, and insisted on putting their demands directly to a member of the government or of the Central Committee. These demands were: a review of the sentences handed down to political prisoners, to be undertaken not by the MVD but rather by members of the Ministry of Justice; the granting of freedom, both to members of Ukrainian, Bielorussian, Moldavian and Baltic nationalist organizations, and also to those prisoners who were "victims of the second world war" (i.e., those imprisoned by Germans in concentration camps, and who on their return to the Soviet Union were given long sentences for espionage or "betraying the nation").[39]

On July 25 four hundred prisoners of the tenth section (mine Nr. 29) refused to leave the mine and to go back to their huts, while the others refused to go to work. On July 26, prisoners of the third section liberated seventy-seven inmates in held solitary confinement. Soldiers fired on prisoners and killed two of them. On July 28 prisoners from section thirteen (mine Nr. 30), learning that in the nearby mine prisoners were on strike, refused to work in order to show their solidarity. Meanwhile, inmates in section number four (mine Nr. 6) joined in the protest. Prisoners on strike by now numbered more than 12,000.

In every section the strike was organized by a committee formed by the heads of the various nationalist groups. Clandestine organizations had obviously played an important part in the election of representatives. Data found in the documents

37. GARF, f. 9413, op. 1, d. 160, l. 130.
38. *Ibid.*
39. GARF, f. 9413, op. 1, d. 160, ll. 260-262.

that we consulted are essentially about committees and organizers of the second and tenth sections.

Feliks Feliksovich Kendezerskii, born in 1912, engineer, ex-officer of the Polish Army, arrested on Soviet territory in 1949, became the head of the strike committee of the second section. He had been sentenced to fifteen years' forced labour, both for being a "traitor to the nation" and also for conducting anti-Soviet propaganda among the prisoners in the camps. Transferred from Kazakhstan in July 1953, he was identified by camp spies as one of the most active supporters of the strike policy. After the disorder he was sentenced a third time for "criminal responsibilities".[40]

Other members of the committee were Vitali Fedorovich Gorev, born in 1922, a Russian, condemned to twenty-five years for being a "traitor to the nation", having been declared guilty of being taken prisoner by Germans "without resisting them",[41] and Anatoli Musaevich Kniazev, born in 1925, a Circassian, who was accused of having collaborated with the Germans when taken prisoner by them, and of having been an agent of the Gestapo. Kniazev was taken prisoner by Italian partisans and handed over to the Americans, who repatriated him to the USSR, where he was sentenced to twenty-five years of forced labour. He was well-known to the Rechlag administration, because he often flouted the detention regime and was also suspected of having killed a spy.[42] Two other prisoners, sentenced as leaders of the disorder among the second section, were Henrikac Jashkynas, born in 1927, who had been sentenced to twenty-five years of forced labour for anti-Soviet propaganda, and because he belonged to a nationalist organization,[43] and Jurii Fedorovich Levando, born in 1925, condemned twice, the first time in 1946 to ten years as a "traitor to the nation", and the second time to be shot, for having killed a prisoner. The latter sentence was commuted twenty-five years forced labour.[44]

Buts, leader of the strike committee of the tenth section, was from Poland too, but the majority of prisoners there were from the Ukraine. It is not without significance that Ukrainians, who were mostly members of OUN, had in this instance chosen a Pole as their leader. The Western Ukrainians hated Poles, because they had been dominated by them until 1939 when their country was invaded by the Red Army. This hatred did not diminish during the years of imprisonment, either in German concentration camps or in the forced labour camps of Stalin. What happened in Vorkuta, where people who hated each other and had fought one another during the war (Poles, Russian, Jews,

40. GARF, f. 9413, op. 1, d. 160, l. 203.
41. GARF, f. 9413, op. 1, d. 160, l. 205.
42. GARF, f. 9413, op. 1, d. 160, l. 206.
43. GARF, f. 9413, op. 1, d. 160, l. 207.
44. GARF, f. 9413, op. 1, d. 160, l. 209.

Ukrainians and Balts) overcame rivalries and became united against the Soviet state, their common enemy, was not a unique episode in the history of resistance in the GULag.

Edgar Antonovich Buts was born in 1926, of peasant origin, and when only fifteen took part in the anti-Nazi resistance. He fought first against the Germans and then against the Soviet Union. In May 1945 he was arrested on Ukrainian territory and sentenced to be shot as a "traitor to the nation". The sentence was commuted to twenty years forced labour.[45]

Ukrainians such as Vladimir Kirillovich Maliuschenko, Vasilii Michailovich Zaiac, Vasilii Vasilievich Grigorciuk, Fedor Semenovich Bolkov, Petr Grigorevich Sobchischchin, were all members of the strike committee. They had all been accused of OUN and UPA militancy and sentenced as "traitors to the nation". Iosif Romanovich Ripetski was also an Ukrainian – and since 1940 an OUN member – who had been sentenced in 1945 to serve fifteen years forced labour. During the strike, he appealed several times to the Central Committee, explaining what it was that his group demanded. He was in fact the only one who had a higher education. Two Russians, Valentin Evstingnevich Vinogradov and Fedor Leontevich Finogenov, were also members of the strike committee. They had been sentenced to twenty-five years[46] for collaborating with the Germans, and also because they had taken part in operations against Soviet partisans. When the strike ended they were all arrested and sentenced for "criminal responsibilities".

The MVD and the Moscow public prosecution office immediately sent a commission of inquiry, the task of which was to investigate and put down the riot. General Maslennikov, a war hero, was the head of the commission formed by eight MVD officers. They went to the sections to talk with prisoners, but the heads of the second and tenth sections refused to talk to them, stating once more that they would negotiate only with a member of the Praesidium of the Central Committee.[47]

The commission reinforced camp security to prevent prisoners escaping. The head of the Rechlag was ordered to make a list of the organizers and most active members of the uprising, so that they could be isolated once order was restored. After deciding on the emergency measures to be adopted, the commission discussed a plan to eliminate resistance within the second and tenth sections, which were the most intransigent. On July 31, at ten o'clock in the morning, soldiers went into the second section and forced inmates to come out in groups a hundred. These groups were then taken to the tundra and "filtered".[48] The

45. GARF, f. 9413, op. 1, d. 160, l. 193.
46. GARF, f. 9413, op. 1, d. 160, ll. 191-196, 201-202.
47. GARF, f. 9413, op. 1, d. 160, l. 230.
48. GARF, f. 9413, op. 1, d. 160, l. 231.

leaders of the strike committee were arrested, and the other prisoners taken back to the camp. The evening shift went to work as usual. Documents fail to reveal the treatment meted out to the arrested inmates, who – as in Norilsk – were beaten and transferred to prison, pending trial.

While soldiers repressed disorder in the second section, the commission went to sections three, four, thirteen and sixteen, where the prisoners were persuaded by threats to return to work. Fearing fresh disorder in this section, the commission decided to isolate activist prisoners "gradually".[49]

On August the first, General Derevianko led operations against the tenth section, following the same plans that had worked so well for the second section. But prisoners armed with knives and staves resisted the escort. The authorities reacted immediately, killing 42 inmates and wounding 138. The leaders of the strike committee were arrested and transferred to prison. During the following days, 883 prisoners, who had been identified by spies as "active participants" in the revolt, were transferred to two special *lagpunkts*. Twenty-nine strike leaders were arrested, while 280 prisoners involved in the revolt were imprisoned.

The public prosecutor of the camp held a further inquiry and stated that the use of weapons during the operations to stop revolts was totally in accord with "soviet legality". The commission from Moscow also stated that the main causes of the strike were partly the incapacity of camp administration to exercize sufficient control (by means of the spy network) and partly the lack of re-education. According to the commission, administrators knew about the critical situation of the camp and the growing influence of clandestine organizations, but had failed to isolate the most dangerous inmates and to prevent the spread of resistance. Constant and illegal acts of "brutality" against both escorts and guards had been tolerated, which had as a result strengthened the solidarity and confidence of the prisoners.[50]

Other and different reasons for the disorder are provided by the testimonies of the surviving inmates. Perhaps the most important of these was the disappointment felt when, after the death of Stalin and the arrest of Beriia, the long awaited amnesty was not granted. Amnesty was granted only to non-political prisoners;[51] when this fact became known to the other inmates, resistance grew stronger. The news of the arrest of Beriia, accused of being an enemy of the people, provoked a sudden escalation of the already serious situation, speeding up the revolt. Because they had been condemned by the MVD – now consid-

---

49. *Ibid.*
50. GARF, f. 9413, op. 1, d. 160, ll. 236-237.
51. Regarding problems arising after the liberation of these prisoners and the problems they caused, see documents published by Werth and Moullec, *Rapports secrèts*, pp. 409-412 and pp. 415-416.

ered as divested of its authority – prisoners in the camps felt entitled to claim a review of their cases.

Although both strikes failed, some of the concessions granted by camp administrators during the disorders were not revoked after they were put down. In August 1953, prisoners of Gorlag, Rechlag and Mineralag (in the Komi Republic) officially obtained the following rights: a working day of no more than nine hours; clothing no longer to have identifying letters and numbers; and the possibility of writing and sending money home once a month, of receiving visits and withdrawing up to three hundred rubles per month from their savings. It was also decided that iron bars would be removued from windows, that doors would be left open at night, and that prisoners could pay visits to inmates living in other huts within the compound. The Vice-minister of the Interior, Serov, and Colonel Kuznetsov, both of whom signed the document containing these concessions, also considered it necessary to reinforce and improve the internal order of the camps. To this end, they asked the Home Office Minister Kruglov to extend these measures to cover all special camps.[52]

Far more meaningful in this regard was the edict issued by the MVD, by the Ministry of Justice, and by USSR public prosecution office "about reviewing sentences of inmates in MVD special camps and prisons of the USSR".[53] The most important demand made by the prisoners had been the review of sentences, and it was this which led to clashes with the Moscow commission. The denial of this demand, together with the refusal to allow inmates to discuss it with a member of the government or of the party, had convinced some prisoners not to yield even to the partial concessions offered by the Moscow commission. But with the order of September 30 1953, all sentences were to be reviewed; those who were not considered as "exceptionally dangerous" were as a result to be transferred to ordinary labour camps.

By November 24, inmates in six out of the ten camps had been reviewed, and of 183,656 prisoners whose cases were examined, 76,750 were transferred to ordinary labour camps.[54]

These measures show, once more, the depth of the crisis affecting the camp system, and the necessity felt by the MVD authorities to stem it so as not to lose control. The MVD had won control after a violent clash with the Justice Ministry in 1934,[55] the year in which the GULag was founded. The running of the camps had a political and economic importance, and it also gave the MVD a significant economic role at the national level. The reorganization of both the political and economic powers of the Ministry of Interior that began immedi-

52. GARF, f. 9414, op. 1, d. 2598, l. 117.
53. GARF, f. 9401, op. 12, d. 513, ll. 110-112.
54. GARF, f. 8131, op. 32, d. 3029, ll. 14-15.
55. Cf. Jakobson, *Origins of the Gulag*, pp. 70-110.

ately after Stalin's death,[56] became irreversible; in the years between 1953 and
1956 the ministry gradually lost, besides its political influence, its economic
empire based on forced labour.

56. Cf. Craveri and Khlevniuk, "Krizis ekonomiki MVD", pp. 108-120.

Marxist and Neo-Classical Approaches to Unfree Labour in India

Wendy K. Olsen

> To understand the process of economic change in a backward agrarian economy, we must try to set it in the context of developments in its social history – the process by which agrarian classes merge and consolidate or decay through steadily gaining or losing in economic strength.[1]

In this paper I examine the usefulness of two viewpoints from economics for the study of free and unfree labour in India. The first viewpoint is at present dominant in the academic discipline of economics, and is represented by the neoclassical writings of Stiglitz.[2] The second viewpoint is that of marxist economists, of whom I take as an exemplar the work of Bhaduri.[3] Before assessing these two schools of thought in sections II and III, I first provide an overview of India's bonded labour situation, with special emphasis on Andhra Pradesh in south India.

I. Introduction

Origins of Bonded Labour in India

Slavery in India has been deeply embedded in the ideology of the Hindu caste system,[4] and has its origins long before the period of colonization by the British and other European powers. People who would now be identified as tribals and as *harijans* (so-called untouchables) were the main groups enslaved in the pre-

---

1. Bhaduri, *Economic Structure of Backward Agriculture*, p. 126.
2. See especially Stiglitz, "New Development Economics", pp. 257-265.
3. Bhaduri, "Study in Agricultural Backwardness", pp. 120-137, "On the Formation of Usurious Interest Rates", pp. 341-352, "Class Relations", pp. 33-46, and "Forced Commerce and Agrarian Growth", pp. 267-272.
4. Sarkar, "Bondage in the Colonial Context", p. 102. For a description of how closely embedded bonded labour is in the caste system in recent times, see the case study by Kamble, *Bonded Labour in India*, p. 128.

colonial period. Slaves were considered non-caste by Hindus, yet caste-like distinctions of purity and status were maintained via customs and rituals among enslaved outcastes as well as among caste Hindus. During British rule the slave systems of India's regions were initially codified and defined through property law, and later (1840 to 1861) abolished.[5] During and after the legal abolition of slavery, existing master-slave relationships went underground. Most were converted into legal forms such as debt bondage. Labour bonded through debt was finally made illegal in India in 1976, but this law is still unenforceable because many such labourers "choose" (through lack of alternatives) to stay in debt bondage. Even in the nineteenth century, there was not a clear delineation of slavery from debt bondage.[6] For instance, under both circumstances the condition of bondage could be inherited from parents; there were diverse sets of obligations (some financial, some in terms of work obligations, and some ritual) varying across castes and regions within the sub-continent.[7]

There were various forms of slavery. For instance, the supply of indentured labourers to tea and coffee plantations in India was a new form, introduced by the British, which involved false promises to prospective migrants and coercion under sub-human conditions for those indentured.[8] By contrast, the use of females as individual slaves for human reproduction and certain kinds of work goes back much further. It is recorded in very early written history and apparently preceded the general enslavement of men and families.[9]

Female slaves often had no right to marriage but might be married to another slave by the owner or made to produce children for the owner. By contrast, male slaves have at times been bought and sold with their wives, whose labour seems to have been an unstated part of the "individual" bargain between two men.[10] In both the pre-colonial and the colonial period, some slaves were owned as individuals, some as families, and yet others lived in a condition of group

---

5. Sarkar, "Bondage in the Colonial Context".
6. Chakravarti, "Of Dasas and Karmakaras", ch. 1, p. 36.
7. Sarkar, "Bondage in the Colonial Context", p. 98.
8. *Ibid.*, pp. 114-116.
9. Chakravarti, "Of Dasas and Karmakaras", pp. 56-62; Lerner makes similar claims with reference to evidence from Assyria, Babylonia, and Mesopotamia. Lerner, *The Creation of Patriarchy*, pp. 76-83.
10. Sarkar, "Bondage in the Colonial Context", p. 105; interestingly Sarkar uses the male gender as universal for slaves and bonded labourers in spite of evidence about women slaves facing different conditions from men. Saldanha says of bonded labourers in the 19th century that "neither the nature of work nor the hours of work were specified [and] the labourers were kept in subjection by sexually oppressing their women and by inflicting physical torture on both men and women [...] the labourers' families too were attached to the master, and bondage was hereditary", Saldanha, "Attached Labour", p. 1122.

enslavement now called corporate bondage.[11] Two examples illustrate the situation in early nineteenth century south Indian agriculture.

Vidyasagar, using primary source material, describes a transition from slavery to bonded labour in southern India over the period from the 10th to the 19th century. In the slave system in villages of what later became South Arcot Dt., Tamil Nadu, whole families of workers in one caste were classified as slaves, with two resulting sets of obligations: (i) the slaves had to work for the caste Hindus on an unpaid, beck-and-call basis, whether male or female, old or young; and (ii) the "community", i.e. caste Hindus, had to support the slave families communally. Ownership of slaves was thus at the village level, not at the household or individual level.[12]

Ramachandran also surveys the south Indian history of bonded labour and concludes that

> an outstanding feature of the class of labourers at the beginning of the nineteenth century was its corporate identity and the condition of corporate bondage; agricultural labourers were bound as a group to the cultivation of wet land in a village [...] the basic remuneration of agricultural labourers [...] was a share of the gross produce of the village (the share varied from village to village), which was handed over to the group.[13]

Out of such systems arose written contracts between male ex-slaves and male owners during the later period of British rule (1850-1947). Vidyasagar reprinted the contract of a male bonded labourer, dated 1916, showing the shift that had occurred toward personal, man-to-man contracts which gradually replaced the slave system.[14] Laws limiting and eventually outlawing slavery did not fully take effect until this and other substitute systems for managing workers had been established.[15]

Dingwaney provides an all-India survey of the legal changes during this period. She says:

> Slavery is the social sanctioning of involuntary servitude by one person or group upon another – the prohibition of slavery was often accompanied by an increasing resort to practices and institutions that attempted to circumvent that prohibition. Hence, substitutes like indentured or contract labour emerged (where there is no ownership of persons, but the right to ownership of labour under exploitative conditions exists).[16]

---

11. The diversity of unfree labour relations in modern India is reflected in the review by Tripathy, *Bonded Labour in India*, esp. chs 2 and 3.
12. Vidyasagar, "Debt Bondage".
13. Ramachandran, *Wage Labour and Unfreedom in Agriculture*, p. 8.
14. Vidyasagar, "Debt Bondage", p. 154.
15. *Ibid.*
16. Dingwaney, "Unredeemed Promises", p. 314.

The worker and his relations in Vidyasagar's example had borrowed for a marriage, and in exchange they promised the labour of one man (or his replacement), "in lieu of interest", for an unspecified period.[17] (At a much earlier stage in Indian history, for which written sources are limited, it seems that slave women were seen as loanable, just as cattle were. The normal rate of interest in kind was one "issue", i.e. a child or a calf.[18] Here we see how far patriarchy preceded capitalism and colonialism; patriarchy has however been adapting to economic conditions and other social structures over the centuries.)

The system of debt-bondage which is the endpoint of Vidyasagar's story is the historical starting-point for a number of other studies of bonded labour in India.[19] As Deshpande points out in the context of tribal workers in the 1970s and 1980s, many such workers are known as "marriage-loan labourers".[20] Deshpande writes,

> the worst part of the contract is that the worker is not free to take work elsewhere without the employer's permission. He therefore cannot take advantage of the opportunity, if available, of earning more money. The contract is not favourable to him, as it entails long hours of work, hard labour, and, in general, humiliating conditions.[21]

Saldanha translates *lagna gadi* as "marriage slave" and reports that the pledge included the family's labour as well as the labour of the male borrower.[22] Deshpande, writing at an earlier date, stressed that the relationship

> is a social informal agreement between a debtor who is invariably a tribal [in the case study area, Thane] and a creditor who is usually a non-tribal [...] usually the creditor extracts work every day. It is a social agreement in the sense that it is recognised and enforced by the sanction of the society, but not by those of law. The society considers it morally binding on the debtor and does not provide any escape to the debtor from the contract. A bonded labourer is thus not given any work by others in the surrounding area, because giving such work is often regarded as unethical.[23]

Deshpande specifies that the creditor gives the marriage advance "on the condition that both husband and wife agree to render personal service or labour for a specific period or for life or till the debt is satisfied".[24] He cites several

---

17. Vidyasagar, "Debt Bondage", p. 154.
18. Chakravarti, "Of Dasas and Karmakaras", p. 63.
19. See for example Saldanha, "Attached Labour", pp. 1121–1127, and Deshpande, *Employment Guarantee Scheme*. Both are based in the Thane Dt. of Maharashtra.
20. Deshpande, *Employment Guarantee Scheme*, p. 112.
21. *Ibid.*, p. 57.
22. Saldanha, "Attached Labour".
23. Deshpande, *Employment Guarantee Scheme*, p. 109.
24. *Ibid.*, p. 110.

examples where the woman's work is implicitly pledged along with the man's among these marriage-labourers.

Persistence of Bonded Labour

Recent research in India suggests that the bonded-labour system persists in various guises in spite of laws that have tried to abolish it. Vidyasagar's 1982 fieldwork provides a case study in which

> While other debts can be paid off and the individual gains his freedom, there exists an understanding that once the master spends money on the marriage of a bonded labourer he gains complete control over the individual until his death.[25]

Note that in this case study the bonded labourer's wife worked as a casual labourer at market wages for other employers.

Action by the Government of India to "free" and "rehabilitate" bonded labourers has had very little success.[26] Many bonded labourers are loath to present themselves to the authorities because of likely reprisals by the employer.[27] In addition some workers feel they voluntarily choose bonded status as preferable to partial unemployment as a "free" labourer. Deshpande paraphrases such respondents saying: "What was the use of freedom if it meant starvation?"[28] Reluctance to break bonds has in some cases been linked by observers to the patronage offered by employers. In addition the "rehabilitation" arrangements made by government have not adequately ensured an income for ex-bonded labourers. DasGupta writes that

> the [rehabilitation] schemes do not meet with much success also because they are not of the choice of the freed bonded labourers [...] but were thrust upon them.[29]

Saldanha says that "delay in rehabilitation facilities often sends the released labourers back to bondage".[30] This is a central Government of India scheme with 125,000 recipients over the five years 1983-1987 at Rs. 6250 each (or Rs. 4000 each before 1987).[31] This scheme does not work, reflecting a serious disjunction between reality and the assumptions of the policy.

---

25. Vidyasagar, "Debt Bondage", p. 150.
26. DasGupta, *Problems of Unorganised Workers*, p. 21.
27. See Deshpande, *Employment Guarantee Scheme*, for as case study reporting the same story at micro level.
28. *Ibid.*, p. 112.
29. DasGupta, *Problems of Unorganised Workers*, pp. 22-23.
30. Saldanha, "Attached Labour", p. 1127.
31. DasGupta, *Problems of Unorganised Workers*, p. 25.

Case Study Evidence from Andhra Pradesh

Recent research in Andhra Pradesh confirms the presence of various types of bonded labour in different regions of the state. R.V. Ramanamurthy has described the terms and conditions under which *paalamuuru* labourers work on 10-month seasonal contracts.[32] The workers, male and female, get individual contracts and large initial advances to work on construction sites such as roads, dams, and other major earthworks. They go far from home, with transport and camps provided by intermediaries called *maistries* and *group-maistries* who each take a cut of the profits. Most of these contracts originate in government funds. As in the other cases described by Brass and by Jodhka in Haryana,[33] most of the workers express hatred for the *paalamuuru* system yet continue to accept contracts and run up debts.

Some workers have escaped the bonded-labour earthworks by becoming seasonal migrants working as casual labourers in Hyderabad city and thereabouts. In "choosing" migration they face insecurity and poor living conditions. Another alternative is to stay at home in their drought-prone and unindustrialized district of Mahabuubnagar in the northern region of the state.

Both *paalamuuru* labourers and casual migrant labourers keep a base in the villages and leave very young and very old members of families there to look after any land they may own or rent. The two months when construction work stops are a time of marriages and ceremonies, and for these more loans are taken. The *paalamuuru* workers' situation has been the subject of concern in national discussions on the condition of rural labourers[34] and in the reports of A.P.'s human rights organization.[35]

Bonded labour is a loose translation of the Telugu word *jeethagaadu*, which would translate literally today into "salaried man". *Jeethagaadu* has been described as it evolved from the 1950s to the 1980s in Guntur District in the coastal region of Andhra Pradesh.[36] Unpublished PhD research by Davaluri Venkateswarlu describes the harassment and social control suffered by *jeethagaadu* workers in the previous generation, with work responsibilities extending to the family of the male bonded labourer. In recent years a system of individual contracting has developed, however, and other family members are free to work for other employers while the *jeethagaadu* is not. In addition the predominance of *jeethagaadu* relationships has fallen and the wages these workers receive are much higher in real terms than they were in the past in this classic "green revolution" district.

32. Ramanamurthy, "Seasonal Labour Migration".
33. See Brass, "Class Struggle", pp. 36-67; and Jodhka, "Agrarian Changes", pp. A-102-A106.
34. Narasimha Reddy, *Rural Migrant Labour*.
35. A.P. Civil Liberties Committee, *Report on Mahboobnagar Civil Rights Situation*.
36. Davaluri Venkateswarlu, unpublished mimeos toward PhD dissertation, Department of Politics, University of Hyderabad, Hyderabad.

The work of Lucia Da Corta provides further evidence of the development of contractual relations over a similar period. Although bonded labour in its classic form had once existed in the villages she studied in 1988/89, it was far less prevalent in 1988 than in the past. However, several forms of labour-tying were found among the landless workers and those with just a little land in the study villages in southern Andhra Pradesh:

(i) tied labour loans, where indebted workers get lower-than-market wage rates and promise to work for the lenders whenever the lenders ask them to ("first-call" on their labour, for short);

(ii) tied labour leasing, where workers get a 50/50 sharecropped plot on the condition that they supply first-call wage labour to the landlord lender (some of these workers have some land);

(iii) tied harvest loans, where the borrower must sell the output to the merchant who loaned them money;[37] and

(iv) tied harvest leasing, where the tenant must sell their harvest to the merchant lender.[38]

The first two arrangements are clearly labour tying. The latter two are arguably indirect ways of exploiting.

Finally the study by Robinson describes the viciously personal and physically violent nature of the relations between workers and their lender-employers in a village in the Telangana region in the 1970s.[39] The village tension level apparently fell after the monopolistic and unchallenged power of certain landlord families was lessened in the aftermath of Panchayati Raj institutions.

There is tremendous diversity in labour contracts and they can include seasonal, annual, till-repayment, and till-death contracts. (I have found few recent reports of the inheritance of debt after Independence, but legal and social factors mitigate against reporting of such situations.) Kapadia has investigated a case of bonded labour among caste Hindus in Tamil Nadu, and there she seems to have found individuated bondage with strong familial (especially female) obligations to repay debts.[40] The evidence offered in this chapter is merely a selection intended to introduce the usual usage of the term *bonded labourer* in Indian contexts. Usually this term is used to refer to a worker who has borrowed, or whose family has borrowed, from an employer, and who must work solely for that employing household, at their beck and call, until the loan is repaid with interest. Legally binding contracts are not necessary for bondage to

37. See also Olsen, "Competition and Power", pp. 83-89, and *Rural Indian Social Relations*.
38. Lucia Da Corta, unpublished mimeos for PhD dissertation, St. Anne's College, Oxford University, Oxford.
39. Robinson, *Local Politics*.
40. Kapadia, "Profitability of Bonded Labour", pp. 446-483.

occur, and social obligations may involve members of the employer's and the worker's families as well as the bonded individuals.

A taxonomy of contractual forms is not the intention of the present work, though some interesting work has been done along these lines.[41] Intriguingly, in Walker and Ryan's report on the long-term village studies done by the International Crops Research Institute for the Semi-Arid Tropics (ICRISAT), Hyderabad, it becomes clear that one of those villages had many out-migrants working as *paalamuuru* (bonded) labourers on large-scale construction works elsewhere in India.[42] However this contractual form does not get attention in the ICRISAT analyses since the migrants were not available for interview most of the year.

Hazy Borders of "Freeness"

The "unfreeness" of the workers to sell their labour elsewhere is only one aspect of the constraints on Indian workers and I wish to point out two additional sets of constraints which need to be allowed for in a revised conceptualization of "free and unfree" labour. Firstly, women as a gender are constrained by their stereotypical domestic responsibilities; and secondly, tenants are constrained by their need for continued access to the land they rent.

In the examples given above we have both a male-centred system of man-to-man contracts and a male-centred mode of reporting. Women's unpaid labour has been mentioned as an incidental component of the bonded labourer's contract, yet women are not seen as bonded labourers by most observers. What is women's position? They can be oppressed in many ways, including through patriarchal authority and through a submissive self-discipline, as well as through direct relations with employers.[43] Casual women workers may nevertheless at times and in some ways fit the classic Marxist definition of free labour: owning their labour power as a commodity and being able to sell it on a labour market.[44] "Free" labour, at one point, was used by marxists as a counterpoint to the unfreeness of land-based peasantries. Leaving the land (by force or by choice) would lead to the creation of a proletariat. Women, who have in many societies not had title to land anyway, could be proletarianised at different times and in different ways from men.

This dimension of "freeness" of women workers has however been curtailed in several ways. Firstly, as agents they are not simply individuals but part of familial and household units with ongoing strategies and shared ideas. Bargaining

41. Rogaly, "Explaining Diverse Labour Arrangements".
42. Walker and Ryan, *Village and Household Economies*, ch. 5.
43. See Olsen and Ramanamurthy, "Analysing Bonded Labour".
44. Miles, *Capitalism and Unfree Labour*, p. 171.

is not really done individually. Secondly, within households they may have responsibilities that reduce their freedom to sell their labour power. Perceived duties create real constraints on action. Thirdly, their kin's debts may restrict their own "freeness", and the marriage debt is one example. In Kapadia's study (which is the only gendered empirical case study of bonded labouring today that I have found) many women had a stronger wish to repay loans than did men.

Here I have raised some questions which merit empirical study as well as some conceptual re-working. Marxist "freeness" only refers to "freedom to sell one's labour power" and should be viewed very sceptically. Such "freedom" may mean only that the shackles are more deeply hidden. Marxists intended the concept of a "free proletariat" to be ironic, anyway, since showing how capitalists hide their exploitative practices is a major aim of marxists. Commodity fetishism and false consciousness are two main concepts that have been invoked, adding a deep critique to the analysis of free labour.

A second type of "free" labour is Lucassen's historical category of independent labour.[45] He means people working on land that they controlled or owned, including peasants, producing for own use. In India today the self-provisioning peasant is hard to find! Many households with small plots of land and perhaps two bullocks also rent in a little land. In upland south India ownership of 1-2 acres of dry land is often combined with renting in from 5 to 50 cents (0.05 to 0.50 acres) of irrigated land. The rice crop resulting from this tiny plot must be shared with the landlord. As already indicated, such rental schemes imply obligations on the tenants' part which may extend to first-call on their labour at crucial times. At ploughing/sowing time a male/female team and two bullocks are requested and this work may delay the tenant family's own sowing work on their own land. Suddenly a group of land-owning marginal farmers no longer look "independent" – they look tied and are indeed unfree to sell their labour power at certain times of year.

So "freeness" is not very free; some aspects of "unfreeness" are not captured by Miles' definition; and the bonded labour definition I gave above is not adequate for the range of attached and tied labour arrangements actually observed in rural India.

The phrase "tied labour" could be used for milder forms of bondage, particularly in the context of rural agriculture where seasonality is great. A tied labourer could be defined as a worker whose debt, or whose family's debt, to an employer leads them to do unpaid or poorly-paid work for that employer, or leads to the employer getting first-call on that worker's labour power at certain times. First-call is a different obligation from beck-and-call. Having first-call means only that at agreed times – presumably the peak season – the worker must work

45. Lucassen, "Free and Unfree Labour in the Twentieth Century, this volume, pp. 45-56.

if called. Having access to labour at the employer's beck-and-call is an obligation that extends over the year(s) and subsumes first-call. In empirical work local terms for such variations must be studied in local languages.

In sum, for future empirical work both classic bonded labour and tied wage labour each have a clear place; of course seasonally attached labour with more or less "freedom" and daily wage labour with more or fewer attached obligations can also be examined. In addition, the degree of individualization of debt-obligations and gender differences in obligations should also be considered. These are the main empirical questions raised by my survey of some literature on Indian bonded labour.

Prakash has developed a more fundamental critique of the free/unfree dichotomy.[46] Prakash argues that calling the sale of wage labour onto markets a "freedom" implicitly concedes much to the dominant way of thinking. Colonial elites, and now capitalist elites, have a vested interest in the label "free labour". Prakash's work supports the usual marxist approach that questions the "goodness" (for workers) of both "free" and "unfree" labour.

Having introduced some historical and conceptual material on bonded labour in a rural Indian context, let me now examine the neoclassical economists' approach to the same question.

II. Neoclassical Economists' Views

Interlinkage of Markets

I turn now to the literature on bonded labour within the academic discipline of economics. Here the phenomenon has been treated as one among several interlinkages between markets. For example, sharecropping is seen as linking the land and labour markets, since payment for labour is made in kind from the produce (see Angelo in this volume).[47] Borrowing from one's landlord is also seen as an interlinkage of markets, in this case the credit and land markets, with the crop potentially acting as security for the loan.[48] The neoclassical literature in this area began as a theory of "interlocking factor markets".[49] The restriction

---

46. Prakash, *Bonded Histories*.
47. Neoclassical studies include Lucas, "Puzzle of Sharecropping", pp. 237-238; Quibria and Rashid, "Puzzle of the Lucas Model", pp. 239-242; Braverman and Stiglitz, "Sharecropping and the Interlinking", pp. 695-715; and Binswanger and Rosenzweig, *Contractual Arrangements*.
48. For a review of studies see Bardhan, *Land, Labour and Rural Poverty*. See also the essays in Bardhan, *Economic Theory of Agrarian Institutions*. For a study in northern India see Bardhan and Rudra, "Interlinkage of Land, Labour and Credit Relations", pp. 367-384.
49. Bardhan, "Interlocking Factor Markets and Agrarian Development", pp. 82-98.

to factor (input) markets has of necessity been removed as economists have realised that the ties extend into the product (output) markets as well. Neoclassical economists wanted to explore the implications of interlinkage for their models which had hitherto assumed that price-quantity equilibria could be predicted for isolated commodities once the supply-demand conditions were known. Marxists, by contrast, concentrate on a wider sense of the words "tying" and "linkages". The agreements connect people and in many cases also link households and kin groups. This personalised approach allows for rich study of inter-household social relations, and includes the social class of families as a major factor influencing their behaviour. Subjective ideas and ideology about economic behaviour have a place in such an analysis, whereas the depersonalised commodity fetishism of the neoclassical approach allows for no such factors. The work of Rosenzweig, Stark, and Becker are examples of the neoclassical approach as applied to marriage.[50]

A brief review of the neoclassical approach may be useful to readers; after that I present a few criticisms.

A Neoclassical Model of Bonded Labour

In the neoclassical approach labourers and employers mutually and voluntarily agree to enter into contracts (written or unwritten). Srinivasan, for instance, has constructed two models of bonded labour in both of which the worker is a male sharecropper (tenant).[51] In the first model, the landlord is the only available lender, and bonded labour is a rational choice for the worker which increases the utility of both parties. In Srinivasan's later model, there is competition in the market for consumer loans.

> A "bonded" labour contract was defined as one in which the landlord provides consumption credit to the sharecropper in return for the latter agreeing to provide labour services (at less than his opportunity cost) to the landlord in the event that the (random) output is inadequate to repay the amount borrowed with accumulated interest.[52]

Using a mathematical model again maximizing the utility of workers and landlords, Srinivasan derives several conclusions beyond the original finding. For instance, credit ceilings on the part of banks are shown to inhibit default of worker/tenant/borrowers, whereas bank lending up to the amount demanded

---

50. See Rosenzweig and Stark, "Consumption Smoothing, Migration and Marriage", pp. 905-926; Becker, "Theory of Marriage: Part I", pp. 813-846; and Becker, "Theory of Marriage: Part II", S11-S26.

51. Srinivasan, "Agricultural Backwardness Under Semi-Feudalism: Comment", pp. 416-419; and Srinivasan, "On Choice Among Creditors", ch. 10.

52. *Ibid.*, p. 203.

might lead to default; (ii) subsidies on bank interest rates could increase (or "at best not decrease") the incidence of bonded labour (leading to a tendency to advocate higher interest rates).[53] Srinivasan's substantive findings are logical implications of the theoretical model. Entry into a bonded labour relationship is seen as a rational choice for both worker and employer.

In general such models have stressed material factors affecting male decision-makers acting to maximize their own utility. Implicitly the neoclassical economists assume these men also maximize the total utility of their households, too, by acting thus. Little correspondence with real-world observations is intended. Srinivasan's models and others like them are intended to be an improvement on much previous economic literature which looked at only one market at a time and which had not allowed for the role social institutions, such as share-cropping, play. Bardhan states, "The models illustrate how some of the tools of advanced economic theory can be fruitfully used in understanding aspects of age-old institutions."[54]

Stiglitz has gone even further in advocating this kind of approach.[55] He argues that the "imperfect information paradigm" is superior to other, in particular marxist, approaches.[56] Stiglitz advocates a form of economics that goes beyond demand-supply and bargaining to allow for differences and dynamics in the information set held by each decision-maker. In his view tied transactions are a way of resolving imperfections in markets. In economic jargon he refers to the "internalization of externalities"; offsetting the "asymmetry of information"; and, like Srinivasan, the lenders' need to alter the incentive structure facing borrowers.[57] In other words low effort levels of workers can be overcome by landlords setting up incentives which cover all possible outcomes and protect employers from the risks attached to their partial ignorance of workers' actions and future production conditions. Stiglitz goes on to argue that this paradigm is superior because of its falsifiability, external completeness, specificity of predictions, predictive power, and generality. "One of its attractive properties [...] is that the information paradigm provides a general framework which is applicable to both developed and less developed economies".[58]

A Critique

My critique of the above approach will cover several areas: the idea that everyone gains through tying; the voluntariness of the act of contracting; the

53. *Ibid.*, pp. 209 and 215.
54. Bardhan, *Economic Theory of Agrarian Institutions*, preface.
55. Stiglitz, "New Development Economics".
56. See also Stiglitz, "Rational Peasants, Efficient Institutions".
57. Stiglitz, "New Development Economics", p. 259.
58. *Ibid.*, p. 262.

absence of certain agents in models up to now; and the ahistoricism and supposed universality of the models.

Tied transactions have been characterised by neoclassical economists as a source of Pareto improvements. A Pareto improvement is any change which leaves no-one worse off and makes at least one person better off. In the neoclassical literature, tied transactions are often assumed to create new economic opportunities and thus, potentially, increase everyone's utility. Utility (or personal satisfaction) is seen as arising from consumption, which in turn depends on the amount produced and/or earned.

The set of all the best possible production combinations given existing assets and technology is called the production possibility frontier (PPF). We can imagine the PPF as a mathematical function that increases when any input is increased, e.g. labour time or fertilizer. From these outputs agents obtain satisfaction, called "utility", and the utilities possibilities frontier (UPF) is the set of optimal combinations of agents' utility levels that are made possible from the PPF output combinations. In both cases society might not be "on" the curve – i.e. optimally placed – but might lie "within" the curve, not maximizing total output (on the PPF) or total utility (on the UPF). The PPF is seen as shifting outward (upward) when a rational bargain is struck.

According to this logic, if the proposed contract did not allow each agent to get at least a little better off, then the bargain would never have been struck. The utility potentially reached by all the parties then also increases, or in technical language we could say the utility possibilities frontier shifts outward (upward).

But utility cannot easily be measured or aggregated, nor can outputs of various products easily be summed up, so this is a wholly unmeasurable theory of contracts. The UPF approach has other serious problems:

(a) In empirical work we never know whether two agents are on the UPF, or somewhere inside it. Economists are not even sure whether real economies operate on their production possibilities frontier or not. We can easily imagine that even if we produced without using any input wastefully (i.e. optimally on the PPF), we could still have *some* people not achieving their maximum potential utility, given the PPF. As a result, increasing output does not necessarily mean both agents get better off. For instance, a rise in crop yields could be associated with tenants' utility falling in spite of an outward UPF shift. This would be described as a movement within the (old or new) UPF – but would not be a Pareto improvement. The theory assumes that the disutility of a tenant's work is fully accounted for using their choice of either tenancy or a market wage. The effect of onerous conditions or feelings of oppression on utility are not allowed for except as unexplained preference differences.[59]

Stiglitz argues that being inside the UPF creates opportunities for state intervention that will be a Pareto improvement.[60] However this is no guarantee that a given intervention is good for everyone. In any case bonded labour today occurs in the informal sector away from state regulation, and agents may quite happily make someone else worse off through their actions.

(b) We are not told what situation the "original" UPF (the hypothetical base case) referred to. Should a sharecropping contract, for instance, be compared to (i) the landlords cultivating the land themselves? (ii) wage labour with no credit? (iii) wage labour with credit? (iv) bonded labour? (v) slavery? The neoclassical models are vague about the pre-contract situation because of their ahistorical, comparative-static approach.

(c) We never know who controls the shape of the UPF. In offering a tied transaction, landlords may simultaneously withdraw other offers such as wage labour. If the landlords can thus alter the UPF in ways that favour their utility and reduce tenants' utility, but not allow the tenant any better alternative, then the landlords' power is enough to force the tenant to accept a contract that leaves them worse off than they were before the offer. The UPF is a construct that masks the social processes of bargaining between parties. It is therefore an inappropriate tool, even as a heuristic device, for analysing village markets.

(d) The UPF is also vague about the time period over which utility is measured. A contract may make a tenant or worker better off today, but worse off in future. Intertemporal utility can be dealt with in neoclassical theory, but the static UPF idea then becomes inappropriate. In regions where there are unstable, multiple interest rates and hidden interest charges, even the algebraic discounting of future utilities becomes a dubious exercize. It can certainly be done in theory, but it is a poor representation of the complex decision-making processes of rich and poor villagers over time. The neoclassical models bear little resemblance to social reality.

Turning now to the voluntariness of the contract, the neoclassical approach has disallowed coercion and power to be exercized. The agents choosing to enter a bonded-labour contract in Srinivasan's model were a male tenant and a male landlord. No attention was paid to the households or the families within which these agents are embedded or the pressures they may come under. Women and

---

59. Folbre recommends extending theory to cover the formation of such preferences, but this is only the beginning of a solution. Folbre, *Who Pays For the Kids?*
60. Stiglitz, "New Development Economics".

children in those families may be forced to comply with terms to which they did not agree. In fact, in Srinivasan's models the entire annual income is seen as being at the man's disposal for repaying loans without any regard to the complex choices people in households make as consumers. Unpaid labour of other household members is ignored, both when done for the landlord/lender and when done for the household of the worker.

But even if we consider the "worker" as an individual choosing for her/himself, neoclassicals do not allow for the interpersonal exercize of power. P. K. Bardhan himself has written:

> In any case, since transaction costs can be as difficult to define and quantify as power, in actual empirical or historical analysis one may sometimes find it hard to unscramble the effects of one from the other.[61]

Power in rural societies has many dimensions, but I shall focus here on the power of lenders to exploit workers. Marxists argue that tying transactions in the land, labour, credit and output markets is a way of re-allocating surplus into landlords' and merchants' hands. This argument can be restated in neoclassical terms: the contracts cause either a movement within the UPF, or a shift in the UPF, or both, that raises landlords' and merchants' utility while decreasing the other agents' utility. In the neoclassical view, workers and tenants enter into tied contracts voluntarily. But we see this as forced commerce.[62] Workers may accept the tied contracts, but

> trading in the credit market in the form of consumption loans, usually induced by a threat to survival, leads to *involuntary* participation in exchange in some other markets.[63]

Involuntariness arises not only from a conscious exertion of power in a pairwise relationship, but also from the structural location of people which is unconsciously reproduced and reinforced through their labour market decisions.[64] The range of choice of each person is constrained by their social class, caste, income, etc.

The use of the adjective "exploitative" for such relationships has a long history. Bharadwaj, B. Harriss, J. Harriss, Srivastava, and Bhaduri are among those who label as exploitative all relations that transfer surplus value from producers' hands into the hands of the owners of the means of production.[65]

61. Bardhan, "New Institutional Economics and Development Theory", p. 1393.
62. Bhaduri, "Forced Commerce and Agrarian Growth".
63. *Ibid.*, p. 269 (italics in the original); see also Bharadwaj, "View on Commercialisation", where a similar point is put.
64. Compare Basu, "One Kind of Power", pp. 259-282, with the arguments of Folbre about structure, in Folbre, *Who Pays For the Kids?*
65. Bharadwaj, "View on Commercialisation"; Harriss, *Transitional Trade and Rural Development*;

The classic use of this term of course refers to exploitation in the process of capitalist production, i.e. directly through wage labour. A case can be made, however, for distinguishing such primary exploitation from secondary exploitation in the sphere of exchange. After all, in most real markets surplus is realised by several intermediaries, some far from the original workers. We could perhaps label the transfer of surplus through exchange as extortion rather than exploitation – noting that pure exchange relations do not create surplus value *per se*, but only realize and reallocate it. In either case, at the end of the marketing chain more resources end up in the lender's hands through the tied lending than would otherwise be the case.

Whatever position one may take about exchange relations and exploitation, a lesson one learns from studies of tied transactions is that the two spheres (production and exchange) are not distinct. Most tied transactions involve obligations that extend over time and that include credit arrangements (loans, promises to pay, etc.). If the system as a whole is judged exploitative, and assuming that the term is defined carefully, the analysis of tied transactions then usefully details certain mechanisms of exploitation. Srivastava's 1989 case study is an example of how such an analysis can be a useful guide to empirical work, without strictly separating the spheres of production and exchange.[66]

Workers would not voluntarily and consciously "choose" to be exploited in either the production or exchange spheres if they had non-coercive alternatives. They are coerced into participating in exploitative economic relationships, often through the absence or withdrawal of acceptable alternatives to bondage. The marxist theory of exploitation through ties thus highlights one of the contradictions between that approach and that of the neoclassical economists. In that sense Stiglitz and Bhaduri are right to focus on their differences. In the third section of the chapter, I comment further on the marxist approach.

A third problem with neoclassical literature is the absence of both merchants and semi-proletarians. Writers from both neoclassical and marxist schools use a simple labelling scheme to describe tied transactions. On the one side are land-lord-lender-employers who have land and/or shops and surplus cash. On the other are worker-tenant-borrowers who are schematically seen as lacking land and surplus cash. This labelling system is a useful simplification which emphasises that market power is concentrated in a very few hands. Group One is a much smaller section of society than Group Two. The particular terms chosen reflect the historical circumstances in which these theories have been developed. The emerging capitalist classes of employer and worker (or bourgeois and proletariat) are only gradually replacing the (originally) feudal classes of landlords and

      Harriss, *Capitalism and Peasant Farming*; and Srivastava, "Interlinked Modes of Exploitation in Indian Agriculture", pp. 493–522.
66. Srivastava, "Interlinked Modes of Exploitation".

tenants. The labels "landlord" and "tenant" are no longer appropriate *class* labels once capitalism has developed, but they are still appropriate labels for particular agents in particular circumstances, especially in house- or land-rental trans-actions. Ultimately the employers of Group One should be assigned their proper name – capitalist farmers – as capitalist relations get well established in villages.

However useful the existing specification of agents, two important classes have been left out of the discussion so far. The first is the semi-proletariat or labouring peasantry. Articles based on 1970s Indian data, particularly, tend to emphasize the absence of full proletarianization at that time in the Indian context.[67] The analysis of tied transactions will improve if we can add a landowning semi-proletariat to the models. Da Corta's detailed family histories in Andhra Pradesh suggest that this group is large and different in crucial ways from landless labourers.

Secondly, merchants are absent from most neoclassical analyses but present in most marxist analyses. Two of Bhaduri's models actually allow for a mercan-tile bourgeoisie, distinct from the landed bourgeois.[68] Separate consideration of the two classes is useful, in the Indian context and perhaps in others.[69] An extreme example of how the merchant class is artificially merged into the landlord-cum-moneylender class is Braverman & Stiglitz's "general model" in which the landlord is simultaneously lender and shopkeeper.[70] Such a model is not appropriate in many Indian contexts. Very few landlords have provisions shops. Parts of precapitalist and capitalist India have had a merchant class which is socially and economically separate from the landed ruling class (different castes and religious communities, without intermarriage). Models of tied transactions can and should take this separate class into account.

Finally, I would question the ahistoricism and claimed universality of the neoclassical approaches. In the neoclassical view "advanced" analysis involves mathematics and grand theory that can be applied universally.[71] The ahistoricism implied by such a conception of social science will be anathema to many people. The same models are applied regardless of the development of classes, the nature of the state, or local norms. The "formalists" of economic anthropology have a legacy in neoclassical economics. The self-conscious superiority of some writers from the latter school reflects their reliance on an unreconstructed positivism. Their lack of concern with linking concepts to real-world structures will be

67. Prasad, "Reactionary Role of Usurer's Capital", pp. 1305-1308; Bhaduri, "Study in Agricultural Backwardness".
68. Bhaduri, "Class Relations", and Bhaduri, *Economic Structure of Backward Agriculture*, ch. VII.
69. Tinberg and Aiyar, "Informal Credit Markets in India", pp. 43-49; and Schrader, "Profes-sional Moneylenders and the Emergence of Capitalism in India and Indonesia", pp. 185-208.
70. Braverman and Stiglitz, "Sharecropping and the Interlinking", p. 699.
71. See Wright Mills, *Sociological Imagination*, for a convincing rejection of both.

opposed by realists of many persuasions, e.g. critical realists such as Sayer and feminist marxists such as Mies.[72] Without advocating a direct correspondence of theory to the material world, we can note that the total lack of any such correspondence makes the neoclassical approach practically useless.

III. Marxist Approaches

Recall that the neoclassical approach to tied transactions had as its main advantage the explanation of how informational asymmetries and incentive structures can generate inter-market linkages. The strength of the various marxist explanations of tied transactions, by contrast, is their firm grounding in the historical origins and social structure of each particular economic situation in which linkages are observed. Each school of thought emphasises a different dimension of the phenomenon: the one, the economic structure at an unspecified point in time; the other, the historical evolution of that structure over time.

A Marxist Model

Marxist theories explain long-term social changes in terms of dialectical materialism, and are therefore inherently society-specific and historical. They recognize that contradictions within a society can persist and grow until a qualitative change in social relations occurs. As Bhaduri put it,

> Conventional economic analysis based upon the notion of "marginal", quantitative changes seems totally inadequate for capturing the consequences of qualitative shifts in class relations that may take place during the process of accumulation.[73]

A marxist model of bonded labour allows qualitative interaction between classes as opposed to only marginal changes. Miles, too, in a series of marxist empirical studies, reveals the links between the material world and means of production, on the one hand, and forms of labour relations on the other.[74] Such claims are so characteristic that they could be seen as a model (involving both material and ideological factors), although not every marxist or neo-marxist would use such an approach.

Bhaduri's work has become well-known for providing marxist models that are in some ways comparable to (and therefore challenging to) the neoclassical models. In 1973 he described how semi-feudal landlords in northern India could exploit workers as a class through tied loans and land rental. In 1983 he pre-

72. Sayer, *Method in Social Science*, and Sayer, *Radical Political Economy*; and Mies and Shiva, *Eco-feminism*.
73. Bhaduri, *Economic Structure of Backward Agriculture*, p. 125.
74. Miles, *Capitalism and Unfree Labour*.

sented more detailed models that could be applied in different empirical settings, stressing the historical specificity of the original schema as outlined in 1973 (which was later criticised). Bharadwaj, Crow and Murshid, B. Harriss, J. Harriss, and Srivastava were meanwhile developing marxist analyses of many other specific situations involving moneylenders and tied transactions.[75] Basu has developed some excellent analyses of dyadic (meaning pairwise, or between individuals) and non-dyadic power in such situations.[76] K. Bardhan reflects one current in marxist thinking in her summary of the historically specific role that tied transactions are playing in India:

> Vertical ties between landowners and labourers have adapted to, not disappeared with, agrarian growth in India, even in eastern India [...] Since a large variety of tying and bondage mechanisms has already been perfected under agrarian feudalism over the centuries, it would be surprizing if capitalist farmers did not harness those time-tested control mechanisms and clientelizing institutions for their profit-making interests merely because they were originally used by absentee landlords and feudal merchants for other purposes.[77]

Here, as in the quote from Bhaduri at the beginning of this paper, we see the exploitation of one class by another highlighted for macro analysis. That phenomenon can in turn be linked to micro power relationships (as Basu has done) thus creating potential links between neoclassical theory and Marxism. K. Bardhan's argument is potentially consistent with both neoclassical and marxist approaches to the question of tied transactions. It shows some complementarity in the two approaches, with neoclassical analysis of capitalists' and workers' motives fitting within a marxist framework of the historical evolution of the socio-economic structure.

Of course fundamental differences in value-orientation and epistemology split the two groups of theorists at present, but both sets of ideas certainly have shed light on bonded labour.

Is This Marxist Model Unfalsifiable?

The marxist approach of Bhaduri does have a few problems. One is that, like the neoclassical theorists, Bhaduri and others have tried to predict interest rates. Their predictions are various, depending on sets of assumed initial conditions, many of which are not measurable. In this they imitate the literature they are

---

75. Bharadwaj, "View on Commercialisation"; Crow and Murshid, "Finance of Forced and Free Markets"; Crow, "Plain Tales From the Rice Trade"; Harriss, "Organised Power of Grain Merchants", pp. A39-A44; and Harriss, *Capitalism and Peasant Farming*.
76. Basu, "One Kind of Power", "Emergence of Isolation", pp. 262-280, and Basu, "Implicit Interest Rates", pp. 145-159.
77. Bardhan, "Poverty, Growth and Rural Labour Markets in India", p. A22.

critiquing. An early strand of neoclassical literature ignored tied transactions altogether in explaining money interest rates.[78] Once linkages were allowed for, the neoclassical models became indeterminate in predicting or explaining interest rates.[79] It became clear that interest may be charged in kind, may be charged at varying monthly (not annual) rates, and may be low or zero when a charge is hidden in some related transaction.

But we find nearly as much indeterminacy in marxist models of interest-rate phenomena. For instance, Bhaduri's initial attempt to explain usuriously high interest rates was later modified by Rao and by Basu to explain low and zero money rates of interest.[80] These theorists would agree on the factors that influence rural interest rates: *personalized collateral valuation; borrowers' and lenders' risk; power of lenders; transfer costs such as the loss of reputation if a worker migrates; and the likelihood of default.* Each of these factors is very hard to measure. Algebraic models don't determine the rural interest rate; they merely explain any observed nominal rate from zero to 200% by varying the hypothesised determining factors. For instance, if the workers' valuation of their collateral is very high, and the employers' valuation very low, then a high interest rate will be agreed (other factors being held equal). However, enquiring about collateral valuations may lead to a change: workers may try to rationalize their response to such a question by stating current market prices instead of their own perceived sense of the worth of the collateral. Thus the marxist multi-variate model can claim to be an improvement on the neoclassical models, but it is quite tricky to turn to empirical evidence to find out how well each claim is borne out.

Bhaduri clarified the analysis by defining the "own rate of interest" on kind loans (which does not vary with price seasonality the way imputed money rates of interest on such loans do) as opposed to money rates of interest.[81] He also never succumbed to the urge to determine the annual (or annualised) interest rate for rural informal credit markets. However these clarifications do not resolve the other measurement problems. Two lessons to be drawn from the marxist literature in this area are:

(i)   supply and demand factors in the grain, credit, labour and land markets vary so much from month to month, in the presence of production seasonality, that annual(ised) interest rates are a nonsensical concept in this context; and

78. Iqbal, "Determinants of Moneylender Interest Rates", pp. 364-377. Tun Wai "Interest Rates Outside the Organized Money Markets", pp. 80-142. Bottomley, "Premium for Risk". Roemer, "Simple Analytics of Segmented Markets", pp. 429-439.
79. Datta *et al.*, "Seasonality, Differential Access and Interlinking of Labour and Credit", pp. 379-393.
80. *Ibid.*
81. Bhaduri, *Economic Structure of Backward Agriculture.*

(ii) in the presence of tied transactions across markets, the search for a single equilibrium interest rate is bound to fail. Multiple informal interest rates and concealed interest charges are to be expected.[82] Kapadia's recent study exemplifies the personalised differences in "interest" nominally extracted from bonded labourers through their wage rates.[83]

Models of interest rate determination that link banks with the informal market are only of limited, heuristic, interest if they do not account for these factors. For example, Roemer analyses the effect on informal savings and interest rates of changes in official policy in the formal sector.[84] The single-market approach ignores important connections with other markets, and could not predict how tied relationships would be affected by the government policies. Worse, aggregated data to test the predictions of these models are not available in India. India's bank interest rates are fixed through intervention by the Reserve Bank of India. There are no published records of informal-market interest rates. We would need to distinguish tied interest rates from untied, monthly rates in one season from those in another, and so on. In other words both the theory and the data collected would have to be adapted to allow for the seasonal and class pattern of credit transactions.

Ironically the marxists face the same problem as the neoclassical economists in having several unquantifiable causal factors in their model. Special problems arise with the quantification of the concept "power of lenders". To use net outcomes as a measure of power would be circular, since power is just one of the posited causal factors. In my view the operationalization of "power of lenders" requires conceptual clarity and substantive empirical analysis but not necessarily quantification – but then falsifying the model in the sense used by Stiglitz in 1986 would not be possible. Research by Brass and Kapadia strongly suggests (as theorists would predict) that power relations are partially internalised and legitimated through ideology, e.g. the duties of fictive kin, and that therefore the outcomes of domination are found not only in material/economic effects but also in the realm of ideas and struggle.[85]

The other causal factors also suffer from similar problems. Quantifying transactions costs is extremely problematic. Risks can only be estimated and

---

82. Basu, "Emergence of Isolation and Interlinkage". Data to support this claim are provided by Kurup, "Price of Rural Credit", pp. 998-1006; and Bhende, "Credit Markets in Rural South India", pp. A119-A124.
83. Kapadia, "Profitability of Bonded Labour".
84. Roemer, "Simple Analytics of Segmented Markets". See also Braverman and Guasch, "Rural Credit Markets", pp. 1253-1267.
85. Brass, "Elementary Strictures of Kinship", pp. 56-68, and Kapadia, "Profitability of Bonded Labour". Knights and Willmott state theoretical reasons for these links in Knights and Willmott, "Power and Subjectivity at Work", pp. 535-558.

there is a paradox here unless uncertainty is assumed to be estimable. However, instead of "testing" the multi-variate models, a special form of inference can be done (called "retroduction" by critical realists). Here one alters the hypotheses in the face of evidence that casts doubt on them, positing factors or mechanisms that could explain the anomalies. One then begins a fresh stage of evidence gathering suited to the restatement.

For marxists the unfalsifiability is not seen as a problem since their approaches are neither positivist nor empiricist. Models are not part of a "factual" analysis, for them. Rather they are part of attempts to grasp the complexity of social relations while at the same time influencing the society. To "explain", for them, means to explain to the people, not to a limited number of experts. For some marxists setting up models to oppose the claims of neoliberals is a polemical task as well as an analytical one. Indeed, since most marxists are concerned not only to know but to change society, they are concerned about the effects of their research. Mies and Shiva point out that in getting to know about something you necessarily change it.[86] The same point has been made at length by Connolly, arguing that where concepts are contested the process of enquiring about them causes re-interpretation and conscientization.[87] For example, asking about risk-aversion might raise consciousness about risks; asking about unfreedom might raise doubts about obligations to employers.

Taken to an extreme, this view might seem to suggest that the marxist approaches needn't be "true" or correspond to reality as long as they ring true to readers/listeners and thus comprise part of practical liberation strategies. We can avoid complete pragmatism through adding two criteria for good explanations. First, models and claims should correspond broadly to the social reality – reality including both the material world and structural phenomena. This approach is acceptable to structuralist, materialist marxists. Secondly, the value position from which marxists start (e.g. that exploitation is bad) can and should also come under scrutiny during the research process.[88] Ideas about what a non-exploitative society would be like can be developed, and the implicit value-positions of both marxists and neoclassicals become the subject of serious consideration. Marxists' usage of the term "exploitation" itself needs further scrutiny, as it seems to have some unquantifiable aspects not allowed for in the labour theory of value. These tasks are being undertaken by current researchers. Delphy and Leonard, for instance, develop a theory of the exploitation of women within marriage that allows for multidimensional exploitation not measured in terms of surplus-value extraction.[89]

---

86. Mies and Shiva, *Ecofeminism*, p. 38.
87. Connolly, *Appearance and Reality in Politics*.
88. See Sayer, *Radical Political Economy*; and Wright, "Explanation and Emancipation", pp. 39-54.
89. Delphy and Leonard, *Familiar Exploitation*, ch. 3.

Have Some Marxists Been Sexist?

In my review of bonded labour in India, several problems have appeared for marxists who use un-gendered models. First, gender blindness can be very detrimental to women because we all live in a patriarchal society with structures that tend to keep many women at home, relatively immobile, economically weak, and dependent. Women's experiences as relatives of male bonded labourers, or as members of bonded households, deserve attention instead of suppression through male-oriented analyses.

Secondly, women's experience of individual bondage and debt needs attention because women's lives differ fundamentally from those of men. In particular the provision of sexual services and domestic caring work need more attention (as shown in the introduction). Furthermore differing meanings are attached to women's "productive" or "public" work, compared with men's, e.g. women's contributions are often devalued or belittled even when they are similar to or more painstaking than men's work.

Thirdly, Bhaduri's model, like others, has not unpacked the household. This gap looms large even in recent writings of marxists. Jodhka for instance quotes a worker saying that being an attached labourer in Haryana is just as bad as being the wife of a [large] farmer: the farmer has complete control of your body and your actions![90] This quote sits ironically with the complete absence of analysis of women in Jodhka's and other marxists' analysis of unfree labour.[91] Folbre argues convincingly that both marxists and neoclassicals need to consider the family, the household, and women as a gender more carefully.[92] In addition Vidyasagar's historical study and recent fieldwork suggest that bondedness of families needs to be considered. Cistorians should be trying to document and explain the development of individuated "bonded" relationships between people, and related private forms of attachment linked thereto. Women's and children's understandings and experiences, related through life histories and oral testimony of older women today, may be helpful here.

Finally, in the study of labour relations marxists can no longer afford to ignore how the reproduction of the labour force is organised. Non-feminist Marxism is inconsistent with marxists' own opposition to oppression. There is an intriguing parallel between the situation of a wife in marriage and that of a bonded labourer. The services provided by the wife or worker are often, on balance, to the advantage of the husband or master, but various ideologies mask the domination and reconstruct it as mutuality. Jodhka's quote vividly draws such an analogy. It might be useful to consider whether conjugal marriage is

---

90. Jodhka, "Agrarian Changes and Attached Labour", p. A104.
91. Miles, *Capitalism and Unfree Labour*.
92. Folbre, "Hearts and Spades", pp. 245-255.

itself a coercive relationship, into which women are forced both through social pressure and economic circumstances. Delphy and Leonard, for example, argue that marriage is exploitative.[93] In their view, men are not forced to marry and are not oppressed within marriage because of their dominant location in patriarchal social structures. Delphy and Leonard's extreme structuralist position differs from that of some feminists, e.g. Folbre, who argue that young men are oppressed by older men and that other structural divisions besides gender complicate the situation.[94] Whatmore, too, would differ from Delphy and Leonard, arguing that through human agency we find substantial deviations from structural starting-points.[95] The actual picture, whether in the west or in India, therefore differs from the stark patriarchal picture drawn by Delphy and Leonard, but discussing the oppressiveness of marriage and kin relationships can be very revealing. The moral obligations felt to be connected with debt, especially marriage debt, may be linked to feelings of obligation to work.[96]

Conclusions

The history of bonded labour in India suggests that questions of familial obligations resulting from male borrowing are an area needing more investigation. I have shown through examples in section I that lenders can wield power over borrowers and their relatives. This "power" has both economic and ideological dimensions. In section II, I pointed out some serious inadequacies in the neoclassical approach to such phenomena (though there are some worthwhile insights in neoclassical writings, too). In section III, I showed that marxist approaches (out of which the free/unfree dichotomy arose) introduce useful elements such as a more complex class structure, historicity, personalised collateral valuations, and the power of lenders. However, nearly all the authors who have developed these insights have avoided a detailed exposition of women's involvement in bonded labouring. A gendered theory of bonded labouring may be needed, and this will require dealing with issues of force and free will, structure and agency. However the marxist approaches have the advantage of allowing for class exploitation, and their methodology calls into question the value-orientation of other analysts who would perhaps wish to be seen as objective.

93. Delphy and Leonard, *Familiar Exploitation*. The authors expressly limit their analysis to western societies, but by handling the case of farming households as well as proletarians they build a model that could be examined in connection with non-western societies, too.
94. Folbre, *Who Pays for the Kids?*
95. Whatmore, *Farming Women*.
96. See also Brass, "Elementary Strictures of Kinship".

I conclude from this analysis that there is a need for feminist research in this area and that marxists can look to feminists (male and female) and to women in villages for help in developing a better understanding of the exploitation that occurs through both "free" and "unfree" labouring.

Free or Unfree? Railway Construction Labour in Nineteenth-Century India[*]

Ian J. Kerr

Introduction

This paper has two purposes. First, to investigate the value of the distinction between free and unfree labour for an understanding of the processes of class formation and class transformation in the advance of capitalism.[1] This investigation will be pursued in two ways: (a) theoretically and, without any attempt at comprehensiveness, historiographically; (b) through the history of the construction workers who built an extensive network of railways in colonial India between 1850 and 1900.[2] It will be argued that the classical view of free and unfree labour adumbrated by Marx has limited value for understanding the trajectories of class formation in the historical or prospective advance of capitalism. At best and ironically, the classical view helps us to distinguish between varieties of coercion. Historically, free labour appears to have had no necessary relationship to the advance of capitalism: unfreedom, at the very least, has been common within capitalism and the achievement of free wage labour uncertain and reversible.[3] Whether or in what ways becoming a free wage labourer

*   Research grants from the Social Science and Humanities Research Council of Canada and the Shastri Indo-Canadian Institute helped to support the research on which this paper is based. I am grateful for the support. I am also grateful to the International Institute of Social History, Amsterdam, which helped to make it possible for me to attend the Free/Unfree Labour Conference. Some parts of this paper are based on material previously published in Ian J. Kerr, *Building the Railways of the Raj, 1850-1900* (New Delhi, 1995).

1.   I adopt the standard definitions. A free wage labourer is one who, lacking ownership in the means of production and being free from direct compulsion, sells his or her labour power for a limited time to someone with capital. Unfree labour is harder to define but is understood to involve "extra-economic coercion". There is merit in the inversionary approach of Steinfeld, *Invention of Free Labor* where he takes a form of "unfree" labour, contractual servitude, to be the normal employment relationship in the Anglo-American tradition until well into the 19th century and thus one of the defining contrasts against which modern free labour is understood.
2.   An excellent collection of South Asian railway statistics is Morris and Dudley, "Selected Railway Statistics", pp. 187-304. In 1901 the route miles in India totalled 24,185, the world's fourth largest railway network.
3.   Thus one can agree with Brass, "Some Observations on Unfree Labour", p. 60, that a central conceptual issue is "to problematize the achievement of free wage labour rather than the existence of unfreedom".

benefitted those who laboured is a question to be answered historically, not teleologically.

An emphasis on unfree/free labour (hence the labour market, i.e., exchange and circulation) shifts the focus away from the labour process, from the realm of production, where the crucial relationship of capitalism (exploitation, the extraction of surplus value) is located and where different issues of freedom and unfreedom arise.

Thus, a second purpose of the paper is to explore the sphere of production, and the interaction of that sphere with the labour market, to identify possibilities for another form of freedom for those who labour. This exploration, located in the collective struggle of workers to control the labour process, will use the history of the Indian railway construction workers to suggest opportunities for, and obstacles to, enhanced worker control over the processes of production and hence more freedom from their exploitation by capital.[4]

Marx left a powerful legacy. Nonetheless, it is not a legacy that is immune to criticism and revision. Indeed, few who write within the Marxist tradition treat it as such. One legacy that needs to be re-examined was Marx's expectation that the advance of the capitalist mode of production involved the ever more extensive commodification of labour power sold on the market by men and women who had been dispossessed (via the processes of primitive accumulation) from the means of production and whose survival had come to depend on their ability to sell to capital the one and only commodity they "freely" controlled: their labour power. The accompanying shift at the level of the labour process, the point of production and of exploitation (i.e., the extraction of surplus value), was marked initially by the formal subsumption of labour under capital which, for Marx, was then replaced by the real subsumption of labour under capital. Increased co-operation, the greater division of labour, "the use of *machinery*, and in general the transformation of production by the conscious *use* of the sciences [...] technology etc. [...]" enormously increased production and relative surplus value.[5] Labour became more thoroughly subordinated to the dictates of capital that could use machinery "to control labour through the production process itself."[6] One might

---

4. See Cohen, "Labour Process to Nowhere", pp. 35-50 for a good argument that valorization and exploitation should be seen as central to an understanding of labour processes and the politics of worker resistance under capitalism. Cohen, p. 41, rightly in my view, does not like the way in which worker control has become the focus of many labour process studies thus obscuring the basic point that we must "understand the labour process as directed centrally at the fundamental project of capitalism, i.e., the generation of surplus value [...]" in which "the central dynamic" is exploitation. My use of "control" encompasses the struggle against exploitation. On the centrality of exploitation also read the ever clear-headed De Ste. Croix, "Class in Marx's Conception", pp. 94-111.
5. Marx, *Results*, p. 1024. See also pp. 1025-1038.
6. Thompson, *Nature of Work*, p. 124.

say that Marx anticipated increased freedom at one level (exchange/circulation: the sale of labour power) and increased unfreedom at another level (production: the use of labour power in the labour process) although that would be to downplay the irony present in Marx's use of the word free.

Part of the problem comes from the words that frame the debate: "unfree" and "free". To juxtapose the two and to see capitalism, itself viewed as a progressive development in its time and place, necessarily calling forth free labour was to privilege in a powerful way a particular conception of freedom.[7] Free and freedom are positive words and the conditions they purportedly describe become self-evidently good. But Marx, of course, understood free labour to be good (necessary might be a better word) only at a certain stage of historical development and he also understood the irony of free labour: economic coercion had replaced extra-economic coercion; the labourer had to sell his or her labour power in the labour market in order to survive.[8] To phrase the debate in terms of the various ways in which labour is coerced to provide labour power and to reduce the unfree/free distinction to, at the most, a device to help to locate the sources of coercion would be to move forward. The best course would be to eliminate unfree/free entirely and to deconstruct a discourse that is both privileged and obfuscating.[9] One might then move to the question of how, if at all, the achievement of the status of economically coerced labour ("free labour") represents a strategic and/or tactical benefit for labour in its struggle with capital.

7. To quote Marx, *Capital*, I, p. 274: "The historical conditions of its [capital's] existence are by no means given with the mere circulation of money and commodities. It arises only when the owner of the means of production and subsistence finds the free worker available, on the market, as the seller of his own labour power. And this one historical pre-condition comprises a world's history. Capital, therefore, announces from the outset a new epoch in the process of social production." There is value in one of the arguments in Prakash, *Bonded Histories*, namely that the discourse of freedom assumed an hegemonic position such that history was (and is) continuously misread in terms of the free-unfree antinomy. Marx recognized that the path, for him the necessssary path to a better future, was full of terrible costs for those caught up in the emerging free labour markets of capitalism but, nonetheless, he privileged the transformation. Marx expected that British rule in India would neither emanicipate the mass of Indians nor mend their social condition but would "lay down the material premises for both". But, he asked, "has the bourgeoisie ever done more? Has it ever effected a progress without dragging individuals and peoples through blood and dirt, through misery and degradation?" See Marx, "Future Results", pp. 36-37. The ambivalent juxtaposition of violence (broadly conceived) and emancipatory progress in Marxism is explored in Parekh, "Marxism and the Problem of Violence", pp. 103-119.

8. A recent attempt to reassert the role of the compulsion of labour in the labour markets of capitalism is Wood, "From Opportunity to Imperative", pp. 14-40. See also Steinfeld, *Invention of Free Labor*, p. 9.

9. *Ibid.*, pp. 8-9, makes a similar argument.

I deny, historically and/or theoretically, any necessary connection between the advance of capitalism and that form of labour Marx labelled free wage labour although I accept that such a connection was conjuncturally present at moments in history. Capital has used, and continues to use, different kinds of labour to generate levels of surplus value acceptable to it and that labour comes to a labour process via a variety of coercive mechanisms designated as unfree and free in the classical formulation.[10] Capital cares little about the freedom or unfreedom of labour at the moment of the purchase of labour power. Capital does care a great deal about the quantity, quality and tractableness of the labour it situationally requires for the purposes of production – hence the current attraction of the "Asian-model" whereby authoritarian regimes help to maximize the efficiency of market economies by seeking to ensure, among other contributions, a tractable labour force. It is at the level of production, the labour process, that capital seeks to realize the value of the labour power it has purchased (i.e., the valorization of labour power whether in the form of absolute or relative surplus value). The advance of capitalism has involved the growth of free markets in labour (but not necessarily free wage labour markets) in which the amounts of labour power required by capital can be bought, but from whom or how, free or unfree, has mattered little to those with capital.

The evidence for the widespread presence of a variety of forms of unfree labour within the capitalist mode of production is substantial. Even a brief glance at the literature turns up repeated examples of the existence of unfree labour in many parts of the globe in the nineteenth and twentieth centuries.[11] Be it in the regions of the developed world where industrial capitalism had bitten long and deep or the underdeveloped world where subsistence peasant agriculture was still widespread, the presence of various forms of unfree labour is striking. Michiel Baud, who has studied unfree labour in the sugar industry in the Dominican Republic, 1870-1935, puts it forcefully: "The reality of the twentieth-century development of capitalism, especially in the so-called Third World, has belied any mechanistic contradiction between capitalist production and the continuing use of unfree labour. Where liberal and Marxist authors prophesied the inevitable disappearance of slavery and other forms of unfree labour with the progress of capitalist production, the opposite was too often the case to be considered an exception."[12] Baud, in fact, goes further and suggests that in parts of the Third World capitalism needed to evade the free labour market in order to develop. Corrigan also makes the latter point but he does not limit it to the

10. I follow Burawoy in believing there is no one form of the labour process unique to a particular mode of production. Thus, one should write about "the labour process in capitalist society" and not about *the* capitalist labour process. Burawoy, *Politics of Production*, p. 14.
11. Miles, *Capitalism and Unfree Labour*, pp. 71-167 surveys some of the literature.
12. Baud, "Sugar and Unfree Labour", pp. 302-303.

Third World when he argues that the expansion of capitalism hinged on the the large-scale presence of "unfree forms of labour which whole generations of historians have seen as simply feudal relics, the sociological equivalent of cultural lags" rather than the effects of the expansion of capitalism.[13]

Other authors have documented the presence of unfree labour in the plantation economies of colonial Asia and Oceania.[14] The latter kind of labourer was often indentured and subjected to an additional bondage that came from his or her transportation to a distant and different land where s/he was economically vulnerable and culturally cut-off. Hugh Tinker was certainly correct to label the movement of indentured Indian labour to places like Fiji, Assam and Malaya "A New System of Slavery".[15] Although not without controversy the "enganche" system of debt bondage in Latin America has been shown to have been pervasive and enduring as have various forms of debt-bonded labour in South Asia and elsewhere.[16] Asian women enmeshed in the webs of domestic servitude in wealthy Middle Eastern households (and, one suspects, more subtly in North American and European households) were, and are, anything but free wage labourers.[17] Black African labourers in the mines of South Africa and the former Rhodesia were certainly involved in capitalist production and just as certainly were not free wage labourers in the classical sense.[18] And, lest we focus over much on the Third World, what of the foreign workers in the Western European bosom of advanced capitalism or the migrant Mexican workers, often illegal aliens (hence doubly vulnerable to the economic and extra-economic coercion of their employers) who continue to provide the cheap labour power for the advanced, capitalist, market-garden agriculture of Southern California?[19]

No, the presence, historically and currently, of unfree labour within the social relations of capitalism is not a matter of controversy. The often intense debates that revolve around the presence of unfree labour within the advance of capitalism rarely argue over the fact of its presence although Tom Brass does

---

13. Corrigan, "Feudal Relics or Capitalist Monuments?", p. 441.
14. Daniel *et al.*, *Plantations, Peasants and Proletarians*.
15. Tinker, *New System of Slavery*.
16. Bauer, "Rural Workers", pp. 34-63; Brass, "Latin American Enganche System", pp. 74-103; Shlomowitz, "Latin American Enganche System", and Brass, "Market Essentialism", pp. 216-244; Patnaik and Dingwaney, *Chains of Servitude*; Breman, "'Even Dogs are Better Off'", pp. 546-608; Brass, "Class Struggle", pp. 36-67; Prakash, *Bonded Histories*.
17. Shah *et al.*, "Asian Women Workers", pp. 464-486. The history of the British working class reveals that domestic service was the major form of female employment well into the 20th century and, in the earlier 19th century, the largest occupational group in the entire economy other than agricultural labourers. See Davidoff, "Mastered For Life", pp. 406-428.
18. Arrighi, "Labor Supplies in Historical Perspective", pp. 180-234; and Pycroft and Munslow, "Black Mine Workers in South Africa", pp. 156-179.
19. Castells, "Immigrant Workers and Class Struggles", pp. 353-379; Miles, *Capitalism and Unfree Labour*, pp. 143-167; and the fine contribution by Krissman in this volume.

suggest that some writers (whose ideological roots he would identify as neo-classical) in effect redefine unfree labour as free.[20] Regardless of that possibility opposed scholars largely agree at the level of description. Shlomowitz and Brass, for example, do not differ much over the description of the "enganche" system but they do disagree over what its presence signified and whether those caught up in the system were free or unfree. The fundamental debate is about the forms and trajectories of class formation; it is a debate, above all, about the nature and course of proletarianization and about the definition of the proletariat itself (can an unfree labourer be a "true proletarian"?). It is, therefore, a debate about the social consequences of the advance of capitalism. Are unfree labourers really unfree?[21] Is the presence of unfree labour a survival of pre-capitalist forms that will disappear once capitalism is fully established? Does the presence of unfree labour represent deproletarianization induced by capital in certain circumstances to ensure the extraction of surplus-value?

The advance of capitalism has increasingly commodified labour power and those who labour, having lost ownership of the means of production, have come increasingly to depend on the sale of their labour power for their survival and reproduction. That much of the classical theory is correct. But there is nothing intrinsic to the working of capitalism that requires free labour or will, of necessity, create the conditions where unfree labour is an anomalous exception. Labour is rarely fully and individually free at the moment of exchange in the labour market when labour power is sold (by the labourer or others who control labourers) to capital or its factotums. In his history of British labour Richard Price states: "Thus the process of proletarianization – of increasing dependence upon the dictates of capitalist relations – was not primarily a matter of subordination to a labour process that was technically driven. Rather it was a process that occurred more in the sphere of market relations and involved an increased exposure to the vagaries of market forces."[22] Indeed, extending Price, one may see the labour market as the mechanism within capitalism that limits rather than enhances freedom as, for example, in the situation where one worker can stand as a reserve for many employers.[23]

Similarly, at the level of a labour process under capitalism workers, despite all their attempts at resistance, are not free: indeed worker resistance is testimony to their lack of freedom or, put another way, to their exploitation by capital. The search for freedom at both levels is, of necessity, a collective activity: workers collectively withhold or withdraw their labour power from capital and

20. Brass, "Market Essentialism", esp. pp. 235-236.
21. Baak in this volume argues for the presence of a good deal of manoeuvering room (qualified freedom?) for plantation coolies within a setting of juridical unfreedom.
22. Price, Labour, p. 21.
23. A process explored in Pentland, "Development of a Capitalistic Labour Market", pp. 450-461.

they collectively seek to enhance their power to do so through the political process. Provided they can resist economic coercion, even temporarily, it is probably to the benefit of labour in its collective struggles with capital to have individual labourers possess the legal status of free wage labour because, if for no other reason, the possession of that status makes withdrawing or witholding labour power easier especially if the collectivity, through devices such as strike funds, can provide striking workers with economic support. Regardless, the juridical status of free wage labourer has been won, historically, through collective, national, political action and not by the inexorable workings of the advance of capitalism.[24] Moreover, the juridical freedom of labour has always been a double-edged sword because its presence has opened the ideological door to the attempt to atomize labour through attacks on labour unions and collective action. If men and women are free labourers, the conservative argument goes, then unions, through such devices as closed-shops, required dues check-off and so on, restrict their freedom – the neo-conservative, politico-legal counter-attack, therefore, takes the shape of "right-to-work" legislation in the United States or similar legislation in Britain in 1980 and 1982 that eliminated the right to the secondary picket and boycott, attacked the closed shop and ended the immunities of trade unions from legal actions for civil wrongs.[25]

Railway Construction in Nineteenth-Century India

The history of the South Asian men, women and children who constructed the railways of the Raj exemplifies well the issues and processes sketched above.[26] Moreover, the some ten million people who built India's railways between 1850 and 1900 represented a fragment of a much larger, world-wide body of workers

24. See Steinfeld, *Invention of Free Labor*, esp. ch. 6, for the "working out of the idea and practice of free labor" in the Anglo-American late eighteenth and nineteenth century context. Sovereign states (often imagined as nations) represent the "terminal communities" of the modern world insofar as identity and political action is concerned, therefore struggles for rights have been largely *intra*-national in character.
25. Price, *Labour*, p. 245.
26. So do, albeit within a different South Asian context and via a different approach, the plantation workers of Southwest India described in this volume by Baak. He and I agree on many specifics, e.g., the roles played by labour contractors (kanganies in Baak's case) and advances in the mobilization and bonding of labour, the legal, extra-legal, economic and extra-economic coercion of workers, and, generally, the mixtures of "freedom" and "unfree-dom" that characterized the reality of most workers' situations. However, I problematize the distinction between unfree and free labour itself. Baak accepts the distinction and then sets out to describe how fluid the unfree-free distinction was in the history of the plantation labour of Southwest India. Baak chooses not to address in a theoretically specific way the consequences of his findings for our understanding of the processes of proletarianization.

within the advance of capitalism, construction workers of all sorts.[27] Railway construction, a world-wide phenomenon by the middle of the nineteenth century, required large numbers of what Marx called the "light infantry of capital".[28] These were nomadic workers, largely rural in origin but whose occupation was industrial, who were thrown from one point to another as needed.

> When they are not on the march they "camp". Nomadic labour is used for various building and draining works, for brick-making, lime-burning, railway-making. etc. A flying column of pestilence, it carries smallpox, typhus, cholera and scarlet fever into the places in whose neighbourhood it pitches its camp. In undertakings which involve a large outlay of capital, such as railways, etc., the contractor himself generally provides his army with wooden huts and so on, thus improvising villages which lack all sanitary arrangements, are outside the control of the local authorities, and are very profitable to the gentleman who is doing the contracting, for he exploits his workers in two directions at once – as soldiers of industry, and as tenants.[29]

Thus, both theoretically and substantively, the construction workers represent an important subject for the investigation of issues of unfreedom/freedom. Substantively, their continuing numerical size and world-wide distribution give them importance. Theoretically, they offer tantalizing prospects both at the level of exchange and at the level of production. These prospects extend to insights into the historical settings within which industrial capitalism unevenly emerged in various parts of the world. Railway construction appeared with its huge demands for labourers into a world where the commodification of labour power was still in its early stages, the processes of industrial work underdeveloped, and labour markets inchoate and poorly integrated. Given the large numbers of workers needed by capital and the widespread physical dispersion of the worksites (even within a given colony or national unit) how were labourers assembled and labour power obtained by capital? Meanwhile, at the level of the labour process railway construction work was characterized by the extensive and persisting presence of the formal subsumption of labour under capital with its continuities to previously existing work practices and technologies.[30] Nine-

---

27. Figures for railway construction employment in India come from Kerr, *Building the Railways of the Raj* revised and extended from estimates published in Kerr, "Constructing Railways in India", pp. 317-339. Construction work continues to provide employment on a large scale in the late 20th century and it continues to be work characterized by uncertainty, seasonality, danger and the need for labour to migrate to, or to circulate to, construction sites.
28. Marx, *Capital*, I, p. 818.
29. *Ibid.*
30. Marx, *Results*, pp. 1026-1027. "Within the production process, however, as we have already shown, two developments emerge: (1) an economic relationship of supremacy and subordination, since the consumption of labour power by the capitalist is naturally supervised and

teenth-century India provides a particularly fertile field in which to address such issues since the context ("colonial backwardness" for lack of a better, brief description) magnified and sharpened the changes and contradictions that accompanied the advance of capitalism everywhere.

The skilled construction workers came from a variety of sources including pre-existing artisan groups. Regardless of origin many skilled workers acquired railway-specific skills within the construction labour process during the first two decades of railway building. It was from those workers, in turn, that subsequent skilled workers were produced and reproduced.[31] The much larger group of unskilled workers including the great mass of the numerically dominant, unskilled earthworkers came from two main sources. The first main source was the tribal groups, landless labourers, poor artisans or poor peasants living in villages close to the line of works. Many of these remained construction workers only for so long as the construction work remained in the vicinity of their villages such that they could easily return to their villages on a daily or weekly basis. Many of these people also considered construction work a seasonal activity to be pursued when the labour requirements of the agricultural cycle, often enforced by village power-holders, permitted. The British records are full of complaints about coolies abandoning railway work in order to plant or to harvest. As one major British contractor, Thomas Glover, put it in 1884: local labour could only be got for the six months of the year when not working in the fields. "After March we never count upon local labour; it is of little use to us in India."[32]

But if Glover and other employers could not depend on locally obtained labour how did they get all the labour they needed? There were other groups in rural India who were not attached to village life in a fashion that demanded their presence at certain times of the year. Yet other groups had no home

directed by him; (2) labour becomes far more continuous and intensive, and the conditions of labour are employed far more economically, since every effort is made to ensure that no more (or rather even less) socially necessary time is consumed in making the product [...]. But the more capitalist production sticks fast to this formal relationship, the less the relation-ship itself will evolve, since for the most part it is based on small capitalists who differ only slightly from the workers in their education and their activities."

31. The following discussion is based closely on Kerr, *Building the Railways of the Raj*, esp. chs 3, 4 and 5 therefore footnoting in this section of this paper is restricted primarily to direct quotations. There was a fourth group – numerically small but crucially important – involved in Indian railway construction: the British engineers, contractors, supervisors and skilled workmen. They numbered less than 1000 across the entirety of Indian railway construction at any point in time. I am only tangentially interested in this group in this paper. They were, however, instrumental in the early decades in transferring to Indians the skilled aspects of railway construction and throughout the period 1850-1900 they managed the construction process.

32. Great Britain, *Parliamentary Papers (Commons), 1884*, Cmnd. 284, 1884, *Report from the Select Committee on East India Railway Communication*, para. 1915.

villages at all. These groups, the second main source of construction labour, plus those from the villages who were inducted into the continuing life of the construction worker, provided labour that the engineers and contractors came to value and to consider more dependable. The sources suggest that this body of circulating labour came increasingly to form the backbone of the unskilled segment of the railway construction workers and that those who comprised this swelling body of workers proved increasingly able to move regionally and then inter-regionally in the search for construction work. Many of these types of workers existed in the pre-railway age. Locally recruited labour never disappeared – and local variations in the extent of its use were considerable – but it became increasingly less important. Two senior railway engineers, Forde and Le Mesurier, with considerable Indian experience gave valuable testimony on this issue as early as 1872. When asked by a committee appointed by Government to examine the feasibility of a railway from Karwar to Gadak: "Is it not the case that most Indian Railways on this side [Western India] are not made with local labour?" both replied that such was largely the case.[33]

Circulating labour had a number of origins but among the most important were people engaged for centuries or longer in earthworking in such forms as the digging of wells, small reservoirs and canals or in the making of roads. For these people railway construction offered opportunities to do on an expanded and more dispersed basis that which they had always done. The evidence suggests they seized the opportunities while the railway builders were happy to utilize their services for in these groups the British found the closest Indian parallel to the British navvy. It was these groups, when available, that formed the most effective excavators at a worksite.

The excavators mentioned most often in the records were a South Indian tribe called Wudders, Wadders, Wodders or Wodars by the British engineers. More formally transliterated they were the Oddar of Tamil, the Odde of Telegu and the Vadda or Vodda of Kannada.[34] The activities of the Wudders can be traced back at least to the sixteenth century in South India.[35] Thurston, the compiler

33. India Office Library and Records, London [hereafter IOL&R], L/PWD/3/280, Bombay Railway Letters, No. 4 of 1873, Enclosures, *Report of the Committee Appointed by Government on the Projected Karwar to Gadak Railway; and Extensions and Alternative Lines* (Bombay, 1873). Henry LeMesurier was the chief engineer for the Jubbulpore extension of the East Indian Railway built in the 1860s and later the Agent of the Great Indian Peninsula Railway. Forde was the chief engineer of the Bombay, Baroda and Central India Railway in the 1850s and later a contractor in India.

34. Richards, *Salem*, p. 187.

35. Burton Stein, personal communication. Buchanan, *Journey From Madras*, I, pp. 310-313, has a description of the "Woddas, or Woddaru [...] a tribe of Telinga origin" who retained that language despite being scattered throughout Tamil and Kannada areas. He says they built roads, tanks, wells and canals and also traded in salt and grain. They also followed armies to supply grain and in peace transported grain, salt, "Jagory" and tamarinds. Some were farmers

of a large, early twentieth century compendium of South India's castes and tribes, discusses them.[36] He suggests they are Telegu people and he presents some of the stories then current among the Wudders to explain their origin and occupation. Various sub-divisions of the tribe are listed of which the two most important were the Kallu or stone-working Wudders and the Mannu or earthworkers. The earthworkers led an itinerant existence and moved from job site to job site near to which they established temporary dwellings of a distinctive conical or bee-hive form. The stone wudders, it appears, had home villages though they would move to a construction site for the duration of a contract. The Wudders had a reputation for hard-drinking and merrymaking in which respect they also paralleled the British navvy. The Wudders, in turn, were but one example, of similar groups found elsewhere in India: the Ods of the Punjab, the Nuniyas of the North-Western Provinces and Bihar, and the Beldars of Bihar and western Bengal.

The 1871 Census called the Wudders the Oddars or Wuddava and labelled them an aboriginal tribe who as gangs took earthwork contracts in which everyone except the very young and very old took part.[37] Women carried the earth in baskets while the men wielded the pick and spade. "They are employed largely in the Public Works Department, and in the construction and maintenance of railways."[38] A North Arcot District *Manual* called them the Wodda, "the navvies of the country, quarrying stone, sinking wells, constructing tank bunds, and executing other kinds of earthwork more rapidly than any other class, so that they have almost got a monopoly of the trade".[39] The Wudders appeared in the railway records from the start of railway construction in South India. The Madras Railway's Chief Engineer, George Bruce, wrote of the operations in 1853: "The earthwork has been performed almost entirely by Wodders – people who work in small gangs, under the guidance of a superior, or maistry, who, being possessed of some trifling capital is raised to that position, as the man of most influence, who can make small advances to the individual labourer, negociate with the employer, and take as his share a certain percentage on the amount paid."[40] They remained an ubiquitous and numerous presence among the railway construction workers in peninsular India and beyond throughout the remainder of the nineteenth century.

but they never hired themselves out as agricultural servants.

36. Thurston, *Castes and Tribes of South India*, pp. 422-436. Nanjundayya and Iyer, *Mysore Tribes*, pp. 659-677 has a useful description of the Vodda (Wudders) with photographs.
37. *Census of the Madras Presidency, 1871*. I: *Report* (Madras, 1874), p. 157.
38. *Ibid.*
39. Cox, *Manual of the North Arcot District*, p. 298.
40. IOL&R, R.2.II, Madras Railway Reports, 1853 to 1855. Madras, *Report of the Railway Department for 1853* (Madras, 1855), pp. 2-3.

Those who laboured to build the railways rarely sold their labour power directly and personally to the British factotums (the engineers etc.) of railway capital. The teleology of British engineers and colonial administrators who expected the advance of capitalism embodied in railway construction to free individuals to sell their labour power in a market "regulated by the natural laws of supply and demand" notwithstanding, the reality was quite different.[41] It was an expectation rarely achieved despite the observation (assertion?) by Chief Engineer Bruce that by offering a fair wage "the people along the course of our line begin to understand the blessings of being able to carry their labour to the best market, without seeking the sanction or caring for the pleasure or ministering to the avarice of some petty tyrant. A result, the beneficial effects of which, in elevating the position of the people, we can scarcely calculate."[42] In fact, landless labourers, village artisans and marginal peasants were attached to villages in ways English contractors and engineers dimly understood although a later Chief Engineer of the Madras Railway, W.G. Smart, came closer to recognizing bondage and coercion when he wrote: "I think, however, the Zemindars and headmen would come forward as Contractors; in which case there would be no want of labour, as they would be interested in procuring it."[43]

Indeed, few among the railway construction workers were individually free wage labourers. Most came to and were kept at construction work as the result

41. The quotation comes from a speech by Bartle Frere, Governor of Bombay Presidency, 1862-1867, at the opening of the Bhore Ghat incline in 1862. Great Britain, *Parliamentary Papers* (Commons), *Report to the Secretary of State for India in Council on Railways in India for the Year 1862-63,* cmd. 3168, sess. 1863, p. 27. A fuller quotation better captures the teleological vision. "We all know what vast sums, chiefly of English capital, have of late years been spent in this country. Let us consider for one moment what has been the effect of all this money being spent, in giving a fair day's wages for a fair day's labour. I can safely say that, as a rule, this was unknown before the commencement of what I may call the Railway Period; not only were wages in most parts of the country fixed by usage and authority, rather than by the natural laws of supply and demand, but the privilege of labour was in general restricted to particular spots, and nothing like the power of taking his labour to the best market practically existed. This was partly due to custom, partly to the absence of any but agricultural employment, partly to long ages of despotic and unsettled government. But the result was, that the condition of the mere laborer was wretched in the extreme, and the past efforts of Government could do but little to raise him above the status of a serf of the soil. All this has now, I am happy to say, changed, mainly as a direct consequence of these vast railway works; and for the first time in history the Indian Cooly finds that he has in his power of labour, a valuable possession, which if he uses it right, will give to him and to his family something better than a mere subsistence, and that there are means open to him of rizing in the world other than by the career of a fortunate soldier, or of the chance favoritism of princes." Classical liberalism and Marxism share, in this matter, a similar teleology. Both ideologies privilege the concept of free labour.
42. IOL&R, V/23/143. *Selections from the Records of the Madras Government.* No. 18: *Report of the Railway Department for 1854* (Madras, 1855), p. 3.
43. IOL&R, L/PWD/3/218, Madras Railway Letters, Collection to Letter 2, 13 Feb. 1864, pp. 15-16.

of extra-economic coercion by those who had *or who came to have* power over them. Some engaged in construction work because those who already commanded their persons, e.g., the tribal Bhils of Khandesh controlled by the landlord Thakurs, made them do so. In that case a pre-capitalist relationship comfortably served the interests of railway capital and the Thakurs. The Wudders and similar bodies emerged from a pre-capitalist past to take group contracts on a piece-work or task-work basis under the "guidance" of a headman who made small advances to individual workers (more likely family work units) and who took a percentage of the group's earnings. Landless labourers and village artisans were made to work at railway construction in ways we can only inferentially reconstruct just as they were similarly called back to village work when local men of power needed their labour. Sometimes the coercion appears to have been quite open. Thus, a contractor building the line from Amritsar to Delhi in the 1860s reported: "The coolie, though fond of money, prefers perfect idleness, and it is frequently necessary to drive him out of his village in the morning to force him to earn a good day's wages on the neighbouring railway works."[44] Meanwhile, especially for those workers who moved to and lived at a construction site for an extended period, the truck system bonded them in debt to petty shopkeepers who also could be petty contractors.[45]

Debt, in fact, was central to most forms of extra-economic coercion applied to the construction workers. It appears most often in the sources as the ubiquitous advance. Advances became and remained a key element in the mobilization and retention of construction labour.[46] For the worker the advance represented the stake necessary to travel to a worksite – or even further in advance to tide the family over the unemployment of a rainy season. From the viewpoint of capital, however, advances helped to mobilize labour and to tie labour to capital.[47] The maker of the advance gained considerable power over the disposition of the labour power of the recipient: the acceptance of the advance meant the loss of the labourer's control over his/her labour power. The advance subordinated the worker to the muccadum and, in the complex hierarchy of

---

44. IOL&R. Tract vol. 592, *Opening of the Meerut and Umballa Section of the Delhi Railway* (London, 1869), pp. 29-30. Note also the colonial discourse of the "lazy native". For a critical examination of that discourse see Alatas, *Myth of the Lazy Native*.

45. "[...] the truck system, commonly discountenanced at home, is beneficial in India." Berkley, *Minutes of Proceedings*, p. 606. At the time of writing Berkley was the chief engineer of the Great Indian Peninsula Railway. For a history of truck see Hilton, *Truck System*.

46. Breman, "Seasonal Migration", pp. 41-70 provides a telling description of the role advances play in the current migration of labour to the sugar factories of Gujarat. Also see the contribution by Baak in this volume.

47. It must be stressed that this use of advances was not unique to India and other third world areas. See Marglin, "What do bosses do?", pp. 26-27.

supervision and direction that characterized Indian railway construction, subordinated muccadum to sub-contractor, sub-contractor to contractor (or to the engineer) and the whole hierarchy to the railway company or to the Government that provided the capital.[48] Individuals who were fully free to sell their labour power were few and far between. As Bayly has observed the changes to India's political economy developing coterminously with the extension of British rule did not initiate a free market or undermine the headman system. Rather, most rights and perquisites came up for sale "but what made the sale worthwhile was that *within* the 'little dominion' which was being put on the market, competition and the free market were still excluded. Here, political muscle, the authority of the headman and the rights of caste rank continued to operate to produce cash, labour or commodities."[49] Railway construction needed lots of waged labour but that labour had to be tapped primarily through various kinds of headmen who, within the ambit of capitalist relationships, functioned as sub-contractors or even sub-sub-contractors. In the case of local, daily-hired labour the "headman" may have been a village power-holder whose good-will was purchased in order to obtain the temporary release of village labour power.

Railway construction meant the presence, however incomplete, of the forces (the labour process) and relationships (especially the commodification of labour power) of capitalism; railway construction penetrated, however temporarily in particular localities, deeply into the Indian countryside. The contractors and the engineers acting as contractors had the task of putting-out capital. But to whom did they put out the capital they owned or which had been entrusted to them? They had to work through would-be petty capitalists, the layers of Indian intermediaries – sub-contractors and muccadums – who had the capacity to mobilize labour but who were themselves only partially enmeshed in the values and relationships of the capitalist order. These lower-level intermediaries, in turn, had to recruit labour from peasant and tribal societies whose linkages to the emerging world of capitalist relationships in the third quarter of the nineteenth century were limited in many dimensions: economic, social and cultural.[50] Free labour had a limited presence in the Indian countryside in the 1850s and 1860s although, partly as the result of railway construction, it grew as the decades passed.[51] Even so labour never became an atomistic entity bargaining

48. Capitalism also subordinates petty capital to large scale capital.
49. Bayly, *Rulers, Townsmen and Bazaars*, p. 317, emphasis in the original. Chakrabarty, *Rethinking Working-Class History*, pp. 112-113 elaborates on the significance of Bayly's observation.
50. Relevant here is Pouchepadass, "Market for Agricultural Labour", pp. 10-27.
51. The recruitment and organization of labour for India's coal industry, whose nineteenth-century development was spurred by the fuel needs of the railways, presents interesting similarities and differences to the case of railway construction labour. See Simmons, "Recruiting and Organizing", pp. 455-485.

directly, freely and solely over wages with would be employers. Extra-economic links bound workers to muccadums and muccadums to sub-contractors.

The crucial question is not whether unfree labour was prevalent in the construction of India's railways – it clearly was – but what that presence signified. How does one account for the persistence of unfree labour within such a substantial project of Victorian capitalism as railways for India? How do we conceptualize the class position of people like those landless labourers, poor artisans and marginal peasants who worked for wages in railway construction for part of the year and then returned to their villages, possibly when commanded to do so by local power holders (and/or from the belief that maintaining a connection with the village economy remained their best guarantee of subsistence), to engage in agriculture or related activities? Do we conceptualize the latter group as semi-proletarians or re-peasantized proletarians or as something else? Or what of groups like the Wudders? Can pre-existing collectivities from a pre-capitalist past who continued to operate in a fashion much like they did before the railway age appropriately be called proletarians just because they started to build the railways?

It is tempting to conceptualize the various forms of unfreedom in the labour market among the railway construction workers as a temporary condition brought on by the uneven advance of the capitalist mode of production articulating in complex ways with pre-existing modes of production.[52] In short, to argue that unfree labour existed because the triumph of the capitalist mode was incomplete. I do not accept this solution. Moreover, the historical and contemporary evidence from India and elswhere does not support the view that unfree labour necessarily disappears with the advance of capitalism. Those who laboured to build the railways entered the relationships of capitalism; they "sold" their labour power to intermediaries who in turn sold that labour power to those who controlled the construction process (which, in the Indian case, came to include state capital). Hybrid solutions, such as semi-feudalism or semi-proletarianization, do not take us very far.[53] However, those workers (or, at least, many of them) did not do so as "free" labour, a form of labour whose existence always has been problematic in the history of capitalism. Forms of unfreedom existing

52. One should not be too quick to label the existing mode in nineteenth-century Indian agriculture pre-capitalist. Banaji has advanced a sophisticated argument, drawing in part on Marx's concept of the formal subsumption of labour under capital, to argue for the presence of "less developed forms" of capitalist agricultural production in the nineteenth-century Deccan. See his "Deccan Districts", pp. 1375-1404.

53. For example, "The collapse of subsistence economies in the face of capitalist penetration has led to the growth of a large group of workers who are ambiguously and simultaneously 'semiproletarians' and 'semi-peasants'." "Introduction", in Cohen et al., Peasants and Proletarians, p. 12. I accepted hybrid solutions in Building the Railways of the Raj but now believe them to be inadequate conceptually and substantively.

in pre-capitalist modes of production were carried over comfortably into the relationships of capitalism; new forms of unfreedom were created through the advance of capitalism: the commodification of labour power with the advance of capitalism is not incompatible with the continued existence of unfree labour at the level of the person. Proletarianization is not the increasing presence of individually free labour; it is the increasing presence of people, dispossessed from the means of production sufficient for survival and reproduction (hence marginal peasants may be included), who participate in the labour processes of capitalist production as, and only as, providers of a commodity, labour power, from which surplus value is extracted. Thus, to answer the question posed above: Wudders and similar groups among the railway construction workers were proletarians.

At the level of the labour process the majority of the construction workers – and certainly virtually all of the earthworkers – existed in the relationship to capital Marx labelled formal subsumption. This was a relationship with which the factotums of railway capital became comfortable as they discovered, some- times as the result of Indian resistance, that existing tools, techniques and ways of working got the job done expeditiously and/or economically. The latter criteria can be considered the engineers' and contractors' working definition of surplus value in the context of Indian railway construction. The use of the same "definition" of surplus value and the juxtaposition of different kinds of labour processes was expressed well by a 20th century engineer in another type of construction work in India, dam building. In the 1930s despite the use of modern machinery some four-fifths of the Mettur Dam in South India was built by hand leading the engineer to observe: "In no other country, perhaps, could such methods have been employed economically or such a high rate of outturn maintained."[54] In railway construction, too, there was mechanization and tech- nological innovation and thus movement towards the real subsumption of labour under capital: electric lighting (which permitted round-the-clock shift work), pneumatic rivetting machines, steam driven dredges and other devices began the process of subordinating labour to the process of production itself.[55] Even in the inchoate world of construction some elements of machino-facture began to intrude but they existed comfortably and side-by-side with much older labour processes. No necessary movement from formal to real subsumption took place.

54. Barber, *History of the Cauvery-Mettur Project*, p. iv.
55. Consider the implications of the following humble example. At the Empress Bridge (opened 1878) across the Sutlej River rivetting proved to be a problem. The engineers and foremen believed the hammermen were bad and the holders-up worse: "a man too listless to hold up for two minutes would spend an hour, if unwatched, in caulking a slack rivet to pass it off as sound." Mr. Macpherson, the foreman riveter, eventually solved the performance problem by devising "an ingenious telescopic dolly to be keyed up to the work by a large cotter". Bell, "Empress Bridge", p. 256.

In the case of railway construction in India as elsewhere capital found that surplus value could be comfortably assured within existing and pre-capitalist ways of work using, if necessary or convenient, unfree labour. The argument of Raphael Samuel that the slow pace of mechanization in mid-Victorian England was a result of "the possibility of increasing productivity within a hand technology, either by the introduction of improved tools, or by a more systematic exploitation of labour, or both" need not be restricted to England.[56] In India, the railway contractors and engineers used existing practices because they got the job done effectively and economically. But, formal or real, construction work was a labour process under capitalism. The labour process was the point where it counted most, the point of production and hence of exploitation, where capital sought to realize the potentiality it had bought in the form of labour power.[57]

What has all of this got to do with freedom? The point of production is, almost by definition, an unfree situation for the worker. Even the free wage labourer in the classic sense gives over to capital the use of his/her labour power. Capital, in turn, seeks to realize surplus value from that labour power.[58] There is nothing benign about this search: it is the central, exploitative relationship of capitalism. Capital embodied in various levels and types of management assumes control of the labour process which means control, within certain limits, of the persons who provide the labour power during the period of work. However, labour resists that control and thus the labour processes become a central terrain of contestation between labour and capital. Leaving aside ineffectual and often individualized acts of everyday resistance one finds workers acting collectively to limit managerial control.[59] Workers seek to contain, to

56. Samuel, "Workshop of the World", p. 49.
57. Where, nakedly to those who see through the mystification, capital's only interest was (is) surplus value. Burawoy, *Politics of Production,* pp. 32-35, discusses mystification in terms of the "obscuring and securing of surplus value".
58. Braverman, *Labor and Monopoly Capital,* p. 57, captures well the fundamental dilemma of the capitalist: "The coin of labor has its obverse side: in purchasing labor power that can do much, he [the capitalist] is at the same time purchasing an undefined quality and quantity. What he buys is infinite in *potential,* but in its *realization* it is limited by the subjective state of the workers, by their previous history, by the general social conditions under which they work as well as the particular conditions of the enterprise, and by the technical setting of their labor. The work actually performed will be affected by these and many other factors, including the organization of the process and the forms of supervision over it, if any." Emphasizes in the original.
59. Let me be clear – I do not deny the existence of "everyday resistance", indeed I practice it myself, and it may be valuable to individuals as a way of coping. I do deny the likelihood, in most instances, that everyday resistance will change things in ways that fundamentally benefit those who labour. Burawoy, *Manufacturing Consent* writes about a form of everday resistance and coping on the shop-floor he labels "making-out". Cf. the contributions in Colburn, *Everyday Forms of Peasant Resistance.* Significantly, the resistance of the plantation

limit, exploitation within the labour process since they cannot, without the overthrow of capitalism itself, eliminate exploitation. The struggle for freedom in the work-place, therefore, always has as its goal the limited freedom of the limiting of exploitation. The wider goal, the overthrow of capitalism, must be fought out in the wider political arena although that same arena may, at some moments in history, offer possibilities for the political or legal strengthening of workers' rights (the 1990s, in most parts of the world, is not one of those moments).

The railway construction workers, standing at the threshold of the emergence of industrial capitalism into India, soon proved willing to act collectively to try to limit the exploitation to which they were subjected: wages – their amount, method of calculation, and their full and regular payment – were the most frequent issue.[60] The strike was the main form of collective action although few were successful. Mounting a strike within the heterogeneous workforces was difficult and combination was necessarily restricted to individual worksites and even to particular groups at worksites. Some idea of the obstacles to worker combination is found in the following mixture of construction workers in Assam in the 1890s: Pathans, Makranis (from the Makran Coast beyond Karachi), coolies from Chapra (west of Patna) and Tirhut; Khols and Santhals from the Central Provinces, and Nuniyas and Sylhetis from Bengal did the earthwork; Nepalese did the dry stonework; carpenters, stonemasons and bricklayers came from the Punjab while Cutch supplied masons and bricklayers; riveters and bridge erectors came from Bombay. Note the horizontal segmentations of region and language, the occupational distinctions and the vertical divisions of unskilled and skilled labour. Success came only in unusual circumstances and particularly eluded the earthworkers for whom replacement workers could usually be obtained. Thus, for example, in an oft repeated response the engineers broke a strike at the Tapti Viaduct construction in February of 1860 by collecting hundreds of replacement coolies from Baroda.

Significantly, most of the recorded strikes in the later decades took place among the skilled workers whose more limited numbers facilitated combination and whose more necessary presence at certain stages in a work process gave them greater leverage. Perhaps, too, their greater subordination to capital heightened their proletarian consciousness. Earthwork coolies had to strike en masse to be effective; relatively few skilled workers, if they chose the right moment (e.g., assembled but loosely bolted bridge girders were vulnerable until riveted), could bring work to a halt at a crucial juncture. Three hundred riveters struck in August 1880 at the Punjab Northern State Railway Bridge across the Sohan but

workers described in this volume by Baak only began – and even then slowly – to have systemic effects when the workers unionized and acted collectively.
60. Kerr, "Working Class Protest", pp. PE34–PE40.

returned to work three days later. Riveters also struck in April, 1903 at the Bengal-Nagpur's coal-line bridge across the Damodar. Divers struck for higher wages during the construction of the Indus Valley State Railways's Jhelum Bridge in the early 1870s and for the same reason on the Punjab Northern's Harro Bridge in the early 1880s. And, in a reprise of the Tapti Viaduct situation some twenty years earlier, a nearly successful strike for higher wages among skilled workmen "whose rates of wages I should otherwise have had very largely to increase" on the Sind-Peshin line in 1889 was put to an end by the arrival of a contingent of Punjabi workmen obtained by a recruiting engineer despatched for the purpose.[61] Even among the more skilled workmen the reserve army of labour could ensure discipline and wages lower than those sought by the workers.

What does this material suggest? First, it shows that even in a setting unfavourable to labour and in the early stage of the transition to capitalism workers did act collectively to try to limit exploitation and thus they sought a limited form of freedom. Significantly, they acted in most cases over issues that directly related to exploitation, namely wages, and not over the "cultural" issues beloved of some theorists. Exploitation was the main source of worker agency. Secondly, it suggests the presence of strategic moments within production processes when the ability of workers to wrest concessions from management was maximized.[62] Thirdly, it suggests an intersection of conditions within the labour process and within the labour market. Particularly as the reserve army of construction labour in India grew and as the labour markets extended and became better integrated (markets that were at first local and poorly integrated became regional and then inter-regional: the operating railways, among other causes, integrated markets by enabling labour to travel further, faster and more easily) workers increased their possibility of success if they struck at a critical moment in a work process when, even if replacement workers were available, management could not recruit them quickly enough to prevent a successful strike. Fourthly, it offers the possibility that proletarianization in the subjective sense (class for itself, consciousness) was exhibited more among those who were more thoroughly enmeshed in the relationships of capitalism, e.g., the skilled workers who became the element more likely to strike in the later nineteenth-century decades of Indian railway construction. What we do not know is whether the kind of coercion, economic or extra-economic, that brought a worker into the labour market affected his or her willingness to act collectively to resist exploitation at the level of the labour process although we can speculate that the unfree workers were less likely to strike unless enouraged to do so by

---

61. IOL&R, Public Works Department, General Proceedings, 18 January 1890, nos 38–42.
62. This is hardly a novel insight. Anyone with any union experience knows that there are usually optimum times to strike.

those who exercized extra-economic coercion over them. One also suspects that those who better approximated the classical definition of the free worker, who may or may not have been the skilled workers, were more likely simply to leave uncongenial work settings provided they could endure the economic consequences of so doing. Conversely, we do know that it was sometimes the petty capitalists who directly commanded the labour power of the unfree workers who encouraged (required?) their workers to strike.

Finally, collective action among the railway construction workers demonstrated their limited ability to achieve freedom through greater control of the labour process. It was particularly limited in their case not only because their condition made combined successful action difficult (their own internal divisions, multiple worksites, and the reservoir of labour) but because the colonial state weighed in on the side of capital. Thus, violence among the construction workers on the Bhor Ghat incline in the late 1850s (brought to a head by wage payments that were both overdue and less than promised) led to the introduction of a bill in the Legislative Council of India "to empower Magistrates to decide disputes between contractors and workmen engaged in railway and other public works".[63] This bill became the Employers and Workmen (Disputes) Act (X) of 1860 in which magistrates were given summary powers to settle wage disputes. Interestingly, an Act initially proposed because of a clear case of maltreatment of workers also came in the course of its formulation to include provisions for fining or imprisoning workers who, having engaged to work for a particular period or to carry out a specific work, failed to fulfill their commitment. No appeal was permitted against a decision passed under the Act.[64] The railways of the Raj, it must not be forgotten, were built with and through the close involvement of the colonial Government of India which was not a neutral, uninterested party standing above the construction process. A legal framework suitable for the advance of capitalism and which reflected the subordination of labour to capital began to be put into place.[65] This subordination came to be expressed in a series of major railway acts (1854, 1879 and 1890) whose labour sections were directed primarily at the employees of the operating railways but whose ambit included permanent employees engaged in construction or reconstruction. These acts and the regulations they spawned were modelled on acts and railway company regulations current in Britain. They gave the railway companies substantial power over their "servants". Colonial despotism gave capital an advantage in the politics of production but colonial situations were

---

63. *Proceedings of the Legislative Council of India, for January to December 1859*, V (Calcutta, 1859), p. 217.
64. The Act is reprinted in Trevor, *Law Relating to Railways*, pp. 347-348.
65. For further explorations of this process see Breman, *Labour Migration*, pp. 60-69 and Burawoy, *Politics of Production*, pp. 214 ff.

only an intense example of the general use of politico-legal power to curb worker power, real or potential, at the point of production.[66]

Conclusion

All of this brings us back to the many issues involved in the concepts of unfree and free labour. I do not deny the existence of these different forms of labour although I do see what they share under capitalism, coercion and exploitation, as more important than that which in the classical formulation differentiates them, extra-economic versus economic coercion: a differentiation, in any case, that is usually continuously graded rather than dichotomous. The centrality of coercion of some sort in both forms of labour also led me to suggest that the very words used to frame the debate, "unfree" and "free", hindered understanding and helped to privilege a certain discourse. I concede that for individual workers and collectivities of workers their status as "unfree" or "free" may have had considerable significance for them in their struggles with capital but I suspect that the significance of the difference has to be understood situationally and historically without reference to general principles. It is certainly not clear to me that the status of individualized free labour, i.e., *a person* has the legal right freely to sell or not to sell his/her labour power, is always an advantage (though it may sometimes be so) for labour. Indeed, such a right can create an ideological barrier to collective action by labour.

I further argued that an emphasis on the marketing of labour power, unfree or free, is misplaced. It unduly emphasizes exchange relationships in the workings of capitalism at the expense of the more fundamental relationships residing in the sphere of production. The driving imperatives of the capitalist market – competition, accumulation, profit maximization and ever higher levels of labour productivity (in short, exploitation based on the extraction of surplus value) – depend fundamentally on capital's control of the labour processes it subsumes. The history of the railway construction workers in 19th century India, like elsewhere, shows that capitalism works comfortably with both unfree and free labour precisely because production, hence realization and valorization, is central to capitalism. Marx's expectation notwithstanding, there appears to be no necessary connection between the advance of capitalism and the increased presence of free labour. Capitalism, after all, is a mode of production; it is not a mode of exchange.

---

66. Washbrook, "Progress and Problems", p. 91 is on the mark where South Asia is concerned: "Political control over the forces of market competition and increasing dominance over labour and its processes of reproduction gave capital a comfortable history in colonial South Asia."

We need, therefore, to rethink the processes of proletarianization. I argue that all Indian railway construction workers were part of an emerging proletariat because their labour power was sold (by themselves or by others) in order that they could survive and because the labour processes in which they were engaged were labour processes under capitalism. The proletariat, or that fraction thereof engaged in railway construction work, included unfree and free labour and both varieties were part of the emerging proletariat. Railway construction enlarged the rural proletariat and accelerated changes from which there was no going back: the further advance of capitalism and the continuing commodification of labour in rural India.

Finally, the paper suggested that the freedom most often sought by the construction workers (and by most workers in any capitalist economy) was not the legal freedom to market their personal labour power but rather the more limited goal of reducing the extent to which they were exploited within the construction labour process. It is a bleak thought but that may be the best labour can do under capitalism. Labour seeks to maximize its control of the labour process in order to reduce exploitation. However, this limited form of freedom (and, again, it comes in various degrees) can only be achieved collectively and situationally. Historians need to study those situations more and worry about the conceptual niceties of unfree and free labour less. Tactically, there are optimum moments for control presented situationally within a production process and by contingent conditions within the labour markets such that replacement workers are not easily found. Strategically, however, the course of action is not to be found in Marx, the profound analyst of capitalism, but rather in the revolutionary Marx who wanted workers to unite in order to emancipate themselves.

Enslaved Ex-Slaves, Uncaptured Contract Coolies and Unfree Freedmen: "Free" and "Unfree" Labour in the Context of Plantation Development in Southwest India

Paul E. Baak[*]

Some Historiographical Reflections

In the literature on plantation development in Asia, the issue of "free" versus "unfree" labour has been much debated. To start with, a first group of scholars argues that from the workers' point of view the decision to work on the plantations seems to have been a rational and conscious choice.[1] They stress that a high degree of social differentiation in the various Asian societies have made low-class people leave their home areas whenever an improvement in their position seemed possible. Most plantation workers came from areas where they had little or no access to the means of production and where many of them were indebted to local landlords and/or moneylenders. For low-caste Indian labourers, the opportunity to work on plantations meant a way out of the disadvantageous conditions in their caste-ridden villages. Town-based labourers also tried to improve their position by accepting work on plantations. Moreover, some of the workers left areas because the latter were plagued by famine. The argument of this first group of scholars is, in short, that the advances and employment offered by the plantations meant *a way out* of difficult circumstances. This is illustrated by the fact that many of the labourers used the advances given by the recruiters to pay off existing debts. Griffiths, for instance, represents this vision very clearly when he maintains that in South India the advances by estates helped to break the system of hereditary serfdom and contributed to ameliorating the indebtedness and depressed conditions of labour.[2] With regard to plantation work itself, these writers do not focus on labour discontent and, often implicitly, stress the consensus between the worker, the overseer and the manager.[3]

Others, however, oppose what might be called the "free choice model". Their vision, termed the "coercion point of view", differs on three major points; the

---

[*] Prof. Dr. Heather Sutherland, Dr. Dick Kooiman (both Free University Amsterdam), Prof. Dr. Frans Hüsken (University of Nijmegen) and Dr. Jos Mooij (Institute for Social Studies, The Hague) contributed by reading an earlier draft of this paper critically.

1. See for example Galenson, "Rise and Fall of Indentured Servitude"; Emmer, "Meek Hindu".
2. Griffiths, *History of the Indian Tea Industry*, p. 39.
3. See for example Graham and Floering, *Modern Plantation in the Third World*.

nature of labour recruitment, the methods of labour control, and the extent of labour resistance.

They stress, for example, that many workers were misled by recruiters, officials and planters. The labourers were given false information about their destination and the nature of plantation work. This explains for example why people with access to land sometimes left for the plantations. But it also means that labourers would have chosen differently had they known about the negative aspects structuring travel to and life on the plantations. Some were even made captive and transported to plantations against their will. In these cases, one cannot speak of "free" choices. In addition, these scholars emphasize that although accepting an advance from a recruiter could mean a way out of bondage, it certainly implicated *a way into* a new one. For example, Breman, speaking about the nature of labour recruitment for plantations on Sumatra in the Dutch East Indies, stresses that intimidation played a major role. According to him, it is therefore "nothing other than a colonial fantasy to maintain that a contract was entered into voluntarily".[4]

Moreover, these authors focus on labour control. They emphasize that the plantations used extra-economic methods in order to determine the lives of the workers. As a consequence, apart from control exercized during work, the social and cultural lives of the labourers were regulated to an overwhelming degree. This was partly related to the system of recruitment. During the second half of the nineteenth century and the first third of the twentieth century, recruitment was structured by the indenture system. Under this, a labourer was bound by a penal contract to serve one particular employer for a specified period. The state enacted penal codes (such as the Workman's/Criminal Breach of Contract Act in British India, and the Coolie Ordinance in the Dutch East Indies) which enabled plantations to track down, sentence and punish runaway labourers. This, however, does not automatically mean that a fundamental difference existed in the labour conditions before the enactment of these legal measures and after their abolition. Although not bound by any written agreement, even non-indentured labourers worked and lived in a state of bondage. This was brought about by the violent treatment of plantation labourers by the planters and the overseers (named respectively *kangany* in south India and on Ceylon/Sri Lanka, *sirdar* in North India and on Mauritius, *tandil* (Chinese foremen) on Sumatra and *mandur* (Javanese foremen) on Java and Sumatra). Also, liquor, opium, gambling and prostitution were permitted by the management, so as to keep their work force indebted and bonded. Moreover, wages were often insufficient for survival, with the result that workers became indebted to the plantation.[5]

---

4. Breman, *Taming the Coolie Beast*, p. 132.
5. Regarding the non-market, coercive aspects of labour control, see for example: Bandarage, *Colonialism in Sri Lanka*, p. 220; Stoler, *Capitalism and Confrontation*, p. 45 (tobacco and rubber

And lastly, these scholars point out that there was no social consensus on the plantations. In support of this view, they point to the existence of conflict on the plantations, and also to many varieties and forms of labour resistance. In this regard, they argue, there was a gradual shift from individual acts (such as desertions and personal revenge) to more organized forms of resistance (like strikes). This change – which was most probably also closely interconnected with the shift from a temporary to a permanent workforce on the estates – was to a large extent effected by an increased solidarity among workers, brought about by the rise of (mostly illegal) political parties and labour unions. On many plantations, class divisions coincided with those of race/ethnicity. In these cases, class struggle often went hand in hand with a national liberation struggle. Interestingly enough, resistance was not always directed towards immediate economic advantages. In Fiji for example, work-gangs of women "coolies" humiliated their European overseers by capturing them, beating them, immobilizing them and urinating on them.[6] Clearly, many of these acts of resistance were intended to break the prestige of the dominant class, race and gender.

To sum up this plantation historiography, it is clear that the nature and meaning of planter/labourer relations in Asia is strongly contested. To place the discussions in a wider political setting, those scholars who focus on the advantages derived by workers recruited for plantations (a way out of indebtedness and other arduous circumstances) can be categorised as the Modernization School, sometimes identified also as the Imperialist or Colonial Group. On the other hand, those who stress the exploitive and violent character of labour recruitment and control are part of the (Neo-)Marxist, Nationalist or Anti-Colonial Tradition.

In my view, two kind of problems arise out of the above debate. The first problem concerns the focus of attention. Though the different interpretations seem totally opposed, both schools have more in common than is apparent at first sight. As I have argued elsewhere,[7] all these studies deal predominantly with the colonial period and with the European-dominated agro-industries. To put it differently, the focus of both these schools is Euro-centric, both in time and in space. Consequently, their debates on the Asian plantation pay insufficient attention to important (and determining) developments which occurred before, during and after the colonial period that were either only partially influenced or not influenced at all by the European presence.

For this reason, the theme of "free" and "unfree" labour in a long-term historical perspective (from the pre-colonial years of the early 16th century to

plantations on Sumatra); Das Gupta, "From Peasants and Tribesman to Plantation Workers", p. PE-3 (tea estates in northeast India); Murray, "'White Gold' or 'White Blood?'", pp. 41-67 (plantations in Indochina).

6. Kelly, "'Coolie' as a Labour Commodity", p. 259.
7. Baak, "Out of the Shadow".

the post-colonial era until the mid-1990s) will be central to my discussion. The focus will be on plantation development in Southwest India, an area ruled successively by the independent (or semi-independent) state of Travancore (since the late 1790s), Travancore-Cochin (since 1949) and Kerala (from 1956 onwards). Moreover, although initiated by European entrepreneurs in the late 1850s, plantation development in Southwest India was dominated by a non-European local elite, the Syrian Christians.[8]

The second problem relates to the nature of the discussions. The heart of the matter seems to be whether or not the plantation labourer was "free" (the modernization school) or "unfree" (the (neo-)marxist tradition). In my opinion, however, the historical reality is more complex: it is not a question of "either [...] or [...]" but of "and [...] and [...]". Indeed, the estate worker was both "free" and "unfree", a paradox which resulted from the often conflicting strategies of labourers, planters and governments. In the case of Southwest India, therefore, the abolition of slavery (1855) did not usher in a period of "free" plantation labour, the introduction of the Criminal Breach of Contract Act (1865) did not establish a completely "unfree" work force, and the abolition of that same act (1935) did not "free" the estate workers.

To prevent any misunderstanding, in this essay "free" refers to "the freedom [...] to choose one's employer and therefore one's labour conditions, or to choose one's means of production".[9] The concept "unfree" covers all elements that restrict one's choice of employer, such as legal obstacles (like slavery or indentured labour), financial hindrances (indebtedness), a segmented labour market (based on, for example, educational and ethnic/communal characteristics) and geographical immobility.

Indigenous Slavery and Foreign Planters

Given that profitability in "New World" plantations was based to a large degree on the import of and control over African slaves, one might expect pre-colonial and early-colonial Southwest India – known for its indigenous slave communities and rigid caste ideology – to be ideally suited for the plantation enterprise.

In Southwest India (including Travancore), the social hierarchy was to a large extent based on caste – at first sight nothing unusual in southern Asia. Like other parts of the subcontinent, the caste status into which one was born greatly influenced one's place in society. Belonging to a specific caste implied a certain

---

8. In 1960 in Kerala the area under the "plantation crops" coffee, tea and rubber amounted to respectively 20,000, 40,000 and 118,000 hectares (*United Planters' Association of Southern India* [hereafter: *UPASI*, 1960, p. 390), providing employment for over 100,000 wage workers.
9. See Lucassen, "Free and Unfree Labour before the Twentieth Century", this volume, p. 47.

religious status and affected one's access to land as well as one's share in political power.

To a greater extent than in other parts of South Asia, however, caste in Southwest India was an all-embracing system. For example, Christians and Muslims were also included in the caste structure, notwithstanding the fact that the latter – in a strictly religious sense – was a social hierarchy based on Hindu writings.[10] Furthermore, the ranking of one's community within the caste system also determined one's access to public roads and temples, and even one's personal appearance. Belonging to a particular caste involved a particular kind of clothing, and determined whether or not one was allowed to wear ornaments or use umbrellas. Day-to-day life was also strongly influenced by precisely defined rules governing the polluting effect of distance, an issue which will be discussed in more detail below. Because of these reasons – the elaborate and explicit nature of caste ranking in southwest India – it can be said that the caste hierarchy was more rigid here than in other parts of southern Asia.[11]

The *Pulayas* and *Parayas* formed the lowest strata of society.[12] The other, higher-ranked castes regarded them as the most impure of all human beings – if human at all – for they were regularly referred to as slaves, their children as calves and their grain as chaff.[13] Indeed, Pulayas and Parayas were considered serfs, and were bought, sold and mortgaged in the same manner as the land on which they dwelt. They were also offered by their masters as presents to friends or as gifts to temples. As humiliating for the Pulayas and Parayas was the fact that members of these so-called slave castes were required to observe practices of subordination in accordance with their ritual status. Maintaining a minimum physical distance from higher castes was one of these requirements. If a person belonging to a slave caste approached someone of a higher caste, thereby transgressing the "pollution distance", the former was punished severely by the latter (a process which might culminate in the death of the subordinate). As the following case demonstrates, this kind of customary practice endured for a very long period. At the beginning of the 16th century, the Portuguese Duarte Barbosa, who accompanied Magellan on his trip around the world, wrote: "When they [the Nayars] walk along a street or road, they shout to the low caste folk to get out of their way; this they do, and if they will not, the Nayre may

---

10. There are four *varna* categories in the Hindu scriptures: *Brahmins* (priests), *Kshatriyas* (warriors), *Vaishyas* (traders) and *Sudras* (menial workers and craftspeople). Those who do not belong to one of these four categories, the *a-varna*, are considered most impure.

11. Alexander, "Caste Mobilization and Class Consciousness", p. 368; and Kooiman, *Conversion and Social Equality in India*, p. 15.

12. For this particular paper, I consider it insufficiently rewarding to discuss the situation of the other communities. In short, the summit of the hierarchy was taken in by *Brahmins*, followed by *Nayars, Syrian Christians, Moplahs* (Muslims), *Ezhavas* and *Shanars*.

13. Alexander, "Caste Mobilization and Class Consiousness", p. 369.

kill him without punishment."[14] Thus the lowest castes were not only considered "untouchables", whose very presence caused members of higher castes to experience ritual impurity, but were virtually regarded as "unseeables", a situation generated by the ideology of pollution-over-long-distances.

Contrary to initial expectations, historical evidence suggests that this particular form of slavery did not arouse the planters' interest. The reason for this, however, is that most British planters avoided Travancore, and preferred to open up coffee estates elsewhere: in Ceylon, the Madras Presidency and Mysore. The only European planter who settled in Travancore, W. Huxham, was faced with many obstacles, not the least of which were land disputes. After having opened up the Camapalle Estate in 1824, Huxham's prime concerns were most probably labour recruitment and control.

Unfortunately, very little information about Huxham's plantations exists. We do know, however, that in 1851 the European planter supervised 9 estates, varying in size from 20 to 611 acres. In that same year, the total area of land brought under cultivation amounted to 2333 acres.[15] Moreover, there is clear evidence which suggests that the chain of command on these plantations was quite rigid. In his letters, Huxham spoke about "the Chief Manager" and "a garden under my own Superintendents".[16] On the other hand, no direct information is provided about the geographical and social background of these overseers and the labourers under their command.

It is useful, therefore, to undertake a comparison in time and space. In 1797, the English East India Company opened up an experimental garden in Randatara in the Malabar district of the Bombay Presidency, cultivating pepper, cotton and coffee among other crops. Murdoch Brown, who was appointed as overseer and manager, experienced extreme difficulties in recruiting local inhabitants and obtaining thereby the 200-300 workers he required daily. He complained about a lack of authority, and requested the Bombay Government to appoint him as the local magistrate and revenue collector. The English officials complied with this request, and gave him the powers that he wanted so as to operate the plantation. When Malabar passed from the Bombay Presidency to the Madras Government, Brown acquired the ownership of the plantation enterprise. Subsequently, he used his juridical and administrative authority to the advantage of the plantation enterprise. The size of his plantation increased from 200 to

14. Cited in Jeffrey, *Decline of Nayar Dominance*, p. 3. And in 1860, the wife of a missionary wrote: "a Nair may approach but not touch a Nambudiri Brahmin; a Chogan Irava must remain 36 paces off, and a Poolayen 96 steps distant. A Chogan must remain 12 steps away from a Nair, and a Poolayen 66 steps off, and a Pariar some distance farther still" (quoted in: *ibid.*, p. 9).
15. *Cover System File, Kerala State Archives* [hereafter: *CSF*], No. 11247.
16. *CSF.*, No. 7253.

3,000 acres, largely as a result of his appropriating the property of local people. He was also able to exercize better control over labourers working on his possessions. Apart from workers from the so-called slave castes, some of which Brown had acquired from Travancore,[17] he used the labour power of those from the Nayar and Mapilla communities. Not surprisingly, his enterprise was seen by the local inhabitants as extremely oppressive. During the Pazhassi revolts all plants and trees on his property were systematically destroyed.[18]

It is probable that Huxham faced similar problems in the recruitment and disciplining of labour in Travancore. Both planters operated in a labour market where most of the agricultural workers were actually bonded to a particular landlord. There was, however, one important difference between Huxham and Brown. Unlike his colleage in Malabar district, the planter in Travancore was neither a magistrate nor a revenue collector: whereas Huxham was merely aided by the British Resident in Travancore, Brown was himself the local representative of the English Government. It was therefore much more difficult for Huxham to settle local affairs to his own advantage, and it is hardly surprising that his enterprise was less successful. In 1852, three years after the separate plots of Huxham's plantation had been incorporated into a single unit (the 10 square miles concession), he transferred his leasehold rights to Binny and Company. The precarious financial position of his enterprise forced him to do this.[19]

The Creation of "Free" Labour: The Abolition of Slavery (1855)

Somewhat surprisingly, the main protests against slave labour did not originate from the single planter in the area – Huxham – but rather from those *who would become* the most influential planters towards the end of the 1850s and the beginning of the 1860s: the European missionaries. In 1847 the missionary societies presented a joint memorandum to the Rajah, requesting the abolition of slavery, and drawing attention to its formal abolition throughout the Indian territories governed by the English East India Company. The high-caste landlords tried to counter-act the influential missionary lobby, fearing that an enforcement of the abolition legislation would create a shortage of workers, especially for the labour intensive process of paddy cultivation.[20] They were to some degree successful, since by 1853 the missionaries' request had only been partially complied with. Although slavery was formally abolished, this was on the proviso that "the slaves as well as all others should clearly understand that

17. Kooiman, "Conversion from Slavery to Plantation Labour", p. 63.
18. Kurup, "Colonial Investment", pp. 188-189.
19. *Papers regarding the Ten Square Miles Concession* [hereafter: *PTSMC*], 1926; *CSF*, No. 11247.
20. Tharakan and George, "Penetration of Capital", p. 207.

there shall be no change in the customs and untouchability in force according to the respective caste etiquettes". Moreover, this regulation did not include provisions for the emancipation of all slaves in Travancore. In contrast to the landlords, therefore, missionaries had no reasons to be satisfied with this ruling. On 26 July 1855, the evangelists informed the Governor in Council of the Madras Presidency that they, "the petitioners, [...] pray for the appointment of a commission of well qualified Europeans", since "this province of Travancore [...] is now bordering on utter disorganization, and in this state of things, the sufferers are the great mass of people".[21] This petition considerably strengthened the missionaries' position vis-à-vis the Travancore landlords. In the same year, additional political pressure from the British Resident and the Madras Government resulted in the enactment of a second ruling by the Travancore Government. Slavery was henceforth completely illegal.[22]

In historiography dealing with Travancore, there is much debate about the extent to which the pressure exercized by missionaries and English officials for the abolition of slavery was motivated by humanitarian/Christian ideals or by economic considerations. Thus Nadar takes the view that slavery was abolished "by the benevolent attitude of the Christian missionaries",[23] while Kurup observes by contrast that emancipation "was closely related to the requirements of the emerging capitalists in Indian agriculture".[24] Kooiman, who based his research on archival materials from the London Missionary Society (LMS), manages to combine both points of view. Unwilling to draw too tight a distinction between humanitarian and economic motives, Kooiman notes that "for the LMS missionaries there was nothing more humanitarian than to enable the people of Travancore to share the blessings of a capitalist development".[25]

I would like to contribute to this debate by suggesting that the links between the abolition of slavery, the religious and economic activities of the missionaries, and the development of the plantations were even more direct than most of the literature indicates. The missionaries were not only lobbying for the abolition of slave labour *before* they themselves had become personally involved in the plantation industry, they were also opposing the employment of bonded labour *during* the period in which they combined their original profession with that of planter. For example, on 18 July 1859 some missionaries, among them John Cox – who was in this period one of the most important planters in the area,

---

21. Signed by among others John Cox, quoted in Yesudas, *British Policy in Travancore*, pp. 87–88.
22. Kurup, "Colonial Investment", pp. 193–195; and Kooiman, "Conversion from Slavery to Plantation Labour", p. 62.
23. Nadar, "Commercialization of Agricultural Products", p. 217.
24. Kurup, "Colonial Investment", pp. 193–94, 196–97.
25. Kooiman, "Conversion from Slavery to Plantation Labour", p. 63.

and who presided for several years over the Travancore Planters' Association[26] – requested the Governor in Council of the Madras Presidency for "the entire removal of slavery [the proclamation of 1855 did not change the situation of the slave labourers immediately], [and] all kinds of forced labour".[27] Clearly, the missionaries' initial religious and humanitarian aversion to slave labour initially only coincided with *what would become* their economic interests (and about which they were at this stage perhaps unaware), but later corresponded with their *current* economic interests (and about which they were only too aware).

Unwilling Wage Workers

The abolition of slavery notwithstanding, the recruitment of workers remained a difficult task for the planters. One would expect that the demand for labour by European planters, who were, according to the Government, "gentlemen sincerely solicitous to deal fairly with their labourers, and to rely upon good treatment and good wages alone for attracting labour",[28] and for whom, according to Mateer, "caste was nothing",[29] would have induced a large number of labourers, especially those with a low-caste background (including the ex-slaves), to leave their poverty-stricken situation in caste-ridden villages. However, quite the opposite was the case. Only in isolated instances, when for example a famine occurred in the Madras Presidency, did workers volunteer en masse for plantation labour. This was especially the case in 1866 and 1877.[30]

The reluctance of the agricultural labourer to accept plantation work is all the more remarkable since reliable historical material suggests that the wages on offer were indeed considerably higher than those paid by landlords in the lower parts of south India. Mateer, for example, notes that in south Travancore during 1859 agricultural labour was obtainable for an anna per day, and that the Public Works Department, which carried out canal works in the region, paid a little over two annas: "The planters, however, were obliged [...] to give at least four annas to induce ordinary coolies to brave the dangers of the hills."[31] Table 1 shows the plantation wages in later years.

26. *CSF*, No. 1760.
27. Cited in Yesudas, *British Policy in Travancore*, pp. 100-101.
28. *Travancore Administration Report* [hereafter: *TAR*], 1040, pp. 22-23.
29. Mateer, *Native Life in Travancore*, p. 236.
30. Government of Travancore, *Adresses*, p. 22.
31. Mateer, *Native Life In Travancore*, p. 235.

Table 1. Daily Plantation Wages in Central Travancore and the Kannan Devan Hills in 1893 and in Travancore in 1896

District	Year	Men	Women	Children
Central Travancore	1893	4 annas	not known	not known
Kannan Devan hills	1893	4.5 annas	2 annas	not known
Travancore	1896	4 annas to 5 annas	3 annas to 3 annas, 6 pies	2 annas to 3 annas

Sources: UPASI Proceedings, 1893; Report South of India Planters' Enquiry Committee [hereafter: RSIPEC], 1896, p. 12.

In their attempts to explain the labourers' unwillingness to work for higher payment, some scholars have incorrectly stressed the "traditional", almost "passive" and "irrational" attitude of the agricultural workforce. Saradamoni, for example, makes the following observation about the freed ex-slaves in the context of plantation work: "By habit and tradition they were unused to leaving their huts and hamlets".[32]

There were, however, many factors which explain the reluctance of agricultural labourers to contract for plantation work. For example, although in a strictly legal sense slavery had been completely abolished in Travancore in 1855 and in the directly ruled territories of the Madras Presidency in 1833,[33] various forms of bonded labour remained in existence throughout South India during the latter half of the 19th century. Legal emancipation notwithstanding, relations between ex-slaves and ex-owners often did not change. Agricultural labourers usually remained attached to a particular plot of land and its owner, particularly as a result of indebtedness.[34] In contrast to other authors who have dealt with this subject, I would like to suggest that these relations between employer and employee, despite their inherent inequalities, were of benefit not just to the landlord. It must be acknowledged that these "unfree" labourers, despite being often cruelly treated, were, at least in some respects, better off than the so-called "free" labourers. The former group of workers, and in particular those attached to paddy lands, were assured of employment and food during the greater part of the year. The latter category of workers was indeed "free" to offer its labour to the highest bidder, but could find neither work nor nourishment in cases of lack of employment or scarcity of food. They were "free to starve", in other

---

32. Saradamoni, *Emergence of Slave Caste*, pp. 114–115; see also Jeffrey, *Decline of Nayar Dominance*, p. 100.
33. *Cambridge Economic History of India* [hereafter: *CEHI*], vol. 2 (1991), pp. 323 and 485.
34. Griffiths, *History of the Indian Tea Industry*, p. 397; Tharakan and George, "Penetration of Capital", p. 207; and Raman, "Labour under Imperial Hegemony", p. 246.

words. For this reason, many attached labourers had no reason to break the bonds with their landlords.

Moreover, many agricultural labourers were able to improve their conditions on the plains. The abolition of slavery and the demand for labour from the planters and the Public Works Department (PWD) – whose establishment in 1860 was closely related with the development of European coffee plantations[35] – gradually strengthened their bargaining positions vis-à-vis their landlords. That again resulted in better working conditions, including higher wages.[36] Indeed, the increase in wages on the plains (see Table 2), brought about in part by the development of plantations in the hills, greatly contributed to the reluctance of many agricultural labourers to opt for estate work.

Table 2. Daily Wages of Agricultural Labourers in some Travancore Taluks[37] in the Period 1880-1895

Taluk	1880-85	1885-90	1890-95
Vaikom	2as. 8p.	3as. 5p.	4as.
Ettumannoor	2as. 8p.	3as. 6p.	4as. 6p.
Kottayam	2as.	2as. 10p.	3as. 6p.
Changanacherry	2as.	2as. 10p.	3as.
Meenachil	2as. 3p.	3as.	4as.

Source: Velu Pillai, quoted in: Tharakan and George, "Penetration of Capital", p. 211.

35. Lovatt, "Short History", p. 51; Menon, History of Travancore, pp. 514-515; and Pandian, Political Economy of Agrarian Change, p. 84.

36. The TAR of 1870/71 stated for example that: "In fact till June 1855, predial slavery existed in Travancore fully recognized by law. [...] The condition of those who thus regained their freedom has since been gradually improving. [...] The law extends to them the same protection as to other members of the community. [...] Compulsion is utterly impossible in these days. [...] The various public works in progress in different parts of the country and the operations of coffee planters have been instrumental in ameliorating the conditions of this class of people, inasmuch as the demand for labour thus created enables them to procure better terms from their old employers" (TAR, 1045, p. 39). In 1883 Mateer observed the same development. "The labour of the previously enslaved castes", he stated, "which had hitherto been almost valueless, being remunerated only by a few measures of rice daily, became of as great money value as that of others; caste was nothing in the eyes of the European planter. [...] The Sudra masters complained of the planters taking away their labourers. But this competition and demand for labour largely ameliorated the condition of the poor. [...] Numbers of the poorest classes of the population were thus [by accepting work on the European estates] removed from the degradation under which they had suffered, and relieved from oppression; while everywhere the landed proprietors were reminded of the necessity of fair and kind treatment to retain the services of their dependents" (Mateer, Native Life in Travancore, pp. 236-237).

37. Taluk: administrative unit beneath a division.

Moreover, for most of the agricultural labourers the journey to the estates, which took about two to three days on average,[38] was something to be feared. As Heather Lovatt, a planters' wife, recalls: "[T]he hills with their dark, dripping forests seemed a fearful place, where only a lucky man could escape the dangers from wild beasts, snakes and shaitans." She concludes that "only extreme poverty and a scarcity of work in their own villages, such as experienced in the two terrible famine years in Madras in the mid-[18]70s, could drive them [the labourers] to this alternative".[39]

Since they were told of this by plantation labourers who returned to the plains, many of the workers were also aware that living conditions on the estates were far from ideal. Lovatt noted the extremely poor health conditions evident during the initial phases of plantation development: "[D]uring the monsoon, when the labourers huddled shivering in their family huts, when the wind whistled through every corner, bronchial diseases took their toll." Besides the latter, illness in the plantation districts was also caused by hookworm, dysentery, smallpox, plague, cholera and malaria – diseases which were often fatal given the limited nature of medical knowledge. In any case, medical breakthroughs did not automatically improve a plantation workers' quality of life: there was often a lack of even the most basic medical facilities on the estates. For instance, even after Ross' discovery of the causes of malaria, "many more years passed before effective steps were taken to reduce this menace". It was no wonder, therefore, that labourers feared the estates, particularly during epidemics. As Lovatt notes: "All the estates along the Periyar were very unhealthy, and when there was a bad outbreak of malaria it was impossible to get any work done."[40]

Most agricultural labourers also realized that caste background continued to play a crucial role on the estates. They feared cruel treatment by higher castes and Europeans. And lastly, many labourers were aware that the wages offered differed from the actual payments. The plantation workers were often paid less than promised.

The Establishment of "Unfree" Labour: The Kangany-System and the Criminal Breach of Contract Act (1865)

The way in which unwilling agricultural labourers were mobilized by the southern Indian planters, those of Travancore included, is clear from the South of India Planters' Enquiry Committee. The latter reported that:

38. Arnold, *Police Power and Colonial Rule*, p. 153; and Devi, *Plantation Economies of the Third World*, p. 81.
39. Lovatt, "Short History", p. 12.
40. *Ibid.*, pp. 12-13, 32.

In securing labour for their estates planters occasionally deal directly with coolies, but these instances are very rare, being limited to engagements made with coolies who have worked for several years on the same plantations or with coolies living close to plantations. But even in such cases the practice is not universal and it may be said that in recruiting imported labour, *maistries*, who answer to the garden sardars of Assam, are invariably employed as the agents between the planters and the coolies. The maistry enters into a contract with the planter and the contract is generally reduced to writing. Such contracts are signed by the maistry, rarely by the planter, and they are seldom, if ever, registered. In the case of old and trusted maistries, informal verbal agreements sometimes take the place of written contracts and in some places, for instance, parts of Travancore, a verbal agreement is supplemented by a promissory note executed by the maistry. Receiving a lump sum in advance, the maistry undertakes to supply a certain number of coolies for plantation work for a certain time. These engagements are made usually in March or April of each year [when the plantation labourers returned to the plains], the time fixed for the commencement of work on the plantations being two or three months later [in June or July]. The period of the contract is usually nine months, sometimes less, and it never exceeds a year [...]. The maistry then proceeds to the village or villages where he collects labour and generally returns to his employer's estate with his gang, though some maistries remain in the villages and send their gangs to the plantations in charge of their representatives as headmen. The average strength of a maistry's gang varies between 20 and 40 adult males, females and children; the average maximum is 100, but in some cases a maistry furnishes as many as 200 or 250 coolies.[41]

In Travancore the labour recruiter, also known as a *kangany*, in his turn "makes [cash] advances to coolies, entering into contracts with them (sometimes in writing, but more often not)".[42] The cash advance offered by the kangany was in many ways of crucial importance. For example, it enabled those workers who were bonded to a particular landlord and/or moneylender to pay off their debts. Many of these labourers, who were often extremely poor, had little reason to refuse a cash advance offered by the kangany, since they had to take care of their immediate basic needs (like food, clothing and shelter). Others, and this group was less significant, used the advances for largescale expenditures, like marriages and other important social events. Generally speaking, recruitment on the basis of cash advances remained very widespread throughout South India during the 19th century. Apart from the disadvantages for the workers, which will be analyzed below, it was for the labourer the only practical guarantee of employment. At the same time, its size gave some indication of the financial power of the new employer and, consequently, about his ability to pay an attractive wage.[43] As can be seen in Table 3, the planters, through their recruiters, were

41. *Report South of India Planters' Enquiry Committee* [hereafter: *RSIPEC*], 1896, p. 12.
42. *Ibid.*, p. 17.
43. *Ibid.*, pp. 18-20.

able to advance relatively large amounts of money. For instance, in central Travancore, where a wage of 4 annas was customary for men (Table 1), an advance of 10 rupees represented pre-payment on 40 days of work.

Table 3. Advances in Central Travancore and the Kannan Devan Hills in 1893

District	Men	Women	Unspecified
Central Travancore	10 rupees	6 rupees	
Kannan Devan hills	unknown	unknown	10 rupees

Source: UPASI Proceedings 1893

Apart from providing cash advances, the kangany was of major importance in other respects as well. For example, the kangany gave workers an exaggeratedly optimistic account about plantation life which, at least partially, decreased their fear of disease, and diminished their concerns about inhuman work conditions and low wages. Uma Devi, who has studied information collected in Travancore on behalf of the South of India Planters' Enquiry Committee, has pointed to the dilemma facing many labourers: either to believe the plantation labourers who returned to the plains, or to have faith in the kangany's picture of plantation life.[44] The recruiters often obtained most of their workers from among their own family and friends. Labourers were thus linked to the kangany not only economically (through cash advances) but also through kinship and/or friendship. Labour recruiters also possessed specialist knowledge: for example, it was they who guided members of their gang through the jungle in order to reach the work destination.

What emerges clearly is that labourers mobilized in this fashion were also immobilised at the same time. Although freed from landlords and moneylenders, therefore, they were subsequently enslaved by their new employers. As already noted, the cash advances offered by labour recruiters were often used immediately by the workers – to pay off already existing debts, to meet basic needs and to defray expenses related to family affairs. Furthermore, the advances were used to pay for expenses incurred in the course of the journey to the plantations, particularly food. Thus even before they had reached the estate, the contract labourers were already in debt to the kanganies, who, in their turn, owed money to the planters for whom they worked.

44. Uma Devi quoted Krishna Iyer, the Tahsildar (government officer in charge of a taluk) of Changanacherry. He stated: "The contractors or maistries before engaging a labourer give him an attractive description of a labourer's life on the plantations, while still under the charm he takes advances and enters into an agreement. Going home, his neighbours, relatives, wife and children describe to him the dark side of the picture and dissuade him from leaving his home" (quoted in: Devi, Plantation Economies of the Third World, p. 82).

The economic situation of most labourers did not improve during their period of contract. Most kanganies were in fact jobbers; apart from the recruitment of workers they supervised "their" gang of labourers on the estates. This meant for example that the kanganies, who apart from their fixed pay as overseers received commission on their gangs' earnings at the end of the year, derived much benefit from keeping their workers indebted. As long as the plantation labourers had to clear their debts, the kanganies could force them to work longer hours than initially agreed, coerce sick workers to fulfil their daily tasks in the fields, and detain labourers beyond the period of contract, all of which contributed to the gross wage paid by the planters, from which the kanganies took their cut. In order to reinforce debt slavery, workers received from the labour contractor a weekly food allowance on credit, together with small cash advances. Only after workers were allowed to return home, which often occurred months after the expiry of their contracts, did they receive the balance of their wages, which in most cases were paid by the kanganies themselves. Not surprisingly, on these occasions the jobbers cheated the often illiterate labourers and kept back for themselves more than their legitimate share of the workers' wages.

Through the kanganies, the planters exercized control over worker indebtedness in order to ensure that their seasonal labour requirements were met. From June/July till March/April about four times as many workers were needed than during off-season.[45] In order to strengthen their grip on the advance system, the European planters in Travancore had successfully requested the *Dewan*[46] to introduce a labour law similar to the British Indian Workman's Breach of Contract Act (Act XIII of 1859). As a result, in 1865 the Criminal Breach of Contract Act (Regulation I of 1040), which was indeed largely modelled on the legislation in force in British India, was enacted. As a well-informed Travancore bureaucrat-cum-historian remarked later, "its object [...] was the protection of the employer against the workmen, of capital against labour".[47] This is also obvious from the legislation itself. For example, article 1 stated that employers could report any breach of contract to any Criminal Court, "and such court shall thereupon issue a summons or a warrant as it shall think proper".[48]

---

45. Griffiths, *History of the Indian Tea Company*, p. 403; Soutar, "High Range", p. 22; Tharakan and George "Penetration of Capital", p. 210; Devi, *Plantation Economies of the Third World*, pp. 80-84; Raman, "Labour Under Imperial Hegemony", p. 248.

46. Dewan: first minister.

47. Pillai, *Travancore State Manual*, vol. IV, p. 340.

48. Article 1 informed: "When any artificer, workman, or labourer shall have received from any master or employer resident, or carrying on business in Travancore, an advance of money on account of any work which he shall have contracted in writing to perform or to get performed by any other artificers, workmen, or labourers, if such artificer, workman, or labourer shall wilfully and without lawful or reasonable excuse neglect or refuse to perform or get performed such work according to the terms of his contract, such master or employer

If the accused was found guilty of the charge, either the money advanced had to be repaid or the terms of the contract had to be fulfilled; if the accused failed to do so, he could be sentenced to a period of imprisonment not exceeding three months (section 2). The purpose of the act, however, was not to punish so much as to compel performance. Apart from defending the interests of the planters vis-à-vis the kanganies, and those of the latter against the workers, the Criminal Breach of Contract Act did not give the employees any form of legal protection against their employers.[49]

Planters also and successfully urged the Travancore Government to install a police force and to appoint magistrates in the plantation districts in order to track down, arrest and sentence absconding labourers. The resulting labour legislation was fully backed by the executive and judicial agencies of the state. For example, in Peermade (central Travancore) a Superintendent and Magistrate of the Cardamom Hills was appointed. It was wholly unsurprising that those appointed to such posts were generally Europeans closely connected with the plantation industry, like Maltby[50] and J.S. Sealy.[51] Even planters, such as J.D. Munro, were allowed to combine their role as estate manager with that of judge. For a brief period, European planters in the Kannan Devan hills jealously watched these developments in central Travancore; as a result of a request made by the

or any such person as aforesaid, may complain to the nearest Zillah Criminal Court, or to the Criminal Court within the jurisdiction of which the contract was entered into or violated, and such court shall thereupon issue a summons or a warrant as it shall think proper, for bringing before it such artificer, workman, or labourer, and shall hear and determine the case."

49. "The Criminal Breach of Contract Act, *Travancore Government Gazette*, 4 February 1865. Clearly, in terms of the law the positions of the labourer (employee/non-European British subject), the kangany (employer and employee/non-European British subject) and the planter (employer/mostly European British subject) were fundamentally unequal. Thus special arrangements were made for the trial of European British subjects committing offences in Travancore. Similarly, the Royal Proclamation of 28 may 1875 stated that "We do hereby divest Our ordinary Criminal Courts of every grade of jurisdiction to try offences committed by European British subjects, and do further declare that such jurisdiction shall [...] be exercized exclusively by Special magistrates, being European British subjects" (section 1). Paradoxically, the special magistrates were authorized to pass, on conviction, any sentence not exceeding three months' imprisonment or fine up to one thousand British Rupees or both (article 3), see *Acts and Proclamations of Travancore* [hereafter: *APT*], 1(1935), pp. 46–47. Breach of contract on the part of a labourer or a kangany was in legal terms judged to be on a par with murder committed by an English planter.

50. Unfortunately, it was impossible to find out whether the Maltby mentioned in *CSF*, No. 1681 and *CSF*, No. 7408, the Superintendent and Magistrate of the Cardamom hills in the late 1880s, was equal or related to F.N. Maltby, the British Resident in the early 1860s. If it was indeed one and the same person, it shows the great importance the Madras government gave to this specific function in Peermade by supporting the appointment of such a politically influential person.

51. *CSF*, No. 1681; *CSF*, No. 2368; *CSF*, No. 7408; *CSF*, No. 11746.

secretary of the North Travancore Land Planting and Agricultural Society,[52] in 1887 a magistrate was also appointed in Devicolam.[53] By the twentieth century, the process of prosecution had itself become easier as a result of taking the workers' thumb prints when they arrived at the estates.[54]

Uncaptured Contract Coolies

Though largely successful, the bonding of labour by estates was not wholly satisfactory from the planters' point of view. For example, if after having received an advance a kangany took no steps to recruit labour for the planter concerned, no court would prosecute the kangany under the penal provisions of the Criminal Breach of Contract Act. As H.M. Knight complained during a planters' meeting:

> [A] man gets an advance for coolies from one planter, he goes back with a gang and starts work on another place in order to get a reputation as a good man who gets coolies without any advances. They know very well that we are powerless to touch them.[55]

Knight did not tell the whole story: the kangany could in fact be prosecuted under civil law. However, such complaints indicated that a kangany ought to meet obligations incurred to a particular planter. Unlike a labourer, a kangany could not be compelled by penal sanction to discharge an undertaking to recruit.

Despite their debts and contractual obligations, individual workers often absconded from the plantation districts. In 1896, Krishna Iyer, the Tahsildar of Changanacherry, stated: "Many of the labourers while in the hills get sick, and they naturally desire to be by the side of their relatives and find their way

52. *CSF*, No. 1681. In 1887, the secretary of the North Travancore Land Planting and Agricultural Society wrote Dewan Rama Rao that "the Cardamom Magistrate resides the greater part of the year at Peermade between which place and Devicolam there is no sort of communication. The Committee venture to suggest that two Cardamom Magistrates should be appointed, one residing always at Peermade [...] and one at Devicolam [...]. The High Range Devicolam and the Unjeenaad Valley with its many villages have at present no magistrate or police. Crimes are frequent – last year by the murder of three people by Pulliars who were arrested after much difficulty – and at present the case of Kristna Iyer which is before Mr Maltby – might be cited as instances" (letter of the secretary of the North Travancore Land Planting and Agricultural Society to Dewan Rama Rao on 8 June 1887, in: *CSF*, No. 1681).

53. Martin, *History of the High Range Planting District*, p. 11.

54. 17th annual general meeting of the UPASI, Bangalore, 1-5 August 1910, in: *UPASI Proceedings*; *Royal Commission on Labour* (1931), vol. VII, Part 2, p. 198; proceedings *Travancore Sri Mulam Assembly* [hereafter: *TSMA*], 24 January 1935.

55. 5th annual general meeting of the UPASI, Bangalore, 8-11 August 1898, in: *UPASI Proceedings*.

home."[56] At the same time, however, Krishna Iyer noticed that many other labourers, who were also discontented, nevertheless did not attempt to abscond. Apart from the fear of being caught, they would also lose any wages due in the event of leaving the plantation in this manner.

The fact that kanganies together with their gang of workers might abscond from a particular estate was for the planters an altogether more serious problem, particularly since it often resulted in irrecoverable debts and a shortfall in labour power. In some cases, the kanganies themselves absconded from a plantation in order to find higher wages and better living conditions nearby, while in others they were encouraged to do this by rival planters who were short of workers.[57] Although planters whose estates were relatively healthy and who paid good wages had nothing to fear from such a situation, the fact that kanganies and labourers could search for the best employer was disadvantageous to all planters: it drove up the price for labour. In order to counteract this development, district planting associations frequently discussed rules which were intended to prevent the crimping of workers.

Perhaps the most serious labour problem faced by planters was that kanganies, together with their labourers, might leave Travancore before the expiry of the work contract. No legal means existed by which a planter could extradite such absconders in order to enforce the contractual obligations.[58] It was probably for this reason that A. Martin, a planter in the Kannan Devan hills, expressed a hatred for most kanganies. During a planters' meeting, therefore, he referred to labour contractors in the following manner: "I think 'sordid, unfeeling, reprobate, degraded, spiritless, outcaste' accurately describes them".[59]

---

56. Quoted in Devi, *Plantation Economies of the Third World*, p. 82.
57. This, for example, quite frequently occurred in the Peermade district. Lovatt stated: "Under these circumstances [a shortage of labour due to among others bolting labourers], every planter did what he could to hold on to his labour, and to gather in new recruits, even if this meant not enquiring too closely from where they came. Poaching labour, or crimping as it was called, was universal and the cause of much bad blood" (Lovatt, "Short History", p. 36).
58. Knight also complained about this. He told his European colleagues in 1898: "our difficulty is to get sufficient gangs of coolies. We have maistries who are up to all sort of tricks. They take money in Travancore and go to British territory, and we never see them again. He knows the law quite as well as the planter and understands that as matters stand at present he cannot be caught" (5th annual general meeting of the UPASI, Bangalore, 8-11 August 1898, in: *UPASI Proceedings*).
59. 11th annual general meeting of the UPASI, Bangalore, 22-24 August 1904, in: *UPASI Proceedings*.

A First Step to "Free" Labour: The Abolition of the Criminal Breach of Contract Act (1935)

The problems faced by Travancore planters with regard to the recruitment and control of workers were certainly not unique. Most planters in south India were confronted with the same kinds of difficulties. Despite the similar nature of their labour problems, it was only during the 1890s that planters finally united on an all-southern-India level. The obstacles to this happening earlier were twofold: the lack of good communications between the various planting districts, and the often individualistic attitude of the planters themselves.[60]

Once united, the planters drew up a a petition outlining their labour problems, and signed by the chairmen and secretaries of the various district associations; this was presented to the Government of India in March 1892. In contrast to the planters' expectations, however, the administration refused to pay serious attention to their difficulties, dismissing the memorandum as coming from "certain planters of the South of India" and stating that the labour problems were created by the planters themselves.[61]

In order to strengthen their lobby to change official policy on labour, the planters formed the United Planters' Association of Southern India (UPASI) in August 1893. In the following years this organization frequently addressed the Governments of India and Madras on the subject of the labour problem and their preferred solutions. Of interest in this regard is the fact that, unlike the Madras administration, the Government of India was opposed to the introduction of new legislation which would strengthen the position of the planter vis-à-vis the kangany and the labourer.[62] In a period when the interests of European workers' were being taken increasing seriously, the Indian administration was more wary of potential criticism from the British parliament than from the Madras Government.

Finally, in December 1895, after a short meeting with representatives of the UPASI, the Viceroy at last agreed that there was a case for an enquiry into the problems of the planters, although, in his view, the remedies proposed were "opposed to the whole spirit of modern legislation".[63] In March 1896 the South of India Planters' Enquiry Committee was convened.

That the enquiry was meant to defend the interests of only the employers was clear from the composition of the committee, the questions to be answered and the nature of the evidence collected. The committee was composed of one representative of the UPASI and two civil servants: neither kanganies nor

60. Mayne, "United Planters' Association", pp. 1-4.
61. *Ibid.*, pp. 4-5.
62. Griffiths, *History of the Indian Tea Industry*, pp. 398-399.
63. Quoted in *ibid.*, p. 399.

labourers – who were also not yet formally organised during this period – were represented officially. The object of the committee was to enquire into (a) the nature of the advance and kangany system, (b) whether or not the latter should continue, (c) the operational problems experienced, and (d) the best method of removing the latter. Clearly, the central issue was to find a solution that would be acceptable both to the planters and to the Governments of India and Madras. Most of the evidence presented to the enquiry committee was collected from the planters themselves: 197 proprietors and managers of estates and 12 secretaries of planting associations answered the questionnaire sent out by the committee. Some 70 officials were also asked to give their views. However, only 14 kanganies and no plantation workers were called upon by the committee to provide evidence. Unsurprisingly, the enquiry accepted the validity of the planters' difficulties and concluded that the kangany system based on cash advances should continue. It recommended not only the enactment of an amended labour law for the Madras Presidency but also that the same legislation should be adopted in the Princely States of Mysore and Cochin.[64]

Although most planters were content with this outcome, subsequent discussions between government officials and planter representatives about the new labour legislation were anything but smooth. The Madras Planters' Labour Act went a considerable way to meet the planters' requirements: for example, kanganies who absconded or failed to account for the advances received from planters were, like labourers, henceforth liable to imprisonment (see clause 24 of the last draft of the bill). It also introduced reciprocity between the Madras Presidency and the Princely States on the matter of warrants issued by each (section 44). At the same time, the planters were unable to prevent the inclusion of some regulations protecting the interests of workers and administrators. Labourers were now entitled to sick pay (article 14), planters were obliged to provide their labourers with house accommodation, water-supply, sanitary arrangements and medical attendance (section 15), and certain officials were allowed to inspect the estates (clause 16). After prolonged deliberations, the Madras Planters' Labour Bill, approved by the representative of the UPASI, was passed in early 1903.[65]

The new legislation was to apply only in the particular areas indicated (article 1). Because of the new welfare provisions, however, it became clear at the 10th annual general meeting of the UPASI that no planting district in the Madras Presidency had any intention of implementing the act. As one planter put it: "We asked for bread and they have given us a stone. [...] I say we should take Act XIII in preference to the new Act."[66] Another planter was even more

64. *RSIPEC*, 1896, pp. 1-5 and 65.
65. The Madras Planters' Labour Act (Act I of 1903), in: *UPASI Proceedings*.
66. The planter's address began thus: "These provisions are not what we asked for. What we did

explicit when he observed that "the house to house inspection is the great block". Unsurprisingly, the Madras Government felt betrayed by the planting community. In a conversation about the introduction of the Madras Planters' Labour Bill, the Governor informed Romilly, a Wynad planter and former Planting Member of the Madras Legislative Council that "[w]e have done all this for you, and if this is all the return we are going to get in the future, you will get precious little from us in the future".[67] At the same time, the Indian administration became increasingly opposed to the old legislation, Act XIII of 1859, for reasons outlined by Stokes, a representative of the Government of India: "That Act was one which, under an unjust Judge, or a stupid Magistrate, might place the cooly in an actual position of servitude." For Romilly there was accordingly no option: "I don't think the Government will force the [new] Act on any District", he cautioned, "but they might take away Act XIII *and then you will have free labour*" (emphasis mine). In 1904 the Nilgiris (apart from Wynad) came under the new legislation; both planting districts were situated in the Madras Presidency.[68]

Since the Indian Government was not interested in the welfare of plantation workers in the Princely States, the Travancore planters had more room for manoeuvre than their above-mentioned colleagues.[69] They were faced with the option of either introducing labour legislation along the lines of the Madras Planters' Labour Act, or keeping the Travancore version of Act XIII of 1859 (the Criminal Breach of Contract Act). To find out the opinion of the planters on this subject, a Select Committee of the Travancore Legislative Council[70] was convened by the Dewan. The Resident, G.T. Mackenzie, detested the proposed

ask for was increased protection against loss by wilful breach of contract. That is what we asked for. We had Act XIII of 1859 and we simply asked that it might be amended so that contracts entered into under it might be enforced and proper punishments meted out for wilful and fraudulent breaches of contract."

67. The Governor began thus: "You ask for an Act. You accept the Act through your Member of Council; and then before you ever give the Act a trial, you ask to have it amended. I will have nothing whatever to say to you in this matter of amendment until you come with a concrete case showing where the Act has caused a hardship. Then we may listen to you and may amend the Act. But to come up before the Act has ever been tested is absolutely illogical and absurd, and is practically putting the Madras Government in a false position."

68. 10th annual general meeting of the UPASI, Bangalore, 3-7 August 1903, in: *UPASI Proceedings*.

69. 11th annual general meeting of the UPASI, Bangalore, 22-24 August 1904, in: *UPASI Proceedings*.

70. The Travancore Legislative Council, inaugurated in 1888, was initially composed of 5-8 members, of whom no fewer than two were men outside government service. These non-official members were nominated by the government and not elected. The council was presided over by the Dewan and functioned solely as an advisory body (Koshy, *Constitutionalism in Travancore and Cochin*, pp. 3-4, 8-9; Sugeetha, *Constitutional Progress in Travancore*, pp. 12-16).

Planters' Labour Bill, and was against the formation of such a committee. His position was not unique, for the committee's report stated that planters "were unanimously of the opinion that the Bill was unnecessary and would destroy the progress of their industry".[71]

The report, however, suggested more of a consensus among the Travancore planters than was actually the case. Thus A.H. Mead, the representative of the planters of central Travancore, was initially in favour of the new legislation, as was H.M. Knight, representing the Cardamom hills, although the latter preferred the existing Criminal Breach of Contract Act if planters were given the power to extradite absconders. By contrast, A. Martin, representing the Kannan Devan hills, thought that "the Act was totally unsuited to labour in south India, and introduced the thin end of the wedge of interference by Government with their [the planters'] labour". He concluded thus: "We do not want inspection." Clearly, the view of Martin, one of the leading figures of the largest plantation company in Travancore, James Finlay and Company, became decisive for the administration. Accordingly, the Madras Planters' Labour Act was never introduced in Travancore.[72]

The Criminal Breach of Contract Act was itself at the centre of the 1913 Slavery Case in the Travancore Highlands. The facts laid before the Sessions Judge, P. Raman Tampi, were as follows. Mylen Chothan, a plantation labourer, complained that Killian Panikan, another estate worker, had kidnapped his twelve-year old son, Kutten. Together with his other son (Azhakan) and nephew (Karumpan), Mylen Chothan himself had been recruited by someone called Chothi to work on the Haileybury estate under the direction of a kangany named Onchi Thevan. Because of a disagreement between the latter and the management, the whole labour gang (including Kutten) subsequently left the Haileybury estate to work on the Kozhikanom estate. Mylen Chothan, however, wished to return home with his children and nephew, and asked the kangany, Onchi Thevan, for permission to do so; the latter stated that this was conditional on the former clearing his debts. While Mylen Chothan was away, his children and nephew found employment on another plantation. When he attempted to return home with them, the new kangany, Abdullah Avukar, and the person who had decoyed the three youngsters, Killian Panikan, were unwilling to release the boys, and threatened Mylen Chotham with violence should they attempt to abscond. He approached the Magistrate's Court of Peermade and registered his complaint.

71. The report stated further "that the Breach of Contract Regulation II of 1080 recently passed would answer their purpose provided a clause was inserted securing to them the privilege of extradition of coolies who run away to British India after receiving advances of money".

72. R/2/903/441; 13th annual general meeting of the UPASI, Bangalore, 13-16 August 1906, in: *UPASI Proceedings.*

It was not the three-month prison sentence passed on Killian Panikan by the Sessions Judge, Raman Tampi, which shocked the European plantation community, but rather the fact that the latter expressed compassion for both the accused and accuser, implicitly condemning the living and working conditions on the plantations. Raman Tampi stated:

> In passing sentence on the prisoner [Killian Panikan] I must not omit to consider the fact that he was a mere tool in the hands of designing persons. He is a victim of circumstances. He was working as a coolie for about three years in Kozhikanom estate, and being ill-paid and under-fed, was anxious to go back to his native village. He had no money to pay his passage expenses. His masters would not willingly release him from bondage. [...] The temptation [receiving a commission by a kangany for bringing 3 labourers] was too strong to be resisted. The boys [...] were working in Kozhikanom Estate and their father was absent. The boys themselves had ceased to be enamoured of highland life and were eager to return home. They were induced to believe that Chothan had arranged for their clandestine departure from the Hills. They at once took the hint and without waiting to ask Thevan [their kangany on Kozhikanom estate] for leave followed the prisoner who had suddenly presented himself before them as deliverer, friend and guide.

Without being explicit, Raman Tampi accused the European planters of creating a financial, judicial and military framework in which bonded labour, especially between worker and kangany, was not only approved of but also encouraged.

> A careful consideration of the evidence in the case lends colour to the impression that slave traffic is carried on with helpless children and credulous adults to their doom. The boy Avutha [alias Kutten Clothan], for instance, was treated to a cup of coffee and sweet meats and decoyed from Manakumam [his home town] without the consent and permission of his mother and elderly brother. Once attached to an Estate as coolies, the defenceless creatures are deprived of all individuality and freedom and looked upon as chattels. [...] It is a pity that such conditions should prevail in modern days when we hear so much about philanthropic endeavours to elevate the depressed classes. The arms of the law are unfortunately not strong enough or long enough to reach the worst offenders. It is permissible to doubt whether the encouragement of the labour contract system by statute is not mainly responsible for this regrettable state of affairs.

Even worse from the planters' point of view was the fact that the case was seized upon by the press. Newspaper headlines and comments, closely following the words of the Sessions Judge, suggested that the plantation workers were indeed slaves.

Alarmed by the Sessions Judge's remarks and the press comment this generated, the managers of the estates concerned and the secretary of the Central Travancore Planters' Association asked the British Resident to take countermeasures. Accordingly, the latter informed the Dewan "that the High Court should draw his attention to the rather lurid language in which the Sessions

Judge has indulged". Some days later, Krishnan Nair, the Chief Justice, admonished Raman Tampi for his comments and unjustified allegations. Fearful for his position, the Sessions Judge retracted his earlier observations.[73]

The real threat to the penal powers of the planters, however, came from outside the state. Initially, this threat was successfully evaded. When the Workman's Breach of Contract Act (Act XIII of 1859) and the Madras Planters' Labour Act (Act I of 1903) were abolished in British India in 1925 and 1929, respectively, the British Resident and the planters in Travancore kept silent about these legal changes so as to prevent the Travancorean legislature from abolishing the Criminal Breach of Contract Act.[74] Similarly, when in 1926 the League of Nations asked whether the slave trade, slavery or similar conditions still existed in Travancore, it received the misleading reply that "there is now no survival in the country or any trace of bondage or compulsory servitude".[75]

By the early 1930s, however, the pressure against the continuance of the Criminal Breach of Contract Act had become more pronounced. In 1930 the International Labour Organization – an institution formed and financed by the League of Nations – discovered that the information it had been given was incorrect, and in 1933 planters in the Princely State of Mysore were deprived of their version of the Workman's Breach of Contract Act. Now that it knew about the opinion of the International Labour Organization and the legal changes in British India and Mysore, the Travancore legislature repealed the Criminal Breach of Contract Act (Regulation II of 1080) in January 1935,[76] thereby ending the situation in which agreements between planter and kangany and between kangany and worker were subject to penal law (Regulation I of 1110).[77] However, agreements which had been entered into before the date of the repealing remained subject to penal clauses until these contracts were completed.[78]

73. For the 1913 Slavery Case in the Travancore Highlands, see file R/2/882/108 and *The Planters' Chronicle* 1913, p. 579.
74. 32nd, 33rd, 34th and 35th annual general meetings of the UPASI, Bangalore, on respectively 17-20 August 1925, 23-26 August 1926, 22-25 August 1927 and 22-25 August 1928, in: *UPASI Proceedings*.
75. Bundle No. 224: 5531/1358.
76. Proceedings *TSMA*, 24 January 1935.
77. *Regulations and Proclamations of Travancore*, vol. VIII, pp. 1-2.
78. *The Planters' Chronicle*, 23 February, 1935, p. 77.

Unfreed Freedmen (1)

Despite the abolition of the Criminal Breach of Contract Act, the situation in which labourers, after having accepted advances, became indebted to recruiters and – because of low wages and dishonest payment – were unable to pay off their debts, continued to exist at least until the early 1960s. Information provided by some elderly workers sheds light on the extent to which they regarded bonded labour as a form of "slavery". Speaking abour the late 1940s and the 1950s, workers emphasized that at the time of recruitment they were misinformed about the reality of plantation life by the kanganies. After arrival on the estate, the level of wages often turned out to be much lower than that promised, and on payday – which took place only occasionally – the majority of workers received a *black* receipt, meaning that they still owed money to the kangany. Often the recruiters-cum-field supervisors disguised their holding back of payment and manipulation of the accounts by informing a worker that he had been lent more than he had actually earned. Moreover, plantation work was much more difficult than workers had expected: kanganies used their position as creditors to force labourers to work long hours, and working days from 5 a.m. until 10 p.m. were not uncommon. To reinforce their control, kanganies also dominated the work force in other ways. In order to teach them to show respect, therefore, kanganies forbade workers from using footware or covering their heads (to protect themselves from the burning sun). Though often regarded as the only way out of these arduous circumstances, absconding (or running away) was not really an option: the Kannan Devan hills, for example, were surrounded by checkpoints, and only those workers who were able to show a *white* receipt were allowed to pass through. Workers who attempted to escape, and were then recaptured, were frequently treated roughly; one labourer recalled that – in front of the other members of the work gang – the runaway labourers were beaten, kicked and covered with agricultural chemicals by the kangany and his helpers.[79]

The same kind of story about this period was repeated by elderly workers from the Peermade/Vandiperiyar district, who recounted the human suffering caused by the violence of kanganies, indebtedness, illiteracy and an (initial) lack of workers' organizations. They added, however, certain details which thus far have not been made known. Many workers, males and females alike, who saw no

---

79. Proceedings *Travancore-Cochin Legaslative Assembly* [hereafter: *TCLA*], 29 March 1955; Labour Bureau, 1964, p. 15; Ramachandran Nair, *Industrial Relations in Kerala*, pp. 240, 245-247; George Jacob, *Labour Conditions in Rubber Estates*, p. 9; interviews: AITUC workers Gudurale estate; Alex Manuel; P. Mathavan; K.T. Thomas and T.J. Joseph; with regard to the continued indebtedness of the plantation labourers after 1960 see for example: Haridasan, *Family Budget and Social Security Benefits*, p. 8.

way out of the cruel labour regime, committed suicide by taking poison or hanging themselves in the labour lines. Informants stressed, moreover, that such occurrences were not isolated incidents, wholly unconnected with plantation life: much rather the contrary, since suicide was not only the cause of death of a great number of workers but it was also directly related to the working and living conditions on the estates.[80]

The Second Step to "Free" Labour: The Abolition of the Kangany-System (1962)

Given the nature and extent of workers' grievances concerning plantation employment during the late 1940s and the 1950s, the growth of trade union organization is unsurprising. Indeed, the slogan "Proletarians Unite!" attracted much support from workers on estates throughout Southwest India. Union complaints and demands focussed on low wages, the harsh working and living conditions and – of crucial importance – the exploitative kangany system. In this regard, a memorandum submitted by the Palappilly Rubber Estate Workers' Congress to the estate managers of Cochin Malabar Estates Ltd, Kerala Calicut Estates Ltd and Malayalam Plantations Ltd is very revealing. The union requested "that the system of recruiting labour through contractors must cease" and demanded direct employment and direct payment by the managements. According to the document, the kangany system was the cause of much of the hardship experienced by workers, and in particular economic privation.[81]

The prolongation of the kangany system as a result of delaying tactics adopted by the planters to prevent abolition greatly antagonized the plantation workers. Initially the planters succeeded in passing a resolution to "defer final decision in the matter until there is an opportunity of consulting the general membership on both sides" (first Tri-Partite Conference – 1950). One year later, they supported the abolition of the kanganies on the condition that a commission was appointed which advised further on that matter (second Tri-Partite Conference – 1951). After having agreed that the kanganies should be replaced by a new cadre of labour supervisors (third Tri-Partite Conference – 1953), the

---

80. Interview with estate workers Pasupara Estate.
81. According to the Memorandum: "It is the labour contractors who benefit. They get from 12 to 16 per cent commission on the total earnings of the labour. [...] The labour contractors enjoy at the cost of poor labour. [...] However experienced be the labourer, and whatever be his service in the estate, there is no security of permanency to his work. His lot is entirely left with the contractor. He can be sent off at any time at the sweet will of the employer and contractor. Labourers who are victims of this sort of treatment are rotting here, as they are penniless and unable to reach their villages and homes." Cf. proceedings *TCLA*, 27 March 1951; proceedings *Travancore Legislative Assembly*, 9 August 1948; proceedings *TCLA*, 6 November 1950; 18 September 1951; and 27 September 1951.

planters encouraged the introduction of a fourth party in the political arena: the kanganies as represented by their own trade union leaders. Subsequently, in 1957 the Government appointed a committee to study the rehabilitation of the kanganies and the payment of compensation to those who were unable to continue estate work. Although the recommendations were slightly modified by the Kerala Government in 1959, planters refused to implement the regulations. Only in September 1962 – that is, quarter of a century after the first plantation workers' unions appeared, 15 years after Indian Independence and four years later than in the neighbouring Madras state – was labour recruitment by kanganies finally abolished.

Unfreed Freedmen (2)

Despite the abolition of the kangany system, labour did not become totally "free". This is most clearly illustrated by the case of Joseph, a plantation labourer in the mid 1990s.

Joseph's family story is most interesting in the context of the above discussion about free and unfree labour. His grandfather, an impoverished landless labourer from Tirunelveli district in the Madras Presidency, was recruited by a kangany for work on the Semini Valley Estate in Peermade/Vandiperiyar district. As time passed, Joseph himself became a kangany, recruiting workers each year when the tea harvesting season began.

The life of Joseph's father was very different from that of his grandfather. The former grew up bilingually, fluently speaking the language of his parents (Tamil) and that of the other, Malayali workers. Joseph's father also settled in the plantation district permanently, working on another estate (though owned by the same company and in the same region) as a supervisor (who did not recruit). During the early 1950s he became active in a trade union affiliated to the Revolutionary Socialist Party, a labour organization which from the early 1960s onwards was instrumental in enhancing workers' self-respect and improving working conditions.

Nowadays, Joseph himself, a bilingual estate worker in his mid thirties, does not see much of a future for himself and his family. Carrying out factory work, pruning tea plants, spraying chemicals and assisting the managers' family, particularly in cooking and gardening, does not satisfy him much, nor are these tasks well-paid. Without an education beyond his 13th year, he is unable to find other, more promising employment elsewhere. Joseph's social networks remain confined to the plantation areas, and his low-caste status does not help him much either in seeking alternative employment. In any case, outside employment would result in the loss of his dwelling on the estate, which is company-owned, as well as other related benefits. Indeed, the segmented labour market and a lack of geographical mobility severely restrict his freedom to choose another employer.

Final Observations

Studying free and unfree labour, both in the context of plantation development in southern India and from a long-term historical perspective, two features appear significant.

First, free and unfree labour alternate with each other. In a strictly legal sense, *unfree labour* (slavery) gave way subsequently to *free labour* (abolition of slavery in 1855), which was followed in turn by *unfree labour* (introduction Criminal Breach of Contract Act in 1865), and then once more by *free labour* (abolition of that same act in 1935 and abolition of the kangany-system in 1962).

And second, at any given moment all labour relations combined aspects of freedom and unfreedom. In the case of southwest India, the abolition of slavery in 1855 did not usher in a period of *free* plantation labour (due to the introduction of contract labour and the kangany system), the introduction of the Criminal Breach of Contract Act in 1865 did not establish a completely *unfree* work force (some workers did find employment elsewhere), and the abolition of the Criminal Breach of Contract Act in 1935 did not fully *free* the estate workers (due to the kangany system, a segmented labour market and geographical immobility).

In order to understand this historical process, it is necessary to consider the conflicting strategies of planters, labourers and officials. Planters were interested in the creation of an unfree work force, and to this end the planting community – European and Indian alike – attempted quite clearly both to influence labour conditions and also to restrict the capacity of labour to choose its employer. Because it enabled planters, policemen and magistrates to track down, arrest and sentence absconders, the Criminal Breach of Contract Act (1865-1935) licensed the intensification of the plantation work regime. Backed up by the threat of trial, conviction and imprisonment, the planters used the law to compel indebted workers to remain on the estate until the debt was cleared and the contract period expired. However, the Act itself only provided a legal context for and thus complemented the central structural component of unfreedom: the kangany system, whereby planters advanced money to labour recruiters (kanganies), who in turn made cash advances to workers.

This system limited the freedom of the labour force in three ways. First, it encouraged debt slavery: kanganies who borrowed money from (and became indebted to) planters used this to recruit workers by means of cash advances for basic needs (food, clothing, travel, etc.). Second, the kangany system encouraged the spread of misinformation about the plantation: interested in bringing as many workers as possible to the estate, recruiters withheld negative details that would enable workers to make a more informed choice. And third, it was structured by various kinds of abuse, including the use of violence. Initially operating as labour recruiters on the plains, and subsequently as overseers on the estates, kanganies derived the major portion of their income from commissions on the earnings of their work gangs. For this reason control was central to the kangany/ worker relation, and control was based ultimately on violence. This sanction was used in many ways: to punish unwilling workers, to ensure that workers repaid debts (both authentic and ficticious), to detain them beyond the contract expiry period, and to make them work long hours (even if they were ill). There can be no question that the kangany system, which was instrumental in in recruiting and disciplining plantation workers, limited the freedom of such labourers in a variety of ways.

On the other hand, workers used or circumvented the planters' rules, depending on the worker's initial situation and his/her ability to deceive the labour recruiter and/or planter. While it is true that at the time of recruitment a group of labourers might be misled by the kangany into regarding the plantation as a place where good wages were paid, did the attractive cash advance offered not indicate that the planter was able and willing to pay a good wage? A large number of workers gave the kanganies and planters the benefit of the doubt, not least because most of these poor, unemployed, low-caste workers could hardly imagine a situation that was worse than their own. The majority of workers, however, probably realised the misleading nature of the information they received and, knowing the hardships of plantation life, still opted for estate work that provided them with a way out, a temporary solution and often a last resort in periods of unemployment and/or food shortages.

Labourers also took advantage of shortcomings in the system. There were instances, therefore, of workers and kanganies who accepted cash advances from planters but subsequently failed to fulfil their contractual obligations. Although they risked severe punishment if caught, labourers and kanganies sometimes absconded, either returning home or going to another estate.

It is precisely these conflicting strategies which help explain the difficulty in characterizing the nature of plantation labour.

Free and Unfree Labour in Australia, 1788-1900

Raymond Markey

The establishment of settler societies, such as the Australian colonies from 1788, offer a unique opportunity to test the various theses concerning the relationship between free and unfree labour systems under an emergent capitalist mode of production. The Aboriginal tribal hunter/gatherers produced no class structure for the control of labour power prior to white settlement. No feudal society or peasantry ever existed in Australia. Consequently, when capitalism was established in the Australian colonies, there were no pre-capitalist forms of production which survived during the early establishment of the capitalist mode (except insofar as traditional Aboriginal society survived beyond the boundaries of settlement), and there was no peasantry to resist the extension of a free labour market, or to be transformed into a proletariat.

Although the Australian colonies were established officially as penal colonies in the late eighteenth century, they were capitalist from the outset, in two important senses. Firstly, they were established as imperial extensions of capitalist society in Britain. Secondly, from an early stage, they were an important source of raw materials, especially wool and precious minerals, for British manufacturers and international markets. The colonies quickly developed free labour markets in this context, but nevertheless, unfree labour remained important until the end of the century.

Unfree labour took two main forms in the colonies. First, with the exception of South Australia, the colonies were originally formed as penal settlements. Convict labour quickly became important, as the military and official caste attempted to establish itself as a landed aristocracy, and they were joined by other entrepreneurs in exploitation of natural resources for the British market. Labour became scarce, particularly with the expansion of the pastoral industry and attempts to establish a small farmer class. Consequently, from the beginning of the nineteenth century free settlers were encouraged, and from the 1850s convict labour was phased out. In the interim, free and convict labour co-existed. The second main form of unfree labour was provided by indentured Melanesian, or "Kanaka", labourers, who serviced the large Queensland sugar plantations from the 1860s to 1901.

Australian convicts and Melanesians were only a small part of a large international flow of unfree labour by forced migration in the nineteenth century. The significance of this flow in many respects rivalled that of free labour, especially to the "New Worlds" of America and Australia, upon which historians of immigration have concentrated. Although Australian historians have tended to treat their convict past as historically exceptional, convict labour systems existed in many countries in the nineteenth century. From 1820 over a quarter of a million Indian, French, and Spanish convicts, as well as those from England and Ireland, were shipped to Australia, New Caledonia, Singapore, French Guinea, Gibraltar, Bermuda, Penang, Malacca and Mauritius, and two million Russians were forced to migrate to Siberia. Bonded or indentured Indians and Pacific Islanders accounted for a further 2.75 million unfree labourers.[1]

Convict labour remained important in the colonies well after the vote by the British parliament in 1792 to gradually abolish the slave trade, after the successful Haitian slave revolt of 1794, and after the ending of the trade in slaves to Spanish possessions in the 1820s, and to Brazil and French possessions in 1830-1831.[2] Indentured labour also became more important internationally after the virtual abolition of the slave trade by about 1850, and in Australia after the abolition of the convict system in the eastern colonies soon afterwards. Slavery had been an important foundation stone for the expansion of mercantilist capitalism in the late seventeenth and eighteenth centuries. As the African slave trade declined, therefore, from the late eighteenth century, new forms of unfree labour provided much of the labour force for the great expansion of capitalism in the nineteenth century.

The Convict Era

"The first settlers of Australia were chosen by the best judges in England."[3] From 1788, when the colony of New South Wales (NSW) was formed, until 1868, almost 160,000 convicts were transported to Australia from Britain and Ireland. The vast majority of these arrived between 1815 and 1835. In the early years of the colony of NSW, the numbers of convicts rose steadily, but slowly. From 1793 to 1810 arrivals averaged about 400 per annum, reaching 1,000 per annum in 1815. After the Napoleonic wars, from 1816-1825, the average number transported reached 2,600 per annum, then climbed to an average of 5,000 between 1826 to 1835, and 6,500 from 1831-1837. Thereafter, numbers

1. See Nicholas and Shergold, "Transportation as Global Migration", pp. 28-42; Eltis, "Free and Coerced Transatlantic Migrations", pp. 251-280; and Tinker, *New System of Slavery*.
2. See Blackburn, *Overthrow of Colonial Slavery*.
3. Inglis, *Australian Colonists*, p. 14.

declined to about 4,000 per annum in the early to mid 1840s, and most of these went to Tasmania (then known as Van Diemen's Land).[4]

Their distribution within the colonies varied a great deal. The original colony of NSW covered all of eastern Australia west to the 135th parallel. The island colony of Van Diemen's Land (later Tasmania) was formed in 1803. Victoria and Queensland were separated from NSW in 1851 and 1859, respectively. All of these colonies, originally as part of NSW, had systems of convict labour from the outset. In contrast, Western Australia did not receive convicts when it was originally settled in 1829 and did not begin to receive them until 1850. South Australia, where settlement began in 1836, never accommodated British convicts, relying entirely upon free settlers. Those colonies which took convicts phased out the importation of convicts at different times, with NSW abolishing further transportation in 1840, followed by Victoria in 1849, Queensland in 1850, Van Diemen's Land in 1853, and Western Australia as late as 1868. However, the great bulk of convicts went to NSW. Western Australia, for example, only received 10,000 in the eighteen years that transportation to that colony operated, although the total population (14,837 in 1861) was so small that convicts (3,846 in 1861) exerted a major impact on society and the labour market.[5]

The sentences of transportation handed out to the convict immigrants were for seven or fourteen years, or life. Most were sentenced for minor crimes against property, although a small minority were found guilty of political crimes. The latter included 464 agricultural rioters (Captain Swing) in 1830-1831, six agricultural unionists (Tolpuddle martyrs) in 1834, 72 Chartists in 1839-1842, 148 North Americans involved in the uprising in Canada in 1840, and many Irish nationalists.[6] Almost two thirds were sentenced to transportation and exile for seven years, with one quarter sentenced to life terms. Many were released or died before their sentence was concluded. However, even sentences of seven to fourteen years effectively meant life exile, because few had the means to return to Britain when freed.[7]

The vast majority of convicts were male; only one in seven were women. Most originated from England or Wales, with about a quarter from Ireland, and few Scots. Some of those from England were also Irish (6,000). The Irish tended to be older, were more likely to be married or female, tended to have fewer prior convictions and shorter sentences, were more frequently from rural areas,

---

4. *Ibid.*, p. 8; Shaw, *Convicts and the Colonies*, pp. 366-368; Crowley, "Foundation Years", p. 4; Roe, "1830-50", p. 119; Fitzpatrick, *British Imperialism*, pp. 69-91, and Fitzpatrick, *British Empire in Australia*, p. 56.
5. Crowley, "Foundation Years", pp. 6-7; and Coghlan, *Labour and Industry*, 1, pp. 556-562.
6. Roe, "1830-1850", p. 120; and Rude, *Protest and Punishment*.
7. Crowley, "Foundation Years", p. 16.

and were more likely to be transported for political crimes. One fifth of the Irish convicts were sentenced for crimes of protest against Britain and/or the land laws.[8] The English and Welsh convicts were mainly unmarried and aged in their twenties, from London and the newer industrial cities of the midlands and the north, and likely to have prior convictions for larceny.

The major motive for establishment of the penal convict system was to relieve the overcrowded prisons of Britain and to punish felons with exile and hard labour. Strategic considerations in relation to French exploration in the region provided a secondary motivation. Initially, there were few, if any, commercial considerations in the decision to establish a penal colony. However, the objectives of the British government and its colonial representatives changed over time. Governor Macquarie (1810-1821) was committed to a program of rehabilitation of convicts whose term had expired or who had been pardoned, through employment in the free labour market. After Macquarie greater emphasis was placed for a time upon the importance of penal servitude as a punishment which would deter crime in Britain.[9]

The free labour market had expanded, gradually at first, and then more dramatically from the 1830s. By then, the demand for labour by the large landholders who produced wool for British mills outstripped the convict supply. Many of these landholders had originally occupied Crown land illegally (and hence, were known as "squatters"), but their importance in imperial trade and industry required various compromises leading to the granting of leaseholds, and they were partly instrumental in gaining a program of assisted immigration for free labour from Britain. This program found further support from those in Britain who wished to send paupers to the colonies, and in the 1830s the Poor Law Commissioners saw opportunities for the removal of excess agricultural labour. At the same time, an attempt was made to make assisted immigration pay for itself through sale of lands in the colonies.[10] In accordance with principles established by the influential British emigration theorist, Edward Gibbon Wakefield, the price for this land was set at a level sufficient to prevent wide-spread land ownership, enabling the retention of a labour force for employment.

In the earliest years of settlement the majority of convicts worked in govern-ment service. The others were assigned as labourers to officers, public servants, free settlers and pardoned convicts who received free land grants.[11] By the 1820s a system of assignment of convicts to private employers became more developed, with private employers signing contracts to employ the convicts for a minimum

---

8. Inglis, *Australian Colonists*, p. 8; and Shaw, "1788-1810", p. 19.
9. Crowley, "Foundation Years", pp. 4, 9; and Fitzpatrick, *British Imperialism*, chs 1-2, 4, 6.
10. Inglis, *Australian Colonists*, pp. 16-17; Hutson, *From Penal Colony to Penal Powers*, pp. 21-22; and Fitzpatrick, *British Imperialism*, chs 7-8.
11. Inglis, *Australian Colonists*, p. 16; Crowley, "Foundation Years", pp. 16, 21.

of twelve months according to certain conditions. From that time, the vast majority of convicts were assigned in this way, at least for part of their sentence. This coincided with a change in land usage and tenure at about this time, with freeholders engaged in cereal production and trade in the settled districts of the colonies becoming displaced numerically and in economic importance by the large wool growers in unsettled districts. The convict system adapted to this change and the new class of employers. Convicts assigned to private employers were employed principally in rural and domestic labour.

The convict labourers employed by government included four main categories: those retained by the authorities because of specific skills or other requirements; those returned by employers to whom they had been assigned because they were considered unfit for service; those re-convicted of further crimes after transportation; and those sentenced to work in irons as a severe form of discipline.

Government convicts were occupied predominantly with building roads, dwellings, wharves, windmills, granaries and other infrastructure, in carting, in brickmaking and vehicle construction, and in stores and hospitals.[12] Skilled mechanics worked at their own trades. As the colony developed, the variety of government employment increased, to include work in coal mining, a brick-yard, lime kiln, lumber yard, quarry and slaughterhouse. With the growth in administrative structures came jobs in government departments, such as the surveyor-general's or engineering departments, or the dockyard. Most women convicts were assigned to private employers as domestics, but from 1810 some were employed in a government clothing factory. In the early 1820s special scrub and bush clearing gangs were employed to assist settlers. They were also employed on government farms to produce food, for until the early 1800s most of the population was fed from government stores, and in 1817 one third of the total population were still dependent upon the government for food. However, this became less important as private landholders became more numerous and established, and in 1832 the last government farm in NSW was closed down. A number of other government activities ceased (for example, the lumber yard) or were reduced at this time, as private enterprise became better established. By the late 1830s over two thirds of convicts in NSW and Tasmania were assigned to private employers. The employment history of most convicts indicated a high degree of mobility, as they commonly moved between government and private employment, as well as between private employers.

Convict labourers were provided with food and clothing by their employer, be they government or private. In the early years of settlement diet was restricted until farms were sufficiently established to provide fresh produce. Lack of vegetables and a reliance on salted meat produced scurvy and dysentry. Food

12. Inglis, *Australian Colonists*, p. 8; and Crowley, "Foundation Years", pp. 16-18.

shortages were so severe in 1802 that it was necessary to reduce normal work loads. However, by mid-1820s farming was sufficiently established to meet the food needs of convicts. Clothing was also very scarce until the 1820s when the government produced its own requirements at a factory for female convicts. Government regulations fixed a minimum weekly ration for assigned convicts in private employment, and employers were expected to provide them with adequate clothing and shelter. However, no official inspections of these conditions occurred. The governors relied upon the convict servants to complain if necessary, and some masters at least could be miserly in these areas. Until 1819 no proper quarters were provided by the government for the great majority of convicts . They were forced to find their own quarters, and to pay rent for them by working in their free hours, or by robbery. For female convicts this situation commonly meant co-habitation with officers, troops or emancipated convicts, or prostitution, since there were few employment opportunities for them.[13]

The organization of working hours for government convicts was forced to recognize their housing situation. For example, from about 1809-1819 these were fixed at sunrise to 8 a.m., and after a meal break, from 9 a.m. to 3 p.m. This amounted to little more than eight hours per day, five days per week, although it had been fixed at ten hours a few years earlier. Saturday working hours amounted to six. Government regulations also stipulated a ten hour working day, five days a week, with six hours on Saturday, for assigned convicts. They could work for themselves outside those hours, although private employers had first call on this extra time if they were willing to pay for it. The government also fixed a yearly wage of 10 pounds per annum for males, and 7 pounds per annum for females, until the mid-1830s. Because of difficulties in obtaining many items, particularly in the countryside, wages were often paid in goods, such as tea, sugar, spirits and tobacco. Some bargaining also occurred to trade-off wages for employer support for a pardon or ticket of leave.[14]

Convicts were able from the beginning to gain a ticket of leave from the governor, exempting them from government or assigned service and allowing them to work for themselves. Tickets of leave were granted as rewards for good conduct or performance of work beyond the normal call of duty in terms of skill, ingenuity or effort. They were granted upon the recommendation of government supervisors or private employers, who frequently recommended their employees in this way. Holders of tickets of leave were meant to become entirely self sufficient, but retained the legal status of convicts, subject to recall where needed by the government, to surveillance, and Sunday musters for church. After the first twenty-five years of settlement, it became uncommon

13. Shaw, "1788-1810", p. 19; Crowley, "Foundation Years", p. 19.
14. Shaw, "1788-1810", p. 19; Coghlan, *Labour and Industry*, p. 176; and Crowley, "Foundation Years", pp. 19, 23.

for convicts to be recalled. In the early 1800s convicts became subject to a standard probation period of three to four years before becoming eligible for a ticket of leave, and in the 1820s this probationary period varied according to the length of the original sentence. By 1837 one quarter of all convicts had tickets of leave.[15]

Conditional or absolute pardons could also be granted to convicts by governors. The total number of beneficiaries of this kind accounted for less than five per cent of all convicts. However, under Governor Macquarie, a higher proportion was granted, as was also the case with tickets of leave. Many of the convicts freed under Macquarie were given land grants of between 30 and 60 acres (depending on the size of their family unit), or entered government service, even as magistrates. However, most of those granted land did not remain on it, ending up in towns as tradesmen or labourers, as they had been in Britain in the majority of cases.[16]

Emancipists who had been pardoned or finished their terms accounted for 20 per cent of the total population in 1828. This proportion actually declined over the next twenty years or so because of a dramatic rise in the proportion of free colonial-born and free immigrants. Table 1 illustrates this transformation of NSW from penal colony to a free society. In 1841, just as transportation to NSW had been abolished, convicts accounted for virtually a quarter of the total population, and convicts and emancipists together accounted for over 70 per cent of the labour force.[17] Ten years later convicts accounted for less than 2 per cent of the population. This had major implications for the nature of the labour market and society.

For the first twenty years of white settlement in Australia fewer than 100 free immigrants were attracted to the colonies (exclusive of military and officials). Most of those who did migrate as free settlers were artisans.[18] North America was generally a more attractive and closer option for British emigrants. Nevertheless, for the last nine years of transportation in NSW (1831-1840), 65,000 free immigrants arrived compared with 50,000 convicts in all Australian colonies.

15. Inglis, *Australian Colonists*, p. 9; and Crowley, "Foundation Years", pp. 27-28.
16. Inglis, *Australian Colonists*, pp. 9, 12-13.
17. Nicholas and Shergold, "Transportation as Global Migration", p. 3.
18. *Ibid.*

Table 1. Composition of the Population of New South Wales 1828-1851[19]

Category %	1828	1841	1851
Convicts	43	23	2
Emancipists	20	16	14
Colonial born	24	24	43
Free immigrants	13	37	41
Total	100	100	100
Total numbers	36,598	116,988	187,243

Source: Ward, *Australian Legend*, p. 15.

Another 100,000 or more arrived in the next decade. Two thirds of the free immigrants from 1831 were assisted in their passage by the government, even though assistance ceased during the depression of the early 1840s, with a consequent slowing of the immigration flow temporarily.[20]

The early free labourers and settlers experienced very harsh living and working conditions, including scarce, poor quality food, and truck and barter payment systems. The skilled were better off, especially since tradesmen were scarce in the early days of settlement. However, even they were subject to a particularly harsh disciplinary code for free labour, underpinned by governors' regulations. There were two reasons for the implementation of these regulations. Firstly, it represented an attempt to control such extremely scarce labour, convict or free; secondly, it was influenced by the harsh methods of the convict system itself, particularly since many free labourers were emancipists. Free labourers do not seem to have been immune from floggings for disobedience or other misbehaviour towards their employers. Various attempts were made by governors' declarations and meetings of magistrates, clergy and colonial gentry to control wages, although with very limited success in the early 1800s, largely because of scarcity of labour and bidding for it by employers. However, magistrates were empowered to settle wage disputes, and their interests were frequently those of an employer. English Master and Servants legislation was applied initially in the colonies from 1828, with a greater emphasis upon the contract to serve, for the reasons already discussed above. Hence, desertion of duty before discharge made workers liable to up to six months imprisonment and forfeiture of all wages due. There were many instances of imprisonment of labourers, and sentencing to the treadmill, under these provisions in the 1830s and 1840s. Free workers were also

19. The figures quoted exclude Van Diemen's Land and the Port Phillip District, which became the separate colony of Victoria in 1850, although they include the Moreton Bay District which became the separate colony of Queensland in 1859. See Coghlan, *Labour and Industry*, p. 561.
20. Inglis, *Australian Colonists*, pp. 16–17.

subject to capricious arrest for suspicion under the Bushranging Act if they wandered far from home. Nor were magistrates very sympathetic to claims for non-payment of wages by employers, which required civil action by the employee, in contrast with the criminal proceedings directed against employees under Master and Servants legislation. Later, the colonies enacted their own legislation, which remained somewhat stricter than the British version.[21]

The Significance of the Convict System

Their importance in creating an economic infrastructure and providing a labour force for the establishment of much of early capitalist activity cannot be denied. Nevertheless, the nature of the convicts has been the subject of considerable debate amongst Australian historians over the years.

From early in the twentieth century a romantic nationalist interpretation viewed the convicts as working class victims of a harsh penal system and a class society in which they were often forced to steal in order to survive, or were political opponents of the British class system (as in the case of the United Irish, the Tolpuddle martyrs, Captain Swing rioters and others), or were involved in organized efforts to defend their position as workers. This background, Russell Ward argued, contributed in a major way to the egalitarian ethos of "mateship" in the Australian working class, and through it to the national characteristics associated with the "typical" Australian.[22] From the 1960s this interpretation was challenged by Manning Clark and others, who argued that the convicts were comprised predominantly of a professional criminal class, and that the "better class" of political convicts were a very small minority. McQueen's new left interpretation also accepted this description of the convicts, in arguing that they represented a lumpenproletariat with a value system which combined hatred of authority with individual acquisitiveness.[23]

However, recent historians of Victorian crime in England and Europe have argued that most crime should not be ascribed to professional criminals, but to workers who supplemented their income by theft, or the unemployed who stole to survive.[24] Consistent with this generalization, their studies indicate that crime was predominantly casual and lacked planning. The most extensive, recent, statistical analysis of the Australian convicts indicates that they were not typically

21. Crowley, "Foundation years", pp. 29-37; Hutson, *Penal Colony to Penal Powers*, pp. 24-25; Merritt, "Development and Application"; and Markey, *Making of the Labor Party*, pp. 122-123.
22. Ward, *Australian Legend*, pp. 1-111.
23. McQueen, *New Britannia*, ch. 11; and Clark, "Rewriting Australian History".
24. Notably Philips, *Crime and Authority*; Jones, *Crime, Protest, Community and Police*; and Rude, *Criminal and Victim*.

professional and habitual criminals, but predominantly working class, fairly typical of the range of occupations found in the British and Irish working class.[25] Most were young, first offenders convicted of petty theft or receiving stolen goods. Many crimes were work-related, involving theft of tools, materials or other possessions from employers. Of the political convicts, 5,000 arrived in the first 25 years, accounting for half of all of the Irish. They thus had a much higher impact on the overall nature of the convict population in the very early years, which was also indicated by the uprising of 300 Irish convicts and emancipists at Castle Hill in 1804.[26]

A number of other characteristics of the Australian convicts confirm these observations and indicate their special usefulness as a labour force in a new colony. The proportion of skilled, semi-skilled and unskilled occupations amongst the convicts was broadly similar to those for the English workforce as a whole in 1841. This wide range of skills proved useful in the creation of a new settlement. Skilled building workers were especially valuable in this regard. Whilst there was a slight urban skill bias amongst the convicts, the proportion of skilled farm workers amongst them was virtually the same as in the British workforce in 1841.[27]

As a whole the convicts were better educated than the working class in Britain. Three quarters of English convicts in NSW could read and/or write, compared with only 58 per cent of all English workers who could sign the marriage register. Those economists who interpret education as a process of human capital formation have argued that a literacy rate of 40 per cent appears to be the threshold level for sustained economic development. The convict labour force of Australia easily attained this level, and surpassed the literacy level of much of the underdeveloped world in the twentieth century.[28]

The Australian convicts were also physically fit and productive. Only healthy convicts were transported on the arduous four-month voyage. Conditions on the convict ships were such that there was low mortality for the times on the

25. Nicholas and Shergold, "Convicts as Migrants", pp. 46-47, and Nicholas and Shergold, "Convicts as Workers", p. 74. This work is based on 19,711 convicts transported to NSW between 1817 to 1840. It admittedly excludes Tasmania, where the recidivist convicts were sent, but these represented a minority of the total. The vast majority of convicts went to NSW and the sample used in this research accounts for 12.5 per cent of all convicts sent to all of the colonies. These observations, and the necessary qualifications expressed here, were the subject of lively debate in review articles and replies published in the *Australian Economic History Review (AEHR)* soon after the work of Nicholas and Sherman was published: Nicholas, "Reinterpreting the Convict Labour Market", pp. 50-66, and Shlomowitz, "Convict Workers", pp. 67-88; and notes from both of these authors in *Australian Economic History Review*, XXXI (1991), pp. 95-109.
26. Shaw, "1788-1810", pp. 22-23.
27. Nicholas and Shergold, "Convicts as Migrants", pp. 62-84.
28. Nicholas and Shergold, "Labour Aristocracy in Chains", pp. 98-110.

voyage (less than 2 per cent, which was lower than for emigrant ships across the Atlantic, and much lower than for African slave ships or for Indian indentured labourers[29]), and the convicts generally arrived in a physically fit state. The convict statistics indicated that they were on average of similar height to other British workers. Height is indicative of nutritional input during the growing years, and a crude indication that the convicts' capacity for labour was as high as that for British workers generally.[30]

Convict health and productivity was partly an outcome of their age distribution. Over 80 per cent of NSW convicts fell within the range of 16 to 25 years. This compared with the alternative labour supply of free immigrants to the eastern colonies between 1829 and 1851, of whom only about two thirds were in the 15 to 35 years age group. Of the free immigrants to North America from 1820 to 1840, 30 per cent were under 15 or over 40 years, compared with the Australian convict equivalent of 10 per cent. The modern Australian Department of Immigration encourages immigrants of 16 to 35 years age, but only 47 per cent fall into that range.

These comparisons indicate the exceptionally high labour force participation rate achieved by the convict labour system. The Australian convicts were predominantly single males, arriving without the very young or the old, to contribute to a participation rate of over 65 per cent in the total colonial population. The age-sex structure of the convict workforce also reduced considerably the call upon dependent services such as schools, trade training, and old-age care for two generations. The workforce structure, therefore, provided unique opportunities for rapid economic growth and the establishment of infrastructure.[31]

The structural efficiency of the convict labour system was further promoted by two other characteristics. First, as a group, convicts had a high degree of experience of migration prior to being transported to Australia. Almost 40 per cent had previously moved county within the British Isles, and 12 per cent of the Irish had previously migrated to Britain. This experience, which correlated to a high degree with skill and a high level of education, facilitated adjustment to the migration experience in Australia, if not to the experience of being imprisoned. Secondly, over 95 per cent of convicts never returned to Britain or Ireland. In contrast, the net immigration level (i.e. the proportion remaining in Australia) for the period 1982-1987 was only 67 per cent of immigrant arrivals. In the parlance of modern immigration policy, the convict system displayed a high degree of "immigration effectiveness".[32]

29. Nicholas and Shergold, "Convicts as Migrants, pp. 47-8; and Shaw, "1788-1810", p. 19.
30. Stephen Nicholas, "Care and Feeding of Convicts".
31. Nicholas and Shergold, "Convicts as Migrants", pp. 43-61.
32. Nicholas and Shergold, "Unshackling the Past", pp. 8-9.

Once established in the Australian colonies, the allocation and organization of convict labour was also relatively efficient. Strictly speaking, it is not possible to refer to a labour market in the classical sense, because the allocation of convict labour was controlled initially entirely by the state apparatus. Nevertheless, the manner in which this occurred would appear to have matched labour market considerations to a relatively high degree. Recent research for NSW in the period 1817-1840 (when most convicts arrived) indicates that skilled urban, rural and construction workers were quite likely to be employed as convicts in similar jobs in NSW to those in which they had been employed in Britain or Ireland: 70 per cent of the urban skilled, 59 per cent of construction trade workers, and 44 per cent of all convicts had their skills matched with their colonial work. This applied equally to the system of assignment by the state, as well as allocation through the labour market. The skills possessed by domestic and unskilled urban workers were less appropriate to the specific labour requirements of the new colony. Consequently, these workers were concentrated in unskilled construction labour, agriculture and public service, all of which they tended to leave once they had gained their freedom. In this way, then, the state operated as an efficient agent of job restructuring according to the needs of economic growth in a new colony.[33]

The organization of public labour under the convict system essentially corresponded to the manner in which it had been organized in Britain. Skilled convict tradesmen, such as carpenters, blacksmiths, wheelwrights, shoemakers and tailors, were organized in workshops, whilst workers employed in building, road construction, land-clearing, ploughing and thrashing were organized in gangs. Much of the supervision of government labour was delegated to superintendents and overseers, originally military, but later including ex-convicts, or even current convicts being rewarded for good service. Road gangs were organized on a self-contained basis in the early years of the system, because they often worked in isolated areas. This created problems of supervision, which were overcome when they came under military supervision in the 1830s, with convicts working in chains.[34]

Notwithstanding some problems of supervision alluded to, a recent study argues that the assignment, supervision and incentive systems which characterized particular work structures were maximized in the organization of convict labour.[35] The main exception to this observation seems to have been the women convicts' factory, where productivity was low in wool and flax spinning, and

---

33. Nicholas, "Convict Labour Market", pp. 111-126; and Dyster, "Public Employment", pp. 127-51. This was also an important aspect of the debate referred to in note 26 above.
34. Coghlan, *Labour and Industry*, pp. 173-177.
35. Nicholas, "Organization of Public Work", pp. 152-166.

payment by result was unsuccessful.[36] "Care-intensive", particularly skilled, labour was mainly motivated by rewards, including extra rations, indulgences (tea, tobacco, rum), preferred work (in some government departments or as supervisors, for example), apprenticeship training, time to work on one's own account, and tickets of leave or pardons. Work which was unsuitable for measurement was tasked, and rewarded in these ways. Supervisors also received bonuses, in extra rations or cash, if they were successful with their convict gangs. On the other hand, "effort-intensive" labour, in scrub clearing and road construction, was more likely to be motivated by fear of pain or punishment.

Punishment could take a number of forms, apart from road gang labour in chains. Flogging was the most common variety. Solitary confinement and restricted rations were also employed. Serious offenders were despatched to special penal settlements, which was the original purpose of the Van Diemen's Land and Norfolk Island settlements (penal settlements within penal settlements). The harshness of these aspects of the system, and the depravity which they often produced, has received considerable attention from historians and nationalist literature. The penal settlements for serious re-offenders were particularly notorious for the cruelty and capriciousness of their commandants. Only magistrates could order corporal punishment; neither supervisors of government convicts nor private employers of assigned convicts could do so unless they held a commission of the peace. However, both government supervisors and private employers could be sadistic or tyrannical.[37] They were also able to determine work loads in ways which could lead convict labourers to commit punishable offences. In unsettled areas especially there was no official supervision of treatment of assigned servants, and those who were mistreated had to appeal to magistrates, who were likely to be employers themselves, and who were more likely to take the word of "respectable citizens" than convicted felons. Absenting themselves from their employer, disobedience, drunkenness, or idleness were all potentially punishable. In NSW between 1826 and 1836 one quarter of all convicts spent some time in a chain gang or at a penal settlement. Between 1833 and 1836 one quarter of all male convicts were flogged each year, for an average of forty lashes each, but some received sentences of up to 500 lashes, and 100 was not unusual.[38]

However, the harshness of the convict system may have been exaggerated by a pre-occupation with the worst horrors and comparison with modern standards, rather than those which prevailed for workers at the time. Physical violence was

---

36. Coghlan, *Labour and Industry*, pp. 177-178; and Oxley, "Female Convicts", pp. 85-97.
37. Crowley, "Foundation Years", pp. 18, 20; and Roe, "1830-50", p. 119.
38. Inglis, *Australian Colonists*, p. 8; Shaw, "1788-1810", p. 19; Roe, "1830-50", p. 119; and Hutson, *Penal Colony to Penal Powers*, pp. 23-24. See also Andrews, *Tales of the Convict System. Selected Stories of Price Warung* ("Price Warung" was William Astley, a prolific writer for the nationalist *Bulletin* in the 1890s).

relatively commonplace in the workplace in the eighteenth and nineteenth centuries, particularly against child and juvenile labourers. A detailed statistical examination of the incidence of corporal punishment in the colonies indicates that the lash was used relatively judiciously, with only one third of all convicts receiving more than one flogging during their period of servitude. The incidence of violence against convicts was probably no greater than that for members of the British army or navy, and certainly less than that for American slaves. Whilst the harshness and suffering of the convict system, and indeed of the working class generally in this time, is undeniable in modern terms, these qualifications suggest that convict workers were not particularly demoralized by the lash, and the relatively good diet and climate experienced in the colonies may even have compensated for transportation to some extent.[39]

All of these characteristics of the convict labour system indicate a more rational, efficient and systematic extraction and application of labour power than has been commonly acknowledged in the historical literature. Until recently, this literature has been more concerned with the social and cultural impact of convictism, than with an examination of its role as a system of labour in a new colony which was developing a capitalist economic infrastructure.

However, the system could not be sustained in the long term because of the contradictions in its aims. We have noted that after Governor Macquarie (1810–1821) the emphasis shifted from rehabilition of convicts, to offering a deterrent for criminality in Britain. The latter meant that the system should operate primarily as a harsh punishment sufficient to be a genuine deterrent. However, that also meant in practice that rehabilitation was simultaneously difficult to sustain. The two major forms of rehabilitation for convicts were their assignment as labourers to private employers, and their establishment as small landowners after gaining early emancipation. Both occurred under Macquarie. Land grants to convicts ceased after his governorship, but assignment actually expanded. That occurred because labour for landowners was scarce, and the British government was concerned with the cost of directly maintaining large numbers of convicts, particularly under the major public works program initiated by Macquarie.

Landowners required convict labour, notwithstanding some difficulties with incentive, because it was relatively cheap, and the flow of free immigrant labour was relatively slow until the goldrushes in the 1850s. The free immigrant labour which did arrive also tended to congregate in the cities, making rural labour even scarcer. This became more problematical as the wool industry grew rapidly from the 1830s. Squatters and other large landowners therefore sought to continue the supply of convict labour, but since they could never obtain enough, they also sought to increase the supply of free immigrant labour.

---

39. Nicholas and Shergold, "Unshackling the Past", p. 11.

However, if the colonies were to operate essentially as punitive penal establish-ments, free labourers would not be easily attracted because of the stigma attached to the convict system. With this understanding, the British government ceased the transportation of convicts to NSW in 1840, so as to encourage the flow of free immigrants. The Royal Commission on Transportation of 1837, which recommended this course of action was also influenced by the perceived failure of transportation as a deterrent to crime in Britain, and by the beginnings of anti-transportation agitation in NSW.

This issue was also linked with land policy. By financially assisting immigrants with their passages to Australia, the British government helped attract them, as well as provide opportunities for the removal of urban and rural unemployed from Britain. This was paid for out of land sales to free immigrants and emanci-pated convicts, with prices set high enough to prevent free immigrants from becoming small landowners too quickly, thus maintaining labour supply for larger landowners. Yet, a larger volume of land sales would fund more assisted immigrants. The government was already committed to an extension of assisted immigration for 1839-1840 when it ceased transportation of convicts to NSW in 1840. But, denied convict labour, the squatters were hampered in their operations and consequent ability to purchase Crown lands which they had occupied. This, together with the squatters' protests, led to a re-opening of the whole issue of transportation.[40]

By the 1840s an anti-transportation political movement grew out of these contradictions, based originally upon radical workers in Sydney and other colonial cities. Although transportation had already ceased in NSW, it continued in other colonies, from whence it was explicitly hoped by the imperial authorities that emancipated convicts would eventually make their way to NSW. The squatters and earlier large landholders consistently lobbied for the re-introduction of transportation because of the problem of attracting sufficient labour. In 1846 the British government instigated a review of the transportation issue by a Select Committee of the NSW Legislative Council, which was dominated by large landholding interests. Under the chairmanship of William Charles Wentworth, a large landholder, the Committee recommended that NSW could accommodate 5,000 convicts per year, provided that the same number of free immigrants came. Great public hostility was aroused by this proposal, particularly since it came during the large-scale depression and unemployment of the 1840s, but in 1850 the Colonial Secretary in Britain indicated that he was seriously considering the re-introduction of transportation. This occurred when the colony was moving towards responsible self-government, which was achieved in 1853. Workers

40. Fitzpatrick, *British Empire in Australia*, pp. 56-61; Hutson, *Penal Colony to Penal Powers*, pp. 22-23; Crowley, "Foundation Years, 1788-1821", pp. 38-40; Coghlan, *Labour and Industry*, pp. 178, 562; and Inglis, *Australian Colonists*, p. 10.

opposed transportation for a number of reasons. First, convicts represented a major threat to free workers in the labour market. Secondly, a high degree of political coherence emerged amongst ex-convicts and the colonial-born (who were predominantly born of convicts or ex-convicts), who were strongly opposed to the re-introduction of the tyrannies of convict labour. While they commonly regarded free immigrants as intruders, their attitudes to transportation coincided.

Finally, because of the coincidence of the threatened re-introduction of transportation with preparations for self- government, the issue became embroiled in a much wider debate concerning the nature of future colonial society. A re-introduction of transportation threatened the democratic basis of the new society to which workers and liberals were committed. Squatters and other large land-holders favoured a high property qualification for the vote in the constitutional negotiations of 1850-1853, as well as transportation. To the disquiet of others, squatters and large landholders were very influential in the NSW Legislative Council which was charged with drawing up a constitution for self-government for recommendation to the British government. From 1842 half of the Legislative Council was elected by propertyholders, the other half being nominated by the governor. Large landholders clearly preferred to maintain this political domination of the colonies. Some even dreamed of themselves as a colonial aristocracy entrenched in a colonial version of the House of Lords.

From 1850 the basis of the anti-transportation movement expanded. Urban business and professional people had been half-hearted in their support previously, because of trade interests with the squatters. Now, however, in the context of political constitution-making and planning for a future society, these groups began to express separate interests from the squatters, based upon attraction of capital to the colony and the development of a free workforce and an expanded market for locally-manufactured goods. They dominated the membership of the Anti-Transportation Association formed in Sydney in 1850, and collected 36,000 signatures for a petition against transportation. This represented almost 20 per cent of the total NSW population.

With the exception of Western Australia, similar rumblings occurred in the other colonies, which were also moving towards responsible self-government. In 1851 the Australasian League for the Abolition of Transportation was formed to co-ordinate these activities on an intercolonial basis. These events were influential in persuading Britain to finally end transportation to eastern Australia. Transportation of convicts to Western Australia began at this time because a high degree of consensus existed in that colony over the need for cheap labour; however, relatively small numbers were involved since the population as a whole was small.[41] The final argument against transportation in the eastern colonies

---

41. Inglis, *Australian Colonists*, pp. 11-12, 16, 46-8; Coghlan, *Labour and Industry*, pp. 553-64;

was the discovery of gold in 1851, and the ensuing gold rushes, which would have placed a convict labour system under enormous pressures. As one abolitionist remarked, "It would be a little too much even for Downing Street philosophy to transport a highwayman or a burglar to a gold mine!"[42]

Indentured Labour and "Kanakas"

The problems associated with attracting sufficient labour for rapid economic expansion in the Australian colonies persisted after the abolition of transportation. Indeed, labour scarcity was exacerbated by the gold rushes of the 1850s, notwithstanding the rapid influx of population to the colonies at that time. In this context, prices rose, even unskilled employees were able to demand large wage increases, and craft trade unions became firmly established.

The creation of democratic self government based upon a male franchise also released the potential for land reform which would "open up the land" to smallholders on a more extensive basis than previously. The dream of independence from wage labour in this way was one of the major attractions to free immigrants. From the beginning of responsible self-government unlocking the land for the creation of a yeomanry of small landholders was a popular political issue. From the early 1860s various legislative attempts were made by the colonies to create this class of small landholders. These efforts enjoyed rather limited success overall, although the colonies varied somewhat in this regard, and precisely because of the limitations of the early legislation, the issue remained politically important until at least the end of the century, and attracted a number of further attempts to extend smallholding. To the extent that some smallholders were settled by these means, this only contributed to the scarcity of labour.

This, in turn, continued to aid the development of a strong trade union movement, which extended beyond craft workers to embrace 20 per cent of the total workforce in the most populous and industrialized colonies of NSW and Victoria by 1890. One of the most prominent of the new unions of the 1880s was the rural-based Australian Workers' Union (originally the Amalgamated Shearers' Union). It succeeded in raising wages for shearers and rural labourers in the 1880s, and was bitterly opposed by the squatters when the opportunity came in the 1890s depression.[43] All of these trends meant that the large landholders' problems with labour scarcity persisted and offered advantages to the unions at the end of the century.

One means of overcoming the problem was the employment of indentured

---

Irving, "1850-70", pp. 133-135; and Hutson, *Penal Colony to Penal Powers*, pp. 22-23.

42. Quoted in Inglis, *Australian Colonists*, pp. 11-12.

43. Markey, *Making of the Labor Party*, pp. 136-170.

labour, particularly since free immigrants continued to gravitate towards the cities later in the nineteenth century. Some landowners had threatened to import Chinese and Indian "coolie" labourers as early as 1836 when cessation of transportation of convicts was first mooted.[44] This was a recurring theme amongst pastoralists and farmers, and some merchants, throughout the 1840s and 1850s, and even later. Pastoralists even formed a Coolie Association in 1837 to promote the importation of indentured labourers.[45]

Colonial governments were initially dubious of such schemes, on the grounds that they would pull down the level of European wages and destroy social homogeneity, both of which would also deter free British immigrants. A petition from over 4,100 persons, "principally of the working classes", endorsed these views, adding that indentured labour systems would degenerate into a form of slavery, and by reducing wages generally, limit the Australian market for British manufactured goods. The British Colonial Office sympathized with these arguments. It refused to pay immigration bounties to employers importing coolies. The British government also instituted a ban on emigration of Indian coolies in 1839 as a result of abuses in their conditions of transport and work in Mauritius and British Guinea, which had imported them to replace slaves. The ban was only lifted in stages between 1842 and 1844 if colonies were prepared to appoint an official Protector of immigrants to monitor conditions, and to pay for supervision in India of contracts and transport arrangements. Australian colonial governments were unwilling to undertake these arrangements.

Nevertheless, small groups of indentured labourers were imported to Australia over the next sixty years, principally by groups of pastoralists. Immediately before the ban over 300 Indians were brought into NSW by and for pastoralists. In 1847 a pastoralist/shipowner recruited about 200 Pacific Islanders under contracts to work in the NSW pastoral industry at about 5 per cent of the wages offered to European shepherds at the time. Allegations of kidnapping were not proved, and supporters of the scheme claimed that the Islanders were being Christianized and prevented from cannibalism and infanticide. However, the NSW government was sufficiently concerned about the spread of a "semi-barbarous or even savage race" that it removed the Islanders from the provisions of the Master and Servants' Act. This effectively ended the scheme because employers then lacked easy means for enforcement of contracts.

In the period 1848-1852 about 3,000 Chinese coolie labourers were also imported to work on pastoral stations and on wharves, under five year contracts, but for wages virtually equivalent to those paid to Europeans. Nevertheless, popular opposition to the scheme was sufficient to produce a Select Committee

44. Fitzpatrick, *British Empire in Australia*, pp. 58-59.
45. The following page is based upon Price, *Great White Walls*, pp. 38-48, 90-92; and McQueen, *New Britannia*, pp. 43-45.

of the NSW Legislative Assembly on Asiatic Labour in 1854. Its recommendations were inconsequential, but the Chinese coolie wave of immigration decreased dramatically as a result of riots in China and the closing of the British Emigration Agency in Amoy in 1854.

Finally, in 1852-1854 about 150 Eurasians, the offspring of British fathers stationed in India, were imported with British government assistance, as shepherds, domestics and tradesmen. However, they were not favoured as sufficiently energetic workers, and the government's financial assistance did not continue, despite the original humanitarian justification for it. The perceived unsuitability of Asian labour, especially in terms of strength, seems to have been a common drawback for the expansion of the indentured labour schemes referred to here, and a disincentive to the widespread recruitment of Aborigines under similar schemes.

Little is known about the eventual fates of these small groups of indentured labourers. Most of the Pacific Islanders returned home within a year. Five year contracts were common for the other groups, many of whose members also eventually returned to their homelands. Generally, however, their conditions of work did not attract official attention, although the main motivation for their importation was to overcome labour scarcity with a cheap labour supply.

There were periodic examples of a similar strategy in specific circumstances involving European labour. For example, coal owners regularly recruited labour in Britain during, or in anticipation of, miners' strikes or lock-outs, usually at lower wages than those prevailing in the high wage economies of the colonies. However, these and other employers who attempted to lock British workers into contracts of this kind commonly encountered difficulties in retaining their imported labourers once they discovered the colonial level of wages and other conditions. Because of continued labour scarcity until the 1890s depression, these immigrants could usually find better-paid work. In order to strengthen employers' legal position in this regard, the NSW government passed an Agreements Validating Act in 1876, specifically directed at contracts signed in Britain. This became a major target of the labour movement thereafter.[46] However, the issue of "Kanaka" labour in Queensland became a far more significant political issue in the late nineteenth century.

From the early 1860s, soon after Queensland gained independence from NSW, Queensland sugar growers began importing Melanesian labourers (known as "Kanakas"). Sugar growers and pastoralists argued that Queensland's needs were exceptional, because of the extreme labour shortage, the large amounts of labour required to develop the sugar industry, and thus attract capital, and the difficult

---

46. See Markey, *Making of the Labor Party*, p. 77; and Coghlan, *Labour and Industry*, 3, pp. 1283-1284.

tropical conditions. The desire for convict labour had been an incentive for seeking separation from NSW. When that proved unavailable, and when the requirements for importing Indian labourers became too complicated and expensive, the sugar growers turned to the Pacific Islands. Their efforts in seeking a ready source of indentured labour were aided by the fact that in the Queensland parliament of the 1860s and 1870s, landowning interests were dominant.[47]

Melanesians were recruited under indenture in their thousands by "black-birders" to service Queensland's sugar plantations in a style reminiscent of feudal serfdom. The plantations were large holdings, requiring a considerably larger workforce than the wool industry. Melanesians were employed because they were readily available nearby, considered docile, they could be paid low wages, and they supposedly had a greater capacity for hard work than did whites under severe, tropical conditions. Whether or not the work was suitable for whites, it is unlikely that the industry could have taken off without the importation of cheap labour, at least while it was organized into large holdings. As an earner of export income, the sugar industry became crucial to the Queensland economy.

However, the Melanesian labour system was subject to a range of abuses. It was commonly alleged by the opponents of the system that the Melanesians were recruited through trickery or force, and at the very least were unlikely to fully understand the conditions of written contracts. In many other respects also, the system of indentured labour was likened to slavery. An Act of 1868 regulated conditions of Melanesian workers for the first time. Nevertheless, abuses, and primitive living and working conditions generally, continued. As a result, the Melanesian death rate was three times that of whites in the 1890s, even though their average age was significantly lower.

As popular opposition to Melanesian labour grew, the government restricted recruitment in 1877 and 1880. In 1885 it legislated for the phasing out of recruitment altogether by 1890. But with the decline in sugar production during the 1890s depression, the government legislated again in 1892 to allow a more gradual ending to the traffic in Melanesians. The campaign against Melanesian labour assumed Intercolonial proportions thereafter, as a result of the movement towards the federation of the Australian colonies, finally achieved in 1901. The new Commonwealth of Australia quickly passed the Immigration Restriction Act, which effectively prevented further recruitment of Melanesians, and in 1906 legislation was enacted for the repatriation of Pacific Islanders.

47. On the nature of the Kanaka labour system, see, Corris, *Passage, Port and Plantation*; Saunders, *Workers in Bondage*; Graves, "The Nature and Origin", pp. 112-139; Shlomowitz, "Melanesian Labor", pp. 327-361, and Munro, "Historiography of the Queensland Labour Trade", this volume, pp. 479-497.

The Impact of Unfree Labour Systems

Both forms of unfree labour were phased out relatively quickly. Nevertheless, they both had a major long-term impact upon free labour. Even after the end of transportation of convicts to NSW in 1840, ex-convicts and their offspring accounted for a majority of the workforce and population for some years afterwards. It has been argued that, at an important formative period in class structure and the national psyche, this convict presence entrenched a general Australian working class disrespect for employers and authority figures, and the egalitarianism commonly depicted as a national trait. Although this may have been exaggerated, the labour movement, which became the principal historical bearer of an egalitarian nationalist ethos from the 1870s, often referred to the continuity from the convict taskmasters of the past to its contemporary opponents amongst employers and the state.[48] The convict system certainly bred traditions of harsh legal regulation of labour, and government intervention in economic relations, well after the colonies gained democratic government from the 1850s.

Opposition to the convict system produced the first mass political organization in the colonies, involving a populist coalition between urban artisans and workers, small business people and merchants. This type of political alliance was to be repeated in opposition to other forms of unfree labour which emerged later. In the meantime, the experience of convict labour produced an extreme wariness of any form of indentured, or "docile" labour on the part of free workers' industrial and political organizations. As late as 1890, when General Booth of the Salvation Army proposed a scheme of colonial emigration for British paupers, the labour movement reacted strongly against it.[49]

Unfree labour systems were opposed by the labour movement for three main reasons. First, they had the potential to subvert free labour conditions. At the very least they would relieve the labour scarcity upon which the Australian labour movement's achievements of high wages and shorter working hours were largely based. Secondly, the labour movement objected on humanitarian grounds to the abuses of indentured labour systems. Both of these motivations were evident in the intercolonial campaign against the "Kanaka" system in the 1890s. It was particularly objectionable on humanitarian grounds, and labour feared that with the impending federation of the colonies the system could spread throughout the nation.[50]

---

48. The title of Hutson's *From Penal Colony to Penal Powers* indicates the modern survival of this linkage.
49. Sydney Trades and Labour Council General Meeting Minutes, 28 November 1890, 8, 22 and 29 October, 12 November 1891; *Australian Workman* (journal of the Labour Council and Labor Party), 3 October 1891; and Markey, "Populist Politics", pp. 68-69.
50. See Markey, *Making of the Labor Party*, pp. 292-293; and *ibid.*, "Australia", pp. 583-584.

Opposition to the "Kanaka" system provided a strong unifying focus for the emergent national labour movement at the turn of the century. However, this opposition was expressed to a large degree in racial terms. It also occurred as the labour movement emerged as the major bearer of Australian nationalism, which became defined increasingly in racial terms. So important was the issue in racial terms that White Australia became the foremost policy of the Labor party as it was established in the 1890s. When this policy was effected in the 1901 Immigration Restriction Act, it was seen in terms of protecting white, unionized labour against "cheap" Asian competition.[51] These trends appear to confirm Brass's theoretical observations concerning the tendency of unfree labour systems to produce "a politically reactionary combination of nationalism and racism",[52] and to hinder the development of proletarian consciousness.

The Australian situation also appears to confirm the thesis of Nieboer (and Wakefield in the 1820s) that the ready availability of land provides a major motivation for unfree labour systems.[53] The reasoning is that, since most people prefer independence from wage labour, where there is an opportunity for this preference to be fulfilled, a labour scarcity will result. Once land is largely appropriated, as a "closed resource", the need for unfree labour systems is negated. These connections existed in the Australian colonies, but in two important respects they were asymptomatic. First, land was never as readily available to small settlers in the colonies as reformers had hoped it would be, because of practical difficulties associated with credit and suitability for particular crops. Secondly, when Melanesian labour was phased out in Queensland from the 1890s, it was as part of a process which broke down the large plantations and replaced them with smallholdings occupied by white farmers. Influential sections of the labour movement were actually committed to a policy of land reform to encourage small farmers.

Finally, the history of unfree labour in the Australian colonies demonstrates clearly that the existence of unfree labour systems cannot be explained in terms of a failure of the capitalist mode of production to triumph over pre-capitalist modes. The phasing out of unfree labour systems in Australia also owed far more to political organization against them, especially by the labour movement, than to any "natural" tendency of the capitalist mode of production to dispense with them.

51. Markey, *Making of the Labor Party*, ch. 10.
52. Brass, "Some Observations on Unfree Labour", this volume, pp. 72 f.
53. Quoted in *ibid*.

The Historiography of the Queensland Labour Trade

Doug Munro

Between 1863 and 1904, some 62,475 contracts of indenture were entered into by Pacific Islanders, overwhelmingly Melanesian and male, for service in Queensland involving a three year period of indenture at a minimum wage of £6 sterling per year (which in practice was usually the actual wage), plus housing, rations, minimal medical care, and the guarantee of a return passage. What started off as a system of circular labour migration, however, came to co-exist with migration of a more permanent nature as an increasing proportion of Melanesians either returned to Queensland (re-engaged workers) or stayed on (time-expired workers). No occupational restrictions were initially placed on Pacific Islander (or Kanaka) labourers to Queensland, but during the 1880s the Kanakas were progressively confined to unskilled field work in the sugar industry. By then the employment of Melanesians in Queensland was living on borrowed time, in the shadow of the White Australia Policy. In 1885 the Liberal government of S.W. Griffith legislated to phase out the introduction of Kanakas in favour of an all-white work force. Although Griffith rescinded the decision when it became evident that this would ruin the ailing sugar industry, the writing was on the wall; and when the Australian colonies federated at the turn of the century, the newly created Commonwealth of Australia government promptly decreed that recruiting would cease in 1904 and, further, that each and every Kanaka be deported by the end of 1906. Planters and Kanakas resisted the extreme application of this legislation to some effect, but over 4,000 Kanakas were compulsorily repatriated. The 2,500 or so who remained were then progressively pushed out the sugar industry by trade union pressure coupled with State and Commonwealth government bounties and other incentives for sugar growers to employ an all-white workforce, culminating in 1913 legislation that excluded all non-white labor from Queensland canefields. In other words, the remaining Kanakas, who had been channelled into the sugar industry during the 1880s by legislative decree were now forced out of their only means of livelihood by another set of rulings; they and their descendants henceforth became an underprivileged minority on the fringes of white Australia.

During the last two and a half decades, the Pacific-wide labour trade has become one of the most important research topics in Pacific Islands history, the Queensland segment most of all. At least 240 publications deal wholly or in part with the labour trade to Queensland. The present paper will focus on the twists and turns of this historiography, tracing the "revisionist" interventions of the late-1960s and early-1970s, the subsequent "counter-revisionist" critiques and the "neo-revisionist" counter thrust. In doing so it attempts to account for the development of a body of writing, showing where the debates lie, and commenting upon them. The intention is to show why the historiography of the Queensland labour trade has the characteristics that it does. Like all exercizes which involve discussion and criticism of colleagues' work, what follows is an avowedly personal view.[1]

Historiographic Background

Until the mid-1960s, the labour trade was largely the preserve of historians of empire. Such studies were concerned with the regulation of the British labour trade, especially the suppression of kidnapping, and how this entered official calculations;[2] and even when the actual plantation experience was considered, for example by O.W. Parnaby, the focus was on the administration of the system rather than on the working lives of the labourers.[3] There was also a heavy emphasis on the violence and fraud that characterised the early years of the recruiting and the almost inevitable side-effect of these studies, some of them thinly researched and inaccurate,[4] was to deprive Islanders of historical agency.

But revisionism was in the air. During the 1950s, a different sort of Pacific history was being developed under the direction of J.W. Davidson at the Australian National University, and thus often termed the "Canberra-school". Reflecting the historiographic currents of the immediate post-War age, Davidson and his colleagues sought above all to replace the role of imperial activity – and the Eurocentrism that this entailed – as the dominant organizing theme in Pacific Islands history and concentrated instead on the proactive role of Pacific Islanders in the shaping of events and their outcomes. In a phrase, Davidson exhorted that Pacific Islands history be studied in terms of culture contacts and "multi-cultural

1. The quantitative details in these two paragraphs have been drawn from Moore, "Labour, Indenture and Historiography", pp. 129-148. For the Pacific-wide context, see Newbury, "Melanesian Labor Reserve", pp. 1-25; Munro, "Pacific Islands Labour Trade", pp. 87-108.
2. E.g., Ward, *British Policy*; Morrell, *Britain in the Pacific Islands*, pp. 171-186; and David McIntyre, *Imperial Frontier*, pp. 240-246, 250-256.
3. Drost, "Forced Labor", pp. 129-143; Parnaby, *Britain and the Labor Trade*, ch. 7; and Bolton, *A Thousand Miles Away*, ch. 7.
4. E.g., Tate and Foy, "Slavery and Racism", pp. 1-21. There have, by contrast, been some thorough empirical articles by economic historians on the role of Kanakas in the Queensland sugar industry. Birch, "Organization and Economics of Pacific Islands' Labour", pp. 53-76; and Shlomowitz, "Melanesian Labor", pp. 327-361.

situations".[5] To this end he encouraged an interdisciplinary approach and he insisted on fieldwork and participant observation so to gain the understanding that derives from a measure of immersion in the culture under study, as well as to counteract the biases and blindspots of documentary records overwhelmingly of European provenance.[6] The new ways of the Canberra-school strengthened in 1966 with the appearance of the *Journal of Pacific History*. Produced within Davidson's own Department and with himself as one of the two editors, the *Journal* performed a comparable function to, say, the *Journal of African History* in providing a publication outlet, a symbol of identity, a means to increased respectability within academia, and a vehicle with which to influence the research agenda. Now in operation for almost thirty years, the *Journal of Pacific History* is standing testimony to the detailed empirical research and a corresponding disdain of theory which has characterised Canberra scholarship.[7]

The Revisionists

The first study of the labour trade to reflect the new ways of the Canberra-school was by Deryck Scarr, a student of Davidson's, in a survey article of seminal importance published in 1967; this in turn emerged from his larger study of the Western Pacific High Commission, which was created in 1877 to control the British labour trade.[8] It was pathbreaking in several respects, particularly in revising the received notions of recruiting as a kidnapping exercize. Instead, Scarr argued that kidnapping was limited to a brief initial period at each new recruiting ground and thereafter assumed a more voluntary guise between two roughly equal parties. He therefore opened the way to relating the labour trade to the Islanders' motivations for engaging for overseas service, seeing it largely as the consequences of pressures from within rather than coercion from without, and in particular he pointed up communities' and kinsgroups' needs for European goods acquired through the participation of young men in the cycle of

5. Davidson, "Problems of Pacific History", p. 21. The transition from imperial history to culture contact history in Pacific historiography bears resemblance to the contemporaneous change in focus in British labour history from institutional history "towards a more rounded *social* history of both labour and 'the people' at large", pioneered by Eric Hobsbawm and E.P. Thompson. See Rudé, *Debate on Europe*, pp. 189-199.
6. Davidson, "Understanding Pacific History", pp. 27-40; and Gunson, "An Introduction", pp. 4-6.
7. It is equally clear that Canberra no longer "owns" Pacific Islands history in the sense that it once did. There are now several epicenters, other specialist journals, and no one dominant approach. See Howe, "Future of Pacific Islands History", pp. 225-231; Hempenstall, "Line of Descent", pp. 157-170.
8. Scarr, "Recruits and Recruiters", pp. 5-25; Scarr, *Fragments of Empire*.

labour migration. Scarr also related the actual recruiting techniques to the fragmented nature of the indigenous political and social structures, and in this respect he highlighted the role of indigenous middlemen (known as passage masters). In sum, Scarr portrayed the labour trade as being less European-dominated and oppressive than had previously been allowed, and he drew the image of a "business", however unruly, hazardous and unprincipled, where tough men on both sides knew the score and drove bargains accordingly.

While Scarr's conclusions reflect the preoccupations of the Canberra-school with its concern for Islander agency, they emerged more directly from his sources. He was the first researcher to use the journals of the Government Agents, whose presence on board Queensland and Fiji labour vessels was required under the terms of the 1872 Pacific Islanders' Protection Act and whose work placed them on an everyday basis at the "coal-face" of the recruiting process. The missionary who pointed out in 1872 that "[t]he real working of the system of recruiting is only to be learnt in the islands where it is carried on"[9] had a point that later historians were slow to heed. Instead of being viewed as a question of legal exegesis or as a narrow moral issue, or as a process where historical agency lay firmly on the European side, the Government Agents' journals enable labour recruiting to be seen in "something approaching its true character".[10]

The demarcation line between the old-style imperial historiography and the new "island-centred" Pacific historiography is represented by the work of Scarr's PhD student, Peter Corris. Based on a combination of documentary research and a cross-disciplinary perspective that included nine months' fieldwork, and interviews with 18 survivors of the labour trade and the descendants of others, Corris's monograph set a standard in approach and methodology that became the yardstick by which subsequent studies on the subject would be judged.[11]

Corris dealt with the recruitment and employment of Solomon Islanders in Queensland and Fiji and the effects of returned labourers on their home communities. He confirmed Scarr's conclusion that recruiting went through stages from outright kidnapping to more settled procedures. His particular empirical advance was to provide detailed information of the Solomon Islanders plantation experience in Queensland (his sections on Fiji are exceedingly thin), with occasional genuflections on New Caledonia and Samoa. It was the first real attempt at applying "history from below" to the Pacific labour trade. Instead of organizing his narrative around the political context of the Islanders' employment or the regulative mechanisms bearing on their working lives, Corris concentrated on the Islanders' actual experiences and attempted to view the labour trade from their standpoint. In addition to oral testimony, he used an

9. Quoted in Morrell, *Britain in the Pacific Islands*, p. 180.
10. Giles, *A Cruise in a Queensland Labour Vessel*, p. 13; Scarr, *Fragments of Empire*, p. 139.
11. Corris, *Passage, Port and Plantation*.

extraordinary array of documentary sources that would characterize much subsequent research into the Queensland segment of the labour trade: Government Agents' journals, administrative reports of inspectors and other government records, naval reports, registers of immigrants, newspapers, individual planters' papers, reports of Royal Commissions and travellers' tales. The only sizeable lacunae in the written sources is the dearth of plantation records; there is little apart from the business archives of the Colonial Sugar Refinery Company.[12]

If Corris's work represents the great leap forward in labour trade studies, it was not without problems that are more evident in retrospect than at the time. *Passage, Port and Plantation* exemplified both the strengths and the weaknesses of the new Pacific historiography: detailed research and sharpness of focus was accompanied by a narrowness of concerns and an over-particularizing empiricism. The spotlight was on the Islander at the expense of wider contexts. In addition, the book reflected a certain imbalance in Pacific historiography which might be termed the success-story syndrome – something which has since been moderated. At the time that Corris was researching and writing, the Canberra-school precept that Islanders were active agents and substantially the arbiters of cross-cultural encounters had hardened into something of an orthodoxy. The very choice of topics encouraged such a tendency. That is to say, if Pacific Islanders were to be accorded the historical agency denied them by the imperial historians of old, it was necessary to concentrate on themes and episodes when Islanders indeed held the upper hand, to the corresponding neglect of encounters to the contrary. Thus Dorothy Shineberg's classic account of the sandalwood trade in Melanesia concludes in the 1860s, precisely when the balance of power was shifting from the Melanesian to the European – a point which she conceded; while Davidson's history of Samoa ends triumphantly in 1962 when Western Samoa finally gained political independence and joined the family of nations.[13]

The success-story syndrome was particularly evident in labour trade studies. During the 1970s a number of writers showed an over-eager acceptance of Scarr and Corris's revisionary interpretations that went well beyond their carefully qualified arguments. For example, what Scarr depicted as a dangerous and disreputable "business" that "throve on cajolery, the dissemination of dissent in island communities, and petty deceit, backed up occasionally by force" is transformed by one writer into "a business conducted on orderly lines, with the principles of the market-place determining whether or not the [...] Islanders signed on".[14] Corris himself contributed to the success-story syndrome simply

---

12. Housed in the Archives of Business and Labour, Research School of Social Sciences, Australian National University. See Lowndes, *South Pacific Enterprise.*
13. Shineberg, *They Came for Sandalwood*, p. 216; Davidson, *Samoa mo Samoa.*
14. Scarr, *Fragments of Empire*, p. 39; Bennett, Review, pp. 234-235. See also Howe, "Tourists, Sailors and Labourers", pp. 22-35; Jackson, "Melanesia, Queensland, Fiji", pp. 61-64;

by dealing with the more-favoured Solomon Islanders, the majority of whom came to Queensland when conditions were at their (relative) best, rather than the less fortunate New Hebrideans, who came in far larger numbers in the earlier years when protective legislation was largely lacking and who therefore had to bear the brunt of recruiting abuses and poor material conditions of employment.[15] With respect to plantation employment, Corris never went so far to say that the Melanesians exercized a large measure of control over their working lives. Like Scarr, however, he drew a deductive link between plantation conditions and voluntary recruiting that has elements of a self-fulfilling prophesy. Their argument is that systematic recruiting over several decades could only have been sustained if conditions on the plantations were at least acceptable to the majority of repatriated workers. By giving the labour trade a clean bill of health, so to speak, the returnees encouraged others to enlist and thus perpetuated the cycle of overseas return labour migration to distant plantations.[16]

Counter-Revisionists

It was a view that was not endorsed by the next two academic researchers, Kay Saunders and Adrian Graves. Neither were products of, nor overly influenced by, the Canberra-school. Graves, to the contrary, was highly critical of the "revisionists", as he styled them. Taking Saunders first, she widened the scope of the inquiry in her various writings by adopting a far broader framework: she viewed the development of the sugar industry in the context of an overall agricultural system, including pastoralism,[17] and linked the use of non-white immigrant labourers (Asians as well as Pacific Islanders) to the demise of the convict system and the drying up of unfree labour from that source; she also contributed to race relations theory by applying the findings of John Rex to the situation in colonial Queensland.[18] In addition, Saunders was concerned to explain the plantation as an institution: the essence of her PhD thesis is the plantation system in Queensland in relation to other plantation systems, and she made a not-overly-successful attempt to compare colonial Queensland with the antebellum United States.[19] However, the various strengths of her work, which

Meleisea, "Last Days", pp. 126-132.

15. See Corris, *Passage, Port and Plantation*, pp. 43, 97. A little-known book in the German language has since been written about New Hebridean (ni-Vanuatu) plantation workers in Queensland and Fiji, but it lacks the sophistication of Corris and has made little impact. Gundert-Hock, *Mission und Wanderarbeit*.
16. See also Gilding, "Massacre of the Mystery", pp. 72-74.
17. See especially Saunders, "Workers' Paradox", pp. 213-259.
18. Saunders, "'Black Scourge'", pp. 147-234.
19. Saunders, "Uncertain Bondage". In the revisions for publication, the comparative material

are underpinned by massive documentary research, are offset to an extent by a lack of supporting fieldwork either in Queensland, where she was based, or in Melanesia.

Central to Saunders', and to a lesser extent Graves', argument is that harsh and oppressive conditions prevailed and that physical coercion of labourers was crucial to the successful operation of sugar plantations. Although Saunders concurred with the Canberra-school's voluntarist depiction of the recruiting process, she then goes on to present an uncomplicated image of almost unrelieved harshness where "violence and coercion were central elements in the operation of the plantation and the pastoral station".[20] It is difficult to know how Saunders arrived at such a conclusion in view of Corris's emphasis on the variability of both plantation conditions and individual worker experience, as does the literature on slavery in the antebellum South, which Saunders consulted.[21] Her interpretation becomes confused because the very next chapter of *Workers in Bondage* is about the "perseverance and ability to adapt to an alien culture [which] was in itself remarkable". To further complicate matters, the following chapter of the same book, concerning strategies of worker resistance, moves yet further from the image of thoroughgoing oppression with the conclusion that the Kanakas displayed "consummate skill" in asserting themselves and resisting "those concerted attempts to render them passive, tractable and fawning lackeys". Her final chapter, moreover, strikes another blow on behalf of a proactive Melanesian workforce with sections on the extent to which Kanakas "were able to organize into effective if informal organizations which could use the tactics of negotiation and effective bargaining", and their ability to force up their wages.[22] In other words, Saunders has "created a contradiction by arguing that successful resistance occurred within a successfully coercive regime".[23] The slides in interpretation and the irreconcilable conclusions point to a methodological problem, namely that Saunders asked what have been termed "yes-type" questions. She asked if workers were oppressed and the sources said "Yes". They also replied in the affirmative when asked if workers resisted the plantation regime – as well they might "because owing to the richness and complexity of the historical record [...] the sources will rarely reply 'No'".[24]

Neither did Adrian Graves engage in fieldwork for his 1979 Oxford doctoral thesis on the political economy of the Queensland sugar industry, and in many other respects his work has similarities with Saunders' in his rebuttal of the

   was omitted. Saunders, *Workers in Bondage*.
20.   Saunders, *Workers in Bondage*, ch. 4 (quotation, p. 76).
21.   Corris, "Pacific Island Labour Migrants", pp. 43-45; Corris, *Passage, Port and Plantation*, p. 97.
22.   Saunders, *Workers in Bondage*, chs 5-7 (quotations, pp. 121, 140, 160).
23.   Moore, "Counterculture of Survival", p. 69.
24.   Kraditor, "American Radical Historians", p. 137.

revisionist interpretations of Scarr and Corris. As befitting the first overtly Marxist interpretation of the labour trade, Graves stresses the use of the coercive apparatus of the state to control and discipline the Melanesian work force, and to maximize their productive capacity, especially after the precipitous fall in world sugar prices in 1883-84. Coming from a quite different intellectual tradition, and influenced by the literature on Southern Africa, Graves took issue directly and contentiously with his predecessors in a singlehanded crusade to discredit the revisionists.

In an early publication concerning the abolition of the Queensland labour trade, Graves questioned the established interpretation and put the view that instead of being an expression of the White Australia Policy, the decision was based on purely economic grounds.[25] To the contrary, there were strong economic incentives to maintain the *status quo* and planters fought to keep their Kanakas. The alternative was an expensive and intransigent white labour force whose employment had to be subsidised by Commonwealth and State government bounties.[26] In dramatic fashion, and in the part of his dissertation that has greatest claim to originality, Graves launched into an explicit assault on the "voluntarist" interpretation of labour recruiting espoused by the Canberra-school and endorsed by Saunders.[27] Instead, he put the view that the incursions of capitalist penetration eroded subsistence agriculture, resulting in a proletarianised people who had nothing but their labour to sell to overseas planters.[28] However, recruiting was slight in areas which experienced capitalist penetration. The communities concerned, because they had European traders in their midst, had access to the desired European goods and therefore engaged in cash-cropping in preference to recruiting.[29] Graves' proposition can thus be turned on its head because nineteenth century capitalist incursions had the effect of *preventing* overseas labour migration.

Overall, Graves' tendency to impose African models on Pacific reality and a shaky basis in empirical research detract from his attempts to revise the revisionists. Nor did his recent monograph on the political economy of the Queensland sugar industry, based on his 1979 doctoral thesis, further that cause. Whereas the revisions were completed by the early 1980s, a series of misadventures delayed its publication until 1993, resulting in a work that had been long superseded by the advances of the "neo-revisionists".[30]

25. Graves, "Abolition of the Queensland Labour Trade", pp. 41-57.
26. Hunt, "Exclusivism and Unionism", pp. 80-95.
27. Graves, "Pacific Island Labour", pp. 112-139, 251-258.
28. This view has been uncritically endorsed by Miles, *Capitalism and Unfree Labour*, p. 114.
29. Scarr, *Fragments of Empire*, pp. 141-142; Corris, *Passage, Port and Plantation*, pp. 29-31 and ch. 6; and Moore, *Kanaka*, pp. 48, 52-55.
30. Graves, *Cane and Labour*. For a different assessment and a critique of my own work, see Brass, "Contextualizing Sugar Production", pp. 100-117; and for my response, see Munro,

Neo-Revisionists

Despite the diversity of intellectual origins, approaches and methodologies, and the sheer volume and variety of their sources, no historians of the Queensland labour trade had applied rigorous quantification to their research. Up to the late 1970s the only statistical exercizes involved tabulating the origins of Pacific Islanders to Queensland, the numbers employed in the colony, a limited run of mortality rates, and the extent of repatriation.[31] This is not the same thing as quantitative analysis, and the Queensland labour trade appeared set to be left untouched in the wake of the Cliometric revolution, spearheaded by Robert William Fogel, that was transforming labour studies in other parts of the world.

In the mid 1970s, however, Ralph Shlomowitz from the Chicago School of Economics, and a student of Fogel, took up a university appointment in Australia and applied his knowledge of labour systems in the postbellum United States to the Queensland labour trade. An outsider's perspective from the vantage point of another discipline can sometimes be revealing, and it was readily apparent to Shlomowitz that the historiography was lacking a systematic study of the operation of the labour market. Of prime importance in this regard was his study of a particular category of Melanesian labourers, the time-expired workers – namely the Melanesians who decided to remain in Queensland upon the expiry of their contracts. Comprizing between one-third and two-thirds of the total Melanesian labour force, and progressively increasing both in numbers and as a proportion of the total Melanesian workforce, the time-expired worker was hardly an unknown figure.[32] But the special niche that he occupied within the labour market was not appreciated and Shlomowitz was the first to recognize this. First, he drew attention to their role in market arbitrage, particularly their ability to bargain for high wages (up to £30 per year) and to express their preferences in other ways, such as working predominantly on small farms rather than on the plantations, and on shorter-term contracts, thus leading to a high incidence of job turnover. For their part, the small farm operators preferred the time-expireds to first-indentured labourers because the former were experienced, required no training, and if more difficult to discipline they were less prone to sickness and death. The time-expireds preference for shorter term contracts also worked to the advantage of the small farm operators because it allowed them to hire Melanesian workers during the crushing seasons and to dispense with their services during the slack months of the year. With a neo-

---

"Revisionism and its Enemies".

31. Parnaby, *Britain and the Labor Trade*, pp. 201-206; Corris, *Passage, Port and Plantation*, pp. 149-150; and Baker, "Origins of Pacific Island Labourers", pp. 106-121.

32. See Corris, "Pacific Island Labour Migrants in Queensland", pp. 54-55; Corris, *Passage, Port and Plantation*, pp. 85-88; and Wyberg Docker, *Blackbirders*, pp. 242-243.

classical flourish, Shlomowitz concluded that the time-expired worker was "not generally exploited" but rather had "the opportunity to express preferences [...] in the marketplace" and thus had "the means to determine much of how he worked and lived in Queensland".[33]

Shlomowitz has also contributed to the demographic aspects of the Pacific Islands labour trade, including Queensland. The question of high worker mortality has never been far beneath the surface of inquiry and the reasons have been largely attributed to harsh and insanitary conditions of plantation life and labour. Historians of the slave trade will probably marvel at the insularity of Pacific labour trade historiography and wonder how scholars in the field could have been oblivious to the relevant works of Alfred Crosby, William McNeill, and more particularly Philip Curtin, who argue that epidemiology provides the answer.[34] In other words, new arrivals from benign disease environments are at risk from a range of unfamiliar infections and viruses against which their immune systems have little or no acquired resistance. In consequence there is a high death rate among imported labourers in the first year, and especially in the first six months, tapering off as the workers gradually become acclimatised to the new range of diseases to which they had been exposed. Shlomowitz's findings support the epidemiological explanation of worker mortality, with variations between different migrant groups largely dependent on the disease environment of their place of origins. Hence, Indian workers in Fiji died from the same diseases as imported Pacific Islanders but their mortality rate was far lower.[35]

Shlomowitz's conclusions on worker mortality have been disputed by Adrian Graves who argues that epidemiological factors take a poor second to treatment in explanatory value.[36] Otherwise, there has been qualification in the context of substantial acceptance. Clive Moore (whose work will be discussed shortly) takes the view that treatment and conditions played a greater role than Shlomowitz allows, and points out that the many deaths by sorcery would have been wrongly attributed; while Doug Munro argues that preventative measures would have had a cushioning effect, a view to which Shlomowitz is more sympathetic

---

33. Shlomowitz first drew attention to the time-expired workers in "Search for Institutional Equilibrium", pp. 102 (Table 1), 107-108. His major statements are "Markets for Indentured and Time-expired Melanesian Labour", pp. 70-91 (quotation, p. 91), and "Time-expired Melanesian Labour", pp. 25-44.

34. Curtin, "Epidemiology and the Slave Trade", pp. 190-216; Crosby Jr, *Columbian Exchange*, ch. 2; and McNeill, *Plagues and People*. An early application of Curtain's work to United States slavery is Wood, *Black Majority*, ch. 3 ("The Sovereign Ray of Health"). The only Australian historian of the Pacific Islands labour trade to have been aware of the epidemiological explanation of mortality was Clive Moore, precisely because he was not trained at Canberra. Moore's attention was drawn to Curtin by his thesis supervisor, who knew about Curtin's work through teaching United States history. Moore, "Kanaka Maratta", pp. 541-542.

35. Shlomowitz, "Differential Mortality", pp. 120-121.

36. Graves, *Cane and Labour*, pp. 81-83.

than previously.[37] A further line of research would be to investigate whether the psychological stresses frequently experienced by newly arrived labourers increased their vulnerability to disease.

Shlomowitz's findings, moreover, suggest that considerable revision of some of Corris's conclusions is in order. Corris was aware of the existence of time-expired workers, noting that they progressively increased as a proportion of the total Melanesian work force. Likewise he noted that mortality rates were higher on the plantations and he explicitly attributed this to conditions being better on the small farms.[38] The lower mortality rates on the farms, however, can be more appropriately attributed to the fact that they were preferred by the time-expired labourers, who had built up an immunity to infectious disease and therefore were less likely to die than the first-indentured labourers. Accordingly, the average annual mortality rate dropped dramatically and in roughly inverse proportion to re-engaged and time-expired labourers as a proportion of the total Melanesian workforce – from 82 per 1,000 in 1879-1887 reducing to 35 per 1,000 in the period 1893-1906.[39]

The other writer in the neo-revisionist category is Clive Moore, a product of the James Cook University of North Queensland, who acknowledges the extent to which his work benefits from the solid quantitative base provided by Shlomowitz. The History Department of this small regional university, until recently under the leadership of Brian Dalton, has a prodigious research output on north Queensland history to its name. Typical of James Cook history graduates of the 1970s and 1980s – and the Canberra-school for that matter – Moore has no rigorous theoretical background. Nor did he start off as a Pacific historian but as a Southeast Asianist. He regards his early training in Indonesian history, schooled in the texts of Clifford Geertz and Benedict Anderson, as a more than useful preparation for ethnohistorical research in Melanesia. This may explain a salient feature of his approach, namely that he attempts to explain and interpret from a Melanesian viewpoint rather than as an outsider looking in.[40] His particular grounding in Southeast Asian history certainly predisposed him to the tenets of the Canberra-school and its stress on Islander agency, which he has taken further than any other historian of the labour trade.

---

37. Moore, *Kanaka*, pp. 244-273; Munro, "Gilbert and Ellice Islanders", pp. 456-458; and Shlomowitz, "Workers and Mortality", p. 126.
38. Corris, *Passage, Port and Plantation*, pp. 74-79.
39. Shlomowitz, "Mortality and the Pacific Labour Trade", p. 53, and "Epidemiology and the Pacific Labor Trade", p. 597.
40. Moore, "Labour, Indenture and Historiography", p. 130; personal communication, 11 May 1991.

Moore's major work, entitled *Kanaka*,[41] differs from that of his predecessors in several respects. First, there is the sharpness of focus and wealth of detail, reminiscent of Geertz's "thick description". Instead of being another colony-wide study, *Kanaka* is concerned with the major sugar producing district of Mackay, where Moore grew up; and rather than taking a Melanesia-wide perspective of recruiting, he concentrates on Malaita, the island which produced by far the largest number of workers. In addition to detailed documentary research, Moore engaged in more extended fieldwork than any other historian, collecting detailed oral testimony ("the most valuable source of all") from descendants of Kanakas in both Malaita and in north Queensland; the latter was obtained with his colleague Patricia Mercer, as part of James Cook University's Black Oral History Project. Moore's work thus invites comparison with historians of plantation life in the antebellum South who have utilised slave narratives and who, too, stress the cultural autonomy of the workers.[42] The slave narratives are crucial, enabling the historians using them to get closer than others to the inner world of the worker.

Far from being an adjunct to the documentary evidence, Moore's oral sources enable him to delve more deeply than previous studies into the Kanakas' private lives – into that hidden world of leadership, magic and religion, housing, diet and health, about which contemporary Europeans knew little or nothing – and to provide correctives to Eurocentric interpretations that emerge from the largely uncomprehending documentary record. Concerning plantation housing, the oral testimony "shows an almost opposite perception to that gained from European documentary sources", and in an early publication he and Mercer demonstrated that Corris had seriously underestimated the incidence of magic.[43] The overall thrust of Moore's argument is that, within the constraints of the framework of the plantation, Kanakas accommodated to life in Queensland largely on their own terms.[44] In adopting an approach firmly grounded in sources close to the firsthand experience of the Kanaka, Moore has gone well beyond his predecessors in addressing the three basic meanings of "treatment" that were identified by Eugene Genovese – namely, the measurable "day-to-day

---

41. Moore, *Kanaka*. The most extensive review of this book is by Leckie, "Melanesian Workers", pp. 62–70.
42. E.g., Blassingame, *Slave Community*; and Rawick, *From Sunup to Sundown*.
43. Moore, *Kanaka*, p. 213; Mercer and Moore, "Melanesians in North Queensland", pp. 66–88. Moore's use of oral sources is discussed explicitly in "Counterculture of Survival", pp. 69–99.
44. One is reminded here of the view that the labour aristocracy in Britain consciously articulated cultural identity: "In so far as the 'aristocrat of labour' did accept certain values held by dominant groups in his society he interpreted and re-formulated them in terms of his own situation, and mediated and diffused them through his own institutions". Grey, "Styles of Life", p. 452.

living conditions", the qualitative "conditions of life", and lastly "access to freedom and citizenship".[45]

The cost in terms of time and commitment of such richly textured research is considerable. Whereas Parnaby, Corris, Saunders and Graves spent three or more years on their PhD dissertations and subsequent revisions, Moore's research represents a full decade's research.[46] The one drawback of his reliance on oral sources is that this data is weighted on the 1890s and early-1900s when plantation conditions had considerably improved. Thus Moore, like Corris and Shlomowitz, tends to present a rather-too-mellow view of the labour trade that derives from the later years and which permits an emphasis on Melanesian agency. Parnaby, Saunders and Graves, by contrast, concentrate on the harsher 1870s and 1880s and accordingly emphasize the structural constraints that affected the Melanesians' working lives. No study has yet managed to bridge this almost binary divide in the historiography.

Issues and Debates

With his emphasis on Melanesian agency, Moore has formulated a sophisticated response to the prevailing kidnapping/whips-and-chains interpretation of the Queensland labour trade that is evident in the writings of the counter-revisionists[47] and in popular accounts, newspaper articles, semi-academic works, school textbooks, films, and even among the descendants of Kanakas in Queensland.[48] Informants on Malaita, by contrast, asserted that their forbearers largely enlisted on a voluntary basis. The insistence by Queensland Kanakas that their

---

45. Genovese, *In Red and Black*, p. 159.
46. Queensland labour trade studies are a good test of the assertion that what individual historians produce is less a matter of the intrinsic requirements of the subject and has more to do with professional opportunities and personal circumstances. Corris provides an example. At a review seminar at the Australian National University, 28 November 1973, which I attended, Corris explained that his original intention, when revizing his thesis for publication, was to incorporate later events and make a much larger book, but he found he neither had the temperament nor the physique (he is diabetic) for the required fieldwork. Moreover, he felt impelled to publish promptly because many of the conclusions from his dissertation were in wider circulation and this would inevitably reduce the impact of the eventual monograph.
47. It will be recalled, however, that Saunders agrees with Corris and Scarr that kidnapping was a transitory phase. See *Workers in Bondage*, ch. 2.
48. The exception is Johnston, *Call of the Land*, pp. 57-64. But see Holthouse, *Cannibal Cargoes*; Docker, *Blackbirders*; Peach, *Peach's Australia*; Bandler, *Wacvie*; Fitzgerald, *History of Queensland*, pp. 180-188, 212-213, 236-256; Toghill, *Ghost Ports of Australia*, pp. 162-166; Matthews, *This Dawning Land*, ch. 6; Horner, "From Slaves to Citizens", pp. 4-10; Goldsmid, *Deadly Legacy*, figure 5.4; Blaikie, "Fine Old Art", p. 21; Camm, "Pacific Islanders", pp. 152-153; and Whittaker, "Old Herby", p. 3. For other references see Moore, *Kanaka*, pp. 337-340.

forbearers were kidnapped still finds an echo in the various attempts to gain retrospective recompense for the plight of Kanakas as a disadvantaged majority on the fringes of White Australia.[49] The irony of the situation is that the case for redress and compensation lies not in the years of the labour trade but in the eight subsequent decades when they were forced out of the sugar industry, their only means to livelihood, by discriminatory legislation to become "a forgotten people, used and discarded by capitalism".[50] Their descendants have since become a minority within a minority in the sense that they have the same underprivileged socio-economic status as Australia Aboriginals and Torres Strait Islanders, yet do not qualify for affirmative action programs in education and housing because of their immigrant as opposed to indigenous status.[51]

There is a parallel between the (neo)revisionist interpretation of the Queensland labour trade and the works of neo-abolitionist scholars of Southern slavery – notably Herbert Aptheker and Kenneth Stampp – during the 1940s and 1950s.[52] More than once it has been remarked that the terms of the latter debate were governed by explicitly moral overtones stemming from the proslavery/antislavery debates of the previous century. Aptheker and Stampp were, in effect, "coerced" by a century old debate; and while they may have won the argument, the terms of the discussion were still being dictated by the ghost of Ulrich Bonnell Phillips (1877-1934), the great Southern apologist of slavery.[53] In similar fashion, the (neo)revisionists of the Queensland labour trade were coerced by the weight of received wisdom – both popular and academic – into presenting a sharp contrast to the prevailing kidnapping/whips-and-chains interpretation. Moore's frequent insistence that indenture cannot be equated with slavery, for example, is an explicit reaction to the oft-expressed view that the Queensland labour trade was Australia's version of slavery.[54]

At the same time, there are significant differences of degree among the various (neo)revisionists. Corris and Moore engaged in fieldwork and gathered oral testimony; Scarr and Shlomowitz did not. Moore and particularly Shlomowitz have been more concerned with quantification than Scarr and Corris. Shlomowitz's work is praised for its empirical strength but his neo-classical leanings and

49. E.g., Evatt Foundation, *Australian South Sea Islanders*.
50. Moore, *Kanaka*, p. 343.
51. Menzies, *Profile of Neglect*; Human Rights and Equal Opportunity Commission, *Call for Recognition*; Murphy, "Slaves to Outcastes", pp. 34-36; "Report Wants Fair Go For Islanders", *Daily Mercury* (Mackay), 23 July 1993, p. 8; Moore and Mercer, "Forgotten Immigrants", pp. 337-340.
52. Aptheker, *American Negro Slave Revolts*; and Stampp, *The Peculiar Institution*.
53. Elkins, *Slavery*, p. 21; Weinstein and Gatell, *American Negro Slavery*, pp. 1-2; Parish, *Slavery: History and Historians*, p. 170.
54. Moore, "Kanakas, Kidnapping and Slavery", pp. 78-92, *Kanaka*, pp. 153-155, 197-199, and "Labour, Indenture and Historiography in the Pacific", pp. 133-134.

depersonalised depiction are atypical. Nevertheless, each has built on the insights of his predecessors, as might be expected. Surprisingly, however, there has been little dialogue between the (neo)revisionists and counter-revisionists despite the potential for fruitful debate. Whilst criticisms have been expressed from time to time – for example Graves' blanket condemnation of the revisionists, Ross Johnston's doubts about the allegedly business-like nature of labour recruiting,[55] and Moore's rebuttal of aspects of Saunders' depiction of plantation life – there has been no debate in the sense of an ongoing two-way engagement. Again the contrast with the historiography of Southern slavery is striking.[56]

It eventually took Shlomowitz, in the early 1990s, to spark a debate in rather unexpected circumstances. It was, moreover, a debate between an economist who was never really in the mainstream of the Canberra-school, and a complete outsider. The essential insularity of Pacific historians could not have been more graphically underlined.[57] The debate, moreover, was between a Chicago economist and a Marxist, meaning that while there could never be any meeting of minds, the underlying assumptions were at last being sharply delineated and explicitly debated. The catalyst was Shlomowitz's critique, in an English journal seldom read by Pacific historians, of an article by Tom Brass, who put the case that the Latin American *enganche* was a system of debt bondage and a coercive mechanism of worker control.[58] The argument spilt over into the Queensland labour trade, and focussed on the utility of the neo-classical approach in analysing unfree labour arrangements. Brass made two basic criticisms with regard to Kanaka labour.[59] First, the occupational restrictions of the 1880s which confined Kanakas to unskilled field labour within the sugar industry negates Shlomowitz's "essentialist belief in the operation of the free market". Brass has to be allowed his point here. Second, Brass attacks Shlomowitz's benign view of the Kanaka's working lives, characterizing this as "the impermissibility of unfree labour", but this argument is less firmly based. Even conceding that Shlomowitz is not overly concerned with the coercive aspects of indentured

55. Johnston, "Captain Hamilton", pp. 58-59. Johnston makes the point that the image of a "business" involves the risk of "imposing too much the rule of reason" on the recruiting process at a time when "[l]egal authority still occupied only a very tenuous place".

56. Clark *et al*, *William Styron's Nat Turner*; Robinson *et al*, *Black Studies in the University*; Lane, *Slavery and Personality*; Butlin, *Ante-Bellum Slavery*; Gutman, *Slavery and the Numbers Game*; David *et al*, *Reckoning with Slavery*; and Gilmore, *Revisiting Blassingame's The Slave Community*.

57. By contrast, much of the literature on U.S. slavery is explicitly comparative. See Kolchin, "Comparing American History", pp. 64-81; and Frederickson, "Planters, Junkers and Pomeschiki", pp. 379-386.

58. Brass, "Latin American *Enganche* System", pp. 73-103.

59. Brass also characterises the employment of European canefield workers in butty gangs as an unfree labour relation because a portion of their wages were deferred, whereas Shlomowitz regards the butty system as an incentive scheme that benefitted employer and employee alike. Shlomowitz, "Team Work and Incentives", pp. 41-55.

service, Queensland was the least oppressive place of employment – at least by the 1890s – for indentured Pacific Islanders.[60] (Some labour trade historians, however, in attempting to show that other areas were deficient in legislative protection and worker conditions by comparison with Queensland, have drawn the distinction too sharply.)[61] At another level, the debate is significant because it draws attention to the need to more precisely conceptualize what is meant by an unfree labour relation and what constitutes exploitation. Disturbingly, each author uses secondary sources in a selective manner. Shlomowitz presses Scarr, Corris and Moore into service whilst Brass invokes Graves and Saunders.[62] The binary character of the literature is seemingly entrenched.

More recently the Scottish economist, T. David Williams, a newcomer to the field, has critiqued Shlomowitz's economic analyses, and in particular his notion that a "well working labour market" was in operation. First, says Williams, Shlomowitz's conclusions depend more on his "often implicit" assumptions than his evidence – and, moreover, his conclusion in support of a well working labour market are often negated by the evidence he presents.[63] It is altogether healthy that different viewpoints are being seriously debated rather than the other side's position being summarily dismissed, as once tended to happen. It is, moreover, fitting that Ralph Shlomowitz, who has always encouraged discussion and debate, is occupying centre stage in this dialogue.

Conclusions

As a field of historical inquiry, the labour trade in Melanesians to Queensland is marked by two dominant approaches in a manner resembling the optimist/pessimist debates surrounding the British Industrial Revolution. There is a group characterised here as revisionists and neo-revisionists who assert worker agency and who provide a benign view of plantation life and labour based largely on the post-1890 experience. They write within the historiographic tradition

60. For comparison, see Gillion, *Fiji's Indian Migrants*, ch. 6; Panoff, "Travailleurs, Recruteurs et Planters", pp. 159-173; Firth, *New Guinea under the Germans*; Takaki, *Pau Hana*, chs 3-5; and chapters on Hawaii, Samoa, Fiji and Solomon Islands in Lal, Munro and Beechert, *Plantation Workers*.

61. E.g., Firth, "German Recruitment", p. 51; Shineberg, "'Noumea No Good, Noumea No Pay'", p. 200.

62. Shlomowitz, "Latin American *Enganche* System", pp. 217-224; and Brass, "Market Essentialism and the Impermissibility of Unfree Labour", pp. 225-244. Shlomowitz has extended his critique to include all Marxian writers on the Queensland labor trade; see his "On Labour Systems", "Marx and the Queensland Labour Trade", pp. 11-17, and "Marx and the Queensland Labour Trade: A Further Note".

63. Munro, Williams and Shlomowitz, "Debate on the Queensland Labour Trade", pp. 105-136.

developed at the Australian National University, typified by a concern for the proactive Pacific Islander *per se*. The counter-revisionists, represented by Saunders, Graves and Brass, tend to set their works in somewhat larger contexts of inquiry, either that of the sugar industry or of unfree labour generally, and within an explicit Marxian framework (except for Saunders who is a social historian interested in class structure and race hierarchy). The counter-revisionists, in common with authors of the popular accounts, stress the authoritarian plantation system and the coercive role of the state, take their examples mainly from the 1870s and 1880s, and emphasize accordingly the harsh and exploitative aspects of plantation life and labour. The popular image of the Queensland labour trade, with its focus on kidnapping and ill-treatment, has considerable congruence with the counter-revisionist stance.

A second characteristic of the historiography is its narrow spatial and temporal focus. The tendency has been to concentrate on Pacific Islanders in the sugar industry, despite large numbers of Asians also being involved in the same employment. Only Saunders escapes this limitation, at least partially. The result, for the most part, is a series of colony-wide studies which commence with the first recruitment of Melanesians in 1863 and end with their deportation in 1908, or soon after. This contrasts markedly with Afro-American historiography where the slavery and the post-emancipation periods constitute an integrated literature.[64]

The limited time-frame is a curious feature of the historiography when one considers that the descendants of the 2,500 or so Kanakas who escaped the deportation order now number anything up to 15,000. The result, in the scholarly historiography, is two discrete literatures with 1906 or thereabouts as the demarcation point.[65] This quality of disjunction and discontinuity is not, interestingly enough, replicated in the more recent accounts by descendants of Kanakas tracing the histories of their families from first recruitment to the present day.[66] The only scholarly account to cover the entire span of time is a recent small monograph on the Rockhampton district by Carol Gistitin which highlights a number of other features of the historiography.[67]

64. In fairness, Mercer and Moore write on the twentieth century experience of the Kanakas and their descendants with a deep understanding of the nineteenth century background. Mercer and Moore, "Australia's Pacific Islanders", pp. 195-213; Mercer, "The Survival", ch. 1.

65. The contrast with Hawaiian historiography is evident. The histories of the various ethnic groups in those islands typically take the long view and see the plantation experience as a prelude to an ongoing saga. E.g., Teodoro Jr, *Out of This Struggle*; Ethnic Studies Oral History Project, *Uchinanchu*; Glick, *Sojourners and Settlers*; Carr, "Puerto Ricans in Hawaii". The experience of East Indians in Fiji provides another contrast. See Mayer, *Indians in Fiji*; Anderson, *Indo-Fijian Smallfarming*; Ali, *From Plantation to Politics*; Subramani, *Indo-Fijian Experience*.

66. Fatnowna, *Fragments of a Lost Heritage*; Edmund, *No Regrets*. See also Moore, *Forgotten People*; Moore, "Noel Fatnowna and His Book", pp. 137-150.

67. Gistitin, *Quite a Colony*.

For one thing, Gistitin provides an implicit reminder of the lack of regional studies and the concentration on sugar, both of which serve to mask the fact that many Kanakas worked in other areas of employment before the occupational restrictions of the 1880s were applied. In the Rockhampton district, sugar was a late starter and small in scale, resulting in most Kanakas being employed in the pastoral industry. Given the extent of inter-district differences, an understanding of the Queensland labour trade, in a manner akin to British Chartism, "must begin with a proper appreciation of regional and local diversity".[68] Yet another contrast with the historiography of Southern slavery comes to mind, namely its variegated character. It has long been recognised that slaves were not confined to cotton, rice, sugar and tobacco plantations but worked in industries and in a variety of other urban jobs, and that a knowledge of slaveholders and the Southern economy is essential to an understanding of slaves and slavery.[69] Queensland labour trade historiography, by contrast, is largely confined to the Melanesian experience, the administrative and legislative framework surrounding it, and the sugar industry. The range of issues studied is equally narrow: only recently, for example, have court records been systematically utilised.[70] Moreover, the employment of Kanakas in Queensland has yet to find its rightful place in the historiography of Australian labour history, where it is presently depicted as a somewhat exotic sideshow.[71]

There is a temptation whenever writing a historiographic essay to focus on gaps and weaknesses, and to lapse into the conventional pleas and injunctions that those concerned rechannel their efforts into various things that they cannot do, do not want to do, or need not do. That said, certain observations can still legitimately be made. A proper appreciation of local diversity, thus far little in evidence, must be accompanied by a wider framework of inquiry. Clive Moore recently voiced his concern about the temporal and spatial focus of the historiography:

> Colonial episodes such as the Queensland labor trade are still unthinkingly bound to firm dates, almost as if the people involved came out of thin air in 1863 and went back into the same ethereal realm in 1908. We need to include as much as possible of the pre-1863 period to provide the context from which the laborers came, and

---

68. Briggs, *Chartist Studies*, p. 2.
69. E.g., Wade, *Slavery in the Cities*; Genovese, *The World the Slaveholders Made*; Starobin, *Industrial Slavery*; Frederickson, *Black Image in the White Mind*; and Oakes, *Ruling Race*.
70. Finnane and Moore, "Kanaka Slaves or Willing Workers?", pp. 141-160. Peter Mühlhäusler of the University of Adelaide is utilizing court records for linguistic analysis. For another dimension, see Gesner, "Maritime Archaeology Approach", pp. 15-20.
71. E.g., Patmore, *Australian Labour History*, pp. 196-199. This contrasts with the comprehensive labour history of Hawaii by Beechert, *Working in Hawaii*.

go beyond 1908 to the 1990s. Immigrant Melanesians have lived in Australia for more than eighty years, double the time the labor trade operated. The 1863-1908 years can be reliably assessed only within a much wider perspective.[72]

To this call for a more rounded approach can be added the observation that explicit comparisons with other coercive labour systems would be equally fruitful, helping to break down the insular nature of Queensland labour history studies. This might also emancipate the historiography from a self-inflicted parochialism and result instead in the subject becoming better known to scholars of other labour systems.[73] Instead of standing largely by itself, the Queensland labour trade could then be incorporated into the wider literature on coercive agrarian labour systems. There is plenty of scope for further research but new directions will increasingly have to be taken. Clive Moore and I represent the two quite different strands of labour trade studies: whilst Moore emphasises the active participation of Melanesians in the labour trade and the extent to which they controlled their working and private lives, I stress more the role of the colonial state and the other larger structures that impinged on the recruitment and employment of workers. Although we have signposted quite different directions for future research, our dissatisfactions with aspects of the current historiography are much the same.

72. Moore, "Revising the Revisionists", p. 74.
73. This point is borne out by Clive Moore's observations about the "Unfree Labour Confer-ence", University of Sydney, 5-6 August 1993, where he presented a paper on the Queens-land labour trade (published as "Methods of Response", pp. 181-207). The conference included sessions on Australian convicts, black immigrants in southern Africa, US slavery, and coerced labour in nineteenth century Indonesia, and Moore found that he was better informed about other participants' areas than they were about his. The others were equally surprised (and perhaps disbelieving) that the Queensland labour trade was a relatively benign example of a coercive labour system, indicating that fruitful comparisons are there to be made. Personal communication, August 1993.

The Origins, Spread and Normalization of Free Wage Labour*

Marcel van der Linden

The previous essays focused primarily on the rise and decline of "unfree" labour; in this context, "free" labour (and "free" wage labour in particular) was treated as the contrasting norm – which, however, itself received very little attention. In this contribution, I want to take the opposite approach, and discuss the apparently self-evident notion of "free" wage labour as a historical category in its own right.

In the late-twentieth century, "free" wage labour is probably the second most important form of labour (after domestic subsistence labour). But how did that come about? Why has slavery – except for some horrific but otherwise rather minor counter-tendencies in Brazil and elsewhere – become a marginal phenomenon? Why do forms of serfdom, for example, not predominate in modern industry? These are questions which historians and social scientists have rarely addressed. Since they are big questions, I cannot pretend to do full justice to them here. My aim in this essay is only to advance some hypotheses and suggestions which could promote further research in the area. I hope that the very shortcomings, gaps and errors of my work will be a challenge to its critics to do more and better.

1. Principles

Capitalism has the tendency to subject more and more parts of human society to the laws of the market. This trend is not only visible geographically, by the ever-decreasing area of the globe that remains untouched by capitalist civilization; it is also clear in the progressive transformation of daily life in the advanced capitalist societies.

"Commodification" means not just that more goods previously produced exclusively for direct consumption, as use-values, are now produced for sale in

* I wish to thank Hans de Beer, Lex Heerma van Voss, Jaap Kloosterman and Jan Lucassen for their comments on an earlier version of this article. I am also grateful to Theo van den Hout and Manfred Schmidt for their suggestions.

the market, with the aim of realizing their exchange-value. It means also that all kinds of things are subjected to the laws of the market which were from the outset not produced for any commercial purpose whatsoever. One major example is nature in its pristine, unexploited state – thus e.g. land which existed already becomes an important object of trade and speculation. Another example is the *human capacity for labour*, the subject of the present discussion.[1]

Human labour power can be turned into a commodity in different ways. The two main forms are chattel slavery and wage labour. In the case of chattel slavery, the labour power of a person is in principle sold once and for all, for the duration of her/his lifetime. The enslaved person thereby loses vital human characteristics, and is treated as an item of fixed capital, similar to cattle or engine. "In the slave relation the worker is nothing but a living labour machine, which therefore has a value for others, or rather is a value."[2]

In the case of wage labour, the capacity for labour is owned by the worker her/himself who, for a limited time, puts this at the disposal of someone else, the employer. Classical Marxism described this process as a temporary sale of labour power. But this seems to be a *contradictio in terminis*; logically one could just as well say that the worker *hires out the right to use* her/his labour power for a limited time to another agency.[3] The free wage earner considers his whole labour capacity "as his property, as one of his moments, over which he, as subject, exercizes domination, and which he maintains by expending it".[4]

1. "Labor is only another name for a human activity which goes with life itself, which in its turn is not produced for sale but for entirely different reasons, nor can that activity be detached from the rest of life, be stored or mobilized; land is only another name for nature, which is not produced by man [...]. None of them is produced for sale. The commodity description [...] is entirely fictitious." Polanyi, *Great Transformation*, p. 72.
2. Marx, *Grundrisse*, p. 465.
3. To my knowledge Franz Oppenheimer was the first to mention the hiring out rather than the temporary sale of labour power. See his *Soziale Frage und der Sozialismus*, pp. 119-122. Compare Eldred and Hanlon, "Reconstructing Value-Form Analysis", p. 44: "[Marx], instead of formulating the relation between capitalist and labourer as one of *hiring* (or, more generally, as a *loan*) simply treats labour power as another commodity, albeit a commodity with special characteristics. The concept of exchange, however, is not adequate to the relation between capitalist and labourer. The exchange of commodity for money is the reciprocal and total surrender of commodity for money and money for commodity; a monetary relation in which the buyer and seller come into momentary contact. With the hiring of labourers, however, the relation is not simply the surrender of something for money. Rather, the capitalist gains the temporary possession of the labourer, a human bearer of labour power, who he can now employ in a labour process producing industrial commodities. The bearer of the labour power is not bought but only hired." See also Lundkvist, "Kritik af Marx' lønteori", pp. 16-18; Burkhardt, "Kritik der Marxschen Mehrwerttheorie", pp. 125-127; and Ruben, "Ist die Arbeitskraft eine Ware?", pp. 167-183.
4. Marx, *Grundrisse*, p. 465.

Contrary to what Marx and many Marxists have argued, *both* modes of exploitation are fundamentally compatible with capitalism.[5] In some cases capital prefers slavery, in other cases wage labour. There exists no theoretical ground for treating the one mode of exploitation as the "true" capitalist form, and the other as an anomalous (though perhaps historically necessary) variation.[6] Gerald Cohen among others has quite correctly pointed out that "either of the two basic modes of exploitation may be conceived to accompany any form of surplus labour".[7]

Although there is no simple one-to-one relationship between modes of exploitation and types of social formations, it is nevertheless the case that a given mode of exploitation can only emerge, or become dominant, under specific circumstances. By way of illustration, consider the case of societies of hunter-gatherers, in some (but not all) of which slavery is simply not a realistic option. Bernard Siegel makes the following observation in the case of the Inuit:

> Life in the Arctic wastelands is extremely hard, social groups are necessarily small and existence often precarious. The keeping of slaves in most cases would be a liability rather than a desired additional source of labor. Although there is private ownership of tools and instruments of production, nomadic life precludes the accumulation of possessions. At best, a man with a strong team of dogs can make a somewhat larger catch, provide better for his wife and children, and allot some work to a less fortunate neighbor. There would still remain the problem of watching after slaves and supervising their household activities or hunting methods. The risks

5. Marx acknowledged that "slavery is possible at individual points within the bourgeois system of production", but he added that in such cases "slavery is then possible there only because it does not exist at other points; and appears as an anomaly opposite the bourgeois system itself". *Grundrisse*, p. 464.
6. Miles, *Capitalism and Unfree Labour*. The resistance of orthodox Marxism against the idea that slavery is a "normal" form of commodification is a consequence of the presumption that the contradiction between capital and labour is the most essential characteristic of capitalism. Contrary to this viewpoint I would follow those authors who give the value form, and not class contradictions, central place in their analysis of capitalism. The contradiction between capital and workers is in that perspective nothing other than a conflict between different groups of commodity owners. See Kurz and Lohoff, "Klassenkampf-Fetisch", pp. 10-41; Postone, *Time, Labor, and Social Domination*. The class analysis approach tends to become tautological rather quickly, i.e. it makes true by definition precisely that which needs to be investigated and explained. A striking example is offered by W.G. Runciman, who states the following definition: "By 'capitalism' I mean a mode of production in which formally free labour is recruited for regular employment by ongoing enterprises competing in the market for profit." So far so good. But then he also argues: "However difficult it may be to say precisely when the transition to a capitalist mode of production occurs in any given society, it is only complete when it can be agreed by observers of all theoretical persuasions that formally free wage labour is dominant in the economy as a whole." Runciman, "'Triumph' of Capitalism", pp. 33-34.
7. Cohen, *Karl Marx's Theory of History*, p. 83.

involved would hardly compensate for the extra benefits, if any. The Eskimos do not measure up to the minimum security necessary for the development of slavery or any other form of extensive servitude.[8]

In numerous societies in which slavery *could* exist, it nevertheless remained marginal for technical, economic and other reasons. Even in a developed class society like Babylon, slavery on a large scale was not yet feasible:

> [In] Babylonia [...], slave labor did not play a decisive role in agriculture and was used on a limited scale in comparison with the labor of free farmers. This explains the action of King Nebuchadnezzar II: having conquered Jerusalem after a prolonged siege, he forcibly deported to Babylonia more than ten thousand inhabitants of that city, but he did not turn them into slaves. The forced labor sector in Babylonia, in contrast to Greek and Roman Antiquity, was not able to absorb such masses of captives.[9]

Conversely, the disappearance of slavery on a mass scale since the nineteenth century leads one to suspect that there exists a kind of historical "upper limit" (a point I will elaborate on below). Certain (to be specified) conditions must be satisfied before a mode of exploitation can be dominant. This applies both for the emergence and for the decline of that dominance.[10] So there appears to be a certain "field of possibilities" (parameters) for distinct modes of exploitation within the historical process; only under specific circumstances can a mode of exploitation emerge, and only under even more specific conditions can it become dominant. Every notion of evolutionism should, incidentally, be avoided in this context: in the course of time a specific mode of exploitation can emerge, become dominant and decline several times in succession.[11]

---

8. Siegel, "Some Methodological Considerations", pp. 360-361. Slavery incidentally did occur in other hunter-gatherer societies. See for example MacLeod, "Debtor and Chattel Slavery", p. 375: "Hereditary chattel slavery was a conspicuous trait of the culture of the non-agricultural North Pacific coast where it has been noted for a continuous area from the Alentian Islands to northwestern California, inclusive. An active intertribal slave trade was carried on."
9. Dandamaev, *Slavery in Babylonia*, p. 652.
10. An attempt at specifying the conditions for the domination of chattel slavery is made by Hahn, "Anfänge der antiken Gesellschaftsformation", pp. 29-47.
11. One may, for instance, think of the resurgence of share-cropping arrangements in the United States. See Wells, "Resurgence of Sharecropping", pp. 1-29.

Figure 1. The "Parameters" of a Mode of Exploitation

Time

Mode of Exploitation

Possible	Dominant	Possible

2. Origins

In the remainder of this essay I will examine the parameters of wage labour more closely. Moses Finley has defended the thesis that the institution of wage labour was a "sophisticated latecomer", because it involved two difficult conceptual steps:

> First it requires the abstraction of a man's labour from both his person and the product of his work. When one purchases an object from an independent craftsman, whether he is free or a slave with a *peculium*, one has not bought his labour but the object, which he had produced in his own time and under his own conditions of work. But when one hires labour, one purchases an abstraction, labour power, which the purchaser then uses at a time and under conditions which he, the purchaser, not the "owner" of the labour power, determines (and for which he normally pays after he has consumed it). Second, the wage labour system requires the establishment of a method of measuring the labour one has purchased, for purposes of payment, commonly by introducing a second abstraction, labour-time.
>
> We should not underestimate the magnitude, speaking socially rather than intellectually, of these two conceptual steps; even the Roman jurists found them difficult.[12]

This interpretation is difficult to sustain – among other things because, in the Antique period, the wage labourer is seen as a "hireling" who did not so much "hire out" (or, if one prefers, temporarily sell) her/his labour power, but who placed her/himself temporarily with her/his whole person in a dependent position.[13] The idea of wage labour as a form of *personal hire* is, as it were, impressed upon us by the ancient sources. Take, for example, the Greek *misthós* (wage, soldier's pay)[14] that via its Indo-European root *mizdho-* is related to the

---

12. Finley, *Ancient Economy*, pp. 65-66.
13. Dreizehnter, "Zur Entstehung der Lohnarbeit", pp. 272-273.
14. *Misthós* can also have other meanings, but "wage" is the most important; see the relevant

Northern High German *Miete* (rent, hire)[15]. *Misthós* was not a wage in the modern sense of the word, but a "personal hire which was finely tuned to the regeneration of labour power, and which hence could be considered equivalent to *trophè* (maintenance)". Labour as such was understood by the Greeks not as "abstract labour", to borrow Karl Marx's term, but as "concrete labour".[16] Wage labour was therefore conceptualized differently than we do today: not as the hire of labour power but as self-hire of a worker and his or her labour performance. The person and labour performance were, to be sure, distinguished[17] but the hire was simultaneously applied to both aspects. The precise terminological development has not been completely clarified, but the most important conclusion is that wage labour existed *before* it was conceptualized in the "modern" way.[18]

section in *Paulys Realencyclopädie*, cols 2078-2095. Edouard Will has stressed that *misthós* can only be translated literally as "wage" when it is a question of paying "the labourer *misthotos*". See his "Notes sur ΜΙΣΘΟΣ", in Bingen *et al.*, *Le monde grec*, pp. 426-438; for additional commentary see Garlan, "Le travail libre", pp. 6-22, 13-15.

15. Benveniste refers to the difference with the other Indo-European word which is relevant in this connection, namely *laun[om]*, from which the German *Lohn* and the Dutch *loon* are derived. "*Laun* is always something different from a salary; it is an act of favour or an advantage obtained by an activity which is not work in the ordinary sense (in which case *mizdo* would be the appropriate term), essentially an 'honorarium' granted or a prize that is won". Benveniste, *Le vocabulaire des institutions indo-européennes*, p. 168. Mauss, "Essai sur le don", pp. 30-186, 155: "Our own word gage is derived from the same source, from *wadium* (cf. the English "wage", salary). Huvelin has already demonstrated that the German *wadium* provides a way to understand the nature of the contracts made, which comes close to the Roman nexus."

16. Rössler, "Handwerk und Lohnarbeit", pp. 73-94, 76. A more extensive treatment is presented by Vernant, *Mythe et pensée chez les Grecs*, pp. 183-247. In Babylonia, "The free hired laborer is designated by the term agru, derived from the verb agaru, 'to hire'." Dandamaev, *Slavery in Babylonia*, pp. 121-122. In Judea, the connection between hire and wage is evident: the Hebrew term for wage labour is *sékér*, derived from *skr* ("hire", "working for wages"). From this root the term *sakîr* ("wage labourer") also is derived. Kreißig, *Die sozialökonomische Situation in Juda*, p. 91; Ben-David, *Talmudische Ökonomie*, pp. 65-66. The Hittite *kuššaniya-* means "to hire", "to take as a day labourer" and is related to *kuššan-*, which means "wage", "pay", "price". Haase, "Dienstleistungsverträge in der hethitischen Rechtssammlung", pp. 109-115.

17. The distinction between the working person and his or her activities developed at an early stage. Kaufmann suggests that the distinction was already present in the Indo-European root *op- (compare Latin *opus*). Kaufmann, *Altrömische Mietrecht*, p. 200.

18. Francine Michaud points out that, as late as the beginning of the fourteenth century AD, contracts were made in Marseille in which wage workers hired out themselves and their labour (*loco me et operas meas*). See her essay "Apprentissage et salariat à Marseille", p. 8. Deschamps has argued that the expression *locatio operarum* ("labour hire") could only be invented because slavery dominated in Rome and wage labour was viewed legally as a parallel working arrangement: not the slaveholder hired out a slave to a client, but the "slave" hired himself out. Deschamps, "Sur l'expression 'locare operas'", pp. 157-179. A similar argument is advanced by Weber, "Agrarverhältnisse im Altertum", pp. 12, 56. Kaufmann, *Das altrömische Mietrecht*, p. 155, strongly criticizes this viewpoint, and tries to show that the term *mercenarius* ("hired worker") was *first* applied to free labourers and only *afterwards* was generalized to hired slaves.

The earliest origins of wage labour are shrouded in darkness. We can imagine that wage labour was already performed on a casual basis among hunter-gatherers, such as among the Inuit described by Siegel where "a man with a strong team of dogs can make a somewhat larger catch, [...] and allot some work to a less fortunate neighbour". The first documented indications are provided by historians in the ancient period. From their work it can be established that there were, in fact, at least four basic variants of early wage labour.

The first form consists of *casual labour*, especially in agriculture but also in building, lumbering, etc. The forms in which this casual labour was organized varied a great deal. In the old Babylonic scripts we encounter, for example, the following formula: "*X* shekels of silver for *x* harvest labourers have been received by the hireling from the hirer. [...] In the harvest season *x* harvest labourers will come. If they do not come, then the royal decrees [apply]". At issue here, however, is the wage that is paid in advance to "harvest labourers, who are demanded seasonally, necessitating this satisfaction beforehand. As a rule it would be the case that larger enterprises are involved here, who could not be conquered with their relatives and family [...]. These harvest labourers were organized in groups under supervisors, leading hands (*waklum*), with whom the contracts were settled."[19]

In other cases, labourers were allocated through a daily market. In Athens there was a space known as *kolonos agoraios* (or *ergatikos* or *misthios*), probably on the West end of the agora, where those who wanted to hire themselves out as land labourer offered their services daily.[20]

The New Testament provides a good example of such a daily market:

For the kingdom of heaven is like a householder who went out early in the morning to hire laborers for his vineyard. After agreeing with the laborers for a denarius a day, he sent them into his vineyard. And going out about the third hour he saw others standing idle in the market place; and then he said, "You go into the vineyard too, and whatever is right I will give you." So they went. Going out again about the sixth hour and the ninth hour, he did the same. And about the eleventh hour

19. Koschaker, Review article, pp. 388-389. The standard work on this material remains Lautner, *Altbabylonische Personenmiete*. See also Klengel, "Soziale Aspekte der altbabylonischen Dienstmiete", p. 41: "The seasonally expanding labour demand, as well as urgent activities in other branches of industry, could often not be satisfied with the regular supply. Since it was not possible to resort to foreign labour on the ground of external economic pressures [...] [an important insight !], not only the labour performed by those in debt but also hired services became significant." As regards the work groups, Hengstl distinguishes two types: (a) the "local groups, which had assembled their members already before the contract was made and then approached the employer"; (b) the labour contract negotiated on behalf of a group: "The individual group member is only the leading hand (subcontractor) for whom labour was performed, while the labour is credited in the accounts to the leading hand." Hengstl, *Private Arbeitsverhältnisse freier Personen*, pp. 102-103.

20. Fuks, "κολωνος μισθιος", pp. 171-173.

he went out and found others standing; and he said to them, "Why do you stand here idle all day?" They said to him, "Because no one has hired us." He said to them, "You go into the vineyard too." And when evening came, the owner of the vineyard said to his steward, "Call the laborers and pay them their wages, beginning with the last, up to the first."[21]

Not always would such casual labour be offered voluntarily. There are many examples in Asian and European history of landlords who oblige their servants to work for a previously determined wage.

The social groups from which the casual labourers were recruited could vary greatly. In his study of the neo-Babylonic age, Muhammed Dandamaev notes that "Sometimes even persons who owned one or two slaves worked as hired labourers."[22] In the Roman period, the agricultural hired labourers in Italy comprized both "cultivators of small farms [...] taking work to supplement a meagre income" and "unemployed and under-employed residents of cities and towns".[23] And for Egypt in late Antiquity (the fourth and fifth century AD) Roger Bagnall concludes: "At harvest time [...] all hands turned out. It is likely that large numbers of men who did something else normally earnt spare cash by helping out at the peak season. Monks poured out of their desert monasteries into the Delta fields to work for a daily wage."[24]

The second form of early wage labour consists of *artisanal* labour, skilled work which had to be carried out now and then, but not continuously (metalwork, carpentry). In the case of Greek Antiquity, Alois Dreizehnter has suggested that because of the small extent of urbanization, "the artisans were for economic reasons initially forced to migrate from farm to farm. Later, when the cities had grown somewhat, the artisans could settle permanently somewhere and begin their own workplace."[25]

The boundary between artisanal and casual labour was therefore initially not sharply drawn, all the more so because certain activities of e.g. harvest labour

21. *Oxford Annotated Bible*, p. 1197 (Matthew 20). See also Churruca, "Gerechte Lohn im Neuen Testament", pp. 131–149.
22. Dandamaev, *Slavery in Babylonia*, p. 121, note.
23. Garnsey, "Non-Slave Labour in the Roman World", p. 42.
24. Bagnall, *Egypt in Late Antiquity*, p. 123.
25. Dreizehnter, "Zur Entstehung der Lohnarbeit".

were also considered skilled labour.[26] In medieval Europe this applied, for example, to the mowers:

> They were the first and most important activity of waged land labourers, which is explained by the significance of harvest labour, primarily grain and hay-cutting, for the agricultural economy. Even for mowing and cutting, the land labourer required a definite ability and work experience. A work team had to be specialized exclusively in this area. [...] The wages of mowers and cutters were generally higher than those of other wage workers.[27]

The third form of wage labour we encounter among the ancient armed forces, in the shape of *military service:* "Already in the late Ancient Empire (around 2290 BC) hirelings were drafted from Nubia and Libya. In the New Empire (1551-1080 BC) there existed settlements of hirelings and forcibly settled foreigners, who likewise were engaged as mercenaries. In the new Syrian legion (in the first half of the tenth century BC) hirelings – partly drawn from the agricultural sphere – played a growing role. In achaimenidic Iran, hirelings are in evidence from the beginning of the fifth century BC. Greek mercenaries played a decisive military role from the Kyros Revolt of 401 BC (retreat of the ten thousand) onwards and, subsequently, in the Revolt of the Satraps, the Secession of Egypt and the war against Philip II of Macedonia and Alexander the Great. The services of hirelings were also used in the later Iranian dynasties. In China, the employment of hirelings probably dates back to the period of the Han dynasty (206 BC to 220 AD)."[28]

Mercenaries formed the first *large* group of wage earners, as G.E.M. De Sainte Croix has correctly pointed out.[29] The wage normally consisted of a basic package of foodstuffs and suchlike, money, or a portion of the war booty.[30] In the Egyptian New Empire, the troops in part consisted of professional soldiers

---

26. Heinz Kreißig gives the example of the brickmakers in Trans-Jordan in the Hellenistic Age: "They carry out any work offered by anyone who can pay, whether a magistrate, or a private customer, or a workshop-owner who receives orders from a third party. These brickmakers may work as hired labourers for a contractor one day, on another day perform services as day-labourers for a private house owner. The contracts might be written or verbal and run for one day, for days, for weeks or until a specific project is complete. The contract might or might not tie the worker to the workshop. Thus the difference between a paid workman and a one-man contractor or entrepreneur can be illusory." Kreißig, "Free Labour in the Hellenistic Age", p. 31. A more extensive analysis is presented in Kreißig's "Versuch über den Status der Lohnarbeiter", pp. 105-113.
27. Hon-Firnberg, *Lohnarbeiter und freie Lohnarbeit im Mittelalter*, pp. 67-68.
28. "Söldner", in Herrmann *et al.*, *Lexikon früher Kulturen*, p. 269.
29. "The first appearance in antiquity of hired labour on a large scale was in the military field, in the shape of mercenary service." Ste. Croix, *Class Struggle in the Ancient Greek World*, p. 182.
30. See among others Corbier, "Salaires et salariat sous le Haut-Empire", pp. 68, 84-85.

("nowadays often but incorrectly referred to as hirelings") and reservists deployed temporarily.[31]

Artisans' *apprenticeships* represent a fourth, probably later, form of wage labour. Apprenticeship contracts differed from other types of contracts because, beyond the employment relationship, a training course was also involved in which the employer took on the obligation to train, and the wage labourer had the duty to learn specific skills.[32]

If we consider these four variants, one common characteristic stands out: free wage labour was engaged above all where the activities were of a *temporary* nature: temporary either in the sense of being carried out during a part of the year only, or during a part of the worker's life (in the case of apprentices). It is worth noting in this context that on dairy farms not wage labour but slavery was the rule, because the activities had a continuous character. This norm is noted e.g. for ancient Greece by Zimmermann: "For seasonal labour on the land, such as the harvesting of olives, free workers were often hired as well. For such short-term activities, buying slaves was not a commercial proposition. [...] The shepherds however were mostly slaves."[33]

But the reverse situation did not hold: by no means all temporary labour was carried out for wages. In thirteenth century England, seasonal operations were most often performed "by means of labour dues of customary tenants".[34] Of importance therefore, is also the extent to which there were other (cheaper?) alternatives to wage labour, such as fatigue-labour.[35]

---

31. "Krieg", *Lexikon der Ägyptologie*, vol. 3, cols 765-782, 776. Very interesting are the origins of the Nubian divisions. Initially prisoners of war were simply put to death on a mass scale (in one such episode of slaughter, this meant the loss of 49,000 lives). Only when "acute labour shortages" occurred in Egypt (during the period of the Old Empire) the policy changed. Then razzias were organized in Nubia (lasting until the end of the Old Empire). "A counter-trend however emerged in the Nubian nations, with which treaties were apparently made requiring them to supply inhabitants as soldiers, who were organized in special ethnically separated units." Later, in the New Empire, predominantly prisoners of war were drafted into the army. "Fremdarbeit", *Lexikon der Ägyptologie*, vol. 2, cols 304-306.

32. Only in recent years has the early history of apprenticeship received more attention. An overview of European research is given by Epstein, *Wage Labor and Guilds*.

33. Zimmermann, "Die freie Arbeit in Griechenland", p. 341. Compare Audring, "Zur sozialen Stellung der Hirten", p. 16: "[Shepherd slavery] indeed can be considered, despite its probably limited occurence, as the first form of economically significant slavery in Greece. [...] in contrast to arable farming and horticulture, [livestock farming] was an area of economic activity in which the amount of labour required remained relatively constant. This created the demand, and favoured the deployment of, a constant number of workers. 'Serfs', but also slaves certainly fitted better into this regime than impoverished free migrants, who in all probability would only consent to contract out their services for a limited period."

34. Postan, *Famulus*, p. 2.

35. For all that, it is thirteenth century England which demonstrates that "free" wage labour was very much related to seasonality. Because apart from serfs who already received a wage (the

3. Spread

Free wage labour in pre-capitalist societies always remained a "spasmodic, casual, marginal" phenomenon.[36] Free wage labour often (but not always) was "an adjunct to other forms of labour and surplus appropriation, often as a means of supplementing the incomes of smallholders whose land – whether owned or held conditionally – has been insufficient for subsistence".[37]

Unfree wage labour for a long time occurred only sporadically, but in a small area of the world became important already before the rise of capitalism. I refer here to the manorial wage labourers, who were essentially nothing but "serf[s] to whom law denied that freedom of contract and movement which it allows to the twentieth-century labourer[s]".[38] Charles Tilly estimates that, in 1500, about 94 percent of all European proletarians were "rural"; even in 1800 it still amounted to 90 percent.[39] The great majority of this group probably consisted initially of unfree wage labourers, and not of more or less "modern" workers.[40] Their existence signals the rapid increase of the cash economy in Europe since the high Middle Ages[41] – a process which first became clearly visible in England.[42]

so-called *famuli* and *famulae*) there existed at that time two groups of "real" wage labourers: skilled artisans, (masons, carpenters) and day labourers. See Middleton, "Familiar Fate of the *Famulae*", pp. 28-29. See also Postan, *Famulus*, p. 18; Hilton, *Bond Men Made Free*, pp. 37-38; Kosminsky, *Studies in the Agrarian History of England*, pp. 305-06. On French jobbing-workers, see Perroy, "Wage Labour in France", p. 236. Actually whether the day labourers were better or worse off then personnel employed on a long-term basis depended heavily on the state of the labour market. After the Plague, which caused major labour shortages and sharply rising food prices, many English labourers "would reject the respectable status of a ploughman, a carter, or a shepherd employed at a yearly wage, for that of a common labourer working by the day, in view of the fact that by such casual labour they could earn far larger sums and yet work entirely where and when they pleased". Kenyon, "Labour Conditions in Essex", p. 431.

36. Finley, *Ancient Slavery*, p. 68.
37. Meiksins Wood, *Peasant-Citizen and Slave*, p. 65.
38. Postan, *Famulus*, p. 23.
39. Tilly, "Demographic Origins of the European Proletariat".
40. Alan Macfarlane suggests this was the case in England. See *Origins of English Individualism*, pp. 148-150.
41. Ricardo Duchesne attempts to explain this monetarization process in "The French Revolution as a Bourgeois Revolution", pp. 288-320. See also Mayhew, "Modelling Medieval Monetization", pp. 55-77.
42. Postan estimates that in thirteenth century England "perhaps as much as a third of the total rural population was available for whole or part-time employment as wage labour". Postan, "England", p. 568. Some scholars interpret this as a reason "to date back the beginning of capitalism in England to the thirteenth century". Gerstenberger, *Subjektlose Gewalt*, p. 51. See further: Weber, "Studie zur Spätmittelalterlichen Arbeitsmarkt- und Wirtschaftsordnung", pp. 358-389; Lütge, *Mitteldeutsche Grundherrschaft*, pp. 216-238; idem, "Das 14./15. Jahrhundert in der Sozial- und Wirtschaftsgeschichte", pp. 281-335, esp. 314-323; and Brown, "Introduction: Wage-labour", pp. 1-27.

The question which arises within the framework of this paper is how and why extensive, more or less free wage labour emerged out of this "spasmodic" free wage labour and extensive unfree wage labour. The oldest group of workers with steady employment probably existed in Egypt. Already early on a small group of artisans developed there who performed wage labour on a permanent basis for the state: the necropole workers. They lived in small purpose-built towns (Kahun, Deir-el-Medina, Tell el-Amarna), where they worked, often generation after generation, on the construction of the tombs of successive pharaos. About the workers in Deir-el-Medina (the eighteenth to the twentieth dynasty) there is a lot of information thanks to archeological research, papyri and ostraka. So we know not only many details of their daily lives, but are also well-informed about their wages:

> The payments were made on the 28th day of the month, for the following month. The basic payment was in grain [...]. The grain included emmer wheat which was ground into flour, and barley which was made into beer. Other payments supplied by the government included fish, vegetables and water; and, for domestic use, wood for fuel and pottery. Less regular deliveries were also made of cakes, ready-made beer and dates, and on festival days or other special occasions, the workforce received bonuses which included salt, natron, sesame oil and meat.[43]

In the twenty-ninth year of the reign of Rameses III (about 1158 BC), these workers staged the first recorded strike in world history because their wages were not paid on time.[44]

Why were these artisans wage labourers rather than slaves? We can only guess at the answer. One possibility is that the activities of these early artisans were originally only of a temporary nature (in an historically still earlier stage) and that, when their employment became permanent, the traditional wage contract continued to exist. Whether this is the correct explanation cannot be assessed from the available sources. But this example does already demonstrate that, beyond economic causes in the strict sense, all kinds of non-economic (cultural, political) factors must be taken into account.

The question of what explains the trend towards permanent wage labour is, to an important extent, bound up with the question of how wage labour could establish itself gradually in increasingly larger economic sectors. Because that expansion had as its inexorable consequence that wage labour no longer comprised mainly temporary activities. In the literature various causal factors are proposed. I will briefly discuss three of them: technological innovation,

---

43. Davis, *Pyramid Builders of Ancient Egypt*, pp. 72-73. Also see Allam, *Verfahrensrecht in der altägyptischen Arbeitersiedlung*; Černy, *Community of Workmen*; Della Monica, *Classe ouvrière sous les pharaons*; Allam, "Familie und Besitzverhältnisse", pp. 17-39; Gutgesell, *Arbeiter und Pharaonen*.
44. Edgerton, "The Strikes in Ramses III's Twenty-ninth Year", pp. 137-145; Janssen, "Background Information on the Strikes of Year 29 of Rameses III", pp. 301-311.

centralization of states and the growing supply of labour. None of these factors, in my view, suffice to explain the problem in hand.

As far as technological innovation is concerned, a frequently cited argument is that modern technology was no longer compatible with unfree labour. This interpretation dates back at least to the nineteenth-century political economist J.E. Cairnes, who, in his influential book *Slave Power,* contended that slave labour was necessarily unskilled labour. The slave, Cairnes wrote, is "unsuited for all branches of industry which require the slightest care, forethought, or dexterity. He cannot be made to co-operate with machinery; he can only be trusted with the coarsest implements; he is incapable of all but the rudest forms of labour."[45] Other authors, including Marx, adopted this interpretation, and accordingly advanced a *technological* explanation of the decline of slavery: the increasingly complex and subtle labour processes supposedly could not be combined with slave labour.[46] Further research however has meanwhile revealed that this argument does not hold water, neither for Antiquity nor for modern capitalism.[47]

In the American South before the Civil War, skilled labour was most definitely performed by slaves, be it with a greater degree of autonomy than the slaves e.g. on cotton plantations. Eugene Genovese quotes a South Carolina planter from 1849 as follows: "Whenever a slave is made a mechanic, he is more than half freed, and soon becomes, as we too well know, and all history attests, with rare exceptions, the most corrupt and turbulent of his class".[48] The underlying logic is made clear by a study which Charles Dew made of an ironmaking enterprise in the Valley of Virginia, at the beginning of the Civil War. Dew describes in detail the reasons why the owner (Weaver) granted his slave-artisans a considerable amount of freedom in their work. Because of the clarity of Dew's account I will quote him at length:

> Weaver, of course, had considerable coercive power at his disposal. He could punish any recalcitrant or troublesome slave, but if he had relied on the whip to achieve satisfactory levels of production, his career as a Virginia ironmaker would have been very short-lived indeed. Excessive use of force certainly would have backfired, and a whipping administered to a skilled slave would, at minimum, leave the man sore and incapable of work. It would probably leave him seething with anger as well and looking for ways to get back at the master. Acts of industrial sabotage could be accomplished with relative ease around a forge. To cite only one example, the huge wooden beams that supported the 500- to 600-pound cast-iron hammerheads in the forge – "helves" was the name given to these beams – occasionally broke in the

45. Cairnes, *Slave Power*, p. 46.
46. Marx, *Capital*, 1, pp. 303-304.
47. Kiechle, *Sklavenarbeit und technischer Fortschritt*.
48. Genovese, "Slave Labor or Free in the Southern Factories", p. 225.

normal course of operations and had to be replaced. The forge would shut down for at least a day, sometimes more, while the forge carpenter installed a new helve. Weaver's foremen could break these helves intentionally whenever they wished, and who could say whether it was or was not deliberate? Another alternative would be for the slave to burn the forge down. On any working day, live charcoal was there to do the job. The slaves, in short, were in a position to do considerable physical and financial damage to Weaver's interests, even if they limited their activities to passive forms of resistance like work slowdowns or slipshod performance of their duties. Not surprisingly, there is no indication that Weaver ever whipped one of his slave forge workers at any time during his forty years in the Valley.

A far greater threat to the slaves was the possibility of sale. Even skilled slaves who tried to run away or who carried their resistance beyond Weaver's level of toleration could be turned over to slave traders and readily sold. Yet no ironmaster would want to part with a trained slave ironworker [...]. Buying or training an immediate replacement would be difficult, if not impossible, and trying to hire skilled slave forge workers was, as Weaver well knew, both uncertain and expensive. It was far better, from Weaver's point of view, to avoid the use of physical coercion to the fullest extent possible and to turn to a weapon like the sale of a slave only in the most extreme circumstances.

The alternative to force was positive incentive. From his earliest days in Virginia, Weaver paid slaves who did extra work. Weaver's artisans had a daily or weekly task to perform, but he compensated them, either in cash or in goods from his store at Buffalo Forge, for anything they turned out over and above the required amount. Payment of "overwork", as this system was called, was a common practice at slave-manned manufacturing establishments throughout the antebellum South, and it was a feature of the labor regime at southern ironworks as early as the mid-eighteenth century.[49]

It is evident from this commentary that slave labour is quite compatible with modern labour processes, provided that the mechanism for extracting labour effort is modified. Technological innovation, while implying the need to offer unfree workers a certain room for manoeuvre, does not logically or practically entail the abolition of the unfree labour relation as such.

A second factor mentioned in the literature is the emergence of modern centralized states, to begin with in England, and afterwards in parts of Western Europe. Robin Blackburn eloquently expresses the relevant point:

In England and France slavery had withered away without ever becoming illegal [...]. It is difficult to believe that the powerful were naturally more gentle and humane in England and France than in other parts of Christendom; in the English case the ferocious Statute of Labourers of 1349-51 certainly suggests otherwise. Therefore it is the possession of other "means" to the same end (presumably, labour control) that must bear the main weight in explaining the eclipse of serfdom and slavery.[50]

49. Dew, *Bond of Iron*, pp. 107-108.
50. Blackburn, *Overthrow of Colonial Slavery*, pp. 39-40.

A similar view is also advanced by Robert Brenner.[51] While undoubtedly containing a kernel of truth, the base of empirical evidence for this interpretation remains rather weak however. At the same time, it is clear that a centralized state creates only the *possibility* of "free" wage labour on a mass scale, and no more. In logical terms, it is a case of a necessary, but not a sufficient condition.

A third factor often introduced in the explanation is the presence of a sufficient supply of labour. Along these lines Maurice Dobb for example wrote that "the transition from coercive extraction of surplus labour by estate-owners to the use of free hired labour must have depended upon the existence of cheap labour for hire (i.e., of proletarian or semi-proletarian elements)".[52] Implied here is that – apparently – the presence of "cheap labour for hire" is sufficient to make the transition from coerced labour to "free" labour possible. But such an inference is far too simplistic. Because the potential employers of this "cheap labour" must from their side be prepared to employ the available labour force *as wage labourers*. In principle at least, however, they could deploy "cheap labour" just as well in a different way; for example, they could contract into e.g. share-cropping arrangements, or introduce a form of slavery (e.g. debt-slavery). That these options are overlooked rather than systematically researched indicates an unacceptable functionalism. With justice Joel Kahn remarks that "Clearly the benefits to capitalism of particular economic forms are on their own no explanation for their existence. One must ask instead whether other forms of economic organization would be equally beneficial to capitalism, whether particular forms benefit capitalism as a whole or only fractions of the dominant class, and, finally, whether there is a possibility of conflict and contradiction within capitalism."[53]

Again, an abundance of workers seeking employment logically only makes "free" labour on a mass scale possible, but not a necessary, inevitable development.

If we now consider these three causal factors as operating in concert, then we have one factor which – in Michael Burawoy's terminology – promotes greater freedom in relations *in* production (technological innovation) and two factors

---

51. "An increasingly centralized state, rooted ever more firmly in broad landed layers, could [...] more effectively undermine the disruptive behaviour of those decreasing numbers of landed elements whose economies still depended upon the application of extra-economic methods [...]. The state which emerged during the Tudor period was, however, no absolutism. Able to profit from rising land rents, through presiding over a newly emerging tripartite capitalist hierarchy of commercial landlord, capitalist tenant and hired wage labourer, the English landed classes had no need to revert to direct, extra-economic compulsion to extract a surplus. Nor did they require the state to serve them indirectly as an engine of surplus appropriation by political means (tax/office and war)." Brenner, "Agrarian Roots of European Capitalism", pp. 297-298.
52. Dobb, "A Reply", p. 61.
53. Kahn, "Mercantilism and the Emergence of Servile Labour", p. 202.

which make greater freedom in relations *of* production *possible* (centralized state power and an abundant labour supply).[54] But that still does not say very much about the specific factors which led to the spread of "free" wage labour. In this respect major gaps in the analysis remain.[55]

Where then should the solution be sought? Under what circumstances is the *possibility* of "free" wage labour converted into a *reality*? In my view, every attempt to answer this question must take account of the interests and choices of both the "employers" and "employees". On both sides economic and non-economic factors play a role. Quite likely it will be useful to distinguish between two kinds of cognitive mechanisms. Firstly, there are *strategic considerations*, i.e. cost-benefit assessments by individuals (or households) of the likely consequences of alternative choices. Secondly, there are also *behavioural norms*, i.e. the application of normative principles to one's own behaviour, and to the behaviour of others.[56] These two mechanisms can operate in concert, and in fact they often do. If an employer decides not to use the services of slaves but of wage labourers, then s/he is conceivably motivated both by strategic considerations ("it is cheaper") and normative considerations ("it is more civilized", etc.).

The critical point to be made is that the combination of these cognitive mechanisms does not always – "automatically" as it were – have the same effect. The same norms and cost-benefit assessments can, in different historical contexts, produce different outcomes. So if we want to explain why, in a given place and time, free wage labour became dominant, then we will have to study the situation in detail and unravel the various motives of "employers" and "employees".[57]

---

54. Burawoy, *Politics of Production*, pp. 13–14.
55. There have been some cautious attempts in this direction in recent times. See for example the micro-historical analysis in Fox, "Servants, Cottages and Tied Cottages", pp. 125–154.
56. These two motivations are described in a somewhat different context in: Burawoy and Olin Wright, "Coercion and Consent in Contested Exchange", pp. 72–87.
57. In the literature, the question of why a specific mode of exploitation is chosen in a given time and place has been dealt with mostly with an *economistic* approach, focusing almost exclusively on employers' motives and interests. Take, for example, the – incidentally very interesting – discussion about the existence and temporal-spatial variation of various types of agricultural firms: share-tenancy, "hired-manager" arrangements, etc. Setting out from the implicit assumption that landowners cannot resort to unfree labour, agricultural economists have developed various models which are supposed to explain the choice for a specific labour regime. An important role is assigned to the "moral hazard" problem of shirking (which is less prevalent with share-cropping than with wage labour) and the corresponding costs of labour supervision. See Eswaran and Kotwal, "Theory of Contractual Structure", p. 361). Keijiro Otsuka, Hiroyuki Chuma and Yujiro Hayami have developed a model in which permanent wage labour in the agricultural sector is, because of the monitoring problem (the difficulty of supervising personnel and prevent shirking), a sort of "last resort" when other options (such as land tenancy) are impossible for legal or social reasons. In line with this hypothesis, the authors explain the frequent occurrence of permanent wage labour in contemporary India, Pakistan and Nepal with reference to the caste system: the lower castes

I will limit myself here to a short summary of possible relevant motives – without pretending to give an exhaustive list. For the *"employers"* three strategic considerations would appear to be of key importance: the immediate costs of the "employee",[58] the flexibility of the supply of labour,[59] and the (effectiveness

are prevented from owning or leasing land, and wage labour was the last option for this reason. The reverse would apply to Indonesia, Malaysia, the Philippines and Thailand. Here "there are no class barriers to becoming tenant or owner cultivators. In such an environment, the land tenancy contract predominates and permanent labor contracts are seldom observed, even though there are many large landowners who could operate sufficiently large farms with permanent workers." (Otsuka, Chuma and Hayami, "Land and Labor Contracts in Agrarian Economies", pp. 2003-2004.) This contrast between South and Southeast Asia has, according to Otsuka *et al.* its counterpart in the history of Japan's agriculture: "In Japan, permanent [wage] labor was preponderant in the early Tokugawa period (the 16th and 17th centuries) under agrarian laws that commanded direct attachment of all tillers to feudal lords and, hence, prohibited landlord-tenant relations to develop below legal peasants (honbyakusho) who were granted usufruct rights on land. This rule was gradually breached by de facto tenancy contracts between the legal peasants and their permanent laborers. The conversion of permanent laborers to tenants was accelerated in the later Tokugawa period (the 18th to 19th centuries) when the feudal lords became less eager to enforce the tenancy regulations as land taxation shifted from the system of variable levy based on crop yield (kemi) to the fixed levy in kind (jomen). The conversion progressed further in the modern era as the Meiji government (1868-1912) granted modern property rights on land, including the right of renting it out, to those who used to have feudal usufruct rights on the land. This process was supported by the development of more intensive cropping systems that required more intensive care and judgment of farm workers and, therefore, could be operated more efficiently by small cultivators who could claim residual profits." (*Ibid.*, p. 2005.) Economistic approaches of this kind certainly make sense when the existence or absence of a specific mode of exploitation is at issue. Actually, the model of Otsuka *et al.* makes it clear that even an economistic explanation cannot do without reference to normative (cultural) factors: the existence or absence of caste-norms among the subaltern population is after all an important consideration in the definition of the possible options open to the employer. But a comprehensive explanation must go further and also explicitly integrate the *normative* aspects.

58. The costs to an "employer" for a single hypothetical producer (either a slave or a worker) comprise at least the following components: *i.* The *acquisition costs* incurred to recruit the producer. These can in the case of the wage labourer be limited to, e.g., the costs of advertising a vacancy. In the case of slave labour, at issue is the price of the slave, or the costs which must be recovered to allow the slave to grow up on the plantation. In general, the acquisition of a slave will cost the employer more than the acquisition of a wage labourer. *ii.* The *reproduction costs* which must be paid to ensure the day-to-day survival of the producer. For the wage-earner, these comprise that component of the gross wage paid to the individual employee, for the slave the naturalia necessary for his/her maintenance. It is not possible to know in advance for which category these costs are the highest. In the antebellum American South, for example, the living standard of slaves was often higher than that of wage-earners. *iii.* The *extraction costs* which must be met to extract labour effort from the producer. These comprise above all the costs of supervision and coercion. Of course, it is not the case that the producers always can do their work *only* on the basis of threats, direct control, etc. In the extraction of labour effort, all sorts of non-material mechanisms promoting compliance can play a role (e.g. notions of fairness), quite apart from financial bonuses etc. which come under the heading of reproduction costs. In the measure that the importance of the latter

of) relevant legislation.[60] The behavioural norms probably relate especially to considerations of humanity and decency, which I will elaborate on below.

For the *"employees"* – in so far as they have a genuine choice in the matter, and are not forced with violence to slavery – two strategic considerations would seem essential: on the one hand, the stability and quality of their standard of life, in other words, material security, and on the other side (in the case of a weak state) the degree of physical protection which an employer can offer. Normative considerations relate especially to questions of personal dignity (whether the proposed employment relation is honourable or an affront to one's status) and distributional justice.[61]

mechanisms increases, the extraction costs will be lower. For an unskilled slave and in the case of time-wages, supervision will probably be higher than for skilled slave labour and piece-rate wages. *iv.* The *costs of non-productivity*, relating to time taken off by the producer because of invalidity or old age. The slaveholder must meet these costs in every case, because a sick slave continues to be part of her/his fixed capital. A different situation pertains when an employer engages wage labour; in many cases s/he can fire the worker in the event of sickness and in this way shift the financial burden on the producers themselves. In mature capitalism, of course, this does not apply as a general norm, since the employer usually has social obligations towards her/his staff.

59. Flexibility is of importance in cases of unpredictable activities. This is very clear in the case of plowing and harvesting: as soon as the weather (not easily predictable) gives cause for it, resolute action is called for. There is then no time anymore for complicated negotiations with potential employees. Hence precautionary measures are required. Already in Mesopotamia attempts at such advance arrangements existed, as noted in the case of harvest labour contracts. See on this issue also Kenyon, "Labour Conditions in Essex", p. 438.

60. A factor which relates both to direct costs and flexibility, and which in most economic analyses only appears in disguise (as the shirking problem), is the degree of organization of potential employees. If the workforce in a given branch belongs to a powerful and militant trade union, then it becomes attractive for a capitalist to look for alternatives to wage labour. Marx already noted that in the United States "every independent workers' movement was paralysed as long as slavery disfigured a part of the republic. Labour in a white skin cannot emancipate itself where it is branded in a black skin." Marx, *Capital*, 1, p. 414. A similar observation about the organizational problems of free wage labour in Antiquity is made by von Pöhlmann, *Geschichte der sozialen Frage*, p. 177.

61. Van der Linden, "Connecting Household History and Labour History", pp. 163-173. Neither strategic considerations, nor behavioural norms imply automatically that unfree workers want to become free wage labourers. A study of serfs in Russian nineteenth-century metallurgical industry observed: "There is no evidence that the serf workers yearned for some condition of 'freedom' or were even aware of the Western concept of freedom. On the contrary, while they at times complained of harsh discipline, they considered the assurance of their basic security to have been an inalienable right, an inherent aspect of the social-economic system in which they lived. [...] The workers so valued this security that some of them received their emancipation in 1861 with dismay at the loss of their 'rights'." Esper, "Condition of the Serf Workers", p. 671.

Figure 2. Some Motives Determining the Choice of Employment Relations

	Strategic considerations	Behavioural norms
Employer	1) direct cost 2) flexibility 3) effective law	1) humanity 2) decency
Employee	1) stability and quality of standard of living 2) protection	1) dignity 2) justice

4. Normalization

Even if we eventually succeeded in developing a coherent theory which describes why employers sometimes do and sometimes do not employ free wage labour, the question still remains as to why wage labour has become the normal form of dependent labour in advanced capitalist societies (leaving domestic subsistence labour out of consideration for the moment). With the term "normal", I mean in this context both that free wage labour has become absolutely dominant, and that all forms of unfree labour are regarded as objectionable and illegal. Once again a purely economic explanation seems insufficient; beyond the immediate material aspects to do with calculations of economic advantage, considerations of morality and legality also play a role.

From an economic standpoint two factors deserve attention. The first (microeconomic) factor was identified already some thirty years ago by John Hicks: the more free wage labour becomes a general phenomenon, unfree labour becomes more expensive, because "they are competing sources: when both are used the availability of one affects the value (wage or capital value) of the other".[62] After all, the maintenance cost of a slave increases as the supply of slaves declines, while conversely an increasing number of wage labourers makes this form of labour cheaper.[63]

The second factor is macro-economic. As is known, capitalism has its roots in the production of luxury goods (textiles, etc.) for the nobility and other wealthy clients. Industrial capitalism took off on this basis, beginning with the

---

62. Hicks, *Theory of Economic History*, p. 132.
63. "When slaves are cheap and easily obtainable, it will pay to keep the sums invested in their maintenance to a minimum; but when slaves are harder to get and more expensive, so that the loss of a slave, or his inability to work, is a serious matter, it will be profitable to undertake expenditure to diminish the risk of its occurrence. [If] labour is abundant [the wage] can fall very low, to something which corresponds to no more than the maintenance of the slave – even to the short-period, or nearly short-period maintenance of the slave." *Ibid.*, pp. 127, 132.

textile industry in the nineteenth century; subsequently it spread in the course of the nineteenth century to a variety of other sectors; in the process *manu*facture gave way to *machino*facture: "The focus of accumulation shifted sharply toward industry, and particularly to the build-up of Department I, including not only factories but also a vast infrastructure of transportation and communications (turnpikes, canals, ports, steamships, railroads, telegraphs)."[64] Gradually however Department II also began to grow, and an increasingly larger part of production in this sector was bought by a growing class of wage earners. Thus a dynamic interaction developed between sectors I and II, which sometimes has been – unjustifiably – theorized as a "Fordist regime of accumulation".[65]

This development is highly important in the context of this analysis, because the growing size of wage earners' consumption showed even in the most abstract and "theoretical" sense the boundaries of mass slavery in the "core" countries. In this connection Marx characterized the difference between slave and wage worker as follows:

> The slave receives the means of subsistence he requires in the form of *naturalia* which are fixed both in kind and quantity – i.e. he receives *use-values*. The free worker receives them in the shape of *money*, *exchange-value*, the abstract social form of wealth. [...] It is the worker himself who converts the money into whatever use-values he desires; it is he who buys commodities as he wishes and, as the *owner of money*, as the buyer of goods, he stands in precisely the same relationship to the sellers of goods as any other buyer.[66]

Padgug has rightly pointed out that "slaves are to a large degree themselves outside of the commodity system as consumers, and therefore do not permit the full development of an internal market".[67] Wage earners by contrast could be integrated in an upward spiral of rising wages and increasing mass consumption.[68] In other words: twentieth century capitalism based on mass consumption

64. Sweezy, "Contradictions of Capitalism", p. 37. Department I is Marx's term for the economic sector producing means of production (equipment goods). Department II is the sector producing consumer goods. See Marx, *Capital*, 2, ch. 20. The reader may be reminded of Hoffmann's theory of industrialization stages: Stage I is characterized by the domination of consumer-goods industries; during Stage II capital goods industries become increasingly important; and during Stage III there is a balance between consumer-goods industries and capital-goods industries with a tendency for the capital-goods industries to expand more rapidly than the consumer-goods industries. See Hoffmann, *Growth of Industrial Economies*.
65. Aglietta, *Theory of Capitalist Regulation*. See also Foster, "Fetish of Fordism", pp. 14–33; Clarke, "Overaccumulation, Class Struggle and the Regulation Approach", pp. 59–92.
66. Marx, "Results", p. 1033.
67. Padgug, "Problems in the Theory of Slavery", p. 20.
68. "To each capitalist, the total mass of all workers, with the exception of his own workers, appear not as workers, but as consumers, possessors of exchange values (wages), money, which they exchange for his commodity." Marx, *Grundrisse*, p. 419. See also Sulkunen, "Individual Consumption in Capitalism", pp. 35–46.

was only possible thanks to the growing buying power of the working classes in the metropoles – and this was only possible because wage labour dominated in the advanced capitalist countries. In fact, the proletarianization of the metropoles was, from this point of view, a *conditio sine qua non* for advanced capitalist prosperity.[69]

These considerations notwithstanding, slave labour remains an economically *conceivable* option in the metropoles as well, be it as a rather marginal phenomenon. That slavery was actually banned in modern capitalist society to a large extent, even where this did not make economic sense from the standpoint of capital accumulation, has less to do with economic contradictions than with the inherently universalistic tendency of bourgeois norms. This brings me to a second, moral aspect of the normalization. In a pathbreaking essay, Thomas Haskell demonstrated some years ago that there exists an intimate relationship between the rise of modern capitalism and the emergence of a humanitarian sensibility: the market wrought changes in perception or cognitive style that underlay "the new constellation of attitudes and activities that we call humanitarianism".[70] According to Haskell an expansion of the market across more and more areas of the globe had two major consequences. In the first place a market can only function effectively if market actors keep their promises, i.e. if they honour their contractual obligations:

> Historically speaking, capitalism requires conscience and can even be said to be identical with the ascendancy of conscience. This "tremendous labor" of instinctual renunciation on which promise keeping rests [...] is an absolute prerequisite for the

69. Ostensibly this is a functional explanation: advanced capitalism demands mass consumption of the working class. But in fact a causal argument is involved: those elements of capitalism dominated by wage labour could realize a higher rate of capital accumulation than those parts where non-economically coerced labour dominated, and thus it acquired the lead in the mutual competition. The importance of this conclusion must not be underestimated. The dominance of wage labour does not imply that it is essentially a question of *free* wage labour. To the contrary: there also exists a tendency in the advanced capitalist countries for a new form of bonding of labour to enterprises. Tom Brass correctly observes that "when labour begins to act individually or to organize collectively in defence of its own interests, by exercizing freedom of movement to secure higher wages, better working conditions, shorter working hours, etc., capitalist employers introduce or reintroduce restrictions on the formation or extension of a labour market with the object of shifting the balance of workplace power in their own direction". Brass, "Some Observations on Unfree Labour", this volume, pp. 74 f. Employers are continually in search of means to tie staff to the enterprise. One of the old ways was the truck system. But even today attempts at bondage occur. Companies possess all sorts of "devices with which to penalize exit, or what amounts to the same thing, reward continuation": deferred payment of premium wages, non-wage compensation (pensions, health insurance, company-provided housing, etc.) and internal promotion ladders. Goldberg, "Bridges over Contested Terrain", pp. 263-264; see also by the same author "Law and Economics of Vertical Restrictions", pp. 91-129, and Dovring, "Bondage, Tenure, and Progress", p. 309.
70. Haskell, "Capitalism and the Origins of the Humanitarian Sensibility", p. 342.

emergence of possessive individualism and market society. [...] Conscience and promise keeping emerged in human history, of course, long before capitalism. [...] But it was not until the eighteenth century, in Western Europe, England, and North America, that societies first appeared whose economic systems depended on the expectation that most people, most of the time, were sufficiently conscience-ridden (and certain of retribution) that they could be trusted to keep their promises. In other words, only then did promise keeping become so widespread that it could be elevated into a general social norm.[71]

The second crucial change accompanying the rise of the market economy was that people learnt to take into account the remote consequences of their actions.

As the prime mover of a promise-keeping form of life, the market established a domain within which human behavior was cut loose from the anchor of tradition and yet simultaneously rendered as stable and predictable as "long chains of will" could make it. The combination of changeability and foreseeability created powerful incentives for the development of a manipulative, problem-solving sort of intelligence.[72]

The combination of these two great cultural changes (promise keeping and recipe knowledge) pushed an initially small, but afterwards gradually growing group from the middle classes over a moral threshold, and allowed them "the extension to strangers of levels of care and concern that were previously confined to family, friends, and neighbours".[73] It enabled them to "place slavery (and much else) on the agenda of remediable evils, making possible the collective action historians call 'humanitarianism'".[74]

The moral, humanitarian impulse was strengthened by a third factor: the fact that capitalism harbours a powerful tendency towards the generalization of formal principles of justice. The cause of this lies in the exchange process which

71. *Ibid.*, pp. 552-553.
72. *Ibid.*, p. 558.
73. Haskell, "Convention and Hegemonic Interest", p. 864. This is a reply to: Davis, "Reflections on Abolitionism", pp. 797-812, and Ashworth, "Relationship between Capitalism and Humanitarianism", pp. 813-828. The importance of promise keeping and a high time-horizon has been stressed before by Gerschenkron in his essay "Modernization of Entrepreneurship", pp. 129-130.
74. Haskell, "Convention and Hegemonic Interest", p. 851. Connected with this problematic is the question why the abolition of slavery occurred in two stages: it begun little by little in feudal Europe, but subsequently slavery was introduced again and on an historically unprecedented scale in the colonial regions and abolished once more in the course of the nineteenth century. For this abolitionism in two stages, no mono-causal explanation exists either. Both for the first phase and for the second phase, a combination of strategic considerations and behavioural norms operated. See for the first phase: Bonnassie, "Survie et extinction du régime esclavagiste", pp. 307-343; Samson, "End of Early Medieval Slavery", pp. 95-124. For the second phase: Drescher, *Capitalism and Antislavery*; Blackburn, *Overthrow of Colonial Slavery*.

penetrates increasingly broader sectors of society. The exchange process is a great "equalizer". If person A and person B want to do business, because A offers a commodity for which B is prepared to pay money, then A and B must recognize each other as equal partners, as owners of private property, each with their own independent will. Freedom and equality are therefore structural elements in the exchange process between commodity owners. More – these ideas have their material basis in the exchange process: "the exchange of exchange values is the productive, real basis of all *equality* and *freedom*. As pure ideas they are merely the idealized expressions of this basis".[75]

The expansion of exchange relations carries the generalization of these notions in its wake. The concept of human equality could only acquire the "permanence of a fixed popular opinion" in a society "where the commodity-form is the universal form of the product of labour, hence the dominant social relation is the relation between men as possessors of commodities".[76] Historically, the idea of equality established itself first among the owners of capital and land, and subsequently also among the owners of labour power, the workers. Together with this generalization also emerges the tendency to regard all relations in which producers did *not* have an independent will (slavery in particular) as unjust.

Even in its phase of generalization, "free" wage labour remains trapped in its central contradiction: unlimited "freedom" continues to mean for workers not just freedom from clientship, bondage and servitude, but also dependence on charity, welfare and the vagaries of an unpredictable labour market.

On the one hand, this leads time and again to attempts to revive bonded relationships, which in extreme cases are also justified with anti-humanitarian and anti-egalitarian arguments (the clearest example being German National Socialism); on the other side, the truly "free" wage earners are very aware of the fact of their lack of rights, and of the uncertainty which their situation brings with it. The struggle for *the emancipatory decommodification of labour power* therefore has lost nothing of its actuality.

---

75. Marx, *Grundrisse*, p. 245.
76. Marx, *Capital*, 1, p. 152. A further elaboration of this idea can be found in the classical text of Pashukanis, "General Theory of Law and Marxism"; see also Stoyanovitch, "Théorie du contrat selon E.B. Pachoukanis", pp. 89-98; Edelman, *Droit saisi par la photographie*; Tuschling, *Rechtsform und Produktionsverhältnisse*; and Balbus, "Commodity Form and Legal Form", pp. 571-588. Prototypical for the tendency towards generalization is of course the French Declaration of Rights of 1789; see Van Kley, "From the Lessons of French History to Truths for All Times and All People", pp. 72-113.

Collective Bibliography

Acuña, Rodolfo, *Occupied America: A History of Chicanos* (New York, 1981).

Adamson, A.H., *Sugar Without Slaves: The Political Economy of British Guiana* (New Haven, 1972).

Adler, Nanci, *Victims of Soviet Terror. The Story of the Memorial Movement* (Westport, 1993)

Agee, Philip, *Inside the Company* (London, 1975).

Aglietta, Michel, *A Theory of Capitalist Regulation*, transl. by David Fernbach (London, 1979).

Agricultural Labor Relations Board, *A Handbook on the California Agricultural Labor Relations Law* (Sacramento, 1990).

Aguirre, Juan Francisco de, "Diario del capitán Juan Francisco de Aguirre (1793-98)", *Revista de la Biblioteca Nacional de Buenos Aires*, 17 (1947), 18 (1948), 19 (1948), and 20 (1949).

Aguirre, Sergio, *Eco de caminos* (Havana, 1974).

Ahlberg, René, "Stalinistische Vergangenheitsbewältigung. Auseinandersetzung über die Zahl der GULAG-Opfer", *Osteuropa*, 42 (1992).

Alatas, Ayed, *The Myth of the Lazy Native* (London, 1977).

Albert, Bill, "The Creation of a Proletariat on Peru's Coastal Sugar Plantations: 1880-1920", in: B. Munslow and H. Finch (eds), *Proletarianization in the Third World* (London, 1984).

Alexander, K.C., "Caste Mobilization and Class Consciousness: The Emergence of Agrarian Movements in Kerala and Tamil Nadu", in: Frankel and Rao, *Dominance and State Power in Modern India*.

Ali, Ahmed, *From Plantation to Politics: Studies on Fiji Indians* (Suva, 1979).

Allam, S., *Das Verfahrensrecht in der altägyptischen Arbeitersiedlung von Deir el Medineh* (Tübingen, 1973).

Allam, S., "Familie und Besitzverhältnisse in der altägyptischen Arbeitersiedlung von Deir-el-Medineh", *Revue internationale des droits de l'antiquité*. Third Series, 30 (1983).

Allegretti Zanoni, Mary Helena, "Os Seringueiros – Estudo de caso de um seringal nativo do Acre" (Ph.D., University of Brasilia, 1979).

Althusser, Louis, "Ideology and Ideological State Apparatuses", in: *Essays on Ideology* (London, 1984).

Alvarado, Juan Antonio, *Tratado de cafecultura práctica*, vol. II (Guatemala, 1936).

Aly, Götz, *et. al.* (eds), *Arbeitsmarkt und Sondererlaß (Beiträge zur nationalsozialistischen Gesundheits- und Sozialpolitik*, Bd. 8 (Berlin, 1990).

Anderson, A. Grant, *Indo-Fijian Smallfarming: Profiles of a Peasantry* (Auckland, 1974).

Anderson, Bridget, *Britain's Secret Slaves: An Investigation into the Plight of Overseas Domestic Workers* (London, 1993).

Andrews, B.G. (ed.), *Tales of the Convict System. Selected Stories of Price Warung* (St. Lucia, 1975).

Andrews, George Reid, *The Afro-Argentines of Buenos Aires* (Madison, 1980).

Andreyev, Catherine, *Vlasov and the Russian Liberation Movement* (Cambridge, 1987).

Angelo, Larian, "Wage Labor Deferred: The Recreation of Unfree Labor in the U.S. South", *The Journal of Peasant Studies*, 23 (1995).

Anjou, Leo d', *Social Movements and Cultural Change. The First Abolition Campaign Revisited* (New York, 1996)

Aparicio, Francisco de, "Relación de un viaje entre Mendoza y Buenos Aires en 1794", *Anales del Instituto de Etnografía Americana*, vol. III (Mendoza, 1942).

Aptheker, Herbert, *American Negro Slave Revolts* (New York, 1941).

Aristotle, "Ethica Eudaimonia", in: *Aristotelis Opera*, ex recensione Bekkeri edidit Akademia Borussica, Editio altera, quam curavit Olof Gigon, Vol. alterum, Berolini, 1972, 1242a.

Aristotle, "Politica", in: *Aristotelis Opera*, ex recensione Bekkeri edidit Akademia Borussica, Editio altera, quam curavit Olof Gigon, Vol. alterum, Berolini, 1972, 1253b-1255b.

Armani, Alberto, *Ciudad de Dios y Ciudad del Sol. El "estado" jesuita de los guaraníes (1609-1769)* (Mexico, 1986).

Armstrong, John A., *Ukrainian Nationalism* (Englewood, 1991).

Arnold, David, *Police Power and Colonial Rule; Madras 1859-1947* (Delhi, 1986).

Arnold, Horace Lucien and Fay Leone Faurote, *Ford Methods and the Ford Shops* (New York, 1919).

Arnot, R., "Soviet Labour Productivity and the Failure of the Shchekino Experiment", *Critique*, 15 (1981).

Arrighi, Giovanni and John S. Paul, "Labour Supplies in Historical Perspective: A Study of the Proletarianization of the African Peasantry in Rhodesia", *The Journal of Development Studies*, 6 (1970). Also in: Giovanni Arrighi and John S. Saul (eds), *Essays on the Political Economy of Africa* (New York, 1973).

Ashton, T.H. and C.H.E. Philpin (eds), *The Brenner Debate* (Cambridge, 1985).

Ashworth, John, "The Relationship between Capitalism and Humanitarianism", *American Historical Review*, 92 (1987).

Assadourian, Carlos Sempat, *El sistema de la economía colonial* (Mexico, 1983).

Audring, Gert, "Zur sozialen Stellung der Hirten in Archaischer Zeit, in: Kreissig and Kühnert, *Antike Abhängigkeitsformen in den griechischen Gebieten*.

Aufhauser, Keith R., "Slavery and Scientific Management", *Journal of Economic History*, 33 (1973).

August, Jochen, "Die Entwicklung des Arbeitsmarkts in Deutschland in den 30er Jahren und der Masseneinsatz ausländischer Arbeitskräfte während des Zweiten Weltkrieges. Das Fallbeispiel der polnischen zivilen Arbeiter und Kriegsgefangenen 1939/40", *Archiv für Sozialgeschichte*, 24 (1984).

Averitt, Robert, *The Dual Economy: The Dynamics of American Industry Structure* (New York, 1968).

Ayers, Edward L., *Vengeance and Justice: Crime and Punishment in the Nineteenth Century American South* (New York, 1984).

Azara, Félix de, *Descripción e historia del Paraguay y del Río de la Plata* (1847), in: *Biblioteca Indiana. Viajes por la América del Sur*, vol. 2 (Madrid, 1962).

Baak, Paul E., "Het Overheidsbeleid van Travancore ten aanzien van de Plantagesector in de Tweede Helft van de Negentiende Eeuw; Achtergronden, Maatregelen en Consequenties" (MA thesis, Free University Amsterdam, 1990).

Baak, Paul E., "The Conference on Capitalist Plantations in Colonial Asia, September 26-29, 1990, Amsterdam", *Archipel*, 42 (1991).

Baak, Paul E., "Planters' Lobby in Late 19th Century: Implications for Travancore", *The Economic and Political Weekly*, 27 (1992).

Baak, Paul E., "Out of the Shadow, Into the Spotlights: The Indigenous Aspects of Plantation Development. The Case of the Emergence of Syrian Christian Planters in Princely Travancore in the First Half of the 20th Century", *Itinerario*, 17-2 (1994).

Baak, Paul E., *Plantation Production and Political Power. Plantation Development in South West India, 1743-1963* (New Dehli, 1997).

Bagnall, Roger S., *Egypt in Late Antiquity* (Princeton, 1993).

Bahro, Rudolf, *Die Alternative. Kritik des real existierenden Sozialismus* (Cologne and Frankfurt/Main, 1977).

Baker, Charles A. with Elizabeth Price, "Origins of Pacific Island Labourers in Queensland, 1863-1904: A Research Note", *Journal of Pacific History*, 11 (1976).

Baks, C., J.C. Breman and A.T.J. Nooij, "Slavery as a System of Production in Tribal Societies", *Bijdragen Taal- Land- en Volkenkunde*, 122 (1966).

Bakunin, Mikhail, *Gott und der Staat*, in: Bakunin, *Gesammelte Werke*, vol. 1 (Berlin, 1975).

Bakunin, Mikhail, *Statism and Anarchy*. Edited by Marshall S. Shatz (Cambridge [etc.], 1990)

Balbus, Isaac, "Commodity Form and Legal Form", *Law and Society Review*, 11 (1977).

Balibar, Etienne and Immanuel Wallerstein, *Race, Nation, Class: Ambiguous Identities* (London, 1991)

Banaji, Jairus, "Deccan Districts in the Late 19th Century", *Economic and Political Weekly*, 12 (1977). Also in: Patnaik, *Agrarian Relations and Accumulation*.

Bandarage, Asoka, *Colonialism in Sri Lanka* (Berlin, 1983).

Bandler, Faith, *Wacvie* (Adelaide, 1977).

Banerjee, Sumanta, *In the Wake of Naxalbari: A History of the Naxalite Movement in India* (Calcutta, 1980).

Barber, C.G., *History of the Cauvery-Mettur Project* (Madras, 1940).

Bardhan, Pranab K., "Interlocking Factor Markets and Agrarian Development: A Review of Issues", *Oxford Economic Papers*, 32 (1980).

Bardhan, Pranab K., "Marxist Ideas in Development Economics: An Evaluation", in: Roemer, *Analytical Marxism*.

Bardhan, Pranab K. (ed.), *The Economic Theory of Agrarian Institutions* (Oxford, 1989).

Bardhan, Pranab K., "The New Institutional Economics and Development Theory: A Brief Critical Assessment", *World Development*, 17 (1989).

Bardhan, Pranab K., "Poverty, Growth and Rural Labour Markets in India", *Economic and Political Weekly*, 24 (1989).

Bardhan, Pranab K. and A. Rudra, "Interlinkage of Land, Labour and Credit Relations: An Analysis of Village Survey Data in East India", *Economic and Political Weekly*, 13 (1978).

Baretta, Silvio Duncan and John Markoff, "Civilization and Barbarism: Cattle Frontiers in Latin America", *Comparative Studies in Society and History*, 20 (1978).

Barrera, Mario, *Race and Class in the Southwest* (Notre Dame, 1979).

Barton, Paul, *L'Institution concentrationnaire en Russie 1930-1957* (Paris, 1959).

Bartz, Hoachim and Dagmar Mor, "Der Weg in die Jugendzwangsarbeit. Maßnahmen gegen Jugendarbeitslosigkeit zwischen 1925 und 1935", in: Lenhardt, *Der hilflose Sozialstaat*.

Barzel, Yoram, "An Economic Analysis of Slavery", *Journal of Law and Economics*, 20 (1977).

Basu, Kaushik, "The Emergence of Isolation and Interlinkage in Rural Markets", *Oxford Economic Papers*, 35 (1983).

Basu, Kaushik, "Implicit Interest Rates, Usury and Isolation in Backward Agriculture", *Cambridge Journal of Economics*, 8 (1984).

Basu, Kaushik, "One Kind of Power", *Oxford Economic Papers*, 38 (1986).

Batchelder, Ronald W. and Herman Freudenberger, "On the Rational Origins of the Modern Centralized State", *Explorations in Economic History*, 20 (1983).

Batchelder, Ronald and Nicolás Sanchez, "The Encomienda and the Maximizing Imperialist: An Interpretation of Spanish Imperialism in the Americas", Working Paper No. 501 (Department of Economics, UCLA, 1988).

Baud, Michiel, "Sugar and Unfree Labour: Reflections on Labour Control in the Dominican Republic, 1870-1935", *Journal of Peasant Studies*, 19 (1992).

Bauer, Arnold J., *Chilean Rural Society from the Spanish Conquest to 1930* (Cambridge, 1975).

Bauer, Arnold J., "Rural Workers in Spanish America: Problems of Peonage and Oppression", *Hispanic American Historical Review*, 59 (1979).

Bayly, C.A., *Rulers, Townsmen and Bazaars. North Indian Society in the Age of British Expansion, 1770-1870* (Cambridge, 1983).

Baysinger, Barry *et al.*, "Mercantilism As a Rent-Seeking Society", in: Buchanan, *Towards a Theory of the Rent-Seeking Society*.

Beachey, R.W, *The British West Indies Sugar Industry in the Late Nineteenth Century* (Oxford, 1957).

Beall, Jo, "Women Under Indenture in Natal", in: Bhana, *Essays on Indentured Indians*.

Bean, Frank D. *et al.*, *Opening and Closing the Doors* (California, 1990).

Bechtle, Günter, *Betrieb als Strategie* (Frankfurt/Main and New York, 1980).

Beck, E.M. and Stewart E. Tolnay, "A Season for Violence: The Lynching of Blacks and Labor Demand in the Agricultural Production Cycle in the American South", *International Review of Social History*, 37 (1992). Also in: Marcel van der Linden and Jan Lucassen (eds), *Racism in the Labour Market: Historical Studies* (Berne, 1995).

Becker, Gary S., "A Theory of Marriage", *Journal of Political Economy*, 81 (1973) and 82 (1974).

Beckles, Hilary McD., *Natural Rebels: A Social History of Enslaved Black Women in Barbados* (London, 1989).

Beechert, Edward D., *Working in Hawaii: A Labor History* (Honolulu, 1985).

Behal, Rana P. and Prabhu P. Mohapatra, "'Tea and Money versus Human Life': The Rise and Fall of the Indenture System in the Assam Tea Plantations 1840-1908", in: Daniel *et al.*, *Plantations*.

Beinart, W., P. Delius, and S. Trapido (eds), *Putting a Plough to the Ground: Accumulation and Dispossession in Rural South Africa, 1850-1930* (Johannesburg, 1986).

Bekker, S. and R. Humphries, *From Control to Confusion* (Cape Town, 1985).

Bell, James R., "The Empress Bridge Over the Sutlej", *Minutes of Proceedings of the Institution of Civil Engineers*, 65 (1881).

Bellon, B.P., *Mercedes in Peace and War: German Automobile Workers, 1903-1945* (New York, 1990).

Belsunce, César García *et al.*, *Buenos Aires: su gente, 1810-1830* (Buenos Aires, 1976).

Ben-David, Arye, *Talmudische Ökonomie*, I (Hildesheim and New York, 1974).

Bennett, Judith A., Review in *Journal of Pacific History*, 14 (1979).

Benveniste, Emile, *Le vocabulaire des instititutions Indo-Européennes*, Vol. 1 (Paris, 1969).

Bergad, Laird W., "On Comparative History: A Reply to Tom Brass", *Journal of Latin American Studies*, 16 (1984).

Bergad, Laird W., *Cuban Rural Society in the Nineteenth Century: the Social and Economic History of Monoculture in Matanzas* (Princeton, 1990).

Berger, Susan, *Political and Agrarian Development in Guatemala* (Boulder, 1992).

Berkley, James John, *Minutes of Proceedings of the Institution of Civil Engineers*, 19 (1859-60).

Bhaduri, Amit, "A Study in Agricultural Backwardness under Semi-Feudalism", *The Economic Journal*, 83 (1973).

Bhaduri, Amit, "On the Formation of Usurious Interest Rates in Backward Agriculture", *Cambridge Journal of Economics*, 1 (1977).

Bhaduri, Amit, "Class Relations and the Pattern of Accumulation in an Agrarian Economy", *Cambridge Journal of Economics*, 5 (1981).

Bhaduri, Amit, *The Economic Structure of Backward Agriculture* (London, 1983).

Bhaduri, Amit, "Forced Commerce and Agrarian Growth", *World Development*, 14 (1986).

Bhagwati, Jagadish, *Free Trade, "Fairness" and the New Protectionism: Reflections on an Agenda For the World Trade Organization* (London, 1995).

Bhana, Surendra (ed.), *Essays on Indentured Indians in Natal* (Leeds, 1988).

Bharadwaj, Krishna, "A View on Commercialisation in Indian Agriculture and the Development of Capitalism", *Journal of Peasant Studies*, 12 (1985).

Bhende, M.J., "Credit Markets in Rural South India", *Economic and Political Weekly*, 21 (1986).

Binswanger, H. and M. Rosenzweig, *Contractual Arrangements, Employment and Wages in Rural Labour Markets in Asia* (New Haven and London, 1984).

Birch, Alan, "The Organization and Economics of Pacific Islands' Labour in the Australian Sugar Industry, 1863-1906", *Business Archives and History*, 6 (1966).

Blackburn, Robin, *The Overthrow of Colonial Slavery, 1776-1848* (London, 1988).

Blackstone, William, *Commentaries on the Laws of England*, 4 vols (Chicago, 1979 [orig. 1765-69]).

Blaikie, George, "The Fine Old Art of Recruiting Help", *Sunday Mail Colour* (Brisbane), 20 May 1984.

Blakeley, A., "Slavery and Slavishness in Rusland and America", *Slavery and Abolition*, 10 (1989).

Blakewell, P.J., *Silver Mining and Society in Colonial Mexico, Zacatecas 1546-1700* (Cambridge, 1971).

Blassingame, John W., *The Slave Community: Plantation Life in the Antebellum South* (New York, 1979).

Blicksilver, Jack, *Cotton Manufacturing in the Southeast: An Historical Analysis* (Atlanta, 1959).

Block, Fred and John Noakes, "The Politics of New-style Workfare", *Socialist Review*, 18 (1988).

Blum, Jerome, *The End of the Old Order in Rural Europe* (Princeton, 1978).

Bolland, O.N., "Systems of Domination after Slavery: The Control of Land and Labor in the British West Indies after 1838", *Comparative Studies in Society and History*, 23 (1981).

Bolland, O.N., "Reply to William A. Green's 'The Perils of Comparative History'", *Comparative Studies in Society and History*, 26 (1984).

Bolton, G.C., *A Thousand Miles Away: A History of North Queensland to 1920* (Brisbane, 1963).

Bonacich, Edna, "A Theory of Middlemen Minorities", *American Sociological Review*, 38 (1973).

Bonnassie, Pierre, "Survie et extinction du régime esclavagiste dans l'Occident du haut moyen âge (IVe-XIe s.)", *Cahiers du Civilisation Médiévale*, 38 (1985).

Bonner, P., "Strikes and the Independent Trade Unions", in: Maree, *The Independent Trade Unions*.

Bottomley, A., "The Premium for Risk as a Determinant of Interest Rates in Underdeveloped Rural Areas", *Quarterly Journal of Economics* 77 (1963).

Boyd, Michael, "The Evolution of Agrarian Institutions: The Case of Medieval and Ottoman Serbia", *Explorations in Economic History*, 28 (1991).

Boyd, Rosalind E., Robin Cohen and Peter C.W. Gutkind (eds), *International Labour and the Third World: The Making of a New Working Class* (Aldershot, 1987).

Bradlow, E., "Capitalists and Labourers in the Post-Emancipation Rural Cape - Part I and Part II", *Historia,* 30 (September 1985).

Brandt, Heinz, "Die soziale Revolution des Nikita Sergejewitsch Chruschtschow", in: Reinhard Crusius and Manfred Wilke (eds), *Entstalinisierung. Der XX. Parteitag der KPdSU und seine Folgen* (Frankfurt/Main, 1977).

Branford, Sue and Oriel Glock, *The Last Frontier - Fighting Over Land in the Amazon* (London, Zed Books Ltd., 1985).

Brass, Tom, "Class Formation and Class Struggle in La Convención, Peru", *Journal of Peasant Studies*, 7 (1980).

Brass, Tom, "Coffee and Rural Proletarianization: A Comment on Bergad", *Journal of Latin American Studies*, 16 (1984).

Brass, Tom, "The Elementary Strictures of Kinship: Unfree Relations and the Production of Commodities", *Social Analysis*, 20 (1986).

Brass, Tom, "Free and Unfree Rural Labour in Puerto Rico during the Nineteenth Century", *Journal of Latin American Studies*, 18 (1986).

Brass, Tom, "Unfree Labour and Capitalist Restructuring in the Agrarian Sector: Peru and India", *Journal of Peasant Studies*, 14 (1986).

Brass, Tom, "Slavery Now: Unfree Labour and Modern Capitalism", *Slavery and Abolition*, 9 (1988).

Brass, Tom, "Class Struggle and the Deproletarianization of Agricultural Labour in Haryana (India)", *Journal of Peasant Studies*, 18 (1990).

Brass, Tom, "The Latin American *Enganche* System: Some Revisionist Reinterpretations Revisited", *Slavery and Abolition*, 11 (1990).

Brass, Tom, "Peasant Essentialism and the Agrarian Question in the Colombian Andes", *Journal of Peasant Studies*, 17 (1990).

Brass, Tom, "Market Essentialism and the Impermissibility of Unfree Labour", *Slavery and Abolition*, 12 (1991).

Brass, Tom, "A-Way with Their Wor(l)d: Rural Labourers through the Postmodern Prism", *Economic and Political Weekly*, 28 (1993).

Brass, Tom, "Migration, Tenancy and Bondage in Purnea District, Bihar", in B.N. Yugandhar and K. Gopal Iyer (eds), *Land Reforms in India*, Vol. I: *Bihar – Institutional Constraints* (New Delhi, 1993).

Brass, Tom, "Contextualizing Sugar Production in Nineteenth Century Queensland", *Slavery and Abolition*, 15 (1994).

Brass, Tom, "Reply to Utsa Patnaik: If the Cap Fits...", *International Review of Social History*, 40 (1995).

Brass, Tom, Review of Patnaik & Dingwaney, *Chains of Servitude*, in *The Journal of Peasants Studies*, 14 (1996), pp. 120-126.

Brass, Tom and Henry Bernstein, "Proletarianization and Deproletarianization on the Colonial Plantation", in: Daniel *et al.*, *Plantations, Proletarians and Peasants*.

Brassey, M., *Labour Relations Under the New Constitution* (Cape Town, 1994).

Braverman, A. and J. Stiglitz, "Sharecropping and the Interlinking of Agrarian Markets", *American Economic Review*, 72 (1982).

Braverman, Harry, *Labor and Monopoly Capital. The Degradation of Work in the Twentieth Century* (New York and London, 1974).

Breman, Jan, "Seasonal Migration and Co-operative Capitalism", *Journal of Peasant Studies*, 6 (1978).

Breman, Jan, *Of Peasants, Migrants and Paupers: Rural Labour Circulation and Capitalist Production in Western India* (Delhi, 1985).

Breman, Jan, *Taming the Coolie Beast: Plantation Society and the Colonial Order in Southeast Asia* (Delhi, 1989).

Breman, Jan, "'Even Dogs are Better Off': The Ongoing Battle Between Capital and Labour in the Cane-Fields of Gujarat", *Journal of Peasant Studies*, 17 (1990).

Breman, Jan, *Labour Migration and Rural Transformation in Colonial Asia* (Amsterdam, 1990).

Breman, Jan, *Koelies, planters en koloniale politiek. Het arbeidsregime op de grootlandbouwondernemingen aan Sumatra's oostkust in het begin van de twintigste eeuw* (Leiden, 1992).

Breman, Jan, *Beyond Patronage and Exploitation. Changing Agrarian Relations in South Gujarat* (Delhi, 1993).

Breman, Jan and Val Daniel, "Conclusion: The Making of a Coolie", in: Daniel *et al.*, *Plantations*.

Brenner, Robert, "Agrarian Class Structure and Economic Development in Pre-Industrial Europe", in: Aston and Philpin, *The Brenner Debate*.

Brenner, Robert, "The Agrarian Roots of European Capitalism", in: Ashton and Philpin, *The Brenner Debate*.

Briggs, Asa (ed.), *Chartist Studies* (London, 1967).

Brintnal, Douglas, *Revolt Against the Dead* (London, 1979).

Brooks, Robert Preston, *The Agrarian Revolution in Georgia 1865-1912* (Madison, WI, 1914).

Brown, Harry Bates, *Cotton: Its History Species, Varieties, Morphology, Breeding, Culture, Marketing and Uses* (New York, 1938).

Brown, Jonathan, *A Socioeconomic History of Argentina, 1776-1860* (Cambridge, 1979).

Brown, Kenneth D., "Introduction: Wage-labour: 1500-1800", in: *The English Labour Movement 1700-1951* (Dublin, 1982).

Brown, W.W. and M.O. Reynolds, "Debt Peonage Re-examined", *Journal of Economic History*, 33 (1973).

Browne, Lynn, "How Different Are Regional Wage Rates", *New England Economic Review*, 10 (1978).

Browning, Christopher R., *Ordinary Men: Reserve Police Battallion 101 and the Final Solution in Poland* (New York, 1992).

Browning, David, *El Salvador: Landscape and Society* (Oxford, 1971).

Buca, Edward, *Vorkuta* (London, 1976).

Buchanan, Francis, *A Journey From Madras Through the Countries of Mysore, Canara, and Malabar*, vol. 1 (London, 1807).

Buchanan, James M. (ed.), *Towards a Theory of the Rent-Seeking Society* (College Station, Texas, 1981).

Buchanan, William, *Understanding Political Variables* (New York, 1980).

Bulmer-Thomas, Victor, "Central America in the Inter-War Period", in: Rosemary Thorp (ed.), *Latin America in the 1930s* (London, 1984).

Bulmer-Thomas, Victor, *The Political Economy of Central America Since 1920* (Cambridge, 1987).

Bunzel, Ruth, *Chichicastenango* (Seattle, 1959).

Burawoy, Michael, *Manufacturing Consent. Changes in the Labour Process under Monopoly Capitalism* (London, 1979).

Burawoy, Michael, "The Functions and Reproduction of Migrant Labor: Comparative Material From Southern Africa and the US", *American Journal of Sociology*, 81 (1981).

Burawoy, Michael, *The Politics of Production. Factory Regimes Under Capitalism and Socialism* (London [etc.], 1985).

Burawoy, Michael and Erik Olin Wright, "Coercion and Consent in Contested Exchange", in: Wright, *Interrogating Inequality*.

Burkhardt, Michael, "Kritik der Marxschen Mehrwerttheorie", *Jahrbuch für Wirtschaftswissenschaften*, 46 (1995).

Burkholder, Mark A. and Lyman L. Johnson, *Colonial Latin America* (New York, 1994²).

Bush, J.A., "'Take This Job and Shove it': The Rise of Free Labor", *Michigan Law Review*, 91 (1993).

Butlin, N.G., *Ante-Bellum Slavery: A Critique of a Debate* (Canberra, 1971).

Cairnes, J.E., *The Slave Power: Its Character, Career, and Probable Designs: Being an Attempt to Explain the Real Issues Involved in the American Contest* (London, 1982).

Cajani, Luigi, "Die italienischen Militär-Internierten im nationalsozialistischen Deutschland", in: Herbert, *Europa und der "Reichseinsatz"*.

Camm, J.C.R., "Pacific Islanders", in: J.C.R. Camm and John McQuilton (eds), *Australians: A Historical Atlas* (Sydney, 1988).

Cardoso, Lawrence A., *Mexican Emigration to the US, 1897-1931* (Arizona, 1980).

Cardozo, Ramón I., *La antigua provincia del Guairá y Villa Rica del Espíritu Santo* (Buenos Aires, 1938).

Carelli, Vincent and Milton Severiano, *Mão Branca Contra o Povo Cinza* (n.p., 1980).

Carlos, Manuel L. and Frida Espinoza, "The International Economic System and the Border Labor Force: The Case of Agricultural Workers from the Imperial-Mexicali Valley Area" (Paper presented at Society for Applied Anthropology meeting in San Diego, 1983).

Carmen Barcia, María del, *Burguesía y abolición* (Havana, 1987).

Carneiro, Robert, "A Theory of the Origin of the State", *Science*, 169 (1970).

Carr, Norma, "The Puerto Ricans in Hawaii, 1900-1958" (Ph.D., University of Hawaii, 1989).

Carr, Edgar H. and Robert W. Davies, *Foundations of a Planned Economy: 1926-1929*, vol. 1 (Harmondsworth, 1974).

Carter, M., "The Transition from Slave to Indentured Labour in Mauritius", *Slavery and Abolition*, 14 (1993).

Carvalho, José Porfirio Fontenele de, *Waimiri-Atroari - A estória que ainda não foi contada* (Brasília, 1982).

Casaldáliga, Pedro, *Uma Igreja da Amazônia em Conflito com o Latifúndio e a Marginalização Social* (São Félix, 1971).

Casaldáliga, Pedro, *Creio na Justiça e na Esperança*, translation by Laura Ramo, Antonio Carlos Moura and Hugo Lopes (Rio de Janeiro, 1978²).

Casanovas Codina, Joan, "Labor and Colonialism in Cuba in the Second Half of the Nineteenth Century" (Ph.D., State University of New York at Stony Brook, 1994).

Castañeda, Antonia, "Soldaderas y Pobladores: Spanish and Mexican Women in Colonial California" (Ph.D., Stanford University, 1990).

Castells, Manuel, "Immigrant Workers and Class Struggles in Advanced Capitalism: The Western European Experience", reprinted in: Robin Cohen *et al.* (eds), *Peasants and Proletarians. The Struggles of Third World Workers* (New York [etc.], 1979).

Castro, Ferreira de, *A Selva* (Rio de Janeiro, n.d.).

Cavazos, Raul, "A View of Farm Labor Contracting in California: Past and Present", in: *Agricultural Labor Research Symposium, June 1991 Proceedings* (Sacramento, 1991).

Caves, Richard, "'Vent-for-Surplus' Models of Trade and Growth", in: Theberge, *The Economics of Trade and Development*.

Cepero Bonilla, Raúl, "Azúcar y abolición (apuntes para una historia crítica del abolicionismo)", in: *Ibid., Escritos históricos*.

Cepero Bonilla, Raúl, "El Siglo" (1862-1868) un periódico en lucha contra la censura", in: *Ibid., Escritos históricos*.

Cepero Bonilla, Raúl, *Escritos históricos* [edited by María Luisa Cepero Fernández] (Havana, 1989; 1948¹)

Černy, Jaroslav, *A Community of Workmen at Thebes in the Ramasside Period* (Paris, 1973).

Chacon, Ramon D., "Labor Unrest and Industrialized Agriculture", *Social Science Quarterly*, 65 (1984).

Chakrabarty, Dipesh, *Rethinking Working-Class History. Bengal 1890-1940* (Princeton, 1989).

Chakravarti, Uma, "Of Dasas and Karmakaras: Servile Labour in Ancient India", in: Patnaik and Dingwaney, *Chains of Servitude*.

Chan, Sucheng, *This Bittersweet Soil: The Chinese in California Agriculture* (Berkeley, 1986).

Chapman, Charles E., *The Founding of Spanish California: The Northwestward Expansion of New Spain, 1687-1783* (New York, 1973).

Chaves, Julio César, "Las ordenanzas de Ramírez de Velasco, Hernandarias y Alfaro", *Historia Paraguaya*, 113 (1969-70).

Chavez, Leo, "Proposition 187: The Nationalist Response to the Transnationalists' Challenge", *Anthropology Newsletter*, 36 (1995).

Chavez, Leo, *Shadowed Lives: Undocumented Immigrants in American Society* (New York, 1992).

Cheng, Lucie and Edna Bonacich (eds), *Labor Immigration Under Capitalism: Asian workers in the United States before World War II* (Berkeley, 1984).

Chopra, Suneet, "Bondage in a Green Revolution Area: A Study of Brick Kiln Workers in Muzaffernagar District", in: Patnaik and Dingwaney, *Chains of Servitude*.

Chossudovsky, Michel, *Towards Capitalist Restoration? Chinese Socialism After Mao* (London, 1986).

Cicero, Marcus Tullius, *De Officis/On Duties*. Edited by Harry G. Edinger (Indianapolis, 1974).

Ciszek, W.J. and D.L. Flaherty, *La spia del Vaticano. 23 anni di attività di un gesuita nell'Unione Sovietica* (Torino, 1978).

Clark, C.M.H., "Rewriting Australian History", in: Thomas Hungerford (ed.), *Australian Signpost* (Melbourne, 1956).

Clark, Colin, "The Economics of Overexploitation", *Science*, 181 (1973).

Clark, John Hendrik *et al*, *William Styron's Nat Turner: Ten Black Writers Respond* (New York, 1968).

Clarke, Simon, "Overaccumulation, Class Struggle and the Regulation Approach", *Capital and Class*, 6 (1988).

Clastres, Pierre, *La société contre l'état* (Paris, 1974).

Cline, Sarah, "Mexican Native Language Documentation and Its Potential for Writing Ethnohistory" (Paper presented at University of California, Santa Barbara, 19 November 1987).

Coats, A.W., "Changing Attitudes to Labour in the Mid-Eighteenth Century", *Economic History Review*, Second Series, 11 (1958-1959).

Coatsworth, John, "Obstacles to Change in 19th Century Mexico", *American Historical Review*, 83 (1978).

Coghlan, Timothy Augustine, *Labour and Industry in Australia*, 4 vols (Melbourne, 1969).

Cohen, G.A., *Karl Marx's Theory of History. A Defence* (Oxford, 1978).

Cohen, Robin *et al.* (eds), *Peasants and Proletarians. The Struggles of Third World Workers* (New York [etc.], 1979).

Cohen, Robin, *The New Helots: Migrants in the International Division of Labour* (Aldershot, 1987).

Cohen, Robin, *Contested Domains: Debates in International Labour Studies* (London, 1991).

Cohen, Sheila, "A Labour Process to Nowhere", *New Left Review*, No. 165 (1987).

Cohen, William, "Negro Involuntary Servitude in the South, 1865-1940: A Preliminary Analysis", *Journal of Southern History*, 42 (1976).

Cohen, William, *At Freedom's Edge: Black Mobility and the Southern Quest for Racial Control, 1861-1915* (Baton Rouge, LA, 1991).

Colburn, Forrest D. (ed.), *Everyday Forms of Peasant Resistance* (Armonk, NY, 1989).

Colby, Benjamin N. and Pierre L. van den Berghe, *Ixil Country: A Plural Society in Highland Guatemala* (Berkeley, 1969).

Commission on Agricultural Workers, "Employment Trends in the US and Seven Key Agricultural States", in: *Case Studies and Research Reports, Appendix I* (Washington, DC, 1992).

Commission on Agricultural Workers, *Report of the Commission* (Washington, DC, 1992).

Conert, Hans-Georg, *Die Ökonomie des unmöglichen Sozialismus. Krise und Reform der sowjetischen Wirtschaft unter Gorbatschow* (Münster, 1990).

Connolly, William, *Appearance and Reality in Politics* (London, 1981).

Conquest, Robert, "Forced Labour Statistics: Some Comments", *Soviet Studies*, 34 (1982).

Conrad, D.C., "Slavery in Bambara Society", *Slavery and Abolition*, 2 (1981).

Consultative Business Movement National Team, *Managing Change* (Johannesburg, 1993).

Cook, Shelburne F., *The Conflict Between the California Indian and White Civilization*, 3 vols (Berkeley, 1943), 1.

Copeland, Melvin Thomas, *The Cotton Manufacturing Industry of the United States* (Cambridge, 1923).

Corbier, Mireille, "Salaires et salariat sous le Haut-Empire", in: *Les "dévaluations" à Rome. Epoque républicaine et impériale*, vol. 2 (Rome, 1980).

Corder, H., *Focus on the History of Labour Legislation* (Cape Town, 1978).

Cornelius, Wayne, "What Role Does Mexican Labor Play in the US Economy Today?" (Paper presented at the Center for US-Mexican Studies, 1987).

Corrigan, Phillip, "Feudal Relics or Capitalist Monuments? Notes on the Sociology of Unfree Labour", *Sociology*, 11 (1977).

Corris, Peter, "Pacific Island Labour Migrants in Queensland", *Journal of Pacific History*, 5 (1970).

Corris, Peter, *Passage, Port and Plantation: A History of Solomon Islands Labour Migration, 1870-1914* (Melbourne, 1973).

Coser, Lewis A., "Forced Labour in Concentration Camps", in: Kai Erikson and Steven Peter Vallas (eds), *The Nature of Work. Sociological Perspectives* (New Haven [etc.], 1990).

Cotlear, Daniel, "El sistema del Enganche del Siglo XX: una versión diferente" (BA thesis in Economics, Universidad Católica del Perú, Lima, 1979).

Cox, Arthur F. (ed.), *A Manual of the North Arcot District in the Presidency of Madras* (Madras, 1881).

Craig Jenkins, J., *The Politics of Insurgency: The Farm Worker Movement of the 1960s* (New York, 1985).

Craton, M.J., "Reshuffling the Pack: Transition from Slavery to Other Forms of Labour in the British Caribbean, ca. 1790-1890", *New West Indian Guide*, 68 (1994).

Craven, Paul and Douglas Hay, "The Criminalization of "Free" Labour: Master and Servant in Comparative Perspective", *Slavery and Abolition*, 15 (1994).

Craveri, M. and O. Khleveniuk, "Krizis ekonomiki MVD konets 1940kh-1950e gody", *Cahiers du monde russe*, 36 (1995).

Creamer, Daniel, "Recruiting Contract Laborers for the Amoskeag Mills", *Journal of Economic History*, 1 (1941).

Croix, Geoffrey de Ste., *The Class Struggle in the Ancient Greek World from the Archaic Age to the Arab Conquests* (London, 1981).

Croix, Geoffrey de Ste., "Class in Marx's Conception of History, Ancient and Modern", *New Left Review*, No. 146 (1984).

Crosby, Alfred W. Jr, *The Columbian Exchange: Biological and Cultural Consequences of 1492* (Westport, 1972).

Cross, Harry E., "Debt Peonage Reconsidered: A Case Study in Nineteenth Century Zacatecas, Mexico", *Business History Review*, 53 (1979).

Crow, Ben, "Plain Tales From the Rice Trade: Indications of Vertical Integration in Rice Markets in Bangladesh", *Journal of Peasant Studies*, 16 (1989).

Crow, Ben and K.A.S. Murshid, "The Finance of Forced and Free Markets: Merchants' Capital in the Bangladesh Grain Trade" (Open University, Development Policy and Practice Working Paper No. 18, November 1989).

Crowley, Frank, "The Foundation Years, 1788–1821", in: Gordon Greenwood (ed.), *Australia: A Social and Political History* (Sydney, 1974).

Crowley, Frank (ed.), *A New History of Australia* (Melbourne, 1974).

Cuevas, Efraím Martínez, *La ganadería en el Paraguay* (Asunción, 1987).

Cunha, Euclydes da, *À Margem da História* (Porto, 1986⁶).

Curthoys, Ann and Andrew Markus (eds), *Who Are Our Enemies? Racism and the Working Class in Australia* (Sydney, 1978).

Curtin, P.D., *Two Jamaicas: The Role of Ideas in a Tropical Colony 1830-1865* (Cambridge, 1955).

Curtin, Philip D., "Epidemiology and the Slave Trade", *Political Science Quarterly*, 93 (1969).

Dallin, David J. and Boris I. Nicolaevsky, *Forced Labor in Soviet Russia* (London, 1948).

Daniel, E. Valentine, Henry Bernstein and Tom Brass (eds), *Plantations, Peasants and Proletarians in Colonial Asia* (London, 1992).

Daniel, Pete, *The Shadow of Slavery: Peonage in the South 1901-1969* (Urbana, 1972).

Daniel, Pete, "The Metamorphosis of Slavery, 1865-1900", *Journal of American History*, 66 (1979).

Das, Arvind N., *Does Bihar Show the Way?* (Calcutta, 1979).

Das Gupta, Ranajit, "From Peasants and Tribesmen to Plantation Workers. Colonial Capitalism, Reproduction of Labour Power and Proletarianisation in North East India, 1850s to 1947", *The Economic and Political Weekly*, 21 (1986). Also in: Ranajit Das Gupta, *Labour and Working Class in Eastern India: Studies in Colonial History* (Calcutta [etc.], 1994).

DasGupta, G., *Report of the Sub-Committee of the Parliamentary Consultative Committee for the Ministry of Labour for Studying and Reporting on the Problems of Unorganised Workers in Agricultural Sector* (Delhi, 1988).

Datta, S.K. *et al.*, "Seasonality, Differential Access and Interlinking of Labour and Credit", *Journal of Development Studies*, 24 (1988).

David, Paul A., *et al*, *Reckoning with Slavery: A Critical Study in the Quantitative History of American Negro Slavery* (New York, 1976).

Davidoff, Leonore, "Mastered For Life: Servant and Wife in Victorian and Edwardian England", *Journal of Social History*, 7 (1974).

Davids, P.A. *et al.*, *Reckoning with Slavery: A Critical Study in the Quantitative History of American Negro Slavery* (New York, 1976).

Davidson, J.W., "Problems of Pacific History", *Journal of Pacific History*, I (1966).

Davidson, J.W., *Samoa mo Samoa: The Emergence of the Independent State of Western Samoa* (Melbourne, 1967).

Davidson, J.W., "Understanding Pacific History: The Participant as Historian", in: Peter Munz (ed.), *The Feel of Truth: Essays in New Zealand and Pacific History* (Wellington, 1969).

Davis, Ann Rosalie, *The Pyramid Builders of Ancient Egypt. A Modern Investigation of Pharaoh's Workforce* (London [etc.], 1986).

Davis, David Brion, *The Problem of Slavery in Western Culture* (Ithaca, NY, 1966).

Davis, David Brion, *The Problem of Slavery in the Age of Revolution 1770-1823* (Ithaca, NY, 1975).

Davis, David Brion, *Slavery and Human Progress* (New York, 1984).

Davis, David Brion, "Reflections on Abolitionism and Ideological Hegemony", *American Historical Review*, 92 (1987).

Davis, Lance, "The Investment Market 1870-1914: The Evolution of a National MArket", *Journal of Economic History*, XXV (1965).

Davis, Shelton, "Land of Our Ancestors" (Ph.D., Harvard University, 1970).

Davis, Shelton, *Victims of the Miracle. Development and the Indians of Brazil* (New York, 1977).

De Canio, Steven J., *Agriculture in the Postbellum South: The Economics of Production and Supply* (Cambridge, MA, 1974).

De Man, Paul, *Allegories of Reading* (New Haven, 1979).

De Wind, Josh *et al.*, "Contract Labor in US Agriculture: The West Indian Cane Cutters in Florida", in: Cohen *et al.*, *Peasants and Proletarians*.

Della Monica, Madeleine, *La classe ouvrière sous les pharaons. Etude du Village de Deir el Medineh* (Paris, 1975).

Delphy, Christine and Diana Leonard, *Familiar Exploitation. A New Analysis of Marriage in Contemporary Western Societies* (Oxford, 1992).

Deschamps, A., "Sur l'expression *'locare operas'* et le travail comme objet de contrat à Rome", *Mélanges Gérardin* (Paris, 1907).

Deshpande, V., *Employment Guarantee Scheme: Impact on Poverty and Bondage Among Tribal Workers* (Pune, 1982).

Dew, Charles B., *Ironmaker to the Confederacy: Joseph R. Anderson and the Tredegar Iron Works* (New Haven, CT, 1966).

Dew, Charles B., *Bond of Iron. Master and Slave at Buffalo Forge* (New York and London, 1994).

Deyo, Frederic C., *Beneath the Miracle: Labor Subordination in the New Asian Industrialism* (Berkeley, 1989).

Dhyani, S.N., *International Labour Organization and India* (New Delhi, 1977).

Dieckmann, Götz, "Existenzbedingungen und Widerstand im Konzentrationslager Dora-Mittelbau unter dem Aspekt der funktionellen Einbeziehung der SS in das System der faschistischen Kriegswirtschaft" (Ph.D., Humboldt Universität Berlin, 1968).

Dingwaney, Manjari, "Unredeemed Promises: The Law and Servitude", in: Patnaik and Dingwaney, *Chains of Servitude*.

Dirección General de Estadística, *Censo de la República de Guatemala, 1921* (Guatemala, 1924).

Dobb, Maurice, "A Reply", in: Hilton, *The Transition from Feudalism to Capitalism*.

Domar, Evesey, "The Causes of Slavery or Serfdom: A Hypothesis", *Journal of Economic History*, 30 (1970).

Domínguez, Manuel, *Expediciones paraguayas al Chaco* (Asunción, 1934).

Douglas, Mary, "Matriliny and Pawnship in Central Africa", *Africa*, 34 (1964).

Dovring, Folke, "Bondage, Tenure, and Progress: Reflections on the Economics of Forced Labour", *Comparative Studies in Society and History*, 7 (1964-65).

Dreizehnter, Alois, "Zur Enstehung der Lohnarbeit und deren Terminologie im Altgriechischen", in: Welskopf, *Soziale Typenbegriffe*, 3.

Drescher, Seymour, *Capitalism and Anti-slavery. British Mobilisation in Comparative Perspective* (New York and Oxford, 1987).

Drescher, Seymour, "Epilogue", in: Oostindie, *Fifty Years Later*.

Drescher, Seymour, "The Long Goodbye: Dutch Capitalism and Antislavery in Comparative Perspective", in: Oostindie, *Fifty Years Later*.

Drobisch, Klaus and Dietrich Eichholtz, "Die Zwangsarbeit ausländischer Arbeitskräfte in Deutschland während des zweiten Weltkrieges", *Bulletin des Arbeitskreises "Zweiter Weltkrieg"*, 3 (1970).

Drost, Richard, "Forced Labor in the South Pacific, 1850-1914", *Iowa Studies in the Social Sciences: Abstracts in History* (Iowa City, 1938).

Duchesne, Ricardo, "The French Revolution as a Bourgeois Revolution: A Critique of the Revisionists", *Science and Society*, 54 (1990).

Dutschke, Rudi, *Versuch, Lenin auf die Füsse zu stellen* (Berlin, 1974).

Dyster, Barrie, "Public Employment and Assignment to Private Masters, 1788–1821", in: Nicholas, *Convict Workers*.

Eagan, Daniel L., *Labor Management Laws in California Agriculture* (Berkeley, 1990).

Edelman, Bernard, *Le droit saisi par le photographie* (Paris, 1973).

Edgerton, W.F., "The Strikes in Ramses III's Twenty-ninth Year", *Journal of Near Eastern Studies*, 10 (1951).

Edid, Marilyn, *Farm Labor Organizing: Trends and Prospects* (Ithaca [etc.], 1994).

Editorial Committee, "Free and Unfree Labour", *International Review of Social History*, 35 (1990).

Edmund, Mabel, *No Regrets* (Brisbane, 1992).

Edwards, Richard, David Gordon and Michael Reich, *Segmented Work, Divided Labor: The Historical Transformation of Labor in the United States* (New York, 1982).

Eggertsson, Thráinn, *Economic Behavior and Institutions* (New York, 1990).

Eichholtz, Dietrich, "Gewalt und Ökonomie", *Jahrbuch für Wirtschaftsgeschichte*, 1964-II/III.

Eichholtz, Dietrich, "Die Vorgeschichte des 'Generalbevollmächtigten für den Arbeitseinsatz' (mit Dokumenten)", *Jahrbuch für Geschichte*, 9 (1973).

Eichholtz, Dietrich, *Geschichte der deutschen Kriegswirtschaft 1939-1945*, vol. II: 1941-1943 (Berlin, 1985).

Eidam, Heinz and Wolfdietrich Schmied-Kowarzik (eds), *Kritische Philosophie gesellschaftlicher Praxis* (Würzburg, 1995).

Eldred, Michael and Marlie Hanlon, "Reconstructing Value-Form Analysis", *Capital and Class*, 13 (1981).

Elias, Norbert, *Über den Prozess der Zivilisation*, 2 vols (Frankfurt/Main, 1976²).

Elkins, Stanley M., *Slavery: A Problem in American Institutional and Intellectual Life* (Chicago, 1959).

Elsner, L., "Foreign Workers and Forced Labor in Germany during the First World War", in: Dirk Hoerder (ed.) *Labor Migration in the Atlantic Economies* (Westport, CT, 1985).

Eltis, David, "Free and Coerced Transatlantic Migrations: Some Comparisons", *American Historical Review*, 88 (1983).

"Em busca de salário e comida (Relato da experiência de subempregados de Teresina no trabalho escravo do Pará)", *Cadernos do Ceas*, No. 95 (1985)

Emmer, Pieter C., *Colonialism and Migration. Indentured Labour Before and After Slavery* (Dordrecht, 1986).

Emmer, Pieter C., "The Meek Hindu: The Recruitment of Indian Indentured Labourers for Service Overseas, 1870-1916", in: Emmer, *Colonialism and Migration*.

Emmer, Pieter C., "Between Slavery and Freedom: The Period of Apprenticeship in Surinam, 1863-1873", *Slavery and Abolition*, 14 (1993).

Engels, Friedrich, "On Authority", in: Karl Marx and Friedrich Engels, *Basic Writings on Politics and Philosophy*, ed. Lewis S. Feuer (Garden City, NY, 1959).

Engerman, Stanley L., "Economic Adjustments to Emancipation in the United States and British West Indies", *Journal of Interdisciplinary History*, 13 (1982).

Engerman, Stanley L., "Servants to Slaves to Servants: Contract Labour and European Expansion", in: Emmer, *Colonialism and Migration*.

Engerman, Stanley L., "Coerced and Free Labor: Property Rights and the Development of the Labor Force", *Explorations in Economic History*, 29 (1992).

Engerman, Stanley L., "Economics of Forced Labor", *Itinerario*, 17 (1993).

Engerman, Stanley L., "The Land and Labour Problem at the Time of the Legal Emancipation of the British West Indies Slaves", in: Richard Lobdell and Roderick McDonald (eds), *West Indies Accounts: Essays on the History of the British Caribbean and the Atlantic Economy in Honour of Richard Sheridan* (Kingston, 1996).

Epstein, Steven A., *Wage-labour and Guilds in Medieval Europe* (Chapel Hill and London, 1991).

Erénchun, Félix, *Anales de la Isla de Cuba. Diccionario administrativo, económico, estadístico y legislativo [...] Año de 1856* (Havana, 1857).

Erickson, Charlotte, *American Industry and the European Immigrant, 1860-1885* (Cambridge, MA, 1957).

Erickson, Charlotte, *Emigration from Europe, 1815–1914: Select Documents* (London, 1976).

Esper, Thomas, "The Condition of the Serf Workers in Russia's Metallurgical Industry, 1800-1861", *Journal of Modern History*, 50 (1978).

Esterci, Neide, "Peonagem na Amazônia", *Dados*, 20 (1979).

Esterci, Neide, "Campesinato e peonagem na Amazônia", *Anuário Antropológico - 1978* (Rio de Janeiro, 1980).

Esterci, Neide, *Conflito no Araguaia - Peões e posseiros contra a grande empresa* (Petrópolis, 1987).

Esterci, Neide, *Escravos da Desigualdade - Um estudo sobre o uso repressivo da força de trabalho hoje* (Rio de Janeiro, 1994).

Estragó, Margarita Durán, *Presencia Franciscana en el Paraguay: 1553-1824* (Asunción, 1987).

Eswaran, Mukesh and Ashok Kotwal, "A Theory of Contractual Structure in Agriculture", *American Economic Review*, 75 (1985).

Ethnic Studies Oral History Project, *Uchinanchu: A History of Okinawans in Hawaii* (Honolulu, 1982).

Evans, Robert, "Some Notes on Coerced Labor", *Journal of Economic History*, 30 (1970).

Evans-Pritchard, E.E., "The Comparative Method in Social Anthropology", in: E.E. Evans-Pritchard, *The Position of Women in Primitive Societies and Other Essays in Social Anthropology* (New York, 1965).

Evatt Foundation, *Australian South Sea Islanders: A Report on the Current Status of South Sea Islanders in Australia* (Sydney, 1991).

Fahrenfort, J.J., "Over Vrije en Onvrije Arbeid", *Mensch en Maatschappij*, 19 (1943).

Fatnowna, Noel, *Fragments of a Lost Heritage.* Edited by Roger M. Keesing (Sydney, 1989).

"Fazendeiro mantém trabalho escravo em Xinguara (PA)", *Aconteceu*, no. 543 (Rio de Janeiro, 1990).

Fellows, Lloyd, *Economic Aspects of the Mexican Rural Population in California, with Special Emphasis on the Need for Mexican Labor in Agriculture* (Los Angeles, 1971).

Fenoaltea, Stefano, "The Rise and Fall of a Theoretical Model: The Manorial System", *Journal of Economic History*, 25 (1975).

Ferencz, B., *Less Than Slaves: Jewish Forced Labor and the Quest for Compensation* (Cambridge, MA, 1979).

Ferretti, Maria, *La memoria mutilata* (Milano, 1993).

Figueira, Ricardo Rezende, *A Justiça do Lobo - Posseiros e Padres do Araguaia* (Petrópolis, 1986).

Figueira, Ricardo Rezende, *Rio Maria - Canto da Terra* (Petrópolis, 1992).

Filtzer, Donald, *Soviet Workers and Stalinist Industrialization. The Formation of Modern Soviet Production Relations, 1928-1941* (London [etc.], 1986).

Fine, R. and D. Davis, *Beyond Apartheid: Labour and Liberation in South Africa* (Johannesburg, 1990).

Finley, M.I., *The Ancient Economy* (London, 1979).

Finley, M.I., *Ancient Slavery and Modern Ideology* (London, 1980).

Finnane, Mark and Clive Moore, "Kanaka Slaves or Willing Workers? Melanesian Workers and the Queensland Criminal Justice System in the 1890s", *Criminal Justice History*, 13 (1992).

First, Ruth, *Black Gold: the Mozambican Miner, Proletarian and Peasant* (Brighton, 1983).

Firth, S.G., "German Recruitment and Employment of Labourers in the Western Pacific before the First World War" (Ph.D., Oxford University, 1973).

Firth, Stewart, *New Guinea under the Germans* (Melbourne, 1982).

Fisher, Lloyd H., *The Harvest Labor Market in California* (Cambridge, 1953).

Fisher, Donald J., "A Historical Study of the Migrant in California" (Ph.D., University of Southern California, 1945).

Fitzgerald, Ross, *A History of Queensland from the Dreaming until 1915* (Brisbane, 1982).

Fitzpatrick, Brian, *The British Empire in Australia, 1834–1939* (Melbourne, 1969).

Fitzpatrick, Brian, *British Imperialism and Australia, 1783–1833* (Sydney, 1971).

Fogel, R.W., *Without Consent or Contract. the Rise and Fall of American Slavery,- Evidence and Methods* (New York and London, 1988).

Fogel, R.W., "Moral Aspects of the Debate over the 'Extra Income' of Slaves", in: Fogel, *Without Consent or Contract.*

Fogel, Robert William and Stanley L. Engerman, *Time on the Cross: The Economics of American Negro Slavery* (London, 1974).

Folbre, Nancy, "Hearts and Spades: Paradigms of Household Economics", *World Development*, 14 (1986).

Folbre, Nancy, *Who Pays For the Kids? Gender and the Structures of Constraint* (London, 1992).

Foner, Eric, *Nothing But Freedom: Emancipation and Its Legacy* (Baton Rouge, LA, 1983).

Foner, Eric, *Reconstruction: America's Unfinished Revolution 1863-1877* (New York, 1988).

Foster, John Bellamy, "The Fetish of Fordism", *Monthly Review*, 39 (1987-88).

Foster-Carter, Aidan, "Can We Articulate Articulation", in: John Clammer (ed.), *The New Economic Anthropology* (New York, 1978).

Fox, H.S.A., "Servants, Cottages and Tied Cottages during the Later Middle Ages: Towards a Regional Dimension", *Rural History*, 6 (1995).

Fox-Genovese, Elizabeth and Eugene D. Genovese, *Fruits of Merchant Capital: Slavery and Bourgeois Property in the Rise and Expansion of Capitalism* (New York, 1983).

Fraginals, Manuel Moreno, *El Ingenio: complejo económico social cubano del azúcar*, 3 vols (Havana, 1978).

Frank, Andre G., *Dependent Accumulation and Underdevelopment* (London, 1978).

Frankel, F.R. and M.S.A. Rao (eds), *Dominance and State Power in Modern India. Decline of A Social Order*, vol. 1 (Delhi, 1989).

Frederickson, George M., *The Black Image in the White Mind: The Debate on Afro-American Character and Destiny, 1817-1914* (New York, 1971).

Frederickson, George M., *White Supremacy: A Comparative Study in American and South African History* (New York, 1981).

Frederickson, George M., "Planters, Junkers and *Pomeschiki*", *Reviews in American History*, 22 (1994).

Freund, Florian, *"Arbeitslager Zement". Das Konzentrationslager Ebensee und die Raketenrüstung* (Vienna, 1989).

Fried, Barbara, "Robert Hale and Progressive Legal Economics" (Unpublished Manuscript, 12/92).

Friedland, William H. and Dorothy Nelkin, *Migrant: Agricultural Workers in America's Northeast* (New York, 1971).

Friedman, S., *Building Tomorrow Today* (Johannesburg, 1987).

Frobe, Rainer, "Der Arbeitseinsatz von KZ-Häftlingen und die Perspektive der Industrie", in: Herbert, *Europa und der "Reichseinsatz"*.

Fröbel, Folker, Jürgen Heinrichs and Otto Kreye, *The New International Division of Labour* (Cambridge, 1980).

Fuente Machaín, R. de la, *El gobernador Domingo Martínez de Irala* (Buenos Aires, 1939).

Fuentes, Moreno de, *Estudios económico-sociales* (Havana, 1865).

Fuentes, Rudy, *Impact of the Immigration Reform and Control Act of 1986 on California Agriculture* (Sacramento, CA, 1988).

Füredi, Frank, *The Soviet Union Demystified. A Materialist Analysis* (London, 1986).

Fuks, Alexander, "κολωνος μισθιος: Labour Exchange in Classical Athens", *Eranos*, 49 (1951).

Fuller, C.J., "Kerala Christians and the Caste System", *Man*, 11 (1976).

Furneaux, Robin, *William Wilberforce* (London, 1974).

Galarza, Ernesto, *Merchants of Labor: The Mexican Bracero Story* (Santa Barbara, CA, 1964).

Galenson, David, *White Servitude in Colonial America* (Cambridge, 1981).

Galenson, Donald, "The Rise and Fall of Indentured Servitude: An Economic Analysis", *Journal of Economic History*, 44 (1984).

Galjart, Benno, "Class and Following in Rural Brazil", *America Latina*, 7 (1964).

Garavaglia, Juan Carlos, *Mercado interno y economía colonial. Tres siglos de historia de la yerba mate* (Mexico, 1983).

Garcia, Mario T., *Memories of Chicano History: The Life and Narrative of Bert Corona* (Berkeley, 1994).

García Galló, Gaspar Jorge, *Biografía del Tabaco Habano* ([Santa Clara], 1959).

Garcilazo, Jeff, "Mexican Railroad Workers in Kansas and the Southwest, 1880-1930" (Ph.D., University of California, Santa Barbara, 1991).

Garlan, Yvon, "Le travail libre en Grèce ancienne", in: Garnsey, *Non-Slave Labour*.

Garnsey, Peter (ed.), *Non-Slave Labour in the Greco-Roman World* (Cambridge, 1980).

Garnsey, Peter, "Non-slave Labour in the Roman World", in: Garnsey, *Non-Slave Labour*.

Genovese, Eugene D., *The Political Economy of Slavery. Studies in the Economy and Society of the Slave South* (New York, 1961).

Genovese, Eugene D., "Slave Labour or Free in the Southern Factories: A Political Analysis of an Economic Debate", in: Genovese, *The Political Economy of Slavery*.

Genovese, Eugene D., *The World the Slaveholders Made: Two Essays in Interpretation* (New York, 1969).

Genovese, Eugene D., *In Red and Black: Marxian Explorations in Southern and Afro-American History* (New York, 1971).

Genovese, Eugene D., *Roll, Jordan, Roll: The World the Slaves Made* (London, 1975).

George Jacob, *Labour Conditions in Rubber Estates* (Kottayam, 1974).

Gerstenberger, Heide, *Die subjektlose Gewalt. Theorie der Enstehung bürgerlicher Staatsgewalt* (Münster, 1990).

Gesner, Peter, "A Maritime Archaeology Approach to the Queensland Labour Trade", *Bulletin of the Australian Institute for Maritime Archaeology*, 15 (1992).

Ghose, Sankar, *Socialism and Communism in India* (Bombay, 1971).

Gilding, Michael, "The Massacre of the Mystery: A Case Study in Contact Relations", *Journal of Pacific History*, 17 (1982)

Giles, W.E., *A Cruise in a Queensland Labour Vessel to the South Seas* (ed. by Deryck Scarr) (Canberra, 1968).

Gillion, K.L., *Fiji's Indian Migrants: A History to the End of Indenture in 1920* (Melbourne, 1962).

Gilmore Al-Tony (ed.), *Revisiting Blassingame's The Slave Community: The Scholars Respond* (Westport, 1978).

Gistitin, Carol, *Quite a Colony: South Sea Islanders in Central Queensland, 1867 to 1993* (Brisbane, 1995).

Glade, William, *The Latin American Economies. A Study of Their Institutional Evolution* (New York, 1969).

Glick, Clarence, *Sojourners and Settlers: Chinese Migrants in Hawaii* (Honolulu, 1980).

Glickstein, J.A., *Concepts of Free Labor in Antebellum America* (New Haven, 1991).

Goldberg, Marta B. and Silvia C. Mallo, "La población africana en Buenos Aires y su campana. Formas de vida y de subsistencia (1750-1850)", *Temas de Africa y Asia* (Buenos Aires, 1993).

Goldberg, Victor P., "The Law and Economics of Vertical Restrictions: A Relational Perspective", *Texas Law Review*, 58 (1979-80).

Goldberg, Victor P., "Bridges over Contested Terrain. Exploring the Radical Account of the Employment Relationship", *Journal of Economic Behavior and Organization*, 1 (1980).

Goldberg y Jany, "Algunos problemas referentes a la situación del esclavo en el Río de la Plata", IV Congreso Internacional de Historia de América, Academia Nacional de la Historia, vol. VI, (Buenos Aires, 1966).

Goldenweiser, E.A., and L.E. Truesdale, *Farm Tenancy in the U.S.: An Analysis of the Results of the 1920 Census Relative to Tenure*, U.S. Census Monographs No. IV (Washington, DC, 1920).

Goldschmidt, Walter, *As You Sow: Three Studies in the Social Consequences of Agribusiness* (Montclair, 1978).

Goldsmid, John, *The Deadly Legacy: Australian History and Transmissible Disease* (Sydney, 1988).

Goodman, David and Michael Redclift, *From Peasant to Proletarian* (Oxford, 1981).

Gordon, David M., Richard Edwards, and Michael Reich, *Segmented Work, Divided Workers: The Historical Transformation of Labor in the US* (Cambridge, 1982).

Government of India, *Report of the Royal Commission on Labour in India* (London, 1931).

Graham, Edgar and Ingrid Floering, *The Modern Plantation in the Third World* (London, 1984).

Graves, Adrian, "The Abolition of the Queensland Labour Trade: Politics or Profits?", in: E.L. Wheelwright and Ken Buckley (eds), *Essays in the Political Economy of Australian Capitalism*, vol. 4 (Sydney, 1980).

Graves, Adrian, "The Nature and Origin of Pacific Island Labour Migration to Queensland, 1864–1906", in: Shula Marks and Peter Richardson (eds), *International Labour Migration: Historical Perspectives* (Middlesex, 1984).

Graves, Adrian, *Cane and Labour: The Political Economy of the Queensland Sugar Industry, 1862-1906* (Edinburgh, 1993).

Graziosi, Andrea, "The Great Strikes of 1953 in Soviet Labor Camps in the Accounts of Their Participants. A Review", *Cahiers du monde russe et soviétique*, 33 (1992).

Green, W.A., *British Slave Emancipation: The Sugar Colonies and the Great Experiment 1830-1865* (Oxford, 1976).

Green, W.A., "The Perils of Comparative History: Belize and the British Sugar Colonies", *Comparative Studies in Society and History*, 26 (1984).

Greenberg, Michael, "The New Economic History and the Understanding of Slavery: A Methodological Critique", *Dialectical Anthropology*, 2 (1977).

Grey, R.Q., "Styles of Life, the 'Labour Aristocracy' and Class Relations in Later Nineteenth Century Edinburgh", *International Review of Social History*, 18 (1973).

Grieb, Kenneth, *Guatemalan Caudillo* (Athens, OH, 1979).

Griffith, David C., "Nonmarket Labor Processes in an Advanced Capitalist Economy", *American Anthropologist*, 89 (1987).

Griffiths, P., *The History of the Indian Tea Industry* (London, 1967).

Groh, George W., *The Black Migration: The Journey to Urban America* (New York, 1972).

Grossman, Jonathan, "Class Relations and the Policies of The Communist Party of South Africa: 1915-1953" (Ph.D., University of Warwick, 1986).

Grossman, Jonathan, "Individualism and Collectivism" (Paper presented to Oral History Conference, New York, 1994).

Gundert-Hock, Sibylle, *Mission und Wanderarbeit in Vanuatu: eine Studie zum sozialen Wandel in Vanuatu, 1863-1915* (Munich, 1985).

Gunson, Niel, "An Introduction to Pacific History", in: Lal, *Pacific Islands History*.

Gupta, Jayoti, "Himalayan Polyandry: Bondage Among Women in Jaunsar Bawar", in: Patnaik and Dingwaney, *Chains of Servitude*.

Gutgesell, Manfred, *Arbeiter und Pharaonen. Wirtschafts-und Sozialgeschichte im Alten Ägypten* (Hildesheim, 1989).

Gutman, Herbert G., *Slavery and the Numbers Game* (Urbana, IL, 1975).

Gutterman, Norbert and Henri Lefebvre, *La conscience mystifiée* (Paris, 1979).

Guy, Donna, "Women, Peonage, and Industrialization: Argentina, 1810-1914", *Latin American Research Review*, 16 (1981).

Hahn, Istvan, "Die Anfänge der antiken Gesellschaftsformation in Griechenland und das Problem der sogenannten asiatischen Produktionsweise", *Jahrbuch für Wirtschaftsgeschichte*, 1971-II.

Hahn, Steven, *The Roots of Southern Populism: The Yeoman Farmer* (New York, 1983).

Hale, Robert, "Coercion and Distribution in a Supposedly Non-Coercive State", *Political Science Quarterly*, 38 (1923).

Hale, Robert, "Force and the State: A Comparison of 'Political' and 'Economic' Compulsion", *Columbia Law Review*, 35 (1935).

Hale, Robert, *Freedom Through Law: Public Control of Private Governing Power* (New York, 1952).

Hall, D., *Free Jamaica 1838-1865: An Economic History* (New Haven, 1959).

Hall, D., "The Flight from the Estates Reconsidered: The British West Indies, 1838-42", *Journal of Caribbean History*, 10-11 (1978).

Hall, Thomas D., "Geographic Factors Shaping Differential Indigenous Incorporation into the European World-Economy: Northern New Spain and La Plata" (Paper presented at the Social Science History Association Meetings, Baltimore, MD, November 5-7, 1993).

Hamburger Stiftung zur Förderung von Wissenschaft und Kultur (ed.), *"Deutsche Wirtschaft". Zwangsarbeit von KZ-Häftlingen für Industrie und Behörden* (Hamburg, 1992).

Hanke, Lewis, *The Spanish Struggle for Justice in the Conquest of America* (Philadelphia, 1949).

Hannington, Wal, *The Problem of the Distressed Areas* (London, 1937).

Hansen, Bent, "An Economic Model for Ottoman Egypt: The Economics of Collective Tax Responsibility", in: A.L. Udovitch (ed.), *The Islamic Middle East: Studies in Economic and Social History* (Princeton, NJ, 1981).

Hansen, Roger D., *The Politics of Mexican Development* (Baltimore, 1971).

Haridasan, V., *Family Budget and Social Security Benefits of Rubber Plantation Workers in India* (Kottayam, 1967).

Harlow, Neal, *California Conquered: The Annexation of a Mexican Province, 1846-1850* (Berkeley, 1982).

Harriss, Barbara, *Transitional Trade and Rural Development* (Delhi, 1981).

Harriss, B., "Organised Power of Grain Merchants in the Dhaka Region of Bangladesh: Comparisons with Indian Cases", *Economic and Political Weekly*, 24 (1989).

Harriss, John, *Capitalism and Peasant Farming: Agrarian Structure and Ideology in Northern Tamil Nadu* (Bombay, 1982).

Hart, Gillian, "Exclusionary Labour Arrangements: interpreting Evidence on Employment Trends in Rural Java", *Journal of Development Studies*, 22 (1986).

Hart, Gillian, *Power, Labor, and Livelihood: Processes of Change in Rural Java* (Berkeley, 1986).

Haskell, Thomas, "Capitalism and the Origins of the Humanitarian Sensibility", *American Historical Review*, 90 (1985).

Haskell, Thomas, "Convention and Hegemonic Interest in the Debate over Anti-slavery: A Reply to Davis and Ashworth", *American Historical Review*, 92 (1987).

Hayes, Peter, *Industry and Ideology: IG Farben in the Nazi Era* (Cambridge, 1987).

Haynes, Douglas and Gyan Prakash (eds), *Resistance and Everyday Social Relations in South Asia* (Delhi, 1991).

Heer, Clarence, *Income and Wages in the South* (Chapel Hill, 1930).

Heinsohn, Gunnar and Otto Steiger, "Geld, Produktivität und Unsicherheit in Kapitalismus und Sozialismus", *Leviathan*, 9 (1981).

Heller, Agnes *et al.*, *Der soujetische Weg. Bedürfnisdiktatur und entfremdeter Alltag* (Hamburg, 1983).

Hemmer, Willi, *Die "unsichtbaren" Arbeitslosen* (Zeulenroda, 1935).

Hemmings, John, *Red Gold: The Conquest of the Brazilian Indians* (Cambridge, MA, 1978).

Hempenstall, Peter, "The Line of Descent: Creating Pacific Histories in Australasia", *Australian Journal of Politics and History*, 41 (1995), special issue.

Henderson, Jeffrey and Manuel Castells (eds), *Global Restructuring and Territorial Development* (London, 1987).

Hengstl, Joachim, *Private Arbeitsverhältnisse freier Personen in den hellenistischen Papyri bis Diokletian* (Bonn, 1972).

Heppel, Monica L. and Sandra L. Amendola, *Immigration Reform and Perishable Crop Agriculture* (New York, 1992).

Herbert, Ulrich, *Fremdarbeiter. Politik und Praxis des "Ausländer-Einsatzes" in der Kriegswirtschaft des Dritten Reiches* (Berlin/Bonn, 1985).

Herbert, Ulrich, *A History of Foreign Labor in Germany, 1880-1980: Seasonal Workers/Forced Laborers/Guest Workers* (Ann Arbor, 1990).

Herbert, Ulrich, "Arbeit und Vernichtung. Ökonomisches Interesse und Primat der 'Weltanschauung' im Nationalsozialismus", in: Herbert, *Europa und der "Reichseinsatz"*.

Herbert, Ulrich (ed.), *Europa und der "Reichseinsatz"* (Essen, 1992).

Hicks, John, *A Theory of Economic History* (London [etc.], 1969).

Hidalgo, Ariel, *Orígenes del movimiento obrero y del pensamiento socialista en Cuba* (Havana, 1976).

Higgs, Robert, *Competition and Coercion: Blacks in the American Economy, 1885-1914* (Chicago, 1977).

Hilton, George W., *The Truck System Including a History of the British Truck Acts, 1465-1960* (Cambridge, 1960).

Hilton, Rodney H., *The Decline of Serfdom in Medieval England* (London [etc.], 1969).

Hilton, Rodney H., *Bond Men Made Free. Medieval Peasant Movements and the English Rising of 1381* (London, 1973).

Hilton, Rodney H. (ed.), *The Transition from Feudalism to Capitalism* (London, 1978).

Hirabayashi, Lane R., *Cultural Capital: Mountain Zapotec Migrant Associations in Mexico City* (Tucson, 1993).

Hjejle, Benedicte, "Slavery and Agricultural Bondage in South India in the Nineteenth Century", *The Scandanavian Economic History Review*, 15 (1967).

Hobsbawm, Eric J., *Labouring Men* (London, 1964).

Hoetink, Harry, *Het patroon van de oude Curaçaose samenleving* (Aruba and Tiel, 1966).

Hoffman, Abraham, *Unwanted Mexican Americans in the Great Depression: Repatriation Pressures, 1929-1939* (Tucson, 1974).

Holt, Wythe, "Labour Conspiracy Cases in the United States, 1805-1842: Bias and Legitimation in Common Law Adjudication", *Osgoode Hall Law Journal*, 22 (1984).

Holt, Wythe, "Recovery by the Worker Who Quits", *Wisconsin Law Review*, 4 (1986).

Holthouse, Hector, *Cannibal Cargoes* (Adelaide, 1969).

Homburg, Heidrun, "Vom Arbeitslosen zum Zwangsarbeiter. Arbeitslosenpolitik und Fraktionierung der Arbeiterschaft in Deutschland 1930-1933 am Beispiel der Wohlfahrtserwerbslosen und der kommunalen Wohlfahrtshilfe", *Archiv für Sozialgeschichte*, 25 (1985).

Hon-Firnberg, Hertha, *Lohnarbeiter und freie Lohnarbeit im Mittelalter und zu Beginn der Neuzeit. Ein Beitrag zur Geschichte der agrarischen Lohnarbeit in Deutschland* (Baden [etc.], 1935).

Honig, Emily, *Sisters and Strangers: Women in the Shanghai Cotton Mills, 1919-1949* (Stanford, CA, 1986).

Horner, Jack, "From Slaves to Citizens - Pacific Islanders in Australia", *St Mark's Review*, 130 (1987).

Howard, Philip A., "Culture, Nationalism, and Liberation: The Afro-Cuban Mutual Aid Societies in the Nineteenth Century" (Ph.D., Indiana University, 1988).

Howe, K.R., "Tourists, Sailors and Labourers: A Survey of Early Labour Recruiting in Southern Melanesia", *Journal of Pacific History*, 13 (1977).

Howe, K.R., "The Future of Pacific Islands History: A Personal View", in: Lal, *Pacific Islands History*.

Hritsiak, E.S., *Istoriia Norilskogo vosstaniia* (Baltimore and Toronto, 1980).

Hudson, Larry E., Jr (ed.), *Working Toward Freedom: Slave Society and Domestic Economy in the American South* (Rochester, 1994).

Human Rights and Equal Opportunity Commission, *The Call for Recognition: A Report on the Situation of Australian South Sea Islanders* (Sydney, 1992).

Hunt, Doug, "Exclusivism and Unionism: Europeans in the Queensland Sugar Industry, 1900-10", in: Curthoys and Marcus, *Who Are Our Enemies?*

Hunt, Shane, "The Economics of Haciendas and Plantations in Latin America" (Discusssion Paper No. 29, Research Program in Economic Development, Woodrow Wilson School, Princeton University, October 1972).

Hunter, Holland, "The Economic Costs of the GULag Archipelago", *Slavic Review*, 39 (1980).

Hutchinson, Edward P., *Legislative History of American Immigration Policy, 1798-1965* (Philadelphia, 1981).

Hutson, J., *From Penal Colony to Penal Powers* (Sydney, 1983).

Indian School of Social Sciences (ed.), *Bonded Labour in India* (Calcutta, 1976).

Inglis, Kenneth Stanley, *The Australian Colonists. An Exploration of Social History, 1788–1870* (Melbourne, 1974).

Innis, Harold A., *Essays in Canadian Economic History* (Toronto, 1956).

Instituto de Historia [...] de Cuba, *Historia del movimiento obrero cubano 1865-1958*, 2 vols (Havana, 1987).

International Confederation of Free Trade Unions, *Stalin's Slave Camps - An Indictment of Modern Slavery* (Brussels, 1951).

Iqbal, F., "The Determinants of Moneylender Interest Rates: Evidence from Rural India", *Journal of Development Studies*, 24 (1989).

Irving, Terrence, "1850–70", in: Crowley, *New History of Australia*.

Jackson, K.B., "Melanesia, Queensland, Fiji: Review Article", *Australian National University Historical Journal*, 10-11 (1973-74).

Jagannathan, N.V., *Informal Markets in Developing Countries* (New York, 1987).

Jakobson, Michael, *Origins of the Gulag. The Soviet Prison Camp System 1917-1934* (Lexington, 1993).

James, C.L.R., *Spheres of Existence* (London, 1980).

Janssen, J.J., "Background Information on the Strikes of Year 29 of Rameses III", *Oriens antiquus*, 18 (1979).

Janvry, Alain de, *The Agrarian Question and Reformism in Latin America* (Baltimore, 1981).

Jaschok, Maria, *Concubines and Bondservants: The Social History of a Chinese Custom* (London, 1988).

Jaynes, Gerald David, *Branches Without Roots: Genesis of the Black Working Class in the American South, 1862-1882* (New York, 1986).

Jeffrey, Robin, *The Decline of Nayar Dominance: Society and Politics in Travancore, 1847-1908* (New Delhi, 1976).

Jenkins, Rhys, "The Political Economy of Industrialization: A Comparison of Latin America and East Asian Newly Industrializing Countries", *Development and Change*, 22 (1991).

Jodhka, Surinder S., "Agrarian Changes and Attached Labour: Emerging Patterns in Haryana Agriculture", *Economic and Political Weekly*, 29 (1994).

Johnson, Charles S., *The Negro in American Civilization: A Study of Negro Life and Race Relations in the Light of Social Research* (New York, 1930).

Johnson, Lyman L., "Estimaciones de la población de Buenos Aires en 1744, 1778, y 1810", *Desarrollo Económico*, 73, 19 (1979).

Johnson, Lyman L., "Manumission in Colonial Buenos Aires, 1776-1810", *Hispanic American Historical Review*, 59 (1979).

Johnson, Lyman L., "Salarios, precios y costo de vida en el Buenos Aires colonial tardío", *Boletin de Historia Argentina y Americana*, 3 (1990).

Johnson, Lyman L. and Susan M. Socolow, "Población y espacio en el Buenos Aires del siglo XVIII", *Desarrollo Económico*, 20-79 (1980).

Johnston, W. Ross, "Captain Hamilton and the Labour Trade", *Journal of the Royal Historical Society of Queensland*, 11-12 (1979-1980).

Johnston, W. Ross, *The Call of the Land: A History of Queensland to the Present Day* (Brisbane, 1982).

Jones, David, *Crime, Protest, Community and Police in Nineteenth Century Britain* (London, 1982).

Juaregui, Antonio Batres, *Los indios: su historia y civilización* (Guatemala, 1893), vol. 3.

Julião, Francisco, *Cambão - The Yoke (The Hidden Face of Brazil)*. Translated by John Butt (Harmondsworth, 1972).

Kahle, Günter and Horst Pietschmann (eds), *Lateinamerika. Entdeckung, Eroberung, Kolonisation. Gesammelte Aufsätze von Richard Konetzke.* (Köln, 1983).

Kahn, Joel S., "Mercantilism and the Emergence of Servile Labour in Colonial Indonesia", in: Joel S. Kahn and Josep R. Llobera (eds), *The Anthropology of Pre-Capitalist Societies* (London and Basingstoke, 1981).

Kahrs, Horst, "Die ordnende Hand der Arbeitsämter. Zur deutschen Arbeitsverwaltung 1933 bis 1939", in: Wolf Gruner *et al.*, *Arbeitsmarkt und Sondererlaß. Menschenverwertung, Rassenpolitik und Arbeitsamt* [Beiträge zur nationalsozialistischen Gesundheits- und Sozialpolitik, vol. 8] (Berlin, 1990).

Kahrs, Horst, "Verstaatlichung der polnischen Arbeitsmigration nach Deutschland in der Zwischenkriegszeit", in: *Arbeitsmigration und Flucht. Vertreibung und Arbeitskräfteregulierung im Zwischenkriegseuropa* [Beiträge zur nationalsozialistischen Gesundheits- und Sozialpolitik, vol. 11] (Berlin and Göttingen, 1993).

Kaienburg, Hermann, *"Vernichtung durch Arbeit". Der Fall Neuengamme. Die Wirtschaftsbestrebungen der SS und ihre Auswirkungen auf die Existenzbedingungen der KZ-Gefangenen* (Bonn, 1990).

Kaienburg, Hermann, "Zwangsarbeit für das "deutsche Rohstoffwunder". Das Phrix-Werk Wittenberge im zweiten Weltkrieg", *1999*, 9 (1994).

Kaiser, Ernst and Michael Knorn, "Die Adlerwerke und ihr KZ-Außenlager-Rüstungsproduktion und Zwangsarbeit in einem Frankfurter Traditionsbetrieb", *1999*, 7 (1992).

Kamble, N.D., *Bonded Labour in India* (New Delhi, 1982).

Kant, Immanuel, *Die Metaphysik der Sitten*, in: Immanuel Kant, *Werke*, vol. 7. (Darmstadt, 1956).

Kapadia, Karen, "The Profitability of Bonded Labour: The Gem-Cutting Industry in Rural South India", *Journal of Peasant Studies*, 22 (1995).

Kapadia, Karen, "Women Workers in Bonded Labour in Rural Industry (South India)", paper presented at the Congress on *Agrarian Questions* held in Wageningen, the Netherlands, during May 1995.

Kaplinsky, Raphael, "Export Processing Zones in the Dominican Republic: Transforming Manufactures into Commodities", *World Development*, 21 (1993).

Karklins, Rasma, "The Organisation of Power in Soviet Labour Camps", *Soviet Studies*, 41 (1989).

Kárný, Miroslav, "'Vernichtung durch Arbeit'. Sterblichkeit in den NS-Konzentrationslagern", in: *Sozialpolitik und Judenvernichtung. Gibt es eine Ökonomie der Endlösung?* [Beiträge zur nationalsozialistischen Gesundheits- und Sozialpolitik, vol. 5] (Berlin, 1987).

Kárný, Miroslav, "'Vernichtung durch Arbeit' in Leitmeritz. Die SS-Führungsstäbe in der deutschen Kriegswirtschaft", *1999*, 8 (1993).

Karsten, Peter, "'Bottomed on Justice': A Reappraisal of Critical Legal Studies Scholarship Concerning Breaches of Labor Contracts by Quitting or Firing in Britain and the U.S., 1630-1880", *American Journal of Legal History*, 34 (1990).

Katz, Friedrich, *The Secret War in Mexico* (Chicago, 1981).

Kaufman, Allen, *Capitalism, Slavery, and Republican Values: Antebellum Political Economists 1819-1848* (Austin, 1982).

Kautsky, Karl, *Terrorism and Communism: A Contribution to the Natural History of Revolution* (London, 1920).

Kautsky, Karl, *The Agrarian Question* , 2 vols (London, 1988).

Kelly, John D., "'Cooly'" as a Labour Commodity: Race, Sex, and European Dignity in Colonial Fiji", *Journal of Peasant Studies*, 19 (1992).

Keneally, T., *Schindler's List* (New York, 1994).

Kennedy, Duncan, "The Role of Law in Economic Thought: Essays in the Fetishism of Commodities", *The American University Law Review*, 34 (1985).

Kennedy, Duncan, "The Stakes of Law, or Hale and Foucault!" *Legal Studies Forum*, 15 (1991).

Kenny, Lorraine, "The Feminization of Immigration: Give Us Your Tired, Your Hungry, Your Poor No More", *Women's Issues Quarterly*, 1 (1995).

Kenyon, Nora, "Labour Conditions in Essex in the Reign of Richard II", *Economic History Review*, 4 (1932-1934).

Kerr, Ian J., "Constructing Railways in India - an estimate of numbers employed, 1850-1880", *Indian Economic and Social History Review*, 20 (1983).

Kerr, Ian J., "Working Class Protest in 19th Century India. Example of Railway Workers", *Economic and Political Weekly*, 20 (1985).

Kerr, Ian J., *Building the Railways of the Raj, 1850-1900* (New Delhi, 1995).

Kim, Kwan S. and Enrique Dussel Peters, "From Trade Liberalization to Economic Integration: The Case of Mexico" (Paper presented at Latin American Studies Association meeting in Los Angeles, 1992).

Kirstein, Wolfgang, *Das Konzentrationslager als Institution totalen Terrors. Das Beispiel des KL Natzweiler* (Pfaffenweiler, 1992).

Klein, Herbert, *Slavery in the Americas. A Comparative Study of Virginia and Cuba* (Chicago, 1967).

Klengel, Horst, "Soziale Aspekte der altbabylonischen Dienstmiete", in: Horst Klengel (ed.), *Beiträge zur sozialen Struktur des alten Vorderasien* (Berlin, 1971).

Klimovich, G., "Vosstanie v Gorlage", *Nezavisimaia gazeta*, 11 (September 1991).

Kloosterboer, W., *Involuntary Labour since the Abolition of Slavery. A Survey of Compulsory Labour throughout the World* (Leiden, 1960).

Knight, Alan, "Mexican Peonage: What Was It and Why Was It?", *Journal of Latin American Studies*, 18 (1986).

Knight, Alan, "Debt Bondage in Latin America", in: Léonie Archer (ed.), *Slavery and Other Forms of Unfree Labour* (London, 1988).

Knight, Franklin W., *Slave Society in Cuba during the Nineteenth Century* (Wisconsin, 1970).

Knights, David and H. Willmott, "Power and Subjectivity at Work: From Degradation to Subjugation in Social Relations", *Sociology*, 23 (1989).

Köbben, André J.F., "Why Exceptions? The Logic of Cross-Cultural Analysis", *Current Anthropology*, 8 (1967).

Köbben, André J.F., "Comparativists and Non-comparativists in Anthropology" in Raoul Naroll and Ronald Cohen (eds), *A Handbook of Method in Cultural Anthropology* (Garden City, NY, 1970).

Koebner, Richard, "Despot and Despotism: Vicissitudes of a Political Term", *Journal of the Warburg and Courtauld Institutes*, 14 (1951).

Köhler, Henning, *Arbeitsdienst in Deutschland. Pläne und Verwirklichungsformen bis zur Einführung der Arbeitsdienstpflicht im Jahre 1935* (Berlin, 1967).

Kösser, Reinhart, "Arbeit und Revolution. Sozialistische Perspektiven", in: Helmut König et al. (eds), *Sozialphilosophie der industriellen Arbeit* (Opladen, 1990).

Kössler, Reinhart, *Arbeitskultur im Industrialisierungsprozess. Studien an englischen und sowjetrussischen Paradigmata* (Münster, 1990).

Kössler, Reinhart, *Despotie in der Moderne* (Frankfurt/Main and New York, 1993).

Kössler, Reinhart, "Trotzki zur Militarisierung der Arbeit oder: Kautskyanismus mit Konsequenz", in: Theodor Bergmann and Gert Schäfer (eds), *Leo Trotzki - Kritiker und Verteidiger der Sowjetgesellschaft* (Mainz, 1993).

Kössler, Reinhart and Mammo Muchie, "American Dreams and Soviet Realities: Socialism and Taylorism", *Capital and Class*, 40 (1990).

Kolchin, Peter, *Unfree Labor: American Slavery and Russian Serfdom* (Cambridge, MA, 1987).

Kolchin, Peter, "Comparing American History", *Reviews in American History*, 9 (1982).

Konetzke, Richard, "La esclavitud de indios como elemento en la estructuración social de Hispanoamérica", in: Kahle and Pietschmann, *Lateinamerika*.

Konetzke, Richard, "La emigración española al Río de la Plata durante el siglo XVI", in: Kahle and Pietschmann, *Lateinamerika*.

Kooiman, Dick, *Conversion and Social Equality in India. The London Missionary Society in South-Travancore in the 19th Century* (Delhi, 1989).

Kooiman, Dick, "Conversion from Slavery to Plantation Labour: Christian Mission in South India, 19th Century", *Social Scientist*, 19 (1991).

Koppenhöfer, Peter, "KZ-Arbeit und Gruppenakkord bei Daimler-Benz Mannheim", *1999*, 9 (1994).

Koschaker, P., [review article], *Zeitschrift der Savigny-Stiftung für Rechtsgeschichte. Romanische Abteilung*, 57 (1927).

Koshy, M.J., *Constitutionalism in Travancore and Cochin* (Trivandrum, 1972).

Kosminsky, E.A., *Studies in the Agrarian History of England in the Thirteenth Century* (Oxford, 1956).

Kotscho, Ricardo, *O Massacre dos Posseiros - Conflitos de terras no Araguaia-Tocantins* (São Paulo, 1981).

Kraak, A., "Human Resources Development and Organised Labour", in: *South African Review*, 6 (1992).

Kraak, Gerald, *Breaking the Chains* (London, 1993).

Kraditor, Aileen S., "American Radical Historians on Their Heritage", *Past and Present*, 56 (1972).

Kreissig, Heinz, *Die sozialökonomische Situation in Juda zur Achämenidenzeit* (Berlin, 1973).

Kreissig, Heinz, "Versuch über den Status der Lohnarbeiter im hellenistischen Orient (Seleukidenreich)", in: *Schiavitu, manumissione e classi dipendenti nel mondo antico* (Rome, 1979).

Kreissig, Heinz and Friedmar Kühnert (eds), *Antike Abhängigkeitsformen in den griechischen Gebieten ohne Polisstruktur und den römischen Provinzen* (Berlin, 1985).

Krissman, Fred, *Removal of the Safety Net: The Piecemeal Approach to Disaster Relief for US Farm Workers* (Unpublished report, 1993).

Krissman, Fred, "The Farm Labor Contractors: Processing Mexico-origin Farm Labor for Californian Agribusiness", *Agriculture and Human Values* (1995).

Krissman, Fred, *Californian Agribusiness and Mexican Farm Workers (1942-1992): A Binational Agricultural System of Production/Reproduction: Californian Agribusiness and Mexico-Origin Farm Workers* (Los Angeles, 1996).

Kruger de Thomas, Hildegard, "Asunción y su área de influencia en la época colonial", *Estudios Paraguayos*, 4 (1978).

Kulkarni, Sharad, "Law and Social Change: The Case of Legislation Relating to Bonded Labour in India", in: D.B. Gupta *et al.* (eds), *Development Planning and Policy* (New Delhi, 1982).

Kumar, Dharma, *Land and Caste in South India: Agricultural Labour in Madras Presidency in the Nineteenth Century* (Cambridge, 1965).

Kurup, K.K.N., "The Colonial Investment and the Abolition of Slavery in South India: A Case Study of Kerala", *Journal of Kerala Studies*, 11 (1994).

Kurup, T.V.N., "Price of Rural Credit: An Empirical Analysis of Kerala", *Economic and Political Weekly*, 11 (1976).

Kurz, Robert and Ernst Lohoff, "Der Klassenkampf-Fetisch. Thesen zur Entmythologisierung des Marxismus", *Marxistische Kritik*, No. 7 (August 1989).

Kuznets, Simon *et al.*, *Population Redistribution and Economic Growth in the United States 1870-1950* (Philadelphia, 1960).

Lacey, Dan, *The White Use of Blacks in America* (New York, 1972).

Lacom, *Freedom From Below* (Durban, n.d.).

Lal, Brij V., "Fiji *Girmitiyas*: The Background to Banishment", in: Vijay Mishra (ed.), *Rama's Banishment: A Centenary Tribute to the Fiji Indians 1879-1979* (Auckland, 1979).

Lal, Brij V., "Kunti's Cry: Indentured Women on Fiji Plantations", in: J. Krishnamurty (ed.) *Women in Colonial India: Essays on Survival, Work and the State* (Delhi, 1989).

Lal, Brij. V. (ed.), *Pacific Islands History: Journeys and Transformations* (Canberra, 1992).

Lal, Brij V., Doug Munro and Edward D. Beechert (eds), *Plantation Workers: Resistance and Accommodation* (Honolulu, 1993).

Lal, Deepak, *The Hindu Equilibrium: II Aspects of Indian Labour* (Oxford, 1989).

Lamar, Howard, "From Bondage to Contract: Ethnic Labor in the American West, 1600-1890", in: Steven Hahn and Jonathan Prude (eds), *The Countryside in the Age of Capitalist Transformation* (Chapel Hill, 1985).

Lambert, R., "SACTU and the IC Act", *South African Labour Bulletin*, 8 (1982).

Lane, Ann J. (ed.), *Slavery and Personality: The Elkins Thesis and Its Critics* (Urbana, 1971).

Laranjeiras, "Horrendous worker enslavement in the State of Paraná", *A Voz do Trabalhador* (Rio de Janeiro, June 1, 1913).

Lasker, Bruno, *Human Bondage in Southeast Asia* (Chapel Hill, 1950).

Latapi, Agustin Escobar, "The Connection at Its Source: Changing Socioeconomic Conditions and Migration Patterns", in: Abraham F. Lowenthal and Katarina Burgess (eds), *The California Connection* (Stanford, 1993).

Lautner, J.G., *Altbabylonische Personenmiete und Erntearbeiterverträge* (Leiden, 1936).

Leckie, Jacqueline, "Melanesian Workers - Myths, History and Reality", *South Pacific Forum* [Suva], 4 (1987).

Leckie, Jacqueline, "Pre-Capitalist Labour in the South Pacific", in: Moore, Leckie and Munro, *Labour in the South Pacific*.

Lefebvre, Henri, *La pensée de Lénine* (Paris, 1957).

Lefebvre, Henri, *La survie du capitalisme: la réproduction des rapports de production* (Paris, 1973).

Lefebvre, Henri, *De l'État*, 4 vols (Paris, 1978).

Legassick, Martin, "South Africa: Forced Labor, Industrialization and Racial Differentiation", in: R. Harris (ed.), *The Political Economy of Africa* (Cambridge, 1975).

Legassick, Martin, "Gold, Agriculture, and Secondary Industry in South Africa, 1885-1970: From Periphery to Sub-Metropole as a Forced Labour System", in: R. Palmer and N. Parsons (eds), *The Roots of Rural Poverty in Central and Southern Africa* (London, 1977).

Lenhardt, Gero (ed.), *Der hilflose Sozialstaat* (Frankfurt/Main, 1979).

Lenin, Vladimir I., *The State and the Revolution*, in: V.I. Lenin, *Collected Works*, vol. 25 (Moscow, 1964).

Leonard, Karen, *Making Ethnic Choices: California's Punjabi Mexican Americans* (Philadelphia, 1992).

Lerner, Gerda, *The Creation of Poverty* (Oxford, 1986).

Letona, Antonio L[ópez] de, *Isla de Cuba: Reflexiones sobre su estado social, político y económico, su administración y gobierno* (Madrid, 1865).

Levi, Margaret, *Of Rule and Revenue* (Berkeley, CA, 1988).

Levi, Primo, *If This is a Man and The Truce*, trans. Stuart Woolf (London, 1987).

Levidow, L. and B. Young (eds), *Science, Technology and the Labour Process*, Volume 1 (London, 1981).

Lewin, Moshe, "The Social Background of Stalinism", in: Robert C. Tucker (ed.), *Stalinism. Essays in Historical Interpretation* (New York, 1977).

Lexikon der Ägyptologie, vol. 2 (Wiesbaden, 1977) and vol. 3 (Wiesbaden, 1980).

Lianos, Theodore P. and Quirino Paris, "American Agriculture and the Prophecy of Increasing Misery", *American Journal of Agricultural Economy*, 54 (1972).

Lichtenstein, Alex, *Twice the Work of Free Labor: The Political Economy of Convict Labor in the New South* (London, 1995).

Lier, Rudolf A.J. van, *Samenleving in een grensgebied. Een sociaal-historische studie van de maatschappij in Suriname* (Den Haag, 1949).

Lieten, G.K., O. Nieuwenhuys and L. Schenk-Sandbergen, *Women, Migrants and Tribals: Survival Strategies in Asia* (New Delhi, 1989).

Linden, Marcel van der, "Connecting Household History and Labour History", in: Marcel van der Linden (ed.), *The End of Labour History?* (Cambridge, 1993).

Linden, Marcel van der, *Von der Oktoberrevolution zur Perestroika. Der westliche Marxismus und die Sowjetunion* (Frankfurt/Main, 1992).

Linder, Marc, *Migrant Workers and Minimum Wages: Regulating the Exploitation of Agricultural Labor in the US* (Boulder, CO, 1992)

Lindo-Fuentes, Hector, *Weak Foundations: The Economy of El Salvador in the Nineteenth Century, 1821-1898* (Berkeley, CA, 1991).

Linhart, Robert, *Lénine, les paysans, Taylor. Essai d'analyse matérialiste historique de la naissance du système productif soviétique* (Paris, 1976).

Lisansky, Judith Matilda, "Santa Terezinha: Life in a Brazilian Frontier Town" (Ph.D., University of Florida, 1980).

Littek, Wolfgang, "Arbeitssituation und betriebliche Arbeitsbedingungen", in: Wolfgang Littek *et al.* (eds), *Einführung in die Arbeits- und Industriesoziologie* (Frankfurt/Main and New York, 1982).

Lloyd, Jack *et al.*, *The Ventura Citrus Labor Market* (Berkeley, CA, 1988).

Lockhart, James, and Stuart B. Schwartz, *Early Latin America: A History of Colonial Spanish America and Brazil* (Cambridge, 1983).

López, Adalberto, "Shipbuilding in Sixteenth Century Asunción del Paraguay", *Mariner's Mirror*, 61 (1975).

Lowndes, A.G. (ed.), *South Pacific Enterprise: The Colonial Sugar Refining Company Limited* (Sydney, 1956).

Lucas, R.E.B., "The Puzzle of Sharecropping: A Piece Refitted", *World Development,* 13 (1985).

Lütge, Friedrich, "Das 14./15. Jahrhundert in der Sozial- und Wirtschaftsgeschichte", in: Friedrich Lütge, *Studien zur Sozial- und Wirtschaftsgeschichte. Gesammelte Abhandlungen* (Stuttgart, 1963).

Lütge, Friedrich, *Die mitteldeutsche Grundherrschaft und ihre Auflösung* (Stuttgart, 1957²).

Lundkvist, Anders, "Kritik af Marx' lønteori", *Kurasje,* No. 37 (December 1985).

Lundrigan, T., "The Grower, the FLC, and the Contract: Co-Employer or Sole Employer?" (Paper presented at FLC Personnel Management Conference in Visalia, California, 1993).

Luxemburg, Rosa, *The Accumulation of Capital* (New York, 1951; reprint 1964).

Lynch, John, *Argentine Dictator. Juan Manuel de Rosas, 1829-1852* (London, 1981).

McBryde, Felix, *Cultural and Historical Geography of Southwest Guatemala* (Washington, DC, 1947).

McCreery, David, "Debt Servitude in Rural Guatemala, 1876-1936", *Hispanic American Historical Review,* 63 (1983).

McCreery, David, "An Odious Feudalism: Mandamientos and Commercial Agriculture in Guatemala, 1853-1920", *Latin American Perspectives,* 13 (1986).

McCreery, David, "Land, Labor, and Violence in Highland Guatemala: San Juan Ixcoy, 1893-1945", *The Americas,* 45 (1988).

McCreery, David, "State Power, Indigenous Communities, and Land in Nineteenth Century Guatemala, 1820-1920", in: Carol Smith (ed.), *Land, Labor, and Community in Guatemala* (Austin, 1989).

McCreery, David, "Hegemony and Repression in Rural Guatemala, 1871-1914", *Peasant Studies,* 17 (1990).

McCreery, David, *Rural Guatemala, 1760-1940* (Stanford, 1994).

McCusker, John J. and Russel R. Menard, *The Economy of British America, 1607-1789* (Chapel Hill and London, 1991).

Macfarlane, Alan, *The Origins of English Individualism* (Oxford, 1978).

McGlynn, F. *et al.* (eds), *The Meaning of Freedom: Economics, Politics and Culture after Slavery* (Pittsburgh, 1992).

Machuca R., Jesus A., *Internacionalización de la Fuerza de Trabajo y Acumulación de Capital: Mexico-Estados Unidos (1970-1980)* (Mexico City, 1990).

McIntyre, W. David, *The Imperial Frontier in the Tropics, 1865-1875* (London, 1967).

McLeod, William Christie, "Debtor and Chattel Slavery in Aboriginal North America", *American Anthropologist*, 27 (1925).

McNeill, William H., *Plagues and People* (Oxford, 1977; reprint 1994).

McQueen, Humphrey, *A New Britannia* (Ringwood, 1970).

McWilliams, Carey, *Factories in the Field: The Story of Migratory Farm Labor in California* (New York, 1939).

Mahar, Dennis J., *Desenvolvimento Econômico na Amazônia - Uma análise das políticas governamentais* (Rio de Janeiro, 1978).

Majka, Theo and Linda C. Majka, *Farm Workers, Agribusiness, and the State* (Berkeley, CA, 1982).

Mandel, Ernest, *Marxist Economic Theory* (New York, 1968).

Mandel, Ernest, "Solzhenitsyn, Stalinism and the October Revolution", *New Left Review*, 86 (July-August 1974).

Mandle, Jay R., *The Roots of Black Poverty: The Southern Plantation Economy after the Civil War* (Durham, NC, 1978).

Mandle, Jay R., *The Plantation Economy. Population and Economic Change in Guyana, 1838-1960* (Philadelphia, 1973).

Mandle, Jay R., "Black Economic Entrapment After the Emancipation in the United States", in: McGlynn *et al.*, *The Meaning of Freedom*.

Mandle, Jay R., *Not Slave, Not Free: The African American Economic Experience Since the Civil War* (Durham, NC, 1992).

Mangum, M., *The Legal Status of the Tenant Farmer in the Southeast* (Chapel Hill, 1954).

Mantelli, Brunello, "Von der Wanderarbeit zur Deportation. Die italienischen Arbeiter in Deutschland 1938-45", in: Herbert, *Europa und der "Reichseinsatz"*.

Marais, J.S., *The Cape Coloured People 1652-1937* (London, 1939).

Maree, J. (ed.), *The Independent Trade Unions 1974-1984* (Johannesburg, 1987).

Maree, J. and D. Budlender, "State Policy and Labour Legislation", in: Maree, *The Independent Trade Unions*.

Marglin, Stephen A., "What Do Bosses Do? The Origins and Functions of Hierarchy in Capitalist Production", in: André Gorz (ed.), *The Division of Labour* (Atlantic Highlands, NJ, 1976).

María de Gordon, Antonio, *El tabaco en Cuba y de Acosta* (Havana, 1901).

Marincowitz, J., "From 'Colour Question' to 'Agrarian Problem' at the Cape: Reflections on the Interim", in: H. MacMillan and S. Marks (eds), *Africa and Empire: W.M. MacMillan, Historian and Social Critic* (London, 1989).

Markey, Raymond, "Populist Politics: Racism and Labor in NSW, 1880–1900", in: Curthoys and Markus, *Who Are Our Enemies*.

Markey, Raymond, *The Making of the Labor Party in NSW, 1880–1900* (Kensington, 1988).

Markey, Raymond, "Australia", in: Marcel van der Linden and Jürgen Rojahn (eds), *The Formation of Labour Movements, 1870–1914. An International Perspective*, 2 vols (Leiden, 1990).

Marla, Sarma, *Bonded Labour in India: National Survey on the Incidence of Bonded Labour (Final Report, January 1981)* (New Delhi, 1981).

Marrero y Artiles, Leví, *Cuba: economía y sociedad*, 15 vols (San Juan and Madrid, 1972-92), vol. 13.

Marrus, Michael R., *The Unwanted: European Refugees in the Twentieth Century* (New York, 1985).

Marshall, W.K., *The Post-Slavery Labour Problem Revisited: The 1990 Elsa Goveia Memorial Lecture* (Mona, 1991).

Martin, Philip L., "Labor in California Agriculture", in: Philip L. Martin (ed.), *Migrant Labor in Agriculture* (Berkeley, CA, 1984).

Martin, Philip L., *Seasonal Workers in American Agriculture: Background and Issues* (Washington, DC, 1985).

Martin, Philip L., "Network Recruitment and Labor Displacement", in: D.E. Simcox (ed.), *US Immigration in the 1980s* (Boulder, CO, 1988).

Martin, Philip L. and J. Edward Taylor, "Immigration Reform and Farm Labor Contracting in California", in: Michael Fix (ed.), *The Paper Curtain: Employer Sanctions', Implementation, Impact, and Reform* (Washington, DC, 1991).

Martin, T., *History of the High Range Planting District, North Travancore* (Bangalore, 1930).

Martínez-Alier (Stolcke), Verena, *Marriage, Class and Colour in Nineteenth Century Cuba: A Study of Racial Attitudes and Sexual Values in a Slave Society* (London, 1974).

Martins, Edilson, *Nossos Índios, Nossos Mortos* (Rio de Janeiro, 1978).

Martins, José de Souza, "A produção capitalista de relações não-capitalistas de produção: o regime de colonato nas fazendas de café", in: *O Cativeiro da Terra* (São Paulo, 1979).

Martins, José de Souza, "A sujeição da renda da terra ao Capital e o novo sentido da luta pela reforma agrária", in: *Os Camponeses e a Política no Brasil* (Petrópolis, 1983).

Marx, Karl, *Grundrisse. Foundations of the Critique of Political Economy (Rough Draft)*. Trans. Martin Nicolaus (Harmondsworth, 1973).

Marx, Karl, *Capital*, vol. 1, trans. Ben Fowkes (Harmondsworth, 1976).

Marx, Karl, *Results of the Immediate Process of Production*, trans. Rodney Livingstone, in: Marx, *Capital*, vol. 1.

Marx, Karl, *Value, Price and Profit* (New York, 1976).

Marx, Karl, *Capital*, vol. 2, trans. By David Fernbach (Harmondsworth, 1979).

Marx, Karl, "The Future Results of the British Rule", in: Karl Marx and Frederick Engels, *The First Indian War of Independence, 1857-1859* (Moscow, n.d.).

Marx, Karl and Friedrich Engels, "Manifesto of the Communist Party", in: Ibid., *Collected Works*, vol. 6 (London, 1976).

Mason, J.E., "'Fit for Freedom': The Slaves, Slavery, and Emancipation in the Cape Colony, South Africa, 1806 to 1842" (Ph.D., Yale University, 1992).

Mason, Timothy W., *Arbeiterklasse und Volksgemeinschaft. Dokumente und Materialien zur deutschen Arbeiterpolitik 1936-1939* (Opladen, 1975).

Massey, Douglas et al., *Return to Aztlan: The Social Process of International Migration from Western Mexico* (Berkeley, CA, 1987).

Mateer, S., *Native Life in Travancore* (London, 1883).

Mathias, Peter, *The Transformation of England: Essays in the Economic and Social History of England in the Eighteenth Century* (New York, 1979).

Mattera, Philip, *Off the Books: The Rise of the Underground Economy* (London, 1985).

Matthews, Tony, *This Dawning Land* (Brisbane, 1986).

Mauss, Marcel, "Essai sur le don. Forme et raison de l'échange dans les sociétiés archaiques", *L'Année Sociologique*, New Series, 1 (1925).

Mayer, Adrian, *Indians in Fiji* (London, 1963).

Mayne, Wilson (ed.), *United Planters' Association of Southern India, 1893-1953* (n.p., 1953).

Mayne, W.W., "United Planters' Association of Southern India", *The James Finlay House Magazine*, Autumn 1974.

Mayo, Carlos, "Estancia y peonaje en la región pampeana en la segunda mitad del XVIII", *Desarrollo económico*, 92 (1984).

Meillassoux, Claude, "Desenvolvimento o Exploraçâo", in: Franz Hinkelammert *et al.*, *Formas Políticas, Econômicas e Sociais de Exploração* (Porto, 1976).

Meillassoux, Claude, *Maidens, Meals and Money* (Cambridge, 1981).

Meillassoux, Claude, *The Anthropology of Slavery. The Womb of Iron and Gold* (London, 1991).

Meleisea, Malama, "The Last Days of the Labour Trade in Western Samoa", *Journal of Pacific History*, 11 (1976).

Melossi, Dario and Massimo Pavarini, *The Prison and the Factory: Origins of the Penitentiary System* (London, 1981).

Menchaca, Martha, "Chicano Indianism: A Historical Account of Racial Repression in the US", *American Ethnologist*, 20 (1993).

Mendez, Rosendo (ed.), *Leyes vigentes de agricultura* (Guatemala, 1937).

Menjivar, Rafael, *Acumulación originaria y desarrollo del capitalismo en El Salvador* (El Salvador, 1980).

Menon, P.S., *A History of Travancore: From the Earliest Times* (New Delhi, 1978).

Menzies, Colin, *A Profile of Neglect: A Background Paper on the Situation of Australian South Sea Islanders* (Sydney, 1992).

Mercer, P.M., "The Survival of a Pacific Islander Population in North Queensland, 1900-1940" (Ph.D., Australian National University, 1981).

Mercer, P.M. and C.R. Moore, "Melanesians in North Queensland: The Retention of Religious and Magical Practices", *Journal of Pacific History*, 11 (1976).

Mercer, P.M. and C.R. Moore, "Australia's Pacific Islanders, 1906-1977", *Journal of Pacific History*, 13 (1978).

Merritt, Alan, "The Development and Application of Master and Servants Legislation in NSW, 1845–1930" (Ph.D., Australian National University, 1981).

Mertz, Paul, *The New Deal and Southern Rural Poverty* (Baton Rouge, 1978).

Michaud, Francine, "Apprentissage et salariat à Marseille avant la peste noire", *Revue Historique*, No. 589 (1994).

Middleton, Chris, "The Familiar Fate of the *Famulae*: Gender Divisions in the History of Wage-labour", in: R.E. Pahl (ed.), *On Work. Historical, Comparative and Theoretical Approaches* (Oxford, 1988).

Miers, Suzanne and Igor Kopytoff (eds), *Slavery in Africa: Historical and Anthropological Perspectives* (Madison, 1977).

Mies, Maria and Vandana Shiva, *Ecofeminism* (London, 1993).

Miles, Robert, *Capitalism and Unfree Labour: Anomaly or Necessity?* (London and New York, 1987).

Mines, Richard, *Developing a Community Tradition of Migration to the US* (La Jolla, 1981).

Mines, Richard and Ricardo Anzaldua, *New Migrants vs. Old Migrants: Alternative Labor Market Structures in the California Citrus Industry* (La Jolla, 1982).

Ministerio de Agricultura, *Memoria-1932* (Guatemala, 1932).

Ministerio de Agricultura, *Memoria-1933* (Guatemala, 1933).

Ministerio de Fomento (Guatemala), *Memorias-1902* (Guatemala, 1902).

Mitchell, Annie, *A Modern History of Tulare County (California)* (Visalia, CA, 1974).

Mittal, S.K., *Peasant Uprisings and Mahatma Gandhi in North Bihar* (Meerut, 1978).

Mitter, Swasti, *Common Fate, Common Bond: Women in the Global Economy* (London, 1986).

Mitter, Swasti, "Industrial restructuring and manufacturing homework: Immigrant women in the UK clothing industry", *Capital & Class*, 27 (1986).

Monroy, Douglas, *Thrown Among Strangers: The Making of Mexican Culture in Frontier California* (Berkeley, CA, 1990).

Monteiro, John Manuel, "São Paulo in the Seventeenth Century: Economy and Society" (Ph.D., Department of History, University of Chicago, 1985).

Monteón, Michael,"The *Enganche* in the Chilean Nitrate Sector, 1880-1930", *Latin American Perspectives*, 22 (1979).

Montesquieu, Ch. de, *Lettres Persanes* (Paris, 1993).

Moore, Clive (ed.), *The Forgotten People: A History of the Australian South Sea Island Community* (Sydney, 1979).

Moore, Clive, "Kanaka Maratta: A History of Melanesian Mackay" (Ph.D., James Cook University of North Queensland, 1981).

Moore, Clive, "Kanakas, Kidnapping and Slavery: Myths from the Nineteenth Century Labour Trade and Their Relevance to Australia's Immigrant Melanesians", *Kabar Seberang: Sulating Maphilindo* [Townsville], No. 8-9 (1981).

Moore, Clive, *Kanaka: A History of Melanesian Mackay* (Boroko and Port Moresby, 1985).

Moore, Clive, Jacqueline Leckie and Doug Munro (eds), *Labour in the South Pacific* (Townsville, 1990).

Moore, Clive, "Labour, Indenture and Historiography in the Pacific", in: Lal, *Pacific Islands History*.

Moore, Clive, "Revising the Revisionists: The Historiography of Immigrant Melanesians in Australia", *Pacific Studies*, 15 (1992).

Moore, Clive, "The Counterculture of Survival: Melanesians in the Mackay District of Queensland, 1865-1906", in: Lal, Munro and Beechert, *Plantation Workers*.

Moore, Clive, "Methods of Response: Melanesian Society in Nineteenth Century Mackay", in: Reynolds, *Race Relations in Colonial Queensland*.

Moore, Clive, "Noel Fatnowna and His Book: The Making of *Fragments of a Lost Heritage*", *Journal of Pacific Studies*, 18 (1994).

Moore, Clive and Trish Mercer, "The Forgotten Immigrants: Australia's South Sea Islanders, 1906-1991", in: Reynolds, *Race Relations in Queensland*.

Mora Mérida, José Luis, "La demografía colonial del Paraguay", *Jahrbuch für Geschichte von Staat, Wirtschaft und Gesellschaft Lateinamerikas*, 11 (1974).

Mora Mérida, José Luís, *Historia Social del Paraguay, 1600-1650* (Sevilla, 1974).

Moraes, Clodomir, "Peasant Leagues in Brazil", in: Rodolfo Stavenhagen (ed.), *Agrarian Problems and Peasant Movements in Latin America* (Garden City, NY, 1970).

Morcha, Bandhua Mukti, *The Crusade Against Slavery* (New Delhi, 1983).

Morrell, W.P., *Britain in the Pacific Islands* (Oxford, 1960).

Morris, David and Clyde B. Dudley, "Selected Railway Statistics for the Indian Subcontinent (India, Pakistan and Bangladesh), 1853-1946/47", *Artha Vijñana. Journal of the Gokhale Institute of Politics and Economics*, 17 (1975).

Morsch, Günter, *Arbeit und Brot. Studien zu Lage, Stimmung, Einstellung und Verhalten der deutschen Arbeiterschaft 1933-1936/37* (Frankfurt/Main, 1993).

Müller, G. *et al.*, "Amazônia, Desenvolvimento Sócio-Econômico e Políticas de População" (São Paulo, 1975).

Munck, Ronaldo, *The New International Labour Studies* (London, 1988).

Mundle, Sudipto, *Backwardness and Bondage: Agrarian Relations in a South Bihar District* (New Delhi, 1979).

Muñiz, José Rivero, "Bosquejo Histórico de la Sociedad de Escogedores de Tabacos de la Habana", *Revista Tabaco*, 1 (1933).

Muñiz, José Rivero, "La lectura en las tabaquerías: monografía histórica", *Revista de la Biblioteca Nacional* [Cuba], Second series, 2 (1951).

Muñiz, José Rivero, "Esquema del movimiento obrero", in: Ramiro Guerra y Sánchez *et al.* (eds), *Historia de la nación cubana*, 10 vols (Havana, 1952).

Muñiz, José Rivero, *Tabaco: su historia en Cuba*, 2 vols (Havana, 1964).

Munro, Doug, "Gilbert and Ellice Islanders on Queensland Canefields, 1894-1899", *Journal of the Royal Historical Society of Queensland*, 14 (1992).

Munro, Doug, "The Pacific Islands Labour Trade: Approaches, Methodologies, Debates", *Slavery and Abolition*, 14 (1993).

Munro, Doug, T. David Williams and Ralph Shlomowitz, "Debate on the Queensland Labour Trade" [symposium], *Journal of Pacific Studies*, 18 (1994).

Munro, Doug, "Revisionism and its Enemies: Debating the Queensland Labour Trade", *Journal of Pacific History*, 30 (1995).

Murphy, Damien, "Slaves to Outcasts", *Bulletin* [Sydney] (August 10, 1993).

Murray, M.J., "'White Gold' or 'White Blood'?: The Rubber Plantations of Colonial Indochina, 1910-1940", *The Journal of Peasant Studies*, 19 (1992).

Musoke, Moses, "Mechanizing Cotton Production in the American South: The Tractor, 1915-1960", *Explorations in Economic History*, 18 (1981).

Nadar, S. Mahadevan, "Commercialisation of Agricultural Products and the New Economic Order in Travancore", *Journal of Kerala Studies*, 7 (1980).

Nanjundayya, H.V. and L.K. Ananthakrishna Iyer, *The Mysore Tribes and Castes*, vol. 4 (Mysore, 1931).

Necker, Louis, "La réaction des Indiens Guarani à la Conquête espagnole du Paraguay, un des facteurs de la colonisation de l'Argentine à la fin de XVIe siècle", *Bulletin de la Société des Américanistes*, no. 38.

Newbury, Colin, "The Melanesian Labor Reserve: Some Reflections on Pacific Labor Markets in the Nineteenth Century", *Pacific Studies*, 4 (1980).

Nicholas, Stephen, "The Convict Labour Market", in: Nicholas, *Convict Workers*.

Nicholas, Stephen (ed.), *Convict Workers. Reinterpreting Australia's Past* (Melbourne, 1988).

Nicholas, Stephen, "The Organisation of Public Work", in: Nicholas, *Convict Workers*.

Nicholas, Stephen, "Reinterpreting the Convict Labour Market", *Australian Economic History Review*, 30 (1990).

Nicholas, Stephen and Peter R. Shergold, "Convicts as Workers", in: Nicholas, *Convict Workers*.

Nicholas, Stephen and Peter R. Shergold, "A Labour Aristocracy in Chains", in: Nicholas, *Convict Workers*.

Nicholas, Stephen and Peter R. Shergold, "Transportation as Global Migration", in: Nicholas, *Convict Workers*.

Nicholas, Stephen and Peter R. Shergold, "Unshackling the Past", in: Nicholas, *Convict Workers*.

Nieboer, H.J., *Slavery as an Industrial System: Ethnological Researches* (The Hague, 1910).

Nieman, D.G., *To Set the Law in Motion: The Freedman's Bureau and the Legal Rights of Blacks, 1865-1868* (Millwood, NY, 1979).

Niess, Frank, *Geschichte der Arbeitslosigkeit. Ökonomische Ursachen und politische Kämpfe: ein Kapitel deutscher Sozialgeschichte* (Köln, 1982²).

Noble, John, *Un americain au Gulag* (Paris, 1972).

North, Douglass C., *The Economic Growth of the United States, 1790-1860* (Englewood Cliffs, NJ, 1961).

North, Douglass C., *Growth and Welfare in the American Past: A New Economic History* (Englewood Cliffs, NJ, 1966).

North, Douglass C., "A Framework for Analyzing the State in Economic History", *Explorations in Economic History*, 16 (1979).

North, Douglass C., *Structure and Change in Economic History* (New York, 1981).

North, Douglass C., *Institutions, Institutional Change, and Economic Performance* (New York, 1991).

North, Douglass C. and Robert P. Thomas, "The Rise and Fall of the Manorial Economy: A Theoretical Model", *Journal of Economic History* (December 1971).

North, Douglass C. and Robert P. Thomas, "An Economic Theory of the Growth of the Western World", *Economic History Review*, Second Series, 23 (1979).

North-Coombes, M.D., "From Slavery to Indenture: Forced Labour in the Political Economy of Mauritius, 1834-1867", in: Saunders, *Indentured Labour*.

Novak, D.A., *The Wheel of Servitude: Black Forced Labor after Slavery* (Lexington, KS, 1978).

Nuti, Domenico, "The Contradictions of Socialist Economies: A Marxist Interpretation", *The Socialist Register 1979*.

Oakes, James, *The Ruling Race: A History of American Slaveholders* (New York, 1982).

Oates, Mary J., *The Role of the Cotton Textile Industry in the Economic Development of the Southeast 1900-1940* (New York, 1975).

Ogburn, W.F., *Social Change* (New York, 1922).

Olitskaia, Ekaterina, *Le Sablier* (Tierce, 1991).

Oliveira, Antonia Alves de (ed.), *Os Nordestinos em São Paulo* (São Paulo, 1982).

Oliveira, José Eduardo Dutra de and Maria Helena Silva Dutra de Oliveira (eds), *"Bóias-frias", uma realidade brasileira* (Academy of Sciences of the State of São Paulo, 1981).

Olsen, Wendy K., "Competition and Power in Rural Markets: A Case Study from Andhra Pradesh", *IDS Bulletin*, 24-3 (July 1993).

Olsen, Wendy K., *Rural Indian Social Relations: A Study of Southern Andhra Pradesh* (Delhi, 1995).

Onselen, Charles van, *Chibaro: African Mine Labour in Southern Rhodesia 1900-1933* (London, 1976).

Oostindie, Gert, "Voltaire, Stedman and Surinam Slavery", *Slavery and Abolition*, 14 (1993).

Oostindie, Gert (ed.), *Fifty years later. Antislavery, Capitalism and Modernity in the Dutch Orbit* (Leiden and Pittsburgh, 1995).

Oostindie, Gert, "Same Old Song? Perspectives on Slavery and Slaves in Surinam and Curaçao", in: Oostindie, *Fifty Years Later*.

Oppenheimer, Franz, *Die soziale Frage und der Sozialismus. Eine kritische Auseinandersetzung mit der marxistischen Theorie* (Jena, 1912).

Otsuka, Keijiro *et al.*, "Land and Labour Contracts in Agrarian Economies: Theories and Facts", *Journal of Economic Literature*, 30 (1992).

Oxley, Deborah, "Female Convicts", in: Nicholas, *Convict Workers*.

Padgug, Robert, "Problems in the Theory of Slavery and Slave Society", *Science and Society*, 40 (1976).

Palerm, Angel, *Modos de Producción y Formaciones Socioeconomicas* (Mexico City, 1976).

Palerm, Juan V., *Farm Labor Needs and Farm Workers in California, 1970-1989* (Sacramento, CA, 1991).

Palerm, Juan V. and Jose I. Urquiola, "A Bi-national System of Agricultural Production: The Case of the Mexican Bajio and California", in: D.G. Aldrich and L. Meyer (eds), *Mexico and the US: Neighbors in Crisis* (San Bernadino, CA, 1993).

Pandian, M.S.S., *The Political Economy of Agrarian Change, Nanchilnadu, 1880-1939* (New Delhi, 1990).

Panoff, Michel, "Travailleurs, Recruteurs et Planters dans l'Archipel Bismarck de 1885 à 1914", *Journal de la Société des Océanistes*, 64 (1979). [English translation in *Journal of Pacific Studies*, 18 (1994).]

Pantín, Santiago Iglesias, *Luchas Emancipadoras (cronicas de Puerto Rico)*, vol. 1 (San Juan, 1929).

Paoli, Juan Bautista Rivarola, *La economía colonial* (Asunción, 1986).

Parekh, Bhikhu, "Marxism and the Problem of Violence", *Development and Change*, 23 (1992).

Parish, Peter J., *Slavery: History and Historians* (New York, 1989).

Parnaby, O.W., *Britain and the Labor Trade in the Southwest Pacific* (Durham, NC, 1964).

Pashukanis, Evgeny, "The General Theory of Law and Marxism" (1924), in: Evgenij Pashukanis, *Selected Writings on Marxism and the Law* (London [etc.], 1980).

Pastore, Carlos, *La lucha por la tierra en el Paraguay* (Montevideo, 1972).

Patmore, Greg, *Australian Labour History* (Melbourne, 1991).

Patnaik, Utsa, "Introduction", in: Patnaik and Dingwaney, *Chains of Servitude*.

Patnaik, Utsa, "The Agrarian Question and the Development of Capitalism in India", *Economic and Political Weekly*, 21 (1986).

Patnaik, Utsa (ed.), *Agrarian Relations and Accumulation: The "Mode of Production" Debate in India* (Bombay, 1990).

Patnaik, Utsa, "On Capitalism and Agrestic Unfreedom", *International Review of Social History*, 40 (1995).

Patnaik, Utsa and Manjari Dingwaney (eds), *Chains of Servitude. Bondage and Slavery in India* (Madras, 1985).

Patterson, Orlando, "Slavery", *Annual Review of Sociology*, 3 (1977).

Patterson, Orlando, *Slavery and Social Death: A Comparative Study* (Cambridge, MA, 1982).

Paulys Realencyclopädie der classischen Altertumswissenschaft, vol. 15-2 (Stuttgart, 1932).

Peach, Bill, *Peach's Australia* (Sydney, 1976).

Pelayo, Agueda Jimenez, *Haciendas y Comunidades Indigenas en el Sur de Zacatecas* (Mexico City, 1989).

Pentland, H.C., "The Development of a Capitalistic Labour Market in Canada", *Canadian Journal of Economics and Political Science*, 24 (1959).

Pérez, Jr, Louis A. (ed.), *Slaves, Sugar, & Colonial Society: Travel Accounts of Cuba, 1801-1899* (Willmington, DE, 1992).

Perroy, E., "Wage-labour in France in the later Middle Ages", *Economic History Review*, Second Series, 8 (1955-1956).

Perz, Bertrand, *Projekt Quarz. Steyr-Daimler-Puch und das Konzentrationslager Melk* (Vienna, 1991).

Petrick, Fritz, *Zur sozialen Lage der Arbeiterjugend in Deutschland 1933 bis 1939* (Berlin, 1974).

Pezuela y Lobo, Jacobo de la, *Diccionario geográfico, estadístico, histórico de la isla de Cuba*, 4 vols (Madrid, 1866).

Philips, David, *Crime and Authority in Victorian England: The Black Country, 1835–60* (London, 1977).

Phongpaichit, Pasuk, *From Peasant Girls to Bangkok Masseuses* (Geneva, 1982).

Pietsch, Anna-Jutta, "Stalinismus als Phänomen der nichtkapitalistischen ursprünglichen Akkumulation", in: Gernot Erler and Walter Süss (eds), *Stalinismus. Probleme der Soujetgesellschaft zwischen Kollektivierung und Weltkrieg* (Frankfurt/Main and New York, 1982).

Pillai, T.K. Velu, *The Travancore State Manual* (n.p., 1940)

Pino, César García del, "La Habana en los días de Yara", *Revista de la Biblioteca Nacional José Martí*, 20 (1978).

Pinto, Lúcio Flávio, *Amazônia: No Rastro do Saque* (São Paulo, 1980).

Pitti, Joseph, "Jorge Ubico and Guatemalan Politics in the 1920s" (Ph.D., University of New Mexico, 1975).

Plant, Roger, *Sugar and Modern Slavery* (London, 1987).

Plasencia Moro, Aleida, "Historia del movimiento obrero en Cuba", in: Pablo González Casanova (ed.), *Historia del movimiento obrero en América Latina*, 4 vols (Mexico City, 1984).

Platteau, Jean-Philippe, "A Framework for the Analysis of Evolving Patron-Client Ties in Agrarian Economies", *World Development*, 23 (1995).

Pöhlmann, Robert von, *Geschichte der sozialen Frage und des Sozialismus in der antiken Welt*, vol. 1 (Munich, 1925³).

Polanyi, Karl, *The Great Transformation. The Political and Economic Origins of Our Time* (Boston, 1957).

Portes, Alejandro *et al.*, *The Informal Economy: Studies in Advanced and Less Developed Countries* (London, 1989).

Portuondo, José Antonio, *"La Aurora" y los comienzos de la prensa obrera en Cuba* (Havana, 1961).

Postan, M.M., *The Famulus. The Estate Labourer in the XIIth and XIIIth Centuries.* Supplement 2, *Economic History Review* n.d. [1954].

Postan, M.M., "England", in: *Cambridge Economic History of Europe*, vol. 1 (Cambridge, 1966²).

Postone, Moishe, *Time, Labour and Social Domination. A Reinterpretation of Marx's Critical Theory* (Cambridge, 1983).

Pouchepadass, Jacques, "The Market for Agricultural Labour in Colonial North Bihar 1860-1920", in: M. Holmstrom (ed.), *Work for Wages in South Asia* (New Delhi, 1990).

Powell, Philip W., *Soldiers, Indians, and Silver: The Northward Advance of New Spain, 1550-1600* (Berkeley, CA, 1952).

Prakash, Gyan, *Bonded Histories: Genealogies of Labor Servitude in Colonial India* (Cambridge [etc.], 1990).

Prakash, Gyan, "Bonded Labour in South Bihar: A Contestatory History", in: S. Bose (ed.), *South Asia and World Capitalism* (Delhi, 1990).

Prakash, Gyan, "Becoming a Bhuinya: Oral Traditions and Contested Domination in Eastern India", in: Haynes and Prakash, *Contesting Power*.

Prakash, Gyan (ed.), *The World of the Rural Labourer in Colonial India* (Delhi, 1992).

Prasad, P.H., "Reactionary Role of Usurer's Capital in Rural India", *Economic and Political Weekly*, 9 (1974).

Prasad, Pradhan H., "Semi-Feudalism: The Basic Constraints of Indian Agriculture", in: Arvind N. Das and V. Nilkant (eds), *Agrarian Relations in India* (New Delhi, 1979).

Prasad, Pradhan H., *Lopsided Growth: Political Economy of Indian Development* (Bombay, 1989).

Price, Charles Archibald, *The Great White Walls Are Built. Restrictive Immigration to North America and Australasia, 1836–88* (Canberra, 1974).

Price, Richard, *Labour in British Society. An Interpretative History* (London, 1986).

Proyecto de Reglamento de la Junta y Ramo de Aprendizaje de la Habana y su Jurisdicción Administrativa (Havana, 1863).

Pycroft, Christopher and Barry Munslow, "Black Mine Workers in South Africa: Strategies of Co-option and Resistance", *Journal of Asian and African Studies*, 23 (1988).

Quibria, M.G. and S. Rashid, "The Puzzle of the Lucas Model: A Reply", *World Development*, 13 (1985).

Raim, Edith, *Die Dachauer KZ-Außenkommandos Kaufering und Mühldorf: Rüstungsbauten und Zwangsarbeit im letzten Kriehsjahr 1944/45* (Landsberg, 1992).

Ramachandran, V.K., *Wage Labour and Unfreedom in Agriculture: An Indian Case Study* (Oxford, 1990).

Ramachandran Nair, K., *Industrial Relations in Kerala* (New Delhi, 1973).

Raman, K. Ravi, "Labour under Imperial Hegemony: The Case of Tea Plantations in South India, c.1914-1946", in: S. Bhattacharya, *The South Indian Economy: Agrarian Change, Industrial Structure and State Policy, c. 1914-1947* (New Delhi, 1991).

Ramanamurthy, R.V., "Seasonal Labour Migration in Semi-Arid Areas: A Case Study of Palamoor Labour" (Ph.D., University of Hyderabad, 1991).

Ramesar, Marianne, "Indentured Labour in Trinidad 1880-1917", in: Saunders, *Indentured Labour.*

Ransom, R., and R. Sutch, "The Lock-In Mechanism and Overproduction of Cotton in the Post Bellum South", *Agricultural History*, 49 (1975).

Ransom, R. and R. Sutch, "Sharecropping: Market Response or Mechanism of Race Control?" in: D.G. Sansing (ed.), *What Was Freedom's Price?* (Jackson, MS, 1978).

Ransom, R. and R. Sutch, "Credit Merchandising in the Post-Emancipation South: Structure, Conduct, Performance", *Explorations in Economic History*, 16 (1979).

Rao, J.M., "Interest Rates in Backward Agriculture", *Cambridge Journal of Economics*, 4 (1980).

Rattray, R.S., *Ashanti Law and Constitution* (Oxford, 1929).

Rawick, George P., *From Sunup to Sundown: The Making of the Black Community* (Westport, 1972).

Rayner, M.I., "Wine and Slaves: The Failure of an Export Economy and the Ending of Slavery in the Cape Colony, South Africa, 1806-1834" (Ph.D., Duke University, 1986).

Reglamento para el aprendizaje de artes y oficios (Havana, 1849).

Reid, Anthony (ed.), *Slavery, Bondage and Dependency in Southeast Asia* (St. Lucia, 1983).

Reid, J.D., Jr, "Sharecropping as an Understandable Market Response: The Post-Bellum South", *Journal of Economic History*, 33 (1973).

Reynolds, Henry (ed.), *Race Relations in Queensland* (Townsville, 1993²).

Riverend Brusone, Julio Le, *La Habana (Biografía de una provincia)* (Havana, 1960).

Riverend Brusone, Julio Le, *Economic History of Cuba* (Havana, 1967).

Riviere, W.E., "Labour Shortage in the British West Indies after Emancipation", *Journal of Caribbean History*, 4 (1972).

Robertson, Claire C. and Martin A. Klein (eds), *Women and Slavery in Africa* (Madison, 1983).

Robinson, Armstead L. *et al* (eds), *Black Studies in the University: A Symposium* (New Haven, CT, 1969).

Robinson, M.S., *Local Politics: Law of the Fishes - Development Through Political Change in Medak District, Andhra Pradesh (South India)* (Delhi, 1988).

Rodney, Walter, *A History of the Guyanese Working People, 1881-1905* (London, 1981).

Rodriguez, Guillermo, *Guatemala en 1919* (Guatemala, 1919).

Roe, Michael, "1830–50", in: Crowley, *A New History of Australia.*

Roediger, David R., *The Wages of Whiteness: Race and the Making of the American Working Class* (London, 1991).

Roemer, John (ed.), *Analytical Marxism* (Cambridge, 1986).

Roemer, Michael, "Simple Analytics of Segmented Markets: What Case for Liberalization?", *World Development*, 14 (1986).

Rössler, Detlef, "Handwerk und Lohnarbeit im Athen des 5. Und 4. Jh. v.u.Z.", *Jahrbuch für Wirtschaftsgeschichte*, 1985-III.

Rohwer, Götz, "Kapitalismus und 'freie Lohnarbeit'. Überlegungen zur Kritik eines Vorurteils", in: Hamburger Stiftung, *"Deutsche Wirtschaft"*.

Rolfi, Lidia Beccaria and Anna Maria Bruzzone, *Le donne di Ravensbrück. Testimonianze di deportate politiche italiane* (Turin, 1978).

Rones, Philip, "Moving to the Sun. Regional Job Growth, 1968 to 1978", *Monthly Labor Review*, 103 (1980).

Root, Hilton, *The Fountain of Privilege. Political Foundations of Markets in Old Regime France and England* (Berkeley, CA, 1994).

Rose, Michael E., *The Relief of Poverty, 1834-1914* (London, 1972).

Rosefielde, Steven, "An Assessment of the Sources and Uses of Gulag Forced Labour 1929-56", *Soviet Studies*, 33 (1981).

Rosenberg, Howard et al., *Farm Labor Contractors in California Agriculture* (Sacramento, CA, 1992).

Rosenzweig, Mark and Oded Stark, "Consumption Smoothing, Migration and Marriage: Evidence From Rural India", *Journal of Political Economy*, 97 (1989).

Ross, H.J., "Difficulty of Obtaining and the High Price of Labour in the West Indies", *The Colonial Magazine and Commercial-Maritime Journal*, New Series, 1 (1842).

Ross, H.J., "Tenantry and Allotment System in the West Indies", *The Colonial Magazine and Commercial-Maritime Journal*, 8 (1842).

Ross, Robert, "Pre-Industrial and Industrial Racial Stratification in South Africa", in: R. Ross (ed.), *Racism and Colonialism. Essays on Ideology and Social Structure* (The Hague, 1982).

Ross, Robert, "The Origins of Capitalist Agriculture in the Cape Colony: A Survey", in: Beinart, Delius, and Trapido, *Putting a Plough to the Ground*.

Ross, Robert, *Beyond the Pale: Essays on the History of Colonial South Africa* (Hanover, 1993).

Ross, Robert, "Emancipations and the Economy of the Cape Colony", *Slavery and Abolition*, 14 (1993).

Rossi, Jacques, *The Gulag Handbook* (New York, 1989).

Rossum, Leo van, "Western Studies of Soviet Labour During the Thirties", *International Review of Social History*, 35 (1990).

Rotermundt, Rainer, Ursula Schmiederer and Helmut Becker-Panitz, *Die Sowjetunion und Europa. Gesellschaftsform und Außenpolitik der UdSSR* (Frankfurt/Main and New York, 1979).

Roth, Karl Heinz, "I.G. Auschwitz. Normalität oder Anomalie eines kapitalistischen Entwicklungssprungs?", *1999*, 4 (1989).

Roth, Karl Heinz, "'Chinawerke' im 'großdeutschen' Herrschaftsbereich. Die Steuerung der Arbeiterpolitik im Siemens-Konzern durch Zwangsarbeit 1938-1945" (Paper at the Second International Conference of the Theresienstadt Initiative, November 25-27, 1992).

Roth, Karl Heinz, "'Vernichtung durch Arbeit' in den nationalsozialistischen Konzentrationslagern. Die Zweite Internationale Tagung der Theresienstädter Initiative vom 25. bis 27. November 1992 in Terezin", *1999*, 8 (1993).

Roulet, Florencia, *La resistencia de los Guaraní del Paraguay a la conquista española, 1537-1556* (Posadas, Argentina, 1993).

Rubbo, Anna and Michael Taussig, "Up Off Their Knees: Servanthood in Southwest Colombia", *Latin American Perspectives*, 39 (1983).

Ruben, Peter, "Ist die Arbeitskraft eine Ware? Ein Beitrag zu einer marxistischen Marxkritik", in: Heinz Eidam and Wolfdietrich Schmied-Kowarzik (eds), *Kritische Philosophie gesellschaftlicher Praxis* (Würzburg, 1995).

Rudé, George, *Debate on Europe, 1815-1850* (New York, 1972).

Rudé, George, *Protest and Punishment: The Story of the Social and Political Protesters Transported to Australia, 1788–1968* (Melbourne, 1978).

Rudé, George, *Criminal and Victim: Crime and Society in Early Nineteenth Century England* (Oxford, 1985).

Rudra, Ashok *et al.*, *Studies in the Development of Capitalism in India* (Lahore, 1978).

Saeger, James Schofield, "Survival and Abolition: The Eighteenth Century Paraguayan Encomienda", *The Americas*, 38 (1981).

Saldanha, Indira Munshi, "Attached Labour: A Historical Overview", *Economic and Political Weekly*, 24 (1989).

Salles, V., *O Negro na Pará sob o Regime da Escravidao* (Rio de Janeiro, 1971).

Salvatore, Ricardo, "Modes of Labor Control in Cattle-Ranching Economies: California, Southern Brazil, and Argentina, 1800-1870", *Journal of Economic History*, 51 (1991).

Salvatore, Ricardo and Jonathon Brown, "Trade and Proletarianization in the Colonial Banda Oriental. Evidence on the Estancia de las Vacas, 1791-1805", *Hispanic American Historical Review*, 67 (1987).

Samson, Ross, "The End of Early Medieval Slavery", in: Allen J. Frantzen and Douglas Moffat (eds), *The Work of Work: Servitude, Slavery, and Labour in Medieval England* (Glasgow, 1994).

Samuel, Raphael, "Workshop of the World: Steam Power and Hand Technology in Mid-Victorian Britain", *History Workshop*, 3 (1977).

San Pedro, Joaquín Rodríguez (ed.), *Legislación ultramarina*, 12 vols (Madrid, 1865-68), vol. 10.

Sanderson, Steven E. (ed.), *The America in the New International Division of Labor* (New York, 1985).

Sansone, Livio, *Schitteren in de schaduw. Overlevingsstrategieën van Creoolse jongeren uit de lagere klassen in Amsterdam* (Amsterdam, 1992).

Santana, Arismendi Díaz, "The Role of Haitian Braceros in Dominican Sugar Production", *Latin American Perspectives*, 8 (1976).

Santos, Roberto, *História Econômica da Amazônia - 1800-1820* (São Paulo, 1980).

Saradamoni, K., *Emergence of a Slave Caste: Pulayas of Kerala* (New Delhi, 1980).

Sarkar, Tanika, "Bondage in the Colonial Context", in: Patnaik and Dingwaney, *Chains of Servitude*.

Sassen, Saskia, *Mobility of Labor and Capital: A Study of International Investment and Labor Flow* (Cambridge, 1988).

Satzewich, Vic, "Unfree Labour and Canadian Capitalism: The Incorporation of Polish War Veterans", *Studies in Political Economy*, 28 (1989).

Saucier, J.F., "Sub Saharan Slavery as Part of a Ranking Process" (unpublished manuscript).

Saunders, C., "Liberated Africans in Cape Colony in the First Half of the Nineteenth Century", *International Journal of African Historical Studies*, 18 (1985).

Saunders, Kay, "Uncertain Bondage: An Analysis of Indentured Labour in Queensland to 1907, with particular reference to the Melanesian servants" (Ph.D., University of Queensland, 1974).

Saunders, Kay, "'The Black Scourge': Racial Responses Towards Melanesians in Colonial Queensland", in: Raymond Evans, Kay Saunders and Kathryn Cronin, *Exclusion, Exploitation and Extermination: Race Relations in Colonial Queensland* (Sydney, 1975).

Saunders, Kay, *Workers in Bondage: The Origins and Bases of Unfree Labour in Queensland, 1824-1916* (Brisbane, 1982).

Saunders, Kay (ed.), *Indentured Labour in the British Empire, 1834-1920* (London and Canberra, 1984).

Saunders, Kay, "The Workers' Paradox: Indentured Labour in the Queensland Sugar Industry to 1920", in: Saunders, *Indentured Labour*.

Saxton, Alexander, *The Indispensable Enemy: Labor and the Anti-Chinese Movement In California* (Berkeley, CA, 1971).

Sayer, A., *Radical Political Economy: A Critique* (Oxford, 1995).

Sayer, Andrew, *Method in Social Science: A Realist Approach* (London, 1992²).

Scarr, Deryck, *Fragments of Empire: A History of the Western Pacific High Commission, 1877-1914* (Canberra, 1967).

Scarr, Deryck, "Recruits and Recruiters: A Portrait of the Pacific Islands Labour Trade", *Journal of Pacific History*, 2 (1967).

Scherer, Heinrich, *Der Aufbruch aus der Mangelgesellschaft. Die Industrialisierung Rußlands unter dem Zarismus (1860 bis 1914)* (Giessen, 1985).

Scheuring, Ann Foley (ed.), *A Guidebook to California Agriculture* (Berkeley, CA, 1983).

Scheuss de Studer, Elena F., *La trata de negros en el Río de la Plata durante el siglo XVIII* (Buenos Aires, 1958).

Schiel, Tilman, "Alltag und Geborgenheit", *Peripherie*, No. 32 (1988).

Schlögel, Karl, *Der renitente Held. Arbeiterprotest in der Sowjetunion 1953-1983* (Hamburg, 1984).

Schmiechen, James A., *Sweated Industries and Sweated Labor: The London Clothing Trades 1860-1914* (London, 1984).

Schrader, H., "Professional Moneylenders and the Emergence of Capitalism in India and Indonesia", *International Sociology*, 9 (1994).

Schroeter, D.J., "Slave Markets and Slavery in Moroccan Urban Society", *Slavery and Abolition*, 13 (1992).

Schwarz, Solomon M., *Labor in the Soviet Union* (New York, 1951).

Scott, Emmet J., *Negro Migration During the War* (New York, 1969).

Scott, James C., *Weapons of the Weak: Everyday Forms of Peasant Resistance* (New Haven, 1985).

Scott, James C. "Domination, Acting, and Fantasy", in: Carolyn Nordstrom and JoAnn Martin (eds), *The Paths to Domination, Resistance, and Terror* (Berkeley, 1992).

Scott, Rebecca J., "Explaining Abolition: Contradiction, Adaptation, and Challenge in Cuban Slave Society, 1860-1886", in: Manuel Moreno Fraginals *et al.* (eds), *Between Slavery and Free Labor: The Spanish-Speaking Caribbean in the Nineteenth Century* (Baltimore, 1985).

Scott, Rebecca J., *Slave Emancipation in Cuba: The Transition to Free Labor, 1860-1899* (Princeton, 1985).

Scully, P., "Criminality and Conflict in Rural Stellenbosch, South Africa, 1870-1900", *Journal of African History*, 30 (1989).

Sellin, Thorsten J., *Slavery and the Penal System* (New York, 1976).

Sen, Samar, Debabrata Panda and Ashish Lahiri, *Naxalbari and After*, vol. 2 (Calcutta, 1978).

Senghaas, Dieter, "Sozialismus. Eine entwicklungsgeschichtliche und entwicklungstheoretische Betrachtung", *Leviathan*, 8 (1980).

Service, Elman R., *Spanish-Guarani Relations in Early Colonial Paraguay* (Westport, CT, 1954).

Service, Elman R., "Indian-European Relations in Colonial Latin America", *American Anthropologist*, 57 (1955).

Sexton, James D. (ed.), *Son of Tecun Uman* (Tucson, 1981).

Sexton, James D., *Campesino* (Tucson, 1985).

Shah, Nasra M. *et al.*, "Asian Women Workers in Kuwait", *International Migration Review*, 25 (1991).

Shankaran, S.R., "Methodology for Identification of Bonded Labour applicable to Telengana Districts of Andhra Pradesh" (Paper presented at the National Seminar on Identification and Rehabilitation of Bonded Labour, organized by the National Labour Institute and the Ministry of Labour, New Delhi, February 7-9, 1983).

Shaw, A.G.L., *Convicts and the Colonies* (London, 1966).

Shaw, A.G.L., "1788–1810", in: Crowley, *New History of Australia*.

Shephard, V.E., "Alternative Husbandry. Slaves and Free Labourers on Livestock Farms in Jamaica in the Eighteenth and Nineteenth Centuries", *Slavery and Abolition*, 14 (1993).

Sheridan, R.B., "From Chattel to Wage Slavery in Jamaica, 1740-1860", *Slavery and Abolition*, 14 (1993).

Sherwood, M., *Many Struggles: West Indian Workers and Service Personnel in Britain 1939-45* (London, 1985).

Shineberg, Dorothy, *They Came for Sandalwood: A Study of the Sandalwood Trade in the South-West Pacific, 1830-1865* (Melbourne, 1967).

Shineberg, Dorothy, "'Noumea No Good, Noumea No Pay': An Aspect of 'New Hebridean' Indentured Labour in New Caledonia", *Journal of Pacific History*, 26 (1991).

Shlomowitz, R., "Markets for Indentured and Time-expired Melanesian Labour in Queensland, 1863-1906", *Journal of Pacific History*, 16 (1981).

Shlomowitz, Ralph, "The Origins of Southern Sharecropping", *Agricultural History*, 53 (1979).

Shlomowitz, Ralph, "The Search for Institutional Equilibrium in Queensland's Sugar Industry, 1884-1913", *Australian Economic History Review*, 19 (1979).

Shlomowitz, Ralph, "Team Work and Incentives: The Origins and Development of the Butty Gang System in Queensland's Sugar Industry, 1891-1913", *Journal of Comparative Economics*, 3 (1979).

Shlomowitz, Ralph, "Melanesian Labor and the Development of the Queensland Sugar Industry, 1863–1906", in: Paul Uselding (ed.), *Research in Economic History*, 7 (1982).

Shlomowitz, Ralph, "Time-expired Melanesian Labour in Queensland: An Investigation of Job Turnover, 1886-1906", *Pacific Studies*, 10 (1985).

Shlomowitz, Ralph, "The Fiji Labor Trade in Comparative Perspective, 1864-1914", *Pacific Studies*, 9 (1986).

Shlomowitz, Ralph, "Mortality and the Pacific Labour Trade", *Journal of Pacific History*, 22 (1987).

Shlomowitz, Ralph, "Planter Combinations and Black Labour in the American South, 1865-1880", *Slavery and Abolition*, 9 (1988).

Shlomowitz, Ralph, "Epidemiology and the Pacific Labor Trade", *Journal of Interdisciplinary History*, 19 (1989).

Shlomowitz, Ralph, "Convict Workers: A Review Article", *Australian Economic History Review*, 30 (1990).

Shlomowitz, Ralph, "Differential Mortality of Asians and Pacific Islanders in the Pacific Labour Trade", *Journal of the Australian Population Association*, 7 (1990).

Shlomowitz, Ralph, "Workers and Mortality", in: Moore, Leckie and Munro, *Labour in the South Pacific*.

Shlomowitz, Ralph, "The Latin American *Enganche* System: A Comment on Brass", *Slavery and Abolition*, 12 (1991).

Shlomowitz, Ralph, "The Genesis of Free Labour in the American Civil War", *Slavery and Abolition*, 13 (1992).

Shlomowitz, Ralph, "On Labour Systems: A Rejoinder to Brass" (Flinders University Working Papers in Economic History, No. 50, Adelaide, 1992).

Shlomowitz, Ralph, "On Punishments and Rewards in Coercive Labour Systems", *Slavery and Abolition*, 13 (1992).

Shlomowitz, Ralph, "Marx and the Queensland Labour Trade", *Journal de la Société des Océanistes*, 96 (1993).

Shlomowitz, Ralph, "Bound or Free: Black Labor in Cotton and Sugar Cane Farming, 1865-1880", *Journal of Southern History,* 50 (1994).

Sholmer, J., *Vorkuta* (London, 1954).

Shugg, Roger W., *Origins of Class Struggle in Louisiana: A Social History of White Farmers and Laborers During Slavery and After* (Baton Rouge, 1939).

Shumuk, Danylo, *Life Sentence* (Edmonton, 1984).

Siegel, Bernard J., "Some Methodological Considerations for a Comparative Study of Slavery", *American Anthropologist*, 47 (1945).

Simmons, C.P., "Recruiting and Organizing an Industrial Labour Force in Colonial India: The Case of the Coal Mining Industry, c. 1880-1939", *Indian Economic and Social History Review*, 13 (1976).

Singleton-Gates, Peter and Maurice Girodias, *The Black Diaries: An account of Roger Casement's life and times with a collection of his diaries and public writings* (London, 1959).

Siwpersad, J.P., *De Nederlandse regering en de afschaffing van de Surinaamse slavernij* (Groningen and Castricum, 1979).

Slack, Paul, *The English Poor Law, 1531-1782* (Houndmills, 1990).

Slatta, Richard W., *Gauchos and the Vanishing Frontier* (Lincoln, NE, 1983).

Slicher van Bath, B.H., *De Agrarische Geschiedenis van West-Europa* (Utrecht, 1960).

Smith, Adam, *An Inquiry into the Nature and Causes of the Wealth of Nations*, 2 vols (Chicago, 1976).

Smith, Robert Freeman, *The US and Revolutionary Nationalism in Mexico, 1916-1932* (Chicago, 1972).

Smith, Waldemar, *The Fiesta System and Economic Change* (New York, 1977).

Sofsky, Wolfgang, *Die Ordnung des Terrors: Das Konzentrationslager* (Frankfurt/Main, 1993).

Solzhenitsyn, Aleksandr, *Archipel Gulag, 1918-1956. Opyt chudozhestvennogo issledovanija*, 3 vols (Paris, 1973).

Soutar, J.B., "The High Range. Ten Years of Transition in Planting", *The James Finlay House Magazine*, Autumn 1974.

Southall, Roger (ed.), *Labour and Unions in Asia and Africa* (London, 1988).

Souza, Márcio, *O Empate Contra Chico Mendes* (São Paulo, 1990).

Spalding Jr, Hobart A., "The Workers' Struggle: 1850-1961", *Cuba Review*, 4 (1974).

Spohn, Wilfried, "Die technologische Abhängigkeit der Sowjetunion vom Weltmarkt", *Probleme des Klassenkampfs*, No. 19-20-21 (October 1975).

Srinivasan, T.N., "On Choice Among Creditors and Bonded Labour Contracts", in: Bardhan, *Economic Theory of Agrarian Institutions*.

Srinivasan, T.N., "Agricultural Backwardness Under Semi-Feudalism: Comment", *Economic Journal*, 89 (1979).

Srivastava, Ravi, "Interlinked Modes of Exploitation in Indian Agriculture During Transition: A Case Study", *Journal of Peasant Studies*, 16 (1989).

Stadelman, Raymond, "Maize Cultivation in Northwestern Guatemala", *Contributions to American Anthropology and History*, 6 (1940).

Stamas, S.H., "The Puzzling Lag in Southern Earnings", *Monthly Labor Review*, 103 (1981).

Stampp, Kenneth M., *The Peculiar Institution: Slavery in the Ante-Bellum South* (New York, 1956).

Starobin, Robert, *Industrial Slavery in the Old South* (New York, 1970).

Stedman, J.G., *Narrative of a Five Years' Expedition against the Revolted Negroes of Surinam* (London, 1796).

Steinfeld, Robert J., *The Invention of Free Labor: The Employment Relation in English and American Law and Culture, 1350-1870* (Chapel Hill, NC, 1991).

Steinfeld, Robert J., "The Myth of the Rise of Free Labor: A Critique of Historical Stage Theory" (forthcoming).

Steinmetz, George, "The Myth and the Reality of the Autonomous State: Industrialists, Junkers and Social Policy in Imperial Germany", *Comparative Social Research*, 12 (1990).

Steward, Julian H., *Handbook of South American Indians*, 7 vols (New York, 1963).

Stichter, Sharon and Jane L. Parpart (eds), *Women, Employment and the Family in the International Division of Labour* (London, 1990).

Stiglitz, Joseph, "The New Development Economics", *World Development*, 14 (1986).

Stiglitz, Joseph, "Rational Peasants, Efficient Institutions, and a Theory of Rural Organization: Methodological Remarks for Development Economics", in: Bardhan, *The Economic Theory of Agrarian Institutions*.

Stoler, Ann Laura, *Capitalism and Confrontation in Sumatra's Plantation Belt, 1870-1979* (New Haven, 1985).

Stoll, David, "Evangelicals, Guerrillas, and the Army: The Triangle Under Rios Mont", in: Robert Carmack (ed.), *Harvest of Violence: The Maya Indians and the Guatemalan Crisis* (Norman, OK, 1988).

Stoyanovitch, K., "La théorie du contrat selon E.B. Pachoukanis", *Archives de philosophie du droit*, 13 (1968).

Street, James H., *The New Revolution in the Cotton Economy: Mechanization and Its Consequences* (Chapel Hill, NC, 1957).

Subramani (ed.), *The Indo-Fijian Experience* (St. Lucia, 1979).

Süss, Walter, *Die Arbeiterklasse als Maschine. Ein industrie-soziologischer Beitrag zur Sozialgeschichte des aufkommenden Stalinismus* (Wiesbaden, 1985).

Sugeetha, G., "The Constitutional Progress in Travancore in the 19th and 20th Centuries", *Journal of Kerala Studies*, 8 (1981).

Sulkunen, Pekka, "Individual Consumption in Capitalism. An Exercise in the Logic of Capital." *Acta Sociologica*, 21 (1978).

Summerskill, M., *China on the Western Front: Britain's Chinese Work Force in the First World War* (London, 1982).

Susnik, Branislava, *El indio colonial del Paraguay* (Asunción, 1965).

Sutch, Richard, "The Treatment Received by American Slaves: A Critical Review of the Evidence Presented in *Time on the Cross*", *Explorations in Economic History*, 12 (1975).

Sutter, Steve, "Agricultural Labor Relations Board Statistics", *Agricultural Personnel Management Program Newsletter* (December 1994).

Sutton, Alison, *Slavery in Brazil - A Link in the Chain of Modernization* (London, 1994).

Sweezy, Paul, "The Contradictions of Capitalism", in: Paul Sweezy, *Four Lectures on Marxism* (New York and London, 1981).

Swianiewicz, S., *Forced Labour and Economic Development. An Enquiry into the Experience of Soviet Industrialization* (London [etc.], 1965).

Syrup, Friedrich, *Der Arbeitseinsatz und die Arbeitslosenhilfe in Deutschland* (Berlin, 1936).

Tadman, Michael, *Speculators and Slaves: Masters, Traders, and Slaves in the Old South* (Madison, WI, 1989).

Takaki, Ronald, *Pau Hana: Plantation Life and Labor in Hawaii, 1835-1920* (Honolulu, 1983).

Tandeter, Enrique, *Coacción y mercado: la minería de la plata en el Potosí colonial, 1692-1826* (Buenos Aires, 1992).

Tate, Merze and Fidele Foy, "Slavery and Racism in South Pacific Annexations", *Journal of Negro History*, 50 (1965).

Tatur, Melanie, *Taylorismus in der Soujetunion. Die Rationalisierungspolitik der UdSSR in den siebziger Jahren* (Frankfurt/Main and New York, 1983).

Taussig, Michael, "Culture of Terror – Space of Death: Roger Casement's Putumayo Report and the Explanation of Torture", *Comparative Studies in Society and History*, 26 (1984).

Taussig, Michael, *Shamanism, Colonialism, and the Wild Man* (Chicago, 1987).

Tax, Sol, "The Municipios of the Midwestern Highlands of Guatemala", *American Anthropologist*, 39 (1937).

Taylor, J. Edward and Thomas J. Espenshade, "Illegal Immigrants in the California Farm Labor Market" (Paper presented at the Center for US-Mexican Studies, 1987).

Taylor, Lewis, "Earning a Living in Hualgayoc, 1870-1900", in: Rory Miller (ed.), *Region and Class in Modern Peruvian History* (Liverpool, 1987).

Taylor, William B., *Landlord and Peasant in Colonial Oaxaca* (Stanford, CA, 1972).

Teixeira, Carlos Corrêa, "O Aviamento e o Barracão na Sociedade do Seringal - Estudo sobre a produção extrativa da borracha na Amazônia" (MSc Thesis, University de São Paulo, 1980).

"Telégrafo Mercantil", *Reflexiones cristianas sobre los negros esclavos*, vol. II (Buenos Aires, 1914).

Temin, Peter, "Freedom and Coercion: Notes on the Analysis of Debt Peonage", in: R. Ransom and R. Sutch (eds), *One Kind of Freedom: The Economic Consequences of the Emancipation* (Cambridge, 1977).

Teodoro Jr, Luis V., *Out of This Struggle: The Filipinos in Hawaii* (Honolulu, 1981).

Tharakan, P.K. Michael and K. Tharian George, "Penetration of Capital into a Traditional Economy. The Case of Tea Plantations in Kerala, 1880-1950", *Studies in History*, 2 (1986).

Tharamangalam, Joseph, "The Penetration of Capitalism and Agrarian Change in South-West India, 1901 to 1941: A Preliminary Analysis", *Bulletin of Concerned Asian Scholars*, 16 (1984).

Theberge, James D. (ed.), *The Economics of Trade and Development* (New York, 1968).

Theron, J., *Rethinking Industrial Councils: What Small Business Signifies for Labour Relations* (Cape Town, 1994).

Thomas, Robert J., *Citizenship, Gender, and Work: The Social Organization of Industrial Agriculture* (Berkeley, CA, 1985).

Thomas, Robert P. and Richard Bean, "The Fishers of Men: The Profits of the Slave Trade", *Journal of Economic History*, 34 (1974).

Thompson, E.P., *The Making of the English Working Class* (London, 1963).

Thompson, Paul, *The Nature of Work: An Introduction to Debates on the Labour Process* (Basingstoke, 1983).

Thurston, Edgar, *Castes and Tribes of South India*, vol. 5 (Madras, 1909).

Ticktin, Hillel, "Towards a Political Economy of the USSR", *Critique*, No. 1 (1973).

Ticktin, Hillel, "The Contradictions of Soviet Society and Professor Bettelheim", *Critique*, No. 6 (1976).

Tilly, Charles, "Demographic Origins of the European Proletariat", in: David Levine (ed.), *Proletarianization and Family History* (Orlando, 1984).

Tinberg, T.A. and C.V. Aiyar, "Informal Credit Markets in India", *Economic Development and Cultural Change*, 33 (1984).

Tinker, Hugh, *A New System of Slavery: The Export of Indian Labour Overseas, 1830–1920* (Oxford, 1974).

Tise, L.E., *Proslavery: A History of the Defense of Slavery in America, 1701-1840* (Athens, GA, 1987).

Tiwary, S.P., "Bondage in Santhal Parganas", in: Patnaik and Dingwaney, *Chains of Servitude.*

Toghill, Jeff, *Ghost Ports of Australia* (Melbourne, 1984).

Tomlins, Christopher L., *Law, Labor and Ideology in the Early American Republic* (Cambridge, 1993).

Trelese, Allen W., *The White Terror: The KKK Conspiracy and Southern Reconstruction* (Westport, CT, 1971).

Trescott, Paul, *Financing American Enterprise: The Story of Commercial Banking* (New York, 1963).

Trevor, Henry Edward, *The Law Relating to Railways in British India* (London, 1891).

Trimberger, Ellen Kay, "State Power and Modes of Production: Implications of the Japanese Transition to Capitalism", *The Insurgent Sociologist*, 7 (1977), No. 2.

Tripathy, S.N., *Bonded Labour in India* (Delhi, 1989).

Trotsky, Leon, *The Defence of Terrorism: A Reply to Karl Kautsky* (London, 1935).

Trujillo, Larry, "Parlier [Fresno County California]: The Hub of Raisin America" (MA thesis, University of California, 1979).

Tsurumi, E. Patricia, "Female Textile Workers and the Failure of Early Trade Unionism in Japan", *History Workshop Journal*, 18 (1984), p. 17.

Tsurumi, E. Patricia , *Factory Girls: Women in the Thread Mills of Meiji Japan* (Princeton, NJ, 1990).

Tuden, Arthur and Leonard Plotnicov (eds), *Social Stratification in Africa* (New York and London, 1970).

Tun Wai, U., "Interest Rates Outside the Organized Money Markets of Underdeveloped Countries", *IMF Staff Papers* (1958).

Turner, William, "No Dice for Braceros", *Ramparts*, 4 (1965).

Tuschling, Burkhard, *Rechtsform und Produktionsverhältnisse* (Frankfurt/Main, 1976).

Twaddle, M., "Visible and Invisible Hands", *Slavery and Abolition*, 14 (1993).

Uma Devi, S., *Plantation Economies of the Third World* (Bombay, 1989).

Van Kley, Dale, "From the Lessons of French History to Truths for All Times and All People: The Historical Origins of an Anti-Historical Declaration", in: Dale van Kley (ed.), *The French Idea of Freedom. The Old Regime and the Declaration of Rights of 1789* (Stanford, CA, 1994).

Vance, Rupert B., *Human Factors in Cotton Culture: A Study in the Social Geography of the American South* (Chapel Hill, NC, 1929).

Veblen, Thorsten, *The Theory of the Leisure Class* (New York, 1953).

Velasco, José María, *Guerra de Cuba. Causas de su duración y medios de terminarla y asegurar su pacificación* (Madrid, 1872).

Velázquez, Rafaél Eladio, "La rebelión de los indios de Arecayá, en 1660", *Revista Paraguaya de Sociología*, 1 (1965).

Velázquez, Rafaél Eladio, "La población del Paraguay en 1682", *Revista Paraguaya de Sociología*, 9 (1972).

Velázquez, Rafaél Eladio, *Breve historia de la cultura en el Paraguay* (Asunción, 1975).

Velázquez, Rafaél Eladio, "Caracteres de la encomienda paraguaya en los siglos XVII y XVIII", *Historia Paraguaya*, 119 (1975-1976).

Velázquez, Rafaél Eladio, "Organización militar de la Gobernación y Capitanía General del Paraguay", *Estudios Paraguayos*, 5 (1977).

Venturi, Franco, "Oriental Despotism", *Journal of the History of Ideas*, 24 (1963).

Vernant, Jean-Pierre, *Mythe et pensée chez les Grecs* (Paris, 1965).

Vidyasagar, R., "Debt Bondage in South Arcot District: A Case Study of Agricultural Labourers and Handloom Weavers", in: Patnaik and Dingwaney, *Chains of Servitude*.

Villarejo, Don, "Elections Signal Revived UFW", *Rural California Report* (1994).

Vries, Jan de, "The Industrial Revolution and the Industrious Revolution", *Journal of Economic Histroy*, 54 (1994).

Wade, Richard C., *Slavery in the Cities: The South, 1820-1860* (New York, 1964).

Wagley, Charles, "Economics of a Guatemalan Village", *American Anthropological Association Memoir*, no. 58 (1941).

Wagner, Regina, "Actividades empresariales de los alemanes en Guatemala, 1850-1920", *Mesoamérica*, 13 (1987).

Wakefield, E.G., *A View of the Art of Colonization* (Oxford, 1914).

Walker, Thomas S. and J. G. Ryan, *Village and Household Economies in India's Semi-Arid Tropics* (Baltimore and London, 1990).

Wallace, David Duncan, *South Carolina: A Short History* (Chapel Hill, NC, 1951).

Wallerstein, Immanuel, *The Modern World-System: Capitalist Agriculture and the Origins of the European World-Economy in the Sixteenth Century* (New York, 1974).

Ward, John M., *British Policy in the South Pacific, 1786-1893* (Sydney, 1948).

Ward, Russel, *The Australian Legend* (Melbourne, 1970).

Warren, Kay, *The Symbolism of Subordination: Indian Identity in a Guatemalan Town* (Austin, 1978).

Washbrook, David, "Progress and Problems: South Asian Social and Economic History, c. 1720-1860", *Modern Asian Studies*, 22 (1988).

Watch, Americas (ed.), *Violencia Rural no Brasil* (São Paulo, 1991).

Watkins, Melville, "A Staple Theory of Economic Growth", *The Canadian Journal of Economics and Political Science*, 19 (1963).

Watson, James B., "Commentary", *Current Anthropology*, 8 (1967).

Wayne, Michael, *The Reshaping of Plantation Society: The Natchez District 1860-1880* (Baton Rouge, LA, 1983).

Weber, Devra Anne, "The Struggle for Stability and Control in the Cotton Fields of California: Class Relations in Agriculture, 1919-1942" (Ph.D., University of California, 1986).

Weber, Max, "Agrarverhältnisse im Altertum" (1909), in: Max Weber, *Gesammelte Aufsätze zur Sozial- und Wirtschaftsgeschichte* (Tübingen, 1924).

Weber, Max, *The Protestant Ethic and the Spirit of Capitalism*, transl. by Talcott Parsons (New York, 1958).

Weber, Max, *General Economic History*, transl. by Frank H. Knight (New York, 1961).

Weber, Max, *The Agrarian Sociology of Ancient Civilizations* (London, 1976).

Weber, Max, "Zur Psychophysik der industriellen Arbeit", in: Max Weber, *Gesammelte Aufsätze zur Soziologie und Sozialpolitik* (Tübingen, 1988²).

Weber, Wilhelm, "Studie zur Spätmittelalterlichen Arbeitsmarkt- und Wirtschaftsordnung", *Jahrbücher für Nationalökonomie und Statistik*, 166 (1954).

Weinstein, Allen and Frank Otto Gatell (eds), *American Negro Slavery: A Modern Reader* (New York, 1968²).

Welskopf, Elisabeth Charlotte (ed.), *Soziale Typenbegriffe und ihr Fortleben in den Sprachen der Welt*, vol. 3 (Berlin, 1981).

Wermel, Michael and Roswitha Urban, *Arbeitslosenfürsorge und Arbeitslosenversicherung in Deutschland* (München, 1949).

Werth, Nicolas and Gael Moullec, *Les rapports secrèts soviétiques 1921-1991* (Paris, 1994).

West, Martin and Erin Moore, "Undocumented Workers in the US and South Africa: A Comparative Study of Changing Control", *Human Organization*, 48 (1989).

Whatmore, Sarah, *Farming Women* (London, 1990).

Wheatcroft, S.G., "Towards a Thorough Analysis of Soviet Forced Labour Statistics", *Soviet Studies*, 35 (1983).

Whigham, Thomas Lyle, *The Politics of River Trade. Tradition and Development in the Upper Plata, 1780-1870* (Albuquerque, 1991).

Whittaker, Paul, "Old Herby Links Australia to Stories of Kanaka 'Slavery'", *Courier-Mail*, Brisbane, 19 April 1989.

Wiener, J.M., R. Higgs and H.D. Woodman, "AHR Forum: Class Structure and Economic Development in the American South, 1865-1955", *American Historical Review*, 84 (1979).

Wiener, Jonathan M., *Social Origins of the New South: Alabama, 1860-1880* (Baton Rouge, LA, 1978).

Will, Edouard, "Notes sur ΜΙΣΘΟΣ", in: Jean Bingen, Guy Cambier and Georges Nachtergael (eds), *Le monde grec. Hommages à Claire Préaux* (Brussels, 1975).

Wilson, Francis, *Labour in South African Gold Mines 1911-1969* (London, 1972).

Wittfogel, Karl August, *Oriental Despotism. A Comparative Study of Total Power* (New Haven [etc.], 1957).

Wolf, Eric R., *Sons of Shaking Earth* (Chicago, 1959).

Wolf, Jan J. de, "Beyond Evolutionism: The Work of H.J. Nieboer on Slavery, 1900-1910", in: Hans F. Vermeulen and Arturo A. Roldán (eds), *Fieldwork and Footnotes. Studies in the History of European Anthropology* (London and New York, 1995).

Wolfe, Humbert, *Labor Supply and Regulation* (Oxford, 1923).

Wolpe, Harold (ed.), *The Articulation of Modes of Production* (London, 1980).

Wood, D., *Trinidad in Transition: The Years after Slavery* (London, 1968).

Wood, Ellen Meiksins, *Peasant-Citizen and Slave. The Foundations of Athenian Democracy* (London and New York, 1988).

Wood, Ellen Meiksins, "From Opportunity to Imperative: The History of the Market", *Monthly Review*, 46 (1994).

Wood, Peter H., *Black Majority: Negroes in Colonial South Carolina from 1670 through the Stono Rebellion* (New York, 1974).

Wood, Stephen (ed.), *The Transformation of Work? Skill, Flexibility and the Labour Process* (London, 1989).

Woodman, Harold D., "Post Civil War Southern Agriculture and the Law", *Agricultural History*, 53 (1979).

Worden, Nigel, *Slavery in Dutch South Africa* (Cambridge, 1985).

Worden, Nigel, "Adjusting to Emancipation: Freed Slaves and Farmers in the Mid-Nineteenth-Century South-Western Cape", in: W.G. James and M. Simons (eds), *The Angry Divide: Social and Economic History of the Western Cape* (Cape Town, 1989).

Worden, Nigel, "Diverging Histories: Slavery and Its Aftermath in the Cape Colony and Mauritius", *South African Historical Journal*, 27 (1992).

Wright, Erik Olin, *Interrogating Inequality. Essays on Class Analysis, Socialism and Marxism* (London, 1994).

Wright, Eric Olin, "Explanation and Emancipation in Marxism and Feminism", *Sociological Theory*, 11 (1993). Also in: Wright, *Interrogating Inequality*.

Wright, Gavin, *The Political Economy of the Cotton South: Households, Markets and Wealth in the Nineteenth Century* (New York, 1978).

Wright, Gavin, *Old South, New South: Revolutions in the Southern Economy Since the Civil War* (New York, 1986).

Wright, Gavin, "The Economics and Politics of Slavery and Freedom in the U.S. South", in: McGlynn *et al.*, *The Meaning of Freedom: Economics, Politics and Culture after Slavery*.

Wright Mills, C., *The Sociological Imagination* (London, 1959).

Wu, Hongda Harry, *Laogai: The Chinese Gulag* (Boulder, CO, 1992).

Wulff, Birgit, *Arbeitslosigkeit und Arbeitsbeschaffungsmaßnahmen in Hamburg 1933-1939* (Frankfurt/Main [etc.], 1987).

Wurdemann, John George F., *Notes on Cuba* (Boston, 1844).

Wyberg Docker, Edward, *The Blackbirders: The Recruiting of South Sea Labour for Queensland, 1863-1907* (Sydney, 1970).

Wysocki, Gerd, *Arbeit für den Krieg. Arbeitseinsatz, Sozialpolitik und staatspolizeiliche Repression bei den Reichswerken "Hermann Göring" im Salzgitter-Gebiet 1937/38 bis 1945* (Braunschweig, 1992).

Yesudas, R.N., *British Policy in Travancore, 1805-1859* (Trivandrum, 1977).

Young, Grace Esther, "The Myth of Being 'Like a Daughter'", *Latin American Perspectives*, 54 (1987).

Young, James P., *Central American Currency and Finance* (Princeton, NJ, 1925).

Zabin, Carol *et al.*, *Mixtec Migrants: A New Cycle of Poverty in California Agriculture* (Davis, 1993).

Zavala, Silvio, *Orígenes de la colonización en el Río de la Plata* (Mexico City, 1977).

Zegeye, A. and S. Ishemo (eds), *Forced Labour and Migration: Patterns of Movement within Africa* (London, 1989).

Zeichner, Oscar, "The Legal Status of the Agricultural Laborer in the South", *Political Science Quarterly*, 55 (1940).

Zelaya Gil, Augusto and Manuel Antonio Lucerno (eds), *Resumen de leyes de la República, clasificados y anotados por secretarías* (Guatemala, 1955).

Zelnik, Reginald E., *Labor and Society in Tsarist Russia: The Factory Workers of St. Petersburg, 1855-1870* (Stanford, CA, 1971).

Zimmerman, Hans Dieter, "Die freie Arbeit in Griechenland während des 5. und des 4. Jahrhunderts v.u.Z.", *Klio*, 56 (1974).

Zlolniski, Christian, "The Informal Economy in an Advanced Industrial Society: Mexican Immigrants in Silicon Valley", *The Yale Law Journal*, 103 (1994).

Index

Notes on Contributors

Larian Angelo is currently the Chief Economist and Special Advisor for the Finance Division of the New York City Council, with primary responsibility for economic and tax revenue forecasting, economic development, labour market policy, and welfare reform initiatives.

Paul E. Baak is currently working as a consultant in the field of Record and Information Management, and free lance India specialist at the Royal Tropical Institute, Amsterdam.

Tom Brass is an Affiliated Lecturer in the Faculty of Social and Political Sciences at the University of Cambridge, and formerly Director of Studies in the Social and Political Sciences at Queen's College, Cambridge. He is an editor of the *Journal of Peasant Studies*.

Joan Casanovas is Professor d'Història d'Amèrica at the Universitat Rovira i Virgilli, Tarragona, Spain.

Marta Craveri is a graduate student at the European University Institute in Fiesole, Italy.

Stanley L. Engerman is John H. Munro Professor of Economics and Professor of History at the University of Rochester, USA.

Jonathan Grossman lectures in the Department of Sociology, University of Cape Town, South Africa. He is involved in developing a Social History and Worker Education Project called Masabelane (Let Us Share).

Lyman L. Johnson is Professor of History at the University of North Carolina at Charlotte.

Ian J. Kerr is a member of the Department of History, University of Manitoba, Winnipeg, Canada.

André J.F. Köbben is emeritus Professor of Anthropology and taught at the Universities of Amsterdam, Pittsburgh, Leiden and Rotterdam.

Reinhart Kössler is Professor and Research Fellow at the Institute of Sociology, University of Münster, Germany.

Fred Krissman is a researcher at University Washington's Center for Labor Studies and funded by the Social Science Research Council.

Jan Lucassen is Head of the Research and Publication Department of the Internationaal Instituut voor Sociale Geschiedenis, Amsterdam, and Professor of International and Comparative Social History, Vrije Universiteit, Amsterdam.

Marcel van der Linden is Senior Research Fellow at the Internationaal Instituut voor Sociale Geschiedenis, Amsterdam, Professor of Social Movement History, Amsterdam University, and Executive Editor of the *International Review of Social History*.

David McCreery is Professor of Latin American History, Georgia State University.

Ray Markey is Associate Professor in the Department of Economics at the University of Wollongong, Australia.

José de Souza Martins is Professor of Sociology at the University of São Paolo (Brazil) and Americas representative in the Board of Trustees of the Voluntary Fund on the Contemporary Forms of Slavery, in Geneva, for three years.

Doug Munro is Reader in History and Politics at the University of the South Pacific, Suva (Fiji).

Wendy Olsen is Lecturer in Quantitative Development Economics at the University of Bradford.

Mario Pastore is Visiting Fellow, Latin American Studies Program, Cornell University, Ithaca, New York.

Karl Heinz Roth medical doctor and historian, is a member of the Hamburger Institut für Sozialforschung, Hamburg.

Ralph Shlomowitz is Reader in History at The Flinders University of South Australia, Adelaide.

Robert J. Steinfeld is Professor of Law at the State University of New York at Buffalo School of Law.

INTERNATIONAL AND COMPARATIVE SOCIAL HISTORY

1. *Racism and the Labour Market: Historical Studies.* Edited by Marcel van der Linden and Jan Lucassen in collaboration with Dik van Arkel, Els Deslé, Fred Goedbloed, Robert Kloosterman and Kenneth Lunn. 1995.

2. *Social Security Mutualism: The Comparative History of Mutual Benefit Societies.* Edited by Marcel van der Linden in collaboration with Michel Dreyfus, Bernard Gibaud and Jan Lucassen. 1996.

3. *The Communist International and its National Sections, 1919-1943.* Edited by Jürgen Rojahn. Forthcoming.

4. *Migration, Migration History, History: Old Paradigms and New Perspectives.* Edited by Jan Lucassen and Leo Lucassen. 1997.

5. *Free and Unfree Labour: The Debate Continues.* Edited by Tom Brass and Marcel van der Linden. 1997.